DISCARD
D0023592

REAL ESTATE FINANCE AND INVESTMENTS

RISKS AND OPPORTUNITIES

Peter Linneman, Ph D

Fourth Edition

Real Estate Finance and Investments: Risks and Opportunities Fourth Edition

Author: Dr. Peter Linneman

Editor: Bruce Kirsch

Assistant Editors: Bharat Nagaswami, Michael Franzese, Jared Karpf

Assistant Editing Team: Christopher Braatz, Robyn Choo, Erez Cohen, Anoop Dave, Manning Feng, James Forman, Michael Givner, Robert Greco, Jason Gruenbaum, Karren Henderson, Avivah Hotimsky Jared Joella, Jeremiah Kane, Chresten Knaff, Adam Leslie, Douglas Linneman, Jared Prushansky, Joshua Schwartz, Brendan Stone, Adi Weinstein, Eugene Wong, Yucheng Tina Xu, Laura Yablon

Project Coordinator: Douglas Linneman

Cover Art: Frances Wan, Eugene Wong

ARGUS Chapter courtesy of:

ARGUS Software Inc., John Lim, Katie Foley

ISBN 978-0-692-48045-8

Linneman Associates
The Victory Building
1001 Chestnut Street, Suite 101
Philadelphia, PA 19107

www.linnemanassociates.com

Linneman Associates is committed to preserving ancient forests and natural resources. We elected to print this title on 30% postconsumer recycled paper, processed chlorine-free. As a result, we have saved:

49 Trees (40' tall and 6-8" diameter)
22 Million BTUs of Total Energy
4,220 Pounds of Greenhouse Gases
22,888 Gallons of Wastewater
1,532 Pounds of Solid Waste

Linneman Associates made this paper choice because our printer, Thomson-Shore, Inc., is a member of Green Press Initiative, a nonprofit program dedicated to supporting authors, publishers, and suppliers in their efforts to reduce their use of fiber obtained from endangered forests.

For more information, visit www.greenpressinitiative.org

Environmental impact estimates were made using the Environmental Defense Paper Calculator. For more information visit: www.edf.org/papercalculator

This book is printed on 30% Post-Consumer Recycled, FSC-Certified Mixed Sources.

Table of Contents

Acknowledgements

We often fail to appreciate the mosaic of people who shape our careers. As such, I must acknowledge a few of the people who have made my career possible.

My greatest professional debt is owed to Lucille Ford, of Ashland University. Lucille is a great teacher, mentor, and friend, who literally changed my life. Without her love and generosity, neither my career nor this book, would not exist. It was also at Ashland that I met Tom Shockney, who has become a lifelong friend, and source of amazement, admiration, and fun.

At the University of Chicago, I was deeply influenced and assisted by many rigorous and creative scholars, including Gary Becker, George Stigler, George Tolley, Jim Heckman, and Milton Friedman. John Abowd was a terrific study mate and colleague.

At Wharton, I was blessed with a wonderful and loving mentor of irreplaceable value in Anita Summers. In addition, Tom Dunfee, Joe Gyourko, Jeremy Siegel, and Susan Wachter found ways to stimulate and challenge me, while Russell Palmer provided the opportunity to lead Wharton's real estate program.

My thought process was unalterably changed by my many friends in the real estate industry over the past 30 years. I continually learn from their creativity, drive, and ingenuity. While it is impossible to identify all of these influences, Dean Adler, Claude Ballard, Peter Bedford, Albert Behler, Marshall Bennett, Chaim Katzman, Ira Lubert, David Marshall, Albert Ratner, Shelly Seevak, A. Alfred Taubman, Ron Terwilliger, Bill Tucker, Samuel Zell, and Michael von Zitzewitz merit special thanks. I marvel at how little I still know, and relish the fact that there is still so much to learn from so many.

I apologize to the innumerable students who suffered in my classes, and hope that they have forgiven my ignorance.

I was blessed to have worked with two wonderful research assistants, Anoop Dave and Jared Prushansky, who worked tirelessly on the first edition of this book. If you find this book is useful, they deserve all of the credit. Christopher Braatz, Robyn Choo, Erez Cohen, Laura Yablon, James Forman, Michael Givner, Robert Greco, Jason Gruenbaum, Avivah Hotimsky, Jared Joella, Jeremiah Kane, Chresten Knaff, Adam Leslie, Bharat Nagaswami, Joshua Schwartz, Adi Weinstein, Eugene Wong, and Tina Xu all provided assistance on earlier editions of this book, as has my brother Douglas Linneman. My former student, Bruce Kirsch, has diligently edited and improved this edition. In addition, Bruce has created a great online interview series to accompany the book, which is available at the Linneman Associates website.

John Lim and Katie Foley of ARGUS Software, Inc. were great co-authors for the ARGUS chapter.

In closing, I thank Felicitas Abel, Lisa Anderson, Kelley Brasfield, Kathy Oberkircher, Jessica Pretzell, Celina Richters, and Leslie von Zitzewitz for being wonderful, loving, and supportive "daughters". Also, special thanks to my assistant, Karren Henderson. And, of course, thanks to my Mother.

Never least, but too often last in my focus, is my soul mate Kathy, who for over four decades has suffered my wanderlust, impatience, and narcissism. My greatest piece of life and career advice is to marry a saint.

Preface

This book explores the key concepts of real estate finance and investment strategy. It is not a formulaic analysis of numbers that yield “the answer” to any and all real estate investment decisions. Instead, this book is designed to help you understand that there is no singular, or simplistic, answer to any real estate finance problem. Rather, real estate finance is fundamentally driven by judgment and experience, with an eye to the numbers. The goal of this book is to help you embark upon the long and unending road of building your judgment.

For basic information on loan amortization, discounted cash flows, net present value, and IRR, refer to the Prerequisite chapters. The chapters in the text assume that you have a mastery of the material in these chapters. But before you start, be absolutely certain that you are comfortable with the materials in these Prerequisite chapters. The Supplemental chapters provide interesting information, but are not essential for you to master the chapters in the text.

This edition also incorporates articles I have written which are related to chapter topics. Though written at earlier dates, they provide breadth and context on the core topics. Each article reflects my thoughts at the time they were written and contain data that was relevant at that time. The formulas and templates found in this book will help you assemble and organize information. However, mastering these tools is merely the beginning — not the end— of real estate finance. This book focuses on what to do after you have mastered the basic financial tools. Just as knowing how to use a hammer and saw is not the same as building a wonderful building that will last the ages, knowing how to build a financial model and calculating the internal rate of return is not the same as making a profitable real estate investment. And no one would ever fly on a plane which has only been modeled. Judgment comes one mistake at a time, and better to make some of those mistakes in this class than “in real life”.

Please note that throughout the text, for the purpose of conveying concepts in a more digestible manner, we will refer to loans and loan debt service with the general assumption that the loan is an interest-only loan, unless otherwise specified.

I hope you enjoy the book.

About the Author

Dr. Peter Linneman is the Emeritus Albert Sussman Professor of Real Estate and Public Policy at the Wharton School of Business, the University of Pennsylvania. For many years he has been one of the nation's top real estate scholars, publishing over 100 papers on topics including real estate capital markets, public real estate companies, corporate real estate, real estate private equity funds, urban markets, and homeownership. His writings and lectures have established him as one of the most influential thought leaders in the real estate industry.

He was the founding co-editor of the Wharton Real Estate Review, and from 1985 – 1998 served as the Director of Wharton's prestigious Samuel Zell and Robert Lurie Real Estate Center. In addition, he was the founding Chairman of Wharton's Real Estate Department. His courses on real estate research and real estate development were popular with Wharton students for over two decades.

As the Founding Principal of Linneman Associates, he has served for over 35 years as a consultant to numerous leading real estate companies and investors around the world. "The Linneman Letter" is one of the most respected economic and real estate market research publications in the industry. In addition, he was Chairman of Rockefeller Center Properties REIT, leading the successful foreclosure and sale of Rockefeller Center in 1995. He has served as a director of numerous public and private corporations. He was Vice Chairman of Amerimar Realty and a Senior Managing Director of Equity Group Investments, and is founder and CEO of the American Land Fund and KL Realty. He has been named one of the "25 Most Influential People in Real Estate" by Realtor Magazine, "One of the 100 Most Powerful People in New York Real Estate" by the New York Observer, and one of the "Most Influential People in Real Estate" by Commercial Property Executive. He also is the recipient of Wharton's Zell-Lurie Real Estate Center's Lifetime Achievement Award and recieved PREA's prestigious Graaskamp's Award for Lifetime Achievement in Real Estate Research. His rare combination of scholarly discipline and industry experience makes him a popular speaker.

Raised in Lima, Ohio, he graduated from Ashland University, before receiving both his Masters and Doctorate degrees in Economics from the University of Chicago. Married for well over 40 years, he remains an avid scuba diver, leading "Peter's Plungers", a consortium of friends and former students. Although childless, he and his wife share their lives with their beloved god-daughters and children, as well as an assortment of nieces and nephews.

Testimonials

"Peter's book brings a much needed blend of theory and practice to the analysis of real estate finance and investment. Too often this field is presented as little more than algebra, with students assembling rows and columns of numbers, but having no idea what they mean."

-Samuel Zell
Chairman of Equity Office Properties and Equity Residential Properties
Chairman of Group Investments

"Linneman's new text provides the best investment analysis of real estate that I have seen. The book is comprehensive, clearly written, and the examples are both relevant and well presented. For students, professors, and young professionals desiring a thorough grounding in real estate finance and investment analysis, this text will provide a compelling and satisfying answer."

-Dr. Joe Gyourko
Martin Bucksbaum Professor of Real Estate and Finance
Wharton School of Business, University of Pennsylvania

"I am currently teaching an MBA class called Real Estate Investment. The class I have developed steps the students through the acquisition process. I find the book well written and easy to follow. I have also gotten good feedback from the students. The book has served as an excellent resource to give them the background necessary to complete the assignments."

Robert Rice
Professor, Concordia University

"I started using Peter Linneman's text with his first edition. The text has proven itself with helping me teach the basics of real estate investment. In fact, I had an outside professional speak to the class who exclaimed that the text was given to all of his agents. He said that it was definitely used in the market, and that it prepares students well for a career in real estate."

Sarah K. Bryant, Ph.D.
Professor of Finance
Shippensburg University of PA

"Peter Linneman's book offers a great blend of theoretical concepts and practical applications. I particularly enjoy the way important concepts are emphasized with examples and empirical findings. The book makes it easy for me to explain how I believe the world should work, and how it actually does. It also offers way to analyze and explain any differences, all with flawless presentation and clear and concise writing."

Andrey Pavlov
Professor of Finance
Beedie School of Business

“Linneman’s text stimulates real analysis, as opposed to just number-crunching. It takes students above and beyond the mechanics of entering data into a spreadsheet and challenges them to think logically and economically about the unique aspects of the commercial real estate market. The combination of the text, the supplemental material and the pre-requisite sections provides a complete package for students at all levels.”

Andrea J. Heuson
Professor of Finance
University of Miami

"Dr. Linneman's book covers commercial real estate from both a macro and micro view. It informs the real estate decision from basic property level modeling, due diligence, and market analysis, through the complexities of finance and the capital markets... I tell my students to keep the book for future reference long after they have finished the class. My students are very complimentary of Dr. Linneman's writing style and the breadth of topics.”

Jerome Sanzo
Adjunct Professor
Shack Institute of Real Estate
New York University

“I’ve now had an opportunity to use Peter’s textbook for teaching graduate level courses in Real Estate Private Equity and Real Estate Structured Finance. In both cases, the book served as an excellent primer on general real estate concepts, in addition to providing in depth analysis of such topics as asset valuation, deal structuring and real estate capital market considerations. The supplemental articles provided great context for discussing the lessons of class, giving the students a much more complete perspective on our industry and it’s unique challenges.”

Thomas Burton
Alex. Brown Realty, Inc.
Adjunct Professor, University of Maryland

“Peter Linneman presents the material in a clear manner, minimizing the use of jargon. The book becomes easy to read and apply, whether among practitioners or advanced graduate students.”

Peter Chinloy
Kogod School of Business
American University

"The Linneman book takes a common sense approach and is an ideal tool for the student interested in building a career in real estate investment and finance".

Richard Powers
Yale College

“Our industry is dynamic, rapidly changing and in need of sound fundamental instruction. Dr. Linneman understands and articulates how sound real estate theory and application collide to make us profitable professionals. His text provides the “must know”, tremendous insight into the “should know” and the occasional “glad I know now”. A must use (and apply) for any real estate professional.”

Daniel Thomas
Partner, St. John Properties, Inc.
Adjunct Professor, University of Baltimore

"It is an excellent textbook that applies the theoretical concepts to the real world with very insightful examples. When looking at the existing textbooks, one is often left with a feeling of being unsure as to how to proceed with actual investment decisions. Quite the contrary here; this textbook fills a huge gap in this respect."

Dr. Martin Hoesli
University of Geneva

"I enjoy using this book because it is straightforward and not afraid to tackle nuances that are often ignored, such as problems with using cap rates to evaluate hotel investments. The structure also allows you to teach at multiple levels within the same class. Topics are covered succinctly in a nuts-and-bolts manner; but there are supplemental chapters that bring more complex analyses within the context of historic events and current markets."

Glenn Williamson
Amber Real Estate LLC
Adjunct Professor, Georgetown University

"Peter Linneman's text is unique in that it teaches students to apply logic and common sense to their quantitative analysis of real estate. I am not aware of any other textbook that does this better. By the end of the course my students were able to analyze and make good judgment calls in complicated real estate case studies. Several have reported back that they are applying the practical tools and skills they acquired in the course to their jobs and internships. Analyzing the risks and opportunities the way Linneman does is what it is all about."

Irene Z. McFarland
Edward J. Bloustein School of Planning and Public Policy
Rutgers, The State University of New Jersey

"The new edition is a great improvement – it incorporates a lot of material that I used supplements for last time...Overall, the tone and level are exactly what I was looking for – something that respects quantitative analysis and explains it clearly while encouraging students to understand its limits."

Marshall Tracht
New York Law School

"I think the new edition of Dr. Linneman's book is an excellent textbook...in commercial real estate investment and finance. It is concise (no-nonsense), easy to read, merging seamlessly the industry practice with academic discipline in a logical way. I found the real world examples and cases refreshing."

Peng (Peter) Liu
Cornell University

"This is the preeminent book on real estate fundamental analysis. It is essential reading."

Amachie K. Ackah
Managing Partner, Argosy Real Estate

"The book contains excellent case studies and examples that are very relevant and insightful for the students. The case studies are very well developed, and illustrate the integration of theories and real world applications."

Tien Foo Sing
National University of Singapore

"Let me compliment you on its clarity and simplicity - a welcome carryover from the second edition. I cannot emphasize that enough because that is what is missing in most real estate texts. Adding contemporary sketches (your articles) about the most recent situation (sub-prime mortgage crisis, etc...) is equally important. It gives the reader a sense of reality and reveals that you and the text are up-do-date."

Alex Garvin
Yale University

"Not surprisingly in view of Peter's experience, this book combines the discipline and breadth of a top scholar, with the feel and judgment of a top industry professional. The book is well written and students will enjoy its style, clear examples, and logical presentation of challenging material."

-Brent Ambrose
Kentucky Real Estate Professor
Gatton College of Business and Economics, University of Kentucky

"This book offers students a rare glimpse into the tools and decision making of real estate finance. Its straightforward exposition allows one to grasp the challenges facing real estate investors, and provides them with an excellent foundation upon which to build their careers. This book will be required reading for new real estate professionals for many years to come."

-Dean Adler
Principal, Lubert-Adler Real Estate Funds

"Dr. Linneman's text has drawn the much needed line between the theoretical world and the real world. The text applies the necessary theory with a large dose of reality. It is concise, well written and the 'real world' examples are invaluable. Students and professionals will profit from this book for many years to come."

-Coleman Rector
Principal, The Rector Companies
Johns Hopkins University, Professor of Real Estate Investments

"It resolves the tension between the "tower" and "street" perspectives as well as any treatment of real estate investment to date. Moreover, it offers any reader—advanced or neophyte—an indispensable guide to enlightened analysis."

-George A. Overstreet
McIntire School of Commerce, University of Virginia

Permissions to Re-print

Chapter 2 Supplement A: International Real Estate Investing reprinted with the permission from the *Wharton Real Estate Review*.

Chapter 4 Supplement A: The Connection Between Capital and Physical markets: Drivers of Real Estate reprinted with the permission from Immobilien Manager Verlag and IMV GmbH & Co. KG.

Chapter 6 Supplement A: Forecasting 2020 U.S. Country and MSA Populations reprinted with the permission from Albert Saiz and the *Wharton Real Estate Review*.

Chapter 6 Supplement B: Regional Growth Variability reprinted with the permission from Deborah Moy and the *Wharton Real Estate Review*.

Chapter 7 Supplement A: A Disconnect in Real Estate Pricing? reprinted with the permission from the *Wharton Real Estate Review*.

Chapter 7 Supplement B: The Equitization of Real Estate reprinted with permission from the *Wharton Real Estate Review*.

Chapter 7 Supplement C: How Should Commercial Real Estate be Priced? reprinted with permission from the *Wharton Real Estate Review*.

Chapter 9 Supplement A: Construction Costs reprinted with permission from Linneman Associates.

Chapter 9 Supplement B: Constructions Costs reprinted with permission from Linneman Associates.

Chapter 14 Supplement A: How We Got to the Credit Crisis reprinted with permission from Linneman Associates.

Chapter 14 Supplement B: The Capital Markets Dissarray reprinted with permission from the *Wharton Real Estate Review*.

Chapter 17 Supplement A: Revisiting Return Profiles of Real Estate Investment Vehicles reprinted with permission from Linneman Associates.

Chapter 17 Supplement B: Understanding the Return Profiles of Real Estate Investment Vehicles reprinted with permission from Deborah Moy and the *Wharton Real Estate Review*.

Chapter 18 Supplement A: The Forces Changing the Real Estate Industry Forever reprinted with permission from the Wharton Real Estate Center.

Chapter 18 Supplement B: The Forces Changing the Real Estate Industry Forever; 5 years later reprinted with permission from the *Wharton Real Estate Review*.

Chapter 19 Supplement A: A New Look at the Homeownership Decisions reprinted with permission from the *Housing Finance Review*.

Chapter 19 Supplement B: Evaluating the Decision to Own Corporate Real Estate reprinted with permission from the *Wharton Real Estate Review*.

Chapter 20 Supplement A: Is This the Worst Ever? reprinted with permission from Linneman Associates.

Chapter 20 Supplement B: Is This the Worst Ever Yet? reprinted with permission from Linneman Associates.

Chapter 20 Supplement C: Will We Need More Office Space? reprinted with permission from the *Wharton Real Estate Review*.

Chapter 21 Supplement A: Some Observations on Real Estate Entrepreneurship reprinted with permission from the *Wharton Real Estate Review*.

Supplemental I Supplement A: The Return Volatility of Publicly and Privately Owned Real Estate reprinted with permission from the *Wharton Real Estate Review*.

Chapter 1
Introduction: Risks and Opportunities

"Saying 'no' is as important as saying 'yes', only tougher".
-Dr. Peter Linneman

RISK AND OPPORTUNITY – THAT'S WHAT IT'S ALL ABOUT

Real estate finance is all about risk and opportunity. There is never opportunity without risks. The value of a property is fundamentally an assessment of the associated risks and opportunities. What happens if everything goes according to plan? More importantly, what can go wrong and what do you do when it does? Identifying the relevant risks and answering such questions will dominate your analysis. While spreadsheets and math will be required, these tools cannot make judgments about risks and opportunities any more than a hammer or saw can decide what type of building to build. There are many "wrong answers", but there is no single "right answer", as different investors have different operating skills and risk profiles. So if you are seeking the "the right decision", look elsewhere.

Suppose you are faced with the opportunity to invest in an office building, Felicitas Tower, leased to the US government for 10 years. Based on your analysis you estimate that net cash flow will be about $3 million each year of the lease. How do you assess what the property is worth? If you have a financial background, you will immediately turn to discounted cash flow analysis (DCF). So you select a discount rate, discount each year's expected net cash flow to the present, and choose a terminal value. Given that this is a 10-year lease to the US government, the 10-year Treasury rate might seem like an appropriate discount rate. But how does the risk of investing in this building differ from that of a 10-year Treasury note? Would you rather own the Treasury note or Felicitas Tower, assuming your annual cash flow projections for both investments were the same? Will your cash flow estimates prove to be accurate? What happens when the current lease expires in 10 years? And what is the discount rate?

Always utilize a risk and opportunity framework in addressing such questions. What risks and opportunities are unique to Felicitas Tower versus your investment alternatives? Are you operationally situated to deal with unexpected challenges?

THE RISKS

Things can happen that you could never imagine. Planes do crash into the mall courtyard two days before Christmas, seemingly great credit tenants like Lehman Brothers, Arthur Anderson, and Enron can disintegrate overnight, and energy prices have doubled in a year, and sometimes these all happen at once.

Operating Cost: You could experience an unexpected increase in operating costs which would decrease the building's net cash flows below your expectations. Utilities, property taxes, maintenance salaries, insurance, and numerous other costs are likely to fluctuate throughout the life of the lease. Although specific contractual lease terms may alleviate some of this risk, you may be unable to pass all operating cost risk to the tenant. And no matter how carefully you analyze these costs, I promise you that your forecasts will be wrong. But "wrong" does not necessarily mean your analysis is meaningless. It just means that you must understand the actual outcomes are not as certain as they appear to be on your beautiful and beloved spreadsheet.

Vacancy: Your income is highly dependent on the US government performing on the lease. There may be intricate wording in the lease — a thick and detailed document — which provides the government with relief from its lease obligation. If the government is the sole tenant and leaves, you face zero income for weeks, months, and perhaps even years. How fast can you re-lease the space if the government is able to get out of the lease and decides to leave? Will you be able to obtain equal or better terms from a new tenant? Will the new tenant require you to remodel or reconfigure the space?

Natural Disaster: Although it may seem remote, there is a chance that a natural disaster may substantially damage the building. In such a case, depending on the lease, you could face zero to significantly reduced income streams. In addition, you will have to spend time and money to renovate the property. For this reason it is particularly important to know whether the space is in a hurricane path or a flood zone. Since property and casualty insurance can reduce the impacts of disasters, you must also evaluate the property's insurance coverage. And in some events, such as terrorist attacks, insurance may be too expensive to realistically purchase.

Leasing: What happens at the end of ten years? With a US Treasury note you get your money back with certainty. With the building you must either extend the government's lease or find another tenant. If you cannot find a suitable tenant, you receive zero income until you successfully re-lease the building.

Liquidity: The building is far less liquid than a government bond. You can sell Treasury bonds in minutes for a small fee, while selling the building may cost you 3% in fees and take 6-8 months. What if you need capital in a hurry? How quickly do you think you could sell the building? What will the real estate market look like when you are ready to sell? All too often, when you are under pressure to sell it is because there is a shortage of interested capital. Thus you run the risk that your attempt to sell will occur in a distressed market.

This is far from a complete listing of the risks associated with the building, yet you can see that the risk is greater for owning the property than for a 10-year US Treasury note.

THE OPPORTUNITIES

On the other hand, while there is no cash flow upside in holding a US Treasury note for 10 years, there may be opportunities to enhance the cash flow from the building.

Operating Costs: You may be able to exploit your management expertise to lower the cost of operating the property, thereby increasing your cash flows. There may also be potential operating cost synergies between this property and other real estate you own.

Terminal Value: The value of the building at the end of the lease may appreciate as a result of economic growth or general inflation, allowing you to sell the property for a considerable profit. Or you may be able to re-lease the property to the government or another tenant for more favorable terms at the end of the initial lease.

Rental Growth: The lease may provide mechanisms to increase total rental payments over the course of the lease. Instead of $3 million per year for 10 years, the lease may call for 3% annual rental increases. Such increasing cash flows need to be factored into your analysis.

Although there are many additional opportunities for increasing the realized return, you can see that the opportunity is greater for owning Felicitas Tower than holding a US Treasury note for 10 years.

Since the property has a greater upside and a greater downside than the 10-year Treasury note, you need to adjust the discount rate accordingly. Conceptually the "right" discount rate to use is always the rate which is reflective of the risk of the anticipated cash flows. How many basis points (100 basis points equal 1 percentage point) you must add to the 10-year Treasury rate is based upon your assessment of the likelihood of the property's risks. But there is no magical website or formula that will tell you the "right" number to use as the discount rate for an office property leased to the US Government for 10 years. If you think the risks are minimal and you are certain you will never sell the building, then you do not require a much higher discount rate than the Treasury rate to offset the added risks of owning the building. By using a low discount rate, you will impute a higher value, and submit a higher bid, increasing your opportunity to acquire the property. Of course, you also increase the risk of overpaying for the building if unexpected negative events occur. Are you right for using the lower discount rate and offering a higher bid? Only time will tell.

On the other hand, you may demand significant compensation for the additional risks of the property. In this case, you will use a notably higher discount rate, and offer a lower price for the building, running the risk of losing the building to a competing bidder. Is this the wise move? Again, only time will provide the answer. Figure 1.1 displays how various discount rates can drastically alter the value of a property.

FIGURE 1.1

Property: Kuo Office						
	Year 1	Year 2	Year 3	Year 4	Year 5	Year 6
Annual Rental Income	$3,000,000	$3,180,000	$3,370,800	$3,573,048	$3,787,431	$4,014,677
Terminal Value (sale of Kuo Office)	$0	$0	$0	$0	$0	$36,497,061
Value if Discounted at 0%	$57,423,017					
Value if Discounted at 3%	$49,364,457					
Value if Discounted at 8%	$38,913,190					
Value if Discounted at 12%	$32,557,251					

Going back to the Felicitas Tower investment opportunity, how would your analysis change if the tenant was a startup company instead of the US government, even if all of the financial terms of the lease were the same? What additional risk and opportunities are associated with this tenancy? To start with, you have to assess tenant credit risk. Will the tenant pay on time? Will the tenant default on the lease? If so, will you be able to re-lease the property for similar terms? How long will it take you to re-lease the space? What costs do you incur when re-leasing the space? You must measure the discount rate based on your assessment of these additional risks as the US government is clearly a better credit tenant. How many basis points should you add? Only you can decide. As you gain experience and expertise you will become better at assessing these risks and opportunities. As this occurs, you will become more accurate in your assessment of value.

WHERE YOU SHOULD FOCUS YOUR ANALYSIS

Now that you know how to think about selecting a discount rate, and realize that there is no magical valuation website, what should you spend time trying to calculate: the future cash flows or the discount rate you apply to those cash flows? The answer is, of course, both. But at the margin, focus on understanding the expected future cash flows. You need to know what can happen at the property, and understand how the property generates its cash streams. After all, how can you analyze the risks of a business if you do not understand the business? Carefully exploring future cash flows is nothing more than trying to understand the business and its risks. Therefore, choose your discount rate wisely, but do not get infatuated with discount rate selection.

Understanding expected future cash flows also helps you understand why you may fail to meet your cash flow projections. This will make you focus on what you will do if the property does not meet your cash flow expectations. You should focus primarily on the downside, because if the property does better than expected, trust me, you will be able to cope with it. Even more important than your cash flow projections, and certainly more important than the discount rate selection, is understanding why things may fail to go according to plan, and what will happen when this occurs. This, and being able to say "no", is what makes a great real estate investor.

MARKET RESEARCH

One of the most important elements of underwriting the purchase, sale, or development of a property is to carefully analyze the market's supply and demand balance. These supply and demand conditions provide the backbone for assumptions about future rents, cost recoveries, marketing costs, time required to lease vacant space, the vacancy rate, operating costs, and ancillary income opportunities.

Focusing first on supply, it is essential that you conduct a detailed evaluation of properties in the market place. What are their strengths and weaknesses? How are they priced? Are they experiencing increasing vacancy? Are their tenants satisfied? Why? Are major leases about to expire at these properties? Have new tenants entered the market? Which tenants have become too large (or too small) for their current space? What ancillary income are owners achieving? What design features and amenity packages at these premises do tenants value most? Least? What marketing techniques are attracting customers? What leasing commissions are they paying brokers? What are their typical tenant improvements (TI) and concession packages? Can these properties be expanded or easily modified to meet additional demand?

In addition, you must carefully check what new properties and property expansions are underway, as well as what building permits have been granted and are soon to be granted. Talk to local brokers and bankers in order to assess who has tentative plans for new properties in the market. Are major property renovations or repositionings anticipated? Which of these projects are most likely to come to fruition, and which are probably pipe dreams? While doing this homework, never forget that talk is cheap, but bricks and mortar are very expensive.

When investigating a property site, aerial photography can help identify other sites which are available for competitive product, as well as provide a perspective on local land use patterns. For larger projects, you may want to helicopter over the area, in order to better understand traffic flows and development patterns. Study the past 30-40 years of local development, in order to see what directions development is going, and at what speed. Figures 1.2 – 1.7 display the development patterns of the rapidly growing Las Vegas metropolitan area over the past 55 years. You need to understand the local zoning ordinances and politics, in order to assess whether new product is easily brought online, and if so, where, and by whom. Carefully assess planned traffic and infrastructure improvements, as well as where the utility backbone extends. Assess whether state or local tax incentives are available to you, your competitors, or key tenants.

FIGURE 1.2

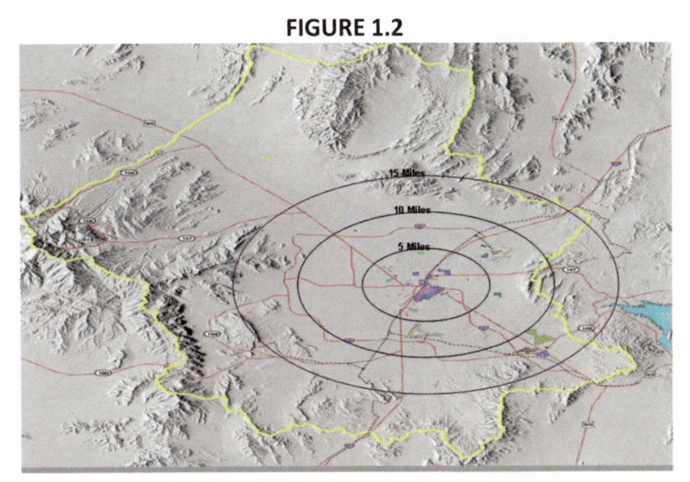

Las Vegas Development – 1950 – 6,906 Acres

FIGURE 1.3

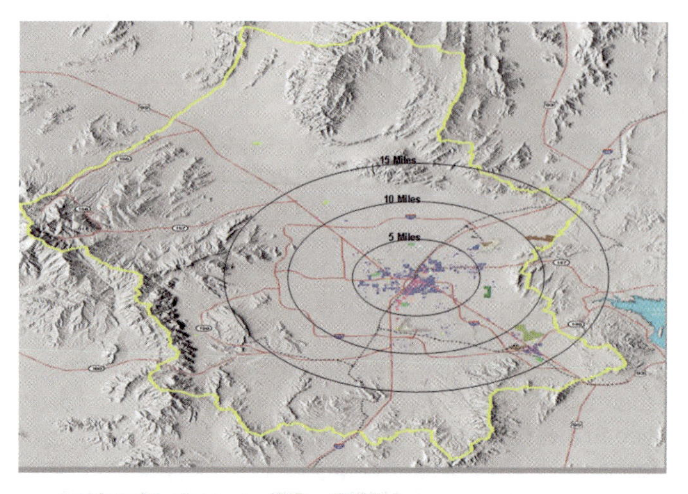

Las Vegas Development – 1960 – 12,972 Acres

FIGURE 1.4

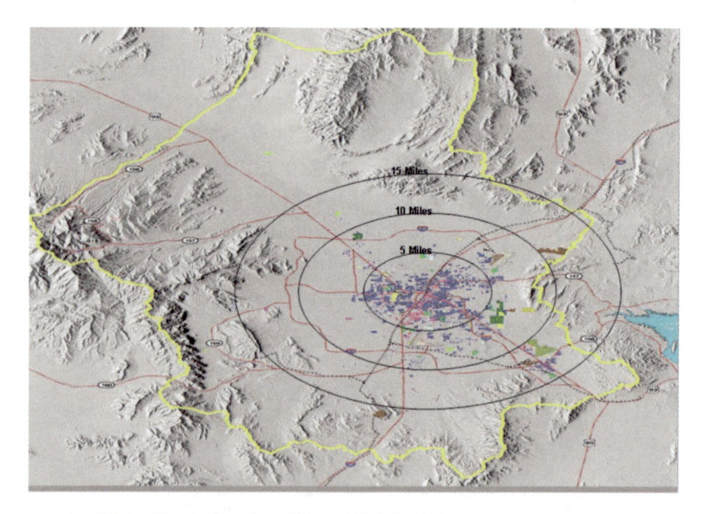

Las Vegas Development – 1970 – 28,211 Acres

FIGURE 1.5

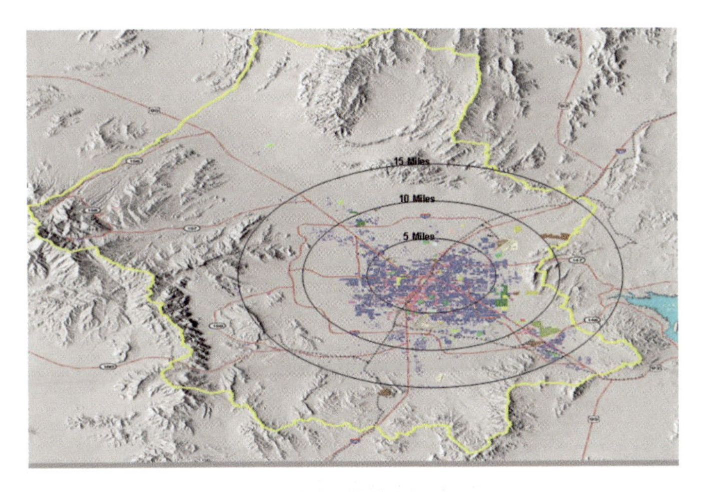

Las Vegas Development – 1980 – 48,250 Acres

FIGURE 1.6

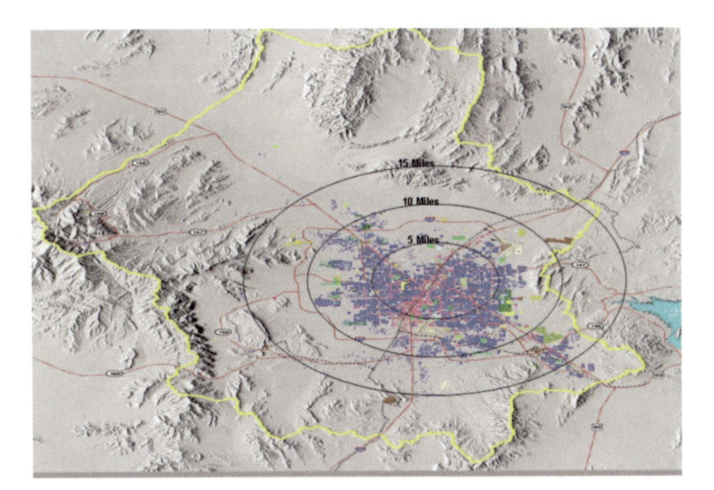

Las Vegas Development – 1990 – 71,630 Acres

FIGURE 1.7

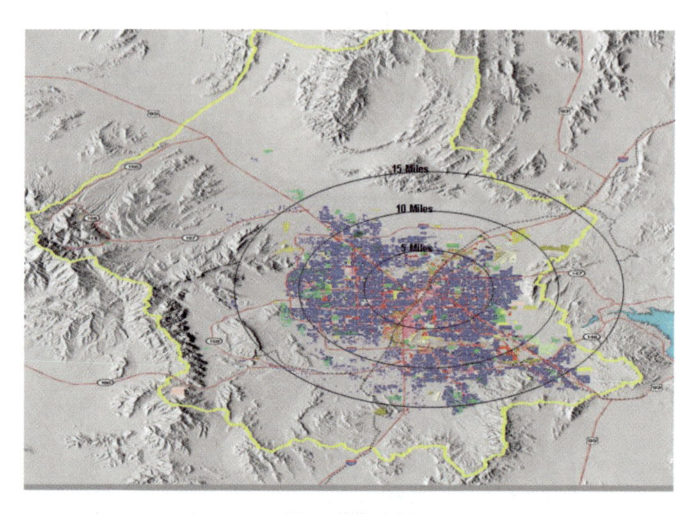

Las Vegas Development – 2003 – 129,752 Acres

Turning to the market demand, do you have a major tenant "in your pocket" that can fill vacant space? Has a major competitor of your tenants, such as Wal-Mart, recently moved into the area? If not, can they easily do so? Where? When? What adjustments can you make at reasonable cost to the property, in order to attract tenants? What design and amenities can you use to more effectively market your property? How do the signage, ingress, and egress aspects of your property compare with others? How do the operating costs, design, and technological capacities of your property compare to competitive properties? Can you increase rents and still remain competitively priced?

In addition, you should study the fundamentals of local, regional, and national growth. To this end, you can utilize research publications such as The Linneman Letter and Rosen Consulting Group analyses to evaluate if, and why, the area will grow, and how it is affected by national and international economic forces, to better assess the risks to the property. Who are the major local employers? Are they growing? What major challenges do they face in their businesses? What type of space do these tenants use? Ask brokers about unhappy tenants looking to relocate. Can their business support the increases in rental costs you project and still remain competitive in their industry?

Always extensively drive and walk your market. Understand who lives in the area, and whether the market is moving up, down, or sideways. The cars in the neighborhood generally provide an excellent predictor of the residents' economic status. In addition, you may purchase a more detailed local market study. But be wary of people selling "the next big thing", as supply frequently has been put in place over the years in anticipation of "next big things" that never happened. Evaluate why projects have failed in your market, as well as why they have succeeded. Ask yourself whether you can provide tenants something better, cheaper, or faster than your competition. If you can, your property will probably succeed over the long term.

Read all available market reports and analysis of competitors. The advent of publicly traded real estate has greatly increased the quality and quantity of such information, as some of your competitors may be public companies. But remember that such information is often conflicting or merely promoting faddish ideas (remember dotcom research?), and is never a substitute for informed judgment.

The best way to know a particular market is to devote your career to a specific product type and geography. Get to the point where literally nothing happens in your market without you knowing about it well before it happens. Obtaining market knowledge is not glamorous, but it pays handsome returns for the diligent. But never forget that there is no shortcut to understanding a market. Becoming a real estate professional entails becoming expert at answering the many questions we have raised, rather than just "assuming" answers. I am frequently asked "is it alright to assume...?" and I respond by saying you can assume whatever you want, but you will ultimately be judged on the accuracy and defensibility of your assumptions.

PERSONAL DECISION

Your investment decision ultimately depends upon who you are, how much risk you are willing and able to take, what expertise and cost synergies you bring to the deal, and your investment goals and experiences. Figures 1.8 - 1.11 provide examples of how personal choices and perspectives can drive real estate investment decisions. Each graph displays the probability distributions of expected returns for four distinct real estate investments. Each of these investments has an expected annual return of 15%. That is, the "pro forma (projected) numbers" for each of these investments are the same, namely a 15% annual return. But the investments are vastly different in terms of the likelihood of the numbers occurring. Consider the unique risk and return profiles of these four investment opportunities. Depending on your expertise, balance sheet, risk preference, experience, and deal flow, these 15% return deals may or may not appeal to you.

Property 1 (*Figure 1.8*), Henderson Office Park, is a fully leased property with a large number of high quality tenants, with lease expirations occurring smoothly over a 20 year horizon. This property offers a 15% expected annual return, with a relatively symmetric chance that the property will perform above and below expectations. The vast majority of the expected return outcomes for this property are very close to the expected return. Finally, this property offers relatively little chance of losing money.

FIGURE 1.8

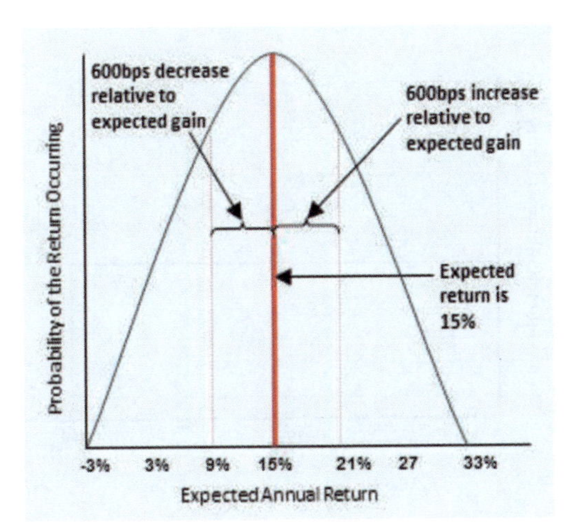

Property 2 (*Figure 1.9*), Jessica Distribution Center, is a build-to-suit property with a long term lease. The tenant has low credit quality, but is growing fast. The property, which also has an expected 15% annual return, basically offers three return outcomes. In *Scenario 1,* the tenant goes out of business and no one else wants to lease the space. In *Scenario 2,* the tenant goes out of business, but you are able to re-lease the space, although at less favorable terms. In *Scenario 3,* the tenant prospers, renews their lease, allowing you to reduce operating costs by

not having additional lease up costs. While the overall expected return is 15%, the return distribution offers a substantial chance that you will lose money, but also a greater upside than Property 1.

FIGURE 1.9

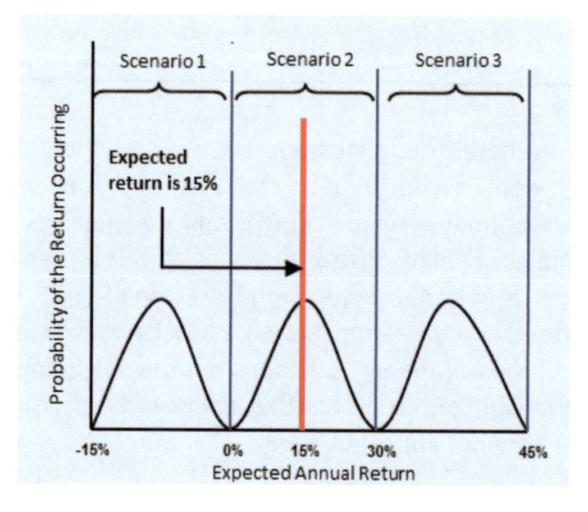

Property 3 (*Figure 1.10*), Celina Gardens, also offers an expected 15% annual return. It is an apartment project located in a "frontier" location with relatively little operating history for your product. Since there is little information that you can use to determine the expected returns, the property seems to offer a fairly uniform opportunity of success and failure. In this case the property offers greater chances of both substantial success and failure than either Property 1 or 2, with less opportunity for mediocre performance.

FIGURE 1.10

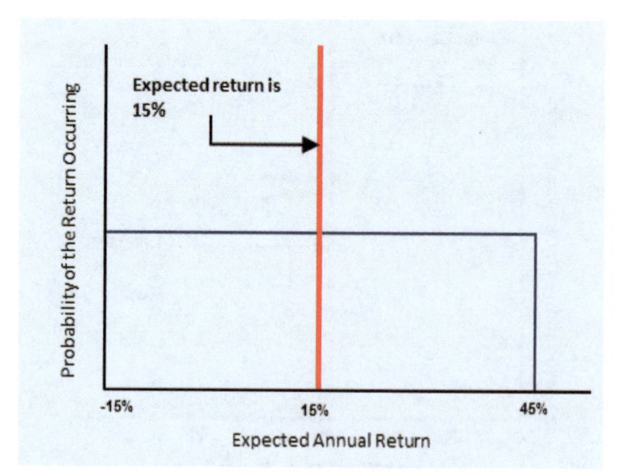

Property 4 (*Figure 1.11*), Leslie Center, is a complicated mixed use property that you hope will revolutionize the market. The property, which also has an expected annual return of 15%, presents two very distinct outcomes. Under *Scenario 2*, the market loves the product and it is a huge success, while under *Scenario 1* the market essentially rejects the product and you may lose a lot of money. But if it succeeds, it makes more money than the other properties.

FIGURE 1.11

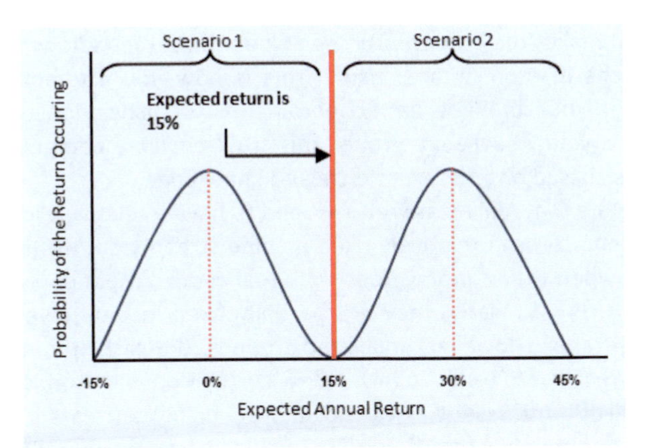

Which of these pro forma "15% return" investments is best for you? Note, these investments look the same based on pro forma returns, but offer radically different real estate and investment propositions. Which, if any, of these investments you make depends on who you are, your investment goals, and your operating expertise. What is right for you will often be wrong for another investor. Never think that the numbers can make investment decisions for you. A mastery of "the numbers" is important, but merely the starting point for investment analysis. So learn how to do "the numbers", but understand that it is just (barely) the beginning.

RISK PARAMETERIZATION

What differentiates these four return distributions for the different properties is not the expected return, but their risk profile around the expected return. Normally, financial economists parameterize investment risk by using the covariance of the return for the asset with the broader set of investable instruments and the standard deviation of the asset's return. While these concepts are appropriate, they are of little assistance to you in evaluating any specific real estate investment. Why not? First, to summarize an investment's risk by its covariance and standard deviation of the expected returns assumes that the returns have a Gaussian Normal Distribution. But as is obvious in our four examples, most real estate deals do not have Normal return distributions. Thus, in our examples the standard deviations and covariances are not sufficient to summarize risks of the investments, as the return distributions are not Normal. This problem is further exacerbated for properties with return distributions that are non-continuous, asymmetric, and highly skewed.

An additional difficulty of utilizing the covariance and standard deviation of returns to summarize risk is that it is almost always impossible to calculate these statistics for most real estate investments. Unlike stocks and bonds, which have long measured return histories which one can use to estimate these risk measures, a typical real estate investment lacks the return history with which to parameterize either the standard deviation or covariance. The problem in this case is not a conceptual one, but a practical one.

A further challenge is that the expected return, the distribution of positive returns, and the covariance of returns with assets can change quickly and dramatically. For example, in the early 1990s and 2007 – 2009 the expected returns for all assets plummeted at the same time due to soaring risk premiums relative to government bonds. As a result, even assets with historically low covariance suddenly experienced near perfect covariance as well as plunging expected returns and much larger left tails in terms of return outcomes. In short, risk is not a fixed concept but rather an ever-changing reality.

As a result, while the notions of standard deviation and covariance as measures of risk are useful intuitions to bear in mind, as a real estate investor you must rely on less parametric analyses of risk. This includes addressing questions like: what makes the property succeed? Can it weather a downturn in the economy? What if a tenant leaves? What happens if interest rates rise? This is how you attempt to measure the risk of the investment. Never forget that your brain is an extraordinarily sophisticated computer, as well as a great synthesizer of information. As your knowledge grows, this truly portable computer becomes more and more sophisticated and calculates risk based on your experience and knowledge.

Bearing this in mind, note that real estate returns tend to have a relatively low correlation with stocks and bonds. This is because they tend to have relatively fixed income streams due to the contractual nature of their lease obligations. As a result, when the economy does well, real estate responds with a lag, as leases expire and renew. The converse is also true. Similarly, they are partially fixed income investments and like a bond are somewhat sensitive to interest rates. However, unlike most bonds, the cash streams and residual value tend to rise with inflation. Therefore, real estate tends to have a low correlation with bonds. But never forget that when capital seeks extreme safety, all of these asset classes become very highly correlated.

It is also important to remember that if you are in the real estate business, you are in the business of taking real estate risks. It is your expertise and core competency. As such, you may want diversification, but that is a luxury afforded primarily to passive investors. As a real estate professional, your business is to exploit your expertise, even though it may not keep you as diversified as you would like. For example, if you have $2 million in capital available to you, and the typical project you specialize in requires $2 million to execute, you will not have enough money to be both diversified and execute the project. Does this fly in the face of portfolio theory? As an investment matter, yes. But it is consistent with the exploitation of your competitive advantage. That is, exploit your core competency, and in doing so maximize your profits.

There is generally a conflict between the desire to diversify your portfolio and exploiting your expertise. You cannot do all the deals you evaluate, even if they are attractive on a risk-return basis. You do not have enough capital, manpower, and resources available. Therefore, you strive to determine which deals deserve a "no", not only because they may have negative net present values, but also because they do not most effectively utilize your skills and meet your investment objectives.

CLOSING THOUGHT

Becoming a successful real estate investor comes very slowly. It is a process of making decisions, dealing with the consequences, and hopefully learning from the experience. You will start your career making relatively small investments because the capital available to you will be limited due to your lack of sophistication and experience. As you become more sophisticated, develop your expertise, become better at managing risks, and learn how to generate returns even when things go wrong, you will find that you will be able to attract a larger investor base and are able to take on larger and more sophisticated deals. Real estate investing is a career rather than a one-time event; a marathon, not a sprint. So if you want to be a successful real estate professional, patience and learning when to say "no" will be your greatest allies.

Chapter 2
What is Real Estate?

"Overnight success almost always took 10-25 years".
-Dr. Peter Linneman

REAL ESTATE IS ABOUT SPACE

Before you can begin to analyze real estate investments, you must gain an understanding of space. How big is the Empire State building? How big is your home, apartment, or the local mall? Figure 2.1 lists typical square footages for several property types.

FIGURE 2.1

Type of Property	Square Feet*
2 Bedroom suburban garden	900 - 1,100
1 Bedroom suburban garden	650 - 850
Typical regional mall	750,000 - 1,250,000
A strip mall	125,000 - 200,000
An acre	43,560
Small studio apartment	500
One floor of a large high-rise	15,000 - 20,000

* The square feet numbers refer to the average area, individual properties will differ significantly

You have been involved with real estate your entire life. Every building and piece of land is owned by someone, with properties such as parks and national forests owned by governments. Other properties are owned by churches and not-for-profit organizations. The office building, hotel, warehouse, and empty building you walked past today are generally owned by for-profit owners.

You should become aware of the different classifications of properties, their design features, and what makes a building good. Walk around with an inquisitive eye: how does your dorm room work, does the supermarket have an efficient floor plan, where do people congregate at the mall, and how does the strip center where you rent movies work?

LAND

Land is perhaps the most basic type of real estate. Greenfield land is undeveloped land, such as farm or pasture. Infill land is located in the city, and generally has already been developed but now it is vacant. Brownfields are parcels of land that had an industrial use and may be environmentally impaired.

Be cautious before developing land, as you would rather have land not generating income, than the extra cost of a non-productive building on top of the land. People often use surface parking lots to generate some revenue while land awaits development. Similarly, cattle grazing flea markets and Christmas markets operate on vacant land in order to generate some cash flow to offset the carrying costs (insurance and tax costs) of vacant land.

The size and location of a parcel of land are important in determining its developability. A common phenomenon in urban areas is that at an earlier point in history someone held out and large buildings were built on either side of the parcel, so nothing functional can be built on the parcel unless one of the adjacent buildings is demolished.

FIGURE 2.2

Brownfield Site

Greenfield Site

RETAIL PROPERTIES

A second type of property is **strip retail centers (strip centers)**. Strip centers may be anchored or unanchored. Having an anchor means the center has one or more large retail stores, such as Walmart, Publix, or Safeway, that attracts customers to the center. Unanchored strips lack such anchors, and are combinations of small stores, ranging from 600-10,000 square feet. Unanchored strip centers have tenants like nail salons, Chinese restaurants, video rental shops, pet grooming salons, dentists, etc. These centers range from 10,000 square feet to about 200,000 square feet. Strip centers tend to be located on major local artery roads, with good ingress and egress. Although a center may be well located, if you are unable to enter or exit the center easily, or you can only enter from a single entrance or direction, its value will be reduced due to its inaccessibility.

Anchored strip centers tend to be larger than unanchored centers because the anchors require a lot of space and are complemented by smaller tenants. You frequently find supermarket anchored strips. Anchor supermarkets typically run 30,000-70,000 square feet, either in the shape of a rectangle or an L. The anchor supermarket will generally have signage visible near the entrance of the center. Anchored centers are generally 50,000-300,000 square feet. Stand alone centers have a single store such as Walmart, Target, or Kmart with no other stores. Often strip centers have **out parcels**, with tenants such as fast food restaurants or a local bank branch located separately and apart from the strip and close to the street. These out parcels may be managed/owned independently from the rest of the center.

FIGURE 2.3

Strip Center with Safeway Anchor

Community retail centers are generally 150,000-350,000 square feet. These centers have several anchors, such as a supermarket and a drugstore, as well as several specialty stores such as Foot Locker and smaller inline stores. These can be laid out as a single center, or as two or three contiguous strip centers. Restaurants will generally be part of the center. These centers are located on local artery roads with excellent ingress and egress, near interstate highway exits.

FIGURE 2.4

Community retail center

A **power center** has few inline stores, but has 3-5 major box retailers such as a Wal-Mart, Home Depot, Fresh Foods, or Staples. These boxes generally are 30,000-200,000 square feet each. The center may also contain out parcels.

There are also individually owned downtown shops. A major problem with such properties is that each shop is interested in maximizing their profit, rather than maximizing the profits for the entire retail environment. In contrast, a shopping center attempts to maximize the entire shopping experience through complementary tenancy, design, shared amenities, and common area maintenance (CAM). As a result, shopping centers are generally a more productive retail format in terms of sales than downtown shops, as they are able to create and internalize positive externalities.

FIGURE 2.5

Power center ground

Power center air

Regional malls run 400,000-2,000,000 square feet and usually have 2-6 anchor stores. These anchors are typically department stores such as Sears, Penny's, and Macy's, as well as big boxes like Barnes & Noble. Mall anchors are generally 60,000-120,000 square feet and may extend one or more levels. The mall is populated with inline stores between the anchors. The strategy is that the anchors draw customers to the center, while the complementary inline stores of 600-12,000 square feet create a rich retailing environment.

FIGURE 2.6

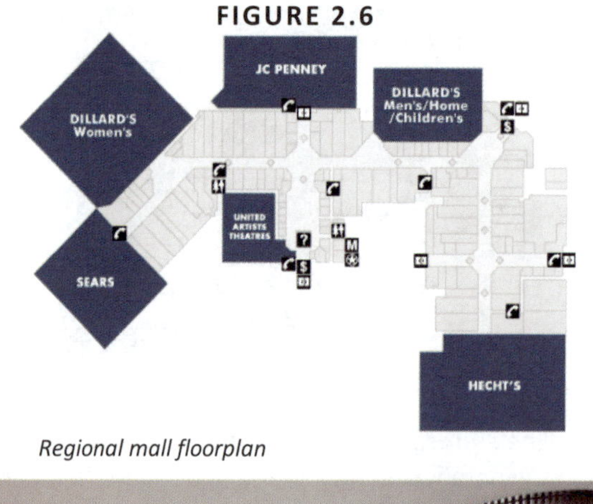

Regional mall floorplan

Regional mall interior

WAREHOUSE AND INDUSTRIAL PROPERTIES

Warehouse properties are used for storage. These are generally simple physical structures, but they may have demanding specifications in terms of floor slope, dust in the air, cooling, humidity, ceiling height and loading dock design. Key design issues are clear height for ceilings and the ease of entry and exit of the property. Clear height is the lowest vertical space which exists without any obstruction such as lights or support beams. A clear height of 30 feet is preferred by large tenants who utilize forklifts to move pallets.

Heavy manufacturing facilities are generally special purpose properties. They are really more of a piece of equipment than a piece of real estate, except for the location dimension. For example, if you own a Kraft cheese manufacturing facility, you will not have an easy alternative use for the property without substantial renovation.

Light assembly space combines warehouse, product assembly, and office space, and may be multi-tenanted. Usually they are fairly simple structures that allow easy reconfiguration. These facilities are generally designed along warehouse principles, with dropped ceilings used for the office component. Light assembly structures will have some parking in front of the building to service the office space. If it is easily convertible, the structure is referred to as a **flex building**. A common construction technique for flex buildings is a slab structure that tilts up to finish the building. Such properties do very well in a strong market because of their flexibility, but in a down market get hurt because there is no shortage of superior office or warehouse space.

FIGURE 2.7

Light industrial/ office flex building

Bulk warehouses are very large buildings that range from 50,000-1,000,000 square feet. These expansive structures are located near the major transportation hubs for ease of truck access. Warehouse users focus on a cubic square footage, as stacking height is critical. The buildings are typically simple rectangular designs, and face the challenges of efficiently processing large volumes of trucks in and out of the property, allowing multiple trucks to enter and exit the docks, and convenient off-loading regardless of truck height and size.

FIGURE 2.8

Warehouse interior

OFFICE PROPERTIES

Central business district (CBD) office space is usually located in a city's central corridor, and has a "Main & Main" orientation related to the transportation network, as well as historic and government nodes. Office space is loosely classified as either Class A, B, or C, but there is no definitive "grading" system. It's like judging who is tall and who is short; it is a matter of context. Someone who is short for the NBA, may be quite tall relative to the normal population. Similarly, what is an A building in Birmingham may be a B building in New York. Be careful when reading reports reporting how much space is Class A, as classification discrepancies frequently exist.

Office buildings in Europe tend to be smaller, shorter, and narrower than buildings found in the US. This is for both regulatory and historical reasons. European highrises also generally have small floorplates, often only 4,000-10,000 square feet per floor. In Europe, a property's location plays a larger role in determining what is Class A than its design, age, or amenities.

A **Class A** CBD office property is relatively new, well located, with modern HVAC systems, modern electrical systems, and quality architecture. A so-called trophy would be among the top 2-3% of the Class A properties, basically the best of the best. **Class B** space is less well located, smaller, older, with fewer modern amenities, and of lesser design. **Class C** space comprises the remainder of the properties.

During a downturn, Class A buildings are generally more resilient and tend to remain better leased, as tenants move up from lesser quality buildings when rents fall. Class B and C properties tend to perform best in strong markets, by focusing on price sensitive tenants.

Class A CBD **highrises** in cities such as Chicago, Philadelphia, and New York typically have floorplates running 15,000-25,000 square feet, with 4-8 corner offices per floor. The Chevron corner design provides eight corners by notching an otherwise rectangular building. Among the challenges facing highrises are efficient vertical transportation and life safety (especially fire). In addition, highrises face security issues since the 9/11 attacks.

FIGURE 2.9

CBD office space *Chevron corners on a CBD office building*

Suburban office buildings are relatively unique to the US. Class A suburban properties tend to be new midrise structures of 80,000-400,000 square feet, with 8,000-14,000 square foot floorplates. Class B and C spaces are older and are not as well located. Suburban office parks provide a campus-like assemblage of office buildings, with the buildings sharing common amenities.

FIGURE 2.10

Suburban office building *Suburban office building*

MULTIFAMILY

Many types of multifamily property exist, including urban highrise, midrise (often infill properties), suburban garden apartments, and small properties. The primary problem with small properties is that a single unleased unit is a large portion of the property. For example, if you own a 2 unit building, you either have 0%, 50%, or 100% occupancy. Smaller properties tend to be owned by "mom and pop" operations with a "do it yourself" mentality. These properties often generate a lot of headaches to tenants due to the lack of expertise on the part of the owners.

FIGURE 2.11

Highrise multifamily *Highrise multifamily*

Suburban garden apartments began in the 1960s and 1970s, as young renters moved to the suburbs. Garden apartments are typically 3-4 story wood structures, with 50-400 units, without elevators, and surface parking. The preferred units are on the top floor because of the vaulted ceilings, or the bottom floor because you do not have to walk up stairs. The middle units tend to be the worst because you do not get vaulted ceilings yet you must walk up stairs.

FIGURE 2.12

Suburban garden apartments

Midrise apartments are 5-9 stories, steel framed, and tend to be an urban infill product. These properties have 30-110 units and are elevator serviced. In a few markets you find multifamily highrises which tend to be professionally operated and entail increased security features. Outside of the US, multifamily tends to be a less important economic property category because housing is often provided either by the government or corporations (for workers). In addition, rent controls transfer many aspects of ownership to renters. Japan is an exception, with an active rental and investment multifamily market.

FIGURE 2.13

Midrise apartments

HOTELS

There are many types of hotels. The full service category includes CBD full service, which may be a high price point operator such as a Four Seasons or Mandarin, or a mid-price point operator like Marriott. Most full service hotels provide room service, restaurants, banquet space, convention services, and food and beverage services. Full service hotels may also provide spas and limited retail.

Limited service urban hotels are usually boutique properties. The distinguishing feature for these hotels is that they are smaller, and do not offer amenities such as room service, restaurants, banquet service, or convention space. This limits overhead and tends to stabilize operating income. The major difficulty with limited service hotels is effective marketing.

The hotel business is an operating business which also involves design and location components. Success hinges on the property's flag and how well that property is operated. In the US, hotels are not generally leased, although in Europe they are frequently leased. In the US the owner either operates the hotel or hires a management company. The typical management contract requires the owner to pay the operator a fixed fee plus a percentage of gross revenues, as well as a fee for business generated by their central reservation system. As a result, if the hotel does poorly, the landlord gets killed. On the other hand, the manager (operator) does adequately even if the hotel is doing poorly. Hotel businesses are heavy fixed cost operations, and while location and design are important, value is created through superior operation.

Another category is **extended stay hotels**, which have larger rooms, small kitchens, and provide limited services. These are designed for people staying a week or more, and attempt to make guests feel like they are home.

FIGURE 2.14

Suburban hotel *Urban hotel*

REAL ESTATE IS MANY DIFFERENT INDUSTRIES

Different property types serve very different users, and require different leases, marketing, design, and engineering. This is why real estate professionals are increasingly specializing in a particular property type. Just because you are very good at marketing multifamily units to 24 year olds does not mean you are good at marketing a CBD office building to corporate America. When you are marketing a bulk warehouse facility, you must know the major manufacturing companies and understand how they operate, while for retail properties you have to know who are the hot tenants and have the clout to convince them that your property is right for them.

GROSS VS. NET LEASABLE

It is generally not possible to lease every foot of a building. Elevator shafts, mechanical space, lobbies, stairwells, and hallways cannot be leased. As a result, there is a distinction between the **gross square footage** of a property and its **net leasable square footage**. The gross square footage refers to the total area of a building, usually measured from inner wall to inner wall, with no deductions for obstructions or non-leasable space. In contrast, net leasable area refers to the floor area that can be leased.

Efficient building design attempts to minimize the loss factor, that is, the difference between gross and net leasable footage. Buildings with enormous lobbies, such as those often found in corporate headquarters, have large loss factors. Similarly, tall buildings with small floorplates have large loss factors as the elevator banks, stairwells, and support columns eat up a larger portion of the space. Faulty design will haunt a property, as once built, a large loss factor is hard to solve.

A similar concept applies to land. How much of the land is economically usable? For example, half of the property may be swampland or environmentally protected, thus limiting the economic use of the property. Also land is needed for roads, sidewalks, and retention ponds.

A property's **floor area ratio** (FAR) is the ratio of a building's above-grade gross floor area (both vertically and horizontally) to the area of the lot upon which the building is constructed. Outside the United States, some countries use the term FSI (Floor Space Index) instead of FAR. You will encounter this concept when analyzing zoning requirements. If the lot is 10,000 square feet and the FAR is one, you have the right to build a structure with one floor that is 10,000 square feet, or a two story structure with 5,000 square feet per floor, etc. Stated differently, with a FAR of one, the total gross square footage of the building cannot exceed the size of the lot. Figure 2.15 and Figure 2.16 illustrate this concept. Of course, each floor does not have to be the same size, as long as the gross square footage does not exceed the lot size multiplied by the allowed FAR.

FAR restrictions are generally accompanied by height and setback restrictions. For example, there may be a maximum allowable height for a building of 100 feet, the building must be set back at least 40 feet from the outer edge of the property boundary, and the FAR is 1.5. In many continental European countries there are also restrictions that dictate that every employee working in the property must have access to natural light. Architects and designers work to maximize a property's economic potential subject to these, and many other restrictions.

FIGURE 2.15

Floor Area Ratio (all area is in square feet)

*For all examples assume the lot size is: **10,000 sf** **10,000 sf**

FAR = 1

*Since FAR = 1, we solve the maximum square feet the structure can have by: Lot size * FAR (10,000 * 1).*

Number of Stories Structure has	1	2	3	4	5
Square Feet per floor	10,000	5,000	3,333	2,500	2,000
Total Square feet of building (Stories * SF Per Floor)	10,000	10,000	10,000	10,000	10,000

FAR = 2

*Since FAR = 2, we solve the maximum square feet the structure can have by: Lot size * FAR (10,000 * 2).*

Number of Stories Structure has	1	2	3	4	5
Square Feet per floor	20,000	10,000	6,667	5,000	4,000
Total Square feet of building (Stories * SF Per Floor)	20,000	20,000	20,000	20,000	20,000

FAR = 3

*Since FAR = 3, we solve the maximum square feet the structure can have by: Lot size * FAR (10,000 * 3).*

Number of Stories Structure has	1	2	3	4	5
Square Feet per floor	30,000	15,000	10,000	7,500	6,000
Total Square feet of building (Stories * SF Per Floor)	30,000	30,000	30,000	30,000	30,000

FIGURE 2.16

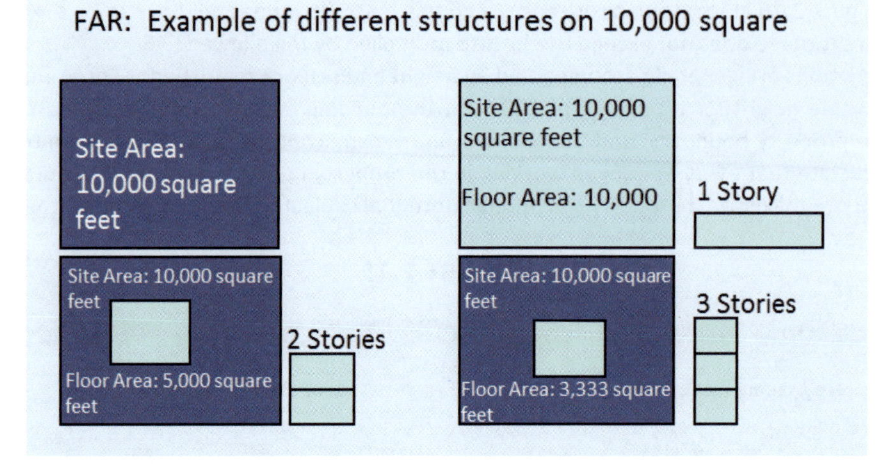

OCCUPANCY AND VACANCY

Another critical distinction is between economically and physically occupied space. **Economic occupancy** refers to space that is currently generating rent. Not all of the space paying rent may be physically occupied. For example, a firm may lease unused space in a building in anticipation of expansion. Or a tenant may have vacated the property, but continue to pay rent in accordance with their lease.

Physical occupancy refers to space that is physically occupied, whether or not the space generates rent. A tenant in bankruptcy may not be paying rent, although it still occupies the space. Or the tenant may occupy the space but not pay rent due to lease concessions, so called "free rent".

FIGURE 2.17

U.S. Vacancy Data for Office Buildings		
	1990	**2002**
Physical Vacancy	18%	16%
Economic Vacancy	30-45%	10-11%

Figure 2.17 displays estimates of physical and economic vacancy rates for US office space in two historically soft market periods. The high economic vacancy rates experienced in 1990 were the result of lease concessions, where 1-2 years of free rent were given to tenants in order to lock them into 4-5 year leases. Thus, while physical occupancy was about 82%, economic occupancy was much lower. In contrast, although in 2002 the physical vacancy rate was similar to 1990, tenants were paying rent on about a third of the vacant space. While landlords received rent on this vacant space, they faced leasing competition from tenants attempting to sublease their empty space.

STACKING PLAN

Tracking vacancy and lease expirations for a property are essential to effective property management. Figure 2.18 displays a stacking plan for Brasfield Tower. The plan notes when leases expire and current rental rates. This information provides the foundation for the leasing strategy.

As of June 2011, this 84,000 foot building had about 14,000 feet vacant, for an approximate 17% vacancy rate. About 14% of the vacancy is associated with the Kuo Corporation leaving the building. Why did this firm leave the property? Was Kuo Corporation having financial difficulty? Were they unhappy with the property services? Was their space too small? Too large? Were rents too high? Could management have been better prepared to deal with Kuo's exit? If Kuo left because their industry, technology, is in trouble, then perhaps BHUMI and Gross Tech, which are in the same industry, may also experience premature vacancies.

Often a firm may leave because their space was inadequate. In this case management must evaluate whether the building needs to be upgraded or marketed to a different tenant base. For example, if the building does not support high speed internet access wires, then it will be very difficult for the management of Brasfield Tower to retain commercial tenants, especially if competitors have installed such technology in their buildings.

CLOSING THOUGHT

Properties come in an infinite variety of designs, shapes, and sizes. Study carefully what drives a property's success, by studying buildings that generate high rents and have consistently high occupancy. Buildings are economic entities that are enhanced by well-conceived design. Whenever you pass or enter a property, ask yourself "does it work?", if not, "why?", "how could it function better?", and "why hasn't anyone done it?" A thorough understanding of space and tenant preferences is the foundation of becoming a great real estate investor.

FIGURE 2.18

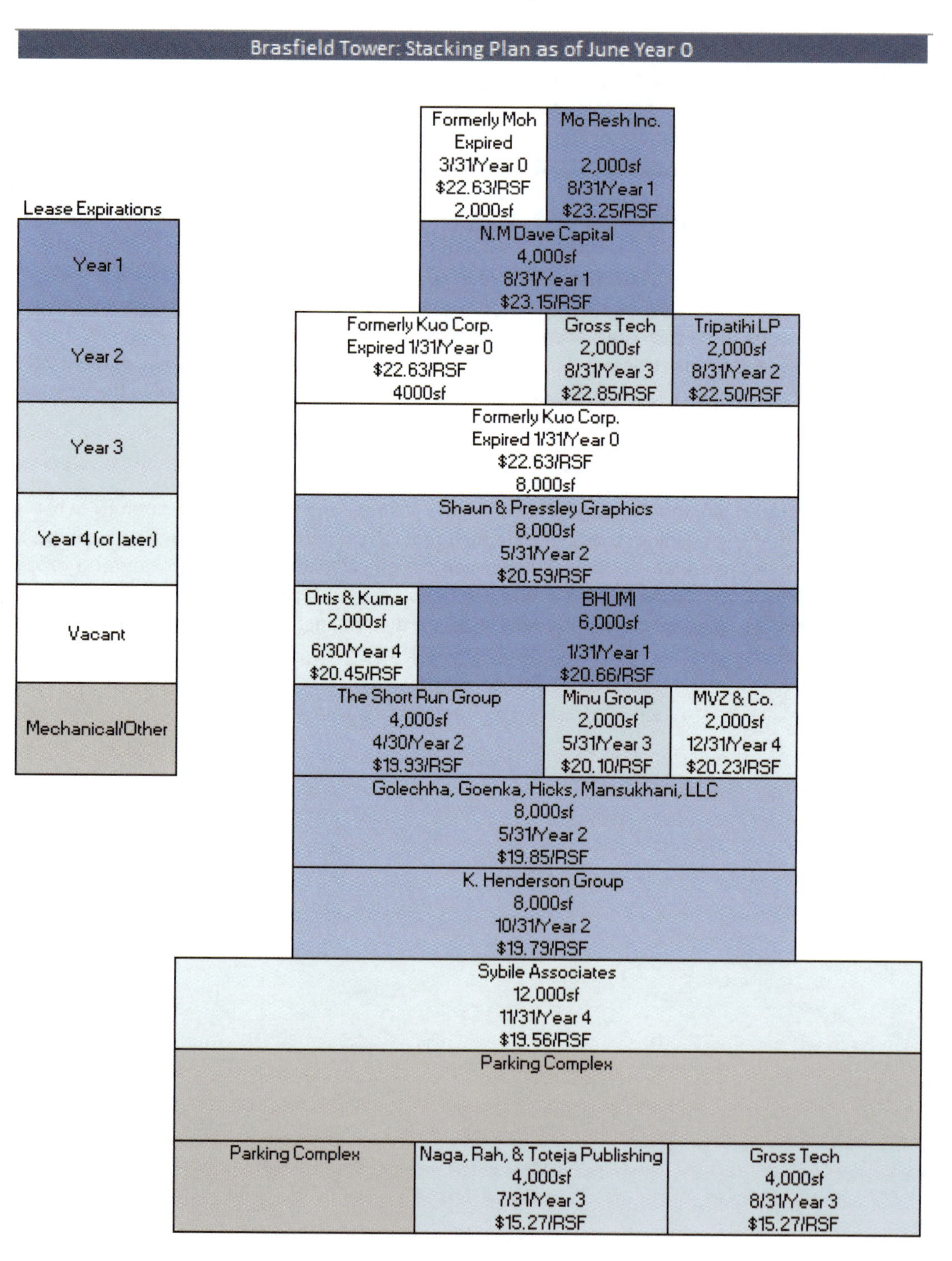
Brasfield Tower: Stacking Plan as of June Year 0
Lease Expirations
Year 1
Year 2
Year 3
Year 4 (or later)
Vacant
Mechanical/Other
Formerly Moh Expired 3/31/Year 0 $22.63/RSF 2,000sf
Mo Resh Inc. 2,000sf 8/31/Year 1 $23.25/RSF
N.M Dave Capital 4,000sf 8/31/Year 1 $23.15/RSF
Formerly Kuo Corp. Expired 1/31/Year 0 $22.63/RSF 4000sf
Gross Tech 2,000sf 8/31/Year 3 $22.85/RSF
Tripatihi LP 2,000sf 8/31/Year 2 $22.50/RSF
Formerly Kuo Corp. Expired 1/31/Year 0 $22.63/RSF 8,000sf
Shaun & Pressley Graphics 8,000sf 5/31/Year 2 $20.59/RSF
Ortis & Kumar 2,000sf 6/30/Year 4 $20.45/RSF
BHUMI 6,000sf 1/31/Year 1 $20.66/RSF
The Short Run Group 4,000sf 4/30/Year 2 $19.93/RSF
Minu Group 2,000sf 5/31/Year 3 $20.10/RSF
MVZ & Co. 2,000sf 12/31/Year 4 $20.23/RSF
Golechha, Goenka, Hicks, Mansukhani, LLC 8,000sf 5/31/Year 2 $19.85/RSF
K. Henderson Group 8,000sf 10/31/Year 2 $19.79/RSF
Sybile Associates 12,000sf 11/31/Year 4 $19.56/RSF
Parking Complex
Parking Complex
Naga, Rah, & Toteja Publishing 4,000sf 7/31/Year 3 $15.27/RSF
Gross Tech 4,000sf 8/31/Year 3 $15.27/RSF

Chapter 2 Supplement A

International Real Estate Investing

Dr. Peter Linneman – Wharton Real Estate Review – Spring 2001 Vol. V No. 1

As a freshman college football player, I was impressed when I read in a press guide that I possessed "great potential". In my naivete I thought that this meant I would be a top-notch college player. However, as I read the press guide more closely I realized that the word "potential" did not appear in the descriptions of the really talented players. "Potential" was just the press guide's way of saying, "He doesn't really have enough talent to play but we're too polite to tell him". This memory comes back to me as I consider the "great potential" of investing in international real estate.

The attractions of international real estate investing are both obvious and alluring. Perhaps as much as 60 percent of investment-quality real estate lies outside the U.S. This real estate is occupied by a rapidly globalizing tenant base, and is financed by capital sources that are increasingly international and integrated. In addition, the prevalence of large, passive owners such as banks, insurance companies, corporate real estate users, and government entities outside the U.S. makes these markets appear ripe — U.S.-style — for entrepreneurial real estate investors and operators.

In spite of these attractions, most efforts to create truly global property investment portfolios have fallen short. Notable disasters include JMB's acquisition of Ranstad (U.K.), Mitsubishi Estate's acquisition of Rockefeller Center, and the expansion of Rodamco. In analyzing why such disasters have occurred, a number of problems with international real estate investment become apparent.

A major problem is that most foreign property markets are not markets in any meaningful sense of the word. Properties rarely if ever trade; information is scarce, distorted and self-serving; many properties are overtly manipulated by (often corrupt) governments; there are only a limited number of capital sources; and, the rules of the game frequently change, often in mid-play. The result is markets with a high degree of uncertainty and inefficiency.

At first blush these inefficiencies appear attractive to "smart" operators, who see an opportunity to realize abnormal returns. On closer inspection, however, these inefficiencies reduce property values and severely limit exit options. When market inefficiencies create excessively high property values, it is hard to harvest one's profits as exit is difficult due to market illiquidity. In fact, many markets are so inefficient that no reliable exit options exist. The inability of investors to short the market in order to pressure property values downward when property values are excessively high means that markets can remain out of balance for prolonged periods. Even entering inefficient markets opportunistically during periods when property values are below economic levels is risky as property values may remain depressed for prolonged periods of time. These risks are particularly severe for outsiders entering markets that possess little in the way of legitimate legal infrastructure.

THE CAPITAL SHORTAGE MYTH

It is commonly believed that foreign real estate markets generally experience shortages of capital. In fact, major foreign markets such as London, Paris, Frankfurt, Madrid, Milan, Zurich, and Amsterdam are no different from New York City, Chicago, and Los Angeles: there is too little capital available 1-2 years out of every 10 years, too much capital 2-3 years out of every 10 years, and the majority of the time the supply and demand for real estate capital are roughly in balance. This is hardly surprising, as all major markets possess substantial financial institutions and participants with a relatively high level of financial sophistication.

The fact that major foreign markets in developed countries are generally in capital supply balance presents a severe problem for outsiders looking to enter, who must possess either a significant value-added operating ability, or access to "hidden" deals, in order to realize above-average returns. Unfortunately, an outsider rarely has access to "hidden" deals, which are generally parceled out to favored insiders with longstanding relations to the country's major financial institutions. In addition, it is difficult for new entrants to add substantial economic value to a property in ways that are not also available to top-quality domestic operators. A notable exception is when a major U.S. based tenant expands into a foreign market and the operator's established relationship with this tenant provides significant value-added ability.

When there is too much capital in major markets, outsiders are welcomed to buy – even in many relatively closed markets. The best evidence of this phenomenon is the inflated price that has been paid over the past twenty years in numerous markets by oil money, thieving third world potentates laundering money, and hapless Japanese investors. Frequently, the smartest locals have sold their prized assets to such outsiders, often repurchasing these assets when the overpaying buyers are squeezed during periods of capital shortages.

Well-developed local infrastructure and information networks are essential to exploit opportunities created by capital shortages. In periods when there is too little capital in real estate markets, it is usually the smart locals — not outsiders — who are the first to spot the best opportunities. Generally, only as a long-depressed market exhibits some upward momentum do outsiders enter, frequently too late to realize the best investment opportunities. A notable exception is when some U.S. opportunity funds have successfully utilized their networks to invest in major markets experiencing temporary capital market shortages. Their experiences in England, France, and Sweden suggest that often these smaller markets experience briefer capital shortage periods than is the case in the U.S.

THE LAND OF THE RISING SUN

The problem of supporting the overhead associated with maintaining an operational and investment infrastructure during times when the markets are not experiencing capital market shortages is paramount. This is why opportunity fund investments have been done primarily through local partners only in the largest and most liquid markets, where internal organizations can be justifiably supported. In this regard, Japan presents a major challenge. The cost of establishing a Tokyo office is very high while the transaction velocity remains very slow. Japan, particularly Tokyo, is a unique situation where real estate has been overvalued for almost two decades. As a result, just as only Japanese investors are willing to invest in Japanese government bonds that pay effectively zero interest rates, only Japanese capital sources have been willing to invest in Japanese properties.

Although Japan is a wealthy, high-income country with a large and diverse property pool, the economic outlook remains murky, and a great deal of structural realignment is necessary before its economic vibrancy will be achieved. Real estate returns available in Japan generally are still too low to justify substantial investments given the lack of transparency, illiquidity, the stagnancy of the economy, and continued low yields. Even though property prices in Japan have fallen by 50-90 percent from their peaks, yields remain in the 5-8 percent range, and even a billion dollars of investment does not go very far in terms of creating a substantial operating base. The main investment opportunities in Japan remain the purchase of distressed loans. These investments are less real estate plays than an exercise in the restructuring of bank debt, where knowing which investors are capable of buying back their notes at restructured terms is more important than the ability to add value to the real estate via operations.

Although Japan is a large, well-developed economy, it will be a long time before there is substantial foreign ownership of real estate. Japan remains insular, with a strong bias against outsiders and deep-rooted socialist tendencies. While it is slowly changing, other parts of the globe will attract foreign real estate investment more quickly.

A RISKY WORLD

Real estate capital is almost always scarce in places where there is high political risk, high economic risk, and an absence of markets with meaningful exit opportunities. Extreme examples are Iraq, Sierra Leone, and Zimbabwe. More relevant examples to investors include South Korea, Thailand, the Philippines, central and eastern Europe, and most of Latin America. While each of these areas offers high returns, each also poses serious risks. For example, although South Korea has experienced a strong rebound from its economic collapse, considerable risk remains in its real estate markets due to the need for substantial structural reforms. These include the elimination of many of the weak subsidiaries of the major *chaebols*. Many of the *chaebols* have attempted to sell some of their secondary properties at 12-15 percent cap rates on 5-year sale-leaseback terms. The buildings being offered are generally new but located in secondary locations, and are occupied by the weakest subsidiaries of the *chaebols*. Even at these yields the pricing for these deals remains unattractive. If South Korea continues its rebound and the subsidiary tenant survives, the buyer will only realize a 12-15 percent return (before taking into account currency risk) as the tenants execute their repurchase option in year 5. If the economy flounders and the weak subsidiary fails, the property (and many others) will remain vacant for some time. In this case, the cash flow will disappear, the repurchase option will not be exercised, and the owner will be stuck with a building in a secondary location with no obvious tenants. Since many of the weakest subsidiaries are in businesses that should never have existed in South Korea, the odds of numerous subsidiary failures are substantial. It is not worth the risk of purchasing these properties merely to receive a 12-15 percent return on an illiquid, low credit-quality "debt" instrument if all goes well, and having to manage a disastrous investment in a foreign country if the subsidiary fails. As in Japan, a substantial loan workout opportunity exists in South Korea in purchasing and restructuring distressed loans. Again, this is a loan restructuring business rather than a real estate business.

In a similar vein, Thailand, Indonesia, and Malaysia are all experiencing shortages of real estate capital. However, these shortages are caused by the multitude of risks presented by these economies. Thailand is the strongest of these economies, but also has experienced the greatest real estate excesses prior to the recent collapse. As a result, a vast quantity of empty (often partially completed) speculative properties remains to be absorbed. Even when they are occupied these properties will not generate sufficient cash flows to justify their construction costs for many years to come. Further, many of these properties are so poorly conceived, located, and executed that they will never be finished, much less occupied. In addition, the business climate remains non-transparent. While the legal infrastructure has improved, it will be a long time before Thailand achieves an effective functioning real estate market.

Indonesia and Malaysia also experienced enormous real estate excesses prior to their collapse. In fact, to a large extent these excesses were a major cause of their economic collapse. In addition, these weak economies have effectively cut themselves off from the mainstream of global capital flows. Add to this the ethnic conflicts and political discontent that bubble beneath the surface in both countries, and it is clear that substantial real estate investments — at almost any price — can only be justified in the most extraordinary situations.

THE OLD SOVIET EMPIRE

The former Soviet Union offers a number of intriguing opportunities for global real estate investors. Unfortunately, the heart of the former Soviet Union, Russia, remains an undesirable location for real estate investors. It is a country where people believe that the road the riches lies in stealing from others — particularly the government and one's partners — rather than by adding value. As a result, newly arrived foreign investors are viewed as prime opportunities for exploitation via fraudulent contracts, self-dealings, and other nefarious acts rather than as partners for value-added operations. The near-term prospects for the Russian economy remain, at best, uncertain while the Russian political and judicial systems show only the faintest signs of evolving into those of a modern liberal democracy. As a result, Russia remains an investment target only for those who are both politically connected and have deep pockets — and strong stomachs.

In contrast, Poland, the Czech Republic, Hungary, and the Baltic states all have undergone considerable economic reforms. They are all rapidly evolving into modern liberal democracies, have turned their backs on Russia, and are showing strong commitment to joining the European community. These countries will continue to integrate into mainstream Europe over the next 10-15 years. However, these countries present two clear difficulties for most global real estate investors. First, with the exception of Poland, they are relatively small. As a result, it is difficult to establish the critical mass of local operations necessary to justify the costs associated with researching the markets, mastering legal and tax structures, etc. Nevertheless, global tenants are rapidly expanding into these countries and demanding global quality space, presenting the opportunity for U.S. real estate operators to leverage their relationships with these tenants.

A second major difficulty faced by foreign real estate investors in Eastern Europe is that for almost a half century the location of commercial, industrial, and retail nodes was arbitrarily fixed by the Soviet planning system. Only over the past decade have market forces been gradually establishing where these activities will occur. However, the transportation and residential infrastructure established by the Soviet system will remain major constraints on the evolution of these markets for many years. As a result, in most cities the ultimate location of the prime residential, commercial, industrial, and retail nodes remains unclear. This substantially raises the risks associated with real estate investments in these markets. In addition, these markets possess few — if any — high quality properties, even a decade after the end of the Soviet empire. Thus, foreign entrants into these markets must assume risks associated not only with real estate, tenant quality, politics, and economics, but also with development. Development risks are compounded by the fact that the political infrastructure required to deal with development is in its infancy. Further, the depth of demand in these markets is uncertain. This phenomenon is often ignored by investors and is vividly displayed in Warsaw, where in the mid-1990s developers were attracted by the very high rents being paid by a very small number of international tenants. These developers calculated that at these rents they could build to western European standards and achieve substantial returns. Unfortunately, as these properties have come on-line developers have discovered that there are few tenants who are willing to pay the required rents. Stated differently, developers developed Mercedes quality properties for a market of Chevy consumers.

The integrating economies of eastern Europe offer the attractive investment bet that over the next decade, although rents may fall over time as new construction continues to bring quality space on the market, the economic integration of these markets into western Europe will result in notably lower cap rates. The bet is that cap rates will fall by more than rents fall over the decade, yielding attractive returns, particularly where leverage is available. If these countries successfully become part of an integrated European economy, Warsaw, Prague, and Budapest, will price at cap rates similar to those found in secondary western European cities, such as Barcelona, Dublin, and Lyon. This would mean that cap rates would fall to roughly 7 percent from their current 10-12 percent levels.

SOUTH OF THE BORDER

Latin America is a very fragmented region, under the shadow of inflation and the return of military dictators. The fear of inflation is analogous to the fear of the Great Depression held by the generation of currently retired Americans, that is, real estate is viewed as a unique asset which provides substantial protection against inflation. In Latin America, this attitude generates real estate prices higher than justified simply on the basis of supply and demand, as many wealthy local investors are willing to pay a premium for the inflation protection offered by real estate. For example, frequently local investors purchase condominium interests in commercial properties or fund new development at returns well below those demanded by foreign investors.

In Argentina, Brazil, and Chile, there are properties yielding 12-15 percent U.S. equivalent returns on investments. But it is difficult to generate returns on equity above these levels due to the absence of long-term debt that is the outgrowth of the political and economic uncertainty of these economies combined with their history of runaway inflation. As a result, most U.S. real estate operators find the risks too high relative to the returns on equity which are available elsewhere, while opportunity funds cannot access sufficient debt to leverage their returns into the range required by their investors.

THE UNITED STATES OF EUROPE

Most cities in western Europe have an excess supply of real estate capital. This is the result of the low returns on equity that remain acceptable to European — particularly French, German, and Italian — banks and insurance companies. These low returns on equity, and the willingness of German open-end fund investors to accept 4-5 percent returns, have fed capital into European real estate as a favored investment class with low yields. This is reflected by the homogeneity of returns in major urban property markets, where high quality properties trade at 5-6 percent cap rates even though the lease structures, the growth prospects, asset liquidity, and tenant quality are very different. Perhaps the most interesting example of this phenomena is Paris, where top-quality office properties trade at 5-6 percent cap rates in spite of the fact that standard leases are 9 years, indexed to the CPI for construction cost, can be broken by the tenants every third year, and give the tenant an absolute right of occupancy at the end of year 9. This lease structure means that if market rents fall, tenants will break their leases every third year, producing returns less than 5-6 percent. Alternatively, if rents rise substantially over the term of the lease, tenants will remain in place and rents will rise only 1-2 percent annually. Active investors in Paris tell themselves that they will receive big rent bumps at the end of the lease, however, this seems to be somewhat wishful thinking, as France remains a fundamentally socialist country. These socialist tendencies make it doubtful that, if market rents tripled over the term of the lease, rents would be allowed to triple at the expiration of the lease.

Observers of western Europe are excited by the unification of European currencies, as well as the integration of economic and regulatory activities. They see the potential for enormous growth driven by integration and the collapse of local protectionism, increased competition, reduced regulations, privatization, and reduced taxes. However, they ignore the flip side of the Euro. Perhaps the most difficult question facing real estate investment in western Europe is how the "local hero" problem will be resolved. For many years, each European country protected its banks, telecommunication companies, automobile companies, airlines, power companies, etc. in order to safeguard jobs from competition — and gain votes. This means that every country houses the headquarters of a carmaker, electronics firm, major telecom, bank, etc. — the local hero — in its major cities. However, as these countries (including portions of the former Soviet Union) continue to integrate, not every country will be able to have a major telecom company, a major electronics company, a major automobile company, etc. In fact, many of these local heroes will be completely eliminated by global competition, while others will be forced to consolidate. As a result, while some cities will see enormous demand growth for headquarters offices, much of the space currently occupied by these noncompetitive local heroes in almost every major European city will be vacated. A similar phenomenon took place in the U.S., when the banking industry, the telecommunications business, electrical supply companies, etc. moved, shrank, or disappeared from many cities, while rapidly expanding in others.

The local hero problem will be exacerbated by political pressures to stop "globalization" since Europeans are generally reluctant to move within their own country, much less across countries. It is difficult enough to move from Cleveland to Dallas, but many times more difficult to move from Copenhagen to Madrid, which involves a change in language, business cultures, governmental structures, tax systems, and legal protections. Western European real estate investments should carry a risk premium for this local hero risk as it remains unclear which cities will be winners or losers in this competitive process. Instead, we see premium pricing for real estate cash flows driven by the availability of capital at local hero banks and insurance companies which are allowed to remain in business by protective governments and corporate governance structures in spite of noncompetitive returns on equity. When these financial institutions are required to achieve higher returns on equity, the adverse reverberations on property prices will be felt throughout European property markets.

FOREIGNERS ARE NOT DUMB

It is often assumed that foreigners are not as smart as U.S. real estate operators. While in many countries local real estate operators are not as adept at sophisticated financial analysis and at the slicing, dicing, and reslicing of real estate cash flows, this is more than offset by the fact that they are intelligent, well-educated, and more importantly, know the rules by which real estate markets operate in their country. And the knowledge of how these local markets work is much more important than in the U.S., as the rules of the game and of transactions are much less predictable and transparent. Not unlike the "old days" in the U.S., local operators generally have a cozy relationship with a friendly local financial institution. In fact, in many cases these operators are the major local banks and insurance companies acting directly as real estate investors. They may not be as nimble or as customer-friendly as the more entrepreneurial U.S. real estate operators, however, tenants in most foreign countries are dominated by large, governmentally influenced institutions, making it more difficult for entrepreneurial U.S. real estate operators to achieve the necessary prestige and clout.

LOCAL PARTNERS

One of the most difficult questions faced when deciding to enter a local real estate market is whether to use a local partner. Local partners bring a wealth of knowledge and expertise. In addition, they know the rules of the game and the major players, as well as which properties have historically been duds (and why). However, these partners generally operate within a different institutional framework than major U.S. real estate operators. They have generally been more reliant on governmental and institutional contacts and inside deals, and less reliant on detailed financial analysis and carefully conceived exit strategies than their U.S. partners.

Particularly in less developed markets a strong local partner is attractive because of extensive contacts and their ability to "make it happen". But this ability often rebounds on the foreign investor when the local partners turn their attention to "making it happen". All too often foreign investors find that their local partners use their powers to restrike their partnership, and that there is little that can be done to stop them. In many markets, particularly less developed economies, the strength of local partners can change very quickly. Perhaps the best example is that for years the Suharto family was the ultimate local partner in Indonesia. Yet overnight they became a liability. Even in more developed and stable economies, this problem exists due to the greater role played by governments.

The alternative to a local partner is to purchase or build a deep local infrastructure. This allows the foreign investor to control his culture and incentive structures, but requires a much greater commitment of capital and managerial effort. Few real estate investment companies can afford to put in place the necessary infrastructure before they have a business. As a result, most global real estate investors choose to use a local partner initially, building their own infrastructure as they generate a sufficient level of business.

CURRENCY RISK

An important issue facing every international real estate investor is currency risk. It is possible that even if the real estate investment performs superbly in terms of local currency, a sufficiently large adverse currency movement can destroy the investment's dollar performance. This risk is not unique to real estate investments, and has been addressed by global corporations for many years. There are several ways that such corporations have historically dealt with currency risks. First, they usually hedge the risks, at least in major currencies, associated with the investment transactions. That is, once a transaction is entered a currency hedge is used to protect against adverse currency movements prior to closing. Such hedges are usually of short duration, and hence relatively cheap. However, in countries with thin currency markets this risk cannot be efficiently hedged, and currency swings between signing and closing are often a contingency for which they may break a deal.

Hedging cash flows associated with the ongoing operation of the properties and the residual value of the asset is much more difficult. This is because even in relatively thick currency markets it is difficult and expensive to hedge long-term currency exposures. Some companies use dynamic hedging models that combine a rolling series of short-term hedges. These models provide adequate hedging coverage on short-term investments but for longer periods their hedging capability greatly diminishes and the expense rises substantially.

An alternative is to underwrite currency erosions that are expected to occur during the investment lifetime process. In the long run, expected changes in currency rates are equal to the difference between expected inflation rates between the two countries. For example, the dollar could be expected to strengthen to the extent that the U.S. expected inflation rate is less than that of the target country. Investors may use the difference in long-term bond rates, adjusted for differences in credit quality, payment mechanics, and liquidity to proxy the differential inflation rates expected by the market. This simple model, while theoretically sound, performs well only in the long run. Even then it is undermined by the fact that inflationary expectations will deviate from actual outcomes. A number of developing countries often quote rents, either legally or de facto, in U.S. dollars in order to offset the volatility and illiquidity of their currency, which greatly reduces the currency risk. However, it does not completely eliminate it because the residual value and the rent renewal cash flows are not in dollars.

The use of local currency debt to partially match the currency exposures of assets and liabilities, thus notably reducing cash flow volatility, is another common risk management technique. Further, to the extent that real estate investors intend to keep their money at work in the country to grow their business, the currency risk is greatly reduced because the returns are made and reinvested in local currency. Thus, even if the currency falls versus the dollar, it still purchases the same amount of new assets and services in the target country. This is the reason why many international corporations do little other than hedge their transactions, leaving their cash flows unhedged, while leveraging in local currency. For most long-term real estate investors this is probably the most efficient long-term strategy.

All of these currency risk management approaches for long-term cash flows are seriously limited. Therefore, the committed international real estate investor must simply accept that currency risks are a part of the risks they accept in order to achieve the performance and diversification advantages of international investing. Currency risks are yet another reason for opportunistically entering foreign markets.

GREAT POTENTIAL?

Will a successful large-scale global real estate investment company ultimately evolve? Despite the perils, the answer is "yes", for the simple reasons that both the tenant base and capital markets are globalizing. It makes sense that banks, automobile companies, electronic companies, accounting firms, and law firms will turn to global space providers. In addition, global capital sources will gravitate to the most efficient real estate firms pulling them into new markets. Further, just as the demise of local banks in the U.S. radically changed the nature of the U.S. real estate market, the demise of local hero banks and life insurance companies will create a demand for global real estate operators who can best service customers and yield the highest returns. As the home of the globalization process, U.S. real estate companies should be among the leaders of this process, and the best opportunistic American firms will ultimately demonstrate that globalized real estate investment is more than just an idea with potential.

[Endnote: This research was supported by a research grant from the National Association of Realtors.]

Chapter 3
The Fundamentals of Commercial Leases

"Analyze first; then leap".
-Dr. Peter Linneman

An essential dimension of real estate finance is understanding leases. With the exception of hotels and multifamily properties, the pro formas we discuss are to a large degree driven by the terms of existing leases. Real estate is a business, and lease terms dictate how many aspects of that business must be conducted. If you, or the property's previous owners, agreed to specific lease terms, those terms dictate the property's performance through the life of the lease. This is true even if the current market would dictate very different lease terms.

The general rationale behind lease negotiations is that the landlord provides the space (the "premises") to the tenant in exchange for rental payments sufficient to yield an adequate return on the real estate. In addition, the tenant should pay all operating and maintenance costs associated with their premises, as those costs are part of the costs of the tenant conducting their business. This simple rationale is complicated by the fact that in weak market conditions, landlords have to compromise in order to attract and retain tenants. Also, reality is complicated by the fact that most properties have operating and maintenance costs associated with the common areas of the property (lobbies, elevators, stairwells, roofs, parking decks, etc.). Are these common costs part of the tenants' cost of doing business? "Yes", as these costs maintain the tenant's general operating environment. But also "no", to the degree that many of these common costs exist whether the tenant is in the building or not. Prevailing market conditions will dictate how these common costs are allocated between the landlord and tenants.

What are the significant aspects of leases, and the reasoning and negotiations that create lease terms? We will primarily focus our discussion on retail leases, as shopping centers and regional mall leases most vividly demonstrate many of the issues that you need to consider. The relevant issues for retail leases tend to be more extensive than for non-retail properties. However, each property type has its own lease nuances.

To understand the rationale of key lease terms, assume that you own a 1 million square foot regional mall, and are negotiating a lease with a potential tenant for 5,000 square foot. What are some of the most important terms you need to address? Bear in mind that the space being leased is only a small part of a large retail property.

RENT

Students invariably suggest the rental rate as the most important lease term. Of course, rent is important as it determines how much money you will collect from the tenant, and to a large extent dictates your revenue stream from that space for the length of the lease. Rent is comprised of three components: base rent; base rent escalations; and, percentage rent. Base rent is the initial rent for the space, while the rent escalation specifies how, if at all, this rent changes during the life of lease. This escalation may be based upon inflation measures, for example, with base rent growing each year proportionate to changes of the Consumer Price Index. Or it may grow at specified dollar or percentage increments over the lease. Or there may be no rent escalations in the lease.

The third component is percentage rent, also known as **overage**, which is unique to retail rents. Percentage rent specifies the percentage of the tenant's revenue that the landlord receives in addition to the base rent and escalations. For instance, the lease may specify that the landlord receives 2% of store revenues in excess of sales of $100 per square foot, monitored monthly. Why is percentage rent used in retail but not in other types of properties? Because the landlord controls store mix and the overall retail environment, and a good store mix and retailing environment can increase tenant sales. In contrast, the productivity of office and warehouse tenants is rarely impacted by their neighbors. In addition, since store sales are relatively easily monitored, it is easy to assess the sales productivity of the space.

Percentage rents helps to align retail tenant interests with those of the landlord. If the landlord has no economic incentive to enhance the tenants' sales, the landlord will primarily focus on leasing the space to whomever will pay the highest base rent. If, on the other hand, the tenant rewards the landlord for their superior sales which result from an enhanced tenant mix, the landlord will focus more on creating a tenant mix that maximizes total center sales. The landlord will attempt to create the optimal mix of tenants by avoiding redundant stores, optimizing the location of tenants, and signing leases with complementary stores. For example, a good tenant mix might be a close proximity of tenants like Bostonian, Brooks Brothers, and Troudeau, as people who shop at one of these stores are likely to shop at the others. Or a Gap, near a Victoria's Secret, near a woman's shoe store. The goal is to generate positive externalities across stores, which the landlord shares with tenants via percentage rents. Percentage rents typically represent 5-10% of a tenant's total rent payment.

MARKETING BUDGET

Shopping centers can be very complicated in their execution as they are operating businesses. For example, centers generally charge anchors a low base rent, while in-line stores, which are the smaller stores located between the anchors, pay notably higher base rents plus percentage rent. Historically, landlords often gave away space to department stores and, to a much lesser extent, supermarkets, even though their stores cost as much as $100 per square foot to build. In return, these anchor stores advertise (including your center's location) and draw customers to the center. Your center's design and in-line tenant mix attempt to channel that traffic to the in-line stores, whose rents are your primary sources of revenue.

Leases will generally require that each tenant pay a share of the center's marketing budget. For example, you will hold promotional days at your center, sponsor a local youth organization, advertise in local newspapers, etc., and each lease will specify how much of these marketing expenses are paid by each tenant.

UTILITIES, INSURANCE, AND PROPERTY TAXES

Another key lease item is the treatment of utility charges. There are two general components of utility costs. The first is the utility expense you as the landlord pay for the **common areas** of the property, including lighting the walkway in front of the stores, water in the public bathrooms, air conditioning for the hallways, etc. These common areas are amenities of the center that benefit all tenants. While the expenses associated with **common area maintenance (CAM)** are not specific to any tenant, they are a critical part of a store's operating environment. You will negotiate how much of these CAM expenses you will pass through to each tenant.

The second component of utility costs relates to expenses that are specific to each tenant's space. In older properties there may not be meters that gauge each tenant's utility usage, but rather only a single meter for the entire property. For such properties you attempt to determine the appropriate allocation of the property's expense for each tenant, with each lease detailing the allocation of these expenses. Modern buildings are metered individually so as to gauge each tenant's usage of water, electricity, gas, etc. Leases in modern buildings generally specify that each tenant is responsible for their own metered utility bills.

Property tax and casualty insurance payments paid by the landlord are part of the cost of the property's operation. Tenants are usually allocated their pro rata share of these expenses based on their share of the property's rentable square footage. However, there are frequently caps specified in the lease that limit the extent to which these items can rise during any single year, or over the term of the lease. These caps, generally referred to as **expense stops**, may be negotiated for any component of operating costs, including utilities, property taxes, and insurance.

Increases in these expense items are frequently passed on only to the extent that they exceed levels at the time the lease is signed (the **base year**). For example, the property tax at the time the lease was signed is $1 per square foot, and the lease specifies that all increases in property taxes are passed through to the tenant, up to a maximum of $0.10 per square foot per year, and not to exceed an increase of $1 per square foot over the 15 year term of the lease. These base year designations, recoveries, and caps are determined by market conditions at the time the lease is negotiated, as well as the risk sharing preferences of the landlord and tenant.

HVAC – HEATING, VENTILATION AND AIR CONDITIONING

In order to save money, a landlord in Phoenix will attempt to turn up the air conditioning, while a landlord in Buffalo will try to turn down the heat. In addition, different tenants have different temperature preferences and usage patterns. As a result, you will negotiate when, and how much, HVAC you need to provide to each tenant, to the common areas, and who pays these expenses. In new buildings, tenants are generally able to control the HVAC in their space. Like individual metering, this makes usage patterns and expense allocation much easier, as the lease generally states that the tenant is responsible for their HVAC usage. However, you still must specify the policy for common areas. In older properties, the lease will specify when heat or air conditioning must be provided (for example, starting at 8 AM on weekdays).

SECURITY AND PROPERTY MAINTENANCE

The lease will specify the type of security provided at the property, and who pays for this security. This is also true of property maintenance, including the common areas and grounds. For example, how often are the grounds and buildings cleaned? How often are windows washed? Who selects the cleaners? Who is responsible for building maintenance? Are security cameras provided in parking areas? Are employees escorted to their cars after hours by security personnel? These, and many similar terms should be addressed in each lease.

TENANT IMPROVEMENTS

Tenant improvements (TIs) include those items necessary to make a tenant's space fully operational. Commonly the landlord provides the tenant with "as is" space. For a new building this will be base space, while for existing buildings it will be the space as left by the last tenant. However, the tenant may want new fixtures, carpeting, a kitchen for restaurants, shelving, etc. in order to run the business. Who pays for these tenant improvements on the space? It depends on the market. In a weak leasing market the landlord may have to provide the tenant with much of the necessary funding for their TIs.

The parties will not only negotiate over who pays for the TIs and how much will be paid, but also who is responsible for completing the work, who the contractor will be, who has rights to the improvements after the lease expires, who pays for the removal of any TIs after the lease expires, etc. Remember that after the lease expires, the space returns to the landlord, irrespective of which party paid for the TIs. Therefore, you have a significant interest in who does the work, how it is done, and what is the quality of the space. Again, the market will dictate which party has the negotiating power in resolving these matters.

Why would you pay for improvements made to a tenant's space? First, consider the case of a building under construction. Rather than paying to paint, install lighting fixtures, erect divider walls, etc. that the tenant may not want, you will say to a tenant (who has the alternative of leasing fully completed space in another property) "why don't I just give you the money to finish the space as you want, instead of me putting money into finishing the space in a way you may not want?" In this way, you attempt to turn your unfinished space from a negative to a positive. In turn, owners of finished (but vacant) space frequently have to offer TIs in order to attract tenants who do not like the current finish of the space.

A second reason you provide TIs is that weak markets force you to offer discounted economics to attract tenants. Why not just reduce rents rather than providing TI dollars up front? After all, aren't you indifferent between offering $35 a foot in TIs up front versus reducing rents over the term of the lease by an equivalent present value? Not really. While tenants may be indifferent between TIs and equivalent NPV rent concessions up to the point where the TIs exceed their desired improvements, TI expenditures go into your building, while rent concessions walk out your door. As a result, if you must give concessions you would rather give TI concessions in order to keep the money in the building, as you hope that these improvements will have some value to future tenants if the current tenant leaves the space.

TIs can run as much as 1-2 years of rent, especially in weak markets with substantial amounts of new empty space coming on the market.

FREE RENT

Free rent is when no rent is paid during the first weeks, months, or years of the lease. In a weak market you may prefer to give a period of free rent, rather than discount rents over the term of the lease by an equivalent NPV amount. This is done in order to keep rents closer to typical rents for when you plan to sell or refinance the property in future years.

CAPITAL COSTS

Leases often specify that the tenant is responsible for all or part of common area **capital costs**, including items such as the repair and maintenance of HVAC system replacements, elevators, parking decks and structural components. This may take the form of a requirement that the tenant pay capital costs as they occur, or that they annually reimburse the landlord for such costs on an amortized basis. Alternatively, the lease may specify that the property be returned at the end of the lease "in commercially acceptable condition" or in its "original condition". The typical lease in London, for example, requires tenants to pay all capital costs as they occur and return the space to its original condition at the tenants' expense.

NET RENT

Net rent means the rent net of all operating costs. The term **triple net lease** generally refers to situations where the tenant pays all operating (and frequently capital) costs, including insurance, utilities, and property taxes in addition to the contractual base rent and escalation payments to the landlord. Net leases shift the risk of increases in such costs from the landlord to the tenant, altering the ownership risk of the property.

Net effective rent is used somewhat ambiguously in the business. Generally stated, it is annual rent, net of: unrecovered maintenance and operating costs (property taxes, insurance, utilities, etc.), the amortized value of free rent, the amortized value of leasing commissions, and the amortized value of TIs. For example, a gross rent of $30 per square foot, with a $5 per square foot cost recovery on $10 per square foot of maintenance and operating costs, yields a net rent of $25 per square foot. If one year free rent was provided on a 10 year lease, this amounts to amortized free rent of $3 per square foot per year ($30 per square foot / 10 years). If $40 per square foot in TIs are provided on this 10 year lease, this amounts to amortized TIs of $4 per square foot per year. If the leasing commissions are 2% of the face value of the 10 year lease, they are $6 per square foot ($30*10*2%), which amortizes to $0.60 per square foot per year. Thus, in this example your net effective rent is $17.40 ($30 + $5 - $10 - $3 - $4 - $0.6) as summarized in Figure 3.1.

FIGURE 3.1

Net Effective Rent Per Square Foot Per Year	
Gross Rent	$30.00 psf
Cost Recoveries	$5.00 psf
Maintenance and Operating Costs	($10.00 psf)
Amortized Free Rent	($3.00 psf)
Amortized Tenant Improvement	($4.00 psf)
Amortized Leasing Commissions	($0.60 psf)
Net Effective Rent	**$17.40 psf**

Note that this approach to net effective rent ignores the time value of money, as TIs, free rent, and leasing commissions are all up front costs, while rents are received in the future. However, since this term is not the basis of valuation or lending calculations, but rather a simple summary statistic, there is no harm in this simplification.

NON-ECONOMIC TERMS

Thus far, we have discussed lease terms which are primarily concerned with payments made by the tenants. These monetary components are generally viewed by students as the most important terms of a lease. But never forget that the tenant is just a small part (in our example 0.5%) of a larger whole. By effectively organizing your space, the center can be worth more than the sum of its parts. In a way, shopping centers are like a sports team. You could have a NBA team made up of just high scoring shooting guards, but the team will be unsuccessful without good defenders, passers, and rebounders. Below are some of the most important lease issues that you must consider, particularly for retail centers. In fact, they can be far more important aspects of retail leases than the monetary issues we have discussed, because if they are not correctly contracted they can destroy your retail environment.

SIGNAGE

One of the most important terms of a retail lease is the location, size, and design of each tenant's signage. If you have no restrictions on signage, each tenant will only be interested in maximizing his or her visibility. For example, a small tenant that sells products geared towards young men might put a huge sign of a naked woman in front of the store absent signage restrictions in the lease. Such a sign might attract young men to that tenant, but is such signage optimal for your overall retail environment? Only if every store in your center is geared towards young men! But usually the bulk of your stores are geared towards children, and young and middle aged women, who will find such signage offensive. Therefore, the lease will carefully regulate the size, location, format, writing, colors, and other details of each tenant's signage.

GOING DARK

What happens if an anchor tenant, who pays little rent, decides to close their store with a lease in effect for 15 more years? For example, the tenant could decide to stop operating in your center and move to a competing center, while still making their minimal lease payments to you. This prevents a potential competitor from moving into their vacated space.

If the lease does not protect against such behavior, known as **going dark**, you will have dramatically reduced the traffic at your property, destroying the performance of your in-line tenants, who are your primary sources of rental income. Therefore, you will try to negotiate terms that prevent a tenant continuing to pay rent but not operating a store in their space. You will try to assure that the anchor operates until the lease expires or until you are able to more productively rent the space.

Wal-Mart, the largest retailer and grocer in America, presents landlords with a particular dilemma. Since Wal-Mart draws shoppers to their stores, you want them in your center, right? Not so fast. Wal-Mart is also the largest tenant of dark space in America, time and again going dark in older stores with low rent long-term leases, in order to move a mile down the road into a larger store. Wal-Mart continues to pay rent on the old store, but the fact that it is not operating destroys your in-line tenants, and hence the center's profitability. So why not simply prohibit them from going dark? Because Wal-Mart may not sign such a lease. If you insist upon this clause, they might go down the road and sign a long-term lease without a go-dark provision at a competitive center, drawing customers from your center. Hopefully, you are beginning to understand the importance of negotiating leverage, especially when you don't have any. The industry has evolved into being damned if you sign Wal-Mart to a long-term lease, or being damned if you don't. Fun business, isn't it?

HOURS AND DAYS OF OPERATION

The lease will specify when the store and center must, or can, be open. If you do not do this, tenants will operate only when they want, and without standardized hours of operations, customers may not experience a rich shopping environment. For this reason, all stores in the mall open and close around the same time, even though not all retailers may like this restriction. For example, certain restaurants may only want to be open at night. But your center needs food available at all hours of operations.

Why do you limit when stores can be open? Because if a store decides to operate very late at night (i.e., in the morning) it may create security issues. Therefore, you may make a decision to restrict the permitted hours of operation to "shopping hours".

LENGTH OF LEASE

You need to specify how long the lease will run. Remember that a long-term lease will impact your revenue and operations for many years. If you sign a long-term lease in a hot market, you will receive a relatively high rent for years. On the other hand, you could suffer for years if you sign a long-term lease at low rents due to a current excess supply environment.

Tenants usually want a very short-term lease with a lot of extension options. With that structure the tenant can walk if business does not go well, a better location arises, or market rents fall. On the other hand, if they want to remain they have the option to stay at the location. Depending on the economic environment, landlords usually prefer the security of a long-term lease. But remember that today's "red hot" retailer may be tomorrow's dud.

EXPANSION RIGHTS

Larger tenants, particularly in office and warehouse properties, want the option to satisfy growth at the same location. Therefore, landlords often sell the option to additional future space near or adjacent to the tenant's current location. In the meantime, the landlord can lease that space to another tenant. The problem is the temporary tenant will have to leave if the option is exercised. As a result, you may have a problem leasing space that is optioned. Frequently you rent option space to short term users, for example, political campaign offices. Juggling option space is an art which can yield unexpected revenues.

USAGE RESTRICTIONS

You do not want to sign a tenant to occupy space as a woman's clothing store and find out the tenant decides to run a slaughterhouse from the space. That is not the retail environment you envisioned! Therefore, the lease must be extremely precise in describing the kind of business the tenant can, and cannot, conduct in the space.

Sublet Rights: Assume that a woman's clothing store has a lease with 15 years to run. Can they sublease their space to another retailer? If the tenant subleases space to a lesser quality store or to a computer repair shop, it can greatly reduce the productivity of your center. Therefore, the lease will specify sublease rights, including whether the landlord has the right to approve all sublease activity.

LOCATION ASSIGNMENT

If you are a retail tenant in a strip shopping center, where do you want to be located within the center? Close to the anchor tenant might be best for your sales. Close to the street might give you more visibility for people driving or walking by the property. The importance of where tenants are located within a property is not unique to retail. In an apartment building, you want a higher floor for a better view, less ground noise, and no neighbors stomping around overhead.

There are unique location dynamics in regional malls that shape mall design. First, you have to understand that there is a tradeoff between land costs and building additional floors for all types of buildings. The incremental hard costs of an additional floor generally increase more than proportionally, with a three story building being more than three times as expensive to build as a one story property. This is because you need more concrete, more steel, more support structures to handle three floors rather than one. Each additional floor you build costs incrementally more than the previous floor. How many floors there are in a building will partially depend on the cost of land. If it costs more to build higher, and land costs are low, you will spread the structure over more land. If land costs are high, such as in Manhattan, you would rather incur the additional costs of building higher in order to spread the cost of the land over more floors. You will use engineers to help analyze this trade off.

Human nature also determines the design of the exterior and interior of a mall. Roughly 90% of the products sold in a regional mall are purchased on impulse. Therefore, you want to maximize the retail stimuli to which a shopper is exposed, as the more stimuli, the more they will tend to spend. Assume your mall is one story. Shoppers will park their cars, walk through your mall, and then walk back through the mall to return to their cars. On the way back, buyers will generally walk faster and shop less than on their initial walk through the mall, because they are seeing "old" stimuli. You will realize lower sales productivity from impulse shoppers on their way out, as they are exposed to few "new" impulses.

To "solve" this problem you could build a two-story mall. With two stories, you are providing additional retail stimuli, as people can walk back through the second floor experiencing entirely new impulse shopping stimuli. If the second floor generates enough impulse buying you can generate enough rent to justify the additional costs of building a second floor. However, you must contend with the fact that most people would rather go down a flight of stairs (unless that flight leads down to a basement) than up a flight of stairs. Why? That's for psychologists to determine. For you it's just an unfortunate fact of life. Therefore, few tenants reliant on impulse shopping want to occupy space on the second floor, as few shoppers will make it to the second story (even with elevators and escalators).

Then why do you see so many two-story regional malls? In some cases it was a dumb development decision. This second story space was surely leased in the financial models for these centers, and justified the cost paid for the development. But retail reality doesn't conform to your ill-conceived pro forma. As a result, there are a lot of centers with vacant second floors.

In other cases it is because clever design addressed the problem. For example, if people won't go up, and they won't go down into a basement, you need to make them think they are on the main floor even though they are on the second floor. Alfred Taubman figured out a way to make people believe they are on the main floor when they enter a mall. To construct a building you have to dig a hole for the foundation. Instead of paying to haul away the dirt from the excavation, he decided to build an embankment with the dirt. As customers drive on to this elevated surface and enter what looks like the first story of a one-story mall, they are actually entering the second floor of a two-story mall. Buyers walk through the mall on the floor they enter, and go down stairs to the first floor for the return trip to their car, because they know it is not a basement. This return trip generates new impulses, hence purchases. With the addition of shoppers that enter on the second floor and are willing to go down the stairs, you are able to generate sufficient productivity for tenants on both floors, particularly if the majority of the tenants enter the second floor. This design, which can also be executed by exploiting natural elevation difference, reduces some of the biases of floor location in a multi-floor mall. Another design solution is to locate "destination", rather than "impulse", stores on the second floor. Examples include food, theatres, bars, doctor's offices, and spas.

Interior design, including corridor width, common areas, and amenities also are important. For instance, if the corridor is too narrow and becomes overly crowded, people will not shop. On the other hand, if the corridor is too wide, the mall appears empty. It's like a comedy club, you don't want to be the only one there and feel obligated to laugh, but you don't want people crowded on top of you. Therefore, regional mall developers seek an optimal corridor design in order to enhance the shopping experience, enhance tenants' revenue, and create more desirable retail space.

DETAILED DESCRIPTION OF THE SPACE

In addition to the location of the space, the lease will include a detailed description of the space to be leased. Further, you must specify what is included in "the space". Is the carpet included? What about the light fixtures, the counter, wiring, windows, shelving, etc.? Do these things stay when a tenant leaves? Do they have to be removed? The lease describes these details.

TENANT MIX

Percentage rents encourage you to create an exciting shopping environment. Some tenants refuse to lease if other similar stores are in the center, as they want complementary stores, but not direct competition. Therefore, you will have to negotiate the terms under which you can lease space to competitors. Many conflicts arise as a result of these clauses. For example, if you signed a lease with a woman's clothing store that states you cannot lease space in the center to another "top quality woman's clothing store," is Burlington Coat Factory a top quality woman's clothing store? They sell clothing for women, but does that make Burlington Coat Factory a "top quality woman's clothing store"? Or does the lease clause prohibiting the presence of a second florist in the center prohibit Walmart from selling poinsettias and Christmas trees during the Christmas season?

In other cases, a tenant will lease only if other tenants remain in the center. As a result of these co-tenancy clauses, a center could lose several tenants if one key tenant goes under, goes dark, or refuses to renew their lease.

On the other hand, the landlord may prohibit the tenant from opening other stores within a certain distance. These **radius restrictions** protect the landlord from the tenant potentially cannibalizing sales at the center. For instance, if an anchor grocery store tenant was not subject to a radius restriction, they could open a new store across the street at a competing center. This would no doubt lower sales for your in-line tenants, reduce your percentage rents, and could even cause in-line tenants to go out of business. That is why landlords seek a radius restriction, particularly for anchor tenants.

PARKING

Tenants are concerned with the amount, location, and maintenance of parking. If there are not enough spaces to service the customers, the stores will lose business. As a result, you will lose percentage rent and/or have tenants vacate the space. In addition, tenants will also want sufficient parking close to their location. If customers cannot park within proximity to their destination, they may not visit the location. The lease may also specify the layout of the parking lot, which may inhibit the redevelopment of the center years from now. In addition, maintenance and lighting of parking lots is of critical importance to tenants.

RECOURSE AND SECURITY DEPOSIT

Who exactly is responsible under the terms of the lease? Is it a new division of a high credit company? If so, and the new division ceases to operate, you are stuck with no tenant and no payment recourse to the high credit parent. This issue frequently arises in office leases. For example, Coca Cola US is a very high credit tenant, but the tenant who leases from you in Moscow is Coca Cola Russia. If they cannot establish a profitable business in Russia, Coca Cola Russia will fold, and you cannot look to Coca Cola US for rent payment. Therefore, you will try to get both the subsidiary and the parent as signatories to the lease. Not surprisingly, the tenant will generally try to keep the parent off the lease.

You will want the individual entrepreneurs and partners of the tenant to be on the lease in addition to their firm. Thus, if the firm goes bankrupt, you can look to these individuals for continued rental payment. Law firms, consulting firms, and accounting firms often must sign the lease as individual partners if they want to get the space they desire.

Alternative forms of recourse are to require that the tenant put up a security deposit or letter of credit, which is only available to you as recourse if the tenant fails to perform on the lease. A problem frequently arises when the tenant goes bankrupt and you attempt to use the security deposit or draw upon the letter of credit, as the bankruptcy court may rule that these are corporate assets that must be used to satisfy the claims of the most senior lenders. But what about the rights specified in your lease? They are generally trumped by bankruptcy law.

CLOSING THOUGHT

We have just scratched the surface concerning the numerous terms that are critical to leases, most of which are non-monetary in nature. Remember real estate is a business, and smart operation is what generates profits over the long term. You must understand the underlying business to successfully negotiate the leases, especially in difficult markets. You also begin to appreciate why leases are so thick.

Chapter 4
Property Level Pro Forma Analysis

"Don't engage in mental masturbation; focus on decisions that matter".
-Dr. Peter Linneman

LEASE BY LEASE ANALYSIS

For many properties the leases provide detailed information about expected cash flows for years to come. Although this incredible detail enhances the accuracy of your future cash flow projections, the task of reading and analyzing numerous leases is tedious. Each lease contains different economic terms, often written by different landlords, drafted in different market and tax environments, and structured to reflect each tenant's and owner's needs at the time the lease was negotiated. Fortunately, software programs such as *Argus* assist the arduous task of creating financial models lease by lease.

Although you use software to assemble and organize lease information into beautiful rows and columns on a pro forma spreadsheet, only you can think about the property's risks and opportunities. For example, what happens when a lease expires? Is the space leasable? To what credit quality tenant? What rent and rent bumps will you receive for the space? What tenant concessions will be required? For how long? How long will it take to lease vacant space? How much of the building will never be leased?

To systematically analyze a property you enter key lease information for each tenant, and effectively create fictional tenants for any vacant space that exists today or in the future. A thorough understanding of the market, product, and tenants is critical for this analysis. If you are too optimistic you will forecast results that cannot come true, and experience severe return shortfalls. But if you are unduly conservative, you will undervalue the property, causing you to be outbid, sell too cheaply, or never do a deal.

LINE ITEM ANALYSIS

With the help of sophisticated property software packages, such as *Argus*, you can create detailed financial pro formas. What is the appropriate time frame to analyze? Pro formas are usually presented on an annual basis, but depending on your investment and information needs, a more detailed time interval may be in order. As an investor you will need to know in great detail when the property generates cash, because you will have monthly operating and debt payments. Small changes in the timing of cash flows may force you to miss payments, causing headaches with employees, vendors, and lenders.

Typically, a detailed pro forma analysis is carried out for 5-7 years. Little value is gained by carrying out the analysis for 50 years, as accuracy rapidly diminishes. In addition, if you have 500 columns in your financial model you will probably lose "bifocal points", as a 500 column spreadsheet will be very difficult to read, and your target user (be it your loan officer, boss, potential investor, or professor) will be unable to read your entries, and may not bother to analyze, let alone approve, your deal. There is no gain from making a spreadsheet too complex to effectively utilize, as in the end it is just simple mathematics. If a major event is about to occur, such as a major tenant vacating the building in the 8th year, or a tax abatement expiring in the 10th year, then it is prudent to carry out the pro forma analysis a year or two beyond such an event. Otherwise, keep your financial model detailed, but simple enough to be useful.

TOTAL RENTAL INCOME

To calculate rental income, you start with the revenue you would receive if the building's leasable space was 100% occupied. This is the **gross potential rental revenue (GPR)**. Gross potential rental revenue is calculated as the base rent multiplied by the property's total leasable square feet. For instance, assume you are the owner of Kathy Center, a 300,000 leasable square foot strip shopping center in Bethesda, Maryland. The average base rent you charge to current tenants is approximately $15 per leasable square foot per year. Thus, your annual gross potential rental revenue is $4.5 million ($15 per square foot * 300,000 total leasable square feet), as summarized in Figure 4.1.

FIGURE 4.1

Kathy Center Gross Potential Rental Revenue Calculation	
Total Rentable Square Feet	300,000
Average Base Rent (per square foot)	$15.00
Gross Potential Rental Revenue	**$4,500,000**

Our use of average base rent is a simplification, as you will charge tenants different rents for their space. Thus, the precise calculation of gross potential rental revenue is a complex lease by lease calculation, estimating the rent you will receive on any vacant space. Based on your existing leases and your expectations for future leasing, Figure 4.2 displays your estimates of the gross potential rental revenue from Kathy Center for the next five years.

FIGURE 4.2

Kathy Center Cash Flow Statement Operating Income	Year 1	Year 2	Year 3	Year 4	Year 5
Gross Potential Rental Revenue	**$ 4,500,000**	**$ 4,590,127**	**$ 4,816,605**	**$ 4,925,280**	**$ 4,958,280**

The interesting thing about real estate cash flows is that the contractual nature of the leases makes revenues easier to predict than for most businesses, as you can model when leases will be renewed, expire, etc. Remember that many leases were signed in market conditions that were very different from the current environment, so in order to accurately forecast revenue you must both incorporate lease specific rental information and estimate future rents. As a result, you will not always see a smooth growth pattern for rental revenue. In fact, if high-priced rental space is vacating into an overbuilt market, rental revenue can decline. In our example, the fluctuations are due to lease terminations and changing market rents.

VACANCY

In the Kathy Center example, three leases expire in January of Year 2. You expect to re-sign two of the three tenants, but think you will not renew the lease for the third space, resulting in 3,000 leasable square feet vacancy (1%) at the end of Year 2. Therefore, you will not receive the projected gross potential rental revenue associated with this 3,000 feet in Year 2. You must subtract the expected gross potential rental revenue associated with the vacant space from the $4.5 million total expected gross potential revenue in Year 2 to calculate the net base rental revenue you expect to receive on occupied space. You perform the same calculation for each year based on your rent and vacancy expectations.

Not all vacancy is equal. Some vacancy exists even in a fully "stabilized" building. For example, a stabilized apartment building will almost always have some empty space, as tenants will be moving in and out as a part of normal tenant turnover. However, vacancy can also extend beyond normal turnover, particularly in weak markets and for vulnerable properties. Such vacancy is often very lumpy, for example, when a corporation that leases half of your office building vacates the property. And some space is effectively non-leasable.

A critical thing to remember about vacancy is its impact on other line items. For instance, as vacancies increase, expense reimbursements will decrease, as there is no tenant to pay reimbursable expenses. A similar relationship generally exists between vacancy and ancillary income, as with fewer people occupying the space, there will be fewer cars parking, decreased washing machine usage, etc. Of course, ancillary income need not diminish with higher vacancy. For example, companies will still pay landlords to utilize rooftops for antennae towers or signage. Therefore, you must carefully analyze each source of ancillary income to determine the appropriate relationship. Also some cost items will vary with vacancy. Bad analysis will generate useless results. You will need to make informed, not capricious, assumptions about likely market outcomes.

The interaction between vacancy and other line items is not limited to those detailed above, but these examples help you understand the interrelated nature of property performance. These interactions mean that sensitivity analyses that simply change one line item ("what if rent is 10% lower") without exploring how it changes other items are meaningless. Real estate is a real business, and you cannot make judgments on its risks and opportunities if you do not understand the business. Real estate is not a spreadsheet, though a spreadsheet is a useful tool of the trade.

FIGURE 4.3

Kathy Center Cash Flow Statement Operating Income	Year 1	Year 2	Year 3	Year 4	Year 5
Gross Potential Rental Revenue	$ 4,500,000	$ 4,590,127	$ 4,816,605	$ 4,925,280	$ 4,958,280
Vacancy	$ -	**$ (45,901)**	**$ (72,249)**	**$ (98,506)**	**$ (148,748)**
Net Base Rental Revenue	$ 4,500,000	$ 4,544,225	$ 4,744,356	$ 4,826,774	$ 4,809,531

OVERAGE/PERCENTAGE RENT

Rent overage usually exists only for retail properties. Retail rent frequently is divided into **base rent** and **percentage rent** (overage). If sales for the tenant exceed predetermined revenue, then a percentage of those sales are paid to the landlord as rent. The sales **breakpoint** is specified in the tenant's lease.

Based on negotiations with tenants you expect the percentage rents from Kathy Center as summarized in Figure 4.4. The total of percentage rents and the net base rental revenue is the total rental income you expect to receive from the property.

FIGURE 4.4

Kathy Center Cash Flow Statement Operating Income					
	Year 1	Year 2	Year 3	Year 4	Year 5
Gross Potential Rental Revenue	$ 4,500,000	$ 4,590,127	$ 4,816,605	$ 4,925,280	$ 4,958,280
Vacancy	$ -	$ (45,901)	$ (72,249)	$ (98,506)	$ (148,748)
Net Base Rental Revenue	$ 4,500,000	$ 4,544,225	$ 4,744,356	$ 4,826,774	$ 4,809,531
Percentage Rents	**$ 93,305**	**$ 66,210**	**$ 66,926**	**$ 64,003**	**$ 65,425**
Total Rental Income	$ 4,593,305	$ 4,610,435	$ 4,811,281	$ 4,890,777	$ 4,874,956

EXPENSE REIMBURSEMENTS (TENANT REIMBURSEMENTS, RECOVERABLE EXPENSES, RECOVERIES)

Tenant reimbursements are payments specified in the leases, made by tenants to the landlord for specified property expenses, such as insurance, property taxes, security, and utilities. These reimbursements are costs initially borne by the landlord, and recovered from tenants as specified in their leases. The specifics of how these costs, including **common area maintenance (CAM)**, are repaid by tenants depends upon market conditions at the time the leases were signed, and on the negotiating strategies of the landlords and tenants. CAM costs are associated with operating and maintaining a property's common space, such as the sidewalks and parking lots of Kathy Center. Costs included in CAM for Kathy Center also include security, utilities, trash removal, landscaping, sidewalk cleaning, janitorial work, parking lot, sidewalk, and signage repair. Your estimates for CAM costs and reimbursements are displayed in Figure 4.5. In our example, the tenants in Kathy Center are expected to reimburse you for all property taxes and common area maintenance.

The local government assesses property taxes on the center based upon the assessed value of the center. They send you a tax bill, which you pay, and then pass it on to your tenants as specified in their leases. This pass-through is often, but not necessarily, based on the tenant's proportionate share of leasable square footage. Your estimates of property tax reimbursements are displayed in Figure 4.5.

FIGURE 4.5

Kathy Center Cash Flow Statement Operating Income					
	Year 1	Year 2	Year 3	Year 4	Year 5
Rental Income:					
Gross Potential Rental Revenue	$ 4,500,000	$ 4,590,127	$ 4,816,605	$ 4,925,280	$ 4,958,280
Vacancy	$ -	$ (45,901)	$ (72,249)	$ (98,506)	$ (148,748)
Net Base Rental Revenue	$ 4,500,000	$ 4,544,225	$ 4,744,356	$ 4,826,774	$ 4,809,531
Percentage Rents	$ 93,305	$ 66,210	$ 66,926	$ 64,003	$ 65,425
Total Rental Income	$ 4,593,305	$ 4,610,435	$ 4,811,281	$ 4,890,777	$ 4,874,956
Expense Reimbursements:					
CAM Billings	**$ 445,368**	**$ 440,267**	**$ 420,196**	**$ 415,895**	**$ 376,894**
Property Tax Billings	**$ 390,428**	**$ 370,123**	**$ 351,126**	**$ 346,681**	**$ 330,128**

Each landlord defines CAM differently and allocates it as specified in the property's leases. Furthermore, while some of the costs such as utilities, security, and trash removal at Kathy Center are common to all properties, some properties incur specific CAM costs. For instance, an office owner may incur costs associated with elevators.

Ancillary Income

Ancillary income is the income generated from all other activities conducted at the property. This may include revenue derived from parking facilities, laundry services, entertainment facilities, storage spaces, communication towers, etc. You will often encounter unbelievable ancillary income forecasts. For example, does the pro forma ancillary revenue forecast require that the parking lot be fully occupied 24 hours a day, 365 days a year? This is not likely, as there will generally be vacant spaces in the parking lot over-night and during holidays. Or will every resident really use the coin operated washer and dryer every day? Such lapses in business logic, or pure deception, are common. When evaluating these forecasts always step back and ask yourself if the numbers make basic business sense. Generally, ancillary income declines as vacancy increases.

FIGURE 4.6

Kathy Center Cash Flow Statement Operating Income	Year 1	Year 2	Year 3	Year 4	Year 5
Rental Income:					
Gross Potential Rental Revenue	$ 4,500,000	$ 4,590,127	$ 4,816,605	$ 4,925,280	$ 4,958,280
Vacancy	**0%**	**1%**	**1.50%**	**2%**	**3%**
Vacancy	$ -	$ (45,901)	$ (72,249)	$ (98,506)	$ (148,748)
Net Base Rental Revenue	$ 4,500,000	$ 4,544,225	$ 4,744,356	$ 4,826,774	$ 4,809,531
Percentage Rents	$ 93,305	$ 66,210	$ 66,926	$ 64,003	$ 65,425
Total Rental Income	$ 4,593,305	$ 4,610,435	$ 4,811,281	$ 4,890,777	$ 4,874,956
Expense Reimbursements:					
CAM Billings	$ 445,368	$ 440,267	$ 420,196	$ 415,895	$ 376,894
Property Tax Billings	$ 390,428	$ 370,123	$ 351,126	$ 346,681	$ 330,128
Ancillary Income	**$ 24,580**	**$ 23,251**	**$ 24,654**	**$ 23,125**	**$ 24,188**
Gross Income	$ 5,453,681	$ 5,444,076	$ 5,607,257	$ 5,676,478	$ 5,606,166

Credit Loss/Bad Debt

Bad debt must be deducted to reflect the anticipated non-payment of rent and other revenues. In quality properties, bad debt will usually be about 1-2% of the expected rental revenue. This percentage rises in a weak economic environment, or as your tenant quality profile deteriorates. While you do not know which tenants will fail to meet their rental obligations, or when, you must have an estimate of the expected default rate. Ask if a tenant has lost a major contract, or taken on a lot of debt, or whether an apartment tenant has lost her job. It will generally be a different tenant every month that does not pay rent. In fact, if it is always the same tenant, it may be time to kick the tenant out of the building. To not allow for bad debt will lead to an overvaluation of the property's revenue capacity. Subtracting expected credit loss from gross income results in **total operating income**.

FIGURE 4.7

Kathy Center Cash Flow Statement Operating Income	Year 1	Year 2	Year 3	Year 4	Year 5
Rental Income:					
Gross Potential Rental Revenue	$ 4,500,000	$ 4,590,127	$ 4,816,605	$ 4,925,280	$ 4,958,280
Vacancy	**0%**	**1%**	**1.50%**	**2%**	**3%**
Vacancy	$ -	$ (45,901)	$ (72,249)	$ (98,506)	$ (148,748)
Net Base Rental Revenue	$ 4,500,000	$ 4,544,225	$ 4,744,356	$ 4,826,774	$ 4,809,531
Percentage Rents	$ 93,305	$ 66,210	$ 66,926	$ 64,003	$ 65,425
Total Rental Income	$ 4,593,305	$ 4,610,435	$ 4,811,281	$ 4,890,777	$ 4,874,956
Expense Reimbursements:					
CAM Billings	$ 445,368	$ 440,267	$ 420,196	$ 415,895	$ 376,894
Property Tax Billings	$ 390,428	$ 370,123	$ 351,126	$ 346,681	$ 330,128
Ancillary Income	$ 24,580	$ 23,251	$ 24,654	$ 23,125	$ 24,188
Gross Income	$ 5,453,681	$ 5,444,076	$ 5,607,257	$ 5,676,478	$ 5,606,166
Credit Loss	**$ (54,537)**	**$ (54,441)**	**$ (56,073)**	**$ (56,765)**	**$ (56,062)**
Total Operating Income	$ 5,399,145	$ 5,389,635	$ 5,551,185	$ 5,619,714	$ 5,550,105

OPERATING EXPENSES

Broadly defined, operating costs are the costs required to effectively operate the property. It is important to understand how and why these costs change over time. The costs of items like security will generally correlate with inflation, while local taxes historically increase more rapidly. Insurance costs can increase dramatically, while utility costs will vary over time depending on both inflation and property vacancy.

REIMBURSABLE EXPENSES

Reimbursable costs are those initially borne by the landlord. For Kathy Center, you expect full reimbursement for all property taxes and CAM costs for occupied space, and subtract these costs, as displayed in Figure 4.8. However, this is not always the case. In particular, you cannot recover costs from vacant space. It is typical, though not required, that tenants pay their pro rata share of these costs. Hence, vacancy generally reduces these recoveries pro rata.

Common Area Maintenance (CAM) Costs: CAM costs refer to upkeep for areas and services that benefit all tenants. Examples include heating or cleaning building hallways, security, and parking lot maintenance. Malls provide a vivid example of CAM costs. Think of all the walking and lounging space that is not leased by *Express*, *Sears*, *JC Penny*, or other retail stores. Someone must clean, maintain, and provide security for such areas for the property to function. Tenants reimburse CAM costs as dictated by their leases.

Property Taxes: Property taxes are collected by the local government and must be paid regardless whether the property generates any revenue. They are calculated based on an assessed tax value. A pro rata vacancy adjustment is made for vacancy non-recovery.

FIGURE 4.8

Kathy Center Cash Flow Statement					
	Year 1	Year 2	Year 3	Year 4	Year 5
OPERATING INCOME					
Rental Income:					
Gross Potential Rental Revenue	$ 4,500,000	$ 4,590,127	$ 4,816,605	$ 4,925,280	$ 4,958,280
Vacancy	$ -	$ (45,901)	$ (72,249)	$ (98,506)	$ (148,748)
Net Base Rental Revenue	$ 4,500,000	$ 4,544,225	$ 4,744,356	$ 4,826,774	$ 4,809,531
Percentage Rents	$ 93,305	$ 66,210	$ 66,926	$ 64,003	$ 65,425
Total Rental Income	$ 4,593,305	$ 4,610,435	$ 4,811,281	$ 4,890,777	$ 4,874,956
Expense Reimbursements:					
CAM Billings	$ 445,368	$ 440,267	$ 420,196	$ 415,895	$ 376,894
Property Tax Billings	$ 390,428	$ 370,123	$ 351,126	$ 346,681	$ 330,128
Ancillary Income	$ 24,580	$ 23,251	$ 24,654	$ 23,125	$ 24,188
Gross Income	$ 5,453,681	$ 5,444,076	$ 5,607,257	$ 5,676,478	$ 5,606,166
Credit Loss	$ (54,537)	$ (54,441)	$ (56,073)	$ (56,765)	$ (56,062)
Total Operating Income	$ 5,399,145	$ 5,389,635	$ 5,551,185	$ 5,619,714	$ 5,550,105
OPERATING EXPENSES					
Reimbursable Expenses:					
Common Area Maintenance	**$ (445,368)**	**$ (463,183)**	**$ (481,710)**	**$ (500,978)**	**$ (521,018)**
Property Taxes	**$ (390,428)**	**$ (406,045)**	**$ (422,287)**	**$ (439,178)**	**$ (456,746)**

NON-REIMBURSABLE EXPENSES

You may incur other operating costs associated with Kathy Center without the right to reimbursement from tenants. Your estimates for each of these non-reimbursable expenses are included in Figure 4.9. The sum of reimbursable and non-reimbursable expenses equals total operating costs expected for Kathy Center. Note that depending on negotiations, different expenses may be reimbursable. For example, while insurance is not a reimbursable expense for Kathy Center, it may be for another property.

Insurance: You will generally obtain insurance to protect the property from natural disasters, tort liability, theft, fire, etc. You may also require each tenant to obtain individual policies for the interior of their space to cover potential liabilities including damage to inventory, customer accidents, employee mishaps, etc. These costs can be very volatile.

Utilities: Utility expenses include water, electric and gas bills. Since most modern buildings have separate utility meters for each tenant, you can easily calculate how much of the total property's utility bill each tenant owes. At

Kathy Center, however, you are responsible for all utilities, excluding those covered under the CAM reimbursement. At another property, these may be recoverable expenses.

Management: Management expense includes all costs associated with providing day-to-day managerial services. This line item represents either the costs associated with in-house management or the fee paid to a third party management company.

FIGURE 4.9

Kathy Center Cash Flow Statement					
	Year 1	Year 2	Year 3	Year 4	Year 5
OPERATING INCOME					
Rental Income:					
Gross Potential Rental Revenue	$ 4,500,000	$ 4,590,127	$ 4,816,605	$ 4,925,280	$ 4,958,280
Vacancy	$ -	$ (45,901)	$ (72,249)	$ (98,506)	$ (148,748)
Net Base Rental Revenue	$ 4,500,000	$ 4,544,225	$ 4,744,356	$ 4,826,774	$ 4,809,531
Percentage Rents	$ 93,305	$ 66,210	$ 66,926	$ 64,003	$ 65,425
Total Rental Income	$ 4,593,305	$ 4,610,435	$ 4,811,281	$ 4,890,777	$ 4,874,956
Expense Reimbursements:					
CAM Billings	$ 445,368	$ 440,267	$ 420,196	$ 415,895	$ 376,894
Property Tax Billings	$ 390,428	$ 370,123	$ 351,126	$ 346,681	$ 330,128
Ancillary Income	$ 24,580	$ 23,251	$ 24,654	$ 23,125	$ 24,188
Gross Income	$ 5,453,681	$ 5,444,076	$ 5,607,257	$ 5,676,478	$ 5,606,166
Credit Loss	$ (54,537)	$ (54,441)	$ (56,073)	$ (56,765)	$ (56,062)
Total Operating Income	$ 5,399,145	$ 5,389,635	$ 5,551,185	$ 5,619,714	$ 5,550,105
OPERATING EXPENSES					
Reimbursable Expenses:					
Common Area Maintenance	$ (445,368)	$ (463,183)	$ (481,710)	$ (500,978)	$ (521,018)
Property Taxes	$ (390,428)	$ (406,045)	$ (422,287)	$ (439,178)	$ (456,746)
Non-Reimbursable Expenses:					
Insurance	**$ (55,548)**	**$ (57,734)**	**$ (60,017)**	**$ (62,389)**	**$ (64,855)**
Utilities	**$ (105,114)**	**$ (109,355)**	**$ (113,755)**	**$ (118,334)**	**$ (123,097)**
Management	**$ (83,580)**	**$ (86,923)**	**$ (90,400)**	**$ (94,016)**	**$ (97,776)**
Total Operating Expenses	$ (1,080,038)	$ (1,123,240)	$ (1,168,169)	$ (1,214,896)	$ (1,263,492)

FIGURE 4.10

Kathy Center Cash Flow Statement					
	Year 1	Year 2	Year 3	Year 4	Year 5
OPERATING INCOME					
Total Operating Income	$ 5,399,145	$ 5,389,635	$ 5,551,185	$ 5,619,714	$ 5,550,105
OPERATING EXPENSES					
Total Operating Expenses	$ (1,080,038)	$ (1,123,240)	$ (1,168,169)	$ (1,214,896)	$ (1,263,492)
NOI	**$ 4,319,107**	**$ 4,266,396**	**$ 4,383,016**	**$ 4,404,818**	**$ 4,286,613**

Net Operating Income (NOI): NOI is perhaps the most discussed performance metric in commercial real estate, and is defined as total operating income less total operating expenses

TENANT IMPROVEMENTS (TIs)

TIs are physical improvements made to make leased space habitable, useful, and pleasant. New office and retail space is usually offered to the tenant as a plain vanilla box with no furnishings, such as light fixtures, carpeting, etc. For completed buildings, the space is generally offered in "as is" condition, i.e., as left by the previous tenant. Tenant improvements make the space operational and acceptable to the tenant. In order to entice a tenant to occupy the space, the landlord will often agree to pay part of the tenant improvements. The negotiations over how much, if any, tenant improvements the landlord pays are dictated by market conditions. If the market is hot and the landlord has several potential tenants wanting the space, they will not have to offer much in the way of TIs. Since TIs are set when the lease is signed, if a cold market suddenly turns hot, the tenant will still receive the agreed upon TIs.

Rarely will a new tenant desire the exact same improvements as the previous tenant. Perhaps the most extreme example of these phenomena is a restaurant. Every restaurant operator has a philosophy on bar and kitchen design, as well as decor. The landlord may spend a lot of money on TIs for a restaurant, and eighteen months later the landlord may have to rip everything out and pay big TIs to attract a new restaurant after the original tenant went bankrupt.

TIs and leasing commissions are relatively predictable, generally coinciding with vacancy. Of course, while unexpected vacancy occurs, you generally know when leases expire. You must estimate when space will be vacant, for how long, at what rent and cost recovery rate, and what TI package and leasing commissions will be required. Renewal leases generally command lower TIs and leasing commissions. Depending upon the tenant and market conditions, people generally model the chance of tenant renewal between 25-75%.

LEASING COMMISSIONS

Leasing commissions are the fees you pay to a broker or leasing company (sometimes a separate firm which you own) that leases your space. Leasing commissions will also generally correspond with your lease expiration schedule, as reflected in the lumpiness displayed in the Leasing Commissions line for Kathy Center in Figure 4.11. For example, the lease turnover in 2012 is expected to result in relatively large leasing commissions. If you do the leasing, these commissions are paid by the property to your management company.

FIGURE 4.11

Kathy Center Cash Flow Statement					
	Year 1	Year 2	Year 3	Year 4	Year 5
OPERATING INCOME					
Rental Income:					
Gross Potential Rental Revenue	$ 4,500,000	$ 4,590,127	$ 4,816,605	$ 4,925,280	$ 4,958,280
Vacancy	**0%**	**1%**	**1.50%**	**2%**	**3%**
Vacancy	$ -	$ (45,901)	$ (72,249)	$ (98,506)	$ (148,748)
Net Base Rental Revenue	$ 4,500,000	$ 4,544,225	$ 4,744,356	$ 4,826,774	$ 4,809,531
Percentage Rents	$ 93,305	$ 66,210	$ 66,926	$ 64,003	$ 65,425
Total Rental Income	$ 4,593,305	$ 4,610,435	$ 4,811,281	$ 4,890,777	$ 4,874,956
Expense Reimbursements:					
CAM Billings	$ 445,368	$ 440,267	$ 420,196	$ 415,895	$ 376,894
Property Tax Billings	$ 390,428	$ 370,123	$ 351,126	$ 346,681	$ 330,128
Ancillary Income	$ 24,580	$ 23,251	$ 24,654	$ 23,125	$ 24,188
Gross Income	$ 5,453,681	$ 5,444,076	$ 5,607,257	$ 5,676,478	$ 5,606,166
Credit Loss	$ (54,537)	$ (54,441)	$ (56,073)	$ (56,765)	$ (56,062)
Total Operating Income	$ 5,399,145	$ 5,389,635	$ 5,551,185	$ 5,619,714	$ 5,550,105
OPERATING EXPENSES					
Reimbursable Expenses:					
Common Area Maintenance	$ (445,368)	$ (463,183)	$ (481,710)	$ (500,978)	$ (521,018)
Property Taxes	$ (390,428)	$ (406,045)	$ (422,287)	$ (439,178)	$ (456,746)
Non-Reimbursable Expenses:					
Insurance	$ (55,548)	$ (57,734)	$ (60,017)	$ (62,389)	$ (64,855)
Utilities	$ (105,114)	$ (109,355)	$ (113,755)	$ (118,334)	$ (123,097)
Management	$ (83,580)	$ (86,923)	$ (90,400)	$ (94,016)	$ (97,776)
Total	$ 244,242	$ 254,012	$ 264,172	$ 274,739	$ 285,729
Total Operating Expenses	$ (1,080,038)	$ (1,123,240)	$ (1,168,169)	$ (1,214,896)	$ (1,263,492)
NOI	$ 4,319,107	$ 4,266,396	$ 4,383,016	$ 4,404,818	$ 4,286,613
CAPITAL & LEASING COSTS					
Tenant Improvements	**$ (36,200)**	**$ (57,629)**	**$ (152,145)**	**$ (46,696)**	**$ (18,629)**
Leasing Commissions	**$ (12,200)**	**$ (41,722)**	**$ (107,561)**	**$ (25,567)**	**$ (18,760)**
Capital Expenditure	**$ (103,400)**	**$ (323,565)**	**$ (190,919)**	**$ (24,947)**	**$ (10,975)**
NOI after normal reserves	**$ 4,167,307**	**$ 3,843,480**	**$ 3,932,391**	**$ 4,307,608**	**$ 4,238,249**

CAPITAL EXPENDITURES

There are many rules of thumb for capital expenditures. For instance, if you operate a property in the northern US, where there are significant weather changes, you will need a higher reserve for cap ex than for a property located in a less extreme climate. Weather changes increase the likelihood of parking lot damage, leakage, roof damage, etc. Or if you operate a property near the ocean you will have higher cap ex needs due to the corrosive effects of salt. Older buildings will generally have higher capital expenditure needs than newer buildings, because it is harder to keep older buildings technologically competitive. Even the type of tenant impacts expected capital expenditures. For example, college students are much more "damage prone" apartment tenants than older adults. Of course, these are not all of the determinants of capital expenditures. But these examples give you an idea of the knowledge and experience you need to accurately forecast future cap ex needs.

The timing of some capital expenditures is predictable. For example, you may know when the elevators will be replaced. But more often you will use your judgment and experience to estimate expected annual expenditures, and incorporate a reserve for normalized capital expenditures.

NOI AFTER NORMAL RESERVES

This adjusted NOI, also known as unlevered cash flow, includes deductions for TIs, leasing commissions, and cap ex. These items are costs associated with operating the property, but are generally not included in NOI as normally defined in conformity with tax rules. Therefore, you will distinguish NOI from "NOI net of usual cap ex, TIs, and commissions". This variance is a common source of differences in reported cap rates, in that you may use NOI before these items, while someone else uses NOI after reserves. In either case, NOI summarizes the property's ability to generate income, irrespective of capital structure, where different owners may be able to achieve different NOIs from the property, depending upon their operating strategy and expertise.

DEPRECIATION VS. CAP EX

It is important to distinguish between "**Depreciation**" and "**Cap ex**". Cap ex reflects the property's actual wear and tear, for which you must spend money to keep your properties in competitive condition. For example, when you replace worn out carpets, money comes out of your pocket to pay for the new carpeting. Depreciation is a fiction created by Congress that governs how you are allowed to deduct the carpet for tax purposes. Depreciation is not a scientific exercise, but rather the result of a highly politicized tax collection process. Remember that age, design, location, tenancy, and luck determine actual capital expenditures in any given year, while tax rules alone determine depreciation.

If you underestimate required cap ex, you will find yourself with a building that is not competitive. To rectify this situation you will need to unexpectedly increase cap ex, substantially reducing your cash flows relative to expectations. So you had better be good at estimating required cap ex. It is common to make simplifying assumptions, such as 3% of gross potential revenue will be required for cap ex. Will cap ex ever be exactly 3% of revenue in any year? Of course not, but it is an educated guess of what cap ex will on average be for a property like Kathy Center . Alternatively, you may use a certain dollar amount per square foot or unit.

Actual cap ex is irregular, with large expenditures in certain years, and smaller amounts in others. For instance, cap ex in a year you replace an elevator, roof, or parking deck will be significantly higher than that for most years. Our model varies cap ex based on reasonable expectations. For example, cap ex in year Year 1 is about 2.3% of gross potential revenue, rising to 7% in Year 2 as that year major renovation is to take place with the electrical and water systems. Cap ex then drops to about 4% in Year 3 as renovations near completion. In the following two years, cap ex is less than 1% since no major maintenance is expected.

A common mistake made in the hotel sector is that whatever is assumed about cap ex, it consistently turned out to be too low, as hotels required ever greater expenditures for lobbies, bathrooms, furnishing, sound systems, technology, etc., in order to remain competitive. It might not seem like a lot of money, but an extra $0.20 per square foot on 300,000 feet is $60,000 per year.

Does forecasted depreciation tell you anything about actual cap ex? No. Future cap ex depends on the deterioration of sidewalks, elevators, carpeting, etc., while future depreciation is determined by Congress, working in concert with the IRS. Do you think that Congress conducted lengthy studies on the actual rate at which carpets need replacement? Of course not. The major discussion in Congress about depreciation was about how to collect the desired tax dollars in a way that gets them re-elected. Re-election is their pro forma! They may have testimony on the cap ex requirements from a variety of trade groups, but ultimately depreciation regulations reflect the political compromises necessary to get re-elected. If depreciation ever matches actual cap ex it is by pure accident, much like "if you give a monkey a typewriter and enough time, it will eventually write *War and Peace*". Forecasted cap ex reflects expectations about future outlays; forecasted depreciation reflects the application of depreciation rules to past outlays.

The taxable income you report to the IRS is net of depreciation. Therefore, the higher your depreciation, the lower your taxable income and tax bill. Depreciation is nothing more than a tax shelter granted by Congress. As a real estate owner you want your allowable depreciation as high possible, as you prefer a lower tax bill for a given pre-tax cash flow. Therefore, every industry lobbies Congress for depreciation tax shields. In contrast, you want your cap ex to be as low as possible while maintaining the property's competitive integrity. In fact, many of the operating expenses you incur are intended to keep future cap ex low. For example, when custodial workers vacuum the carpets it reduces the damage dirt does to your carpets, and extends their useful life.

In most countries, but not all, you are not allowed to depreciate land. Does land actually depreciate in value? It can. For example, what if you bought land thinking that a planned highway exit ramp would greatly improve access to your property, and the ramp is subsequently canceled? You bought the land believing you could develop a warehouse. However, without an exit ramp it is not a viable warehouse site, and the land is worth much less than you paid. That is economic depreciation of land. Nevertheless, Congress says that you cannot depreciate land, even in such instances.

How is future depreciation estimated? A (very) simple example illustrates the process. Assume you bought Kathy Center at a 9 cap on Year 1 NOI, for $48.5 million purchase price. Since you want your allowable depreciation to be as large as possible, you attempt to attribute as little of the $48.5 million purchase price to land as the IRS will allow. You could allocate none of the $48.5 million purchase price to land, and hence maximize your tax shield. But if you are audited, the IRS will retroactively make a "correct" land allocation and charge you interest and penalties on the taxes you saved due to your excessive depreciation. You will probably use an expert to select a "defensible" land allocation that is consistent with IRS norms.

Assume that your tax expert says that 20% of the total purchase price must be allocated to land. This means you can only depreciate 80% of the total purchase price for tax purposes. Of that 80%, you need to distinguish the allocation of value between structure and improvements, as well as specific allocations within the improvement category, as each has a different allowable depreciation rate. Structure generally refers to the building's frame, foundation slab, steel, brick, mortar, etc. Tax law requires you to depreciate the physical structure over a 27.5 (for residential) or 39 (for all other property types) year period. Note that a depreciable 39-year life means that $1/39^{th}$ (2.6%) of the value allocated to the structure is depreciable each year for 39 years. After that you can depreciate 0%. Improvements include elevators, furniture, carpeting, woodwork, lighting, etc. Tax law may allow you to depreciate such improvements over shorter periods. A 3-year depreciation allowance for improvements means that 33.33% of the allocated value is taken as depreciation each year for 3 years, and 0% thereafter.

You want to allocate as much of the $38.8 million depreciable value to improvements, but the IRS is vigilant about allocations. Your tax expert will establish the "correct" allocation based on IRS norms.

Figure 4.12 displays the allocation of the property purchase price for Kathy Center and associated depreciation. Our example allocates 20% to land, 50% to structure (39 year depreciation), 20% to 7-year improvements, and 10% to 3 year improvements.

FIGURE 4.12: KATHY CENTER

Kathy Center						
Purchase Information						
Purchase Price		$48.5 million				
Percentage allocations						
Land (20%)		$9.70 million				
Structure (50%)		$24.25 million				
7-year items (20%)		$9.70 million				
3-year items (10%)		$4.85 million				
Depreciation: Formula = Cost/Time						
		Year 1	Year 2	Year 3	Year 4	Year 5
	Calculation					
Land	0	$0.00 MM	$0.00 MM	$0.00 MM	$0.00 MM	$0.00 MM
Structure (over 39 yrs)	=24.3 MM/39	$0.62 MM	$0.62 MM	$0.62 MM	$0.62 MM	$0.62 MM
7-year items (over 7 yrs)	=9.7 MM/7	$1.39 MM	$1.39 MM	$1.39 MM	$1.39 MM	$1.39 MM
3-year items (over 3 yrs)	=4.9 MM/3	$1.62 MM	$1.62 MM	$1.62 MM	$0.00 MM	$0.00 MM
Total		**$3.62 MM**	**$3.62 MM**	**$3.62 MM**	**$2.01 MM**	**$2.01 MM**

The price you paid for the property reflects expected cash flows, including expected cap ex. Rarely do you approach the valuation of your property the way the IRS views it. Namely, how much is the land worth, how much is each improvement worth, and how much is the structure worth. It would be like asking "how much of a cake's value is due to the sugar?" Or flour? Or milk? It is the mix that creates the value of the cake, not the component parts. Your interest is the property's cash flow, while the IRS is interested in the ingredients.

The depreciation exercise is merely to calculate your tax shield. It is essential to understand that depreciation and capital expenditures are two totally different things. It is as if you have one department filled with tax accountants who know nothing about the building's operation who constantly try to minimize your taxes by carefully selecting the best depreciation allocations, and another department that is filled with real estate engineers who focus solely on minimizing the costs of the physical deterioration of your building. And the two departments do not socialize! As the owner, you care about what both departments have to say, but for very different reasons.

TIs, CAP EX AND DEPRECIATION

In addition to the depreciation of the purchase price, the IRS requires you to capitalize TIs and cap ex (to capitalize means to add the value of an expense to the balance sheet as a liability). Thus, for tax purposes instead of expensing these cash outflows as they occur, you must depreciate them over the appropriate depreciable lives. In general, cap ex will fall under the improvement category and each asset purchased or constructed using these funds will have a different depreciable life. As such, you will need to keep separate records for each asset acquired or constructed in each year. Obviously this type of depreciation exercise quickly becomes tedious. Assume that all cap ex is depreciable over 7 years.

TIs are depreciated differently, as for tax purposes landlords write-off TIs as follows: 50% of TIs in the first year, with the remainder amortized over the life of the lease, which we will assume to be 7 years. As a result, you expect to depreciate deductions for TIs and cap ex as summarized in Figure 4.13.

FIGURE 4.13

Kathy Center Depreciation Schedule: TIs & CAPEX					
	Year 1	Year 2	Year 3	Year 4	Year 5
Depreciation From:					
Total TIs	**$18,100**	**$31,831**	**$83,892**	**$43,846**	**$33,704**
Cap ex	**$14,771**	**$60,995**	**$88,269**	**$91,833**	**$93,401**
Total Annual Depreciation Expense	$32,871	$92,826	$172,161	$135,679	$127,105

Thus, the total depreciation deduction you can take over this five year period is the sum of the depreciation from TIs, cap ex. and the depreciation of the purchase price, as displayed in Figure 4.14.

FIGURE 4.14

Kathy Center Total Depreciation						
Purchase Information						
Purchase Price		$48.5 million				
Percentage allocations						
Land (20%)		$9.7 million				
Structure (50%)		$24.3 million				
7-year items (20%)		$9.7 million				
3-year items (10%)		$4.9 million				
Depreciation: Formula = Cost/Time						
		Year 1	Year 2	Year 3	Year 4	Year 5
	Calculation					
Land	0	$0.00 MM	$0.00 MM	$0.00 MM	$0.00 MM	$0.00 MM
Structure (over 39 yrs)	=24.3 MM/39	$0.62 MM	$0.62 MM	$0.62 MM	$0.62 MM	$0.62 MM
7-year items (over 7 yrs)	=9.7 MM/7	$1.39 MM	$1.39 MM	$1.39 MM	$1.39 MM	$1.39 MM
3-year items (over 3 yrs)	=4.9 MM/3	$1.62 MM	$1.62 MM	$1.62 MM	$0.00 MM	$0.00 MM
Total from Purchase		$3.624 MM	$3.624 MM	$3.624 MM	$2.008 MM	$2.008 MM
Total TIs		$0.018 MM	$0.032 MM	$0.084 MM	$0.044 MM	$0.034 MM
Total Cap Ex (rounded from Fig. 4.13)		$0.015 MM	$0.061 MM	$0.088 MM	$0.092 MM	$0.093 MM
Total		$3.657 MM	$3.717 MM	$3.796 MM	$2.143 MM	$2.135 MM

UNLEVERED NET CASH FLOW

To calculate net cash flow, subtract the total operating expenses and the cap ex, TIs, and leasing commissions from total operating income. The resulting **unlevered cash flow** reflects the net cash inflow from Kathy Center before any financing or tax liabilities, as displayed in the bottom line in Figure 4.15.

LEVERED CASH FLOW

If Kathy Center is unencumbered by debt and you were a tax-exempt entity, there would be no need for additional analysis. Also, if you were only interested in the property level performance, as opposed to cash flows to equity, there would be no need to incorporate financing or tax considerations. However, since you are a taxable owner and probably will use debt financing to complete your purchase of Kathy Center, you will also want to know the expected after tax cash flows to equity. To estimate cash flows to equity you need to incorporate debt and tax liabilities into your analysis.

Debt Financing: Loan points, amortization, and interest payments resulting from use of debt financing have an impact on the calculation of after tax equity cash flow. Assume you purchased Kathy Center for $48.5 million, using an 80% LTV or "Loan to Value" ($38.8 million), interest only, 5% interest rate mortgage in addition to your $9.7 million equity. The loan has a 7 year term.

FIGURE 4.15

Kathy Center Cash Flow Statement					
	Year 1	Year 2	Year 3	Year 4	Year 5
OPERATING INCOME					
Rental Income:					
Gross Potential Rental Revenue	$ 4,500,000	$ 4,590,127	$ 4,816,605	$ 4,925,280	$ 4,958,280
Vacancy	$ -	$ (45,901)	$ (72,249)	$ (98,506)	$ (148,748)
Net Base Rental Revenue	$ 4,500,000	$ 4,544,225	$ 4,744,356	$ 4,826,774	$ 4,809,531
Percentage Rents	$ 93,305	$ 66,210	$ 66,926	$ 64,003	$ 65,425
Total Rental Income	$ 4,593,305	$ 4,610,435	$ 4,811,281	$ 4,890,777	$ 4,874,956
Expense Reimbursements:					
CAM Billings	$ 445,368	$ 440,267	$ 420,196	$ 415,895	$ 376,894
Property Tax Billings	$ 390,428	$ 370,123	$ 351,126	$ 346,681	$ 330,128
Ancillary Income	$ 24,580	$ 23,251	$ 24,654	$ 23,125	$ 24,188
Gross Income	$ 5,453,681	$ 5,444,076	$ 5,607,257	$ 5,676,478	$ 5,606,166
Credit Loss	$ (54,537)	$ (54,441)	$ (56,073)	$ (56,765)	$ (56,062)
Total Operating Income	$ 5,399,145	$ 5,389,635	$ 5,551,185	$ 5,619,714	$ 5,550,105
OPERATING EXPENSES					
Reimbursable Expenses:					
Common Area Maintenance	$ (445,368)	$ (463,183)	$ (481,710)	$ (500,978)	$ (521,018)
Property Taxes	$ (390,428)	$ (406,045)	$ (422,287)	$ (439,178)	$ (456,746)
Non-Reimbursable Expenses:					
Insurance	$ (55,548)	$ (57,734)	$ (60,017)	$ (62,389)	$ (64,855)
Utilities	$ (105,114)	$ (109,355)	$ (113,755)	$ (118,334)	$ (123,097)
Management	$ (83,580)	$ (86,923)	$ (90,400)	$ (94,016)	$ (97,776)
Total Operating Expenses	$ (1,080,038)	$ (1,123,240)	$ (1,168,169)	$ (1,214,896)	$ (1,263,492)
NOI	$ 4,319,107	$ 4,266,396	$ 4,383,016	$ 4,404,818	$ 4,286,613
CAPITAL & LEASING COSTS					
Tenant Improvements	$ (36,200)	$ (57,629)	$ (152,145)	$ (46,696)	$ (18,629)
Leasing Commissions	$ (12,200)	$ (41,722)	$ (107,561)	$ (25,567)	$ (18,760)
Capital Expenditure	$ (103,400)	$ (323,565)	$ (190,919)	$ (24,947)	$ (10,975)
UNLEVERED CASH FLOW	**$ 4,167,307**	**$ 3,843,480**	**$ 3,932,391**	**$ 4,307,608**	**$ 4,238,249**

Loan Points: Loan points are the fee paid to the lender to compensate for underwriting costs. You were required to pay the lender a 50 basis point loan fee at closing. Thus, you paid the lender 0.5% of the face value of the loan, or $194,000 ($38.8 million * 0.5%), an immediate cash outflow at closing. You will not recognize any additional cash outflows associated with loan points. It does, however, have an impact on your future tax payments, as for tax purposes you must amortize this fee over the term of the loan.

Interest Payments: The loan carries a 5% fixed interest rate, resulting in a $1.94 million annual interest payment ($38.8 million mortgage * 5% interest rate). You deduct this annual interest payment from your estimated unlevered cash flow, as you must make this payment to the lender each year in order to retain control of Kathy Center. Figure 4.16 displays the cash outflows associated with this debt financing. Given this information, you can now calculate before tax **levered cash flow**, which is the unlevered cash flow minus interest payments and amortization, as summarized in Figure 4.16.

FIGURE 4.16

Kathy Center Cash Flow Statement Levered Cash Flows					
	Year 1	Year 2	Year 3	Year 4	Year 5
Unlevered Cash Flows	$ 4,167,307	$ 3,843,480	$ 3,932,391	$ 4,307,608	$ 4,238,249
Loan Points	$ (194,000)	$ -	$ -	$ -	$ -
Interest Payment	$ (1,940,000)	$ (1,940,000)	$ (1,940,000)	$ (1,940,000)	$ (1,940,000)
Before Tax Levered Cash Flows	**$ 2,033,307**	**$ 1,903,480**	**$ 1,992,391**	**$ 2,367,608**	**$ 2,298,249**

Taxable Income: The final step in determining your after tax levered (equity) cash flow for Kathy Center is the calculation of your expected annual tax liability. Assume that you purchased Kathy Center using a limited partnership structure. This is a pass-through entity, which means the tax liability is calculated for the property and literally passed through to the partners in the limited partnership. If you were a non-taxable entity such as a pension fund or a university, there would be no need to calculate the resulting tax liability that is passed through. You, however, are a taxable individual and as such are extremely interested in your expected tax bill to the IRS.

To determine your expected tax liability you must calculate your taxable income, which is the income you receive from the property according to IRS rules. While you might expect taxable income to equal your before tax cash flow (i.e. the actual money you receive from the property), the IRS sees it differently. Instead, several adjustments to the before tax cash flow are necessary to derive taxable income. Why? Because in some cases lobbyists were able to achieve beneficial rulings that help lower taxable income, while in other cases the government passed laws to generate tax revenue which result in higher taxable income. As a taxpayer you want taxable income as low as possible because your tax liability is calculated as your taxable income times your tax rate. Thus, the lower your taxable income, the lower your tax liability in that year.

DEPRECIATION, CAP EX, AND TIs

Depreciation expense serves as a tax shield because you are allowed to deduct the expense without a corresponding cash outflow, as seen in the adjustment to before tax cash flow in Figure 4.16. Tax law requires you to capitalize cap ex and TIs rather than expense them. As such you have to add back the costs of cap ex and TIs as demonstrated in Figure 4.17, to avoid double counting the expenses since they were previously deducted from NOI to get to unlevered cash flow.

FIGURE 4.17

Kathy Center Cash Flow Statement Taxable Income	Year 1	Year 2	Year 3	Year 4	Year 5
Before Tax Levered Cash Flows	$ 2,033,307	$ 1,903,480	$ 1,992,391	$ 2,367,608	$ 2,298,249
Adjustments:					
Less: Depreciation (Purchase Price)	$ (3,624,176)	$ (3,624,176)	$ (3,624,176)	$ (2,007,509)	$ (2,007,509)
Less: Depreciation (TIs)	$ (18,100)	$ (31,831)	$ (83,892)	$ (43,846)	$ (33,704)
Less: Depreciation (CAPEX)	$ (14,771)	$ (60,995)	$ (88,269)	$ (91,833)	$ (93,401)
Plus: CAPEX	**$ 103,400**	**$ 323,565**	**$ 190,919**	**$ 24,947**	**$ 10,975**
Plus: TIs	**$ 36,200**	**$ 57,629**	**$ 152,145**	**$ 46,696**	**$ 18,629**

POINTS AMORTIZATION

The last adjustment necessary to calculate taxable income for Kathy Center is the amortization of loan points. For tax purposes you have to capitalize the cost of the loan points, which are to be deducted (usually equally) over the life of the loan. The total loan fee was $194,000, amortized over 7 years, so you can deduct $27,714 annually from before tax cash flow, as displayed in Figure 4.18.

FIGURE 4.18

Kathy Center Cash Flow Statement Taxable Income	Year 1	Year 2	Year 3	Year 4	Year 5
Before Tax Levered Cash Flows	$ 2,033,307	$ 1,903,480	$ 1,992,391	$ 2,367,608	$ 2,298,249
Adjustments:					
Less: Depreciation (Purchase Price)	$ (3,624,176)	$ (3,624,176)	$ (3,624,176)	$ (2,007,509)	$ (2,007,509)
Less: Depreciation (TIs)	$ (18,100)	$ (31,831)	$ (83,892)	$ (43,846)	$ (33,704)
Less: Depreciation (CAPEX)	$ (14,771)	$ (60,995)	$ (88,269)	$ (91,833)	$ (93,401)
Plus: CAPEX	$ 103,400	$ 323,565	$ 190,919	$ 24,947	$ 10,975
Plus: TIs	$ 36,200	$ 57,629	$ 152,145	$ 46,696	$ 18,629
Plus: Principal Amortization	-	-	-	-	-
Less: Points Amortization	**$ (27,714)**	**$ (27,714)**	**$ (27,714)**	**$ (27,714)**	**$ (27,714)**

AFTER TAX EQUITY CASH FLOW

After making all of these adjustments to before tax cash flow, you can derive your taxable income from Kathy Center, as summarized in Figure 4.18. You then apply the federal tax rate that corresponds to your income bracket to the expected taxable income from Kathy Center. For simplicity, assume your entire taxable income will be taxed at the highest marginal tax rate of 38.6%. This simplification ignores the marginal tax system that is actually used in calculating the income tax liability. The resulting tax liability for Kathy Center is calculated below in Figure 4.19. Subtracting the tax liability from pre-tax cash flow yields your after-tax equity cash flows.

FIGURE 4.19

Kathy Center Cash Flow Statement Taxable Income	Year 1	Year 2	Year 3	Year 4	Year 5
Before Tax Levered Cash Flows	$ 2,033,307	$ 1,903,480	$ 1,992,391	$ 2,367,608	$ 2,298,249
Adjustments:					
Less: Depreciation (Purchase Price)	$ (3,624,176)	$ (3,624,176)	$ (3,624,176)	$ (2,007,509)	$ (2,007,509)
Less: Depreciation (TIs)	$ (18,100)	$ (31,831)	$ (83,892)	$ (43,846)	$ (33,704)
Less: Depreciation (CAPEX)	$ (14,771)	$ (60,995)	$ (88,269)	$ (91,833)	$ (93,401)
Plus: CAPEX	$ 103,400	$ 323,565	$ 190,919	$ 24,947	$ 10,975
Plus: TIs	$ 36,200	$ 57,629	$ 152,145	$ 46,696	$ 18,629
Plus: Principal Amortization	$ -	$ -	$ -	$ -	$ -
Less: Points Amortization	$ (27,714)	$ (27,714)	$ (27,714)	$ (27,714)	$ (27,714)
Taxable Income (Loss)	$ (1,511,855)	$ (1,460,042)	$ (1,488,596)	$ 268,348	$ 165,525
Less: Application of Suspended Losses	$ -	$ -	$ -	$ (268,348)	$ (165,525)
Net Taxable Income (Loss)	$ (1,511,855)	$ (1,460,042)	$ (1,488,596)	$ -	$ -
Less: Tax Liability (38.6%) *	$ -	$ -	$ -	$ -	$ -
Plus: Depreciation (Purchase Price)	$ 3,624,176	$ 3,624,176	$ 3,624,176	$ 2,007,509	$ 2,007,509
Plus: Depreciation (TIs)	$ 18,100	$ 31,831	$ 83,892	$ 43,846	$ 33,704
Plus: Depreciation (CAPEX)	$ 14,771	$ 60,995	$ 88,269	$ 91,833	$ 93,401
Less: CAPEX	$ (103,400)	$ (323,565)	$ (190,919)	$ (24,947)	$ (10,975)
Less: TIs	$ (36,200)	$ (57,629)	$ (152,145)	$ (46,696)	$ (18,629)
Less: Principal Amortization	$ -	$ -	$ -	$ -	$ -
Plus: Points Amortization	$ (194,000)	$ -	$ -	$ -	$ -
After-Tax Cash Flows	**$ 2,033,307**	**$ 1,903,480**	**$ 1,992,391**	**$ 2,367,608**	**$ 2,298,249**

* Note: Profitable real estate properties without a tax shelter must pay income taxes annually. In this example, losses are sustained in years 1 through 3, and income is fully sheltered in years 4 and 5 from suspended loss carry-forward. Consequently, tax liability is $0 in all years shown, and before and after tax cash flows in each year are equal to one another.

THE 1980s

This depreciation discussion provides some insight into the craziness of the 1980s real estate tax law. If you purchased a property in the 1980s for a 9% cap rate, and allocated 20% of the purchase price to land, with the remainder allocated to structure and improvements as above, the IRS Code allowed you to take roughly 8% of the purchase price as depreciation each year. With a 9% NOI return each year, you only had a 1% tax exposure (9%-8%), excluding any tax shield from interest expenses. If you had any debt on the building you generated significant tax losses, even though the building was cash flow positive. Further, you were allowed to sell these tax losses to third parties from 1981 through 1986. This led property owners to create tax losses which were sold to people seeking to shelter taxable income (doctors, lawyers, etc.). The income derived from the sale of these tax losses lowered the effective acquisition cost for the property owner.

Real estate quickly became a business of manufacturing tax losses rather than satisfying tenant demand for space. It is hardly surprising that an incredible excess supply occurred during the 1980s, as it paid well to lose money!

Figure 4.20 demonstrates the 1980s scenario for a residential property, Leslie Heights. This property was bought for $100 million with 90% leverage. This high level of debt allowed the owner to acquire the property with little (if any) of their own money at risk. An $8 million depreciation allowance was taken. The profit derived purely from selling the tax credits. In particular, the owner could generate their equity requirement ($10 million) for the purchase essentially from the sale of the first two years of tax losses ($4.4 million annually). Note that the

$600,000 pre-tax profit (also the after tax profit) represents a 6% return on the $10 million equity. In addition, if the property appreciated at the rate of inflation (which was roughly 10%) for 3 years, if you sold your property at the end of Year 3, the pre-tax annual equity IRR is seemingly 67% (see figure 4.21). Note that all of this occurs in spite of the fact that annual interest payments exceed stabilized NOI by $1.8 million.

FIGURE 4.20

Leslie Heights with Pre-1986 Tax Shelters		
Purchase Price		$100 MM
Interest Calculation		
Debt		$90 MM
Interest Rate		12%
Interest Payment		10.8 MM
Tax Calculation		
NOI		$9 MM
Depreciation		(8.0 MM)
Interest		(10.8 MM)
Taxable Income		**(9.8 MM)**
Value of excess tax shelter at 50% tax bracket		
Taxable Income		(9.8 MM)
Tax Bracket Rate		50%
Value	9.8 * .5	**4.9 MM**
Cash Flow from Operation		
NOI		$9.0 MM
Cap Ex		(2 MM)
Interest		(10.8 MM)
Tax Shelter Sales	90 cents on the dollar: (4.9*.9)	4.4 MM
Net Cash Flow from Operation		**$0.6 MM**

The industry collapsed once these tax shelters were eliminated and banks disciplined their lending. Figure 4.22 displays the same deal treated in the current tax framework. With the tax practices of old you could achieve a 6% pre-tax return, while under today's structure you could realize a negative 38% return! Not surprisingly, development of new space quickly aligned to meeting property demand (rather than selling tax losses). Actually, the atmosphere of that time was even more ridiculous, in that the developer was paid for all future tax losses up front, rather than as they occurred. So, the developer cashed out very early in this sort of deal. Let's hope that those days never return.

FIGURE 4.21

Leslie Heights Return on Equity Calculation (in MM)	
Calculation showing sale of property	
Proceeds From Sale *(property grows at inflation: 100*1.1^3)*	$ 133.00
Debt Payment	$ (90.00)
Net Cash Flow from Sale	$ 43.00

Developer's Cash Outflows and Inflows (in MM)				
	Year 0	**Year 1**	**Year 2**	**Year 3**
Purchase Price	$ (10.00)			
Net Cash Flow From Operations		$ 0.60	$ 0.60	$ 0.60
Cash Flow From Sale				$ 43.00
Total	$ (10.00)	$ 0.60	$ 0.60	$ 43.60
IRR on Equity	**67%**			

FIGURE 4.22: POST-1986 TAX FRAMEWORK COMPARED WITH PRE-1986 TAX FRAMEWORK

Leslie Heights with Pre-1986 Tax Shelters		
Value of Property		$100 MM
Interest Calculation		
Debt		$90 MM
Interest Rate		12%
Interest Payment		10.8 MM
Tax Calculation		
NOI		$9 MM
Depreciation		(8.0 MM)
Interest		(10.8 MM)
Taxable Income		**(9.8 MM)**
Value of excess tax shelter at 50% tax bracket		
Taxable Income		(9.8 MM)
Tax Bracket Rate		50%
Value	9.8 * .5	**4.9 MM**
Cash Flow from Operation		
NOI		$9.0 MM
Cap Ex		(2.0 MM)
Interest		(10.8 MM)
Tax Shelter Sales	90 cents on the dollar: (4.9*.9)	4.4 MM
Net Cash Flow from Operation		**$0.6 MM**

Leslie Heights post 1986	
Value of Property	$100 MM
Interest Calculation	
Debt	$90 MM
Interest Rate	12%
Interest Payment	10.8 MM
Tax Calculation	
NOI	$9 MM
Depreciation	(4.0 MM)
Interest	(10.8 MM)
Taxable Income	**(5.8 MM)**
(Tax losses no longer apply)	
Actual Expenditures Calculation	
NOI	$9.0 MM
Cap Ex	(2.0 MM)
Interest	(10.8 MM)
Tax Shelter Sales	.0 MM
Net Cash Flow from Operation	**(3.8 MM)**

CLOSING THOUGHT

You must remember that your property level pro forma must be a careful business analysis. It should be a preliminary assessment of the most likely net operating income outcomes. Have some humility and understand that even when carefully analyzed, the most likely outcomes are highly unlikely to occur. If things turn out better than expected, you can easily live with it. But if they are worse, it will be a problem. Addressing why and when it will be worse, and how you will deal with such situations, is much more important than just assembling "the numbers".

Numbers are easily manipulated to look good on paper. The difficult part is making them a reality, even for the most likely outcome. Football plays always work on paper. The playbook reads that Prushansky blocks Elliott while Galloway throws a perfect spiral to Ferreira. But what really happens? Prushansky slips and misses the block. Under pressure, Galloway throws a wobbly pass, which Brasfield intercepts and runs for a touchdown! That is not in the playbook – but it happens. And it is all happening in inclement weather conditions. A playbook cannot tell you that Prushansky has a metal plate in his leg making it difficult for him to make that block. You have to know your players' weaknesses and strengths, and understand what can go wrong, and how you will adjust your strategy and personnel to deal with shortfalls. Likewise, to be a successful real estate investor you must intimately know your personnel, market, property, and tenants. And just as in football, achieving the expected outcome requires tremendous planning, knowledge, diligence, energy, concentration, adaptability, and luck. Being average is hard work and a fulltime job.

Chapter 4 Supplement A

The Connection Between Capital and Physical Markets: Drivers of Real Estate

Immobilien Manager Verlag, IMV GmbH & Co. KG – Handbook Real Estate Capital Markets - 2008

COMMERCIAL REAL ESTATE AS MAJOR ASSET CLASS:

Commercial real estate is a major asset class. Every building and every piece of vacant land is owned by someone. In some cases it is a commercial interest that owns the property, while others are owned by a governmental agency or charitable organization. But in each instance, capital flows to these assets.

For commercial properties owned by for-profit enterprises, value is determined by the present value of the property's expected cash flows. But what risk is appropriate to reflect in the discount rate, and what are the future cash flows into perpetuity? This valuation exercise is typically redefined as one of evaluating the future cash flow of the property over the next 5-10 years, presuming the property is sold at the end of this period for a multiple of then expected cash flow. These expected cash streams are then discounted at a single discount rate which reflects the risk embedded in the property's cash stream and the property's illiquidity.

STARTING POINT OF FORECASTING ARE LEASES:

When forecasting future cash streams, the starting point is in place leases. These leases are of varying length, were negotiated with a variety of tenants, at a number of different points in time, often by previous owners. Some of the markets in which these leases were negotiated were strong landlord markets, while others were strong tenant markets. In either case, the negotiated terms determine current rental payments. Some leases may be at rents below current market rates, while others may be above what the space would fetch today. But as long as the tenant is bound by the lease, and does not go out of business, it is obligated to pay the agreed upon rents and expenses for their space.

Existing leases often have bumps in their rent during the term of the lease, as landlords and tenants rarely negotiate a flat lease for the entire period of the lease. This allows rents to move upward over time, reflective of inflation. Sometimes these rental increases are gradual, perhaps 1-3% annually, while in other cases they are structured with no increases for several years followed by large rental or expense increases.

LEASES, NOT INFLATION, DICTATE WHAT OCCURS:

The analysis of real estate is both simpler and more difficult than most businesses, as in place leases often determine a large portion of future income. Thus, contrary to most businesses, when analyzing real estate, one cannot simply assume that cash streams rise annually at roughly the rate of inflation, as in place leases to a large degree dictate what occurs. As a result, arduous and painstaking analysis of in place leases occurs when valuing a property. There is no shortcut. The result is that the valuation of real estate tends to be much more accurate than for most businesses, as "forward sales contracts" — leases — allow greater precision. However, it also means that the valuation differences among bidders tend to be smaller, as all bidders generally have access to detailed lease information. The more space that is subject to long-term in place leases, the narrower will be the bidding range [1].

OPERATING COSTS:

A key element of in place leases is the extent to which operating costs are borne by tenants. This is not a matter of theoretical assumption, but rather an arduous process of reading the terms of the in place leases. Generally tenants are responsible for the operating costs for their space, plus their pro rata share of the costs associated with local taxes, insurance, and the maintenance of common areas such as lobbies, parking lots, and general security. However, each lease dictates the precise terms. Sometimes all costs are paid by the tenants, while other times these costs are not paid at all by tenants. In other cases, they are paid in arrears; other times they are paid in advance. Often they are capped in terms of how much they can rise in a particular period of time. And vacant space never pays a share of common expenses and taxes. Thus, empty space hurts real estate not only in the loss of rental income but also by not absorbing its share of the costs associated with operating a property.

TENANT'S USAGE AND CANCELLATION RIGHTS:

A key element of in place leases is the tenant's usage and cancellation rights. For example, the tenant may have the right to cancel their lease if their business is sold or if the ownership of the property changes. Or the usage of the space may be restricted by the lease. Once again, there is no substitute for carefully examining the rights of in place tenants described in the lease.

When leased space is vacant or is expected to become vacant, one must estimate the nature of the lease that is expected to be signed for this space. This is generally done for each separate parcel of space in the building. Models such as Argus make this a relatively painless mechanical task, wherein one specifies for each currently empty or future unleased space, the length of time the property will be vacant, how much will be paid in leasing commissions, what the rent will be, what expenses will be borne by the tenant, etc. This process amounts to creating a "what will happen" lease, and modeling it as if it were an in place lease. Of course, in place leases are more certain than "what will happen" leases. By combining in place lease information with "what will happen" lease information, one constructs an expected revenue and cost structure for the property for each time period.

You must also add all sources of ancillary income, such as parking, temporary kiosks, signage, communication towers, etc. Some of the sources of income will be related to occupancy (e.g. parking), while others are not (e.g. signage income).

Total income expected for the property in each time period is the sum of in place income streams plus expected income from empty space, plus ancillary income, minus property operating costs and losses associated with poor credit. That is, not all tenants always pay their rent on time or in full. This generates a stream of expected net operating income (NOI) for the property.

NOI VERSUS CASH FLOWS:

An important distinction to remember is that NOI and cash flow are very different things [2]. NOI does not include the costs associated with ongoing capital expenditures by the landlord. For example, lobbies have to be re-outfitted, parking decks have to be resurfaced, roofs have to be replaced, and elevators must be replaced. These capital expenditures regularly occur, though their precise timing is generally irregular and lumpy. When underwriting a property, you must evaluate when these expenses are expected to occur. In the absence of detailed engineering information regarding their precise timing, it is generally assumed that these expenses occur smoothly over time. However, it is important to remember when evaluating the risk of cash flows that while a reserve for these items may be smooth, the actual outlays are not. Thus, the riskiness of future cash flows are higher than is generally obvious when one models cash flow as NOI minus standardized capital expenditures, leasing commissions, and TIs. Leasing commissions and tenant improvements relate to signing new leases. Thus, when evaluating the value of a property one has to analyze these additional costs as occurring as empty space is occupied. These costs will often be quite large in the year following a lease's execution. As a result, although NOI rises as empty space is leased, cash flow will generally decline for a year or so. The link between capital markets and property markets requires one to understand these subtleties.

PROPERTY'S RESIDUAL VALUE:

Turning to the residual value of the property, that is the value of the property when it is sold, one typically uses the stabilized NOI 5-10 years from now, and applies a cap rate to calculate the perpetuity value of this income stream. This is equivalent to applying a valuation multiple to the stabilized future NOI. In some instances, a property's residual value is better viewed as the redevelopment value of the property rather than the value of ongoing cash streams. This is particularly the case as a building approaches the final stage of its useful life.

CHOICE OF CAP RATE:

Which cap rate should be used when calculating residual value? Typically one uses the cap rate for comparable buildings which prevails in the current capital market, with perhaps an upward adjustment to reflect the slope of the yield curve. Such an adjustment reflects the capital market's anticipation that alternative returns are higher (or lower) in the future. Also, the exit cap rate must be adjusted to capture the fact that the building will be older and perhaps less competitive when it is sold in 5-10 years.

Having specified the expected future cash streams, including the residual value of the property, these cash streams are subjected to a discount rate reflective of the risk inherent in the expected future cash streams. The risk reflects the tenant's credit, as well as operating risks associated with the property. It also reflects the differential liquidity of owning the property versus benchmark assets such as government bonds.

The riskiness of a cash stream, and hence the discount rate, may vary as the tenancy and the competitive circumstances of the property change. An obvious example is when a building goes from being leased by the US government to being leased by corporate tenants upon lease expiration. While the rent paid may (or may not) be higher than the rent paid by the government, the risk of corporate tenants is higher, as these tenants are inferior credit risks. Another example is that the risk associated with in place leases that have rents well below prevailing market rents is less than if leases are at rents which are well above market rates. This is because if the tenant ceases to operate, the below market rate lease sets a better floor on revenues, and rents may rise once the tenant vacates. In contrast, an above market rent is less likely to remain in place if the tenant ceases to lease the space.

COMPARABLE RISK CHARACTERISTICS:

In assessing discount rates, it is helpful to think about the risk of the cash flow compared to assets with roughly comparable risk characteristics. For example, if the tenant is the US government, a comparable risk is a US government bond with an adjustment reflecting the differential liquidity of government bonds. Or if the property houses high-grade corporate tenants in a mid-town Manhattan office building, the comparable risk is a portfolio of high-grade corporate bonds, again adjusted for the relative illiquidity of the real estate. Remember that there is no magic to picking discount rates. In fact, markets are such that the bidder who assigns the lowest risk to cash streams tends to prevail, as they derive the highest valuation expectation.

THE "GORDON" MODEL:

If a property's NOI is stabilized, that is no major deviations are expected to occur, a very simple valuation model evolves as a special case of the discounted cash flow model. This is the "Gordon" model [3], which notes that the value of a perpetuity stream of stabilized cash flows (*CF*) growing at a rate of g and a risk discount rate of r, is equal to:

$$V = CF / (r - g).$$

That is, the value of a property is equal to its cash flow in the first year of ownership divided by the cap rate, where the cap rate for a perpetuity cash flow stream is equal to the discount rate minus the cash flow growth rate. The Gordon model only works if cash streams are such that the discount rate is significantly higher than the perpetuity cash flow growth rate. It also applies only if the cash streams grow relatively smoothly at the rate of g.

The Gordon model highlights the theoretical underpinnings for the valuation of real estate. That is, it depends upon current cash flow, the discount rate (assuming it is constant over time), and the perpetuity cash flow growth rate. For example, if the discount rate is 8%, and the growth rate is 2%, then the cap rate is theoretically 6% (that is, $r - g$). This provides a powerful, yet simple, mechanism for approximating cap rates. The Gordon model is much easier to use than conducting a full discounted cash flow analysis. But it must be used with care, as it is only applicable if the discount rate and growth rate are basically constant and the property is stabilized.

The discount rate is equal to the government bond rate, plus the additional risk increment associated with the building's cash flow risk, plus an illiquidity premium associated with the property relative to government bonds. In general, one expects the cash flow growth rate into perpetuity to be equal to, or slightly less than, the economy's general rate of inflation. This is because as the building ages its cash stream should increase at approximately the rate of inflation, with perhaps a modest reduction due to the fact that as the building ages, ever larger capital expenditures will be required to keep it competitive.

The Gordon model underscores the fact that as the base rate of interest falls, so too should the cap rate. Similarly as tenant credit risk or the liquidity of the real estate improves, the discount rate falls. Finally, as the sustainable growth rate of cash flows rises, the cap rate also falls.

PROPERTY AND CAPITAL MARKETS:

In sum, a disciplined approach to the valuation of real estate is an intersection of the characteristics of the property and capital markets: leases; operational conditions; the local market; property liquidity; tenant quality; and the returns on alternative investments. Of course, actual markets at any point in time will deviate from theoretical pricing constructs. In particular, markets are always right at the moment, though over the long run they will gravitate to theoretical norms. A vivid example of prolonged mispricing relative to theoretical norms was the market valuation of dot-com companies. Ultimately, theory proved correct, but not until several years of bizarre pricing prevailed. So too is the case in real estate.

<1990: US REAL ESTATE AS DEBT FINANCED BUSINESS:

Real estate in the US, the most transparent and liquid real estate market in the world, was substantially underpriced from 1990 through early 2006. This reflected a prolonged capital market adjustment following the meltdown of US real estate which took place in the very early 1990s. Up to that time US real estate was almost totally a debt financed business. When debt sources evaporated, pricing was far out of line with risk metrics. Instead, market pricing was established by distressed sales conducted by distressed sellers to a very limited set of buyers who possessed the requisite equity. This condition prevailed well into the 1990s. As debt capital returned to real estate, the tech bubble caused equity investors to lose sight of the appropriate pricing of cash streams. As a result, real estate (like all other cash flow businesses) saw cap rates rise irrespective of the fundamentals of risk and cash flow growth.

This led to long period of under pricing of U.S. real estate, which began to end when the tech bubble burst. After the bubble burst, cap rates fell. Yet it took approximately 5 years of falling cap rates to finally get real pricing in line with risk. Finally, in early 2006, US real estate pricing was approximately in line with risk. Interestingly, when market pricing is about correct, it means that approximately half of the real estate is overpriced, and approximately half is underpriced.

CAPM TO EVALUATE PRICING:

A simple way to evaluate correct risk pricing is to apply the Capital Asset Pricing Model (CAPM) [4]. For example, the beta for real estate is roughly 0.5, so for a risk-free rate of 4.8%, and a market expected return of 8.8%, the total expected return for real estate is 6.8%. Since the cash stream of real estate is expected to increase at about the rate of inflation (approximately 2.5%), this means that the current cash flow yield for a typical piece of real estate should be approximately 4.3%. That is, the total return expectation of 6.8% for real estate is achieved by 4.3% current cash flow, and a 2.5% annual appreciation at a constant cap rate [5].

At this pricing, the cash flow yield is less than the risk-free rate. This reflects the fact that with a beta of 0.5 and a 2.5% growth rate, real estate serves to improve portfolio diversification while also providing income growth. It also reflects that while a government bond realizes 100% of its return through its coupon, real estate achieves approximately one-third of its return through appreciation.

COMPARISON TO BONDS AND EQUITY:

Another way to consider real estate pricing is to compare the expected return for real estate with the expected return on corporate bonds and equity. Specifically, BBB corporate debt generally prices at a return of approximately 180 basis points in excess of government bonds [6]. Corporate equities have an expected return of approximately 8.8% in an environment of 2.5% inflation. But the return expected for real estate must be lower than that for corporate equities, as the risk of lease payments is less than that of an equity claim for the corporate tenants. That is, the leases and the equity claims are being paid by the same corporations, as are the debt obligations on corporate bonds. Thus, real estate occupied by a pool of BBB credit tenants, which is approximately the typical tenant quality in a major US corporate real estate portfolio, should have an expected return much less than the equity returns expected of those tenants.

The lease claims are also safer than the debt claims, as the vast majority of the time both debt and lease claims will be paid by tenants. And when the tenant only has enough resources to pay one of these claims, they are more likely to pay their lease claim than their debt claim. This means that the total expected return of the lease claim, that is real estate, should be modestly lower than that of the debt claim. As a result, real estate pricing over the long run should move in relation to the returns on corporate equities, as well as government bonds.

We have conducted a study of the relative underpricing of commercial real estate in the US based on a very simple CAPM for 1990-2007. This model demonstrates that until early 2006 commercial real estate was massively underpriced, reflective of the collapse of real estate debt markets and the tech bubble. However, today pricing is generally in line with risk (see figure 4A.1).

FIGURE 4A.1

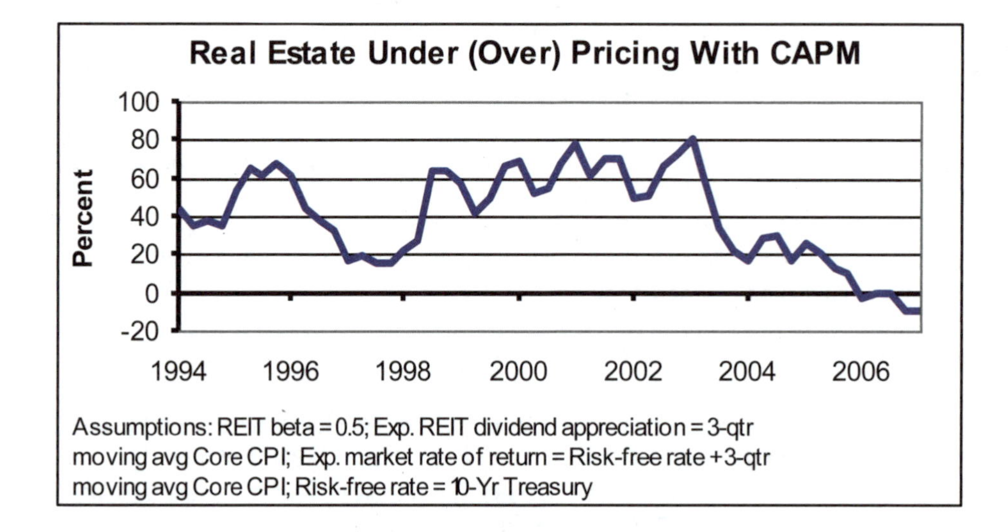

REAL ESTATE PRICING TO BECOME MORE INTEGRATED:

Real estate pricing is becoming more integrated across major real estate markets as capital flows between borders. More importantly, real estate pricing is integrating with other global assets. Increasingly, real estate is just another type of cash stream with associated risks. In this regard, multifamily buildings are just high quality consumer credit receivables, higher quality than credit card or auto receivables as tenants are more likely to pay their rents than to pay these other credits. Similarly a portfolio of shopping centers is basically a pool of retailers' debt claims, while a portfolio of major office properties should be priced roughly similar to the claims on corporate debt [7].

Capital now moves around the world, as more and more investors move their money quickly and with relative transparency into real estate across borders. This money comes in the form of REITs, real estate private equity funds, high wealth investors, and investments by institutions such as banks and pension funds. On the debt side, CMBS have provided transparency and risk pricing that links the pricing of real estate debt to comparable credit on corporate and government instruments. While banks and life companies continue to be major sources of direct real estate lending, their pricing is now intimately linked to the transparent pricing on CMBS. And real estate in markets in Western Europe and Japan are less and less priced on the basis of "who once slept here" or its architectural uniqueness, but rather based on cash flow potential and risk.

MARKETS BETTER PRICED THAN EVER:

While markets remain far from perfect, they are massively more integrated and better "pricers" of risk than has ever been in the case. Every day, major investors wake up with trillions of uncommitted dollars in search of risk arbitrage. This footloose money compares risk, liquidity, and cash flow growth opportunities across a vast array of investments of different structure, geography, and sector. Increasingly, real estate is just one more asset category they examine.

INTEREST IN GERMAN APARTMENT PORTFOLIOS:

The recent interest in German apartment portfolios underscores this linkage. These portfolios had for a long time been poorly managed by both government and corporate owners. They were privatized via sales dominated by non-German private equity funds, who receive their money from university endowments, foundations, pension funds, and high wealth individuals. These private equity investors invested their money in apartments resided in by working class Germans.

The debt for these purchases was provided by CMBS offerings and global bank syndications, involving investors from across the globe. The pricing for these portfolios reflected the fact that the risk of the underlying German apartment cash streams is extremely low, as the tenants have lived in these properties for many years, and there are few viable alternatives for them to move in to, particularly given the fact that their current rents are well below market rents due to rent controls. Thus, in an environment where German government bonds yield 3.5%, a 150 basis point total return premium for such a low risk consumer receivable is a healthy premium. This implies the total return expectation need only be roughly 5%, of which 3% comes from current dividends, and 2% from expected appreciation as the cash streams grow by approximately inflation.

PROPERTIES AS HIGH-GRADE CONSUMER RECEIVABLES:

A 5% total expected return may seem absurd by historical standards. But upon reflection, these properties are nothing more than very high grade consumer receivables. From this perspective, and given alternative returns, the pricing seems rock solid. This is why billions of dollars of global debt and equity gravitated from around the globe to these humble German properties. The miracle of capital market integration has taken extremely localized real estate assets, and moved them into the pricing of liquid and transparent cash streams. Welcome to the wonderful world of modern real estate!

Bibliography:

[1] Linneman, P. D., Real Estate Finance and Investments: Risks and Opportunities, 2nd edition, Linneman Associates, Philadelphia, PA, 2004.

[2] ib.

[3] ib.

[4] Linneman, P. D., The Equitization of Real Estate. Wharton Real Estate Review, Vol. X, 2006, No. 2.

[5] Linneman, P. D., The Linneman Letter, first quarter 2007, Vol. 7, Issue 1.

[6] Linneman, P.D., The Linneman Letter, second quarter 2007, Vol. 7, Issue 2.

[7] Linneman, P. D., The Linneman Letter, fourth quarter 2007, Vol. 6, Issue 4.

Chapter 5
Financial Modeling

"A 26.24% IRR is silly; no one is 200 basis points accurate, much less 24 basis points accurate".
-Dr. Peter Linneman

WHAT IS FINANCIAL MODELING?

Financial modeling is the systematic analysis of expected outcomes for an investment to assist in evaluating its risks and opportunities. A detailed financial model provides a microscopic view of the financial elements of the property. Remember that the rows and columns in your financial model are only as useful as the quality of the information and judgment behind them. Just because they look authoritative on paper does not make them insightful, much less correct. Always be skeptical of your financial model, especially when you are inexperienced in the business. Be sure that you, not the rows and columns, make your investment decisions.

If a property's economics are very complex, even after comprehensive analysis experts may not agree on the value of a property. Smart investors, armed with similar information, frequently arrive at drastically different valuations because they perceive different degrees of risk and opportunity in the property. Value, like beauty, is in the eye of the beholder. And execution, not financial modeling, ultimately is the source of your returns.

THINGS CHANGE FOR A REASON

Students and young professionals generally put too much emphasis on the numbers, and too little on the reasoning behind the numbers. As a result, meaningless "sensitivity tests" are often run, where the young analyst arbitrarily increases vacancy by 10%, or decreases rental growth by 1%, or raises the exit cap by 100 bp, without ever pausing to think about what the world needs to look like for such a change to happen. Have you ever been shown false sympathy? Remember how easily you recognized it, and how much it irritated you? A financial sensitivity analysis done without sincere thought is much the same.

Before you change the vacancy rate, ask yourself why would the vacancy rate increase? Is it because the economy is weak? Or has a big firm moved out of the area? Or is the property poorly located or of inferior design? Or are the rents too high? Like a good doctor, treat the disease, not the symptoms.

LESLIE COURT APARTMENTS

FIGURE 5.1

Leslie Court Apartments								
		Decline			Recovery		Stable	
	Year 0	Year 1	Year 2	Year 3	Year 4	Year 5	Year 6	Year 7
Base Rental Revenue Growth			**-6.0%**	**-3.0%**	**-1.0%**	**2.0%**	**3.0%**	**3.0%**
Base Rental Revenues		$1,100,305	$1,034,287	$1,003,258	$993,226	$1,013,090	$1,043,483	$1,074,787
Expense Reimbursement Revenue		$0	$0	$0	$0	$0	$0	$0
Gross Revenues		$1,100,305	$1,034,287	$1,003,258	$993,226	$1,013,090	$1,043,483	$1,074,787
Vacancy % Gross Revenues		**7.0%**	**10.0%**	**14.0%**	**10.0%**	**7.0%**	**5.0%**	**5.0%**
Less: Vacancies		($77,021)	($103,429)	($140,456)	($99,323)	($70,916)	($52,174)	($53,739)
Net Base Rental Revenue		$1,023,284	$930,858	$862,802	$893,903	$942,174	$991,309	$1,021,048
Ancillary Income Growth			**-8.0%**	**-7.0%**	**-3.0%**	**5.0%**	**3.0%**	**3.0%**
Plus: Ancillary Income		$6,052	$5,568	$5,178	$5,022	$5,274	$5,432	$5,595
Effective Gross Income (EGI)		$1,029,335	$936,426	$867,980	$898,925	$947,447	$996,740	$1,026,643
Operating Expense Growth			**-2.0%**	**-1.0%**	**0.0%**	**4.0%**	**3.5%**	**3.0%**
Less: Operating Expenses (Insurance, Utilities, Etc.)		($102,934)	($100,875)	($99,866)	($99,866)	($103,861)	($107,496)	($110,721)
Less: Real Estate Taxes		($110,031)	($113,331)	($116,731)	($120,233)	($123,840)	($127,556)	($131,382)
Less: Replacement Reserve		($49,514)	($46,543)	($45,147)	($44,695)	($45,589)	($46,957)	($48,365)
Total Expenses		($262,478)	($260,749)	($261,744)	($264,795)	($273,290)	($282,008)	($290,468)
NOI		$766,858	$675,676	$606,236	$634,131	$674,157	$714,732	$736,174
Change In Cap Ex			**-8.9%**	**8.5%**	**3.6%**	**19.5%**	**-21.9%**	**-2.4%**
Less: Cap Ex		($75,264)	($68,541)	($74,354)	($77,000)	($92,000)	($71,850)	($70,125)
Change In TI			**8.6%**	**10.4%**	**-9.9%**	**-10.0%**	**-8.2%**	**-8.2%**
Less: TI		($35,000)	($38,000)	($41,950)	($37,812)	($34,012)	($31,209)	($28,658)
Change In Leasing Commissions			**27.0%**	**10.8%**	**18.0%**	**-1.7%**	**-14.8%**	**-3.3%**
Less: Leasing Commissions		($20,458)	($25,981)	($28,795)	($33,987)	($33,404)	($28,456)	($27,514)
Adjusted Net Operating Income (NOI) *		$636,136	$543,154	$461,137	$485,332	$514,741	$583,217	$609,877
Less: Loan Points	($50,250)	$0	$0	$0	$0	$0	$0	$0
Less: Debt Service Payment		($404,947)	($404,947)	($404,947)	($404,947)	($404,947)	($404,947)	($404,947)
Before Tax Levered Cash Flows		$231,189	$138,208	$56,190	$80,385	$109,795	$178,271	$204,931
Less: Depreciation of Building		($201,818)	($201,818)	($201,818)	($201,818)	($201,818)	($201,818)	($201,818)
Less: Tenant Improvements Depreciation		($35,000)	($38,000)	($41,950)	($37,812)	($34,012)	($31,209)	($28,658)
Less: Capital Expenditures Depreciation		($10,752)	($20,544)	($31,166)	($42,166)	($55,308)	($65,573)	($75,591)
Plus: Capital Expenditures		$75,264	$68,541	$74,354	$77,000	$92,000	$71,850	$70,125
Plus: Tenant Improvements		$35,000	$38,000	$41,950	$37,812	$34,012	$31,209	$28,658
Plus: Principal Amortization		$53,197	$56,920	$60,905	$65,168	$69,730	$74,611	$79,834
Less: Points Amortization		($7,179)	($7,179)	($7,179)	($7,179)	($7,179)	($7,179)	($7,179)
Taxable Income (Loss)		$139,901	$34,129	($48,713)	($28,609)	$7,219	$50,162	$70,302
Less: Application of Suspended Losses		$0	$0	$0	$0	($7,219)	($50,162)	($19,941)
Net Taxable Income (Loss)		$139,901	$34,129	($48,713)	($28,609)	$0	$0	$50,361
Less: Tax Liability	38.6%	($54,002)	($13,174)	$0	$0	$0	$0	($19,439)
After-Tax Cash Flows		$177,187	$125,034	$56,190	$80,385	$109,795	$178,271	$185,492
After-Tax Net Proceeds From Sale								$2,285,509
Initial Equity Investment	($1,725,250)							
Total Cash Flows **	($1,725,250)	$177,187	$125,034	$56,190	$80,385	$109,795	$178,271	$2,471,001

* Also known as Unlevered Cash Flow

** Also known as After-Tax Levered Cash Flow

IRR:	10.78%
NPV @ 15%:	($333,125)

Total Positive Cash Flows	$3,197,862
Net Sales Proceeds/Total Positive Cash Flows	71.47%

To illustrate the interaction of different line items in a good financial model, consider Leslie Court, a 100 unit residential property. You are considering purchasing the building for $6.7 million, using a $5.025 million mortgage with annual (vs. monthly) payments for simplicity of calculations. The building is located in Colonial Heights, Virginia. After a recent boom, Colonial Heights' market is rapidly weakening due to the recession and overbuilding. As a result, you believe the property's performance will weaken for the next three years before rebounding.

FIGURE 5.2

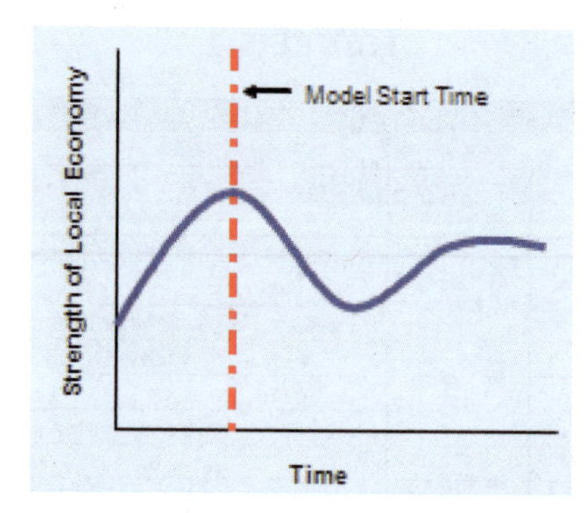

After careful analysis, you conclude that the market will worsen over the next three years as new supply continues to exceed demand. You do not believe this pattern will reverse until the fourth year. Young analysts often only adjust the vacancy rate to reflect the changing market fundamentals. Figure 5.1 reveals that there are many variables which change as market conditions change. A well-constructed financial model allows you to change these items and have the pre-wired financial model run the mathematics implied by your assumptions. The affected line items are outlined.

BASE RENTAL REVENUE

FIGURE 5.3

Leslie Court Apartments								
		Decline			Recovery		Stable	
	Year 0	Year 1	Year 2	Year 3	Year 4	Year 5	Year 6	Year 7
Base Rental Revenue Growth			**-6.0%**	**-3.0%**	**-1.0%**	**2.0%**	**3.0%**	**3.0%**
Base Rental Revenues		$1,100,305	$1,034,287	$1,003,258	$993,226	$1,013,090	$1,043,483	$1,074,787
Expense Reimbursement Revenue		-	-	-	-	-	-	-
Gross Revenues		$1,100,305	$1,034,287	$1,003,258	$993,226	$1,013,090	$1,043,483	$1,074,787

One thing always hit by weak market conditions is rent. In soft markets, tenants will have to be enticed to your property through lower rents and other concessions. These concessions may be free rent, lower deposits, toasters, etc. Note that the change in base rent revenues is not smooth, with the biggest drops occurring as one moves from a hot to a cold market. During the decline, base rental revenue falls rapidly until new supply shuts down, and demand begins to absorb the excess space. Upon stabilizing, you expect rent to grow at 3%, roughly the rate of long term economy-wide expected inflation. Of course, there could be a big rent pop of say 6 – 9% if the economy recovers quickly or robustly. These assumptions will vary on the deal and market.

VACANCY

FIGURE 5.4

Leslie Court Apartments								
		Decline			Recovery		Stable	
	Year 0	Year 1	Year 2	Year 3	Year 4	Year 5	Year 6	Year 7
Base Rental Revenue Growth			**-6.0%**	**-3.0%**	**-1.0%**	**2.0%**	**3.0%**	**3.0%**
Base Rental Revenues		$1,100,305	$1,034,287	$1,003,258	$993,226	$1,013,090	$1,043,483	$1,074,787
Expense Reimbursement Revenue		-	-	-	-	-	-	-
Gross Revenues		$1,100,305	$1,034,287	$1,003,258	$993,226	$1,013,090	$1,043,483	$1,074,787
Vacancy Percentage		**7.0%**	**10.0%**	**14.0%**	**10.0%**	**7.0%**	**5.0%**	**5.0%**
Less: Vacancies		($77,021)	($103,429)	($140,456)	($99,323)	($70,916)	($52,174)	($53,739)
Net Base Rental Revenue		$1,023,284	$930,858	$862,802	$893,903	$942,174	$991,309	$1,021,048

Vacancy generally moves inversely with the strength of the market. That is, the weaker the market, the higher the vacancy. In lesser quality buildings, this is more pronounced, as tenants move up to higher quality buildings because better buildings are available at rents at or below what the tenants are currently paying. While vacancy decreases Net Base Rental Revenue, its indirect effects are also felt on other line items.

ANCILLARY INCOME

FIGURE 5.5

Leslie Court Apartments								
		Decline			Recovery		Stable	
	Year 0	Year 1	Year 2	Year 3	Year 4	Year 5	Year 6	Year 7
Base Rental Revenue Growth			**-6.0%**	**-3.0%**	**-1.0%**	**2.0%**	**3.0%**	**3.0%**
Base Rental Revenues		$1,100,305	$1,034,287	$1,003,258	$993,226	$1,013,090	$1,043,483	$1,074,787
Expense Reimbursement Revenue		-	-	-	-	-	-	-
Gross Revenues		$1,100,305	$1,034,287	$1,003,258	$993,226	$1,013,090	$1,043,483	$1,074,787
Vacancy Percentage		**7.0%**	**10.0%**	**14.0%**	**10.0%**	**7.0%**	**5.0%**	**5.0%**
Less: Vacancies		($77,021)	($103,429)	($140,456)	($99,323)	($70,916)	($52,174)	($53,739)
Net Base Rental Revenue		$1,023,284	$930,858	$862,802	$893,903	$942,174	$991,309	$1,021,048
Ancillary Income Growth			**-8.0%**	**-7.0%**	**-3.0%**	**5.0%**	**3.0%**	**3.0%**
Plus: Ancillary Income		$6,052	$5,568	$5,178	$5,022	$5,274	$5,432	$5,595
Effective Gross Income (EGI)		$1,029,335	$936,426	$867,980	$898,925	$947,447	$996,740	$1,026,643

Notice how the 3% increase in the vacancy rate in the first two years causes an 8% drop in ancillary income. This is not unexpected, for two main reasons. First, amenities such as your health club are predominantly used by your tenants. Hence, as vacancy increases, there are fewer tenants to join the club. Second, if the increased vacancy is due to a weak economy (rather than excess building), tenants may not renew their memberships due to having less disposable income. During more prosperous times, such as the recovery period, the opposite is true. As a result, ancillary income often moves with greater volatility than rental income.

OPERATING EXPENSE

FIGURE 5.6

Leslie Court Apartments								
		Decline			Recovery		Stable	
	Year 0	Year 1	Year 2	Year 3	Year 4	Year 5	Year 6	Year 7
Base Rental Revenue Growth			**-6.0%**	**-3.0%**	**-1.0%**	**2.0%**	**3.0%**	**3.0%**
Base Rental Revenues		$1,100,305	$1,034,287	$1,003,258	$993,226	$1,013,090	$1,043,483	$1,074,787
Expense Reimbursement Revenue		-	-	-	-	-	-	-
Gross Revenues		$1,100,305	$1,034,287	$1,003,258	$993,226	$1,013,090	$1,043,483	$1,074,787
Vacancy Percentage		**7.0%**	**10.0%**	**14.0%**	**10.0%**	**7.0%**	**5.0%**	**5.0%**
Less: Vacancies		($77,021)	($103,429)	($140,456)	($99,323)	($70,916)	($52,174)	($53,739)
Net Base Rental Revenue		$1,023,284	$930,858	$862,802	$893,903	$942,174	$991,309	$1,021,048
Ancillary Income Growth			**-8.0%**	**-7.0%**	**-3.0%**	**5.0%**	**3.0%**	**3.0%**
Plus: Ancillary Income		$6,052	$5,568	$5,178	$5,022	$5,274	$5,432	$5,595
Effective Gross Income (EGI)		$1,029,335	$936,426	$867,980	$898,925	$947,447	$996,740	$1,026,643
Operating Expense Growth			**-2.0%**	**-1.0%**	**0.0%**	**4.0%**	**3.5%**	**3.0%**
Less: Operating Expenses (Insurance, Utilities, Etc.)		($102,934)	($100,875)	($99,866)	($99,866)	($103,861)	($107,496)	($110,721)
Less: Real Estate Taxes		($110,031)	($113,331)	($116,731)	($120,233)	($123,840)	($127,556)	($131,382)
Less: Replacement Reserve		($49,514)	($46,543)	($45,147)	($44,695)	($45,589)	($46,957)	($48,365)
Total Expenses		($262,478)	($260,749)	($261,744)	($264,795)	($273,290)	($282,008)	($290,468)
NOI		$766,858	$675,676	$606,236	$634,131	$674,157	$714,732	$736,174

While operators always attempt to lower costs, this is particularly true during a recession. An inspection of Figure 5.1 reveals that in years 3 and 4, the property barely generates enough to cover debt service. In fact, if the debt covenants require a debt coverage ratio (NOI divided by total debt service expense, also known as DCR) of 1.2, there would be a violation in these years. As a result, you will seek ways to squeeze out every dime of costs.

In weak markets, the increased vacancy reduces some operating expenses ("variable" expenses). Utilities expense, for example, will not be as high because there are not as many tenants using computers, hot water, lights, etc. In addition, you may reduce certain operating expenses by mowing the lawn yourself instead of using a gardener, or maybe mowing once every three weeks instead of every two weeks. Other operating expenses, such as insurance, will not change with the state of the market ("fixed" expenses). But cost cutting measures should be assessed carefully. If the property deteriorates from a lack of maintenance, you may have greater repairs to contend with in the future, attract lower quality tenants, or destroy the image of a brand that you spent years building.

As the market strengthens, operating expenses will increase. For example, you may need more staff to deal with the greater tenant demand. It will take time to train these people, and you may not hire the right people, so some may need to be replaced. These inefficiencies need to be reflected in your model.

CAP EX

If the building requires a new roof or new plumbing system, capital expenditures will be quite large. In weak markets, you may not have enough capital to pay for these essential, but expensive repairs. As a result, in weak markets, you postpone as much cap ex as possible. In the Leslie Court Apartments model, $10,000 of cap ex due to water damage is not made in year 2. Therefore, it is expected that in year 5, the typical $70,000 in cap ex is instead $92,000 to make up for this deferral. What if the damage is worse than expected and it is necessary to make repairs in year 3? You may default on your loan! Also, if the water damage causes unhappiness with tenants, your vacancy may further increase.

FIGURE 5.7

Leslie Court Apartments								
		Decline			Recovery		Stable	
	Year 0	Year 1	Year 2	Year 3	Year 4	Year 5	Year 6	Year 7
Base Rental Revenue Growth			**-6.0%**	**-3.0%**	**-1.0%**	**2.0%**	**3.0%**	**3.0%**
Base Rental Revenues		$1,100,305	$1,034,287	$1,003,258	$993,226	$1,013,090	$1,043,483	$1,074,787
Expense Reimbursement Revenue		-	-	-	-	-	-	-
Gross Revenues		$1,100,305	$1,034,287	$1,003,258	$993,226	$1,013,090	$1,043,483	$1,074,787
Vacancy Percentage		**7.0%**	**10.0%**	**14.0%**	**10.0%**	**7.0%**	**5.0%**	**5.0%**
Less: Vacancies		($77,021)	($103,429)	($140,456)	($99,323)	($70,916)	($52,174)	($53,739)
Net Base Rental Revenue		$1,023,284	$930,858	$862,802	$893,903	$942,174	$991,309	$1,021,048
Ancillary Income Growth			**-8.0%**	**-7.0%**	**-3.0%**	**5.0%**	**3.0%**	**3.0%**
Plus: Ancillary Income		$6,052	$5,568	$5,178	$5,022	$5,274	$5,432	$5,595
Effective Gross Income (EGI)		$1,029,335	$936,426	$867,980	$898,925	$947,447	$996,740	$1,026,643
Operating Expense Growth			**-2.0%**	**-1.0%**	**0.0%**	**4.0%**	**3.5%**	**3.0%**
Less: Operating Expenses (Insurance, Utilities, Etc.)		($102,934)	($100,875)	($99,866)	($99,866)	($103,861)	($107,496)	($110,721)
Less: Real Estate Taxes		($110,031)	($113,331)	($116,731)	($120,233)	($123,840)	($127,556)	($131,382)
Less: Replacement Reserve		($49,514)	($46,543)	($45,147)	($44,695)	($45,589)	($46,957)	($48,365)
Total Expenses		($262,478)	($260,749)	($261,744)	($264,795)	($273,290)	($282,008)	($290,468)
NOI		$766,858	$675,676	$606,236	$634,131	$674,157	$714,732	$736,174
Change In Cap Ex			**-8.9%**	**8.5%**	**3.6%**	**19.5%**	**-21.9%**	**-2.4%**
Less: Cap Ex		($75,264)	($68,541)	($74,354)	($77,000)	($92,000)	($71,850)	($70,125)

TIs AND LEASING COMMISSIONS

If you experience high vacancy, you will focus a great deal of energy on trying to attract tenants. One way to accomplish this is to increase marketing efforts. You may increase the leasing commissions to motivate your sales force, hire additional leasing agents, or you may increase your advertising. For this reason, leasing commissions generally increase as vacancy increases.

TIs for office and retail properties will also increase with greater vacancy, as when tenants leave, you have to pay to attract tenants to re-lease the space. If leases are renewed, you will pay lower TIs than for new leases. For apartments, you may give away toasters, TVs, DVD players, etc. in order to attract customers, and as the market recovers these costs will drop substantially. Again, these costs must be shown in your analysis.

FIGURE 5.8

Leslie Court Apartments								
		Decline			Recovery		Stable	
	Year 0	Year 1	Year 2	Year 3	Year 4	Year 5	Year 6	Year 7
Base Rental Revenue Growth			**-6.0%**	**-3.0%**	**-1.0%**	**2.0%**	**3.0%**	**3.0%**
Base Rental Revenues		$1,100,305	$1,034,287	$1,003,258	$993,226	$1,013,090	$1,043,483	$1,074,787
Expense Reimbursement Revenue		$0	$0	$0	$0	$0	$0	$0
Gross Revenues		$1,100,305	$1,034,287	$1,003,258	$993,226	$1,013,090	$1,043,483	$1,074,787
Vacancy % Gross Revenues		**7.0%**	**10.0%**	**14.0%**	**10.0%**	**7.0%**	**5.0%**	**5.0%**
Less: Vacancies		($77,021)	($103,429)	($140,456)	($99,323)	($70,916)	($52,174)	($53,739)
Net Base Rental Revenue		$1,023,284	$930,858	$862,802	$893,903	$942,174	$991,309	$1,021,048
Ancillary Income Growth			**-8.0%**	**-7.0%**	**-3.0%**	**5.0%**	**3.0%**	**3.0%**
Plus: Ancillary Income		$6,052	$5,568	$5,178	$5,022	$5,274	$5,432	$5,595
Effective Gross Income (EGI)		$1,029,335	$936,426	$867,980	$898,925	$947,447	$996,740	$1,026,643
Operating Expense Growth			**-2.0%**	**-1.0%**	**0.0%**	**4.0%**	**3.5%**	**3.0%**
Less: Operating Expenses (Insurance, Utilities, Etc.)		($102,934)	($100,875)	($99,866)	($99,866)	($103,861)	($107,496)	($110,721)
Less: Real Estate Taxes		($110,031)	($113,331)	($116,731)	($120,233)	($123,840)	($127,556)	($131,382)
Less: Replacement Reserve		($49,514)	($46,543)	($45,147)	($44,695)	($45,589)	($46,957)	($48,365)
Total Expenses		($262,478)	($260,749)	($261,744)	($264,795)	($273,290)	($282,008)	($290,468)
NOI		$766,858	$675,676	$606,236	$634,131	$674,157	$714,732	$736,174
Change In Cap Ex			**-8.9%**	**8.5%**	**3.6%**	**19.5%**	**-21.9%**	**-2.4%**
Less: Cap Ex		($75,264)	($68,541)	($74,354)	($77,000)	($92,000)	($71,850)	($70,125)
Change In TI			**8.6%**	**10.4%**	**-9.9%**	**-10.0%**	**-8.2%**	**-8.2%**
Less: TI		($35,000)	($38,000)	($41,950)	($37,812)	($34,012)	($31,209)	($28,658)
Change In Leasing Commissions			**27.0%**	**10.8%**	**18.0%**	**-1.7%**	**-14.8%**	**-3.3%**
Less: Leasing Commissions		($20,458)	($25,981)	($28,795)	($33,987)	($33,404)	($28,456)	($27,514)
Adjusted Net Operating Income (NOI) *		$636,136	$543,154	$461,137	$485,332	$514,741	$583,217	$609,877
Less: Loan Points	($50,250)	$0	$0	$0	$0	$0	$0	$0
Less: Debt Service Payment		($404,947)	($404,947)	($404,947)	($404,947)	($404,947)	($404,947)	($404,947)
Before Tax Levered Cash Flows		$231,189	$138,208	$56,190	$80,385	$109,795	$178,271	$204,931
Less: Depreciation of Building		($201,818)	($201,818)	($201,818)	($201,818)	($201,818)	($201,818)	($201,818)
Less: Tenant Improvements Depreciation		($35,000)	($38,000)	($41,950)	($37,812)	($34,012)	($31,209)	($28,658)
Less: Capital Expenditures Depreciation		($10,752)	($20,544)	($31,166)	($42,166)	($55,308)	($65,573)	($75,591)
Plus: Capital Expenditures		$75,264	$68,541	$74,354	$77,000	$92,000	$71,850	$70,125
Plus: Tenant Improvements		$35,000	$38,000	$41,950	$37,812	$34,012	$31,209	$28,658
Plus: Principal Amortization		$53,197	$56,920	$60,905	$65,168	$69,730	$74,611	$79,834
Less: Points Amortization		($7,179)	($7,179)	($7,179)	($7,179)	($7,179)	($7,179)	($7,179)
Taxable Income (Loss)		$139,901	$34,129	($48,713)	($28,609)	$7,219	$50,162	$70,302
Less: Application of Suspended Losses		$0	$0	$0	$0	($7,219)	($50,162)	($19,941)
Net Taxable Income (Loss)		$139,901	$34,129	($48,713)	($28,609)	$0	$0	$50,361
Less: Tax Liability	38.6%	($54,002)	($13,174)	$0	$0	$0	$0	($19,439)
After-Tax Cash Flows		$177,187	$125,034	$56,190	$80,385	$109,795	$178,271	$185,492

* Also known as Unlevered Cash Flow

RESIDUAL VALUE

The analysis of the value upon sale is critical, as a dominant portion of your building's value derives from disposition. As Figure 5.9 reveals, over 71% of the present value is due to its residual value. To understand this residual value, and how it is impacted by market conditions, it is necessary to determine how Net Proceeds from Sale are calculated.

FIGURE 5.9

Leslie Court Apartments									
		Decline			Recovery		Stable		Forward
	Year 0	Year 1	Year 2	Year 3	Year 4	Year 5	Year 6	Year 7	Year 8
Base Rental Revenue Growth			**-6.0%**	**-3.0%**	**-1.0%**	**2.0%**	**3.0%**	**3.0%**	**3.0%**
Base Rental Revenues		$1,100,305	$1,034,287	$1,003,258	$993,226	$1,013,090	$1,043,483	$1,074,787	$1,107,031
Expense Reimbursement Revenue		$0	$0	$0	$0	$0	$0	$0	$0
Gross Revenues		$1,100,305	$1,034,287	$1,003,258	$993,226	$1,013,090	$1,043,483	$1,074,787	$1,107,031
Vacancy % Gross Revenues		**7.0%**	**10.0%**	**14.0%**	**10.0%**	**7.0%**	**5.0%**	**5.0%**	**5.0%**
Less: Vacancies		($77,021)	($103,429)	($140,456)	($99,323)	($70,916)	($52,174)	($53,739)	($55,352)
Net Base Rental Revenue		$1,023,284	$930,858	$862,802	$893,903	$942,174	$991,309	$1,021,048	$1,051,679
Ancillary Income Growth			**-8.0%**	**-7.0%**	**-3.0%**	**5.0%**	**3.0%**	**3.0%**	**3.0%**
Plus: Ancillary Income		$6,052	$5,568	$5,178	$5,022	$5,274	$5,432	$5,595	$5,763
Effective Gross Income (EGI)		$1,029,335	$936,426	$867,980	$898,925	$947,447	$996,740	$1,026,643	$1,057,442
Operating Expense Growth			**-2.0%**	**-1.0%**	**0.0%**	**4.0%**	**3.5%**	**3.0%**	**3.0%**
Less: Operating Expenses (Insurance, Utilities, Etc.)		($102,934)	($100,875)	($99,866)	($99,866)	($103,861)	($107,496)	($110,721)	($114,042)
Less: Real Estate Taxes		($110,031)	($113,331)	($116,731)	($120,233)	($123,840)	($127,556)	($131,382)	($135,324)
Less: Replacement Reserve		($49,514)	($46,543)	($45,147)	($44,695)	($45,589)	($46,957)	($48,365)	($49,816)
Total Expenses		($262,478)	($260,749)	($261,744)	($264,795)	($273,290)	($282,008)	($290,468)	($299,182)
NOI		$766,858	$675,676	$606,236	$634,131	$674,157	$714,732	$736,174	$758,259
Change In Cap Ex			**-8.9%**	**8.5%**	**3.6%**	**19.5%**	**-21.9%**	**-2.4%**	**0.0%**
Less: Cap Ex		($75,264)	($68,541)	($74,354)	($77,000)	($92,000)	($71,850)	($70,125)	($70,125)
Change In TI			**8.6%**	**10.4%**	**-9.9%**	**-10.0%**	**-8.2%**	**-8.2%**	**0.0%**
Less: TI		($35,000)	($38,000)	($41,950)	($37,812)	($34,012)	($31,209)	($28,658)	($28,658)
Change In Leasing Commissions			**27.0%**	**10.8%**	**18.0%**	**-1.7%**	**-14.8%**	**-3.3%**	**0.0%**
Less: Leasing Commissions		($20,458)	($25,981)	($28,795)	($33,987)	($33,404)	($28,456)	($27,514)	($27,514)
Adjusted Net Operating Income (NOI) *		$636,136	$543,154	$461,137	$485,332	$514,741	$583,217	$609,877	$631,962
Less: Loan Points	($50,250)	$0	$0	$0	$0	$0	$0	$0	
Less: Debt Service Payment		($404,947)	($404,947)	($404,947)	($404,947)	($404,947)	($404,947)	($404,947)	
Before Tax Levered Cash Flows		$231,189	$138,208	$56,190	$80,385	$109,795	$178,271	$204,931	
Less: Depreciation of Building		($201,818)	($201,818)	($201,818)	($201,818)	($201,818)	($201,818)	($201,818)	
Less: Tenant Improvements Depreciation		($35,000)	($38,000)	($41,950)	($37,812)	($34,012)	($31,209)	($28,658)	
Less: Capital Expenditures Depreciation		($10,752)	($20,544)	($31,166)	($42,166)	($55,308)	($65,573)	($75,591)	
Plus: Capital Expenditures		$75,264	$68,541	$74,354	$77,000	$92,000	$71,850	$70,125	
Plus: Tenant Improvements		$35,000	$38,000	$41,950	$37,812	$34,012	$31,209	$28,658	
Plus: Principal Amortization		$53,197	$56,920	$60,905	$65,168	$69,730	$74,611	$79,834	
Less: Points Amortization		($7,179)	($7,179)	($7,179)	($7,179)	($7,179)	($7,179)	($7,179)	
Taxable Income (Loss)		$139,901	$34,129	($48,713)	($28,609)	$7,219	$50,162	$70,302	
Less: Application of Suspended Losses		$0	$0	$0	$0	($7,219)	($50,162)	($19,941)	
Net Taxable Income (Loss)		$139,901	$34,129	($48,713)	($28,609)	$0	$0	$50,361	
Less: Tax Liability	38.6%	($54,002)	($13,174)	$0	$0	$0	$0	($19,439)	
After-Tax Cash Flows		$177,187	$125,034	$56,190	$80,385	$109,795	$178,271	$185,492	
After-Tax Net Proceeds From Sale								$2,285,509	
Initial Equity Investment	($1,725,250)								
Total Cash Flows **	($1,725,250)	$177,187	$125,034	$56,190	$80,385	$109,795	$178,271	$2,471,001	

* Also known as Unlevered Cash Flow

** Also known as After-Tax Levered Cash Flow

IRR:	10.78%
NPV @ 15%:	($333,125)

Total Positive Cash Flows	$3,197,862
Net Sales Proceeds/Total Positive Cash Flows	71.47%

FIGURE 5.10

Leslie Court Apartments		
Gain on Sale Accounting Analysis		
Gross Sales Price: =(Year 8 Adjusted NOI/Cap Rate)		$7,899,531
Less Brokerage Commission	2%	($157,991)
Net Sales Price		$7,741,540
Less Adjusted Basis:		
Acquisition Cost	$6,700,000	
Loan Points	$50,250	
Application of Replacement Reserve	$326,810	
Accumulated Depreciation	($1,960,467)	
Accumulated Cost Amortization	($50,250)	
	$5,066,343	
		$5,066,343
Gain-on-Sale		$2,675,198
Less Application of Unutilized Suspended Losses		$0
Net Book Gain-on-Sale		$2,675,198
Tax on Accum Depreciation	25%	$490,117
Capital Gains Tax Liability	15%	$401,280
Tax Liability		$891,396
Net Sales Proceeds: Cash Flows		
Gross Sales Price		$7,899,531
Less Brokerage Commission		($157,991)
Net Sales Price		$7,741,540
Less Tax Liability		($891,396)
Less Outstanding Mortgage Balance		($4,564,635)
Net Sales Proceeds		$2,285,509

GROSS SALE PRICE

The gross sales price is generally estimated by capping future stabilized NOI. Analysts often mistakenly use the same cap at exit as for their purchase. The problem with this approach is that the building is older and perhaps not as competitive. It also can justify crazy pricing. For example, use a 1% cap both in and out, it seems like a good deal. But, as the Japanese buyers of the 1980s found out, no one may exist who is willing to pay the same crazy cap rate as you. So if you enter at a 1 cap, and exit at an 8 cap, you are dead.

For a stabilized property, the exit cap rate is generally somewhat higher than your going in rate, reflective of it being an older and less sought after building. Interestingly for Leslie Court Apartments, the going-in cap is a 9.5 while the exit cap is an 8. Isn't this contrary to what we just said? No. Specifically, you are purchasing while income is low and falling, and exiting after the building is stabilized. That is, your entry cap rate is for a non-stabilized property, while your exit cap is for a stabilized property.

You will often search in vain for cap rates for comparables, as comparable transactions may not exist particularly in weak markets. Plus, not all comps will be at the same cap rate, and there is no guarantee you will realize the mean or median cap. Further, no website or professor can tell you exactly what to assume. Yet you must assume something intelligent (which will be wrong), understand what can go wrong, and live with it. As Figure 5.11 shows, just a 50 bps increase in your exit cap can reduce your equity IRR by over 200 bps.

FIGURE 5.11

	Year 0	Year 1	Year 2	Year 3	Year 4	Year 5	Year 6	Year 7
Total Cash Flows	($1,725,250)	$177,187	$125,034	$56,190	$80,385	$109,795	$178,271	$2,083,924

IRR:	8.56%
NPV @ 15%:	($478,642)

Total Positive Cash Flows	$2,810,785
Net Sales Proceeds/Total Positive Cash Flows	67.54%

BROKERAGE COMMISSIONS

FIGURE 5.12

Leslie Court Apartments		
Gain on Sale Accounting Analysis		
Gross Sales Price: =(Year 8 NOI/Cap Rate)		$ 7,899,531
Less Brokerage Commission	**2%**	**(157,991)**
Net Sales Price		7,741,540

Brokerage commissions are generally taken as a percentage of the gross sales price. Two percent is used for this analysis, but if the building is a hard sale, this can increase significantly. A difficult market or property may not be the only reason for the hard sale. If you have considerable deferred cap ex, or have done a poor job of leasing the property, you may need to pay larger brokerage fees in order to sell the building.

CLOSING THOUGHT

Never simply change a single line item or entry and think you are conducting sensitivity analysis. True insight requires a clear understanding of the ramifications and interdependencies between various line items. Focus on the "disease" that causes things to be worse, and carefully work through each line item in view of the disease. You will focus more on bad outcomes, because you can always live with things turning out better than expected. But even meaningful analysis, complete with well-conceived scenarios, will never be right. You will either be too low or too high. But your model allows you to systematically think about the property in a critical manner. As you gain business experience, you will be better at evaluating what to be wary of, and how to best use financial models. Be patient. You'll get better over time.

Chapter 6
Real Estate Due Diligence Analysis

"Strive to explain complex things simply".
-Dr. Peter Linneman

WHAT IS DUE DILIGENCE?

Real estate courses often fail to cover due diligence, focusing instead on esoteric financing possibilities and option pricing models. But if you enter the real estate business you will quickly find yourself engaged in due diligence efforts, as it is the foundation of real estate investments.

Due diligence is the investigation made by an investor prior to committing to making an investment. It involves analyzing both the facts about the property and the robustness of the assumptions made for your financial model. As such, due diligence serves as both a reality check and a challenge to your financial model. It also provides important insights concerning the property's risks.

There are many things to investigate before acquiring or developing a building. Where do you start? A due diligence checklist helps, but creativity and awareness of the unique risks of each property are critical.

Assume you have developed a financial model for the next eleven years for your investment target. This pro forma summarizes expected revenues, expenses, capital improvements, leasing expenditures, interest payments, etc. A critical aspect of due diligence is challenging your pro forma assumptions. Are the leases such that rents can grow by 5% in the third year? Can you sell the property when you want? How long will it take to sell the building? Will there be large capital expenditures? When can tenants get out of their leases? How? Are back-taxes owed? Are tenants actually paying the contracted rents? Are there hidden legal liabilities? Is the property insurable? Addressing these types of questions is what due diligence is all about.

Will the assumptions in your pro forma ever happen? Of course not! That is where careful analysis and risk management come into play. When real dollars are riding on your assumptions, you want to be extremely careful. In the end, the due diligence process provides information which helps you determine whether the risks of acquiring or developing a property are more than offset by the opportunities it offers you.

When you see a pro forma where a $2 million NOI in year 4 doubles to $4 million by year 7, you should be very curious about how this fortunate increase will be achieved. What specific factors make the increase possible; are they sustainable? Do the assumptions which yield this result make sense given the leases, the age of the property, and the market?

Mistakes are costly. Often young professionals fall in love with the complexity and elegance of their financial models and neglect carefully analyzing the property and its market. This invariably leads to expensive mistakes.

Sometimes your mistakes are apparent immediately. But more frequently they will not show up until 12-36 months after you have closed the deal. Everything is running smoothly, when suddenly NOI begins to head south. Perhaps this is because the people in the area have moved elsewhere due to the local factory closing. Had you thoroughly performed due diligence you would have been aware of the weak state of the factory and either bid less or walked away from the deal. At a minimum, it should have been an outcome you considered when forming your bid. Of course everyone makes mistakes. If you have not made any, it just means you have not done any deals. But if you make serious mistakes too often, you had better find another career.

So what exactly goes into the due diligence process for real estate? A basic breakdown is:

- Title, Survey, Environmental, and Legal
- Revenue
- Operating Expenditures
- Capital Expenditures
- Loan Documents
- Neighborhood and Market.

TITLE, SURVEY, ENVIRONMENTAL AND LEGAL

When you prepare to buy a property it is important to know exactly what you are buying. Who owns it? What exactly do they own? Has it been owned before? Are there competing ownership claims? The way you obtain this information is by ordering a title search. Title companies compile title reports by searching public records. Knowing who owns the property is essential, because if you do not have each owner's title you may not own what you think you bought. The title search contains information on what each person owns, along with detailed legal property descriptions. A title document also contains additional information about the property, including its previous usage and ownership.

In the due diligence process it is your responsibility to understand what all this information means. This entails reading all of these documents, as well as referenced materials that describe restrictions placed on the property. Deciphering all of this information is complex work that generally requires legal assistance. But reviewing and questioning your attorney's work is essential, as in the end it is your money at risk.

When you purchase real estate you can purchase it either **encumbered** or **unencumbered**. Encumbered real estate has a lien, charge, or other liability attached to the property. For example, the owner owns a mortgaged property, but the lender has a security interest on the property as long as the mortgage is outstanding. While encumbrances do not generally prevent the transfer of title, you had better know what encumbrances you are accepting before you acquire the property. There may also be physical encumbrances, such as telephone poles, or utility towers on your property. All known encumbrances will be listed on the property's legal property description.

A **title survey** is created from this information. This description will display where improvements have been made, as well as what can potentially be added. **Easements** which have been granted will also be noted on this description. Easements are the right to do something on the property. It may be an appurtenant easement, such as the right for someone to cross through the property for transportation, ingress, or egress purposes. Another common easement is called easement "in gross", which is for the benefit of a person or company, rather than the benefit of another parcel of land. An example is an easement for public utilities. When performing due diligence it is important to know who has rights and what easements exist.

A hot topic in real estate is environmental contamination. If you are purchasing a residential property, chances are the owner has not been engaged in activities that cause severe environmental damage. So why do you have to be concerned about the potential environmental contamination of your property and the surrounding area? Because it may have had a "dirty" use before becoming residential, or surrounding contamination may have entered the property. For example, a gas station operated a block away from the site for many years before going out of business. It is possible that the gas tanks leaked and leached onto the property, contaminating both the site and the local aquifer. According to the current Superfund Law you are liable for the damage regardless whether or not you were the source. Why? Because Congress decided to have things cleaned up first, and only then can you sort out if you can collect from the original polluter later via a tort claim. These costs can be huge, and due diligence helps determine if these problems exist before you purchase the property.

There are several ways to conduct environmental studies: you search the public record; talk to people familiar with the property; hire consultants; and run your own investigations. If you walk the site and the grass is orange, it is not a good sign. When contracting people to conduct your investigations, you must be diligent of their cutting corners. They may not interview enough people or not sample enough sites on the property. Your money is at risk, so it is your job to supervise them. Even if the seller says he has already checked everything and guarantees everything is fine, you must still perform your own due diligence, as the seller may not have sufficient assets to cover the damages they guarantee. Moreover, it is costly and difficult to prove that the seller engaged in fraudulent activity. Remember that the more severe the problem, the more likely the seller will try to convince you not to worry.

Just as you have to check for potential environmental defects, you also need to watch for structural defects. For example, some tall buildings have placed swimming pools on the top floors of their buildings. While beautiful, this can cause problems as it enhances mold spore growth. Mold problems are now being compared to the asbestos problem of two decades ago, even though analysts have yet to quantify the extent of the mold problem. Other questions to consider are: Is the roof in good shape? How about the HVAC system? The elevators?

A property should pass a Possible Maximum Loss (PML) test in terms of structural integrity. If the score is greater than 19, it will be hard to find a lender. A warehouse is built like a big box, so if an earthquake occurs the entire structure may fall like a stack of pancakes. Such a structural defect gives the building a PML in excess of 19, and bracing is required to provide sufficient support. If the PML is greater than 20, you may not want to purchase the structure because the cost of earthquake proofing the property may be prohibitively high. Sometimes less sophisticated investors do not get the PML ratings in time, and therefore lose substantial amounts of time and money bidding on a non-financeable asset.

You will also need to conduct legal diligence in order to determine if there are outstanding legal claims associated with the property. This includes worker injury claims, "slip and fall" claims, lawsuits filed by tenants, vendors or customers, etc.

REVENUES, EXPENSES, AND CAPITAL EXPENDITURES

REVENUES

After the physical aspects of the property have been thoroughly investigated, it is necessary to challenge your beliefs about how much cash flow your investment in the property can generate. Revenue can be broken into three components: creditworthiness of the tenant, current leases, and the long term competitiveness of the property. For this last consideration, the location, design durability, and the flexibility of the property are critical, as these factors allow the value of the property to be maintained over time. The property may be currently leased to a great tenant at great terms, but the space may be difficult to re-lease because of poor design or location. For example, with an industrial warehouse, you want to make sure that the floors are truly flat, so when tenants stack boxes they do not lean. Also, is it easy for trucks to enter and exit the facility? Does the property have good clear height? Is it near a major highway interchange?

Is there a book or website that tells you what is a good location or design? No, but common sense and experience are good guides. You need to understand how the building will be used and the tenant's operating needs. Truck drivers, for example, generally cannot drive for more than an 8 hour shift. If your warehouse facility takes 30 minutes to enter and exit, the tenant will not be happy because that time could have been spent making deliveries.

Your surroundings play a major role in property design, so there are no set rules of design. But experience dictates some lasting design elements. What is considered a "hot" design today may be passé in 10 years. As firms grow more sophisticated, and their operations change, so too will their design requirements. For this reason, it is important to be aware of the property's expansion and redevelopment options.

Contracts also play a large role in determining your revenues. If you own a strip center, your revenue will be largely dependent upon your tenant mix. If the property has a strong anchor, like Wal-Mart, you will want to know if they have the right to terminate the lease or go dark. If so, under what circumstances? If a key tenant can go dark, then other tenants who have co-tenancy agreements may also leave the center. Since much of the center's profits derive from the smaller tenants, a dark anchor can destroy a center.

A different problem can occur in an office building. The property may have Citi as a major tenant, and at the end of their lease they have the option to renew the lease for 15 years at 95% of "fair market value". What happens if the lease expires in a down market? Then you have no choice but to lock in the tenant at very low rents for another 15 years. This problem is exacerbated if the current lease states that the landlord provide tenant improvements at $50 per square foot upon renewal.

A careful review of accounts receivable indicates who is in arrears, and for how long. If receivables are high, one or more of your tenants may be facing bankruptcy. Will they void their leases in bankruptcy? Is their weakness an indicator of an economic decline in the area? Or perhaps a major tenant has a dispute with the current owner. A major problem with gathering receivables information is that the seller is usually slow to show you who is paying and who is not, as they want to collect as much as they can of these receivables before selling. Further, they are hesitant to expose the weaker aspects of their property. Oftentimes, receivables data are among the last data you will receive.

How do you learn about the demand side of the real estate business? Talk with tenants, local leasing agents, and brokers. In fact, working for a broker can be a great way to learn about tenants and their leasing needs. You will also gain some experience in what design features are relevant for tenants.

EXPENSES

You should carefully explore the last 3-5 years' property expense reports and tax returns. Carefully reading the leases is also critical because they articulate who pays for what. Will the tenant pay for utility bills or does the landlord? In a shopping center, tenants usually pay a share of all costs. For offices, each tenant tends to have a base year expense stop that reflects market conditions at the time the lease was signed.

Assume you want to construct Henderson Arms in downtown Philadelphia. Based on your work in the Philadelphia suburbs, you think that $125/square foot is a reasonable estimate of construction costs. If you do not perform careful due diligence, you will be in for quite a shock when you realize it costs closer to $200/square foot to build the structure! Why? Philadelphia is a union town. Union wages and work rules ramp up costs significantly. If you attempt to avoid union labor, you may find your project halted due to strikes or labor shortages. If you are building a medical facility and must install a multimillion dollar CAT scan machine, you will probably want the manufacturer of the machine to install it to avoid breaching the warranty. In this situation you may have to pay for a union member to stand and watch the installation process. Does the union worker add any value? No. Do you have to pay him? Yes. For this reason you will have to adjust your pro forma expenditures accordingly.

After the September 11 attacks, insurance coverage and premiums changed for many properties. This means that coverage which was acceptable 15 years ago is not adequate today. These changes will increase your insurance expenditures and decrease your NOI.

Another government policy that will alter expenditures is property taxes. When were they last raised? Are they up for revision? If the local government is looking for a quick way to increase revenues, they may consider increasing local property taxes. These increases will take away from your cash stream. You must assess the likelihood that your purchase triggers a new assessment and perhaps petition against it.

Sometimes the property may be over assessed. If your due diligence discovers this problem, then you will want to see if you can get a property tax reduction by a reassessment.

CAPITAL EXPENDITURE NEEDS

Capital expenditure reserves are the cash reserves set aside for future capital expenditures. These contingencies reflect the fact that you know things will occur, but not precisely when. These expenditures may result from severe damage due to a tornado or an unexpected collapse of the roof. The reserves also cover routine capital expenditures. How do you determine if your pro forma reserve is large enough? Go out and look at the structure, and make a detailed analysis of what costs you think will occur. A reserve that is too small will make it difficult to get a loan or will squeeze you when you need money most.

LOAN DOCUMENTS

When buying a property, you may find that it is encumbered by debt. In certain cases the debt is not transferable, which means the current owner cannot sell the property without paying off the debt. If the current owner needs cash right away to pay off the debt, then you probably will not be able to pay the owner in installments over time.

In some situations the debt may be transferable, meaning that you can take on the previous owner's debt. If you choose to do that, you must be wary. There may be covenants on the debt that prohibit certain operations you may wish to perform. If you are building a retail center and a covenant states that you cannot have parking lots, you will not be able to go ahead with your plans. Sometimes the debt has an "equity kicker," where if the property generates a profit over some pre-determined amount, the lender receives a portion of the upside. If you do not want to share your profit, you may want to pay off the debt. But the loan may have a pre-payment penalty. If the debt is due in the distant future and it is locked in at a high rate, this penalty can be quite large.

NEIGHBORHOOD AND MARKET

When you purchase a property, you are purchasing a part of the community. For this reason, you must be aware of what is happening in the community. If the area has experienced phenomenal growth due to the opening of a biotechnology firm, you must investigate whether the biotechnology firm and industry are solid. Otherwise, you may put growth numbers in your pro forma that are impossible to achieve. Performing a neighborhood demographic analysis includes gathering data on income, traffic patterns, population trends, and employment trends. All of this aids you in doing a supply and demand analysis of the area (for example, if the city has a population of 400,000, is estimated to grow at 5% over the next 5 years, there is no new construction, the city has about 40 million square feet of retail, and the market currently has only about 100 square feet/person of shopping space). A crude rule of thumb is that a market can support up to about 200 square feet/person of shopping space. Thus, this town may be underserved in terms of retail space. If the town is an upper middle class town, and incomes are expected to grow, perhaps an upscale shopping venue is most appropriate. To determine the prime location of this center, traffic patterns are evaluated to assess where people congregate or pass. Gathering credit card receipt data from the town hall is another efficient means of determining where people shop. Always drive or walk around the neighborhood and observe the homes, cars, and stores in the area. And do this on different days and times, as the character and activity may differ depending upon day and time.

CLOSING THOUGHT

All of this information is not nicely organized on some website. You must get out, walk around, talk to brokers, read reports, drive or helicopter the area, and visit the property and town both at night and during the day. You may engage consultants. Doing your homework will require substantial creativity and dedication. In addition, you must be skeptical of what you read and hear. If you find a report saying that population is expected to double in three years, question that report, even if it is by a major firm. Their mistakes and typos can cost you a lot of money!

Chapter 6 Supplement A

Forecasting 2020 U.S. County and MSA Populations

Dr. Peter Linneman and Albert Saiz – Wharton Real Estate Review – Fall 2006 Vol. X No. 2

Whether relying upon explicit statistical models, recent information on the evolution of local markets, conversations with friends, the latest headlines in the local newspaper, or gut feelings, real estate entrepreneurs are constantly guessing the future demand for their product. Population growth is associated with increased residential demand, increased demand in the office and distribution sectors, and more shoppers to patronize local retail. In short, population growth drives real estate development opportunities.

We examine the key statistical determinants of population growth in U.S. metropolitan counties, identifying characteristics that are important predictors of subsequent population growth. From our statistical analysis we gain a better understanding of the conceptual underpinnings of the population growth across U.S. metropolitan counties during the last 30 years. In addition to learning what makes cities "tick", we are also able to make predictions of population growth for all metropolitan counties in the United States.

It is perilous to predict the future. However, our model accurately describes the population growth that took place from 1980 to 2000, and past growth forecasts future growth relatively accurately. We therefore believe that our estimates for 2000 to 2020 population growth will prove to be not too far off the mark. Nevertheless, our statistical work fails to account for about a quarter of all the variation in county population growth. That is, growth surprises do occur, and in some cases they matter a lot. In the 1950s, who would have predicted that Benton County, Arkansas, would emerge as the center of the biggest commercial empire in world history? Spurred by the phenomenal growth of Wal-Mart, Benton County makes the Census list of top 70 counties by population growth. The point is that our statistical analysis cannot predict who the next Sam Walton will be, and where he or she will be based.

POPULATION GROWTH

1980-2000

Regression analysis allows us to identify some of the key variables that predict future population growth. We explore a variety of variables at the county level. Examples include demographic variables (such as the percentage of individuals older than 65), fiscal variables (such as taxes) and geographic factors (such as local weather and elevation). These variables have predictive power for several reasons. First, they capture attributes of an area that cause it to grow economically, and therefore attract employees. Firm productivity varies across locales for several reasons: the skills and education of their population; accessibility to markets and transportation nodes; the impact of local public finances (taxes and expenditures); and agglomeration economies. The latter refers to firms becoming more productive if they locate closer to similar firms, enabling them to share information, infrastructures, and a pool of relevant workers, and to reduce the transportation costs of their common input and output transactions.

Other variables predict how attractive an area is for prospective inhabitants due to local amenities. Research by Edward Glaeser, Jed Kolko, and Albert Saiz demonstrates that cities are becoming as important in terms of *consumption* as they used to be in terms of traditional *productivity*. The capacity to generate and retain amenities adds considerably to the appeal of a city. Some cities will attract high-income residents by offering varied shopping experiences, proximity to attractive activities, good schools, and a strong social milieu that is conducive to both work and play. The attraction to a city on the basis of its physical and social environment represents a major paradigm shift; whereas people formerly followed jobs, jobs now also follow workers.

Thanks to information and ethnic networks, people tend to move to areas where they have social contacts. Thus, metropolitan areas with large immigrant populations, for example, tend to attract yet more immigrants. In addition, the characteristics of the population of a county can predict population growth for simple biological reasons: younger populations tend to be more fertile, while the elderly experience higher mortality rates. Finally, some variables are good predictors of population growth even though they are difficult to measure: a vibrant lifestyle, an openness to entrepreneurs, a good climate, and so on.

This study focuses on "metropolitan counties" as defined by the Office of Management and Budget (OMB) in 2000. These are counties that belong to OMB-defined metropolitan areas that are major population centers. We limit ourselves to the continental United States, excluding Hawaii, Alaska and Puerto Rico. The 804 counties that we examine in our analysis represent 76 percent of all U.S. population in 2000.

The U.S. population has grown by about 10 percent every decade since 1970, and is predicted to continue doing so through 2020 (Figure 6A.1). In 2000, the population was estimated to be 282 million, and by 2020 it is expected to grow to 336 million. This means that between 2000 and 2020 the population will increase by a staggering 53.7 million. Where will these people live? Our statistical model addresses this question by analyzing county population growth across all metropolitan counties between 1980 and 2000. The focus is on long-term urban population growth.

FIGURE 6A.1: U.S. population, 1970 to 2020

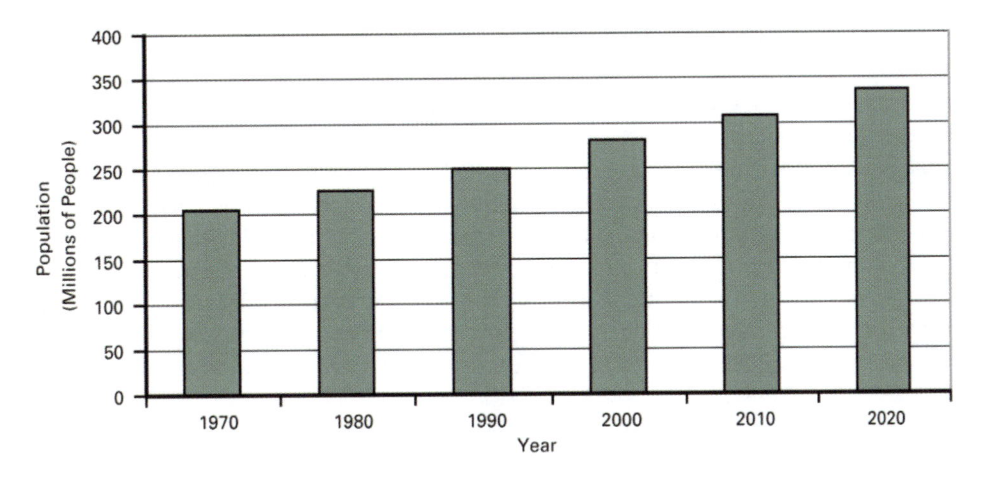

Whereas most of the previous research on city growth has focused on percentage of population growth, we use a more relevant growth metric that recognizes that in very small counties, growth rates can be extremely high although the actual number of new people moving into the area is very small. We calculate the share of county population as a percentage of total U.S. population, and use the change in that share between 1980 and 2000 in our statistical analysis. To the best of our knowledge, this is the first time this particular variable has been used in the context of long-term growth. Since this measure is relative to the total size of the population, we combine our regression results with Census projections of future population growth to forecast local growth. Figure 6A.2 shows the results of a regression analysis of the change in total population share from 1980 to 2000 as a function of a number of county characteristics in 1980.

The dependent variable in the regressions is multiplied by 10,000 so that our regression coefficients do not display an inordinate number of decimal positions. Figure 6A.2 presents the results, including a variable that has high forecasting power: the "population market share capture" of the county from 1970 to 1980 (growth in the recent past). Thus, we find that recent past growth forecasts future growth. This regression accounts for 75 percent of the variability in county growth.

Our model is rich in specification, including 26 local economic, demographic, political, climatologic, geological, and housing variables. We will focus primarily on describing the impacts of the variables that are most statistically significant, although we will comment on a few variables that we expected to be more important. We begin by noting the importance of recent growth. Our results confirm this result of previous research that used data from different countries, and different geographic definitions (for example, city level forecasts), population growth definitions, and time periods. Everyone (including us) finds that, even after controlling for a variety of other variables, population growth is extremely persistent; absent other information, the best way to predict a county's population growth is to look at how much it grew in the past decade. It appears that the forces that shape an area's attractiveness have persistent impacts.

Immigration has become a primary driver of population growth. In the 1960s, most Americans claimed European or African ancestry, and the number of foreign-born households was relatively low. Between now and 2050, immigrants and their offspring will account for about half of the total growth in U.S. population, and Americans of European and African origin will become *primi inter pares* in a country of Mexican-Americans, Chinese-Americans, Korean-Americans, Indian-Americans, Filipino-Americans, and many others.

It is obvious that immigration will be a key element of county-level growth, but can we forecast where immigrants will settle? The answer to the question is a qualified yes. Immigrants tend to concentrate wherever previous immigrants have settled. Kinship ties, shared language, and the existence of common amenities and public goods make "immigrant enclaves" attractive to subsequent immigrants. Thus, a county's share of the foreign-born in 1980 was an important predictor of population growth from 1980 to 2000. And so it will be in the future.

Previous research by Edward Glaeser and Albert Saiz has shown that during the last century local educational achievement has been an important explanatory factor for population growth in cities. In short, smart cities grow faster. We find the same to be true at the county level. Specifically, counties with lower shares of high-school dropouts grew more quickly. However, education is a weaker predictor of county growth than of metropolitan growth, especially when one includes previous growth trends. This means that education has an important long-run impact, but that short-term changes in education levels are not powerful predictors of short-term changes in growth patterns. Metropolitan areas with highly educated individuals are more productive, allowing them to pay higher wages, which attracts population inflows. On the other hand, highly educated populations are typically more effective in curtailing local residential development at the local level, and may be a counter-influence on population growth.

The age distribution of the population is another predictor of future growth; that is, very young and very old populations tend to grow more slowly. Specifically, we find that population growth is negatively related to both the share of people younger than 25 and the share of people older than 65, reflecting that households in their prime earning years are typically older than 25, and younger than 65. Moreover, areas with a major proportion of older residents are less attractive to younger generations.

Tax rates are not uniform for different municipalities. We use data from the Census of Governments on local taxation (municipal and county) to create two measures of fiscal burden: income taxes and the sales tax. Furthermore, since different individuals typically face different tax rates depending on their location, income, and type of business, we use total tax revenues per capita divided by income per capita to measure a county's tax burden. A high degree of taxation may make a county less attractive to taxpayers and entrepreneurs. On the other hand, higher tax revenues may be associated with better public schools and public services. Our statistical analysis reveals that the local sales tax burden is generally associated with slower population growth. Since all tax measures are strongly associated, we tentatively conclude that higher taxation discourages local growth. We suspect, however, that the efficiency of local government in spending sensibly and government efficiency in providing key public services are also important. Determining the factors that are associated with local mismanagement or good government remains a topic for future research.

FIGURE 6A.2: U.S. metropolitan county growth model

	US Population Share Change 1980-2000
Share foreign-born in 1980	12.621*
% with bachelor's degree or higher in 1980	-0.132
% with less than a high school diploma in 1980	-0.188
% white in 1980	0.184
% over 65 years old in 1980	-10.873*
% under 25 years old in 1980	-9.035*
ncome tax per capita / Income per capita in 1980	34.189
Sales tax per capita / Income per capita in 1980	-23.86*
Log population density in 1980	0.512
Log density squared in 1980 -0.050	
Presidential election vote over 55% Republican in 1980	-0.193
Presidential election vote below 45% Republican in 1980	0.317*
All state senators Republican in 1980	-0.407
All state senators Democrat in 1980	-0.195
Log average precipitation	-0.681
Log average snowfall	-0.238
Log January average temperature	0.282
Log average January sun days	1.101*
Share housing older than 30 years	3.040*
Share housing newer than 11 years	5.206*
=1 if county borders an ocean or a Great Lake	-0.684*
Hills or mountains in county	-0.079
Northeast	-0.349
South	-0.357
West	0.351*
U.S. population share change 1970-1980	1.026*
Constant	-2.011
Observations	805.00
R-squared	0.76
Robust standard errors in parentheses	
*Significant at 10%	

We find that population density also matters, although in a complex way. Counties with very low densities tended to grow more slowly. But above a certain threshold, higher density is associated with slower growth. This threshold population density corresponds with a median county density of 60 persons per square mile. Therefore, density increases growth up to about 60 people per square mile, after which amenity levels drop and population growth diminishes.

The impact of demography on politics is a hotly debated topic by political scientists and media pundits. Observations on the growth of "red" states and the demise of "blue" states are commonplace. If we run our analysis with politics as the only variable, we find that Republican-dominated counties (based upon presidential and senatorial election data from early 1980s) do tend to grow faster. However, this can be explained by other variables. Republican-dominated counties were already rapidly growing, so it is possible that the new rapidly growing areas are attracting individuals with a more libertarian or conservative outlook. Moreover, many of the metropolitan areas in "red" states have geographic attributes that are associated with growth. When we control for these other factors, we find that political orientation is not strongly associated with growth. There is a weak link, however, between the 1980 presidential results and subsequent county growth. Almost half of the counties in our sample of 804 metropolitan counties had between 45 percent and 55 percent support for Ronald Reagan. A number of counties were more polarized, with more than a 55 percent share for either Reagan (about 40 percent) or Carter (about 12 percent). These strongly Democratic counties grew significantly faster between 1980 and 2000, controlling for a host of other variables. It is unclear why.

Some of the most powerful predictors of county population growth during our sample years are weather-related. Briefly put, Americans are rapidly leaving cold, damp, and snowy areas for sunnier and drier climates. Both a West regional indicator and "good weather" variables are strong predictors of population growth. All of the weather variables (snowfall, precipitation, temperature, and sun days) are interrelated, with the number of sun days in January being the variable that comes out more strongly in our analysis. In short, people are moving to "the bright side". We speculate that there may be a geopolitical economic shift from the Atlantic to the Pacific area, motivated by changing trade links and the emergence of China and India as global powerhouses. The impact of globalization on population growth remains an understudied topic for future exploration.

The age distribution of the county's housing stock also has some predictive power, confirming previous research by Edward Glaeser and Joseph Gyourko. Areas with large amounts of new housing have three important attributes that favor growth: they are favorably inclined to development; they have a large recent demand relative to pre-existing housing; and their housing stock is more in line with modern housing preferences. Interestingly, there is some (weak) evidence that having a very old housing stock is mildly correlated with relatively faster growth than would otherwise be the case. The very old housing stock that has survived was generally built for high-income families, and hence are of good quality. Since declining cities such as New Orleans, Detroit, and Buffalo have massive and valuable housing stocks, reduced housing demand translated into lower housing prices and made these cities a bit less unattractive. All things equal, areas with older housing stocks experienced slower decline than expected.

Counties adjacent to the coastlines of the Atlantic, Pacific, and Great Lakes tend to grow more slowly than inland counties. Coastal areas in the west and northeast often have restrictive zoning, which raises prices and discourages growth. However, there appears to be no relationship between the altitude of a county and its growth. This is a somewhat surprising finding, as mountain areas are generally popular.

A LOOK AT 2020

Combining county characteristics with our statistical growth model and Census projections of total population in 2020, we obtain county and MSA population forecasts for 2020. Figure 6A.4 details the counties that are the biggest projected population losers. Also displayed are their MSAs, our estimate of population losses (expressed in both levels and as a percentage of the 2000 population), our estimate of population levels in 2020, and previous population gains or losses from 1980 to 2000. Because we used the change in the shares of the total population, five counties display negative population predictions for 2020, which we replace by zero. Our expectations for these counties are bleak, notwithstanding the fact that we do not know exactly how many people will actually be living there.

Baltimore has the dubious honor of being ranked the biggest loser by 2020. That city (which is also a county) is forecast to lose about 100,000 residents, or about 15 percent of its year 2000 population. Most other counties that we expect to decline are in the Rustbelt.

Interestingly, 10 percent (five out of 50) of the bottom counties are in the New Orleans metropolitan area—and this is without factoring in the impact of Katrina. In other words, New Orleans was the rare case of a Sunbelt area that was losing population like a Rustbelt area. According to research by Donald Davis and David Weinstein, who used data from the bombing of Japanese cities during World War II, the impact of major disasters on a city's population growth tends to dissipate over time. Remarkably, Davis and Weinstein found that the cities that lost more population during the war grew faster afterwards, and their populations after 20 years were at the point that one would have predicted by looking at pre-war growth trends. Thus, we are very pessimistic about New Orleans' growth over the next 20 years, irrespective of what aid flows to this area.

Figure 6A.5 displays the "winners" in terms of forecasted county growth. Big counties in major metropolitan areas tend to dominate. Insofar as the U.S. population is growing, and the share of population captured by a county is not declining too quickly, big counties are expected to grow because of general population growth trends. However, Figure 6A.5 also captures the massive expected growth of relatively new areas, such as Maricopa County, Ariz., the top county in terms of expected population growth in 2020. It is apparent that most of the big growth counties are in the West, the Sunbelt, and the Southern I-85 corridor linking Atlanta with Raleigh, N.C. Our results reveal that prospective real estate developers had better buy a good pair of sunglasses and some sunblock.

The map (Figure 6A.3) displays the expected population growth for all metropolitan counties. Since we are measuring overall population growth numbers, rather than percentage growth, the Northeastern metropolitan counties are shown to expect considerable growth in numbers even if percentage growth there will be relatively slow. Otherwise, growth will be concentrated in California, Arizona, New Mexico, Florida, the greater Seattle metropolitan area, Salt Lake City, the Denver North-South corridor, Texas, the Atlanta-Charlotte-Raleigh corridor, and the Chicago-Madison region.

FIGURE 6A.3: Expected population growth in metropolitan counties, 2000-2020

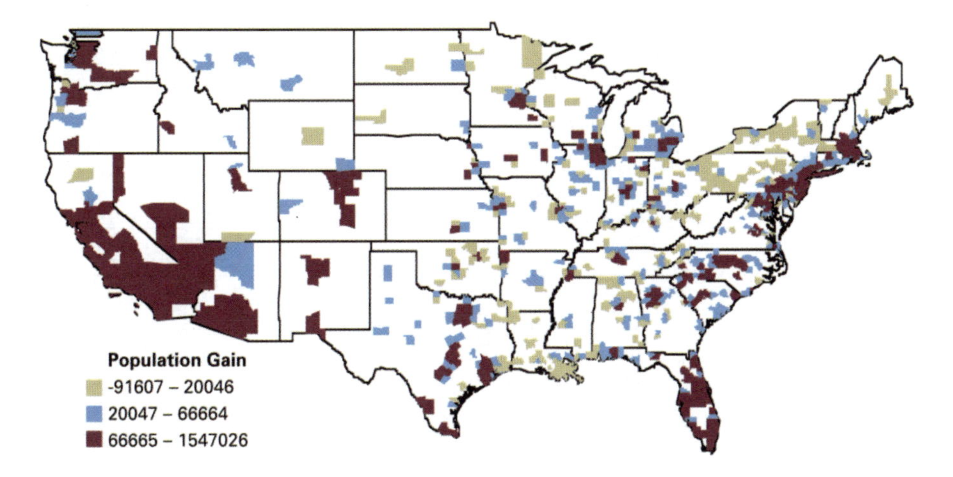

Lastly, Figure 6A.6 displays our population growth forecasts for all U.S. metropolitan areas used in our analysis, based upon our county-level forecasts and year 2000 MSA definitions. In this case, we rank metropolitan areas according to their expected population gains (or losses). A small number of major metropolitan areas are forecasted to lose population by 2020: New Orleans, Syracuse, Rochester, Buffalo, Pittsburgh, and Youngstown-Warren.

FIGURE 6A.4: Largest population loss counties, 2020 forecast

Rank	County Name	Metropolitan Area	Population Loss 2020-2000	Forecast: Population in 2020	Loss as Percentage of 2000 Population	Population Loss/Gain 2000-1980
1	Baltimore	Baltimore, Md.	-91,607	556,950	-14.1%	-137,751
2	Oswego	Syracuse, N.Y.	-62,809	59,728	-51.3%	8,762
3	Herkimer	Utica-Rome, N.Y.	-59,174	5,217	-91.9%	-2,272
4	Cayuga	Syracuse, N.Y.	-56,550	25,388	-69.0%	1,986
5	Chautauqua	Jamestown, N.Y.	-49,891	89,698	-35.7%	-7,372
6	Allegheny	Pittsburgh, Pa.	-48,588	1,231,395	-3.8%	-168,271
7	Cambria	Johnstown, Pa.	-48,233	103,997	-31.7%	-30,756
8	St. Charles	New Orleans, La.	-48,196	0	-100%	10,713
9	Terrebonne	Houma, La.	-47,720	56,804	-45.7%	9,541
10	St. Bernard	New Orleans, La.	-47,531	19,484	-70.9%	2,620
11	Lafourche	Houma, La.	-41,959	47,996	-46.6%	6,621
12	Erie	Buffalo-Niagara Falls, N.Y.	-40,544	908,823	-4.3%	-64,847
13	St. John the Baptist	New Orleans, La.	-39,592	3,547	-91.8%	10,852
14	Grand Forks	Grand Forks, N.D.-Minn.	-38,635	27,233	-58.7%	-403
15	Erie	Erie, Pa.	-38,486	242,201	-13.7%	644
16	Ashtabula	Cleveland-Lorain-Elyria, Ohio	-37,191	65,579	-36.2%	-1,249
17	Somerset	Johnstown, Pa.	-36,894	43,131	-46.1%	-1,261
18	Oneida	Utica-Rome, N.Y.	-36,758	198,450	-15.6%	-18,352
19	Madison	Syracuse, N.Y.	-36,066	33,378	-51.9%	4,187
20	Belmont	Wheeling, W.V.-Ohio	-34,829	35,290	-49.7%	-12,345
21	St. Louis	St. Louis, Mo.-Ill.	-33,793	312,975	-9.7%	-104,344
22	Orleans	Rochester, N.Y.	-33,150	11,028	-75.0%	5,652
23	Acadia	Lafayette, La.	-32,338	26,489	-55.0%	2,196
24	Mercer	Sharon, Pa.	-32,073	88,113	-26.7%	-8,019
25	Ouachita	Monroe, La.	-31,782	115,441	-21.6%	7,569
26	Schoharie	Albany-Schenectady-Troy, N.Y.	-30,077	1,516	-95.2%	1,886
27	Webster	Shreveport-Bossier City, La.	-29,886	11,849	-71.6%	-1,923
28	Rapides	Alexandria, La.	-28,461	97,952	-22.5%	-9,009
29	Douglas	Duluth-Superior, Minn.-Wisc.	-28,419	14,988	-65.5%	-1,156
30	Livingston	Rochester, N.Y.	-27,988	36,395	-43.5%	7,298
31	Plaquemines	New Orleans, La.	-26,746	0	-100%	645
32	Tioga	Binghamton, N.Y.	-26,731	25,021	-51.7%	1,821
33	Ohio	Wheeling, W.V.-Ohio	-26,563	20,771	-56.1%	-14,010
34	Columbia	Scranton-Wilkes-Barre-Hazleton, Pa.	-26,520	37,585	-41.4%	2,036
35	Strafford	Boston-Worcester-Lawrence, Mass.-N.H.	-26,439	86,241	-23.5%	26,746
36	Carroll	Canton-Massillon, Ohio	-26,412	2,467	-91.5%	3,288
37	Chemung	Elmira, N.Y.	-25,628	65,413	-28.1%	-6,402
38	Niagara	Buffalo-Niagara Falls, N.Y.	-24,756	194,829	-11.3%	-7,476
39	Calhoun	Anniston, Ala.	-24,576	86,764	-22.1%	-8,676
40	Wayne	Rochester, N.Y.	-24,492	69,276	-26.1%	8,996
41	Onondaga	Syracuse, N.Y.	-24,414	434,030	-5.3%	-5,288
42	Morton	Bismarck, N.D.	-24,052	1,273	-95.0%	99
43	Wayne	Huntington-Ashland, W.V.-Ky.-Ohio	-23,953	18,958	-55.8%	-3,136
44	Polk	Grand Forks, N.D.-Minn.	-23,628	7,752	-75.3%	-3,423
45	Genesee	Rochester, N.Y.	-23,423	36,901	-38.8%	828
46	Lawrence	Huntington-Ashland, W.V.-Ky.-Ohio	-21,975	40,308	-35.3%	-1,459
47	Sequoyah	Fort Smith, Ark.-Okla.	-21,946	17,114	-56.2%	8,282
48	Broome	Binghamton, N.Y.	-21,465	178,829	-10.7%	-13,414
49	Philadelphia	Philadelphia, Pa.-N.J.	-21,309	1,492,375	-1.4%	-171,750
50	St. James	New Orleans, La.	-21194	0	-100%	-370

FIGURE 6A.5: Largest population gain counties, 2020 forecast

Rank	County Name	Metropolitan Area	Population Gain 2020-2000	Forecast: Population in 2020	Gain as Percentage of 2000 Population	Population Gain 2000-1980
1	Maricopa	Phoenix-Mesa, Ariz.	1,547,026	4,643,369	50.0%	1,575,503
2	Los Angeles	Los Angeles-Long Beach, Calif.	1,414,155	11,000,000	14.8%	2,038,470
3	Clark	Las Vegas, Nev.-Ariz.	1,120,793	2,513,962	80.4%	923,984
4	Harris	Houston, Texas	958,645	4,373,626	28.1%	976,442
5	Orange	Orange County, Calif.	853,954	3,710,400	29.9%	908,379
6	Miami-Dade	Miami, Fla.	722,061	2,982,303	31.9%	617,110
7	Riverside	Riverside-San Bernardino, Calif.	681,484	2,241,310	43.7%	890,353
8	Broward	Fort Lauderdale, Fla.	677,134	2,309,574	41.5%	606,378
9	Dallas	Dallas, Texas	642,464	2,867,806	28.9%	659,694
10	San Diego	San Diego, Calif.	634,780	3,459,858	22.5%	949,458
11	Queens	New York, N.Y.	610,051	2,840,947	27.3%	336,600
12	Cook	Chicago, Ill.	604,597	5,981,749	11.2%	128,274
13	San Bernardino	Riverside-San Bernardino, Calif.	569,074	2,288,002	33.1%	815,972
14	Santa Clara	San Jose, Calif.	497,900	2,184,374	29.5%	384,959
15	Tarrant	Fort Worth-Arlington, Texas	480,496	1,934,957	33.0%	586,130
16	Palm Beach	West Palm Beach-Boca Raton, Fla.	466,127	1,601,782	41.0%	549,913
17	Gwinnett	Atlanta, Ga.	443,177	1,039,634	74.3%	427,113
18	Collin	Dallas, Texas	438,551	938,606	87.7%	353,516
19	Orange	Orlando, Fla.	433,910	1,336,228	48.1%	427,576
20	Travis	Austin-San Marcos, Texas	424,739	1,244,583	51.8%	397,846
21	King	Seattle-Bellevue-Everett, Wash.	424,664	2,163,580	24.4%	462,391
22	Kings	New York, N.Y.	413,431	2,879,690	16.8%	232,473
23	Alameda	Oakland, Calif.	412,117	1,862,524	28.4%	340,476
24	Hidalgo	McAllen-Edinburg-Mission, Texas	396,458	970,381	69.1%	287,383
25	Wake	Raleigh-Durham-Chapel Hill, N.C.	392,122	1,025,270	61.9%	329,792
26	Pima	Tucson, Ariz.	380,615	1,229,259	44.8%	312,864
27	Bexar	San Antonio, Texas	374,932	1,772,749	26.8%	402,676
28	Contra Costa	Oakland, Calif.	358,894	1,312,457	37.6%	294,780
29	Mecklenburg	Charlotte-Gastonia-Rock Hill, N.C.-S.C.	349,854	1,050,071	50.0%	293,722
30	Fulton	Atlanta, Ga.	331,074	1,148,117	40.5%	224,253
31	Montgomery	Washington, D.C.-Md.-Va.-W.V.	326,464	1,204,245	37.2%	295,728
32	Hillsborough	Tampa-St. Petersburg-Clearwater, Fla.	321,649	1,324,731	32.1%	351,249
33	San Francisco	San Francisco, Calif.	315,630	1,092,232	40.6%	95,772
34	Fresno	Fresno, Calif.	315,146	1,117,160	39.3%	284,335
35	Cobb	Atlanta, Ga.	307,450	920,222	50.2%	312,184
36	Sacramento	Sacramento, Calif.	302,821	1,532,860	24.6%	441,764
37	Denton	Dallas, Texas	301,085	739,896	68.6%	293,360
38	Kern	Bakersfield, Calif.	297,696	961,370	44.9%	257,267
39	Bronx	New York, N.Y.	297,217	1,631,465	22.3%	165,845
40	San Mateo	San Francisco, Calif.	292,084	1,000,422	41.2%	119,896
41	El Paso	El Paso, Texas	285,652	967,352	41.9%	197,989
42	Salt Lake	Salt Lake City-Ogden, Utah	284,412	1,185,036	31.6%	276,617
43	Fort Bend	Houston, Texas	283,281	642,237	78.9%	225,689
44	Will	Chicago, Ill.	279,533	787,760	55.0%	183,253
45	Douglas	Denver, Colo.	277,818	458,222	154.0%	154,785
46	Ventura	Ventura, Calif.	269,157	1,025,782	35.6%	223,798
47	San Joaquin	Stockton-Lodi, Calif.	268,931	837,094	47.3%	217,859
48	Washington	Portland-Vancouver, Ore.-Wash.	266,919	715,361	59.5%	200,680
49	DeKalb	Atlanta, Ga.	262,934	931,246	39.3%	184,219
50	Washoe	Reno, Nev.	259,487	600,804	76.0%	145,945

FIGURE 6B.5: Greatest population losses, 2020 forecast

MSA Code	MSA Name	Population Gain 2020-2000	Forecast: Population in 2020	Gain as Percentage of 2000 Population	Population Gain 2000-1980
5560	New Orleans, La. (MSA)	-214,098	1,122,720	-16.02%	28,407
8160	Syracuse, N.Y. (MSA)	-179,839	552,524	-24.56%	9,647
8680	Utica-Rome, N.Y. (MSA)	-95,932	203,667	-32.02%	-20,624
6840	Rochester, N.Y. (MSA)	-91,710	1,007,018	-8.35%	66,504
3350	Houma, La. (MSA)	-89,678	104,801	-46.11%	16,162
3400	Huntington-Ashland, W.V.-Ky.-Ohio (MSA)	-88,634	226,593	-28.12%	-21,159
3680	Johnstown, Pa. (MSA)	-85,127	147,128	-36.65%	-32,017
9000	Wheeling, W.V.-Ohio (MSA)	-73,815	79,035	-48.29%	-32,490
7560	Scranton-Wilkes-Barre-Hazleton, Pa. (MSA)	-72,260	551,352	-11.59%	-35,478
1280	Buffalo-Niagara Falls, N.Y. (MSA)	-65,300	1,103,652	-5.59%	-72,323
2985	Grand Forks, N.D.-Minn. (MSA)	-62,264	34,984	-64.03%	-3,826
6280	Pittsburgh, Pa. (MSA)	-61,107	2,295,862	-2.59%	-211,721
3610	Jamestown, N.Y. (MSA)	-49,891	89,698	-35.74%	-7,372
960	Binghamton, N.Y. (MSA)	-48,197	203,849	-19.12%	-11,593
7000	St. Joseph, Mo. (MSA)	-41,008	61,579	-39.97%	839
2240	Duluth-Superior, Minn.-Wisc. (MSA)	-39,580	204,258	-16.23%	-22,633
2360	Erie, Pa. (MSA)	-38,486	242,201	-13.71%	644
2975	Glens Falls, N.Y. (MSA)	-32,592	91,755	-26.21%	14,622
7610	Sharon, Pa. (MSA)	-32,073	88,113	-26.69%	-8,019
5200	Monroe, La. (MSA)	-31,782	115,441	-21.59%	7,569
3880	Lafayette, La. (MSA)	-28,768	357,055	-7.46%	52,901
220	Alexandria, La. (MSA)	-28,461	97,952	-22.51%	-9,009
2335	Elmira, N.Y. (MSA)	-25,628	65,413	-28.15%	-6,402
3580	Jackson, Tenn. (MSA)	-24,707	82,844	-22.97%	19,997
450	Anniston, Ala. (MSA)	-24,576	86,764	-22.07%	-8,676
7680	Shreveport-Bossier City, La. (MSA)	-23,940	368,342	-6.10%	14,338
8080	Steubenville-Weirton, Ohio-W.V. (MSA)	-20,951	110,720	-15.91%	-31,674
1010	Bismarck, N.D. (MSA)	-20,688	74,143	-21.82%	14,629
2340	Enid, Okla. (MSA)	-18,395	39,277	-31.90%	-5,507
1320	Canton-Massillon, Ohio (MSA)	-16,106	390,848	-3.96%	2,589
280	Altoona, Pa. (MSA)	-15,994	113,050	-12.39%	-7,399
6020	Parkersburg-Marietta, W.V.-Ohio (MSA)	-15,946	135,126	-10.56%	-6,776
1480	Charleston, W.V. (MSA)	-14,445	236,971	-5.75%	-18,306
2180	Dothan, Ala. (MSA)	-11,659	126,386	-8.45%	15,067
9320	Youngstown-Warren, Ohio (MSA)	-10,774	583,313	-1.81%	-49,736
1900	Cumberland, Md.-W.V. (MSA)	-10,504	91,339	-10.31%	-6,025
733	Bangor, Maine (NECMA)	-9,402	135,483	-6.49%	7,657
6240	Pine Bluff, Ark. (MSA)	-7,693	76,526	-9.13%	-6,503
2650	Florence, Ala. (MSA)	-7,273	135,726	-5.09%	7,677
4800	Mansfield, Ohio (MSA)	-6,860	168,820	-3.90%	-5,510
5990	Owensboro, Ky. (MSA)	-3,181	88,423	-3.47%	5,512
6323	Pittsfield, Mass. (NECMA)	-2,750	132,059	-2.04%	-10,272
870	Benton Harbor, Mich. (MSA)	-2,459	160,152	-1.51%	-8,677
8050	State College, Pa. (MSA)	-1,221	134,758	-0.90%	22,848
4640	Lynchburg, Va. (MSA)	-408	31,486	-1.28%	2,766
840	Beaumont-Port Arthur, Texas (MSA)	-392	384,345	-0.10%	9,940

FIGURE 6A.6: Forecasts for metropolitan areas, 2020

MSA Code	MSA Name	Population Gain 2020-2000	Forecast: Population in 2020	Gain as Percentage of 2000 Population	Population Gain 2000-1980
1350	Casper, Wyo. (MSA)	703	67,253	1.06%	-5,973
6660	Rapid City, S.D. (MSA)	788	89,559	0.89%	18,287
2030	Decatur, Ala. (MSA)	1,420	147,481	0.97%	25,626
9140	Williamsport, Pa. (MSA)	1,433	121,368	1.19%	1,664
2880	Gadsden, Ala. (MSA)	1,475	104,775	1.43%	188
2290	Eau Claire, Wisc. (MSA)	1,881	150,490	1.27%	17,204
3605	Jacksonville, N.C. (MSA)	1,881	152,104	1.25%	36,708
4243	Lewiston-Auburn, Maine (NECMA)	1,882	105,747	1.81%	4,334
160	Albany-Schenectady-Troy, N.Y. (MSA)	2,442	878,789	0.28%	51,127
3960	Lake Charles, La. (MSA)	4,423	187,943	2.41%	15,466
8600	Tuscaloosa, Ala. (MSA)	5,708	170,773	3.46%	27,234
2620	Flagstaff, Ariz.-Utah (MSA)	5,737	128,455	4.67%	43,101
2040	Decatur, Ill. (MSA)	7,833	122,316	6.84%	-16,722
6690	Redding, Calif. (MSA)	8,631	172,457	5.27%	47,236
3870	La Crosse, Wisc.-Minn. (MSA)	8,783	135,790	6.92%	17,311
3285	Hattiesburg, Miss. (MSA)	9,167	121,271	8.18%	21,665
8360	Texarkana, Texas-Texarkana Ark. (MSA)	9,616	139,348	7.41%	16,353
4420	Longview-Marshall, Texas (MSA)	10,000	218,747	4.79%	27,002
5280	Muncie, Ind. (MSA)	11,638	130,312	9.81%	-9,720
9080	Wichita Falls, Texas (MSA)	12,167	152,500	8.67%	11,442
7620	Sheboygan, Wisc. (MSA)	13,685	126,439	12.14%	11,847
8003	Springfield, Mass. (NECMA)	17,322	626,271	2.84%	26,257
4200	Lawton, Okla. (MSA)	18,354	132,918	16.02%	1,643
8940	Wausau, Wisc. (MSA)	18,751	144,653	14.89%	14,656
1890	Corvallis, Ore. (MSA)	19,450	97,609	24.88%	9,688
8750	Victoria, Texas (MSA)	19,492	103,509	23.20%	14,640
3700	Jonesboro, Ark. (MSA)	20,235	102,721	24.53%	19,182
6340	Pocatello, Idaho (MSA)	20,306	95,888	26.87%	9,932
6980	St. Cloud, Minn. (MSA)	20,384	188,460	12.13%	34,294
2520	Fargo-Moorhead, N.D.-Minn. (MSA)	20,567	195,253	11.77%	36,707
920	Biloxi-Gulfport-Pascagoula, Miss. (MSA)	21,056	385,880	5.77%	63,706
6800	Roanoke, Va. (MSA)	21,649	52,215	70.83%	7,255
1560	Chattanooga, Tenn.-Ga. (MSA)	21,785	487,506	4.68%	46,910
860	Bellingham, Wash. (MSA)	22,245	189,847	13.27%	60,380
5523	New London-Norwich, Conn. (NECMA)	22,822	282,282	8.80%	20,232
4320	Lima, Ohio (MSA)	24,528	179,689	15.81%	308
2190	Dover, Del. (MSA)	25,697	152,793	20.22%	28,816
40	Abilene, Texas (MSA)	25,700	152,162	20.32%	14,645
2200	Dubuque, Iowa (MSA)	26,027	115,285	29.16%	-4,443
8920	Waterloo-Cedar Falls, Iowa (MSA)	26,620	154,522	20.81%	-10,111
7200	San Angelo, Texas (MSA)	27,165	131,107	26.14%	18,619
1680	Cleveland-Lorain-Elyria, Ohio (PMSA)	27,723	2,278,531	1.23%	-25,649
3710	Joplin, Mo. (MSA)	27,996	185,698	17.75%	29,857
7640	Sherman-Denison, Texas (MSA)	28,292	139,304	25.49%	20,894
6403	Portland, Maine (NECMA)	28,451	294,410	10.70%	49,563
8440	Topeka, Kan. (MSA)	28,967	199,014	17.03%	14,913

MSA Code	MSA Name	Population Gain 2020-2000	Forecast: Population in 2020	Gain as Percentage of 2000 Population	Population Gain 2000-1980
6600	Racine, Wisc. (PMSA)	29,126	218,111	15.41%	16,006
8140	Sumter, S.C. (MSA)	29,953	134,694	28.60%	16,005
1580	Cheyenne, Wyo. (MSA)	30,914	112,623	37.83%	12,715
3180	Hagerstown, Md. (PMSA)	32,076	164,188	24.28%	19,108
5140	Missoula, Mont. (MSA)	32,153	128,235	33.46%	19,967
8320	Terre Haute, Ind. (MSA)	32,857	181,911	22.04%	-6,247
1400	Champaign-Urbana, Ill. (MSA)	33,029	212,994	18.35%	11,085
8760	Vineland-Millville-Bridgeton, N.J. (PMSA)	33,559	179,933	22.93%	13,286
580	Auburn-Opelika, Ala. (MSA)	33,587	149,045	29.09%	38,848
2720	Fort Smith, Ark.-Okla. (MSA)	34,256	242,220	16.47%	44,880
3740	Kankakee, Ill. (PMSA)	34,494	138,371	33.21%	991
3040	Great Falls, Mont. (MSA)	34,777	114,960	43.37%	-444
1660	Clarksville-Hopkinsville, Tenn.-Ky. (MSA)	35,214	242,826	16.96%	57,025
8400	Toledo, Ohio (MSA)	35,767	654,012	5.79%	1,080
1740	Columbia, Mo. (MSA)	36,451	172,276	26.84%	35,049
6015	Panama City, Fla. (MSA)	36,533	184,776	24.64%	49,925
3520	Jackson, Mich. (MSA)	36,797	195,527	23.18%	7,176
6580	Punta Gorda, Fla. (MSA)	36,808	179,076	25.87%	82,796
743	Barnstable-Yarmouth, Mass. (NECMA)	38,089	261,331	17.06%	74,395
3850	Kokomo, Ind. (MSA)	38,952	140,478	38.37%	-2,033
7800	South Bend, Ind. (MSA)	40,572	306,433	15.26%	24,509
3800	Kenosha, Wisc. (PMSA)	41,300	191,369	27.52%	27,126
1880	Corpus Christi, Texas (MSA)	41,498	422,188	10.90%	52,875
2281	Dutchess County, N.Y. (PMSA)	42,223	323,059	15.03%	35,499
1020	Bloomington, Ind. (MSA)	42,526	163,219	35.23%	21,486
4600	Lubbock, Texas (MSA)	42,590	285,480	17.53%	30,773
5910	Olympia, Wash. (PMSA)	42,768	251,132	20.53%	83,039
1260	Bryan-College Station, Texas (MSA)	43,073	195,875	28.19%	57,397
4150	Lawrence, Kan. (MSA)	44,253	144,435	44.17%	32,137
2980	Goldsboro, N.C. (MSA)	44,584	157,914	39.34%	16,016
880	Billings, Mont. (MSA)	45,375	174,928	35.02%	20,977
5160	Mobile, Ala. (MSA)	46,107	587,572	8.52%	96,328
6960	Saginaw-Bay City-Midland, Mich. (MSA)	47,027	450,122	11.67%	-18,197
6120	Peoria-Pekin, Ill. (MSA)	48,334	395,520	13.92%	-18,716
2400	Eugene-Springfield, Ore. (MSA)	48,683	372,096	15.05%	47,705
8800	Waco, Texas (MSA)	48,814	262,815	22.81%	42,547
2995	Grand Junction, Colo. (MSA)	49,649	167,124	42.26%	34,679
3620	Janesville-Beloit, Wisc. (MSA)	49,866	202,404	32.69%	13,269
3720	Kalamazoo-Battle Creek, Mich. (MSA)	50,234	503,553	11.08%	31,992
1040	Bloomington-Normal, Ill. (MSA)	50,680	201,556	33.59%	31,522
8640	Tyler, Texas (MSA)	51,100	226,508	29.13%	46,092
1620	Chico-Paradise, Calif. (MSA)	51,120	254,890	25.09%	58,942
2640	Flint, Mich. (PMSA)	51,640	488,593	11.82%	-12,178
7880	Springfield, Ill. (MSA)	55,160	256,724	27.37%	13,784
3660	Johnson City-Kingsport-Bristol, Tenn.-Va. (MSA)	56,740	468,693	13.77%	42,787
2655	Florence, S.C. (MSA)	59,507	185,300	47.31%	15,272

MSA Code	MSA Name	Population Gain 2020-2000	Forecast: Population in 2020	Gain as Percentage of 2000 Population	Population Gain 2000-1980
2750	Fort Walton Beach, Fla. (MSA)	60,088	231,048	35.15%	60,281
3080	Green Bay, Wisc. (MSA)	60,104	287,361	26.45%	51,522
3150	Greenville, N.C. (MSA)	60,770	194,859	45.32%	43,509
1303	Burlington, Vt. (NECMA)	60,991	260,487	30.57%	44,066
2960	Gary, Ind. (PMSA)	61,366	693,187	9.71%	-9,798
240	Allentown-Bethlehem-Easton, Pa. (MSA)	61,877	700,751	9.69%	87,073
760	Baton Rouge, La. (MSA)	64,219	668,478	10.63%	107,056
1150	Bremerton, Wash. (PMSA)	64,615	297,141	27.79%	83,764
2920	Galveston-Texas City, Texas (PMSA)	66,336	317,061	26.46%	53,697
3500	Iowa City, Iowa (MSA)	67,275	178,637	60.41%	29,213
6680	Reading, Pa. (MSA)	67,888	442,355	18.13%	61,451
80	Akron, Ohio (PMSA)	69,506	765,426	9.99%	35,586
5240	Montgomery, Ala. (MSA)	69,693	403,185	20.90%	60,187
6820	Rochester, Minn. (MSA)	69,929	194,773	56.01%	32,491
3240	Harrisburg-Lebanon-Carlisle, Pa. (MSA)	73,652	703,441	11.69%	72,233
2000	Dayton-Springfield, Ohio (MSA)	73,749	1,024,036	7.76%	8,136
560	Atlantic-Cape May, N.J. (PMSA)	75,220	430,570	21.17%	78,030
120	Albany, Ga. (MSA)	75,257	196,045	62.31%	7,942
6895	Rocky Mount, N.C. (MSA)	75,297	218,350	52.64%	19,590
2440	Evansville-Henderson, Ind.-Ky. (MSA)	75,351	371,650	25.43%	19,832
1540	Charlottesville, Va. (MSA)	75,660	111,255	212.56%	17,614
9280	York, Pa. (MSA)	76,931	459,651	20.10%	69,121
3440	Huntsville, Ala. (MSA)	77,994	421,489	22.71%	99,875
2330	Elkhart-Goshen, Ind. (MSA)	78,776	262,283	42.93%	46,215
2560	Fayetteville, N.C. (MSA)	79,882	382,720	26.38%	54,942
1360	Cedar Rapids, Iowa (MSA)	80,226	272,448	41.74%	22,572
4040	Lansing-East Lansing, Mich. (MSA)	80,470	528,894	17.95%	28,315
3200	Hamilton-Middletown, Ohio (PMSA)	80,717	414,402	24.19%	74,153
6560	Pueblo, Colo. (MSA)	81,719	223,557	57.61%	15,826
5660	Newburgh, N.Y.-Pa. (PMSA)	82,869	472,546	21.27%	110,789
7920	Springfield, Mo. (MSA)	84,046	410,871	25.72%	98,242
480	Asheville, N.C. (MSA)	84,180	310,850	37.14%	48,544
1145	Brazoria, Texas (PMSA)	89,454	332,674	36.78%	72,371
3840	Knoxville, Tenn. (MSA)	89,876	779,010	13.04%	140,732
8560	Tulsa, Okla. (MSA)	90,396	895,332	11.23%	143,935
320	Amarillo, Texas (MSA)	90,801	309,186	41.58%	43,855
7760	Sioux Falls, SD (MSA)	90,809	264,347	52.33%	49,967
3920	Lafayette, Ind. (MSA)	91,505	274,816	49.92%	29,799
1960	Davenport-Moline-Rock Island, Iowa-Ill. (MSA)	95,229	454,124	26.53%	-26,173
7460	San Luis Obispo-Atascadero-Paso Robles, Calif. (MSA)	96,291	343,969	38.88%	90,892
4000	Lancaster, Pa. (MSA)	96,896	568,550	20.54%	108,234
4360	Lincoln, Neb. (MSA)	97,268	348,458	38.72%	57,591
4890	Medford-Ashland, Ore. (MSA)	103,137	284,977	56.72%	48,911
2900	Gainesville, Fla. (MSA)	107,987	326,282	49.47%	66,072
1800	Columbus, Ga.-Ala. (MSA)	108,793	383,768	39.56%	20,348

MSA Code	MSA Name	Population Gain 2020-2000	Forecast: Population in 2020	Gain as Percentage of 2000 Population	Population Gain 2000-1980
8480	Trenton, N.J. (PMSA)	113,600	465,180	32.31%	43,784
5800	Odessa-Midland, Texas (MSA)	113,645	349,877	48.11%	35,223
3560	Jackson, Miss. (MSA)	114,708	556,539	25.96%	78,649
5330	Myrtle Beach, S.C. (MSA)	115,446	313,473	58.30%	95,558
9200	Wilmington, N.C. (MSA)	116,943	351,356	49.89%	94,427
7840	Spokane, Wash. (MSA)	118,094	536,767	28.21%	75,734
7520	Savannah, Ga. (MSA)	119,243	412,557	40.65%	61,623
9260	Yakima, Wash. (MSA)	122,911	345,620	55.19%	49,591
6080	Pensacola, Fla. (MSA)	125,081	537,832	30.30%	120,921
5790	Ocala, Fla. (MSA)	126,184	386,474	48.48%	136,072
7720	Sioux City, Iowa-Neb. (MSA)	126,855	250,982	102.20%	6,502
460	Appleton-Oshkosh-Neenah, Wisc. (MSA)	128,178	487,724	35.65%	67,908
500	Athens, Ga. (MSA)	132,142	286,186	85.78%	48,677
3060	Greeley, Colo. (PMSA)	133,687	316,851	72.99%	59,397
2670	Fort Collins-Loveland, Colo. (MSA)	134,548	387,486	53.19%	102,847
2710	Fort Pierce-Port St. Lucie, Fla. (MSA)	134,951	455,511	42.10%	166,790
4680	Macon, Ga. (MSA)	135,454	458,665	41.91%	49,550
2760	Fort Wayne, Ind. (MSA)	136,513	639,661	27.13%	58,955
7080	Salem, Ore. (PMSA)	138,556	486,786	39.79%	97,381
4720	Madison, Wisc. (MSA)	140,455	568,854	32.79%	104,045
1000	Birmingham, Ala. (MSA)	143,657	1,066,520	15.57%	107,179
3810	Killeen-Temple, Texas (MSA)	143,878	458,080	45.79%	98,244
9040	Wichita, Kan. (MSA)	144,657	690,690	26.49%	101,636
4900	Melbourne-Titusville-Palm Bay, Fla. (MSA)	145,575	623,407	30.47%	202,168
1440	Charleston-North Charleston, S.C. (MSA)	151,196	701,561	27.47%	116,750
8200	Tacoma, Wash. (PMSA)	151,866	855,827	21.57%	215,207
9160	Wilmington-Newark, Del.-Md. (PMSA)	156,082	744,400	26.53%	129,200
7485	Santa Cruz-Watsonville, Calif. (PMSA)	156,829	412,611	61.31%	66,477
3283	Hartford, Conn. (NECMA)	157,093	1,307,965	13.65%	97,414
6520	Provo-Orem, Utah (MSA)	160,268	531,128	43.22%	150,967
9340	Yuba City, Calif. (MSA)	161,321	300,829	115.64%	37,120
9270	Yolo, Calif. (PMSA)	167,084	336,850	98.42%	55,975
6483	Providence-Warwick-Pawtucket, R.I. (NECMA)	167,874	1,132,863	17.40%	97,869
8240	Tallahassee, Fla. (MSA)	169,427	454,505	59.43%	93,533
7480	Santa Barbara-Santa Maria-Lompoc, Calif. (MSA)	170,907	570,653	42.75%	99,555
3980	Lakeland-Winter Haven, Fla. (MSA)	173,954	659,358	35.84%	161,366
8780	Visalia-Tulare-Porterville, Calif. (MSA)	174,369	543,214	47.27%	121,419
5880	Oklahoma City, Okla. (MSA)	176,642	1,262,292	16.27%	219,202
6880	Rockford, Ill. (MSA)	177,111	549,290	47.59%	45,928
2700	Fort Myers-Cape Coral, Fla. (MSA)	177,526	621,315	40.00%	235,739
4400	Little Rock-North Little Rock, Ark. (MSA)	180,592	765,784	30.86%	109,751
4100	Las Cruces, N.M. (MSA)	180,911	355,891	103.39%	77,968
1125	Boulder-Longmont, Colo. (PMSA)	180,944	473,917	61.76%	102,038
1240	Brownsville-Harlingen-San Benito, Texas (MSA)	181,585	518,369	53.92%	124,840
2580	Fayetteville-Springdale-Rogers, Ark. (MSA)	182,824	496,307	58.32%	134,430

MSA Code	MSA Name	Population Gain 2020-2000	Forecast: Population in 2020	Gain as Percentage of 2000 Population	Population Gain 2000-1980
4280	Lexington, Ky. (MSA)	183,128	663,890	38.09%	109,151
5080	Milwaukee-Waukesha, Wisc. (PMSA)	188,685	1,690,777	12.56%	105,433
7510	Sarasota-Bradenton, Fla. (MSA)	197,219	789,935	33.27%	237,992
2020	Daytona Beach, Fla. (MSA)	199,448	694,990	40.25%	222,894
7500	Santa Rosa, Calif. (PMSA)	200,535	660,873	43.56%	158,752
3290	Hickory-Morganton-Lenoir, N.C. (MSA)	204,666	547,659	59.67%	71,925
6740	Richland-Kennewick-Pasco, Wash. (MSA)	205,560	398,206	106.70%	47,131
2120	Des Moines, Iowa (MSA)	206,664	664,268	45.16%	89,491
600	Augusta-Aiken, Ga.-S.C. (MSA)	213,036	691,067	44.57%	113,691
4080	Laredo, Texas (MSA)	213,157	407,818	109.50%	94,180
4940	Merced, Calif. (MSA)	215,010	426,643	101.60%	76,008
5345	Naples, Fla. (MSA)	217,819	471,890	85.73%	166,567
1720	Colorado Springs, Colo. (MSA)	222,520	742,011	42.83%	207,448
3000	Grand Rapids-Muskegon-Holland, Mich. (MSA)	223,359	1,315,681	20.45%	249,302
4520	Louisville, Ky.-Ind. (MSA)	223,650	1,251,377	21.76%	73,783
7490	Santa Fe, N.M. (MSA)	224,125	372,235	151.32%	54,646
5483	New Haven-Bridgprt-Stamfrd-Danbry-Wtrbry, Conn. (PMSA)	225,394	1,934,985	13.18%	138,822
7120	Salinas, Calif. (MSA)	228,776	631,809	56.76%	110,627
1760	Columbia, S.C. (MSA)	229,297	767,509	42.60%	126,531
5720	Norfolk-Virginia Beach-Newport News, Va.-N.C. (MSA)	230,045	1,013,710	29.35%	295,293
4920	Memphis, Tenn.-Ark., Miss. (MSA)	230,618	1,369,085	20.26%	200,074
9360	Yuma, Ariz. (MSA)	236,192	396,899	146.97%	69,314
5190	Monmouth-Ocean, N.J. (PMSA)	242,004	1,372,732	21.40%	278,713
3640	Jersey City, N.J. (PMSA)	242,171	851,548	39.74%	50,785
5920	Omaha, Neb.-Iowa (MSA)	244,940	963,811	34.07%	112,370
5170	Modesto, Calif. (MSA)	247,120	696,910	54.94%	181,938
6720	Reno, Nev. (MSA)	259,487	600,804	76.03%	145,945
440	Ann Arbor, Mich. (PMSA)	261,703	843,700	44.97%	126,842
8120	Stockton-Lodi, Calif. (MSA)	268,931	837,094	47.33%	217,859
8735	Ventura, Calif. (PMSA)	269,157	1,025,782	35.57%	223,798
2320	El Paso, Texas (MSA)	285,652	967,352	41.90%	197,989
680	Bakersfield, Calif. (MSA)	297,696	961,370	44.86%	257,267
1080	Boise City, Idaho (MSA)	317,238	753,305	72.75%	178,033
8720	Vallejo-Fairfield-Napa, Calif. (PMSA)	331,254	853,006	63.49%	184,965
7040	St. Louis, Mo.-Ill. (MSA)	337,622	2,944,132	12.95%	191,189
3160	Greenville-Spartanburg-Anderson, S.C. (MSA)	366,869	1,332,334	38.00%	217,831
5380	Nassau-Suffolk, N.Y. (PMSA)	369,709	3,130,120	13.39%	154,617
8520	Tucson, Ariz. (MSA)	380,615	1,229,259	44.85%	312,864
4880	McAllen-Edinburg-Mission, Texas (MSA)	396,458	970,381	69.08%	287,383
875	Bergen-Passaic, N.J. (PMSA)	399,718	1,776,350	29.04%	82,277
6760	Richmond-Petersburg, Va. (MSA)	406,660	1,077,913	60.58%	256,517
5360	Nashville, Tenn. (MSA)	416,861	1,652,993	33.72%	383,221
7160	Salt Lake City-Ogden, Utah (MSA)	420,031	1,758,405	31.38%	421,078
3600	Jacksonville, Fla. (MSA)	421,801	1,525,501	38.22%	377,695

MSA Code	MSA Name	Population Gain 2020-2000	Forecast: Population in 2020	Gain as Percentage of 2000 Population	Population Gain 2000-1980
1640	Cincinnati, Ohio-Ky.-Ind. (PMSA)	425,905	2,076,104	25.81%	181,274
200	Albuquerque, N.M. (MSA)	437,323	1,151,941	61.20%	196,532
1840	Columbus, Ohio (MSA)	447,346	1,993,370	28.94%	328,268
5015	Middlesex-Somerset-Hunterdon, N.J. (PMSA)	447,355	1,621,940	38.09%	286,127
3760	Kansas City, Mo.-Kan. (MSA)	455,683	2,238,064	25.57%	330,831
8960	West Palm Beach-Boca Raton, Fla. (MSA)	466,127	1,601,782	41.04%	549,913
720	Baltimore, Md. (PMSA)	467,127	3,024,426	18.27%	353,914
2840	Fresno, Calif. (MSA)	478,510	1,404,155	51.69%	344,006
5640	Newark, N.J. (PMSA)	491,983	2,526,593	24.18%	71,462
7400	San Jose, Calif. (PMSA)	497,900	2,184,374	29.52%	384,959
2160	Detroit, Mich. (PMSA)	531,480	4,977,649	11.95%	72,320
6920	Sacramento, Calif. (PMSA)	538,971	2,177,470	32.89%	645,335
7240	San Antonio, Texas (MSA)	560,660	2,159,863	35.06%	503,432
8280	Tampa-St. Petersburg-Clearwater, Fla. (MSA)	587,691	2,991,828	24.44%	777,162
3120	Greensboro-Winston-Salem-High Point, N.C. (MSA)	600,863	1,856,583	47.85%	302,124
6160	Philadelphia, Pa.-N.J. (PMSA)	604,153	5,708,962	11.83%	319,909
7320	San Diego, Calif. (MSA)	634,780	3,459,858	22.47%	949,458
2800	Fort Worth-Arlington, Texas (PMSA)	652,796	2,366,071	38.10%	713,971
3480	Indianapolis, Ind. (MSA)	662,227	2,275,157	41.06%	305,763
7600	Seattle-Bellevue-Everett, Wash. (PMSA)	667,900	3,087,827	27.60%	758,548
2680	Fort Lauderdale, Fla. (PMSA)	677,134	2,309,574	41.48%	606,378
5000	Miami, Fla. (PMSA)	722,061	2,982,303	31.95%	617,110
5775	Oakland, Calif. (PMSA)	771,010	3,174,980	32.07%	635,256
7360	San Francisco, Calif. (PMSA)	776,304	2,508,855	44.81%	240,335
6440	Portland-Vancouver, Ore.-Wash. (PMSA)	834,721	2,760,577	43.34%	587,047
6640	Raleigh-Durham-Chapel Hill, N.C. (MSA)	837,397	2,031,703	70.12%	526,350
640	Austin-San Marcos, Texas (MSA)	843,168	2,107,774	66.67%	675,024
5945	Orange County, Calif. (PMSA)	853,954	3,710,400	29.90%	908,379
1520	Charlotte-Gastonia-Rock Hill, N.C.-S.C. (MSA)	884,449	2,393,562	58.61%	533,119
1123	Boston-Worcester-Lawrence-Lowell-Brocktn, Mass.-N.H. (NECMA)	927,833	7,000,417	15.28%	725,956
5960	Orlando, Fla. (MSA)	932,809	2,589,134	56.32%	843,100
5120	Minneapolis-St. Paul, Minn.-Wisc. (MSA)	1,062,726	4,043,656	35.65%	774,385
2080	Denver, Colo. (PMSA)	1,161,122	3,283,739	54.70%	683,792
6780	Riverside-San Bernardino, Calif. (PMSA)	1,250,558	4,529,312	38.14%	1,706,325
4120	Las Vegas, Nev.-Ariz. (MSA)	1,353,348	2,935,680	85.53%	1,047,239
8840	Washington, D.C.-Md.-Va.-W.V. (PMSA)	1,389,616	4,762,682	41.20%	832,437
4480	Los Angeles-Long Beach, Calif. (PMSA)	1,414,155	11,000,000	14.82%	2,038,470
3360	Houston, Texas (PMSA)	1,552,407	5,753,543	36.95%	1,414,017
1920	Dallas, Texas (PMSA)	1,624,924	5,168,165	45.86%	1,472,984
6200	Phoenix-Mesa, Ariz. (MSA)	1,739,038	5,016,813	53.06%	1,665,593
1600	Chicago, Ill. (PMSA)	1,912,411	10,200,000	23.06%	1,044,858
5600	New York, N.Y. (PMSA)	1,969,280	11,300,000	21.11%	1,044,813
520	Atlanta, Ga. (MSA)	2,653,713	6,798,925	64.02%	1,898,202

The central cities of many other Rustbelt MSAs will continue to lose population. However, modest gains in their suburbs will offset further population decline from their MSAs. Notwithstanding mild positive metropolitan area growth, Cleveland, Philadelphia, Detroit, Milwaukee, New Haven, and Saint Louis are all expected to lag behind general U.S. population growth patterns through 2020.

Atlanta, Chicago, Phoenix, New York, Dallas, Houston, Los Angeles, Orlando, and Denver are all predicted to experience substantial population inflows. However, if we look at percentage growth in the biggest metropolitan areas, the forecasts single out Las Vegas, driven by good weather, gambling, tourism and an easy lifestyle. The group of major metropolitan areas with very high expected growth rates includes Phoenix, Dallas, Houston, Denver, Orlando, Charlotte, Austin, and Raleigh-Durham-Chapel Hill, all of them in the Sunbelt.

CONCLUSION

Population growth at the county level can be predicted using widely available demographic and economic data. Past recent growth, the presence of immigrants, the fraction of population older than 25 and younger than 65, low taxes, and good weather are all positively associated with population growth. Our forecasts reveal that most growth and real estate development will occur in the West, the Sunbelt, and along the Southern I-85 route. However, our model only accounts for 75 percent of the variance in growth experiences between 1980 and 2000, with the other 25 percent explained by "surprise" events. Many unexpected places will be winners or losers in the game of future local real estate development.

A companion spreadsheet of our population predictions at the county level (metropolitan counties) is available in the Working Paper section of the Zell-Lurie Real Estate Center website, http://realestate.wharton.upenn.edu.

Chapter 6 Supplement B

Regional Growth Variability

A study of the level of municipal regulations and how they affect real estate development.

Dr. Peter Linneman and Deborah Moy- Wharton Real Estate Review- Spring 2007 Vol. XI No. 1

At 7:46 a.m. on October 17, 2006, America's population reached 300 million. Unlike McDonald's 100 millionth customer, who was showered with confetti, the 300 millionth American remains unknown. Was it a man or woman, boy or girl? A first-, second-, or fifth-generation native? Or was it an immigrant — legal or illegal — in search of a better life? It took more than fifty years for the U.S. population to grow from 100 million to 200 million in 1967, and not quite forty more to reach today's historic threshold. According to current Census estimates, it will take less than thirty-five years to reach 400 million.

Based on research done with Wharton colleague Albert Saiz (see "Forecasting 2020 U.S. County and MSA Populations," *WRER*, Fall 2006), we estimate that the U.S. population will grow by roughly 65 million (22 percent) over the next twenty years. These 65 million new citizens will represent some 25 million additional households, of which approximately nine million will be immigrants. As we noted in the earlier paper, "Baby Boomers will be solidly in their retirement years by the end of the next twenty years, while the Baby Echo will be entering early middle age. To put things in perspective, 65 million people amount to the combined state populations of California, New York, and New Jersey, or the entire current population of France".

Unlike most European nations, as well as Japan and China, the United States has a growing population, and one that shows no sign of slowing. Real per capita income, too, will rise over the next twenty years, from about $25,000 to $39,000 (Figure 6B.1). Similarly, real wealth per household will increase from about $425,000 to nearly $665,000. Over the next twenty years, many consequences will flow from a burgeoning and increasingly prosperous population. The United States will see increasing demand across all consumer-related goods and (particularly) services, since people will require more of everything: real estate and infrastructure, public education and cosmetic surgery, iPods and Xboxes.

Figure 6B.1: Increasing spending power

	2005	2025 Est.
Real GDP (billions)	$12,790	$24,248
Real income per capita	$25,026	$39,053
Real net worth per household	$424,861	$663,000

Where will this larger and richer population choose to live, work, play, and retire? The research of Linneman and Saiz found, "higher real incomes and real wealth will propel the demand to live near oceans, major lakes, mountains, and in the best areas of our best urban centers". "Best" means safe and attractive neighborhoods. As Baby Boomers age with greater wealth and income than any previous generation, they will desire easy-to-navigate, warm, safe communities with access to the best medical facilities in the world.

HISTORY LESSONS

The Linneman-Saiz research provides detail concerning the precise geographic location of long-term population growth in the United States over the next twenty years. As this growth takes place, the national and local economies will go through hot and cold periods. This raises an important question: as the U.S. economy moves through cycles, which MSAs will over-react, and which will under-react? Those that over-react will be great places to be on the up-cycle (around trend growth), but will disproportionately suffer during down-cycles, while those that under-react will grow more steadily around their trends over the cycle.

We examined more than forty-five years of historical data on job growth and unemployment rates, and more than fifteen years of single-family home price appreciation in the thirty-nine largest MSAs (Figure 6B.2). We performed a simple regression analysis of how each MSA's percentage employment growth covaries with U.S. percentage job growth (a metric of office-demand variability); how each MSA's unemployment rate covaries with the U.S. unemployment rate (a metric of retail and warehouse demand variability); and how each MSA's median real single-family home price covaries with the national median real single-family home price (a metric of local household wealth volatility).

For each MSA, we estimated a "beta" that summarizes how a 100 basis point (bps) change at the national variable affects the local indicator. The beta for the United States as a whole is defined as 1. Thus, an MSA with a beta of 1 registers (on average) an increase of 100 bps in employment growth (around its trend), when national employment rises by 100 bps. A beta of 0.5 means that local growth rises by 50 bps (above trend) when the national rate increases by 100 basis points. If an MSA's beta is 1.5, it means that when national employment rises or falls by 100 basis points, the local area responds 50 percent more (around its mean). Hence, a beta that is less than 1 indicates that the MSA does not boom (or bust) to as great an extent as the national economy. The estimated betas are a simple indicator of how coincident each MSA's economy is with movements of the national economy. They provide insight into the demand volatility around trend (pro forma) during unusual boom or bust times (which occur, but are never modeled in pro formas).

We also examined whether an MSA has the same beta when the national economy is booming, or when it experiences a bust. That is, an MSA might react differently depending on whether the national economy is growing or shrinking. For example, it is possible that as U.S. employment growth increases, an MSA may have a beta of 1.5, but when the employment growth is negative, the MSA's employment decline may grow slower than that of the nation; for example, with a beta equaling 0.8.

The estimated employment growth rate betas are shown in Figure 6B.3. For each MSA, the relationship between MSA employment growth rate and that of the nation is statistically significant at standard confidence levels. In the case of a rising national employment growth rate, a positive beta indicates that when national employment grows, the MSA employment growth rate increases as well. This is the case for all MSAs.

The last column in Figure 6B.3 indicates how local employment growth changed in the face of a 100 bp decline in national employment. A negative entry indicates declining employment in this MSA when national employment weakened (a positive beta). All but four MSAs experienced (on average) negative job growth when national employment is negative. However, Austin, Fort Lauderdale, San Diego, and West Palm Beach all exhibit statistically significant job growth (though at lesser rates), even when the nation's job growth rate is negative. The positive demand-side responses of these four MSAs indicate that these local economies basically always continued to grow. That is, while they slow, they have been (statistically) recession-proof. West Palm Beach in particular has a high beta of 3.28, meaning that even when the national employment growth rate is negative, a 100 basis point U.S. decline results in job growth of 328 bps in West Palm Beach. Similarly, Fort Lauderdale grows by 210 bps, even as the United States declines by 100 bps.

Long Island, Dallas, Denver, and Northern New Jersey exhibit employment growth rate betas closest to 1.0, indicating that local employment growth patterns moved closely in tandem with the nation (Figure 6B.4). New

York City, Philadelphia, Houston, St. Louis, and Washington, D.C. have the lowest betas. Employment growth rates in these MSAs move with lower amplitude than the nation, although in the same direction.

Figure 6B.2: Historical MSA performance

MSA	Average Employment Growth %	Average Unemployment Rate %	Real (2006$) Median home price CAGR %
Atlanta	3.53	4.39	1.58
Austin*	4.89	3.94	3.28
Boston	1.17	5.00	3.30
Charlotte	3.01	4.40	1.80
Chicago	1.27	6.78	3.43
Cincinnati	1.88	4.69	1.25
Cleveland	0.50	6.36	1.12
Columbus	2.53	4.05	1.42
Dallas/Ft. Worth	3.10	5.08	0.19
Denver	2.02	4.32	3.86
Detroit	1.01	7.38	1.67
Fairfield County*, Conn.	0.86	4.42	5.73
Fort Lauderdale	5.22	5.50	n/a
Houston	2.83	5.73	2.27
Indianapolis	2.21	3.61	0.48
Las Vegas	6.26	5.25	5.26
Long Island, N.Y.	2.34	n/a	2.94
Los Angeles-Long Beach	1.38	7.14	3.32
Miami	2.70	7.27	6.14
Minneapolis	2.17	3.56	2.94
Nashville	2.93	4.02	1.77
New York City	0.40	8.14	n/a
Northern-Central N.J.**	0.95	6.29	2.75
Orange County	5.13	4.45	n/a
Orlando	5.74	4.73	4.38
Philadelphia	1.03	5.34	2.43
Phoenix	5.16	4.29	4.44
Portland	2.34	5.40	5.89
Raleigh-Durham	4.02	3.48	1.60
Riverside-San Bernardino	4.06	7.13	4.00
San Diego	3.57	5.18	4.63
San Francisco	0.96	4.55	3.71
San Jose*	2.73	5.46	6.21
Seattle	2.50	5.50	5.96
St. Louis	1.36	5.10	0.91
Tampa Bay	3.70	4.70	4.27
Washington, D.C.	3.20	3.72	4.49
Westchester County, N.Y.	1.48	7.16	2.83
West Palm Beach	5.21	6.59	n/a

* Home price data are calculated 1989-2006 with the following beginning year exceptions: Austin (1991); Fairfield County (2001); San Jose (2002).

** Home price appreciation covers the entire N.Y. metropolitan area, including NYC

Figure 6B.3: MSA employment growth betas

MSA	Average growth	Capital city	Reaction to rising national employment	Reaction to falling national employment
U.S.	1.98		1.00	-1.00
Atlanta	3.53	C	1.28	-1.28
Austin	4.89	C	1.65	1.30
Boston	1.17	C	1.65	-1.65
Charlotte	3.01		1.40	-1.40
Chicago	1.27		1.08	-1.08
Cincinnati	1.88		0.95	-0.95
Cleveland	0.50		1.06	-1.06
Columbus	2.53	C	0.95	-0.95
Dallas	3.23		1.03	-1.03
Denver	2.02	C	1.02	-1.02
Detroit	1.01		1.74	-1.74
Fairfield County	0.86		1.11	-1.11
Fort Lauderdale	5.22		2.53	2.10
Houston	2.83		0.79	-0.79
Indianapolis	2.21		1.19	-1.19
Inland Empire	4.06		0.89	-0.89
Las Vegas	6.26		1.08	-1.08
Long Island	2.34		0.99	-0.99
Los Angeles	1.38		1.13	-1.13
Miami - Hialeah	2.70		0.99	-0.99
Minneapolis	2.17		1.16	-1.16
Nashville	2.93	C	1.26	-1.26
New York City	0.40		0.76	-0.76
Northern-Central N.J.	0.95		1.03	-1.03
Orange County	5.13		1.35	-1.35
Orlando	5.74		1.49	-1.49
Philadelphia	1.03		0.77	-0.77
Phoenix	5.16	C	1.36	-1.36
Portland	2.34		1.27	-1.27
Raleigh-Durham	4.02	C	1.08	-1.08
San Diego	3.57		1.42	0.21
San Francisco	0.96		0.87	-0.87
San Jose	2.73		1.47	-1.47
Seattle	2.50		1.22	-1.22
St. Louis	1.36		0.81	-0.81
Tampa Bay	3.70		1.19	-1.19
Washington, D.C.	3.20	C	0.84	-0.84
West Palm Beach	5.21		2.53	3.28
Westchester County	1.48		0.87	-0.87

Figure 6B.4: Reaction to change in national employment growth rates

0.5 < or = |beta| < 0.9	0.9 < or = |beta| < or = 1.1	1.1 < |beta| < or = 1.5	|beta| > 1.5
New York City	Columbus	Fairfield County	Boston
Philadelphia	Cincinnati	Los Angeles	*Austin*
Houston	Miami-Hialeah	Minneapolis	Detroit
St. Louis	Long Island, N.Y.	Indianapolis	*West Palm Beach*
Washington, D.C.	Denver	Tampa Bay	*Fort Lauderdale*
San Francisco	Dallas	Seattle	
Westchester County	Northern-Central N.J.	Nashville	
Inland Empire	Cleveland	Portland	
	Las Vegas	Atlanta	
	Raleigh-Durham	Orange County	
	Chicago	Phoenix	
		Charlotte	
		San Diego	
		San Jose	
		Orlando	

Italics indicate growing MSA employment when national employment falls; categorized by rising employment betas

Note: Italics indicate growing MSA employment when national employment falls; categorized by rising employment betas

At the other end of the spectrum, Fort Lauderdale, West Palm Beach, Detroit, Austin, and Boston exhibit the relatively highest betas, indicating job growth volatility notably greater than the nation. Detroit, Austin, and Boston generally booms when the nation adds jobs, but suffers badly on the downside.

We conducted a statistical analysis of MSA employment growth betas to determine if capital cities and high average employment rate growth MSAs have systematically different betas, but found no statistically significant relationship.

UNEMPLOYMENT RATE VOLATILITY

Estimates of unemployment rate betas are displayed in Figure 6B.5. Once again, the relationship between MSA unemployment rates (a proxy for the general health of the MSA, and hence retail and warehouse demand), and that of the nation is statistically significant, and exhibits stronger relationships (much higher R-squared values) than is the case for the employment growth rate betas.

Figure 6B.5: MSA employment growth betas

MSA	Average unemployment rate	Capital city	Reaction to rising national unemployment	Reaction to falling national unemployment
U.S.	4.80		1.00	1.00
Atlanta	4.39	C	0.78	-0.78
Austin	3.94	C	0.44	-0.31
Boston	5.00	C	1.63	-1.59
Bridgeport	4.42		1.20	-1.20
Charlotte	4.40		0.78	-0.78
Chicago	6.78		1.29	-1.29
Cincinnati	4.69		0.75	-0.80
Cleveland	6.36		1.30	-1.35
Columbus	4.05	C	0.59	-0.59
Dallas-Fort Worth	5.08		1.06	-1.00
Denver	4.32	C	0.80	-0.80
Detroit	7.38		1.95	-1.95
Fort Lauderdale	5.50		1.40	-1.33
Fort Worth	5.05		1.14	-1.09
Houston	5.73		0.86	-0.95
Indianapolis	3.61		0.58	-0.58
Las Vegas	5.25		0.83	-0.78
Los Angeles	7.14		0.74	-0.81
Miami	7.27		0.99	-0.99
Minneapolis	3.56		0.65	-0.59
Nashville	4.02	C	0.56	-0.49
New York City	8.14		0.74	-0.74
New York Metro Area	6.29		1.22	-1.28
N.Y.-Westchester County	7.16		1.24	-1.32
Orange County	4.45		1.16	-1.21
Orlando	4.73		1.42	-1.33
Philadelphia	5.34		1.09	-1.09
Phoenix	4.29	C	0.85	-0.79
Portland	5.40		0.58	-0.58
Raleigh-Durham	3.48	C	0.53	-0.41
Riverside-San Bernardino	7.13		1.78	-1.91
San Diego	5.18		1.30	-1.39
San Francisco	4.55		0.95	-0.95
San Jose	5.46		1.35	-1.35
Seattle	5.50		0.81	-0.85
St. Louis	5.10		0.82	-0.77
Tampa	4.70		1.30	-1.23
Washington	3.72	C	0.68	-0.68
West Palm Beach	6.59		1.75	-1.75

In the case of a rising national unemployment rate (that is, a weakening national economy), a positive beta indicates that when the national unemployment rate increases, the MSA unemployment rate also rises. This is the case for all MSAs. That is, no MSA is immune from rising unemployment when the national unemployment rate rises. Stated differently, all local economies suffer when the national economy declines, and gains when the national economy grows. Thus, even in the four recession-proof areas in terms of job growth (Austin, Fort Lauderdale, San Diego, and West Palm Beach), during times of rising national unemployment, the labor force expands more rapidly than jobs are created, weakening job prospects in the market. This reflects the phenomena that labor force growth expands at basically trend levels, while even though these MSAs add jobs, they are not added fast enough to offset the expanding local labor force during national downturns.

Nearly 60 percent of the metropolitan markets in our study have statistically different unemployment rate betas in the face of rising and falling national unemployment rates. That is, while all of the MSA unemployment rates move in the same direction as that of the nation, the extent to which they move frequently differ, depending upon whether the national unemployment rate is rising or falling.

Figure 6B.6 (increasing unemployment rates) and Figure 6B.7 (decreasing unemployment rates) group the MSAs by the absolute values of their betas. In some cases, MSAs are in different groupings, depending on whether the national unemployment rate is increasing or decreasing. In other cases, MSAs are in the same beta grouping regardless of the national trend, but had moved up or down within that category in relation to the reactions of the other markets. Ten markets, led by Riverside-San Bernardino, Houston, San Diego, Westchester County, and Los Angeles, show statistically greater reactions when the national unemployment rate is declining than when it is increasing. Specifically, Riverside-San Bernardino's "increasing unemployment" beta is 1.78, but its "decreasing unemployment" beta is 1.91. That is, while it always overreacts, it does so more in up-cycles than in down-cycles. Thirteen MSAs have asymmetric unemployment rate betas where their reaction is statistically more pronounced to a rising national unemployment rate. Some of these include Austin, Raleigh, Orlando, Fort Lauderdale, and Phoenix. The largest differential response is Austin, with 13 basis points.

Figure 6B.6: Reaction to rising national unemployment rates

$\|beta\| \leq 0.5$	$0.5 \leq \|beta\| < 0.9$	$0.9 \leq \|beta\| \leq 1.1$	$1.1 < \|beta\| \leq 1.5$	$\|beta\| > 1.5$
Austin	Raleigh	San Francisco	Fort Worth	Boston
	Nashville	Miami	Orange County	West Palm Beach
	Indianapolis	Dallas-Fort Worth	Bridgeport	Riverside-San Bernardino
	Portland	Philadelphia	New York Metropolitan Area	Detroit
	Columbus		N.Y.-Westchester County	
	Minneapolis		Chicago	
	Washington		Tampa	
	Los Angeles		Cleveland	
	New York City		San Diego	
	Cincinnati		San Jose	
	Atlanta		Fort Lauderdale	
	Charlotte		Orlando	
	Denver			
	Seattle			
	St. Louis			
	Las Vegas			
	Phoenix			
	Houston			

Figure 6B.7: Reaction to falling national unemployment rates

$\lvert \text{beta} \rvert \leq 0.5$	$0.5 \leq \lvert \text{beta} \rvert < 0.9$	$0.9 \leq \lvert \text{beta} \rvert \leq 1.1$	$1.1 < \lvert \text{beta} \rvert \leq 1.5$	$\lvert \text{beta} \rvert > 1.5$
Austin	Indianapolis	Houston	Bridgeport	Boston
Raleigh	Portland	San Francisco	Orange County	West Palm Beach
Nashville	Columbus	Miami	Tampa	Riverside-San Bernardino
	Minneapolis	Dallas-Fort Worth	New York Metropolitan Area	Detroit
	Washington	Philadelphia	Chicago	
	New York City	Fort Worth	N.Y.-Westchester County	
	St. Louis		Orlando	
	Las Vegas		Fort Lauderdale	
	Atlanta		San Jose	
	Charlotte		Cleveland	
	Phoenix		San Diego	
	Cincinnati			
	Denver			
	Los Angeles			
	Seattle			

San Francisco, Miami, Dallas-Ft. Worth, and Philadelphia are among the MSAs that moved roughly in concert with U.S. unemployment rates, while Austin, Raleigh-Durham, and Nashville reveal the lowest betas. Detroit, Riverside-San Bernardino, West Palm Beach, and Boston have the highest unemployment rate betas, indicating substantially greater movements (both up and down) at the MSA than at the national level. With a beta of almost two, Detroit is the most "boom-and-bust" MSA. That is, when the national unemployment rate was improving, it is generally very good in Detroit, but when national unemployment increases, Detroit really feels the pain.

We also conducted a statistical analysis of the MSA unemployment rate betas as a function of their average unemployment rate, and whether they are a state capital. We found no statistically significant impact of the average local unemployment rate, but state capital MSAs had unemployment rate betas that are on average 32 basis points lower (and statistically significant). That is, capital MSAs are much less cyclical in their unemployment rates than other MSAs.

HOME PRICE APPRECIATION VOLATILITY

Real national housing prices are an indicator of the interaction of housing supply and demand, and capture the volatility of the main component of household wealth. Specifically, we estimated MSA betas for median real (in 2006 dollars) single-family home prices. The estimated betas are displayed in Figure 6B.8. In general, there is a strong correlation between MSA and national median real home prices, although to a lesser extent than for unemployment rate betas. However, the betas are statistically significant for all MSAs. On average, capital cities had lower home price betas by 1.4 basis points per every 10 percent increase in job growth, in comparison to non-capital cities.

Figure 6B.8: MSA vs. U.S. single family home price reactions

MSA	Capital city	Average median price ($000s)*	REAL HOME PRICES Reaction to rising national home prices	Reaction to falling national home prices
U.S.		224.8	1.00	1.00
Anaheim		403.0	0.79	-0.79
Atlanta	C	144.8	0.52	-0.52
Austin	C	150.6	0.48	-0.48
Boston	C	297.0	2.00	-2.00
Bridgeport		461.3	0.84	-0.84
Charlotte		158.4	1.11	-1.11
Chicago		201.6	0.92	-0.92
Cincinnati		138.5	0.56	-1.48
Cleveland		137.5	1.02	-2.18
Columbus	C	141.8	1.02	-1.02
Dallas-Fort Worth		140.2	0.87	-0.87
Denver	C	192.1	0.65	-0.65
Detroit		148.6	1.08	-1.08
Hartford	C	210.5	1.10	-1.10
Houston		124.1	0.50	-1.96
Indianapolis		125.6	1.02	-1.02
Las Vegas		178.2	0.50	-0.50
Los Angeles		313.8	0.77	-0.77
Miami		187.4	0.77	-0.77
Minneapolis-St. Paul		169.1	0.71	-0.71
Nashville	C	141.7	0.73	-0.73
New Haven		211.4	1.13	-1.13
New York Metro		285.7	0.72	-0.72
N.Y.-Westchester Cnty		322.6	0.90	-0.90
Norwich		223.1	0.68	-0.68
N.Y.-Edison, N.J.		243.9	0.94	-0.94
N.Y.-Nassau		282.0	0.52	-0.52
N.Y.-Newark		295.1	1.24	-1.24
Orlando		143.2	0.97	-0.97
Philadelphia		168.6	1.71	-1.71
Phoenix	C	152.7	0.85	-0.85
Portland		178.0	0.67	-0.67
Raleigh	C	169.5	0.16	-0.16
Riverside-San Bernardino		205.3	0.58	-0.58
St. Louis, Mo.		127.0	1.58	-1.58
San Diego		334.5	0.75	-0.75
San Francisco		467.2	0.85	-0.85
San Jose		705.1	0.52	-0.52
Seattle		218.1	1.63	-1.63
Tampa Bay		128.6	1.02	-1.02
Washington	C	247.9	2.57	-2.57

* Average of median home prices from 1Q89-2Q06.

Our results reveal that when real median home prices are rising nationally, all of the MSAs in our study experience positive local home price appreciation, while when real national home prices are declining, home prices in all MSAs also decline. Thus, no MSA housing market is immune from the effect of a weak housing market.

Most MSAs exhibit symmetrical reactions to rising and falling real national home prices. That is, most MSA home prices correlate by the same magnitude, whether the national housing market is strengthening or weakening. However, Cincinnati, Houston and Cleveland exhibit statistically asymmetric housing price betas. In these cases, the betas are larger for falling national home prices. The disparities range from 90 basis points (Cincinnati), to as much as 154 bps (Cleveland) greater in a declining national housing market versus a strengthening national market.

Figure 6B.9 reveals that the majority of MSA home prices have a slightly dampened reaction to that of the nation. New York, Orlando, and Columbus are among the MSAs that roughly moved in concert with the national housing market. In contrast, Raleigh-Durham and Austin are among those with the lowest betas, meaning that real home prices in those MSAs move to a lesser degree than national real home price appreciation or depreciation. Washington, D.C. real home prices, on the other hand, with a beta of nearly 2.6, experience hyper-reactions relative to national cycles.

Figure 6B.9: Reactions to changing real national home prices

$\lvert beta \rvert \le 0.5$	$0.5 \le \lvert beta \rvert < 0.9$	$0.9 \le \lvert beta \rvert \le 1.1$	$1.1 < \lvert beta \rvert \le 1.5$	$\lvert beta \rvert > 1.5$
Raleigh	Las Vegas	N.Y.- Westchester Cnty.	Charlotte	Saint Louis, Mo.
Austin	N.Y.: Nassau	Chicago	New Haven	Seattle
Houston	San Jose	N.Y.-Edison, N.J.	N.Y.-Newark	Philadelphia
Las Vegas	Atlanta	Orlando		Boston
	Cincinnati	Tampa Bay		Washington
	Riverside- San Bernardino	*Cleveland*		
	Denver	Columbus		
	Portland	Indianapolis		
	Norwich	Detroit		
	Minneapolis- St. Paul	Hartford		
	New York Metro			
	Nashville			
	San Diego			
	Miami			
	Los Angeles			
	Anaheim			
	Bridgeport			
	Phoenix			
	San Francisco			
	Dallas-Fort Worth			

Italics indicate assymetric results. Rising national home price scenario is shown.

CONCLUSION

Our analyses provide basic insights into how MSA demand fundamentals respond to national trends, and clarify how local markets prosper and lag in comparison to the nation's economy. Taken together, they provide a picture of both long-term growth trends and the risk of economic variability around these trends as the U.S. economy cycles. We observe that the San Jose, San Diego, and New York MSAs have unemployment rate betas that are significantly greater than their housing price betas. What does this mean? They are housing-supply constrained, and hence housing prices do not fall as rapidly as the economy slows. On the other hand, the housing betas for the Seattle, Philadelphia, and Washington, D.C. MSAs are greater than their respective unemployment rate betas, suggesting that housing prices in those markets are more volatile than their local economies. All are relatively less supply-constrained.

These analyses have important consequences for investors. Specifically, when the national economy is in a strong expansion phase, targeting office development in high employment beta MSAs will provide the greatest space-demand upside. As previously indicated in Figure 6B.9, when national employment grows, Fort Lauderdale, West Palm Beach, Detroit, Austin, and Boston exhibit the highest employment growth betas, and thus will experience the greatest regional percentage growth above that of the nation. During a national recession, on the other hand, low employment beta MSAs, such as New York, Philadelphia, Houston, St. Louis, and Washington, D.C., provide greater downside demand-risk protection.

Similarly, unemployment is a metric of retail and warehouse demand variability, and therefore focusing on the unemployment beta analysis for those sectors is most relevant. Referring back to Figure 6B.6 and Figure 6B.7, when national unemployment rates rise (a weakening economy), Detroit, the Inland Empire, West Palm Beach, and Boston unemployment rates have all historically increased to a much greater magnitude than the nation—indicating the greatest risk of experiencing a retail and warehouse demand bust. On the other hand, when national unemployment declines (a strengthening economy), those same markets would be expected to provide the greatest upside in retail and industrial demand.

By the same token, the housing price beta analysis provides a metric of local household wealth, given that one's home has accounted for an increasing share of personal net wealth. Thus, depending on risk tolerance, in strong economies, homebuilders may target markets (Washington, D.C., Boston, and Philadelphia) with high home price betas, but low beta markets (Raleigh, Austin, and Houston) on the downside. By the same token, it follows that when perceived household wealth increases, purchasing power will also increase, positively affecting retail and warehouse demand.

In summary, these beta estimates provide some insight into MSA reactions to movements of the national economy, and into the demand variability and risk of each MSA as the national economy moves through a cycle. They provide a metric with which to manage risk expectations around generally smoothly growing pro forma analyses of local demographics.

The authors extend thanks to Manhong Feng for the statistical analysis.

Chapter 7
The Use and Selection of Cap Rates

"'What is the bet?' is the critical question".
-Dr. Peter Linneman

BASIC VALUATION

For existing properties you will usually begin your valuation analysis with simpler tools than DCF. It is much like how you carefully sketch a building before you build it. This is partly for speed and simplicity, and partly because the distant future is difficult to forecast accurately (even though on a spreadsheet, each column looks equally authoritative). A standard simple valuation method is income multiple analysis, which estimates the value of a property by multiplying next year's "stabilized" NOI by the price-to-NOI multiple for which comparable properties are selling today.

Capitalization, or cap rates, rather than income multiples, are generally quoted in real estate valuation analysis. The cap rate is the inverse of the multiple, that is, it is defined as stabilized NOI divided by property value (purchase price, either actual or anticipated). The real estate industry's usage of cap rates reflects its historic linkage to the bond market, as real estate derives its income from future promissory income streams. So just as the bond market commonly quotes yield, as opposed to multiple, when valuing bonds, the real estate industry generally quotes cap rates.

FIGURE 7.1

Cap Rate Calculation
Cap Rate = Stabilized NOI/Value = 1/Multiple
Multiple = Value/Stabilized NOI = 1/Cap Rate
Value = Multiple*Stabilized NOI = Stabilized NOI/Cap Rate
Note an "8 cap" = .08 = 8% = 12.5 Multiple

In order to quickly calculate the value of a stabilized property, divide the property's "stabilized" NOI by the cap rate. However, the cap rate (or multiple) valuation method is only used when NOI is flat or growing relatively smoothly, generally referred to as "stabilized" NOI. If you cap an unstabilized NOI, that is an NOI which is not indicative of the property's long-term future performance, this calculation generates nonsense values. For such properties, you must do a full DCF valuation.

For a stabilized property you normally apply the cap rate to next year's NOI, as this is the first full-year cash flow you will receive as the owner. Therefore, the most commonly utilized equation for the cap rate is the property's NOI in year 1 divided by the property's value.

FIGURE 7.2

Cap Rate Calculation
Cap Rate = Stabilized NOI (yr 1)/Value
Value = Stabilized NOI (yr 1)/ Cap Rate

Illustration: Let's revisit our earlier example property, Felicitas Tower, with the 10 year lease to the US government that is expected to generate $3 million annually in NOI. Assuming that the 10 year Treasury bond carried a yield of 3.6%, and that based on your judgment of the risk of Felicitas Tower's future cash streams, you determine that an additional 100 basis points expected return is required for the added risks presented by a property with a 10 year lease to the US government. Hence, you apply a 4.6% cap rate (a 21.7x multiple) to the property's stabilized NOI, as you feel you need a 4.6% NOI yield in order to invest in the property. This 4.6% cap rate is generally referred to as a 4.6 cap. With the property's stabilized NOI of roughly $3 million and a 4.6 cap rate, you estimate a value of $65.2 million ($3 million / .046) via the cap rate valuation methodology. Understand that your assessment of the property's opportunity and risk are reflected in this value calculation via the $3 million stabilized NOI, and the 4.6 cap rate.

FIGURE 7.3

Summary	
<u>**Information**</u>	
Yield on 10 Year T Note	**3.60%**
Risk Premium	**100 basis points (bp)**
Cap Rate	3.6%+100bp = **4.6**
Multiple	1/.046 = **21.7x**
NOI	**$3MM**
<u>**Valuation**</u>	
With Cap Rate	3/.046 = **$65.2MM**
With Multiple	3 * 21.7 = **$65.2MM**

As the buyer, you desire high cap rates (that is, a low multiple) for given property risk. This is because the higher the cap rate, the lower is the purchase price for the stabilized income stream. On the other hand, the seller desires a low cap rate (high multiple), as the seller wants the highest price possible for the stabilized income stream they are selling.

NOT EVERYONE AGREES

It is common to have discrepancies between the "seller's" cap rate and "buyer's" cap rate. Why? Assume you bought the building in our example for $65.2 million. The seller of the building, who received the $65.2 million, might brag that they sold you the building for a 4.6 cap. However, you might say you got it for a 5.6 cap. How is this possible? Is someone lying? Maybe, but not necessarily.

There are several reasons purchase cap rate quotes can differ. For example, the seller and the buyer may have very different estimates of next year's NOI. Remember that each party derived their estimate of next year's

NOI based on their independent analysis, and in most cases different parties will arrive at different NOI estimates. In addition, the seller and the buyer may apply different definitions of stabilized NOI, as the term stabilized NOI is a bit ambiguous. Also different investors may categorize different costs as "operating expenses". Specifically, are reserves deducted from NOI for normalized cap ex, TIs, and leasing commissions? Or the seller and the buyer may be using the NOI from different years in their calculations. Thus, although next year's NOI is the industry convention, the seller may quote the cap rate using this year's actual NOI, while the buyer may quote the cap rate for their purchase using next year's expected NOI. Further, the buyer and seller may use different definitions of "stabilized". For example, the buyer might view next year's NOI as indicative of the stabilized performance of the property, while the seller may feel that NOI is not stabilized for 3 years. These examples demonstrate that you must be careful when comparing "market" cap rates.

When correctly applied to a stabilized property, this simple cap rate valuation approach produces roughly the same valuation estimate for a property as a more complex DCF analysis. However, if the property's expected NOI stream is complex, with irregular rental growth and substantially changing NOI, only DCF analysis can yield a credible value estimate.

REPLACEMENT COSTS

The denominator of the cap rate is the value (or sale price) of the building. In the case of our example, you used the cap rate to estimate a value of $65.2 million. In conducting your analysis, should you care what it cost to build Felicitas Tower? For example, if it cost $100 million to build the property three years ago, should this have any bearing on your assessment of the property's risk and opportunity? Probably not, as it is ancient history. In some ways, it is like your birth weight: interesting, but not terribly descriptive of who you are today. As a result, you will generally focus on conditions today, rather than historic cost.

An important exception is a property's **replacement cost**. What if Felicitas Tower cost $100 million to develop three years ago, and total development costs today are about the same? Your valuation of the property's stabilized cash flows indicates that the building is only worth $65.2 million. If your valuation is correct, it means that you are purchasing the property for a 35% discount to replacement cost. As a result, rents must increase by roughly 53% before they will be high enough to justify new construction. That is quite a cushion before new competition appears. But if Felicitas Tower was built in expectation of a less than competitive return, or if the development costs were significantly above market, you cannot use the $100 million cost as an estimate of replacement cost. For example, if the developer was inefficient, or substantially overpaid for land, or if no one will ever again build such a "white elephant", the original cost does not reflect the relevant replacement cost.

Of critical importance when calculating a property's replacement cost is the cost of land. If the original owner massively overpaid for the land, the relevant replacement cost must reflect realistic land costs. Developers frequently overpay for land in the euphoria of a booming market. An extreme example occurred in Tokyo in the 1980s, where developers paid $90 million for land while it cost just $10 million to build the structure. The land cost for a comparable site today is only $8 million, and the structure costs remain $10 million. Hence the relevant replacement cost is $18 million, not the original $100 million cost. At an $18 million replacement cost, competition can profitably enter the market at an $18 million cost basis, while you are preparing to bid $65.2 million for a comparable building. If the government breaks their lease or fails to renew their lease upon expiration, who will rent from you at a rent which justifies your valuation when they can build a new property for about 73% less? In this case you will be seriously concerned that competition will enter the market at a lower cost basis which allows them to offer lower rents, and still generate an adequate return on their cost.

If, on the other hand, the structure is not a "white elephant" and structure costs are about $90 million, and land cost was originally $10 million, even in the unlikely case that the land is completely worthless today, the property's replacement cost is $90 million. If you can acquire the building for $65.2 million, you acquire the property for a $24.8 million discount to replacement cost. Will the building ever be worth replacement cost again? Who knows? But there is some comfort in the fact that entrants cannot profitably build a competitive property for less than your purchase price.

GORDON MODEL: SIMPLE CAP RATE ESTIMATION

Returning to the Felicitas Tower opportunity, assume that NOI grows modestly each year. For example, the government lease contains provisions that dictate a roughly 1% increase in rent each year. In addition, assume that you believe the government will renew the lease at roughly similar terms forever. Will this really happen? Probably not, but based on your analysis you may reasonably expect a 1% growth rate in NOI each year basically forever. As shown in Figure 7.4, the so-called Gordon Model, named after Myron J. Gordon converts perpetuity DCF analysis for a cash stream growing at a constant rate into a simple cap rate approximation by dividing stabilized NOI by the difference between the property's discount rate (r) and the NOI growth rate (g).

FIGURE 7.4

Growth and Discounting*
Value = (NOI) / (discount rate – growth rate) = NOI/Cap
Therefore: CAP = (r - g)
**Unless stated otherwise assume Stabilized NOI*

How do you apply this formula to value the government leased office building with an expected 1% annual rental growth? Recall that you based your original assessment of the property's risk assuming that there was no rental growth (g=0), and added 100 basis points to the 3.6% 10 year Treasury yield to obtain a 4.6% discount rate. For this property, the Gordon Model yields a cap rate of 3.6% (a 27.8X multiple).

FIGURE 7.5

Summary	
Information	
Discount Rate	**4.6%**
Growth Rate	**1.0%**
Gordon Calculation	1/(.046-.01) = 27.8
Multiple	**27.8x**
Cap Rate	.046-.01 = .036 = 3.6%

Applying this cap rate to next year's NOI of $3.03 million (1% higher than today's $3 million) generates an estimated value for Felicitas Tower of $84.2 million. The Gordon Model cap rate for a 1% growth in rent is lower than the 4.6% cap used for the zero NOI growth example. But it makes sense that a property that has NOI growing by 1% every year should be worth more than a property with no future NOI growth. Alternatively, if you decide that the property's discount rate should be 100 basis points higher, (5.6% rather than 4.6%) the Gordon Model yields a 4.6 cap for an expected 1% NOI growth, for an estimated property value of $65.8 million. Thus, the 100 basis point risk factor increase lowered the estimated value by 21.8%.

These examples demonstrate how opportunity (that is, NOI and NOI growth) increases value, while risk (the discount rate) decreases value. In our example, a 1% NOI growth rate increases estimated value by 29 percent. That is, even a little growth adds a lot to value, especially for low risk cash streams.

FIGURE 7.6

Summary	
Information	
Discount Rate	**5.6%**
Growth Rate	**1.0%**
Multiple with growth	**[1/(r-g)]=1/(.056-.01)=21.7x**
Multiple with no growth	**[1/r]=1/.056=17.9x**
NOI this year	**$3 MM**
Valuation	
NOI next year	$3 MM * 1.01 = **$3.03 MM**
With Multiple and growth	3.03 * 21.7 = **$65.8 MM**
With Multiple and no growth	3 * 17.9 = **$53.7 MM**

Instead of using the Gordon Model you could conduct a full DCF analysis of the steadily growing NOI, going out as many columns as possible, and discounting them at your selected discount rate. The Gordon Model provides a "quick and dirty" alternative value estimation calculation that generates almost the same answer as a full DCF analysis, as long as the property's NOI growth rate is fairly steady (stabilized) and is small relative to the selected discount rate. If, however, the property does not meet these "stabilized" criteria, you must conduct a full DCF analysis to accurately assess its value.

Caveats: Looking at the Gordon Model formula, do you see any problems? For example, what if you think that NOI growth rate is greater than the discount rate? Using the Gordon Model yields a negative cap rate, and hence a negative value for the property, even though it has rapid income growth and low risk – clearly a nonsense result. Similarly, if the NOI growth rate is equal to the appropriate discount rate, the Gordon Model yields value as infinite! Not likely. Using this model with a very high growth rate generates nonsense, as it is inconceivable that an asset's NOI can grow well in excess of the economy forever. Eventually the property's NOI will be larger than the economy!

You must pay careful attention to NOI growth forecasts and the reasonableness of the assumptions utilized. I was once in a meeting where a non-real estate firm was pitching its very optimistic growth expectations. I asked how they intended to meet the sales objectives. The response was they would hire enough sales people to meet their goals. As I listened, I estimated the sales volume an experienced sales person could reasonably be expected to achieve, and how many such sales people the firm would need over the next two years to achieve their forecasted sales. The number was 840 successful sales reps, without taking into account that some sales people would quit or die, or that it takes time to train the sales people, and that some will be unqualified, quit, or die. And, oh yes, the firm currently had two sales people. I quickly concluded that no matter how good their product was, it would be impossible to grow as projected, as they could never hire, train, and retain 8 qualified sales reps a week, every week, for the next two years. But such nonsense projections abound, frequently going unchallenged.

To effectively employ the Gordon Model to assess value, the discount rate must significantly exceed the NOI growth rate. If the property's NOI is expected to experience substantial growth in the next few years, as the market recovers or below market leases rollover, after which NOI will stabilize at a lower growth rate, it is not appropriate to use the Gordon Model. Simple valuation metrics are powerful, but like a pair of shoes, one size does not fit all. If you have a size 10 foot, then do not wear size 3 shoes! If NOI is not stabilized, do not use cap rate models to assess value. And always make sure your NOI growth and discount rates are sensible.

MARKET CHANGE

Thus far we have been using a 3.6% yield for the 10-Year US Treasury bond. However, over the past decade, this rate has ranged from 2.5% to 5.4%. How does a higher risk-free rate impact real estate valuation analysis? Go back to the selection of the discount rates for Felicitas Tower. You began with the Treasury rate, and adjusted for the additional risks associated with the property. If the long term Treasury rate increased by 100 basis points, your discount rate should also rise. If the long term Treasury rate decreases by 4 basis points, your discount rates will remain unchanged for all practical purposes, as smart real estate investors only respond to significant changes in long term Treasury interest rates rather than continually changing their discount rates for minor movements.

In addition, depending upon investors' level of fear and greed, the risk premium over Treasury yields vary substantially. For example, in February 2007 investor optimism ruled, and risk premiums were minimal (perhaps 50 basis points). A brief 18 months later in September 2008, risk premiums skyrocketed (to perhaps 900 basis points) as investor greed turned to total fear.

How do cap rates respond to changing long term Treasury rates and risk premiums? Look at the Gordon Model. At lower discount rates and relatively unchanged growth rates, you would expect cap rates to fall. Intuitively, the return required to compensate for risk has decreased, while your long term NOI stream has remained roughly the same. In fact, market cap rates for solid cash streams decreased by roughly 100 basis points for almost all property types as the long term Treasury rates fell between 2002 and 2004. They fell even further as risk premiums fell from 2004 through early 2007. Cap rates then exploded (rose) in 2007 through 2009 in spite of falling Treasury rates due to an explosion in risk premiums.

Figure 7.7 provides the approximate cap rates for stabilized properties as of early 2010. These rates changed as the risk-free rate, property risk premiums, and expected NOI growth rates changed.

FIGURE 7.7
TYPICAL CAP RATES AS OF EARLY 2010

Description	Cap Rate
Office: Downtown office, prime towers, well located, well designed, top of the market, big building, lots of quality tenants, smooth lease expiration	7-8
Office: Suburban, good, smaller, fewer tenants, not as well located, not quite as liquid.	7.5-9
Office: Second tier city, suburban, small, two tenants, medium quality credit tenants, less liquid, lumpy lease expiration **Comment:** There is a large spread on the second tier office buildings. The city in which the property is located will have a significant impact on the property's cap rate.	8.5-12
Garden Apartments (A quality): Good location, recent design, no individuals will have credit, but tenants as a whole have good credit.	7-8

Garden Apartments (B quality): Usually has a good market	8-9.5
Garden Apartments (C quality): Usually has a good market **Comment**: There is a significant increase in the cap rate for lower quality, B and C, properties. In a tough market, like the current environment, the A quality properties will be able to maintain occupancy. Although owners may have to lower rents in order to keep tenants, the building will have roughly the same occupancy. At lower rents, more people will be able to afford the A quality property and will move into the best buildings. As more and more people move to quality buildings, the lower quality buildings will experience an increase in vacancy rates. With this higher risk, investors have historically required a higher return on these lower quality buildings, thus a higher cap rate. There is no exact definition for these quality rankings. This is just a phraseology the market uses to describe certain properties. It is just like saying someone is short. There is no pure definition of short.	9-12
Shopping Centers (A): Good supermarket anchored tenant with Wal-Mart already in the competing market, so no fear of sudden entry and decline in customers	7.5-8.5
Shopping Centers (B): Pretty good strip center	8.5-11
Shopping Centers (C): Empty Kmart, not well located	10-14
Warehouse: Great location, near a major highway or exit ramp that leads to the property with ease.	8-9.5
Warehouse: Poor location, no easy access to the highway **Comment:** Warehouses tend to have higher cap rates than other property types. This is due to the fact that warehouses tend to have lower growth rates. Growth rates are lower because you can build a warehouse in roughly 8 months. A warehouse is generally a fairly simple structure to build. Therefore, demand can rarely exceed supply by a great margin for an extended period of time. If rents start to increase, developers can quickly build new product that will satisfy the demand. Furthermore, there is additional risk with a warehouse property. Specifically, warehouses only rent to a few large tenants, GE, Wal-Mart, etc. Although those companies have excellent credit, your profitability is completely concentrated with a few tenants. If the tenant decides to leave, you are faced with an empty building and no cash flow. With no diversification your tenant risk is incredibly high.	9-12

Hotels: Hotels are difficult to value due to their operating leverage. Hotels are essentially all fixed costs. Regardless of the occupancy from night to night, you are going to incur costs to continue to operate and maintain the hotel, the soap, the electricity, the marketing costs, etc. Therefore, a decrease in demand will cause a quick decline in prices. Hotels will be willing to lower prices to draw as many people as possible to cover as much of the fixed cost as possible. If you don't cut your prices, you will remain empty. If you do cut, you will have lower income. This is a good example where cap rates and multiples are inappropriate valuation metrics because of unstablized income. This is also an example of the numbers serving as a starting point. You could perform a DCF analysis on a hotel property right now. However, you are really going to have to start thinking about the risks and opportunities beyond the DCF. There is no way the model will be able to accurately capture the possible outcome for the property. You will have to consider how quickly tourism will recover, the likelihood of war, the impact war would have on air travel, how much lower rates will decrease, etc. The numbers will only show you the expected outcome. You will have to analyze the multitude of additional factors that will ultimately determine your success or failure. If you really think about it, hotels are really an operating business not real estate.	n/a

RESPONDING TO THE MARKET

Do you always have to adjust your discount and cap rates for significantly lower long-term Treasury rates or altered market risk premiums? Not if you believe the changes are unjustified and you believe the market is wrong. You have every right to your view of the world. The only time you have to bid like everyone else is when you want to buy. Just as a baseball player does not have to swing at a pitch just because the pitcher throws the ball, even if it is a strike, you do not have to value things like other market participants. In fact, the truly great hitters know when to "take" a pitch, swinging only at pitches they believe they can successfully hit. In real estate, not bidding or purposefully offering a non-market bid is often the wise move.

A non-real estate example is the valuation of WorldCom. Although WorldCom was not a real estate company, the same valuation issues apply. Historically, WorldCom had maybe a discount rate of 35% and a growth rate of 17%, which implied an 18% cap rate, or a 5.6 multiple. During the Tech bubble in the late 90s, the market thought WorldCom had little risk and would conquer the world. As investors started to lower the discount rate to 20% and increase the long term-growth rate to 20%, WorldCom's market value exploded. If you held a view of the world that they were overvalued, you did not change your valuation of World Com and did not buy more shares, and hopefully sold or even shorted the stock. As the bubble burst, the market value of WorldCom collapsed, as the discount rate soared and growth estimates plummeted. The point is that you must always have a rational view of the world. At times you may find yourself swimming against the current, but that may prove to be smarter (though lonelier) in the end.

A LOOK AT THE PAST

Figure 7.8 displays the history of cash flow cap rate (that is [r-g] from the Gordon Model estimate) "spreads" (margins) over the 10 year US Treasury yield. This cap rate spread over treasury reflects the general pricing of real estate relative to government bonds. In the early 1980s, when you bought real estate, you not only acquired its income growth potential and risk, but also accessed enormous tax benefits, as well as the option to massively over-leverage the property. As a result, the value of a property reflected the value of future operating income, plus the value of the tax benefits, plus the value of the option to over-leverage the property. During this period, cash flow cap rates for all property types were very negative, as their cash flow risk and potential were swamped by the value of the overleveraging option and tax benefits. Cash flow cap rates in the early 1980s were consistently 400-800 basis points lower than 10-year Treasuries, in spite of the fact that high (and rising) vacancy meant there was little hope for near term cash flow growth. In this era, "forward" (based on future expectations) cash flow cap rate spreads were not about real estate, but rather about purchasing the option to over-leverage and accessing to tax benefits.

When real estate's tax benefits were eliminated in 1986, forward cash flow cap rate spreads rose almost overnight by roughly 400 basis points for all property types. Nonetheless, forward cash flow cap rate spreads remained 200-400 basis points below Treasury yields, in spite of weak property fundamentals, due to the continued presence of the option to over-leverage. That is, purchasing a property provided operating income risk and opportunity, as well as the option to receive grossly mispriced non-recourse debt. During this period, variations in spreads across product types grew, with retail and office cap rate spreads being roughly 200 basis points lower than for apartments. This gap reflected the greater perceived credit quality of retail and office tenants.

In the early 1990s, real estate debt evaporated (as shown in Figure 7.9), and real estate no longer included an option to over-leverage. Instead, purchasing real estate included the requirement to under-leverage. Thus, even as construction ceased, and property fundamentals began modestly improving, forward cash flow cap rate spreads exploded, rising by nearly 400 basis points. Retail and office forward cash flow spreads remained the lowest, while spreads for apartments remained the largest, at nearly a 200 basis point spread over Treasury.

By the mid-1990s, not only were real estate fundamentals improving, but real estate capital markets were returning to equilibrium due to capital flows to CMBS, REITs, and opportunity funds. As a result, the period from late 1994 through the August 1998 Russian ruble crisis saw forward cash flow cap rate spreads for apartments moderate to 50-100 basis points. Retail spreads remained the narrowest, at –100 basis points, while office and industrial spreads were roughly zero.

FIGURE 7.8
CAP RATES NET OF 10 YEAR TREASURY

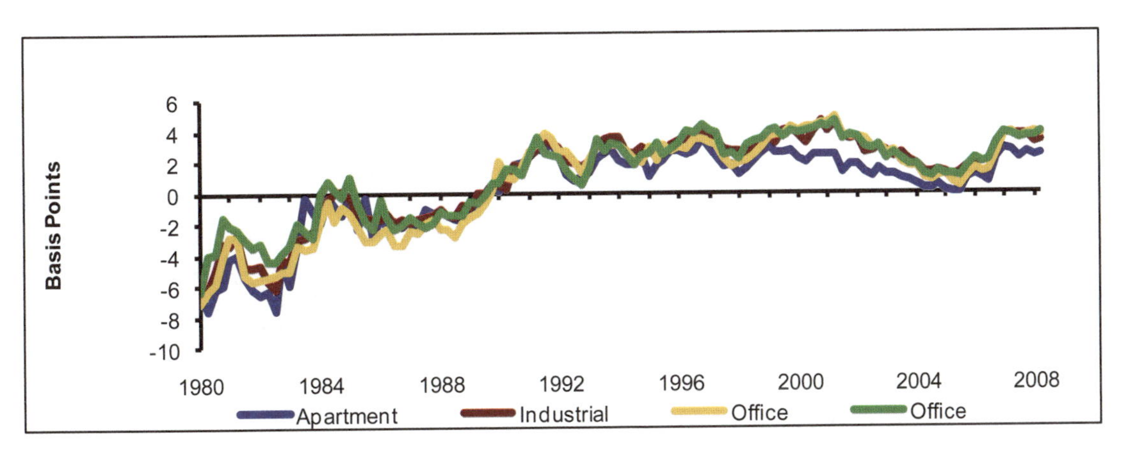

FIGURE 7.9
NET DEBT FLOWS TO REAL ESTATE

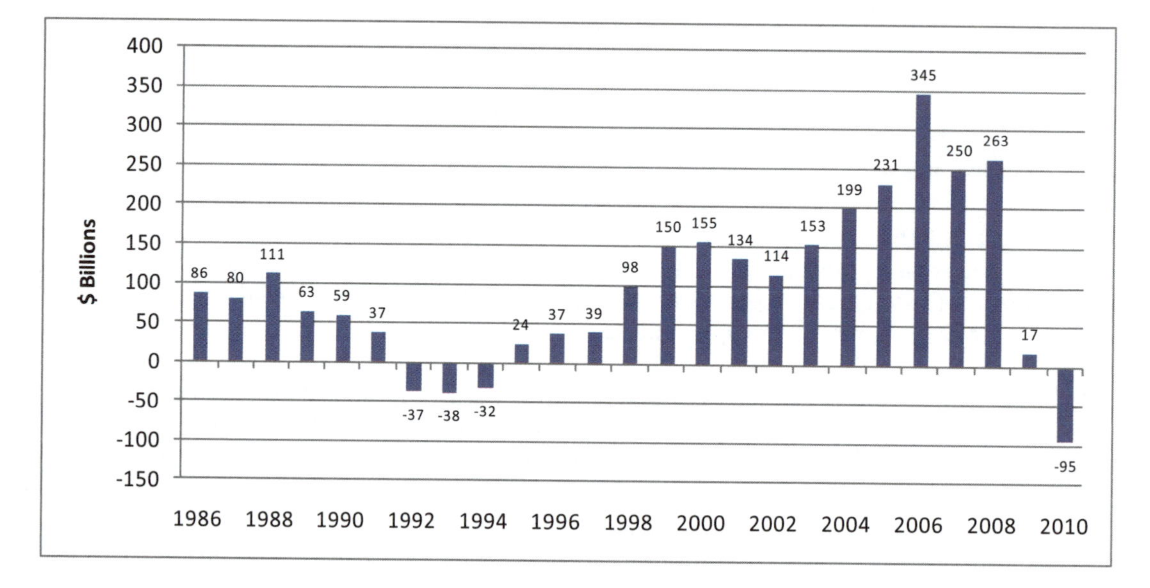

The late-1998 Russian ruble crisis, which had nothing to do with real estate, caused cap rate spreads to rise by 100-200 basis points, as real estate capital markets were now connected with broader global capital flows. Hence, as global capital fled to safety, it abandoned relatively risky assets, including real estate. This pattern continued even as global capital markets stabilized, as the tech bubble made cash flow seem passé.

As the tech bubble burst in 2001, cap rate spreads narrowed, falling by 50-75 basis points as cash flow became king. As property market fundamentals weakened following 9/11, cash flow cap rate spreads rose temporarily. Cap rate spreads subsequently fell by 150-300 basis points across the board through early 2007, in spite of weakening property fundamentals. Then as risk premiums exploded during the credit crisis, cap rate spreads soared, seriously depressing property valuations.

What is the historic relationship between cap rates and long-term Treasuries? If we focus on the "modern" real estate era, when real estate capital markets are connected to global capital markets, and ignore the Russian ruble crisis, the tech bubble, and the credit crisis, the answer appears to be that cap rate spreads for institutional quality multifamily properties are 50-100 basis points. But it is only these brief periods of the past 25 years which are reflective of true real estate pricing, as opposed to an option to over-leverage, access to tax benefits, and abnormal capital markets. Thus, we generally expect cap rate spreads of approximately 50-100 basis points for stabilized portfolio of institutional quality multifamily properties, as the greater risk of these properties relative to long-term Treasury bonds is roughly offset by their cash flow growth potential. But substantial variations around this norm are generated by capital market abnormalities.

CONTRACTUAL INFORMATION

The analysis of real estate is more substantive and challenging than for most industries as real estate NOIs are often driven by existing leases. If you value a typical company, say a bubble gum company, you must make some very broad predictions about future income streams. For example, you may assume that sales will increase with inflation, a reasonable though imprecise assumption. With long leased properties you can much more precisely predict future cash flows, as the leases are contractual obligations. These lengthy leases provide detailed information that to a large degree specify the operating costs, rental income, and many other critical aspects of future income. Once signed, these documents determine payment streams even if markets radically change. Hotels and multifamily properties are notable exceptions, as the contract between the tenants and the landlord cover a much shorter period, making assessment of future cash flows much like that of a bubble gum company.

Numerous assumptions are necessary to reasonably forecast future real estate cash flows. For instance, you need to make assumptions regarding inflation, rents, vacancy, property taxes, utility costs, the time needed to re-lease, etc. Your research, experience, and judgment drive the selection of these unknowns. As you gain experience, usually by making mistakes, your analysis will become more than just a spreadsheet game; it will become the sophisticated analysis of a business.

The reward for this tedious analysis is that you will have a much clearer picture of the future income streams derived from a real estate asset than for most other companies. As a result, the spread on bids for real estate tends to be much tighter than those for most assets, as serious bidders generally have access to the same detailed lease information.

CLOSING THOUGHT

Despite the fact that real estate investors often have access to more substantive information about future income streams than exists for most companies, successful property investors must work desperately hard just to get actual outcomes remotely close to projections. Once you have estimated property value, determined a plan of action, and successfully purchased the property, you will work hard everyday to execute that plan. Execution is where your skills and experience really come into play. Do you have expertise in running an office building? Do you have good tenant contacts? Are you familiar with the area? When the numbers fail to come to fruition, and tenants start to leave, or problems with the building arise, expertise with the property type and local market are critical in determining the success or failure of your investment.

The real estate investment process is like a football game. You may have a perfect game plan, but translating that plan on to the field is a very different story. Saying you are going to block a superstar 300 pound defensive lineman is a lot easier than doing it! And completing a pass in the rain, on the run, as three defenders grasp your quarterback is much more difficult than the pass appeared in the playbook. Remember that the great ones only make things look effortless; they really are very hard.

The numbers are just the start of true real estate finance and investment analysis. That is why the analyst calculating the numbers gets a relatively meager salary, while the CEOs get the big bucks!

Chapter 7 Supplement A

A Disconnect in Real Estate Pricing?

Real estate pays a price for being connected to broader capital flows.

Dr. Peter Linneman- Wharton Real Estate Review- Spring 2004 Vol. VIII No. 1

Hardly a day goes by without talk of today's "disconnect" in the pricing of commercial real estate. The disconnect concerns the historic lows of cap rates, despite weak property fundamentals. As a result, while property cash flows decline, property prices remain high. The best example is the General Motors Building in New York City, which recently traded at a near 5 percent cap rate. However, this phenomenon is not limited to New York trophy office properties; it extends to strip shopping centers and suburban garden apartments.

WEAK FUNDAMENTALS

How weak are property market fundamentals? Focusing on publicly traded real estate companies, for which the best data is available, average funds from operations (FFO) are down over the past year by roughly 4 percent for office REITs and 5 percent for industrial REITs, while apartment REIT FFO are down by 7 percent. Only retail REITs have experienced FFO increases over the past year (6 percent). Over this period, "same store" NOIs are down by even more at apartment, office, and industrial REITs, with only retail REITs registering positive "same store" growth. These declines (for all but retail) are reflective of the rapid increases in property vacancy rates as the bubble economy exploded. [Figure 7A.1]

FIGURE 7A.1: U.S. VACANCY TRENDS BY SECTOR

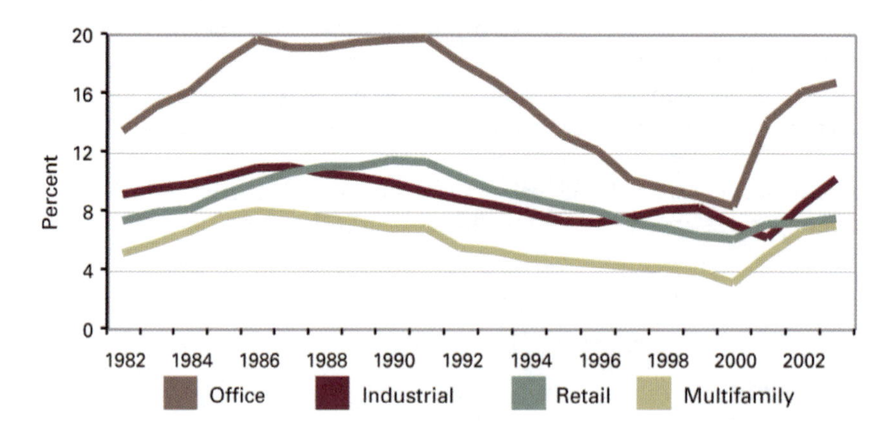

This weakness is also witnessed by the fact that the Linneman Real Estate Index stands at approximately 125, some 25 percent above a condition of market supply and demand balance. [Figure 7A.2]

FIGURE 7A.2: LINNEMAN REAL ESTATE INDEX

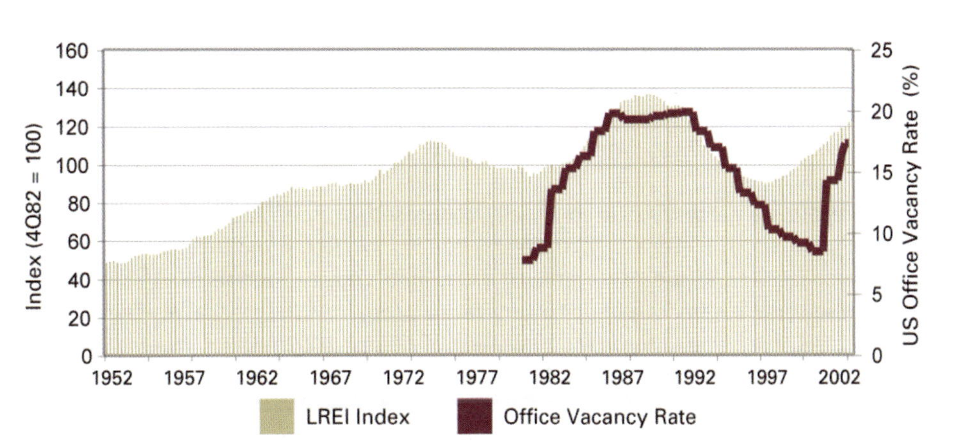

While this is lower than a decade ago, it is substantially higher than in 1999, and indicates substantial excess supply.

HOW STRONG IS PRICING?

Based upon NCREIF data, cap rates are roughly 20 percent lower today than roughly 18 months ago. This represents a cap rate decline of 160 to 200 basis points for core properties over this period. While NCREIF data series are notoriously flawed due to lags induced by appraisal bias, it is clear that a substantial movement downward in cap rates has occurred over the past two years, precisely as property markets have been generally falling apart.

Turning to the valuations of public companies, implied cap rates for the major office industrial, retail, and apartment companies have also declined by roughly 20 percent over the past 18 months. This decline of roughly 160 to 200 basis points is consistent with the NCREIF data. In fact, it is surprising that the retail cap rates have fallen the least, despite their NOI fundamentals remaining strong. Instead, cap rates have fallen most dramatically for those property sectors where fundamentals have deteriorated the most, namely office and apartments. Over the past year, changes in the market pricing for private assets are generally in line with the pricing in public markets, with estimates of REIT market value relative to Net Asset Value (NAV) remaining in the range of 100, with the exception of modest public market premiums for retail.

These pricing patterns are clearly discernible among the day-to-day pricing of well-located, relatively well-leased properties owned by major REITs and institutional investors. However, the pricing for "questionable" properties in weak markets such as Silicon Valley, Austin, Texas, South of Market in San Francisco, Downtown Dallas, and severely challenged retail, indicates that "pure property" has not achieved the same type of strong pricing. In fact, it has been difficult to find bidders for such market-challenged properties, as low short-term interest rates have allowed their owners to keep their reservation prices high, in the hope that things will get better before their loans mature. Transactions for these weak properties have generally been on a "by the pound" basis, trading well below replacement cost of the property.

WHAT IS A CAP RATE?

A cap rate is the "stabilized" NOI generated by a property, divided by its value. This metric is relevant only for properties with stabilized NOI. If NOI is not stabilized, this concept lacks meaning as a valuation metric. For stabilized properties, the theoretical cap rate approximately equals a property's discount rate minus its long-term stabilized NOI growth rate. For example, if a property has a 10 percent discount rate and a 2 percent long-term stabilized NOI growth rate, its cap rate should theoretically be approximately 8 percent. This is the so-called Gordon Rule. Using this approximation of the theoretical cap rate for a stabilized property allows us to examine how the cap rate should have moved over the past two years, and to compare actual cap rate movements with the theoretically predicted movements. This, in turn, allows us to evaluate whether there is a disconnect in market pricing.

The discount rate for a property is theoretically composed of three factors: the long-term risk-free rate (approximated by the yield on a 10-year U.S. Treasury bond); the risk premium associated with unexpected outcomes in the property's NOI; and the risk premium associated with the property's illiquidity relative to a 10-year Treasury bond. These three elements add up to generate a property's theoretical discount rate.

Figure 7A.3 reveals that as recently as the beginning of August 2002 (90-day moving average), the yield on the 10-year Treasury bond was 5 percent. [Figure 7A.3]

FIGURE 7A.3: 10-YEAR TREASURY (3-MONTH MOVING AVERAGE)

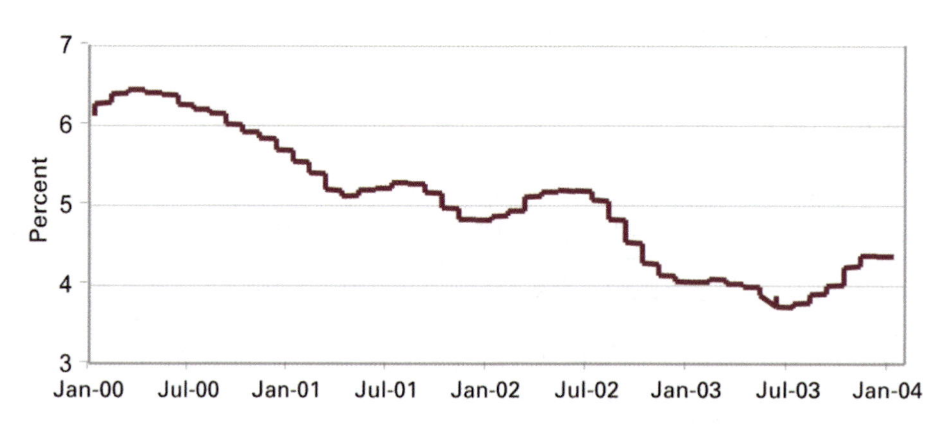

In contrast, from December 27, 2002 through October 9, 2003, the yield remained below 4 percent. The 10-year Treasury yield hit a low of 3.07 percent in early June 2003. In sum, over the past 14 months, the yield on the 10-year Treasury has been an average of roughly 110 basis points lower than during the previous two years, without any notable change in inflationary expectations. This decline in the yield on long-term Treasury bonds primarily reflects investor "flight to safety" in the face of the bursting stock market bubble and a string of financial scandals. In short, the combination of the global recession, 9/11 psychological trauma, corporate scandals, and the bursting of the stock market bubble worked to generate a cyclically high demand for relatively risk-free cash streams, of which the 10-year Treasury bond is the poster child. And while demand has surged for relatively risk-free investments, the supply of relatively risk-free assets experienced a cyclical reduction, as corporate cash flows and credit weakened throughout the recession. Thus, the declining yields on long-term, relatively risk-free assets reflect a relatively rare combination of an abnormally high demand for risk-free cash streams and a cyclically low supply of such cash streams.

The second element of the discount rate, the property-level NOI risk premium, has been differently impacted depending upon the nature of the property. To the extent that the property is fully leased on long-term leases to relatively strong-credit tenants, this risk premium has been largely unaffected by the current property market weakness. This is the case for properties like the General Motors Building, strip centers anchored by strong retailers, and office buildings leased to credit tenants with little lease rollover in the foreseeable future. In contrast, as property markets weakened, properties with significant lease rollovers, such as apartment buildings, have experienced notable increases in their NOI risk premium over the past two years. While it is impossible to know exactly how much higher the NOI risk premium should be, we suspect that it should be roughly 50 basis points higher. Finally, for properties facing major lease rollovers or with large amounts of vacant space, the NOI risk premiums have risen to such an extent that they are no longer stabilized properties. As such, cap rate valuation analysis is irrelevant for these properties.

With respect to the third component of the discount rate, namely the liquidity premium associated with the property, this continues to decline modestly for all but the most challenged real estate. This reflects the fact that as real estate becomes ever more connected to broader capital markets via CMBS debt funding, the public equity financing of REITs, and the continued investment of investors in real estate private equity funds, the real estate liquidity premium continuously declines. This connectivity means that for the first time in history, capital has remained available even as property fundamentals have weakened.

Combining these three factors suggests that the theoretical discount rates for properties have declined by 135 basis points for safe properties and 85 basis points for more typical properties. [Figure 7A.4]

FIGURE 7A.4: THEORETICAL DISCOUNT RATE CHANGES (BASIS POINTS)

Theoretical Discount Rate Changes (Basis Points)			
	Safe Property	Typical Property	Destabilized Property
Risk Free	(110)	(110)	(110)
Property Specific Risk	0	50	150
Liquidity	(25)	(25)	0
Total Change	(135)	(85)	40

Thus, in spite of weakening fundamentals, the greater connectivity with global capital markets, combined with massively reduced long-term risk-free rates, has generated notable declines in real estate discount rates for all but the weakest properties.

The improved connectivity of real estate with global capital flows means that not only has real estate capital remained available, but also real estate has been a preferred asset class. Real estate's status as a preferred asset class over the past several years is vividly demonstrated by the fact that "mom and pop" private REIT syndicators have raised more than $10 billion over the past two years, in spite of approximately 15 percent front-end load factors. This is the Webster's Dictionary definition of a preferred asset class.

Real estate has been a preferred asset class despite its weakening property fundamentals, because global capital flows to the sector that performs relatively—not absolutely—best. Thus, although real estate fundamentals have deteriorated over the past three years, compared to the collapse of the tech sector, the soaring default rates on corporate bonds, the shock of corporate malfeasance, and the poor performance of the broad stock market, real estate debt and equity has been a relatively attractive safe harbor. As a result, capital has flowed to real estate, as real estate's fundamentals were better than could generally be found elsewhere. This is a benefit real estate has earned by finally connecting with global capital markets. However, this connectivity can also work against real estate. There will soon come a time when, despite better real estate fundamentals, real estate will not be improving as rapidly as other sectors. The result will be a capital rotation into other sectors, even as real estate fundamentals improve.

The stabilized, long-term NOI growth rate, the second component of the theoretical cap rate, has remained largely unchanged over the cycle for properties with long-term leases to high-credit tenants. These "safe" properties have had the good fortune of not having leases rolling over into the current softness, or into the softness that will prevail in the next several years. For these "safe" properties, their lease structure protects them and, as a result, their stabilized NOI growth rate has been unaffected by the current market softness.

For more typical properties, with existing vacancies and notable lease rollovers during the next five years, long-term NOI growth rates are actually modestly higher today than several years ago. This is because by late 2001, it was apparent that substantial excess supply would occur in most property markets, and that NOI growth rates would weaken. But the worst years of this NOI deterioration have already occurred. Looking forward, the long-term expected NOI growth rate is modestly higher than two years ago. "The worst is behind us" effect means that over the past year, stabilized annual NOI growth rates for typical properties have risen by 50 to 100 basis points. While this may seem counterintuitive, it is obvious that expected long-term NOI growth rates are higher as one moves through the down phase of a cycle relative to the peak.

Returning to the Gordon model of the theoretical cap rate, namely the discount rate minus the long-term stabilized NOI growth rate, for "safe" properties the theoretical cap rate is roughly 185 basis points lower than prior to 14 months ago, while for more typical properties it is approximately 160 basis points lower. It is important to note that many properties that were considered "stabilized" two years ago are no longer remotely stabilized, and the cap rate valuation approach is irrelevant. The most notable examples are the once "hot" properties in Silicon Valley or the Boston tech corridor.

Our analysis suggests that, theoretically, cap rates should have fallen for most stabilized properties by roughly 20 percent over the past 14 months, in spite of weakening property fundamentals. Such movements do not reflect a "disconnect" in pricing, but rather a new connectivity with the theoretically expected outcome. [Figure 7A.5]

FIGURE 7A.5: THEORETICAL CAP RATE CHANGES (BASIS POINTS)

Theoretical Cap Rate Changes (Basis Points)			
	Safe Property	Typical Property	Destabilized Property
Theoretical Discount Rate	(135)	(85)	40
Minus: Long Term NOI Growth	50	75	N/A
Equal: Theoretical Cap Rate Change	(185)	(160)	N/A

Importantly, the movements in actual cap rates over the past 14 months are basically in line with this expected movement.

Of course, this does not mean that every real estate transaction has been correctly priced. In fact, we suspect that some aggressive property buyers are incorrectly focusing their valuation analysis on short-term interest rates, which have declined by roughly 300 basis points. These purchasers are either knowingly or unknowingly using real estate to make a highly leveraged bet on short-term rates remaining at their historic lows. This may (or may not) prove to be a profitable bet. However, this is not real estate pricing, but rather the use of real estate as the vehicle through which to execute a highly leveraged yield curve arbitrage. This seems to explain the more "disconnected" transactions we have seen. But in general, we conclude that the broad pricing of both public and private real estate is "connected" today.

WHERE DO WE GO FROM HERE?

There are clouds on the horizon. The most notable cloud is that we expect long-term risk-free rates to rise 60 to 100 basis points over the next 12 months. In addition, as real estate begins its slow move through the upside of the cycle, the long-term stabilized NOI growth rate will modestly decline. Together, these factors suggest that cap rates will revert by 75 to 125 basis points over the next 12 to 24 months. This will be somewhat mitigated by the continued improved liquidity of real estate via public markets, securitized debt, and large liquid private equity funds. However, we believe that as other sectors of the economy improve, there will be a rotation out of relatively safe cash streams (including real estate) and into riskier assets. Stated differently, we expect a cyclical decline in the demand for relatively risk-free cash streams, at the same time that a cyclical increase in the supply of relatively risk-free cash streams occurs. This should result in a widespread cap rate reversion of roughly 100 basis points. This is the price that real estate pays for being connected to broader capital flows. We expect that this cap rate reversion will be widely heralded as a new "disconnect" in real estate pricing. People will ask, "How is it that as real estate fundamentals slowly improve, pricing is deteriorating?" The answer will be that in interconnected capital markets it is not enough to "do better;" rather, one must do better than the alternatives.

Chapter 7 Supplement B

The Equitization of Real Estate

What return does real estate deserve?

Dr. Peter Linneman- Wharton Real Estate Review- Fall 2006 Vol. X No. 2

At the beginning of 1990, federal bank regulators fanned out across the country in search of excessive real estate loans. Shocked by the poor underwriting and excessive loan-to-value ratios (LTV) that had been discovered in Texas, they had orders to impose sanity on the capitalization structure of real estate. Up to that point, real estate was basically a 100 percent debt business, with small amounts of equity required to get a project under way, and a history of abusive tax syndicates in the early 1980s. But equity underwriting of future cash streams was a rare commodity in the real estate industry as these regulators began to scrutinize banks and savings and loans across the country.

The regulators, armed with new federal lender regulations, were surprised at what they found at nearly every federally insured depository. Many lenders had provided real estate loans, particularly for development projects, at 100 percent of loan-to-cost, often with minimal underwriting and documentation. This meant that real estate owners had no equity invested, yet had 100 percent of the upside. This capital structure made no sense, and could be found in no other sector of the economy. Yet it was the common practice in commercial real estate, which represented one of the world's largest asset pools. Under intense regulatory pressure, banks announced that they were no longer making new loans, and many outstanding loans were in breach of covenants and must be repaid. Finding a 50 percent LTV loan was hard, even for properties with strong cash flow, and there was little hope of rolling over maturating debt. With the withdrawal of the industry's major capital source, property sales became almost nonexistent, and property values plummeted, although it was difficult to assess what "value" was, as so few properties were trading. This problem was exacerbated by the fact that the only properties on the market were being sold under duress by foreclosing lenders and government agencies, rather than by traditional property owners. As the 1990s dawned, the era of debt ended, and the era of real estate equitization began.

For a $2 trillion industry, this meant that as much as $500 billion of equity was necessary to replace debt and put the real estate industry's capital structure on par with other asset-rich, cash-flow businesses in terms of capital structure. The immediate reaction of most real estate owners was to view the problem as temporary and hope that lenders would soon revert to their old ways. But the more prescient realized that the world had changed, and that access to substantial equity would be required in this new era.

The obvious source of fresh equity should have been cash-rich pension funds. But those that had invested in real estate (remarkably, with little or no debt in an era when debt was massively underpriced) stood on the sidelines, as the value of their real estate portfolios plunged. Most had lost faith in their core real estate managers, who had repeatedly assured them that their properties could not fall in value. The open-end funds in which they invested were frozen as investors ran for the exits, and many managers were rocked by scandals involving properties being assigned artificially high valuations. Pension fund investors seeking to sell properties could do so only at substantial capital losses. In this environment, it was practically impossible for pension fund investors to commit additional funds for real estate. Quite simply, real estate lacked the transparency and track record to attract new money from these funds. Thus, at a time when these funds should have been aggressively purchasing real estate, most were looking to exit.

The equitization of real estate was seriously hampered by real estate having become a four-letter word—deservedly so, as it had almost brought down the U.S. financial system. This, combined with serious global equity investors having never followed real estate, meant that it was going to take time to develop a solid equity following. In addition, for most people real estate was synonymous with development. Hence, most global equity investors did not realize that real estate ownership involved relatively predictable operating cash streams for mature properties.

As the search for equity began in earnest, an obvious source was leveraged buy-out (LBO) funds. But these funds lacked real estate underwriting expertise and were hesitant to enter the industry at a time when a recession was under way. Further, LBO funds faced issues with their existing investments due to the recession. Another potential source for equity was high-net-wealth individuals. But most knew little about real estate and lacked the real estate underwriting expertise required to evaluate real estate opportunities in a meltdown environment. Their entry was further handicapped by the absence of an appropriate investment vehicle, and realistically there was not sufficient capital available through high-wealth individuals to replace the half trillion dollars of debt trying to exit real estate.

A logical source of equity for any capital-intensive industry is public markets. Over the years, public markets have invested in nearly every industry that provides a sufficient risk-return trade-off. But public market investors lacked an understanding of real estate, as they had never underwritten real estate in the era of 100 percent debt and tax gimmicks.

During the 1990s, real estate investment opportunities improved, since prices plummeted as distressed owners teetered on the brink of financial disaster. Not only were these owners going to lose their properties through foreclosures, but they would also lose the management fee streams associated with their properties, and faced enormous tax liabilities. Many owners went bankrupt, while even more faced the prospect of bankruptcy.

EQUITIZATION

A modest equitization effort was under way through real estate private equity funds modeled after LBO funds. The first two funds were Zell-Merrill Fund I and Goldman Sachs' Whitehall Fund I. But these funds were small and difficult to raise, and absorbed much of the available high wealth and institutional equity seeking to enter at that point. Several visionary real estate players, led by Kimco, understood that the stabilized cash streams associated with their stabilized properties were quite safe when delivered, and that safe cash streams could be relatively easily valued by the stock market. Thus arose the alternative of an initial public offering (IPO), which allowed sponsors to avoid bankruptcy. The execution of an IPO was daunting, time-consuming, and expensive, and the outcome uncertain. But if successful, the sponsor could use the offering proceeds (net of expenses) to reduce debt to 40 percent to 50 percent LTV (loan-to-value) and avoid personal recourse.

A successful IPO also salvaged the fee stream from properties that would otherwise have been lost to sale or foreclosure. These fee streams were converted into a value equivalent via shares in the newly public company. In addition, if properly structured as an UPREIT, the sponsor avoided punitive tax liabilities. Finally, with their low LTVs, the newly public company could obtain a corporate line of credit, which could be used to purchase properties from foreclosing financial institutions and distressed owners.

This new era of real estate equitization has four critical events: in 1989, the Zell-Merrill Fund I raised $409 million; in 1991, Goldman Sachs' Whitehall Fund I raised $166 million; Kimco's IPO in November 1991 raised $135 million; and Taubman's IPO in December 1992 raised $295 million. These four transactions set the tone for the modern real estate private equity fund and the modern REIT, respectively.

At the beginning of the 1990s, REITs were an obscure, capital market backwater. Out of roughly $2 trillion in industry value, equity REITs accounted for a mere $5.5 billion. In the early days of equitization, real estate pricing was tenuous at best. Burdened with a bad reputation, a poor track record, unproven sponsors, and complex investment vehicles, it is not surprising that public execution occurred at high cap rates relative to the risk. This pricing was consistent with the private pricing of real estate, which was dominated by distressed sales. For example, the typical REIT dividend yield at the end of 1993 was 6.2 percent. This implied an expected total return of roughly 10 percent for REITs, compared with a 5.8 percent ten-year Treasury rate, a 7.4 percent yield on

BBB long-term bonds, and a roughly 9 percent total return expectation for diversified stock holdings. Thus, as 1993 ended, the expected total return for real estate investments was well in excess of those available for either stocks or bonds. This return premium was necessary to attract uninformed equity into real estate. As the initial REITs succeeded in avoiding bankruptcy while maintaining tax protection and management fee stream value, more IPOs occurred. At the same time, the success of the initial real estate private equity funds also attracted entrants.

FIGURE 7B.1: U.S. REIT EQUITY OFFERING PROCEEDS

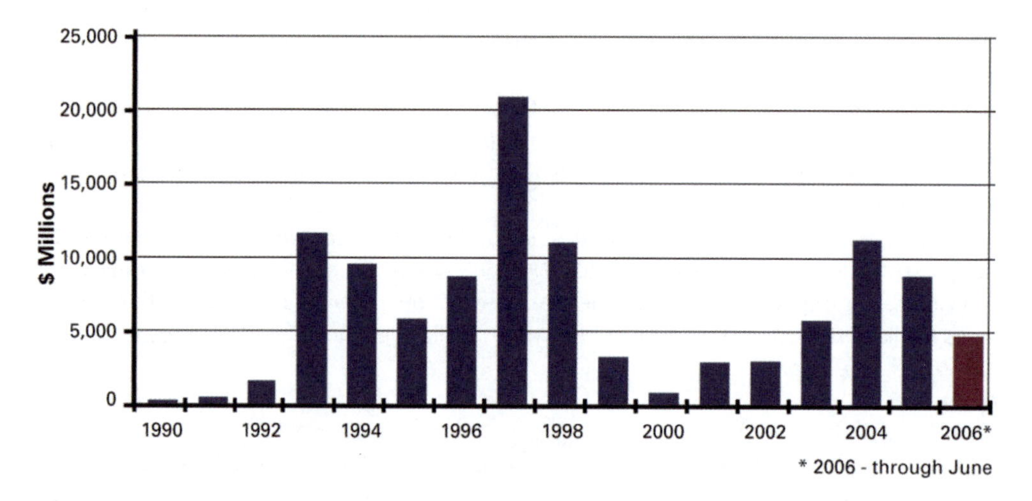

FIGURE 7B.2: U.S. EQUITY REIT MARKET CAPITALIZATION

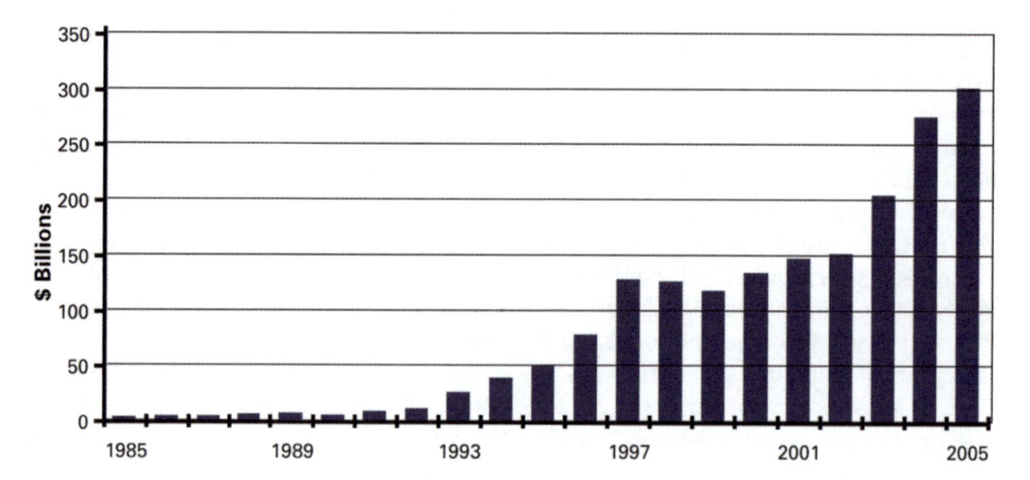

FIGURE 7B.3: NET INFLOWS TO REAL ESTATE MUTUAL FUNDS

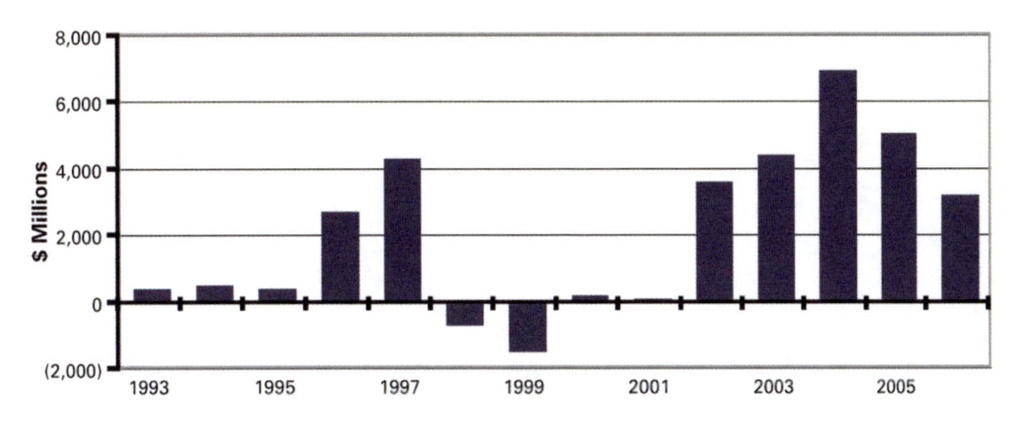

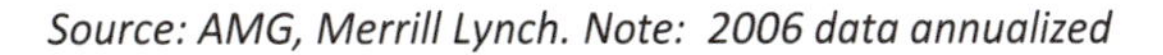
Source: AMG, Merrill Lynch. Note: 2006 data annualized

In a massive debt-for-equity swap, some $58.2 billion was raised by public companies from 1992 through 1997, with an additional $30 billion entering via real estate private equity funds. By the end of 1997, debt was returning to real estate markets, though in a very different form, and with lower LTVs. Specifically, commercial mortgage-backed securities (CMBS) were the primary debt vehicle, pooling individual mortgages that were cut into risk tranches and sold as securities into global debt markets. These debt securities were also initially mispriced as global bond investors and rating agencies lacked an understanding of real estate underwriting. As a result, the spreads on CMBS debt were much higher than their corporate counterparts, despite the fact that relatively transparent hard assets backed these instruments. CMBS issues also had high subordination levels, causing real estate debt to remain expensive relative to the underlying risk. This was the price that was paid for the misconduct of real estate lenders in the previous decade. Typical CMBS LTVs were 50 percent to 70 percent, and equity was required in every project.

FIGURE 7B.4: HISTORICAL U.S. CMBS ISSUANCE

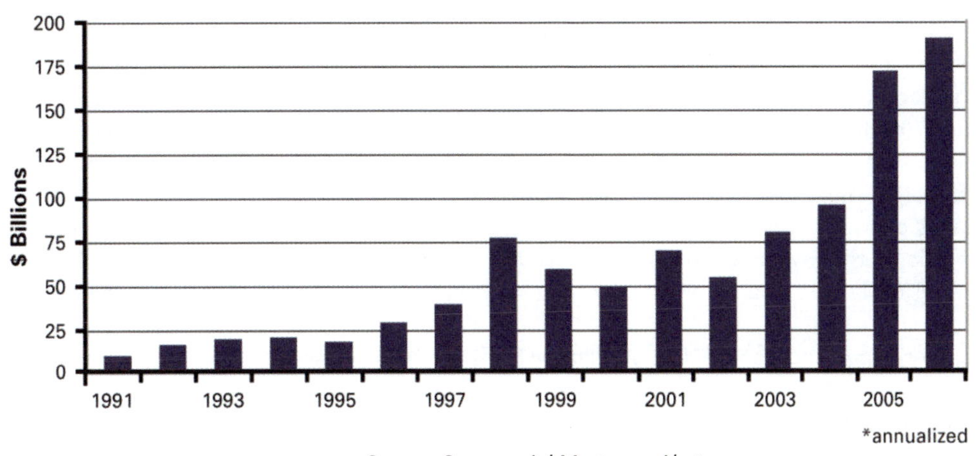

Source: Commercial Mortgage Alert

FIGURE 7B.5: CAPITAL FLOWS IN REAL ESTATE

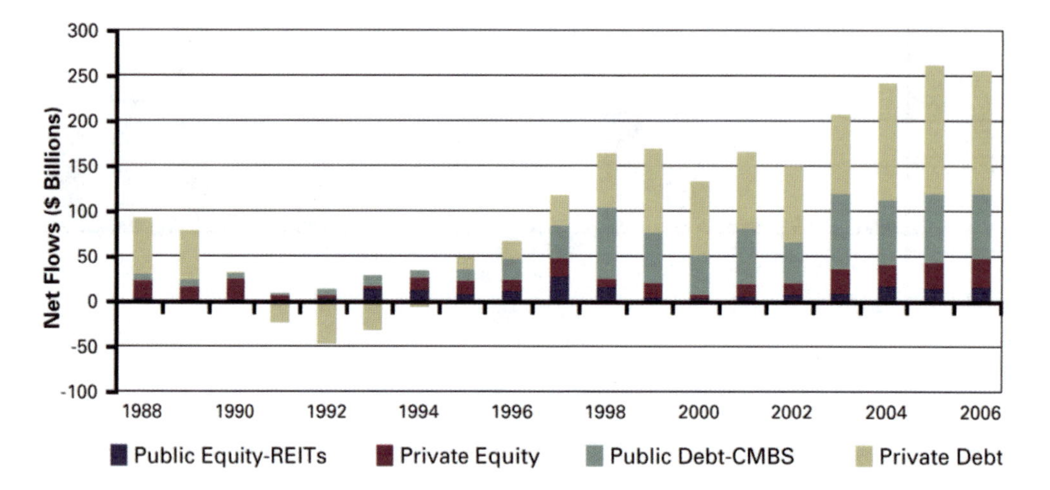

By the end of 1998, the first phase of the equitization of real estate was a success. Equity had tentatively entered real estate via real estate private funds and REITs, while CMBS brought debt back to real estate with disciplined underwriting. And these vehicles had withstood the capital market dislocation of the Russian ruble crisis.

WHAT RETURN DOES REAL ESTATE DESERVE?

Real estate cash flow cap rates for both public and private real estate fluctuated between 8 percent and 10 percent from 1993 to the end of 2001. Since the end of 2001, they have steadily fallen, to approximately 4.7 percent today. In addition to this initial cash flow return, one anticipates receiving an appreciation return roughly equal to the expected rate of inflation. Over the past decade, this inflation has generally been 2 percent to 3 percent. Some observers have argued that real estate cap rates will revert to their historic norms of the past ten to fifteen years. But to answer whether cap rates will rise, one must address the risk-adjusted return for real estate.

Investors have three alternatives in terms of deploying their capital. First, they can invest in the equity claims on the corporations of the world. If we focus our analysis on the equity claims of U.S. corporations, the expected return for this claim is proxied by the expected returns for the broad U.S. stock market. Second, investors can invest in the debt claims of the same corporations, as well as various levels of government (state/local/federal). These debts claims are best proxied by the long-term BBB bond yield. Third, they can invest in the lease claims on the corporations and governments of the United States. These lease claims are primarily the lease claims held by the owners of real estate leased to government and corporate tenants. These lease claims, including the residual value, can be proxied by the ownership of a broad pool of cash flowing real estate such as the REIT index.

From a risk perspective, the debt and lease claims are far less risky than the equity claim, as corporations will pay their lease and debt claims prior to paying equity claims. As a result, the ownership of the debt and lease claims should command a substantially lower expected return than the ownership of the equity claim. Research by Jeremy Siegel of the Wharton School indicates that the expected return on the equity claim of U.S. corporations over the long-term is approximately 6 percent plus expected inflation. Thus, in a world of expected inflation of 2.5 percent, the total expected return for the ownership of the equity claim on U.S. corporations is today approximately 8.5 percent. Since no anticipated appreciation exists in the pricing of most debt claims, their total expected return is proxied by the BBB bond yield. In contrast, the ownership of the lease claim has both a cash flow component and an appreciation component reflective of expected appreciation.

Which is riskier, the debt claim or the real estate claim? Approximately 95 percent of the time, tenants will pay both their lease and debt claims in full. However, the remaining 5 percent of the time they will not fully honor these claims due to bankruptcy. Our analysis suggests that in bankruptcy the loss factor for real estate is slightly less than the loss suffered on the debt claim. To be conservative, we assume that bankruptcy losses are equal for the debt and the lease claim. This means that the total expected returns for the debt and the lease claims must be approximately equal. For example, if BBB bond yields are 7 percent, then the total return for real estate must also be 7 percent, comprised of 2.5 percent expected annual appreciation from inflation and 4.5 percent in current cash flow yield. Stated differently, the risk appropriate total expected return requires that the real estate cash flow return must be below the BBB yield by expected inflation.

Since BBB bond yields are 180 to 225 basis points over the ten-year Treasury yield, for today's 2.5 percent rate of expected inflation, the cash flow cap rate for real estate should be below the ten-year Treasury yield by appropriately price 25 to 70 basis points. That is, if real estate cash flow cap rates exceed the ten-year Treasury yield, real estate is underpriced!

Alternatively one can analyze the appropriate pricing of real estate using the Capital Asset Pricing Model (CAPM). CAPM states that the total expected return for an asset is equal to the risk-free rate (ten-year Treasury yield), plus beta times the market return net of the risk-free rate. Due to the longevity of real estate leases, and the differential supply and demand dynamics of real estate relative to other sectors of the economy, long-term real estate betas are 0.4 to 0.5. Since real estate reduces portfolio return volatility by not being perfectly correlated with market returns, the total expected real estate return should be less than for stocks, and above the ten-year Treasury, to the extent that beta exceeds zero. For example, for today's ten-year Treasury yield of 5 percent, and an expected stock market return of 8.5 percent, the total expected return for a real estate beta of 0.5 is 6.75 percent. Note that for a 2.5 percent expected rate of inflation, the cash flow cap rate for real estate must be approximately 4.25 percent; that is, the total expected return minus expected appreciation (in this example, 6.75 percent minus 2.5 percent). Note that this yields a cash flow cap rate that is 75 basis points below the ten-year Treasury rate.

These alternative approaches to analyzing the total expected return one deserves for real estate generate almost identical results. Namely, the total expected return on real estate should be roughly equal to the yield on BBB bonds, and the typical real estate cash flow cap rate should be 25 to 100 basis points below the ten-year Treasury yield. Higher expected returns mean that real estate is underpriced, while expected returns below this level indicate that real estate is overpriced.

Some argue that this analysis is correct for a diversified pool of real estate, but does not hold for any single property. But this is also the case for every individual stock or bond. Since diversification can be achieved at the investor portfolio level, the total expected returns are reduced to the point where the analyses above applies for each asset class. This is particularly relevant for real estate, which prior to the equitization of real estate did not offer large diversified investment opportunities. But investors today can diversify their ownership across a broad pool of REITs, real estate equity funds, and direct investments, and in doing so, push down expected real estate returns. This outcome is perhaps one of the greatest benefits of the equitization of real estate.

REAL ESTATE PRICING IN THE ERA OF EQUITIZATION

Throughout the era of equitization, the ownership of real estate has been substantially underpriced. In fact, from 1990 through 2002, the cash flow cap rate for real estate (that is, ignoring any expected appreciation) exceeded the total expected return for stocks. This was the case even though the equity claim is notably riskier than the lease claim. Underpricing continued through mid-2004, as the total expected return on real estate (cash flow cap rate plus inflationary appreciation) exceeded that of stocks. Only in the past two years, as cap rates have plunged, has this not been the case.

Figure 7B.6 displays the estimated cash flow cap rate spreads relative to the ten-year Treasury yield for differing types of real estate. Due to the appraisal lag in NCREIF data, these cap rates are lagged 18 months to provide a more accurate presentation of the timing (Figure 7B.7). Note that cash flow cap rate spreads were significantly negative in the early 1980s, when owning real estate was about purchasing not only cash flow but also access to mispriced debt and substantial tax write-offs. As the tax breaks were eliminated at the end of 1986, real estate cash flow cap rate spreads rose. However, the access to mispriced debt meant that real estate investors were willing to pay well in excess of the risk-adjusted price associated with the cash streams alone. As the 1990s dawned, cash flow cap rate spreads exploded, as not only were the cash streams more questionable in the recessionary economic environment, but also the ownership of real estate meant the lack of access to fairly priced debt.

Throughout the 1990s, real estate remained substantially underpriced as debt attempted to exit the market. During this period, anyone with access to equity and courage in their convictions realized a once-in-a-lifetime purchasing opportunity. As the equitization of real estate evolved into the mid-1990s, cash flow cap rates spreads narrowed, but remained positive. However, by the end of the 1990s, real estate cash flow cap rate spreads moved upwards, as cash streams fell out of favor during the Tech Bubble. Only when the bubble burst five years ago did cash flow cap rate spreads begin to fall. Yet as recently as a year ago (the most recently available data given the appraisal lag), cash flow cap rates spreads were generally positive. This stands in stark contrast to theoretically justified negative spreads.

Figure 7B.8 displays estimates of average REIT total expected returns, calculated as the dividend yield plus expected appreciation (measured by the three-quarter moving average inflation rate.) Also displayed are the BBB bond yield, the ten-year Treasury yield, and the expected stock market return (measured by 6 percent plus expected inflation). Figure 7B.9 displays the spread between the average REIT dividend yield and the U.S. corporate BBB bond yield, while Figure 7B.10 shows the REIT AFFO yield over the ten-year Treasury. In the early days of the equitization of real estate, expected returns were 35 percent to 40 percent higher than deserved. By the time of the Russian ruble crisis, the mispricing had narrowed to about 20 percent, but as the bubble set in, underpricing soared to as much as 70 percent. In fact, between September 1997 and December 2000, expected real estate returns rose by 217 basis points, even as real estate operating fundamentals were improving. At the same time, Treasury yields fell by 48 basis points. This created a staggering period of mispricing. REIT implied total returns reached a high of 10.2 percent just before the bubble burst, at a time when ten-year Treasury yield stood at roughly 4.9 percent, BBB bond yields were at 7.5 percent, and expected stock returns were at 8.6 percent.

FIGURE 7B.6: CAP RATE SPREADS OVER 10-YEAR TREASURY

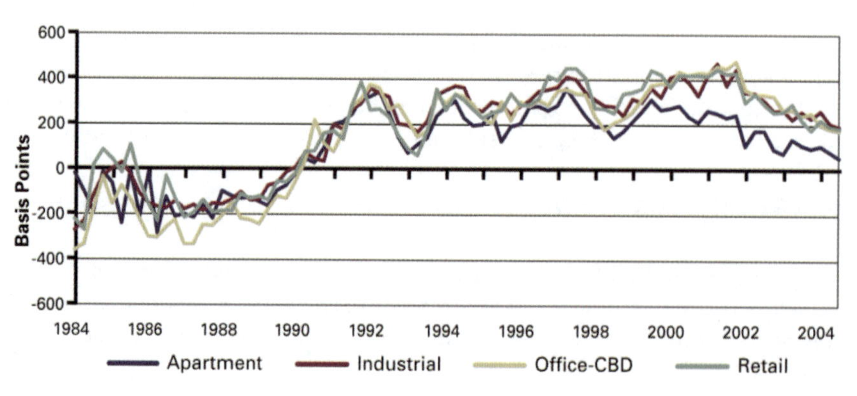

FIGURE 7B.7: NCREIF CAP RATES LAGGED 18 MONTHS

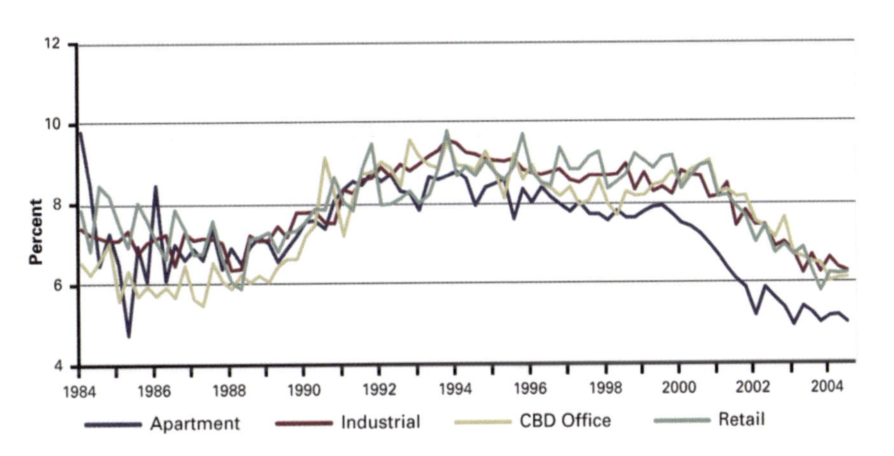

FIGURE 7B.8: YIELD COMPARISON

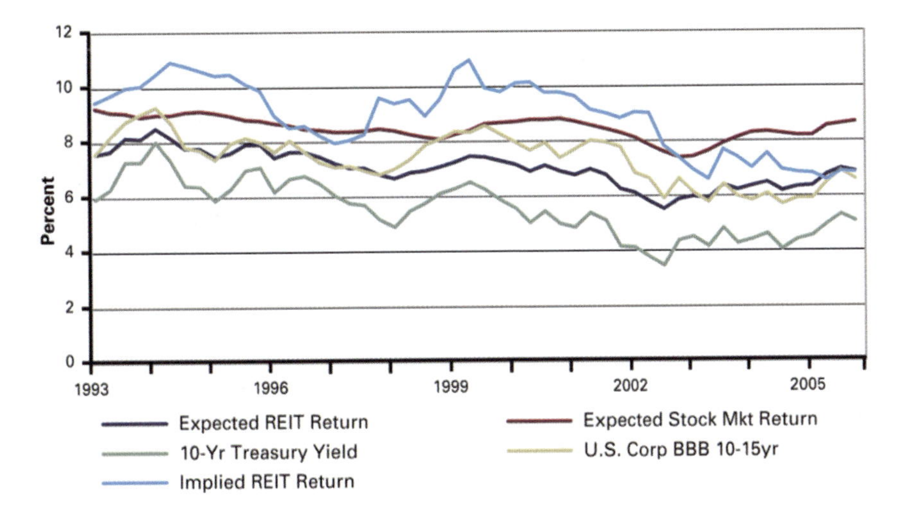

FIGURE 7B.9: DIFFERENCE BETWEEN REIT DIVIDEND YIELD AND AVERAGE U.S. CORPORATE BBB

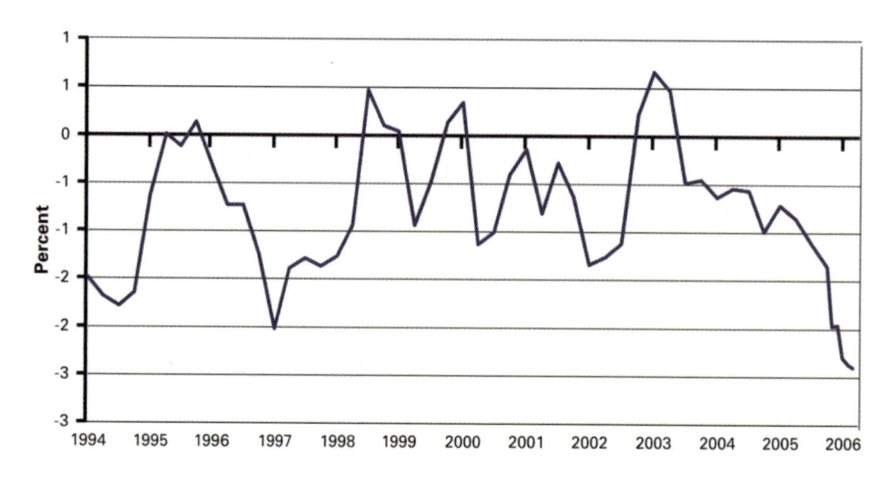

After the bubble burst, expected real estate returns steadily fell. But as expected real estate returns fell, BBB bond and ten-year Treasury yields also fell rapidly. As a result, between December 2000 and June 2003, real estate expected return rates fell by 232 basis points, while ten-year Treasury yields fell by 211 basis points, leaving real estate pricing still substantially out of alignment with the risk. Not until September 2003 did the expected real estate cash return equal the total expected return on stocks, and not until March 2006 did it approach the BBB bond yield. That is, until March 2006, real estate was underpriced in spite of four years of large and continuous declines in cap rates.

FIGURE 7B.10: DIFFERENCE BETWEEN REIT AFFO YIELD AND 10-YEAR TREASURY YIELD

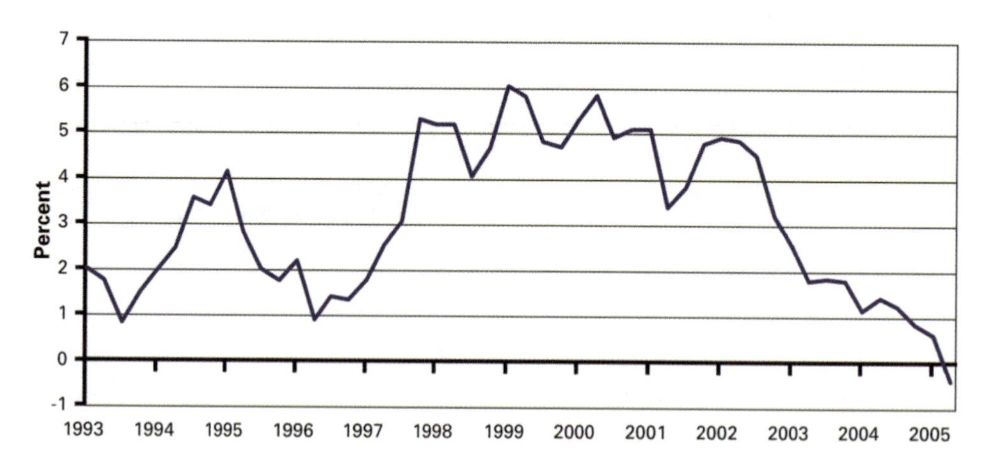

Over the past two years, real estate cash flow cap rates have continued to drift downward. At the same time, stock return expectations have risen modestly as inflation rose, while Treasury yields have risen by 90 basis points and BBB bond yields rose by 60 basis points. And only recently have cash flow cap rate spreads turned modestly negative. We believe that this modest negative cash flow cap rate spread will fall by another 25 to 50 basis points over the coming year. But for the first time in 16 years, real estate is not massively underpriced.

Figure 7B.11 displays the extent of real estate underpricing based upon CAPM, using a beta of 0.5 and an expected long-term dividend growth rate equal to the three-quarter moving average inflation rate. This more structured methodology yields the same story of considerable underpricing in the early-1990s, as equity began to flow into real estate. Underpricing lessened until the bubble. But CAPM reveals that during the bubble, there was enormous underpricing, disappearing only with the recent run-up in ten-year Treasury yields and the ongoing decline of cash flow cap rates. Figure 7B.12 illustrates an under-(over-)pricing matrix, assuming a beta range of 0.3 to 0.6 and long-term annual dividend growth of 2-3.5%.

FIGURE 7B.11: REIT UNDER- (OVER-) PRICING BASED ON CAPM

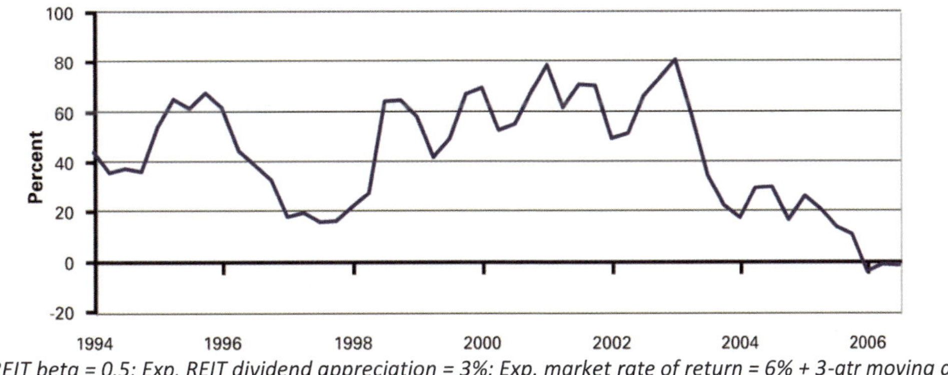

Assumptions: REIT beta = 0.5; Exp. REIT dividend appreciation = 3%; Exp. market rate of return = 6% + 3-qtr moving avg Core CPI; Risk-free rate = 10-Yr Treasury

Theoretically, capital market adjustments occur instantaneously, as there is always enough "smart money" to arbitrage any mispricing caused by capital outflows. But the experience of the real estate industry reveals that the answer to the question, "How long will it take real estate equity to efficiently price real estate cash streams?" is "About 15 years". This capital market adjustment took so long because knowledge was a rare commodity, and courage of investment convictions even more rarely met knowledge.

FIGURE 7B.12: REIT UNDER- (OVER-) PRICING THROUGH JULY 28, 2006

		vLong-Term Annual Dividend Growth			
		2.0%	2.5%	3.0%	3.5%
Beta	0.3	1.7%	15.9%	34.6%	60.6%
	0.4	-6.3%	5.6%	20.9%	41.4%
	0.5	3.2%	-3.1%	9.7%	26.4%
	0.6	-19.1%	-10.4%	0.4%	14.2%

WHAT ABOUT MORTGAGE PRICING?

An interesting corollary is that if real estate expected total return should approximately equal BBB bond yields, then real estate debt (which holds the second loss position on real estate cash streams) should price substantially better than BBB bonds. Yet, until very recently, real estate debt was priced at a premium—not the expected discount—to BBB debt. Only recently has this reversed, as global debt markets have slowly come to better understand real estate. Not surprisingly, if real estate debt was substantially overpriced, real estate was underpriced.

Another way to see the mispricing of real estate debt over the last fifteen years is to note that the spreads on comparably rated CMBS tranches have generally been wider than comparable corporates. This reflects the lack of comfort with these instruments among both ratings agencies and investors, particularly in the early days when real estate was a four-letter word. But, as real estate demonstrated that the high default rates of the late 1980s and early 1990s were not reflective of the risks of underlying cash streams, but rather excessive leverage, real estate debt pricing improved. This is also seen in declining subordination levels for CMBS.

A further demonstration of the mispricing of real estate debt is that REIT corporate debt has generally been rated around BBB. But this cannot be correct pricing if the underlying cash streams of real estate held by these companies is basically BBB in quality, and these REITs have only 40 percent to 50 percent LTVs. Instead, REIT debt was substantially overpriced due to systematic underrating by the rating agencies. This underrating is seen in the fact that there have been no defaults on REIT debt, while equivalently rated corporate debt has seen both defaults and transitions to lower ratings.

Given current leverage, it is likely that most REIT corporate debt should be rated A+ to AA. These ratings, and attendant pricing, will come in time. As it does, the advantages to being a public company will increase, as companies will be able to access fairly priced corporate debt.

WHY ARE REITS GOING PRIVATE?

Why are so many REITs going private (Figure 7B.13)? If today's REIT pricing is roughly correct, it is not that these private buyers are exploiting enormous underpricing. In fact, that opportunity was largely passed over by private equity players until recently, as their funds were too small to take on these opportunities. It is noteworthy that pricing today offers little in the way of positive leverage opportunities. In fact, negative leverage is often the case. In addition, the debt that private borrowers use costs approximately the same as public company debt. If anything, public companies can access debt more cheaply than private entities. In addition, the equity return required by most private buyers is generally the same or higher than that required by public equity. So if there is no major return capital market arbitrage achievable by going private, why have so many companies gone private in the past eighteen months?

FIGURE 7B.13: RECENT REIT PRIVATIZATION

Acquired Entity	Buyer	Price ($Mil)
CarrAmerica (pending)	Blackstone Group	$5,600.0
Arden Realty (pending)	GE Real Estate	$4,800.0
Centerpoint Properties	Calpers, LaSalle	$3,400.0
Capital Automotive REIT	DRA Advisors	$2,960.8
Gables Residential	ING Clarion	$2,313.7
Storage USA	Extra Space, Prudential	$2,300.0
CRT Properties	DRA Advisors	$1,501.4
Town & Country Trust	Morgan Stanley, Onex	$1,500.0
Kramont Realty	Centro Properties	$1,103.9
Bedford Property (pending)	LBA Realty	$796.7
Prime Group Realty	Lightstone Group	$662.0

Source: Linneman Associates

The answer is threefold. First, many of these going-private REITs are sponsors who never wanted to go public, and did so only to avoid bankruptcy. A decade later, these sponsors have aged, and most found that the public arena (particularly with Sarbanes-Oxley [SOX] headaches) is difficult. These entrepreneurial spirits were never comfortable operating a public company, with their requirements for reporting, strategy, and governance. Absent the bizarre world of the early 1990s, these sponsors would never have gone public. But the complete absence of debt and the need for large pools of equity drove them to survive by going public in the 1990s. Having survived, many had little appetite for the public world.

Interestingly, most of the going-private REITs are exits for these original sponsors. Most will pursue entrepreneurial deals funded either from their own capital or via equity provided by private equity firms. These entrepreneurs always felt hamstrung by the low debt levels imposed on REITs. Their exit is proof that real estate pricing has finally improved to the point where it is roughly in line with its risk, as otherwise these savvy real estate players would not have cashed out. Having achieved full value for their properties, they can gracefully exit the public playing field having served their—and their shareholders'—interests. To have sold when real estate was so obviously mispriced would have been a breach of their fiduciary and personal responsibility. Stated differently, these private transactions are evidence that real estate pricing is today in line with risk.

These going-private acquisitions also reflect that private real estate equity pools have finally grown to the point where they can make such purchases, as until recently private equity pools were insufficient to execute a meaningful going-private transaction. A further reason for going-private transactions is that as real estate pricing has come in line with the risk, private equity players have found it harder to achieve returns in excess of risk simply by acquiring real estate. As a result, some are now resorting to highly leveraged buyouts (LBOs), making a highly levered "bet" that cash flows will improve at 5 percent to 6 percent annually for the next three years, and cap rates will remain stable. These are classic LBOs of strong cash-flow streams. If they are right, and cap rates remain low while cash flows increase substantially, these going-private transactions will yield the 20 percent or greater equity IRRs they are seeking. If they are wrong, these transactions will underperform.

Going-private LBOs reflect the maturation of real estate capital markets, as LBOs have existed for years in other sectors. Just like traditional LBO funds, going-private REIT purchasers are willing to accept the risk of higher debt levels than the public market finds acceptable. If the behavior of LBO firms is an indicator, many of the acquired properties will enter public hands as the business plan is achieved.

Finally, some going-private transactions reflect that some of these REITs have missed opportunities to reposition their properties. This is because their entrepreneurial sponsors were so absorbed with the process of running a public company that they were sometimes unable to focus on the blocking and tackling of real estate. The private buyers hope to treat these assets with "loving care" or sell them to owners who will pay for the right to add value.

Nevertheless, there remains a major role for public real estate companies. In fact, new public REITs have entered the market even as others have gone private. The most creative public companies have demonstrated that, as we argued eight years ago, there is very little that a well managed public company cannot do in terms of its capital structure that a private company can do; but there are things that a public company can do that a private company cannot. Thus, the best REITs are pursuing joint ventures with private capital, managing third-party assets, and operating value-added funds. These REITs have become efficient operating companies and the public market has provided them with unparalleled access to both public and private capital with a speed that is hard to match. Consider that a large REIT can raise a billion dollars in days, versus the months it takes even the best private equity funds to raise the same amount.

CHALLENGES REMAIN

Public real estate firms must resolve a number of issues. Foremost among these is to establish executive compensation structures that reward value creation, and assure that top-quality management can be attracted and retained. This problem arises because the REIT IPOs in the 1990s squeezed compensation in order to achieve every penny in valuation. However, this created executive compensation schemes that were unsustainably low. While REIT compensation has improved, it has not kept pace with the opportunities available in the private market. Thus, much of the best talent remains private, or at public companies in other sectors (such as financial services).

Another problem is that only a few REITs have successfully incorporated meaningful value-add platforms. This includes not only development, but also leveraged subsidiaries, high-risk activities, and other value-creation activities. This reflects that most REIT management teams have been slow to demonstrate that they can create value. Similarly, they have been slow to move into alternative property types. As a result, unlike the best private equity players, most REITs are restricted to a single property strategy. While this is appropriate for some, others must convince public capital providers that they can successfully allocate capital and operate across property types. Further, while management fees may not be as stable as property cash flows, a successfully created management fee stream is extremely valuable. One need only look at the trading multiples associated with investment management companies. A major problem that arises in this context is the resolution of the inherent conflict of interest in fee management relationships. However, as REIT managers gain investor trust, they should be able to deal with these.

Chapter 7 Supplement C

How Should Commercial Real Estate Be Priced?

Commercial real estate pricing needs disciplined and systematic analysis of the data.

Dr. Peter Linneman - Wharton Real Estate Review- Spring 2008 Vol. XII No. 1

Commercial real estate pricing is like the weather: everyone talks about it, but few understand it. Most observers base "appropriate" real estate pricing on historical norms. The cap rate—an indicator of value relative to stabilized net operating income (NOI) before capital expenditures, tenant improvement, and leasing commissions—is the most commonly used metric of real estate pricing. But cap rates have been largely unresponsive to alternative rates of return available to investors, with the exception of BBB bonds, throughout most of the past twenty-five years (Figure 7C.1). Such a relationship defies investment theory, as real estate pricing should change as property risks and the returns of alternative investments change.

FIGURE 7C.1: CAP RATE CORRELATIONS

	Cap Rate Correlation With:*		
	10-Year Treasury	BBB Corp Bond Yield (10-15 yr)	S&P Dividend Yield
Multifamily	0.187	0.771	0.068
Industrial	-0.221	0.748	-0.307
CBD Office	-0.449	0.694	-0.458
Retail	-0.181	0.649	-02.58

* Based on 25 years of data for the 10yrT & S&P DivYld; and 14 years for BBB.

FIGURE 7C.2: NCREIF CAP RATES vs. 10-YEAR TREASURY

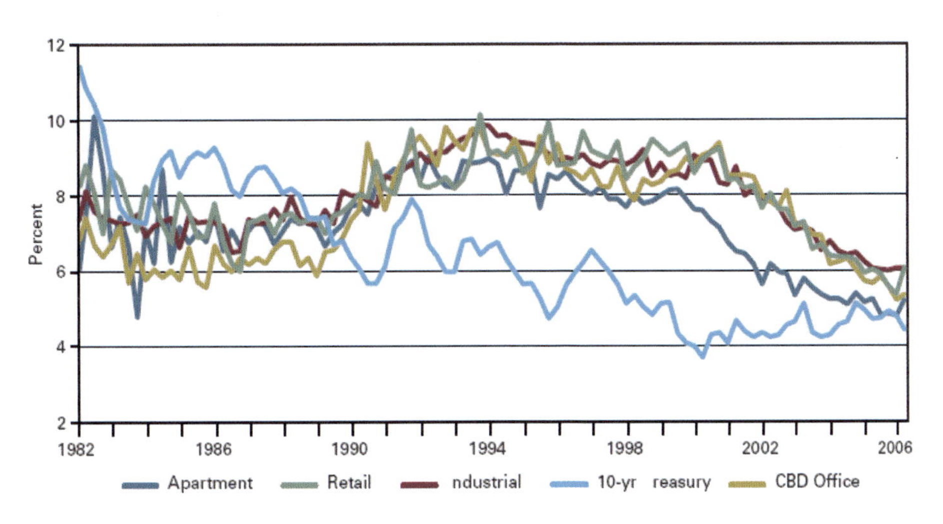

Figure 7C.2 displays NCREIF cap rates by property type compared to the ten-year Treasury yield. Because the National Council of Real Estate Investment Fiduciaries (NCREIF) cap rate data is seriously flawed due to appraisal lags, it is presented in Figure 7C.3 with an eighteen-month lag. This data provides an overview of the pricing of institutional quality real estate. Figure 7C.3 reflects these cap rates net of the ten-year Treasury yield. Since cap rate spreads are highly correlated across property types (Figure 7C.4), we can speak of "cap rates" without reference to property type with little loss of insight. Cap rate spreads were negative in the early to mid-1980s, when purchasing real estate was more about investing in tax losses than real estate cash streams. When tax laws dramatically changed in 1986, cap rate spreads rose, though they generally remained negative due to the availability of excess leverage through 1990 and projections of strong cash flow growth, in spite of weak fundamentals.

FIGURE 7C.3: NCREIF CAP RATES vs. 10-YEAR TREASURY

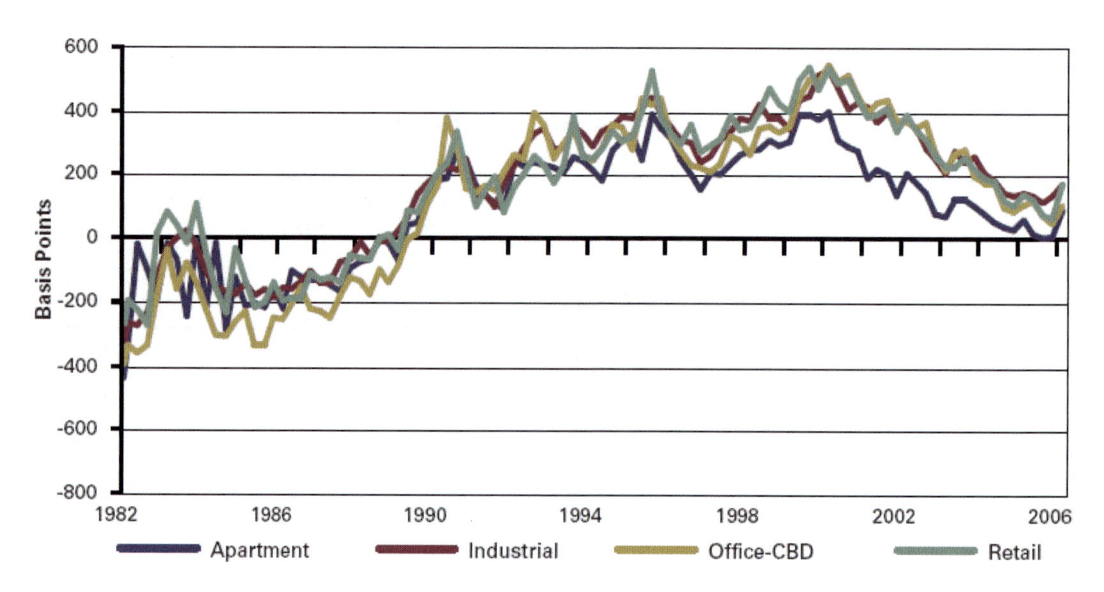

FIGURE 7C.4: CORRELATIONS OF SPREADS BY PROPERTY TYPE

	Correlation of Cap Rate Spreads Over Treasury		
	Multifamily	Industrial	CBD Office
Industrial	0.937		
CBD Office	0.924		
Retail	0.922	0.969	0.964

Throughout the first two-thirds of the 1990s, spreads substantially widened as capital abandoned real estate. Spreads further widened in the latter part of the 1990s, as investors scorned cash flow during the tech bubble and treasury rates drifted downward. As the tech bubble burst, cap rate spreads steadily compressed, recently falling to approximately zero. And if NOI cap rate spreads are roughly zero, cash flow cap rate spreads (after reserves for tenant improvements, leasing commissions, and capital expenditures) are well below zero.

This compression of cap rates and cap rate spreads over the past five years has generated enormous wealth for real estate owners. In fact, the combination of cheap debt and cap rate compression covered a multitude of property underwriting errors made during the past five years, as neither cap rate compression nor narrowing debt spreads were part of original pro forma models. This cap rate spread compression offset weak cash flows in a post-recessionary economy from 2002 to 2005, while continued compression, combined with improved cash flows, pushed property values skyward in 2006 through mid-2007.

Cap rate compression reduced the importance of the ability to add value. After all, if all you had to do to make money was to leverage to the hilt while cap rates fell, why take on the extra work and risk of attempting to add value? Stated differently: Why print money if it is laying everywhere on the streets?

In Figure 7C.5 and Figure 7C.6, we demonstrate the power of cap rate compression via very simple pro forma cash flow analyses that assume Year 1 NOI of $100; a going-in cap rate of 9 percent; an LTV of 70 percent; and an interest rate of 7 percent. Within each figure, we display two scenarios, which vary based on NOI growth assumptions. Scenario I assumes that NOI grows by 3 percent per year, while Scenario II assumes a value-add NOI growth of 20 percent between years two and three.

The only other difference between Figure 7C.5 and Figure 7C.6 is in residual cap rates, which are assumed to be 6 percent and 9 percent, respectively. Based on these assumptions, we calculate the equity IRRs. It is clear that cap rate compression is a significant factor in driving returns. That is, cap rate compression from 9 percent to 6 percent increased IRR on leveraged stabilized properties by 250 percent, to a staggering 57 percent. Who needs to take on value add risk at this return for stabilized assets?

In the early 1980s, money was made in real estate by mastering the creation and syndication of tax gimmicks. In the late 1980s, one made money by mastering bank and S&L connections to over-leverage. In the early 1990s, one made money in real estate by having access to equity—the more the better. During the late 1990s, one made money from real estate by realizing large spreads between cap rates and debt costs. And, over the past five years, the way to make money in real estate was to own real estate on a highly leveraged basis as cap rates plunged.

The classic asset pricing model is the capital asset pricing model (CAPM). CAPM is a simple, yet elegant, model that relates asset pricing to the risk-free rate (F), the ability of an asset to reduce portfolio variance (B), and the expected rate of return on the market bundle of investable assets (M). CAPM is far from perfect, but provides a crude benchmark for asset pricing, around which discrepancies and novelties arise. Specifically, CAPM states that an asset's price is set such that the expected return for an asset

$$(R) \text{ is } R = F + \beta\,(M-F).$$

If beta equals one, it means that the asset's return moves in coincidence with the market return, providing no ability to reduce portfolio expected return volatility. As a result, the expected return for such an asset should gravitate toward the return on the market portfolio.

If beta is greater than one, the asset's return increases more than the market return, and falls more than the market return. Such an asset accentuates the return volatility of a portfolio, as it rises or falls more than the market. In order to accept this increased portfolio volatility, the expected return must exceed the expected return for the market portfolio. Similarly, if beta is less than one, the expected return for the asset should be less than the market rate of return, as the asset is able to reduce portfolio risk. In fact, an asset that is uncorrelated with the market ($\beta = 0$) should price such that it need only generate the risk-free rate of return.

FIGURE 7C.5: PRO FORMA CASH FLOW, 9 PERCENT RESIDUAL CAP RATE

Scenario I with 9% Residual Cap Rate					
NOI Growth Rate			3%		
Going-in Cap Rate			9%		
Implied Purchase Price (Direct Cap Yr 1 NOI)			$1,111		
Loan-to-Value			70%		
Equity Financing			$333		
Debt Financing			$778		
Interest Rate			7%		
Residual Cap Rate			9%		
	Year 0	Year 1	Year 2	Year 3	Year 4
NOI		$100	$103	$106	$109
Ann Int (Interest Only)		($54)	($54)	($54)	
Debt Repayment				($778)	
Residual Value (Cap next year's NOI)				$1,214	
Net Cash Flow	($333)	$46	$49	$488	
Scenario I Equity IRR	23%				

Scenario II with 9% Residual Cap Rate					
Going-in Cap Rate			9%		
Implied Purchase Price (Direct Cap Yr 1 NOI)			$1,111		
Loan-to-Value			70%		
Equity Financing			$333		
Debt Financing			$778		
Interest Rate			7%		
Residual Cap Rate			9%		
	Year 0	Year 1	Year 2	Year 3	Year 4
NOI		$100	$100	$120	$120
Ann Int (Interest Only)		($54)	($54)	($54)	
Debt Repayment				($778)	
Residual Value (Cap next year's NOI)				$1,333	
Net Cash Flow	($333)	$46	$46	$621	
Scenario II Equity IRR	32%				

FIGURE 7C.6: PRO FORMA CASH FLOW, 6 PERCENT RESIDUAL CAP RATE

Scenario I with 6% Residual Cap Rate					
NOI Growth Rate			3%		
Going-in Cap Rate			9%		
Implied Purchase Price (Direct Cap Yr 1 NOI)			$1,111		
Loan-to-Value			70%		
Equity Financing			$333		
Debt Financing			$778		
Interest Rate			7%		
Residual Cap Rate			6%		
	Year 0	Year 1	Year 2	Year 3	Year 4
NOI		$100	$103	$106	$109
Ann Int (Interest Only)		($54)	($54)	($54)	
Debt Repayment				($778)	
Residual Value (Cap next year's NOI)				$1,821	
Net Cash Flow	($333)	$46	$49	$1,095	
Scenario I Equity IRR	57%				

Scenario II with 6% Residual Cap Rate					
Going-in Cap Rate			9%		
Implied Purchase Price (Direct Cap Yr 1 NOI)			$1,111		
Loan-to-Value			70%		
Equity Financing			$333		
Debt Financing			$778		
Interest Rate			7%		
Residual Cap Rate			6%		
	Year 0	Year 1	Year 2	Year 3	Year 4
NOI		$100	$100	$120	$120
Ann Int (Interest Only)		($54)	($54)	($54)	
Debt Repayment				($778)	
Residual Value (Cap next year's NOI)				$2,000	
Net Cash Flow	($333)	$46	$46	$1,288	
Scenario II Equity IRR	65%				

Applying CAPM to real estate provides dramatic insights about the history of real estate pricing, as it says that real estate returns should reflect real estate's beta, the expected market return, and the risk-free rate. Since real estate generates its return through a combination of current cash flow and expected appreciation, we need to measure both at various points in time in order to evaluate actual real estate pricing versus expected pricing indicated by CAPM.

As the proxy of real estate's current cash flow return, we use the dividend yield on REITs, and proxy the expected perpetuity real estate appreciation rate by the three-year moving average of the core inflation rate (excluding food and energy). This highly simplified model suggests that at any moment in time the expected return for holding real estate equals the current REIT dividend rate (which is near 100 percent of cash flow post-reserves) plus the three-year moving average rate of inflation (that is, the long-term cash flow growth equals inflation). At each point in history, we compare the actual dividend yield (grossed up for six months of growth) to the dividend yield implied by CAPM, assuming a beta of 0.5. This tells us how much real estate prices would have had to have risen (or fallen) for this implied real estate return to be equal to the return indicated by CAPM. For example, at year end 2006, the actual dividend yield (grossed up for six months of growth) was 3.74 percent, while CAPM implied real estate deserved a 4.16 percent dividend yield. This was an indication that the price of real estate was 10 percent too high, as the current return expectation fell short of expectations implied by CAPM.

The blue line in Figure 7C.7 plots the extent of real estate overpricing based on the weighted average dividend yield of all publicly traded equity REITs from 1993 through the first quarter of 2008. Since beta equals 0.5 (in line with historic norms) in this analysis, real estate returns are correlated with market returns, but only half as volatile. As a result, real estate return expectations should be less than the return expectations for the market portfolio. In a simple example, if the risk-free rate is 5 percent, beta is 0.5, and the expected market rate of return is 9 percent, the expected return for real estate lies midway between the risk-free rate and the market rate, at 7 percent. For real estate to generate a 7 percent return expectation in a world of 2.5 percent inflation (hence expected appreciation), real estate cash flow cap rates need to be 4.5 percent. If real estate requires a 25 percent reserve for capital expenditures, leasing commissions, and tenant improvements, it must price at a 6 percent cap rate on stabilized NOI in order to generate a 4.5 percent cash flow return. That is, the implied required cash flow cap rate must be grossed up by the extent of capital reserves to obtain the expected NOI cap rate.

FIGURE 7C.7: REAL ESTATE (UNDER) PRICING THROUGH MARCH 28, 2008

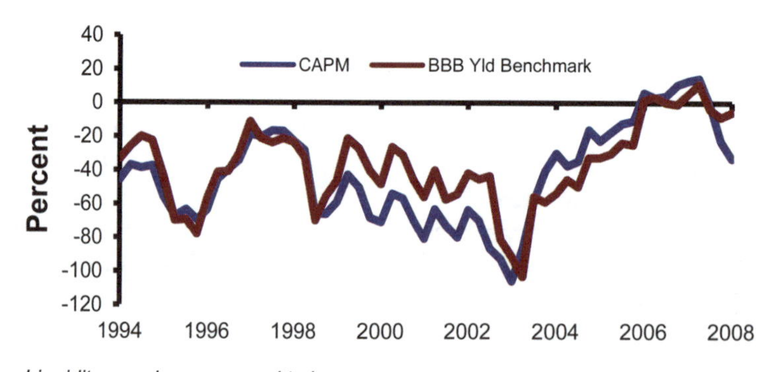

Liquidity premium assumed to be zero.

FIGURE 7C.8: LONG TERM ANNUAL DIVIDEND GROWTH

		Long Term Annual Dividend Growth			
		2.0%	2.5%	3.0%	3.5%
BETA	0.3	-66.8%	-100.7%	-152.0%	-238.3%
	0.4	-43.7%	-68.2%	-102.7%	-155.0%
	0.5	-26.2%	-44.7%	-69.5%	-104.7%
	0.6	-12.5%	-27.0%	-45.7%	-70.9%

Reviewing the blue line in Figure 7C.7 reveals that in the early 1990s, when capital abandoned real estate during the real estate depression, real estate was massively under-priced. This is consistent with the fact that most knowledgeable real estate players desired to buy real estate during this period, but lacked an essential ingredient: equity. As capital returned to real estate in the form of real estate private equity funds, REITs, and securitized debt, the extent of real estate under-pricing fell. Thus, by early 1998, it was "only" about 20 percent underpriced. But as the tech bubble drove real estate cap rates upward even as treasury yields fell, real estate under-pricing on the order of 60 percent to 80 percent resulted. This under-pricing of real estate was consistent with the under-pricing of most cash flow businesses during the tech bubble, when strong cash flow was shunned in favor of "clicks". Recall that this was a time when Warren Buffett supposedly had lost his touch because he refused to invest in dotcoms, preferring out-of-favor cash flow investments. As the tech bubble burst in 2001, and cap rate spreads compressed, the under-pricing slowly but steadily evaporated. By mid-2006, pricing had come roughly in line with CAPM expectations for a beta of 0.5.

Subsequent to the euphoria associated with the EOP and Archstone going private transactions, real estate pricing swung to 15 percent to 20 percent overpriced based upon CAPM. As interest rates rose, loan-to-value (LTV) ratios tightened, and CMBS spreads widened from April 2007 through August, REIT pricing reacted, with prices falling in line with those predicted by CAPM. In fact, as of mid October, CAPM analysis indicates that REIT pricing was about right. However, as the depth of the credit crisis unfolded, real estate became increasingly out of favor. As of the end of March 2008, CAPM indicates that REITs are 36 percent undervalued.

An alternative approach to pricing real estate is what we call the "it tastes like chicken" (ITLC) approach. Though less elegant than CAPM, this approach states that real estate should price comparable to comparable risk claims. For example, quality apartments should generate the same general return as other high-quality consumer receivables, as apartment ownership is a high-quality consumer receivable, and renters will generally pay rent before they pay their credit card and car debt. Since credit cards and car loans are widely sold on the capital markets, by comparing real estate returns to these consumer receivables, ITLC provides a crude approximation of expected apartment pricing.

Similarly, office properties in world class CBDs are dominated by a diverse set of corporate tenants (including banks, insurance companies, corporations, law firms, etc.). ITLC implies that these properties should generate a return roughly commensurate with the long-term debt claims on these tenants. This is because stabilized office properties in these markets are perpetuity lease claims on this tenant base, and tenants will honor these lease claims about the same as their debt claims. The debt claims on corporate tenants, which are widely sold in the capital markets, provide an approximation of the return one deserves for such office properties.

The credit quality of the office tenants affects the expected real estate return, just as debtor quality affects the expected pricing of their debt. For example, ITLC suggests that for quality office properties located near the White House, which will always be occupied by the U.S. government and high-quality tenants who need to be near the government, real estate returns should be roughly comparable to AAA to AA debt. For midtown

Manhattan office buildings, with their diverse portfolio of high-grade corporate tenants, pricing should be roughly commensurate with high-grade corporate debt (A to BBB+). For lesser tenant quality properties and markets, the pricing should be higher reflective of the lower credit quality of tenants (BBB to B+).

An adjustment should be made reflective of the differential liquidity of real estate versus debt claims. Although not as liquid as debt claims (i.e., bonds), as real estate investments have become more liquid via REITs, deeper markets, greater transparency, and more diversified investor holdings, real estate pricing should have improved.

Some object to ITLC, noting that unlike a portfolio of bonds, real estate ownership provides a real asset (the property) at the end of the lease. But at the end of the lease, this ownership simply means that the owner refills the property with new tenants, effectively repeating this exercise into perpetuity. If the prospective tenant pool is dominated by tenants of roughly comparable credit as that of existing tenants, the ownership of the property is effectively a perpetuity lease claim of comparable risk to the perpetuity debt claims on tenants.

If the property is of insufficient quality to merit leasing to comparable tenant quality upon lease expiration, stabilization pricing analysis is inappropriate. For example, if the market is comprised of low-quality tenants, while the current tenant is a high-quality credit who is only on the lease for a few years, the pricing of the property must reflect a blended credit quality. Thus, the ITLC approach to real estate pricing is most easily applied to buildings with tenants who are representative of the market's tenant pool. The beauty of ITLC is that it allows the use of the tenant, building, and market quality to assess the relevant credit against which expected real estate returns are evaluated. This expected total return is composed of the current cash flow and expected appreciation.

If the debt claims of the tenants dominating the typical commercial market are BBB, and BBB debt yields 7 percent, and the expected real estate cash flow appreciation rate is approximately the 2.5 percent economy-wide inflation rate, then the expected cash flow cap rate for the properties in that market is approximately 4.5 percent. That is, a 4.5 percent current cash flow plus a 2.5 percent expected appreciation return, yields a 7 percent total expected return for real estate, roughly equal to the 7 percent yield on the BBB debt. If reserves for TIs, capital expenditures, and leasing commissions are approximately 25 percent of NOI, a 6 percent NOI cap rate is appropriate for a BBB tenant pool property, as a 6 percent NOI cap rate yields a 4.5 percent cash flow cap rate.

The red line in Figure 7C.7 applies ITLC to real estate pricing, where BBB debt is used as the relevant tenant pool. The extent of overpricing is derived in the same manner as was described for CAPM. ITLC reveals the same basic pricing history, though the extent of under-pricing during the tech bubble is somewhat less than indicated by CAPM, with substantial under-pricing lasting somewhat longer into the 2000s based upon ITLC.

The Gordon model for valuing a perpetuity cash flow yields a simple, yet powerful, solution for expected cash flow cap rates. This model states that the cap rate is the difference between the property's discount rate and perpetuity cash flow growth rate. So if the discount rate reflective of the risk of the property is approximately 8 percent, and the perpetuity growth rate of its cash streams is approximately 2.5 percent (general inflation), then the cash flow cap rate should be approximately 5.5 percent. If reserves are 25 percent of cash flows, the theoretically expected NOI cap rate is 7.3 percent.

The Gordon model, like CAPM and ITLC, highlights the fact that the cap rate should vary with returns on alternative investments, as the discount rate reflects the risk-free rate plus the risk premium associated with real estate, plus the illiquidity premium. The risk-free rate is proxied by ten year Treasury, while the additional premium for alternative assets is reflected by risk spreads that the capital market assigns to alternative investments with similar risk characteristics. The risk-free rate rises and falls with inflation, while the risk spread required on alternative assets will vary as investor risk perceptions change. Liquidity premiums vary as capital markets evolve and deepen.

These alternative approaches underscore that real estate returns should vary as alternative investments opportunities change over time, as well as inflation, growth, risk, and liquidity change.

Armed with these general models of pricing, we demonstrate how different types of office properties should price using ITLC, based upon the risk-free rate, the nature of the tenant pool, building quality, the operated cash flow growth rates, reserve gap between NOI and cash flow, and illiquidity.

Figure 7C.9 summarizes our analysis for office buildings in four distinct quality markets. In each case, we focus on a property that is of typical quality for that market category, with typical reserves and typical long-term expected growth rate for each market. The markets differ in terms of the reserve gap between NOI and cash flow, due to the variable expenses associated with tenant releasing costs. We utilize proprietary data on the history of properties in a variety of markets to estimate these gaps. Markets also vary in terms of their long-term cash flow growth rates, and liquidity.

The strongest markets, which include midtown New York, Washington, D.C., and the San Francisco CBD, have approximately a 19 percent gap between NOI and cash flow. At the other extreme, poor markets have a 38 percent reserve gap. This is reflective of greater tenant improvement costs, leasing commissions and capital expenditures relative to market rents in poor markets. Adjustments are also made to reflect that cash flow will decline as a property's capital expenditures rises over time, resulting in a higher NOI cap rate upon exit. That is, a building that is new today will not trade at the cap rate of a new building ten years from now, but rather the NOI cap rate for a ten-year-old building, which is slightly higher since the ten-year-old building has less cash flow for a given NOI due to higher capital expenditure requirements.

FIGURE 7C.9: REAL ESTATE PRICING EXPECTATION MODEL

Real Estate Pricing Expectation Model	Strong	Good	Typical	Weak
10-Year Treasury	4.70%	4.70%	4.70%	4.70%
Tenant credit premium	1.75%	2.00%	2.00%	2.25%
Liquidity premium	0.25%	0.50%	0.50%	1.00%
Expected total return (IRR)	6.70%	7.20%	7.20%	7.95%
Less expected appreciation	-3.00%	-2.75%	-2.50%	-2.50%
Expected cash flow cap rate	3.70%	4.45%	4.70%	5.45%
Cash flow as percent of NOI	81%	76%	70%	62%
Implied NOI cap rate	4.57%	5.86%	6.71%	8.79%
Capital adjustment for 10-year hold*	0.12%	0.29%	0.52%	0.88%

**This is to suggest that after 10 years, one should apply a higher residual cap rate because the next buyer will incur greater capital costs on the then-older building.*

We begin this pricing analysis with the risk-free rate, which is 4.7 percent (reflective of the ten-year Treasury rate at the time of writing). We add to this return a risk premium reflective of the pool of local tenants. Since BBB credit historically trades at roughly 200 basis points over treasury, the risk premium for most markets is 200 basis points. The third line in Figure 7C.9 reflects the fact that liquidity is greater in stronger/deeper markets. This premium ranges from 25 to 100 basis points across markets.

Adding these three components generates the total expected return that investors should require for stabilized properties in these markets, which range from 6.7 percent to 7.95 percent. Note that these expected returns will change as treasury rates, tenant credit premiums, and liquidity change. The expected appreciation for most markets is 2.5 percent (the expected rate of inflation). However, supply constrained markets will have somewhat higher growth rates since supply will generally lag demand. Thus, if a 6.7 percent total return is required in a strong market, and 3 percent derives from appreciation, the expected cash flow cap rate is 3.7 percent. For weak markets, a cash flow cap rate of 5.45 percent is required to achieve the expected 7.95 percent return.

Adjusting these cash flow cap rates upward to get to the NOI cap rate implied by typical market TIs, leasing commissions and capital expenditures, generates the implied NOI cap rate. In the case of strong markets, this is approximately 4.57 percent, while in the case of weak markets it is 8.79 percent. Note that because of the greater deduction associated with reserves in weak markets relative to strong markets, the gap between NOI cap rates notably exceeds that of cash flow cap rates. That is, high NOI cap rates do not necessarily generate higher cash flow returns.

The next line indicates that as the property ages ten years, the NOI cap rate should rise, reflective of the fact that there is higher capital expenditure required for older buildings. Based on proprietary information, we estimate that this component amounts to 12 to 88 basis points, depending upon market category. Not surprisingly, this adjustment is greatest in weak markets, as relative fixed capital expenditures amount to a greater proportion of low rents. Hence, if one enters at a strong market 4.5 percent cap rate, the expectation is that they will leave at approximately a 4.67 percent cap rate a decade later. For a property in a weak market, the ten-year change is from 8.79 percent to 9.67 percent. Conducting similar analysis of earlier times is consistent with the patterns indicated by CAPM and ITLC. Specifically, we have gone from a period of massive under-pricing of the real estate to a period of modest overpricing of real estate.

A disciplined and consistent approach to pricing real estate exists, which prices on the basis of market alternatives, property and tenant profiles, liquidity, and cash flow growth expectations. This analysis provides a beginning step to a more systematic and disciplined analysis of real estate pricing than has historically been the case.

Chapter 7 Supplement D

What Determines Cap Rates?

Dr. Peter Linneman – Linneman Letter- Summer 2015 Vol. 15, Issue 2

In corporate finance, equity valuation is summarized by the price-earnings (P/E) ratio, which is the ratio of a firm's value (e.g., stock price per share) divided by its earnings. In real estate, valuation is generally described by the capitalization rate (familiarly, cap rates), rather than income multiples. The concept of the cap rate is simply the inverse of the traditional valuation multiple. That is, the cap rate is the income return of real estate, and is defined as stabilized net operating income (NOI) divided by the value of the property (purchase price, either anticipated or actual). The real estate industry's usage of cap rates reflects its historic linkage to the bond market, as real estate derives its income from future tenant promissory income streams. So just as the bond market commonly quotes yield, as opposed to multiples when describing bond values, the real estate industry generally refers to cap rates.

The cap rate (C) for a stabilized property can be shown to theoretically equal the discount rate (r) for the property's cash stream minus the perpetuity growth rate (g) of those cash streams.

$$C=r-g$$

The discount rate (r) is equal to the real long-term risk-free rate (Rf), plus expected economy-wide inflation (p), plus the operating risk of the asset (o), plus the liquidity premium associated with the asset's illiquidity versus the risk free rate (l):

$$r=Rf+p+o+l$$

The expected long-term cash-flow growth rate (g) is expressed as the expected real cash-flow growth rate (c) plus economy-wide inflation (p):

$$g=c+p$$

Thus, basic algebra reveals that the cap rate is theoretically defined as:

$$C=Rf+o+l-c$$

Note that economy-wide inflation cancels out, as it is an equal component of both the risk-free rate and expected long-term cash-flow growth. Thus, inflation does not theoretically affect cap rates per se, as inflation increases both the discount rate and the cash-flow growth rate by the same amount. The cap rate is therefore equal to the real long-term risk-free rate, plus the property's operating risk and liquidity premiums, minus the real perpetuity expected cash-flow growth rate.

In analyzing these four components, the real perpetuity expected cash-flow growth rate (c) is the least volatile component of the cap rate. This is because "perpetuity" is, by definition, a very long time. The property-specific operating risk component (o) is tied closely to the macro or regional economy and is generally counter-cyclical. Specifically, cap rates tend to fall due to a decline in operating risk as the economy moves through the recovery phase of the business cycle. Turning to interest rates, historically, the real long-term risk-free rate (Rf) has been fairly constant at 200-250 bps, but has been abnormally low, and at times, even negative during the Financial Crisis. This reduction of 200-275 bps is historically unique, reflecting both the extraordinary flight to safety during the Financial Crisis, as well as unprecedented monetary policy activism. When the real return rose by about 100-

150 bps in July 2013, it created upward pressure on cap rates, which was observed in both REIT and high-quality private asset pricing. However, our assessment is that the major movements of cap rates are attributable to changes in the liquidity premium (I). This component is highly counter-cyclical, plunging as the economy and capital markets boom and skyrocketing when they contract.

In 2015, we were among a minority that believes that cap rates, and equity multiples in general, would basically hold, even as interest rates rise. As support for this position we note that when value multiples were at similar levels in late 2006 and early 2007, the short-term rate was 5.3% and the 10 year yield was at 4.7%. That is, low cap rates (and high multiples) can co-exist with high interest rates. But for this to be the case, there must be an increased flow of funds, particularly of debt.

People correctly argue that, all other things being equal, a rise in interest rates should cause cap rates to rise by increasing the weighted cost of capital. But it is important to understand that "other things" do not remain equal as interest rates rise. In particular, as interest rates rise from artificially low levels, borrowers have a reduced incentive to borrow, while lenders have a notably increased incentive to lend. This incentive to lend manifests itself by changing "other things", including offering higher loan-to-value ratios, slower amortization, longer periods of interest-only payments, reduced covenants, narrower debt spreads, reduced underwriting standards, etc. These factors result in an increased flow of debt as rates rise from artificially low levels. This results in a reduced weighted cost of capital and more investor money chasing a limited supply of NOI and properties, resulting in higher prices. This was the case in 2006- 2007, when high interest rates stimulated a dramatic flow of debt.

When there is an extraordinary amount of liquidity pent-up in the largest money center banks, as interest rates rise these banks will notably increase lending incentives in order to increase the volume of loan originations. The resulting flood of debt, based on our research, more than offsets any negative impact of higher interest rates on cap rates.

The problem is that when the flow of debt eventually comes to an end, the process dramatically reverses. The contraction of debt is felt dramatically in the real estate sector, even when real estate is in supply-and-demand balance. This is because mortgage loans are roughly 60% of the real estate capital stack. As lenders pull back on originations, prospective buyers, as well as owners seeking to refinance are negatively and dramatically affected. If they are unable to refinance, existing owners face a capital shortfall, which is simply too large to be "instantaneously" filled. And to the extent it is filled, it is with expensive equity rather than cheap debt. This causes the cost of capital to temporarily skyrocket, forcing transactions to halt. As transactions cease, and loans default, the only transactions occurring are at temporarily depressed values to opportunistic equity buyers. These low value marks (i.e. high cap rates), in turn, further discourage lending, creating a feedback loop.

Given real estate's high overall leverage, even a 5-10% cyclical pullback in outstanding debt is simply too large to be absorbed without a severe impact on liquidity and pricing. This phenomenon underscores the fact that the flow of debt funds – more so than interest rates – is the dominant determinant of real estate pricing, as even very low rates cannot offset the absence of debt in terms of the weighted averaged cost of capital.

The Fed's artificially low interest rate policy resulted in a lot of frustrated "would be" investors. These are people and firms who would like to borrow at these low rates, but find that they are not credit worthy, and hence are unable to get loans. Most have become so frustrated that they have stopped trying. As the Fed allows rates to rise, we will see an upward movement along the debt supply curve, and lenders will have greater incentive to lend. Thus, higher interest rates result in more funds flowing to borrowers. The result will be fewer frustrated "would be" borrowers, more outstanding debt, and a great flow of debt that will offset any impact of rising interest rates on cap rates (and equity multiples). Hence, it is not hard to understand why even as rates rise from artificially low levels, more debt will be issued.

Chapter 8
Development Pro Forma Analysis

"Be prepared to adjust".
-Dr. Peter Linneman

DEVELOPMENT

We next turn our attention to the creation of properties, i.e. development. While the previously discussed concepts directly apply to development, development also presents its own unique risks and opportunities.

Figure 8.1 summarizes the development pro forma for Celina Gardens, a 250 unit suburban garden apartment complex being built for sale as condominiums. While this pro forma lists the major cost categories, a full pro forma would include more detailed cost categories.

FIGURE 8.1

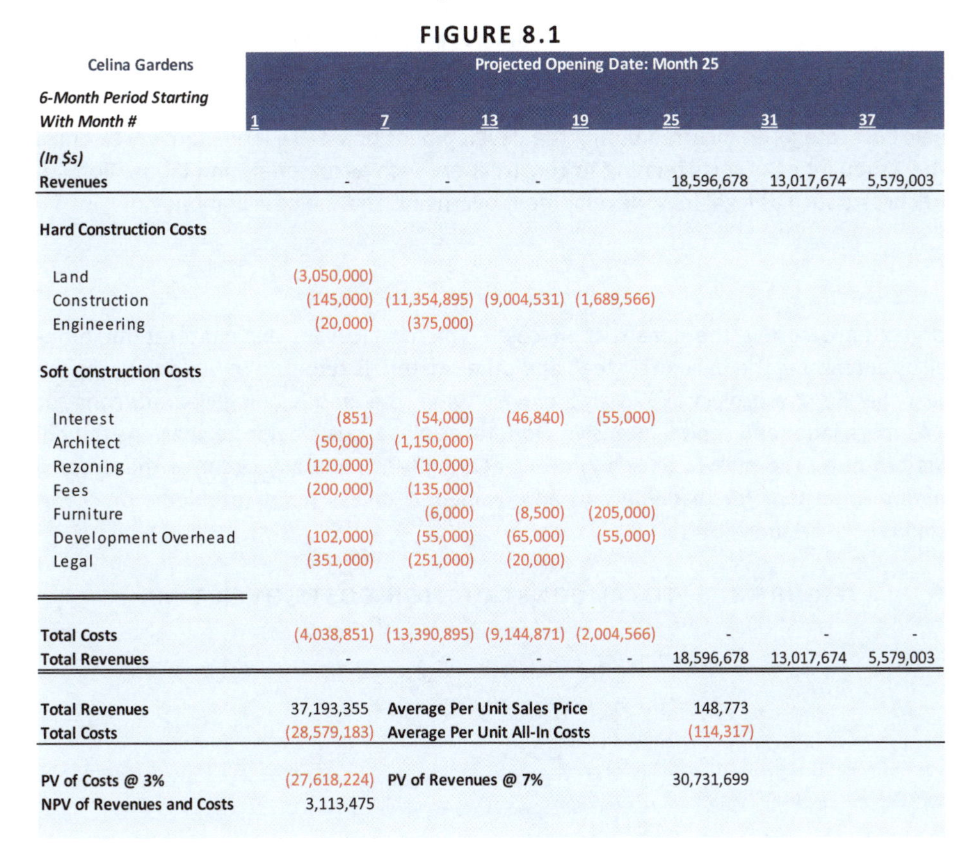

Celina Gardens	Projected Opening Date: Month 25						
6-Month Period Starting With Month #	1	7	13	19	25	31	37
(In $s)							
Revenues	-	-	-		18,596,678	13,017,674	5,579,003
Hard Construction Costs							
Land	(3,050,000)						
Construction	(145,000)	(11,354,895)	(9,004,531)	(1,689,566)			
Engineering	(20,000)	(375,000)					
Soft Construction Costs							
Interest	(851)	(54,000)	(46,840)	(55,000)			
Architect	(50,000)	(1,150,000)					
Rezoning	(120,000)	(10,000)					
Fees	(200,000)	(135,000)					
Furniture		(6,000)	(8,500)	(205,000)			
Development Overhead	(102,000)	(55,000)	(65,000)	(55,000)			
Legal	(351,000)	(251,000)	(20,000)				
Total Costs	(4,038,851)	(13,390,895)	(9,144,871)	(2,004,566)	-	-	-
Total Revenues	-	-	-	-	18,596,678	13,017,674	5,579,003

Total Revenues	37,193,355	**Average Per Unit Sales Price**	148,773
Total Costs	(28,579,183)	**Average Per Unit All-In Costs**	(114,317)
PV of Costs @ 3%	(27,618,224)	**PV of Revenues @ 7%**	30,731,699
NPV of Revenues and Costs	3,113,475		

The Celina Gardens development project consists of two very different business activities. The first business is the planning and construction of the building. In our example, the planning and construction phase was expected to take about 18 months. Figure 8.2 summarizes typical time frames for the planning and construction of different buildings types.

FIGURE 8.2

Asset Type	Planning & Construction Time
Warehouse	9-18 months
Garden Apartments	1-2 years
Suburban Office	18-36 months
CBD Office and High Rise Residential	2-4 years
Strip Center	18-30 months
Regional Mall	3-6 years

The planning and construction process entails many steps, including feasibility analysis, the design process, the planning process, the approval process, site preparation, infrastructure installation, and physical construction. Upon completion of construction, the second business begins. Specifically, the property changes to the business of operating a building. This reflects the time it takes to sell or lease the property and for it to achieve market acceptance. In the case of Celina Gardens, you believed you would sell out the condos in months 24 through 36.

The main cost categories incurred during the development phase are land, hard costs, and soft costs. The hard costs are best thought of as costs relating to construction, such as materials and labor. Soft costs are broadly defined as indirect costs such as legal fees, development overhead, and the cost of money.

HARD COSTS

The largest hard cost is the construction cost. This cost covers expenditures for hiring construction workers, as well as purchasing the concrete, steel, and other materials required to build the property. These costs tend to flow over the life of a project like in an S curve. When the land is being cleared, construction costs are relatively low. As more labor and capital intensive work takes place, costs begin to soar. As the finishing touches are added, costs top out. The bulk of design and engineering fees generally occur at the onset of the process. These functions are important for planning and approvals, but unless major problems or changes occur they become less significant over time.

FIGURE 8.3: TOTAL CONSTRUCTION COSTS OVER TIME

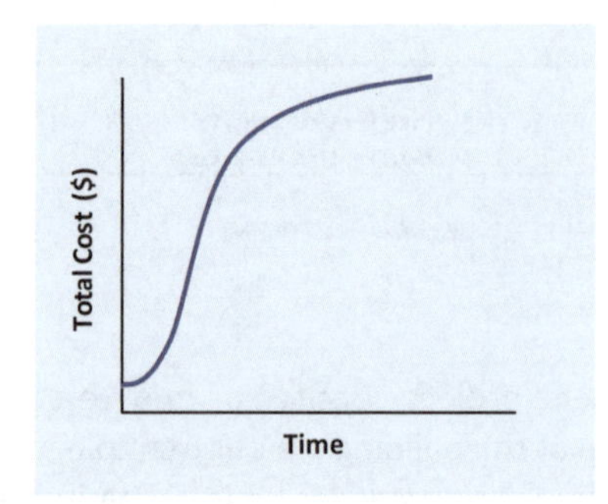

SOFT COSTS

The largest soft costs are generally architects, engineers, and interest costs. The property will not generate any significant revenue until construction is completed and a large share of the development costs will be paid with borrowed funds. With this debt comes interest incurred on the outstanding loan balance. As more money is borrowed to pay for construction costs, interest costs rise. But how can this interest be paid if there is no revenue? The answer is that the interest on the construction loan accrues. Effectively, the lender loans the developer money to pay the interest which is due. This additional borrowing is added to the principal balance, with interest charged on this accrued interest. As a result, the loan principal increases until the property generates enough cash flow to service the debt. This type of loan is referred to as a **negative amortization loan** (see pp. 435-436).

Development overhead encompasses things such as project manager salaries, back office work, accounting, etc. The construction process also requires lawyers performing due diligence analysis, such as checking titles and deeds. If complex environmental issues arise, legal fees rise substantially. A more detailed pro forma would describe these fees with much greater specificity. For example, fees will be incurred for obtaining the construction loan as well as for leasing.

Rezoning costs are associated with changing zoning ordinances or if any variances are sought for the use of land. Land is often optioned to reduce the developer's risk while zoning is sought. Specifically, the developer options, rather than purchases, the land during the approval phase in order to reduce the risks and costs. An option amount of 3-10% of the total land price is typically paid up front, with the remainder due at the developer's option at some future date. Often the option requires that all approvals be in place before the developer must exercise the option.

During its early stages, a development generates negative cash flows, as a great deal of money is paid out for the creation of the building, while little or no revenue is generated. For example, during the first 18 months, you will pay contractors for construction, lawyers to finalize zoning and approvals, and architects to draw up plans, but until you have an occupied property, you have no income to offset these outflows. By itself this is a bad business! It is development's "second" business, that is, operating a completed property, which is expected to yield substantial positive cash flows that can make development attractive.

PHASE I: THE NEGATIVE CASH FLOW BUSINESS

Which part of development's cash flow is more certain: the planning and construction phase, or the unit sales or operation of the completed product? Unfortunately, the outlays associated with the planning and construction phase are much more certain than the NOI which occurs upon completion. As a developer, you know you must expend a lot of money in order to plan and construct the building by month 18. Since these costs are relatively certain to occur, the appropriate discount rate for this negative cash flow phase is quite low, as the discount rate always represents the riskiness associated with the corresponding cash flows. As a result, buying the land, renting construction equipment, paying lawyers and architects and other planning and construction costs should be discounted at roughly the 2 year Treasury rate, as this is roughly the risk free rate for the 18 month planning and development phase. In the case of Celina Gardens, we use the two-year Treasury rate plus a 100 basis point risk premium as the discount rate for these costs. If the 2 year Treasury rate is 2%, it yields a 3% discount rate for the development costs.

Another way to understand why a very low rate is the appropriate discount rate for the development phase is to consider a developer who asks, "How much money do I need to set aside today in order to be absolutely certain I will be able to cover all development costs by liquidating this money plus the interest it earns?" In order to be certain that no payment shortfall occurs during the development phase, the money must be invested in very low risk instruments, like short term Treasuries. For example, to cover the final payment of

$2,004,566 in the six - month period starting in month 19 the developer needs to set aside about $1,965,187 in month 1, and with the interest earned on the 2 year Treasury (starting in month 1) making up the $39,379 difference. As a result, a low discount rate must be applied to the relatively certain planning and construction costs.

PHASE II: POSITIVE CASH FLOW BUSINESS

In contrast to the relatively certain planning and construction expenses, the positive cash flows derived from operating the property upon completion are much less certain. The business of forecasting the building's NOI two years into the future is difficult. This is not to say that the property will not be very successful, but there may be cost overruns, construction delays, weakened market conditions, or leasing problems which hurt future cash flows. This future cash flow uncertainty requires that you apply a notably higher discount rate to the operating phase than is used to discount the negative cash flows incurred during planning and construction phase. Of course, if the development process took two days, you could apply the same discount rate to the positive cash flow business as to the negative cash flow business with little harm. However, longer development projects necessitate varying discount rates in order to accurately estimate the present value of the development. It also means that development IRRs are meaningless, as the IRR calculation inappropriately assumes a single discount rate applies to all years. Yet, developers and lenders use it because of its mathematical elegance (or perhaps because ignorance is bliss).

In some cases the risks of future operating cash flows can be partially mitigated. Recall that revenue generated from a building derives primarily from the rent and cost recoveries paid by tenants. For example, if you lease the building to GE or the US Government you are leasing to high credit tenants, and hence reduce the risk of not being paid. Thus, for future revenue derived from tenants like GE you should employ a relatively low discount rate. In contrast, if you plan to lease the building to Wish & A Prayer, Inc., you should utilize a much higher discount rate. As the tenant mix for a property changes over time, the appropriate discount rate applied to future cash flows should change accordingly.

FIGURE 8.4: DIFFERENT QUALITY TENANTS AND DISCOUNT RATE RISK

	Wish & A Prayer, Inc.			GE		
	Year 1	Year 2	Year 3	Year 4	Year 5	Year 6
Rent	1000	1000	1000	1000	1000	1000
Appropriate Discount Rate	12%	12%	12%	8%	8%	8%

Another possible strategy to mitigate risk involves leasing before the building is complete, so-called "pre-leasing". The advantage of pre-leasing is that some of the uncertainty of future cash flows and tenant credit risk is mitigated. Offsetting this advantage is that rents are locked in several years in advance, meaning that if market rents rise over time (which is probably the developer's expectation), the developer cannot take advantage of the higher rents.

Note how at the bottom of Figure 8.5 the NPV of the project differs across the two methods. If the development costs are incorrectly discounted at the same 7% rate as the condo sales cash flows, the costs will be understated, and the project appears more attractive than it actually is by over $1,100,000. If you do not analyze your costs and revenues properly, development projects will appear more lucrative than reality, and you can end up entering a thin-margin deal or even lose money. Celina Gardens is financially feasible under both discounting methods, but misleadingly so when discounting costs too aggressively.

FIGURE 8.5: CELINA GARDENS PRO FORMA NPV CALCULATIONS

Celina Gardens Pro Forma *(In $s)*		Projected Opening Date: Month 25	
Total Revenues	37,193,355	**Average Per Unit Sales Price**	148,773
Total Costs	(28,579,183)	**Average Per Unit All-In Costs**	(114,317)
PV of Costs @ 3%	(27,618,224)	**PV of Revenues @ 7%**	30,731,699
PV of Costs @ 7%	(26,432,544)		
Correct Method		Incorrect Method: Understates Costs	
NPV of Revenues and Costs at different discount rates	3,113,475	**NPV of Revenues and Cost both at 7%**	4,299,156

FORECASTING

One of the problems of development is the difficulty of accurately forecasting future NOI or property sale proceeds. Who is going occupy the space? What will market rent and TIs be in two years? Five years? What will operating expenses be? What will be the credit of the tenants? When will rental payments begin? What new competitive product will come online in the meantime? How will the economy perform over the next several years? Simply stated, it is easier to analyze and forecast such operating issues for the present than for several years into the future. Even the best analyst has a clearer picture of today, than tomorrow, or next week, or next year, or ten years from now.

In order to assess the leases or expected condo sale proceeds several years into the future, you carefully study the supply and demand for competitive space. In addition, you may execute pre-leases or pre-sales. Such contracts are much riskier than leases or sales for existing properties. For example, a pre-lease merely obliges the tenant to sign a pre-agreed lease if the building receives a certificate of occupancy by a specified date, is built in accordance with the agreed upon design specifications, and has an agreed upon tenant profile. Only if all of these numerous conditions are met is the tenant legally obligated to sign the actual lease. In addition, the pre-lease tenant must still be in business when it is time to start paying rent. For example, during the dotcom boom, many start-ups had Candy Land dreams and signed pre-lease agreements for large blocks of office space. But as the bubble burst, most dissolved, and their pre-leased space went vacant. The surviving few found themselves committed to space at rents well above market. In the face of their dire circumstance, these firms scrutinized their pre-lease agreements to find ways of getting out of their obligations, claiming they did not have to comply with the pre-lease agreement because: the building was completed late, or the design was not exactly as anticipated, or perhaps the developer did not get enough "quality" firms to lease the building. Hence, while pre-leasing and pre-sales can reduce your development risk, it can also lull you into a false sense of security.

Your ability to pre-lease critically depends upon market conditions. For example, if there are an abundance of leases expiring in existing buildings over the next two years, successful pre-leasing is easier. But remember that if a tenant leases in an existing building it does not have to worry about the developer finishing construction on time. In order to attract pre-lease tenants in a weak market, you will need to offer substantial concessions. For example, in addition to cutting rents, you may have to offer the tenant better space in the building, or alter designs to meet the tenant's desires. On the other hand, if the market is tight and space is not readily available, you may receive a premium, as in such a market you help solve the tenant's business problem–the lack of sufficient operating space.

Pre-leasing and pre-sales strategies are less relevant for multifamily properties (excluding condo pre-sales). Retail space, in contrast, is generally pre-leased. Everything else falls somewhere in between.

CONSTRUCTION DELAYS

Assume you are able to find a tenant who is willing to pre-lease. If the property is ready for occupancy on time and meets all of the pre-lease specifications, the tenant executes the lease upon building completion, provided that the tenant is not bankrupt. But if the completion is delayed, even by a few months, the tenant may no longer be obligated to execute the pre-agreed lease. Two years may seem like sufficient time to get the development done. However, many things can happen during development, and most of them are bad. Developers must carefully plan for the foreseeable and perhaps more importantly, unforeseeable delays.

A developer generally works with more than fifteen regulatory bodies to obtain all of the necessary planning and construction approvals. This process is expensive and time consuming, as regulatory bodies on the state, municipal, and Federal levels often have more pressing priorities than your development. In addition, these regulatory bodies often have conflicting missions, opinions, and agendas. A month, week, or even a day delay beyond the time you allotted for a particular regulatory process can snowball into additional delays and costs, perhaps resulting in the loss of a pre-leased tenant. Remember that the time pressures created by pre-leases are your problems, not the regulators', as you were the one who agreed to the pre-lease arrangements.

In addition to numerous regulatory approvals, a developer must also worry about the timing involved with financing the property. In order to help cover construction costs you will almost certainly obtain a construction loan. How long will it take to close this loan? If you have trouble finding suitable construction financing, you risk pre-lease negotiations breaking down, or delaying completion and hence losing a pre-leased tenant.

Assuming that you find a lender that will lend 65% of the development costs, the lender will demand that your equity money go in first. This is because if anything goes wrong during the development, your equity is completely at risk. By requiring the equity to go in first, the lender attempts to align the developer's incentives with their interests. Keep in mind that the equity investors receive all of the upside if the project succeeds. The construction loan covers costs only after all equity is completely drawn.

When thinking about what can go wrong with financing a development, ask questions like: "What if the loan officer in charge of your loan goes on vacation during the week you need to close your loan?"; or "What if the loan officer has a family or medical emergency that renders them unavailable for a month?" You were expecting the loan to close in the next 5 days, but these factors may delay the loan closing. Construction will generally not commence until you have a construction loan in place to assure that checks can be written for the concrete, steel, bricks, contractors, construction workers, and other construction costs. Your time constraints are your problem, not the lender's. A good developer understands and plans for the human aspects of the development process that can destroy their timeline.

Another human aspect of development is the interaction you will have with numerous vendors, including contractors and construction trades. For example, if business is hot for contractors, they may accept more projects than they can service, creating costly delays for your project. On the other hand, in a slow construction environment, contractors and construction workers may purposely delay the construction process in order to prolong their employment. A classic example is discovering that concrete was "accidentally" poured into the plumbing after it has been installed. In order to rectify this "mistake" the construction company will have to replace the fixtures and pipes. This will not only increase your costs, but the delayed completion may cause you to miss pre-lease deadlines.

Another risk is that your contractors may go bankrupt. For example, you have made a down payment on the electrical work, and your electrician files for bankruptcy two weeks into their work. You simply become another unsecured creditor of the electrical contractor hoping (in vain) to re-coup payment. In addition, you must spend time and money finding another electrical contractor on short notice. The result is a cost overrun and damaging delay.

Completion delays are damaging even if you do not have pre-leases, as you cannot collect rent until the building is completed. Hence, the longer it takes you to finish, the longer it takes to realize positive cash flows from the project, plus you will incur additional interest costs and suffer "image" problems ("behind schedule", "in trouble", etc.).

Another risk is that even if you meet every pre-lease requirement, the tenant may go bankrupt. In bankruptcy, the tenant can void the lease, leaving you with vacant space and a negative cash flow project. In fact, absent the pre-lease you may not have developed the building.

OPPORTUNITY

Why take on these, and many other, development risks? Because development, if done in a timely and efficient fashion, can compensate you handsomely for the risk. Development is the attempt to make the final product (a building) more valuable than the ingredients (land, steel, concrete, labor, and other materials). As such, successful development is true value creation.

If the developer can, for example, "**build to** a 10" and "**sell to** an 8," they create a lot of value. What does this mean? Build to an *X* means that projected NOI for the property upon stabilization divided by the expected total development cost equals *X* percent. So to build to a 10 means that your stabilized annual NOI return is 10% of total development cost. Remember that expected stabilized NOI is in the eye of the beholder. Some buildings are considered stabilized only when they reach 97% occupancy, others when they achieve 92% occupancy, and still others when they are at 88% occupancy. Stabilized NOI is contingent upon the market, location, type of building, as well as who is using the term. Most simply, think of a stabilized building as one that has not only completed construction, but has also had sufficient time to achieve economic maturity.

Let's go through the simple mathematics of calculating the developer's expected "build to" return on cost, often referred to as the **going in cap rate**. Figure 8.6 shows that if you have a total projected development cost of $10 million, and expect $1 million stabilized NOI, the "build to" return is 10%.

FIGURE 8.6

Going In Cap Rate		
Return on Cost	=	Projected Stabilized NOI / Projected All in Costs
Build to a 10	=	$1 Million / $10 Million

It is highly unlikely that the total development cost for the building will end up equaling the projected $10 million. Similarly, it is unlikely that actual stabilized NOI will be the projected $1 million. Yet, these are your informed expectations. In the end, the concrete will be more expensive than you thought, the steel cheaper than expected, and rents will be above your expectations. Even for the most experienced and diligent developer, these numbers are merely estimates, not guarantees, of what will happen.

To "sell to an X" means that stabilized NOI divided by your projected sales price upon stabilization is X percent. Note that your projected stabilized NOI is the same as that used in calculating your expected return on cost. The concept of "sell to an 8" is the same as a **going out cap rate of 8**.

FIGURE 8.7

Going Out Cap Rate

$$\text{Sell to an X} = \frac{\text{Projected Stabilized NOI}}{\text{Projected Sale Price}}$$

$$\text{Sell to an 8} = \frac{\$1 \text{ Million}}{\$12.5 \text{ Million}}$$

In our example, if the projected stabilized NOI is $1 million and the "sell to" rate is 8, the expected sale price upon stabilization is $12.5 million. This means you expect a $2.5 million value creation from the development, that is, the difference between the $10 million in projected development costs and the $12.5 million expected sales price. Value creation in development is no different than baking a cake. You combine the ingredients for a cake (sugar, eggs, flower), and hope that you create a cake that is sufficiently more valuable to customers than the ingredients to make it worth your effort. Development is taking a collection of inputs (steel, wood, land, and labor) and creating a building which you hope tenants will find sufficiently useful to generate enough value creation to compensate you for the risks.

The "build to" and "sell to" calculations are critical calculations for a developer. While you will utilize detailed spreadsheets to summarize projected revenues and costs, these "build to" and "sell to" calculations effectively summarize the developer's assessment of value creation potential. These calculations will almost always yield the same results as complex net present value spreadsheet calculations. In fact, if they do not, you should carefully examine your spreadsheets.

The $2.5 million expected value creation on the $10 million in projected costs in our example, means that you expect a gross development profit margin of 25% for the project.

FIGURE 8.8

Gross Development Profit Margin Calculation

Expected development profit margin = (Expected Cap rate on cost /Expected cap rate on sale) – 1

= (Expected Cap rate on cost /Expected cap rate on sale) – 1 = (Expected value at sale/Expected cost) - 1

= (10/8) - 1 = .25 = 25%

The opportunity to achieve a meaningful profit margin is why developers accept the risks of development. Expected gross profit margins for development projects are typically 15-25%. This is significantly higher than the returns on Treasury notes, but so are the risks. Your assessments of risk and opportunity are critical in deciding whether to develop. Who you are, the development experience and expertise you possess, your investment criteria, your comfort with specific types of risks, sources of capital, and how well you can cope with the many problems that will occur during the development process, determine whether you will undertake a development. In fact, these considerations are far more important than the expected returns, as if you lack the ability to resolve the many headaches that arise during development, your pro forma profit will quickly disappear.

Thus far we have not discussed financing structure. This is because it is essential to understand the "business" of real estate before you can contemplate how best to finance it. While leverage can dramatically increase returns on equity, it also substantially increases equity risk. Remember, if a development project is a bad business idea, financing is almost never going to save it. A bad piece of real estate is almost always a bad development deal.

OPTIONS AND DEVELOPMENT

Development is in many ways like an option. When you own or control a parcel of land, its value increases as the likelihood of profitable development increases. For example, a tenant may come to you and ask you to develop a building for them. Or a change in zoning may make your site more valuable as a development. Or the construction of a highway exit ramp near your property may put the development value of your land "in the money". A substantial, and elegant, theoretical literature of option models for real estate development has evolved. The spirit of this literature is that while there is no (or little) cash stream from raw land, future growth and the volatility of future growth creates development value for land. To value this option, this literature uses variations of the Black-Scholes option pricing model. When valuing development land with such models, the value is higher: the greater the growth in the local economy; the longer the hold time period; and, the greater the volatility of local growth.

Unfortunately, these parameters are basically impossible to measure for development parcels. Take growth volatility as an example. You may know that Philadelphia is a market with relatively little growth volatility, while Houston has a great deal of growth and growth volatility. So, other things equal, land in Philadelphia tends to be worth less than land in Houston because there is a chance that a sharp economic upswing will occur in Houston. But how much less for your particular Philadelphia site? You cannot answer this question, because there is no reliable data with which to estimate the volatility facing your property, both because properties are very idiosyncratic, and because return data does not exist for your site. As a result, while development option pricing is a nice intuition to bear in mind, concentrate on understanding the risks and opportunities offered by your property. Your brain is a powerful portable computer, and as you gain experience and information from watching others, reading, thinking, and succeeding or failing on the projects, you will formulate a sophisticated approach to development valuation.

CLOSING THOUGHT

If after weighing the risks and opportunities of development you still want to be a developer, the next questions are: "Where should I start?" and "How should I start?" If you really want to be a developer, perhaps you should not go to Midtown Manhattan to start your career, even though Manhattan is a fun and exciting place. After all, it is already built! A developer is in the business of servicing population, economic, and political growth. Therefore, the best opportunities are where there is sustained growth. This means places like Chester, Virginia, or Victorville, California, or Albuquerque, New Mexico. These places may not be the sexiest, but they are where the greatest development opportunities are located. Just as if you want to be a dairy farmer, it is unlikely that you will find great opportunities in Manhattan, so too with development.

Assuming you pick an appropriate location to launch your development career, how do you start your career? In order to succeed in developing new products it is essential that you understand the market's product offerings. If you wanted to create a new beer, you would taste a lot of beer. You would also study brewing and fermentation processes, and how they have changed over time. You would study the labeling, advertising, and marketing strategies of beers. That is, you would learn the beer business from the ground up. In the same way, if you want to develop real estate, get close to the tenants and the operation of properties in order to understand what works, why, and what product niches are underserved. Understand that any idiot can develop a "unique" product. For example, develop a structure without doors or windows! A successful developer knows what works and generally makes minor improvements on successful products. Rarely do they create a "unique" product. To be a successful developer, copy what works and strive to do it cheaper, faster, and better.

Perhaps the most common question I hear is some variation of, "Can't I start my career in investment banking, so I can enjoy Manhattan and make those big Wall Street bucks?" The short answer is that working at a prestigious investment banking firm is a great place to learn finance, but probably not be the best place to become a developer. Imagine that you want to someday be the head coach of the Philadelphia Eagles. Would you start your career in the entertainment group at Morgan Stanley? Very doubtful. You would probably start as an assistant coach for a high school or college team, and work your way up. Similarly, if you someday want to be a great developer, work with a firm that specializes in the ownership, operation, or creation of property. Many great financiers, but very few great developers, began their careers at investment banks. If you want to become a developer, go to a good local, regional, or national real estate firm and start learning the business from the ground up one day at a time.

Chapter 9
Development Feasibility Analysis

"In the battle between fear and greed, greed wins about 80% of the time".
-Dr. Peter Linneman

DEVELOPMENT FEASIBILITY ASSESSMENT

Now that you better understand the risks and opportunities present in development, you can analyze specific developments. As with existing properties, a spreadsheet is merely a helpful tool to organize information. Remember that numbers are just informed guesses. As such, your spreadsheet serves as a template to challenge your beliefs, and against which to assess the risks and opportunities. Before you begin the arduous task of modeling the detailed cash flows for a development project, you should always perform a simple financial feasibility analysis. If the development does not work based upon this simple analysis, I promise you that it will not work any better after hours, days, and weeks of arduously modeling rows and columns. If the simple analysis suggests it could work, then create a detailed spreadsheet, and begin your in depth market analysis.

SIMPLE CALCULATIONS

Assume that as a developer of office buildings in downtown Phoenix, you have decided that you need to build to a 10 (i.e., a 10% expected stabilized NOI return on expected total costs) in order to undertake the Muk Office Plaza development project summarized in Figure 9.1. This reflects your belief that comparable existing stabilized properties are selling at 8-8.5 cap rates, and you feel a 15-20% development profit margin is required to offset the risks of development. Take a moment to study Muk Office Plaza, paying special attention to the space **loss factor**. You only receive rent on leasable space, which depends upon the building's design. Space used for elevators, lobby, mechanicals, and stairwells does not generate income because it cannot be leased. The loss factor, that is, how much of gross square footage is unleasable, also depends upon your leasing strategy. For instance, if you decide to split a floor in the office building between six tenants rather than rent the entire floor to a single tenant, the loss factor rises as you must provide hallway access for the tenants. With one tenant, common area hallway space is reduced and you can collect rent on more of the space.

FIGURE 9.1: DEVELOPMENT EXPECTED COST SUMMARY

Muk Office Plaza	
Land	$30 per gross foot
Hard Costs	$90 per gross foot
Soft Costs	$30 per gross foot
Total Cost Gross	$150 per gross foot
Rent	$30 per leaseable foot
Operating Cost	$10 per gross foot
Occupancy	95% of leaseable footage
Loss Factor	30% of gross footage

Based upon your knowledge of the market, you anticipate that total development costs will be about $150 per gross square foot of the building. Included in this figure are land, hard costs and soft costs. Thus, in order to generate at least the necessary 10% return on total development costs, the property must generate an expected stabilized NOI of $15 per gross square foot.

FIGURE 9.2: BUILD TO CALCULATION

Build to Calculation
Build to 10% = Expected Stabilized NOI / Expected Total Costs = $15 / $150

What NOI can you expect from the property? The key top line component of NOI is expected rental income, which is primarily determined by market conditions. Unless this is an enormous project, you will probably not significantly impact market rent. But remember that your building adds to market supply, and will place some downward pressure on market rents. Assume that based on your knowledge of the local market, you determine the expected rent is $30 per leasable square foot. However, you do not expect to receive $30 per square foot on every leasable foot due to stabilized vacancy. As a result, you must adjust the rent per leasable square foot to reflect vacant space. Assuming a 95% occupancy upon stabilization, you estimate rental income of $28.50 per leasable square foot (95% of $30). Ancillary income (not shown in this calculation) derived from things like parking, video games, and vending machines must also be included if it is expected to be a major source of revenue. Remember, the higher your stabilized vacancy, the fewer people in the building to park their cars, use vending machines, etc.

FIGURE 9.3: RENT PER LEASABLE FOOT CALCULATION

Rent on Leasable Space
Rent per Leasable Foot = Expected Market Rent * % Occupancy + Rent Received on Vacant Space * % Vacant Space
Rent on occupied leasable space = 30 * .95 + 0 * .05 = $28.50 per occupied foot

Based upon your knowledge of local operating costs (utilities, real estate taxes, insurance), you estimate annual operating costs net of tenant recoveries of approximately $10 per square foot. You will have to pay roughly $10 per square foot even if the space is vacant as you must pay real estate taxes, insurance, snow removal, and other costs regardless of whether or not you are fully occupied. For consistency in calculating NOI per square foot, you must convert rents per leasable foot (net of stabilized vacancy) to rent per gross foot. Alternatively, you could convert operating and construction costs to cost per leasable foot. If only 70% of the property is leasable, a $28.50 rent per leasable foot is equivalent to $19.95 rent per gross foot.

FIGURE 9.4: CONVERTING LEASABLE RENT TO GROSS RENT

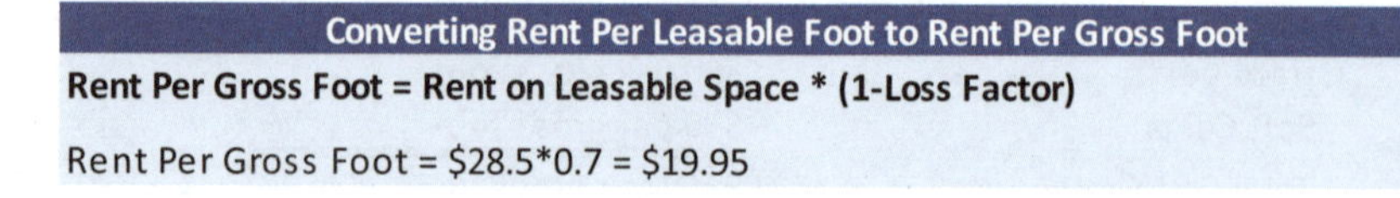

Converting Rent Per Leasable Foot to Rent Per Gross Foot
Rent Per Gross Foot = Rent on Leasable Space * (1-Loss Factor)
Rent Per Gross Foot = $28.5*0.7 = $19.95

With expected rental income of $19.95 per gross square foot, and expected operating costs net of recoveries of $10 per gross square foot, you expect stabilized NOI per gross square foot of $9.95. This implies an expected return on total development costs (the build to return) of 6.6%, i.e., $9.95/$150.

FIGURE 9.5: STABILIZED NOI (PER GROSS FOOT)

Stabilized NOI Calculation (Per Gross Foot)
Stabilized NOI = Rental Revenues – Operating Costs
Stabilized NOI = $19.95-$10 = $9.95

FIGURE 9.6: RETURN ON TOTAL DEVELOPMENT COST

Expected Return on Total Development Cost
Expected Stabilized NOI / Expected Total Costs = $9.95 / $150 = 6.63% < 10%

So does this project pass an initial examination? Not if you require a 10% stabilized NOI return on cost to compensate for taking on development risks. Based on this simple analysis, the project does not offer enough potential return to make it worth the risk. If you undertake the project, you expect an unacceptable compensation for the development risks. Stated bluntly, why would you take on all of the risks of development, when you can buy comparable existing stabilized buildings for an 8-8.5 cap? By the way, note that this analysis took you less time than you need to warm up your PC for a full spreadsheet analysis.

SOLVE BACKWARDS FOR REPLACEMENT RENT

How high does the market rent have to be for the Muk Office Plaza to be potentially viable? You can solve backwards for this replacement rent.

Since stabilized NOI must equal $15 per gross foot for you to expect to receive a 10% return on total costs of $150 per gross foot, market rents per gross foot must rise to $25 if expected operating costs are $10 per gross foot.

FIGURE 9.7

Build to Calculation
Replacement Rent per Gross Foot= (Build To Return * Expected Total Cost) + Expected Operating Costs
Replacement Rent per Gross Foot = (10%)*($150) + $10 = $15 + $10 = $25

How does required gross rent per square foot translate into rent per leasable foot (which is how market rents are generally quoted)?

FIGURE 9.8

Replacment Rent per Leasable Foot
Rent per Leasable Foot = Replacement Rent per Gross * (1/(1-Loss Factor))*(1/(1-Vacancy))
Rent per Leasable Foot = $25 * (1/0.7) * (1/0.95) = $37.59

Since 30% of the building is unleasable, and 5% of the leasable space will be vacant, rent per leasable foot must be $37.59 for the expected return on costs to be 10%.

Since the rent per leasable foot must be at least $37.59 for the project to generate your required returns, market rents must rise by roughly 25% before replacement rent is achieved. If rents rise 3% per annum, this will take 7.6 years to achieve. Of course, since operating costs, rent, construction costs, and other factors change daily, while $37.59 per leasable foot may be sufficient to justify development today, it may not be adequate tomorrow. As a result, developers regularly re-evaluate projects to determine their feasibility.

This simple feasibility analysis is fast, accurate, and with a little practice can be done in your head. If your spreadsheets produce significantly different results from this analysis, carefully check the rows and columns on your spreadsheet, as they are wrong. This analysis saves you a lot of time and trouble performing the detailed analysis only to find that you cannot remotely achieve your desired profitability given current market conditions.

A COMMON MISTAKE

Avoid simply extrapolating rental trends. Developers frequently lose sight of the fact that rent is driven by supply and demand fundamentals rather than trend lines. Assume that you passed on our example development in Year 2 because you felt that the $30 market rent was too low. You continue to monitor rents over the next several years, and the pattern shown in Figure 9.9 evolves.

FIGURE 9.9: INCORRECT RENTAL PROJECTIONS

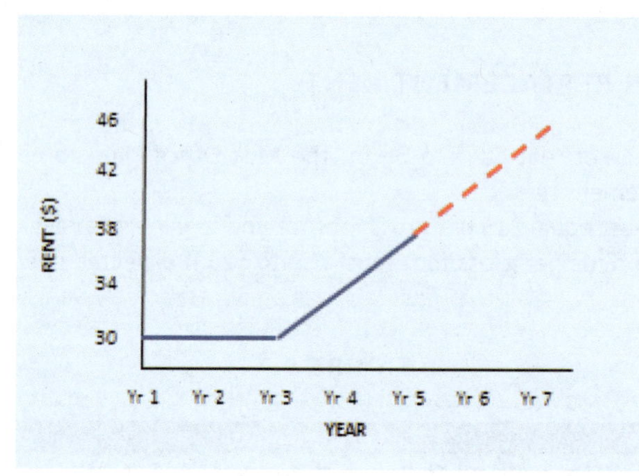

Specifically, after flat rents of $30 per leasable foot in Years 1 through 3, as the economy picked up, rents rose to $34 in Year 4 and to $38 in Year 5. While rents in Year 4 remained too low to justify development, by early 2005 rents had risen above replacement rent.

Looking at this rental trend (in early Year 5) you might infer that since over the past two years market rent increased by $8 per square foot, or 26.7%, while inflation over that same time period was only about 2-3% per year, this must be a great market with great rental growth potential, and project continued rental growth through Year 7, as indicated by the dotted line in Figure 9.9. Forecasting market rent of $42 per square foot in Year 6 and $46 per square foot in Year 7, you decide if you start development now (in early Year 5), when completed in Year 7 you will receive rent of roughly $46 per leasable foot. This forecasted rent is well in excess of the $37.59 per leasable foot replacement rent. Deciding it is time to build, you note that if necessary you can pay more than the $30 per gross foot for the land you originally assumed and still generate your 10% target return.

Does this analysis make sense? Of course not. Once rents rise above replacement rent, developers will do what they do best: Develop! Just as you see development opportunity, so too will other developers. If it makes sense for you to build, it will make sense for others as well. Thus, as demand growth pushes rents above replacement rent, supply will increase with a lag. As this new space comes online, rents will tend to revert to replacement rent, rather than continue the upward trend. To believe that rents will continue to rise well beyond replacement rent ignores the basics of supply and demand. In fact, if enough developers use this faulty analysis to justify development, rents will fall below replacement rent, as excessive development will occur. Figure 9.10 depicts realistic rental growth patterns. Note, that rental growth should taper off as rents approach replacement rent. The upper line reflects an overshot of rents as supply lags demand, while the lower path reflects a pattern of an overshoot of rents followed by a fall due to excessive development.

FIGURE 9.10

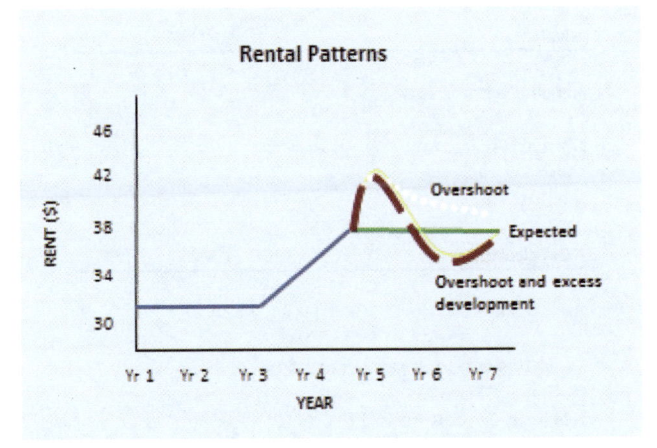

Although it may seem an obvious error in a classroom, this type of rental trend analysis is common practice. Would a rational person accept this trend analysis? No. But neither would a rational person drink to excess and sleep with their head on the toilet. Yet some of you do it! In the morning you say that you will never do it again, yet next weekend some of you do it yet again. In the same way, no matter how obvious it may appear, if you are overly anxious to develop, you will frequently neglect market dynamics. It happens time and time again.

LAND COST

Where analytic sloppiness costs you, as a developer, is in the price you pay to purchase the development site. Based on the faulty trend analysis you believe you will receive $46 per square foot for your office space when completed in Year 7. In your haste to take advantage of this "great opportunity," you may overpay for land. Recall that your original analysis indicated that you would pay about $30 per gross foot of the building for the land. To assure that you are not outbid for the "can't miss" development site, you submit a higher bid for the land, raising your development costs. When market rents turn out to be $38, rather than $46 per leasable foot, your realized return falls below your 10% return on cost threshold.

You must always carefully calculate what you can afford to pay for a development site as a function of the market environment and your required expected return. Just as with replacement rent, you can determine the maximum amount you are able to pay for the development site by making land cost the unknown variable and solving for the maximum you can pay and still receive your targeted 10% return on total development costs. Using the Muk Office Plaza example, if market rent is $38 per leasable foot, and all else is as previously described (Figure 9.1), the expected rent per gross foot is $25.27 [($38*0.7)*(0.95)]. At $10 per gross foot operating cost, expected NOI per gross foot is $15.27 ($25.27-$10). Given soft costs of $30 per gross foot, and hard costs of roughly $90 per gross foot, and your 10% required return on total costs, total cost can be as high as $152.70 per gross foot. Thus, you can pay up to $32.70 per gross building foot for the development site. Note that to the extent you borrow to pay the extra $2.70 per gross foot for the land, your interest costs, hence your soft costs will be very modestly higher. Specifically, if you borrow 65% of the total costs at a 6% interest rate, your soft costs will be $0.11 ($2.70*0.65*0.06) per gross foot higher than your original $30 per gross foot soft cost estimates.

FIGURE 9.11

Solving for Maximum Land Price
Given
Required Return: 10%
Leaseable space: 70%
Vacancy: 5%
NOI Calculation
Rent per gross foot: ($38*0.7)*(1-.05) = **$25.27**
Operating costs per gross foot = **$10**
NOI = $25.27 - $10 = **$15.27**
Costs
Soft costs per gross foot = **$30**
Hard costs per gross foot = **$90**
Land costs = **X**
10% = $15.27/($30+$90+$X)
(10%)($120+$X) = $15.27
$12+($X/10) = $15.27
($X/10) = $3.27
Land Cost = $X = $32.70

If the FAR is 1, the maximum land price of $32.70 per gross foot, means you can pay $1,424,412 per acre. If FAR is 2 you can pay up to $2,848,824 as you can build twice as much footage, and if FAR is 0.5 you can only afford to pay up to $712,206.

FIGURE 9.12

FAR and Land Costs			
Land Cost Per Gross Foot of Building	$32.70	$32.70	$32.70
FAR	1	0.5	2
Gross Square Footage	43,560	21,780	87,120
Price Able to Pay (Land Cost * SF)	$1,424,412	$712,206	$2,848,824

Regardless of the landowner's asking price or competing bids, $32.70 per gross building foot is the most you should be willing to pay for the site in this example. This simple backwards arithmetic helps avoid the mistake of overpaying for land.

Do the calculations above mean that land should, or will, be sold for $32.70 per gross foot? That's not your decision. It is up to the landowner. But if you cannot buy the land for less than $32.70 per gross foot, don't do the deal! If you pay more, you are punishing yourself. And never forget that the other bidders for the land may be idiots.

AN EXAMPLE: ANOOP COURT

Let's consider the development budget for a 258 unit multifamily development project, Anoop Court. You can create similar pro formas using software like Argus. These projections can be made quarterly, monthly, or even daily depending on your information needs.

FIGURE 9.13: ANOOP COURT BUDGETED TOTAL COSTS

	Anoop Court	
	Total	Per Unit
Total Costs	$30,000,000	$116,279

The budgeted total cost for the project is $30,000,000 or $116,279 per unit. If comparable units in the market are selling for $95,000, does it make sense to build? Of course not, as building would destroy value. If you built in this scenario, the cake would be worth less than the cost of the ingredients. You would only build if after careful study you felt that the units were worth at least 15-20% above your cost.

INTERIM INCOME

Not all parts of the development process are necessarily cash outflows, as it is possible to have income during the interim stages of construction. For example, construction sites can lease billboards to generate revenues, or have a surface parking lot that generates some income. In our example, Anoop Court generates no interim income.

FIGURE 9.14: ANOOP COURT SOURCES AND USES OF FUNDS SHEET

Anoop Court		
Sources		
	Total	**Per Unit**
Construction Mortgage	$ 23,513,000	$ 91,136
Interim Income	$ -	$ -
Equity	$ 6,487,000	$ 25,143
Total Sources	$ 30,000,000	$ 116,279
Uses		
Land	$ 2,326,923	$ 9,019
Hard Costs		
Rezoning Costs	$ 150,000	$ 581
Construction	$ 21,500,000	$ 83,333
Arch/Engineering/Tap Fees	$ 1,850,000	$ 7,171
		$ -
Subtotal	$ 23,500,000	$ 91,085
Soft Costs		
Owner Allowances	$ 150,000	$ 581
Construction Loan Fee	$ 176,348	$ 684
Permanent Conversion Fee	$ -	$ -
Lending Inspection	$ 50,000	$ 194
Transfer/Recordation	$ 259,457	$ 1,006
Capitalized Real Estate Taxes	$ 200,000	$ 775
Capitalized Insurance	$ 23,420	$ 91
Capitalized Marketing	$ 200,000	$ 775
Furniture	$ 350,000	$ 1,357
Borrower Legal	$ 50,000	$ 194
Lender Legal	$ 50,000	$ 194
Development Overhead	$ 750,000	$ 2,907
Contingency	$ 800,000	$ 3,101
Subtotal	$ 3,059,225	$ 11,857
Construction Interest	$ 1,113,852	$ 4,317
Total Uses	$ 30,000,000	$ 116,279

HARD COSTS

FIGURE 9.15: ANOOP COURT HARD COSTS

Anoop Court		
	Total	Per Unit
Hard Costs		
Rezoning Costs	$ 150,000	$ 581
Construction	$ 21,500,000	$ 83,333
Arch/Engineering/Tap Fees	$ 1,850,000	$ 7,171

Hard costs include items such as rezoning costs, construction, and architectural fees. These are costs related to the material and labor costs of constructing a building. Rezoning costs are incurred if you want the property to be used in a manner that does not conform with current zoning. Such rezoning not only raises the cost of development, but also raises the risk. This is because it extends the approval process and there is always a chance that your rezoning request will be denied. You may sometimes see these costs listed as soft costs, demonstrating that the exact classification of costs is less critical than being certain to account for all costs.

While hard costs are impacted by the market prices of drywall, steel, and labor, your costs are also the outcome of value engineering and your project oversight. Too often developers incorporate costly features for which tenants are unwilling to pay. Such developments regularly win design awards as their developers go bankrupt.

How do you estimate hard costs? By going out and seeing what has been built, what succeeded, what mistakes were made, who are the high quality but low cost contractors and vendors, etc. If you are developing a 20,000 foot building, find out how much similar buildings have cost to construct and study how you can build it cheaper yet better. Generally, you will engage a specialist to estimate these costs. But the better you understand the property type and local market, the more accurate and lower will be your development hard costs.

SOFT COSTS

Soft costs are indirect development costs. There are many categories of indirect costs, including development fees, transfer and recording fees, and a contingency reserve. The contingency reserve is basically, "I don't know what unexpected event is going to happen, or when, but I had better set something aside, because experience says that I had better expect the unexpected". You never know what will go wrong with your development, but something surely will. More complicated developments will generally require larger contingency reserves. Similarly, redevelopments of older properties generally require larger contingency reserves than new developments, as you never know what lurks behind those walls.

When estimating costs you need to carefully assess each cost category. This is a tedious, yet essential task for even small developments, much less a $30,000,000 development.

FIGURE 9.16: ANOOP COURT SOFT COSTS

Anoop Court	Total	Per Unit
Soft Costs		
Owner Allowances	$ 150,000	$ 581
Construction Loan Fee	$ 176,348	$ 684
Permanent Conversion Fee	$ -	$ -
Lending Inspection	$ 50,000	$ 194
Transfer/Recordation	$ 259,457	$ 1,006
Real Estate Taxes	$ 200,000	$ 775
Insurance	$ 23,420	$ 91
Marketing	$ 200,000	$ 775
Furniture	$ 350,000	$ 1,357
Borrower Legal	$ 50,000	$ 194
Lender Legal	$ 50,000	$ 194
Development Fee	$ 750,000	$ 2,907
Contingency	$ 800,000	$ 3,101
Total	**$ 3,059,225**	**$ 11,857**

TIMING

Your lenders will require you to inject your equity before drawing upon your loan. Your loan officer will ask the following questions:

- "What is the money for?"
- "How much equity is ahead of my loan?"
- "How large a loan do you want?"
- "When exactly do you need the money?"
- "When and how do I get paid back?"

The "when do you need the money" and "when am I going to get repaid" are particularly key questions.

Capital sources need to know precisely when you expect to incur the development costs in order to track the timing of your loan. You do not draw on the loan before you need the money because as soon as you take the money, the interest clock starts ticking. If you have a cash shortage during development, things can get very messy. Construction can grind to a halt as you cannot pay your bills, you default on your loan, and the entire project may be dead.

The costs during a development project are not the same every week. Typically the run rate, that is, how much is being spent daily (or weekly, or monthly) is low in the beginning, rising as the construction gets in full swing, before stabilizing upon completion at your interest carry cost. Figure 9.17 is a graphical portrayal of the costs.

FIGURE 9.17: DEVELOPMENT COST DAILY RUN RATE

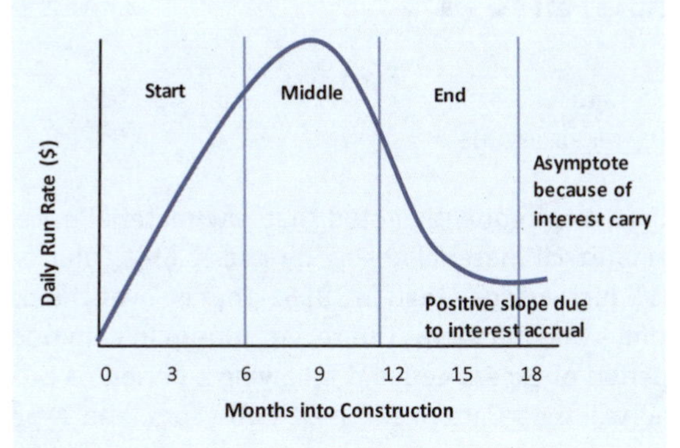

DESIGN

Property design is an important aspect that affects both your costs and revenues. How do you decide what floorplans to use? Should you offer one or two bedroom units? A mix of both? Big kitchens or big bathrooms? A large lobby or a small one? How many elevators are needed? Where are they located? What types and sizes of windows? Should the property include a pool? What type of HVAC system? Plus a million more such questions. The answers are not found in a book or on a magical website. And while architects can design what you need, they will rarely know what you need. So how do you discover the right design? Get in your car (or walk) and visit competitive properties in the area. See what works and why. Constantly visit apartment complexes and tell the leasing agent, "I am interested in a one-bedroom unit. May I see them? What is the rent? What are their best selling features?" Speak with potential tenants and see what they want, and are willing to pay for. This will give you an idea of what is selling and what is not. Looking at a blue print or photos of a kitchen is different from seeing it. In short, immerse yourself in the product.

Design affects your loss factor, that is, how much space is unleasable. How efficiently you create space substantially impacts your costs and income. Sometimes design will affect how many rooms you build. Suppose you have 600 feet of "extra space" after creating the perfect design plan. Perhaps you can turn that space into a studio unit, or make a superior 2 bedroom unit. Be creative and explore alternative solutions in your head and on paper before committing to construction. It is cheap to throw away paper, but very expensive to rectify design flaws once they are built.

CLOSING THOUGHT

What is the most important aspect of a development to analyze? Development cost? Interest rates? The return on cost? Market rent? Your detailed pro forma? The dynamics of the local economy? NPV? IRR? The answer is everything and a lot more. When real money is at stake, you need to research and analyze the factors influencing the risks and opportunities. Asking which "one" to focus on is like asking which characteristic to use in drafting a basketball player. Is it a person's height, arm span, speed, jumping ability, strength, endurance, shooting ability, motivation? To only focus on any one such characteristic would be ludicrous. It is the entire package of skills (and luck) that ultimately determines success on the court. Real estate development is no different. If the project appears to yield negative or minimal returns, walk away. But once a deal meets this most basic test, everything matters.

Each property type, geographic region, and street location offers specific challenges. What makes a great developer is avoiding properties for which you have no viable design solution, and more efficiently delivering better designed space than your competitors. That is, just like any other business, if you give the customer a product they want, faster, cheaper, and better than the competition, you will generally succeed.

Chapter 9 Supplement A

Construction Costs

Dr. Peter Linneman – The Linneman Letter – Fall 2006

In the context of inflation, it is frequently noted that raw material prices have soared over the last five years, with spot prices for raw industrial materials rising by nearly 65%. But what is not reported is that raw material prices are only about 11% higher today than in 1995. That is, over the past 11 years, raw material prices have risen by far less than economy-wide inflation. The recent run-up in commodity prices is another cyclical run in materials prices, reflecting a period of excess demand following a period of excess supply. We believe that the current period of excess demand will moderate in the next two years, and expect falling commodity prices for about five years thereafter.

FIGURE 9A.1

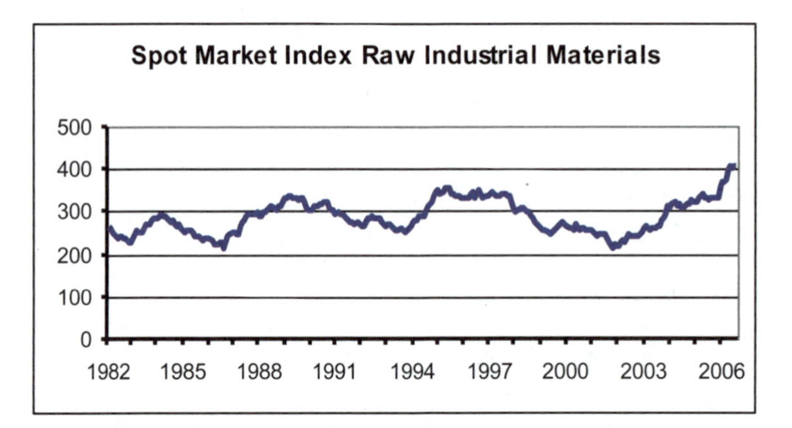

Commercial real estate valuations in the U.S. have been increasing for the past several years. We have argued that the phenomenon is a result of the integration of the real estate sector into the broader capital markets. Real estate is no longer a backwater, "mom and pop" asset class, but rather a full-fledged investment alternative in the eyes of the global investment community. We believe that current commercial real estate pricing is basically correct, while residential valuations will experience some short-term softness, but will not fall significantly.

Yet the talking heads continue to herald the imminent collapse of real estate. Not only do these analysts ignore supply and demand, as well as investment theory, but they also ignore replacement cost. And ultimately, the valuation of real estate will track replacement cost.

To that end, we evaluate the cost of several major inputs into real estate construction: lumber, steel, gypsum, concrete, and labor. When the increase in replacement cost is considered, the recent appreciation of real estate values is justified.

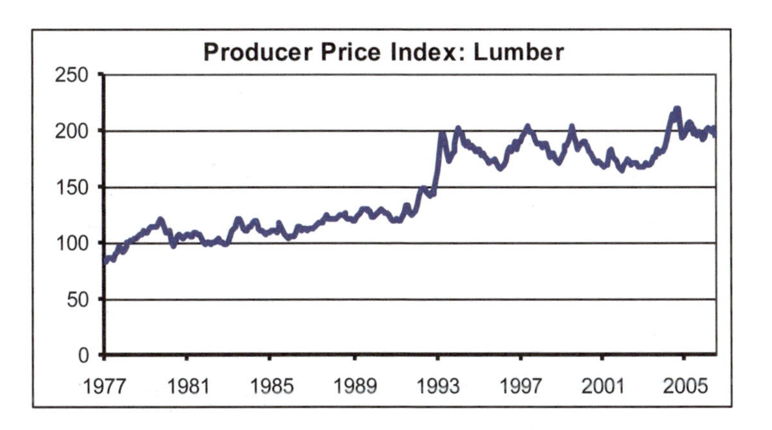

Lumber prices have increased on average by 1.5% per annum since 1995, and 4.2% per annum since 2001. This growth has occurred with significant volatility, with lumber prices declining by 17% between 1999 and 2003, and rising by 17% over the past four years.

FIGURE 9A.3

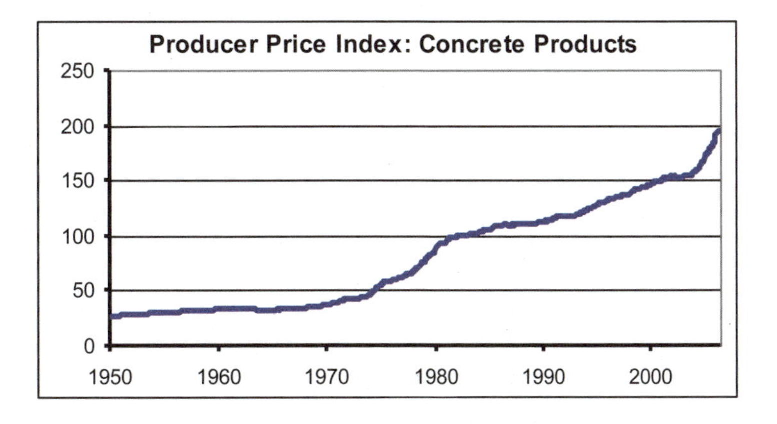

Concrete products have increased by an average of 3.4% per annum since 1995, and 4.6% per annum since 2001. On a cumulative basis, concrete products have increased in price by 40% since 1995, with half of that growth (20%) occurring since 2001.

FIGURE 9A.4

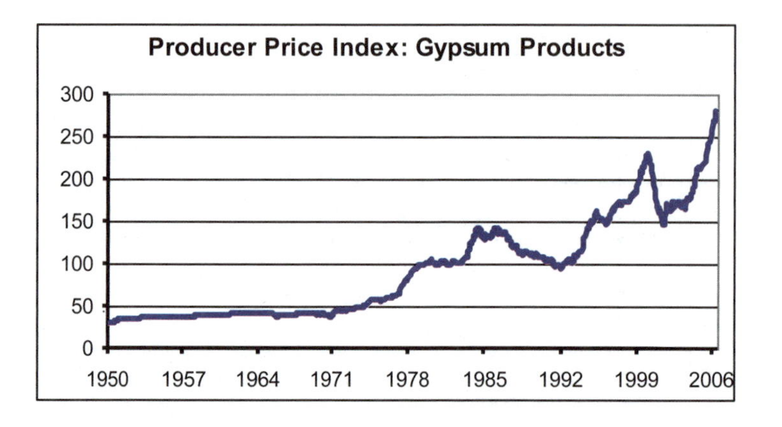

Gypsum prices have increased by 5.3% per annum since 1995, and by more than 10.3% annually since 2001. As a result, gypsum products (including plaster and drywall) have increased by over 52% since 2001. However, note that gypsum prices have often fallen sharply and remain depressed for extended periods. For example, between 1986 and 1992, the price of gypsum dropped by 32%, or 6.2% per annum.

FIGURE 9A.5

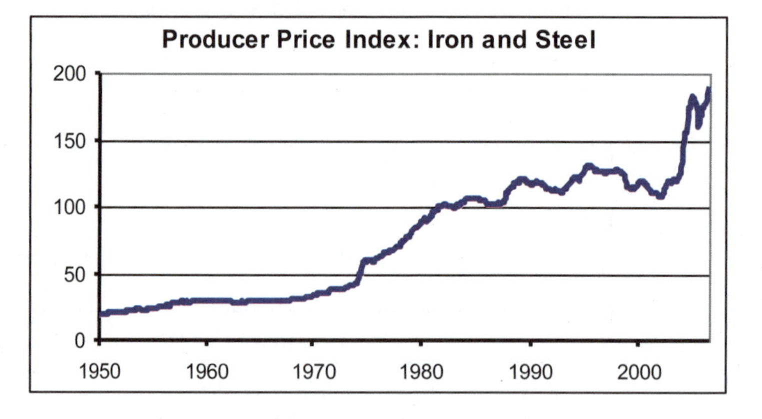

Steel prices have increased over 12.3% annually since 2001, yielding a cumulative growth rate of over 62% since 2001. But like lumber and gypsum prices, steel prices have a history of occasional sharp and prolonged price declines. For example, from 1995 to 2002, steel prices declined by 17.7%. As a result, steel prices have only increased by 37.2% over the last 10 years, or an average of just 3.2% per annum, versus an overall (CPI) inflation rate of 2.6% per annum over this 10-year period.

FIGURE 9A.6

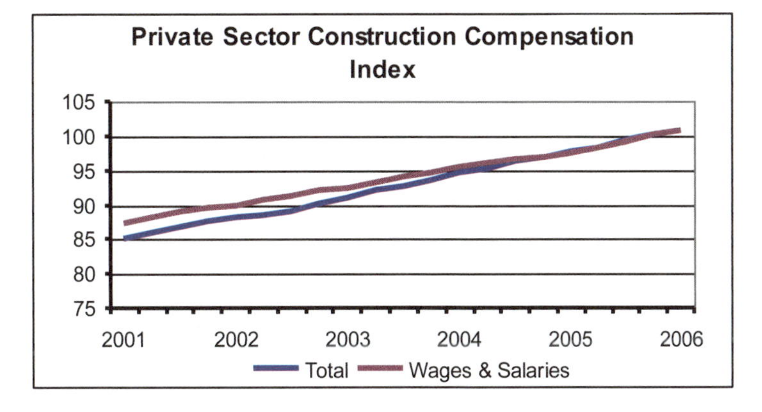

FIGURE 9A.7

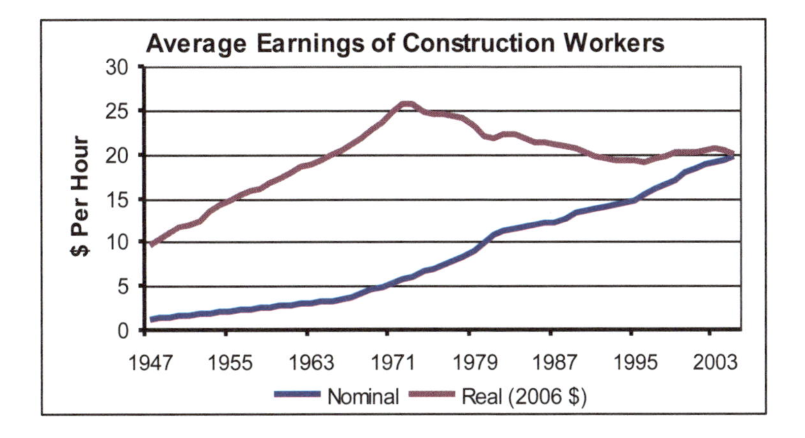

FIGURE 9A.8

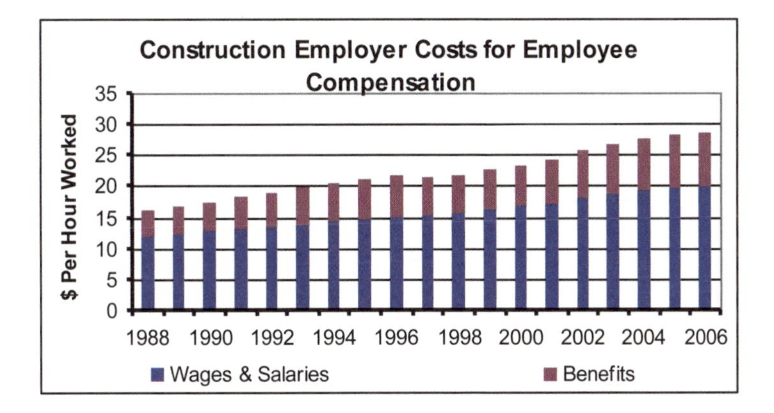

FIGURE 9A.9

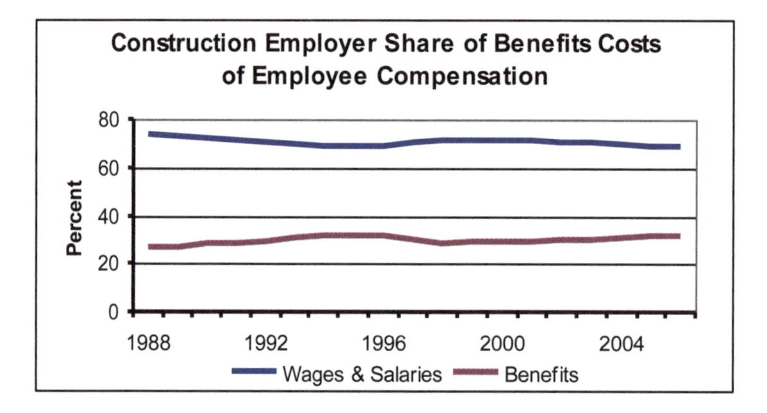

FIGURE 9A.10

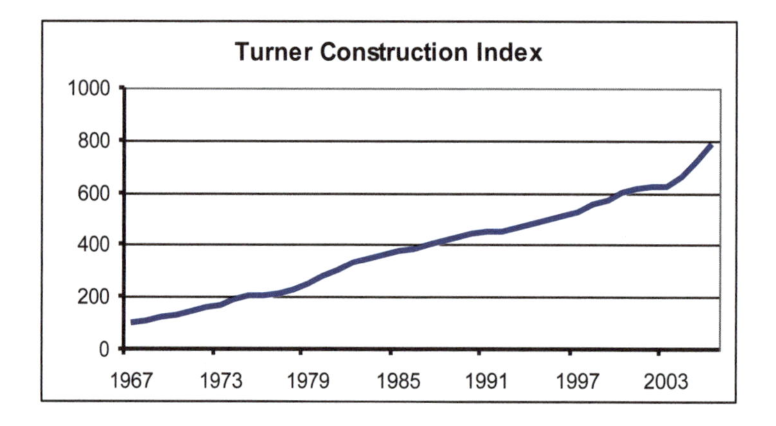

FIGURE 9A.11

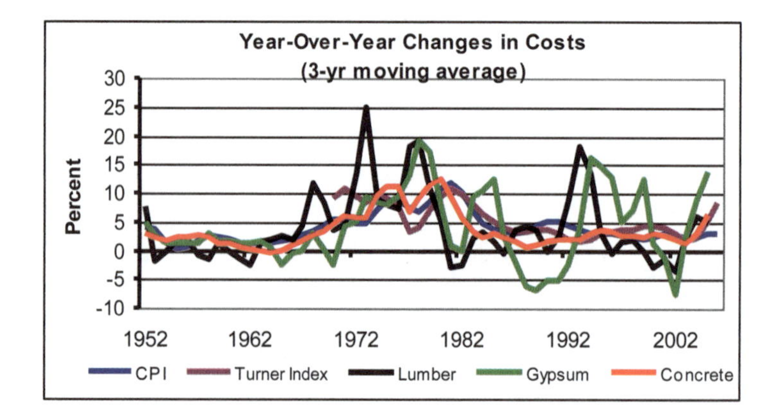

Total compensation paid to the construction workforce increased by 4.1% per annum since 2001, yielding a cumulative growth rate of 17.5%. Since 1995, compensation expense has grown by 34.5%, or an average annual increase of approximately 3%. Benefits growth far exceeded wage growth since 2001, with benefits accounting for an ever increasing share of total employee compensation.

The Turner Construction Index for building costs tracks the overall cost of construction on a national basis, taking into account major construction cost categories like material, labor and productivity. Year-to-date through June 2006, the Turner Index had a cumulative increase of 28% and 60% since 2001 and 1995, respectively. These growth rates include a 9.8% increase over the last year.

We also created a construction cost index based on a hypothetical building consisting of lumber (5%), concrete (5%), gypsum (10%), steel (10%), labor (50%), and land (20%). We assume that land value increases by core CPI. Our results indicate that this Linneman Construction Cost Index increased at an average annual rate of 7.3%, and a cumulative rate of 23.6%, from 2002 through year-end 2005.

FIGURE 9A.12

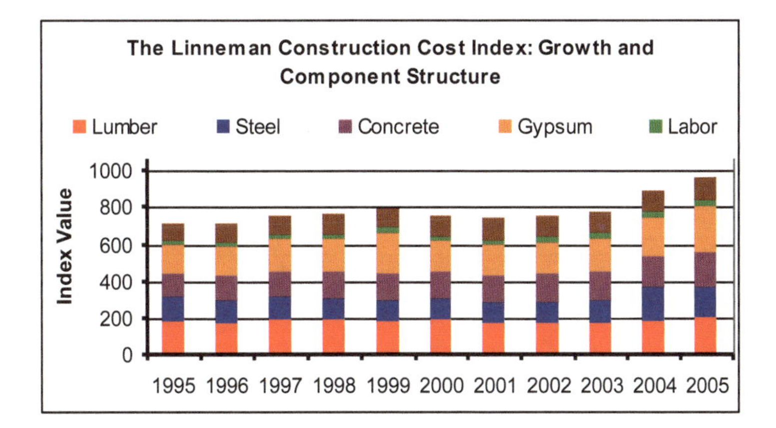

Interestingly, viewed over the long term, since 1988, both the Turner and Linneman Construction Cost indices have risen almost exactly in line with inflation. Thus, although construction costs have extended periods where they lag or outrun economy-wide inflation, over time these costs track general inflation. We are experiencing a period where construction cost increases exceed economy-wide inflation, which comes after an extended period where they lagged behind inflation.

Construction costs today must be viewed from the perspective of history, as construction component prices are volatile, both on the upside and the downside. This latter fact is all too often forgotten. As demand grows more quickly than expected, as has recently been the case in India and China, steep component price increases occur. As suppliers attempt to capitalize on the price increases by expanding capacity, overcapacity results and component prices drop. The recent increases in construction costs are not anomalies, but rather another cycle. In all, while nominal construction costs have risen significantly over the last 20 years, according to both the Linneman and the Turner Construction Cost Indices, real construction costs, though volatile, have not experienced real increases.

FIGURE 9A.13

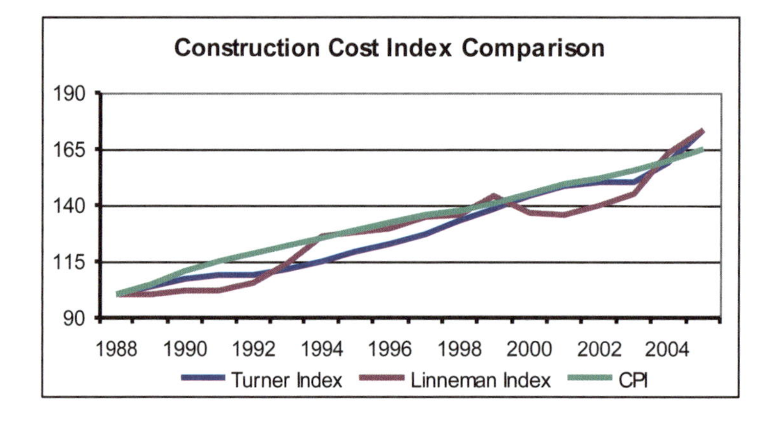

FIGURE 9A.14

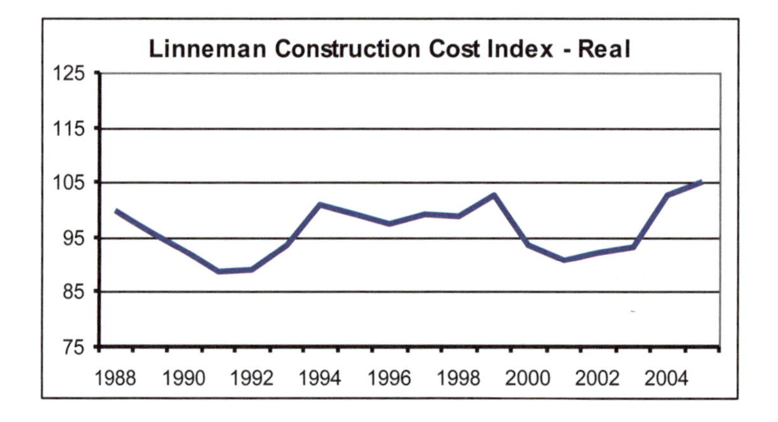

FIGURE 9A.15

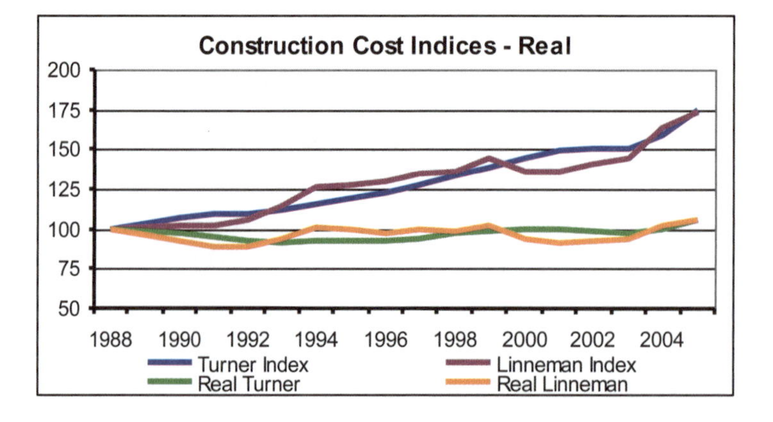

Armed with this perspective on construction costs, we can evaluate how changes in construction costs reinforce the recent appreciation in real estate values. Since 1990, the MIT Real Estate Price Index has risen by a cumulative 53%. Over the same time frame, the Linneman Construction Cost Index rose by 70% – 17 percentage points more than is needed to sustain current real estate prices. That is, construction costs have risen by more than values, suggesting that a valuation cushion exists even if construction costs fall by 17%.

FIGURE 9A.16

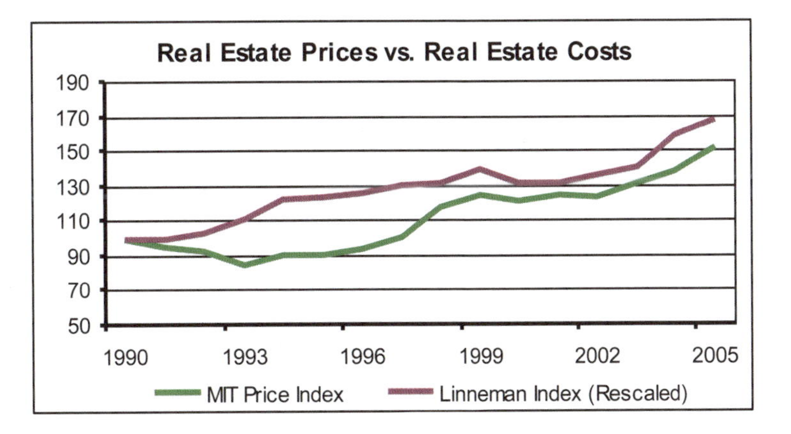

In short, real estate is subject to the economic principles of supply and demand. While in the short run, supply and demand imbalances cause significant price volatility, over the long run, inflationary construction cost increases underpin real estate prices.

Chapter 9 Supplement B

Construction Costs

Dr. Peter Linneman – The Linneman Letter – Summer 2010

After a brief rise to 31.7 million square feet of commercial and industrial contracts awarded in December 2009, the two-year downward trend resumed, standing at 22.8 million square feet in March 2010. We expect construction levels to remain low through 2011, due to the lag in demand for space after the overall economy picks up momentum, high vacancy rates, and an absence of construction debt. Year-over-year through April 2010, commercial construction trends began to stabilize, and surprisingly, showed modest month-to-month increases in the industrial and hotel sectors. In real dollars, year-over-year construction growth was down across the board: -38% ($16.7 billion) in the office sector; -34% ($32.9 billion) in the industrial sector; -58% ($21 billion) in the multifamily sector; -43% ($19.3 billion) in retail; and -61% ($18.8 billion) in lodging.

FIGURE 9B.1

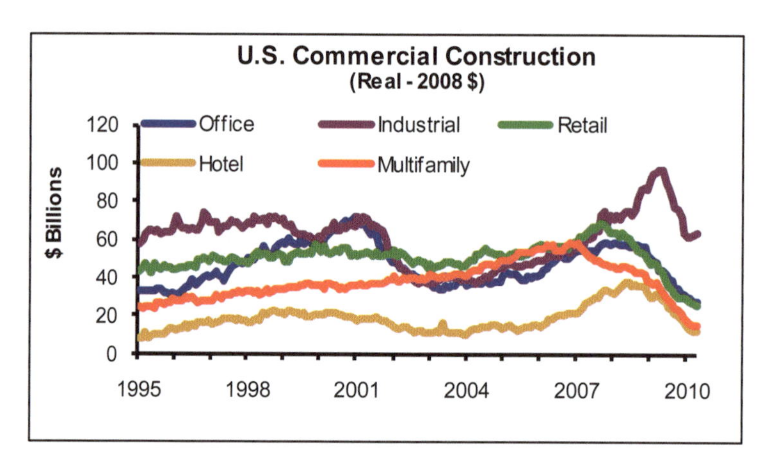

FIGURE 9B.2

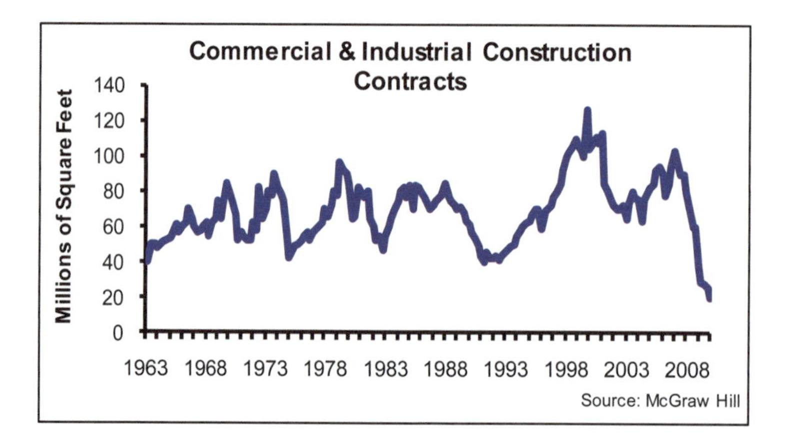

FIGURE 9B.3

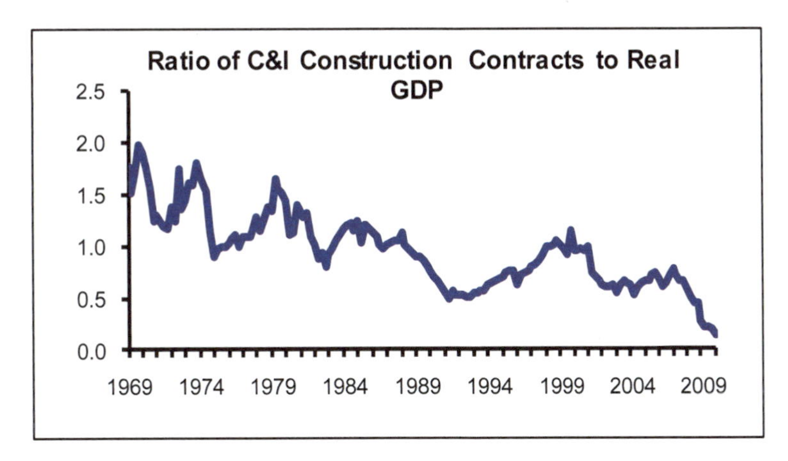

The Linneman Construction Cost Index (LCCI) is based on a hypothetical building consisting of lumber (5%), concrete (5%), gypsum (10%), iron and steel (10%), labor (50%), and land (20%). We track the costs of all of these components except land using producer price indices from the U.S. Bureau of Labor Statistics. For land, we set the 1995 base value to 100 and assume that it has increased by CPI (all goods) over time. We add up all of the nominal values of the component indices to arrive at the nominal LCCI, and then convert to a real basis using CPI.

In comparison, the Turner Building Cost Index (TBCI), published by Turner Construction, tracks the overall cost of construction on a national basis, taking into account major construction cost categories such as "material prices, labor rates, productivity, and the competitive condition of the marketplace". As with the LCCI, we converted the TBCI to a real basis using core CPI.

FIGURE 9B.4

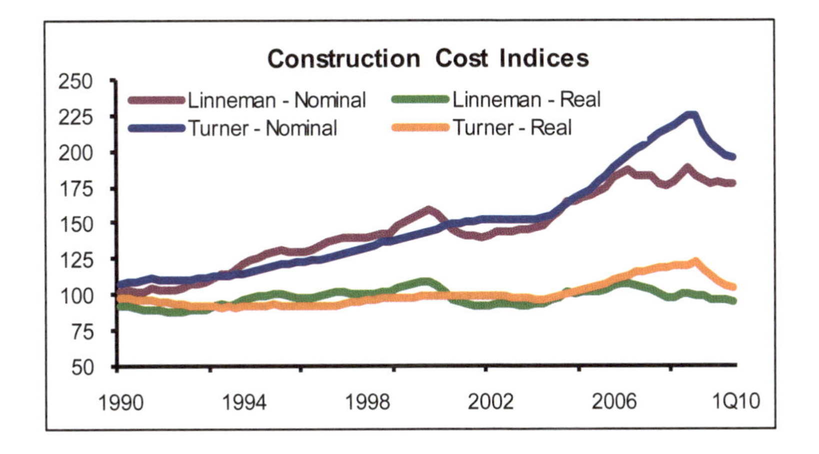

FIGURE 9B.5

Change in Cost Indices
Through 1Q10

	Y/Y	Q/Q	Over 3 Yrs	20-Yr CAGR
LCCI (Nominal)	-1.2%	0.0%	-3.0%	2.8%
LCCI (Real)	-3.5%	-0.4%	-8.9%	0.1%
Turner Index (Nominal)	-7.7%	-0.5%	-3.9%	3.1%
Turner Index (Real)	-9.8%	-0.9%	-9.7%	0.4%
Lumber	6.9%	2.9%	-10.7%	1.1%
Concrete	-2.8%	-0.5%	4.3%	3.2%
Gypsum	-11.1%	-2.4%	-23.8%	3.2%
Iron & Steel	7.3%	2.4%	0.6%	3.2%
Labor (Benefits + Wages)	-0.2%	-0.5%	9.1%	3.0%
CPI (all items)	2.3%	0.4%	6.4%	2.7%

Source: Bureau of Labor Statistics, Linneman Associates, Turner Construction

On a real basis, both the LCCI and the Turner Index exhibited 20-year compounded annual growth rates of just 0.1% and 0.4%, respectively. Thus, even as costs were surging in the short term, we maintained that construction costs would revert back to the long-term trend. In the first quarter of 2010, the real LCCI declined by 3.5% year-over-year and 0.4% since the previous quarter. The 8.9% drop in the LCCI over the last three years has been driven by two steep input-factor declines. First, the gypsum producer price index dropped by nearly 30% from its mid-2006 peak through the February 2009 low point. More recently, the cost of iron and steel rose sharply through August 2008, but then dropped by 43% through April 2009.

FIGURE 9B.6

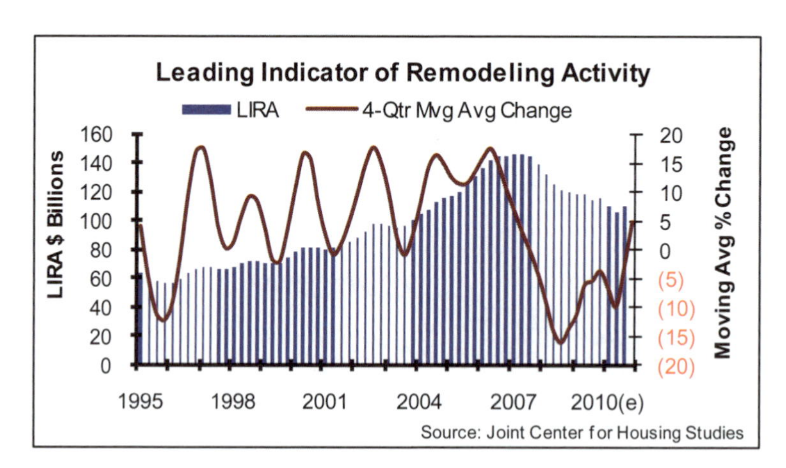

FIGURE 9B.7

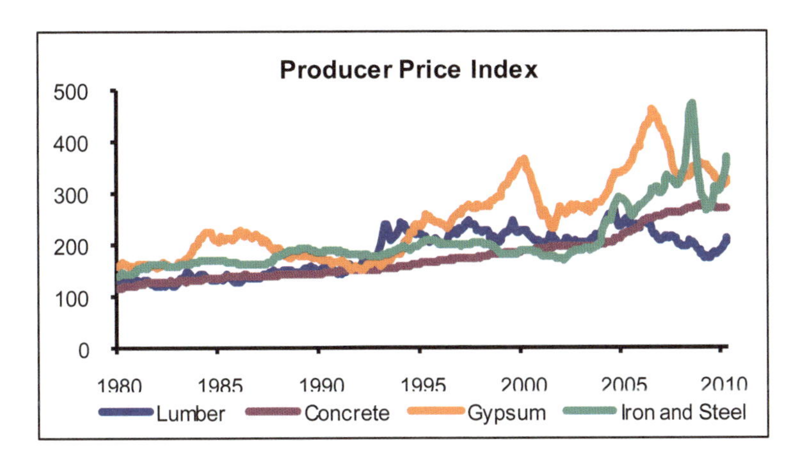

The lumber price index peaked in the third quarter of 2004 and declined by nearly 33% through the second quarter of 2009, but increased by 9.2% over the last three quarters. Concrete prices have been on an upward trend for the last 20 years through mid-2009, but have declined by about 2% since then. On a year-over-year and quarter-over-quarter basis through the first quarter of 2010, the gypsum producer price index declined by 11.1% and 2.4%, respectively. Current gypsum pricing reflects a 31% decline since its peak in the third quarter of 2006.

Chapter 10
Real Estate Company Analysis

"People are the ultimate assets".
-Dr. Peter Linneman

Assume you manage FJCL real estate company, which owns 70 properties, each similar to the properties we have discussed, and you are asked by your shareholders to value the company, and to produce a consolidated financial report. To that end, you roll-up the 70 property level pro formas, with each line item reflecting the sum of the revenues, the expenses, and debt across the properties. How will this aggregate pro forma differ from what you saw at the property level?

DIFFERENCES

The first significant difference is company level overhead. At the property level there is no line item reflecting the costs of running your company, although the property level analyses reflect the administrative expenses related to operating each building. However, you must pay your corporate staff, rent corporate office space, and engage outside accountants and lawyers. This overhead is referred to as **corporate general and administrative (G&A)** expense.

Some line items may occur both on the property and company level pro formas, but will have different meanings. For example, cap ex on a company level reflects both the sum of property level cap ex as well as company level cap ex for desks, chairs, computers, and other things at your corporate offices. Likewise, depreciation on the company pro forma reflects both property level depreciation as well as depreciation on carpets, lamps, furniture...etc at your administrative offices.

If you have corporate level debt in addition to individual property debt, these obligations will not appear on a property level pro forma but must appear in the entity level analysis. In contrast to a mortgage, which is secured by a building as collateral, you may also have debt that is not secured by real estate. The risk of such unsecured debt reflects the risk of the company's net cash flows, as well as its operating and financial reputation.

There may also be income generated at the company level that is not related to property revenue. For example, the company may derive income from stocks, bonds, or other non-real estate assets. Or perhaps you have been able to license your company's name for merchandising. For example, if you are able to license your name to a golf ball or bottled water manufacturer, this income stream will appear at the company level. You may also receive management fees, development fees, and leasing commissions from your properties or third party properties you service.

These examples reveal that you must first roll up the 70 property pro formas, and then incorporate corporate level line items in order to properly analyze your real estate company.

FIGURE 10.1

FJCL Annual Model (in $000s)						
	Year 1	Year 2	Year 3	Year 4	Year 5	Year 6
Forecasting Variables						
Acquisitions during period	$0	$11,200	$20,000	$30,000	$30,000	$30,000
Developments during period	$0	$22,500	$37,800	$50,000	$50,000	$50,000
Rate of return on new acquisitions	0%	8.5%	8.5%	8.5%	8.5%	8.5%
Rate of return on new development	0%	8.0%	8.0%	8.0%	8.0%	8.0%
Dispositions during period	$0	($30,000)	$0	$0	$0	$0
Cap rate on dispositions	NA	9.2%	9.0%	9.0%	9.0%	9.0%
Revenue growth **(Internal)**	0.0%	5.3%	4.4%	3.3%	2.9%	2.9%
Income Statement						
Rents - Existing properties	$287,450	$302,612	$316,097	$331,527	$347,983	$364,674
Rents - New acquisitions	$0	$952	$1,700	$2,550	$2,550	$2,550
Rents - New developments	$0	$1,800	$3,024	$4,000	$4,000	$4,000
Rent - Dispositions	$0	($2,760)	$0	$0	$0	$0
Subtotal	**$287,450**	**$302,604**	**$320,821**	**$338,077**	**$354,533**	**$371,224**
Parking	$12,712	$11,501	$11,501	$11,789	$12,016	$12,415
Other	$6,301	$6,305	$6,308	$6,965	$7,601	$8,409
Properting operating	($100,605)	($97,009)	($103,418)	($112,604)	($121,918)	($131,666)
Property NOI	**$205,858**	**$223,401**	**$235,213**	**$244,227**	**$252,232**	**$260,383**
Fees from noncombined affiliates	$1,508	$1,609	$1,618	$1,656	$1,649	$1,618
Interest income	$4,012	$2,502	$2,000	$2,000	$2,000	$2,000
General and administrative	($11,564)	($13,113)	($12,912)	($13,645)	($14,578)	($15,356)
EBITDA	**$199,814**	**$214,399**	**$225,919**	**$234,238**	**$241,303**	**$248,645**
Interest expense	($72,876)	($82,519)	($82,253)	($84,802)	($88,305)	($92,523)
Amortization of financing costs	($500)	$0	$0	$0	$0	$0
Depreciation	($57,500)	($68,200)	($69,712)	($73,218)	($75,300)	($78,209)
Impairment on securities and assets held for sale	($12,685)	$0	$0	$0	$0	$0
Net income before minority interest	**$56,253**	**$63,680**	**$73,954**	**$76,218**	**$77,698**	**$77,913**
Minority interest in OP	($7,612)	($10,136)	($10,085)	($10,800)	($11,998)	($12,118)
Minority interest in partially owned assets	($812)	($500)	($500)	($500)	($500)	($500)
Income from investment in limited partnerships	$6,908	$10,712	$6,600	$6,800	$7,000	$7,200
Gain (loss) on sale of real estate	$0	$8,125	$0	$0	$0	$0
Net income before pref div and extra items	**$54,737**	**$71,881**	**$69,969**	**$71,718**	**$72,200**	**$72,495**
Preferred dividends	($5,700)	($5,600)	($4,500)	($4,500)	($4,500)	($4,500)
Net income before extraordinary items	**$49,037**	**$66,281**	**$65,469**	**$67,218**	**$67,700**	**$67,995**
Performance Indicators						
Rental expense as percentage of revenues **(Internal)**	35.0%	32.1%	32.7%	34.0%	35.0%	36.1%
NOI Growth		8.5%	5.3%	3.8%	3.3%	3.2%
Growth in EBITDA		7.30%	5.37%	3.68%	3.02%	3.04%

Figure 10.1 presents the pro forma model for FJCL, which owns 70 properties, comprising about 12 million square feet of US office space. When FJCL produces an internal consolidated financial analysis, it rolls-up the detailed information they possess for each property. In contrast, a "Wall Street" analyst model does not possess the detailed information for each of FJCL's properties necessary to perform a roll-up. Why doesn't the Wall Street analyst just ask FJCL for the detailed data required for each property level pro forma and then roll them up? Because FJCL will not provide such detailed private information, as one of its most coveted assets is this detailed

information. Armed with this information, competitors could replicate FJCL's marketing and tenant retention strategy. For example, if competitors knew exactly when FJCL's tenants' leases expire and at what rents, they would know exactly when and how to pounce. Wall Street analysts must rely on publicly available information to model future performance. But this is not the same quality information which is available for internal purposes. As a result, Wall Street analyses provide relatively imprecise financial descriptions of companies.

ASSUMPTIONS

Let's examine a few of the key assumptions (Forecasting Variables) that are used to produce a company financial pro forma.

Acquisitions and Development: A company can generate growth beyond that achieved at existing properties via acquisitions and development. For example, as FJCL acquires properties, it adds both revenues and expenses. FJCL may also develop new properties that generate additional income. For example, $11,200,000 is FJCL's estimate of their acquisitions during Year 2. Will $11,200,000 be the actual amount? Of course not. It is merely an educated guess. If they acquire more, the line item "Rents – new acquisitions" will be higher than expectations, and vice versa. Similarly, if FJCL develops more properties than their $22,500,000 estimate for Year 2, the line item "Rents – new developments" will be higher than currently forecasted.

Rate of return on new acquisitions and developments: In addition to the amount of acquisition and development activity expected, you need to project the expected return on these activities in order to forecast the future income of these properties. Applying the expected return to the forecasted level of acquisitions and developments, and using assumptions about FJCL's cost structure, you forecast the expected rental income and expected operating costs associated with expansion activities.

Dispositions during the period: This line item represents the expected property sales activity of FJCL, which will impact expected future cash flows. First, FJCL receives the cash proceeds from the sale of a property as an immediate cash inflow. But after the property is sold it generates no future NOI, lowering expected future rental income, operating costs, interest payments on secured debt, and depreciation.

Revenue growth – existing properties: This reflects the anticipated rental growth for FJCL's existing properties. Absent detailed lease information, Wall Street analysts can only make guesses of future rental growth that in the long run are roughly equal to expected inflation. There is absolutely no chance that FJCL will actually achieve such smooth rental growth. This vividly demonstrates how detailed lease information enhances careful real estate analysis. Without such information Wall Street simply performs "bubble gum company" analysis. Such analysis, when well done, works best for apartments and hotels, as they have short leases. However, this type of analysis is less well suited for office, warehouse, and retail properties, where long term leases determine the timing of revenue changes.

The pro forma displays the results obtained from applying the assumptions to base year information.

Rents – new acquisitions and developments: The rents from the new property will grow based on the additional space that is acquired or developed. For example, in Year 2 FJCL only receives the revenue from the $11,200,000 in acquisitions made that year. As you add more properties, this line item continues to be populated.

Fees from non-combined affiliates: FJCL also receives some fees from certain partners and co-investors for managing properties. For example, they may own 25% of a property they manage, with unrelated investors owning the remainder. The fees they derive for such management services are reflected here.

EBITDA (earnings before interest, tax, depreciation and amortization): EBITDA is not the same as NOI. NOI is the rental revenue from existing and net new properties, plus any ancillary income from the properties, minus property operating costs. EBITDA also reflects fee income and interest income from non-real estate assets, and company level G&A expenses.

Interest Expense: After calculating EBITDA, you need to incorporate the effects of financing. The company's total interest payments are the sum of the interest payments made for each existing property, plus the interest expenses which are associated with additional debt the company expects to undertake for new developments and net (of dispositions) acquisitions. In addition, some of the existing debt will mature. Therefore, you must estimate how much new debt and refinancing the company will undertake, and what the terms will be for this debt. You must also incorporate interest payments for existing and future corporate level debt.

Minority interest: Generally Accepted Accounting Principles (GAAP) states that for assets in which the company owns a controlling share, the company must report those assets on the balance sheet as if they owned 100% of the assets. Given the company really owns less than 100%, companies must make an adjustment to reflect the portion of assets and income they receive. Similarly, unconsolidated minority positions need to be added.

Depreciation and Cap Ex: The depreciation line item for FJCL reflects depreciation on existing assets, plus depreciation on newly acquired and developed properties, plus depreciation on corporate assets like chairs, desks, computers and other assets. Furthermore, there is depreciation on anticipated future cap ex, TIs, and leasing commissions net of the discontinued depreciation of the assets sold.

Cap ex occurs not only at existing properties but also at newly developed and acquired properties, and corporate assets. This amount has to be adjusted for disposed assets. It is common to assume that X% of gross revenues will be required for cap ex, with the percentage varying by property type, geography, age, and other factors. This method will not fully capture the realities of cap ex, but is generally the best that one can do.

VALUE OF A COMPANY

The value of a company can be greater or less than the value of its properties. This is because when you own a company, you own both its properties and its management. If management adds value beyond the value of the properties, the value of the company is greater than the properties. The converse is also true.

While all management believes they add value, this is simply not the case. A good example is that properties in England generally have a very low risk lease structure. Specifically, the leases run for 25 years, are triple net, the tenant is responsible for all cap ex, and tenants must return the property in its original condition or better. The tenant can escape the lease only by liquidation bankruptcy, and rental rates are adjusted every five years to market rents. However, rents can only be adjusted upward upon these reviews. This means if market rents have fallen since the last rent review, rents remain at their current level for the next five years; if rents have risen, they are adjusted upward to market rates.

A company which owns a large portfolio of properties leased in this manner to high credit tenants provides a very safe income stream. Yet British property companies generally trade at substantial discounts to their property values. Why? It is because the management of many of these public companies often destroys value by reinvesting these relatively safe cash streams in high risk developments. By investing in high risk developments, management believes that they are creating value. But in fact they may be destroying value, as investors who desire low risk cash streams avoid these property companies for fear that their safe cash streams will be lost in high risk developments. In the extreme, imagine the discount at which a government bond fund would trade if the cash flows from these bonds were invested in biotech start-up firms.

In the case of real estate, particularly when it is well-leased, high quality, and well-located, management's value-added potential is relatively limited. After all, how much can you improve the value of a fully leased building which has the US Government as its tenant for the next twenty years? Sure you can control your costs a little better, and exploit favorable refinancing opportunities, but compared to typical operating businesses, the scope for management value added is relatively small.

The primary ways in which management can add value beyond the properties are: execute strategies involving substantial lease up; property repositioning; development; opportunistic acquisitions or dispositions; improving operations through cost controls and efficient leasing strategies; and, taking advantage of favorable financing windows. A high value-added real estate strategy successfully executed, such as development or redevelopment, can add about 15-20% in value. A well-executed cost control and refinancing strategy for a fully leased building can probably add 5-15% to value. While these margins are small compared with businesses such as high-tech companies, when executed with leverage and on a large asset base, the value enhancements are substantial. For example, if the value added by efficient management of publicly traded real estate companies is 10% of their $400 billion asset value, this amounts to $40 billion in value enhancement. Similarly, on a $1 billion private equity fund, a 20% value-added margin represents $200 million.

FFO

FIGURE 10.2

FJCL Annual Model (in $000s) FFO Calculation

	Year 1	Year 2	Year 3	Year 4	Year 5	Year 6
Capital Expenditures as % of rental revenues **(Internal)**	5.4%	6.9%	7.2%	6.1%	6.9%	6.9%
Subtotal: (Rents from existing properties, new acquisitions, new developments, dispositions)	$287,450	$302,604	$320,821	$338,077	$354,533	$371,224
Adjustments to Derive FFO:						
Net income before extraordinary items	$49,037	$66,281	$65,469	$67,218	$67,700	$67,995
Minority interest in OP	$7,612	$10,136	$10,085	$10,800	$11,998	$12,118
(Gain) loss on sale of real estate/other adj.	$0	$8,125	$0	$0	$0	$0
Real estate depreciation (incl jv deprec)	$61,300	$71,800	$73,300	$75,900	$78,800	$81,800
Impairment on assets held for sale	$218	$0	$0	$0	$0	$0
Other adjustments	$0	$77,514	$0	$0	$0	$0
Funds from Operations	$118,167	$233,856	$148,854	$153,918	$158,498	$161,913
Estimated Capital Expenditures	($15,619)	($21,025)	($23,014)	($20,736)	($24,594)	($25,725)
Straightline rent adjustment	($6,616)	($7,900)	($7,900)	($7,900)	($7,900)	($7,900)
Adjusted Funds from Operations (FAD)	**$95,932**	**$204,931**	**$117,940**	**$125,282**	**$126,004**	**$128,288**

Funds from operations (FFO) refers to funds from operations which are available to equity owners. It is equal to NOI, plus other income, minus overhead, minus interest payments but before depreciation, amortization and tax considerations. It is a non-audited metric often used instead of earnings. This is because depreciation for real estate is so large that analysts seek a metric that is not skewed by historically determined depreciation. While FFO does this, it fails to reflect cap ex requirements, tenant improvements, and leasing commissions that are a normalized part of operations. Consequently, two companies with the same FFO may have very different free cash flows, as their cap ex, leasing commissions, and TIs may be significantly different.

FAD

Funds available for distribution (FAD) is FFO less expected recurring cap ex, leasing commissions, and TIs. Again, this is a non-audited number used to measure a real estate company's cash available for distribution to shareholders without a deterioration of its asset base.

DCF VALUATION

When evaluating the value of a real estate company, you value the company's ability to generate recurring cash streams. This is no different from valuing any other company. Thus, you forecast future cash streams for the company, including growth in net cash flow, derived from net acquisitions, refinancings, and development, and discount these future cash streams at the appropriate discount rate. The discount rate will generally be modestly lower than that for individual properties, particularly for a large company, as the law of large numbers makes the expected returns statistically more likely for the company's portfolio than for any individual property. This company value reflects the ability of existing assets, as well as management's ability to add value. To obtain the value of the equity of the company, deduct the value of liabilities. Figure 10.3 displays the estimated value via DCF for FJCL.

FIGURE 10.3

A Simple DCF Example (in $000s)						
	Year 1	Year 2	Year 3	Year 4	Year 5	Year 6
EBITDA	$199,814	$214,399	$225,919	$234,238	$241,303	$248,645
Cap Ex, TIs, & Commissions	($15,619)	($21,025)	($23,014)	($20,736)	($24,594)	($25,725)
Cash Flows	$184,195	$193,374	$202,905	$213,502	$216,709	$222,920
					Terminal value:	$2,786,494
					CF Year 6/.08	
PV of Cash Flows @ 11%	$2,349,452					
Average Debt Outstanding (in Year 6)	($1,027,810)					
Equity Value	$1,321,642					

Figure 10.3 calculates the equity value by first calculating the expected cash flows of FJCL. If FJCL does not generate enough cash to cover all expenses, it will not be able to pay its operating obligations. To approximate the cash flows, take EBITDA and adjust for expected cap ex, TIs and leasing commissions. The expected cash flows are discounted by an 11% rate, while the terminal value is calculated using an 8% cash flow cap rate (aka Gordon model, an 11% discount rate and a 3% growth rate). This residual value is then converted into present value at an 11% discount rate. Note that EBITDA takes into account the value of management by incorporating the income generated from new acquisitions, dispositions, and capital improvements.

If you value FJCL without taking into account future acquisitions, developments, refinancings, and dispositions you will be ignoring the potential value added by management. If good management chooses lucrative acquisitions, prudent dispositions, and profitable development which contribute to the growth of profits, they add value to the firm. This is reflected via the Rents – new acquisitions, Rents – new developments, and Rents – dispositions entries. This shows that the firm's value will be greater than just what existing properties generate. If you do not take these factors into account, the equity value will be less than the $1.32 billion amount that Figure 10.3 calculates.

CAP RATE APPROACH

Capping Year 3 stabilized EBITDA adjusted for cap ex at an 8 cap, yields an equity value of $1.43 billion, as shown in Figure 10.4. The debt in Year 3 is subtracted, because Year 3 EBITDA is used. Realize that both cap rate (or multiple) approach is reliant on the risk and growth assumptions for the company. You attempt to use market comparables when selecting the cap rate to use. The cap rate approach is a good approximation for the equity value of the firm. Currently, the multiple approach values FJCL at an 8.27% premium over the DCF valuation, which is in the same ballpark.

FIGURE 10.4

Cap Rate Approach ($ in thousands)		
Stabilized EBITDA		$234,238
Less: Cap Ex		($20,736)
Stabilized NOI in Year 4		$213,502
Cap Rate (discount- growth)	(11%-3%)	8.0%
Capped Stabilized NOI		$2,668,772
Debt in Year 4		($1,237,790)
Equity value with cap rate approach		**$1,430,982**
Equity value with DCF		**$1,321,642**
% Difference between Equity Values		**8.27%**

NET ASSET VALUE (NAV)

NAV is a commonly used approach to valuing a real estate company. This approach assumes that management neither adds nor subtracts value. Figure 10.5 presents a calculation of NAV for FJCL.

As displayed in Figure 10.5, there are a number of value sources in the company. First are its existing properties. Their value is estimated by capping their (stabilized) NOI, which assumes that on average the NOI for all properties is stabilized. The company may also derive net income from property management or development services that are being offered to third parties. The value of these income streams is achieved by applying a market multiple for such businesses to their stabilized net income from these activities. These activities will merit different multiples from those used to value the real estate. For example, the property management services business may be a 2-5x multiple business while the property ownership multiple is 9-11x. The reason why the management service multiple is lower is that management contracts are usually cancelable on 30 day notice. If you had a development for fee or a management for fee business, you would similarly value each net income stream separately.

Total company value is then the sum of: the capitalized value of the properties; the capitalized value of the management business; the capitalized value of the development business; the value of land; and your cash position. To calculate NAV, you deduct the value of the company's debt and other liabilities.

Unfortunately, NAV is not as precise as it seems. NAV analysis is very sensitive to the cap rates and multiples chosen to convert the incomes into value. As figure 10.6 reveals, a 50 bp shift in the cap rate or multiple alters FJCL's value considerably. Since no one knows the exact multiple or cap rate to use for these different value sources, two intelligent and meticulous analysts could disagree by a small amount and the NAVs would differ substantially. Further, this approach ignores the value of management.

FIGURE 10.5

Sample NAV Components and Calculation ($ in thousands)	Baseline
NOI Stabilized in Year 4	$244,227
Property Ownership Cap Rate	9.0%
Value of property portfolio	**$2,713,631**
Other Income in Year 4	
Parking	$11,789
Parking Multiple	4.7 X
Fees from Noncombined Affiliates	$1,656
Fees from Noncombined Affiliates Multiple	4.8 X
Other	$6,965
Other Multiple	5.6 X
Value of management or fee income	**$102,361**
Add other assets:	
Development project underway	**$50,000**
Land held for future development or sale	**$6,762**
Other investments in unconsolidated subsidiaries (Year 4)	**$10,800**
Cash and equivalents	**$8,452**
Other miscellaneous assets	**$10,142**
Gross value of assets	**$2,902,148**
Deduct:	
Total liabilities	$1,447,031
Preferred stock	$16,000
Net Asset Value	**$1,439,117**
DCF Equity Value	**$1,321,642**
% Difference between NAV and DCF	**8.89%**

FIGURE 10.6

Sample NAV Components and Calculation ($ in thousands)			
	Baseline		
	9.00%	8.50%	9.50%
NOI Stabilized in Year 4	$244,227	$244,227	$244,227
Property Ownership Cap Rate	9.0%	8.5%	9.5%
Value of property portfolio	**$2,713,631**	**$2,873,256**	**$2,570,808**
Other Income in Year 4			
Parking	$11,789	$11,789	$11,789
Parking Multiple	4.7 X	4.7 X	4.7 X
Fees from Noncombined Affiliates	$1,656	$1,656	$1,656
Fees from Noncombined Affiliates Multiple	4.8 X	4.8 X	4.8 X
Other	$6,965	$6,965	$6,965
Other Multiple	5.6 X	5.6 X	5.6 X
Value of management or fee income	**$102,361**	**$102,361**	**$102,361**
Add other assets:			
Development project underway	**$50,000**	**$50,000**	**$50,000**
Land held for future development or sale	**$6,762**	**$6,762**	**$6,762**
Other investments in unconsolidated subsidiaries (Year 4)	**$10,800**	**$10,800**	**$10,800**
Cash and equivalents	**$8,452**	**$8,452**	**$8,452**
Other miscellaneous assets	**$10,142**	**$10,142**	**$10,142**
Gross value of assets	**$2,902,148**	**$3,061,773**	**$2,759,325**
Deduct:			
Total liabilities	$1,447,031	$1,447,031	$1,447,031
Preferred stock	$16,000	$16,000	$16,000
Net Asset Value	**$1,439,117**	**$1,598,742**	**$1,296,294**
DCF Equity Value	**$1,321,642**	**$1,321,642**	**$1,321,642**
% Difference between NAV and DCF	**8.89%**	**20.97%**	**-1.92%**
% Difference from baseline NAV	**NA**	**11.09%**	**-9.92%**

The only way you will ever know what the "correct" cap rates or multiples are for the firm is to liquidate it, as it is only worth as much as somebody is willing to pay for it. Liquidating a firm could take 6 months to 2 years, depending on the size of the company. When selling the firm, you would also be selling management (for better or worse).

NAV also fails to reflect hidden tax, debt, and environmental liabilities. For example, pre-payment penalties associated with debt are not deducted. Nor are substantial capital gains taxes that must often be paid by the company upon sale. Also, there may be environmental liabilities or employee severance contracts associated with liquidation. As a result, if carefully calculated NAV is more than 10-15% different from the market value of the assets, there is a possibility that the assets are substantially over or under priced. But if the estimated NAV is within 10-15% of the market value, the market value is probably a better indicator of value.

CLOSING THOUGHT

What makes a property company potentially more valuable than the value of their properties? In short, it is the ability to squeeze even more income out of these properties than competitors (who establish market values), and the ability to find and successfully execute value enhancing transactions. That is, people! When you own a pool of properties you only have the claim on those assets, while when you own the company you also own the claim on the creativity and execution skills of the people at the company. These people may either create or destroy value. So when approaching the valuation of a property company, you must look to the value of all its assets, including the people.

Chapter 11
Real Estate Bankruptcy Basics

"Have both a professional and private life to balance the ups and downs that occur on either side".
-Dr. Peter Linneman

What happens if the property you own underperforms and you are unable to meet the terms of your loan agreement? Or if, as happens during capital crunches, you are unable to refinance your debt upon maturity or you are unable to pay off the loan via cash funds or sale. You can declare bankruptcy. Bankruptcy law is a mechanism by which a debtor, who is unable to meet the terms of his or her credit agreements, attempts to resolve its debts and other liabilities.

A lender has contractual rights to the cash flow and collateral throughout the life of the loan. For example, a first lien lender generally has the right to **foreclose** on the property if the borrower violates, or **breaches**, the terms of the loan agreement. In foreclosure, a lender with a first security position can theoretically take control of the property and auction it off. The first payments from the sale go to the government to settle any outstanding tax or environmental claims against the asset, as the government always has a "super position". A distressing element of bankruptcy is that a bankruptcy sale is treated as the sale of the asset, hence triggering capital gain taxes, even though debtor generally receives no income from this "sale". Imagine having to come up with millions of dollars in tax payments but having no source of income with which to pay these taxes! This is the so-called phantom income problem.

Remaining sale proceeds are used to pay off the lawyers and brokers used in the foreclosure and sale process. Finally, the lender theoretically receives all principal and interest owed to them. After these obligations are satisfied, any money left goes to repay the owners of the next priority position. This process continues until all creditors with lower positions (junior creditors) are paid off, assuming there is sufficient value received from the sale. The last party to receive proceeds from the sale are the common equity holders. Each lender only has the right to any remaining principal and interest that is owed (plus related expenses).

Bankruptcy law varies significantly across countries. For instance, Canada and the U.K. are extremely unforgiving to a defaulting borrower. At one time, borrowers in the U.K. who were unable to meet loan agreements were considered criminals, as not fulfilling a loan agreement was viewed as a form of fraud. In the U.K. today, borrowers do not go to jail for violating the terms of a loan agreement, but the bankrupt borrower will be quickly replaced by a trustee who operates the entity with the sole objective of maximizing recovery for the debt holders. This creates a strong bankruptcy framework for lenders.

In contrast, the "defaulting criminals" that fled the U.K., came to America and established a more borrower friendly system. Their view was that their bankruptcy was not due to their malfeasance, but rather due to unexpected temporary setbacks. Thus, historically the United States has had a relatively forgiving bankruptcy framework for borrowers. There are two basic types of bankruptcies, Chapter 7 and Chapter 11, named after the respective sections of the IRS Code. In a Chapter 7 bankruptcy, the debtor ceases all operations, goes completely out of business, and a trustee is appointed to sell the property and attempts to pay off obligations through this liquidation. Chapter 11 bankruptcy law was created in 1978 to formalize the business reorganization framework. This codified the view that reorganization of the business is generally preferred to liquidation. As such, the US Chapter 11 bankruptcy process attempts to conserve going concern value, generally requiring a consensual plan of reorganization. This reflects the nation's social policy to protect equity holders from temporary setbacks. These laws are the underpinning of all contracts, including mortgages, leases, and labor contracts. As such, it is incumbent under the law for management to use the full force of bankruptcy in order to protect equity owners from temporary setbacks.

Perhaps not surprisingly in view of this history, one of the key provisions of the US bankruptcy code is that once a borrower enters into Chapter 11 bankruptcy, secured lenders cannot immediately seize their collateral. This is why people refer to "seeking bankruptcy protection". Why, if the loan document says the lender can seize their collateral, are they unable to do so? Simply stated, because bankruptcy law trumps the loan contract. Once US bankruptcy is declared, bankruptcy law effectively dictates the terms of the loan agreement.

US bankruptcy law allows the defaulting borrower to remain in control of business decisions (subject to bankruptcy court oversight) until the point is reached where the bankruptcy court rules that either a successful reorganization has occurred or that a successful reorganization is impossible. Instead of assigning a trustee to work on behalf of the lenders, US bankruptcy law works with the borrower in an attempt to regenerate value beyond liabilities. To this end, US bankruptcy law provides a 180 day exclusivity period, during which time only the debtor is allowed to submit a reorganization plan. This exclusivity period will be extended beyond 180 days as long as the bankruptcy court feels that a reorganization by the borrower is not futile. As a result, the defaulting borrower is entrusted with creating a plan to save the company for at least 180 days, and perhaps several years. This framework is much less lender friendly than U.K. bankruptcy law.

BORROWERS' RIGHTS

US bankruptcy law also allows for **debtor in possession** financing (DIP). This allows the defaulting borrower to subordinate existing debt claims to new debt which is taken on to operate the business while it attempts a successful reorganization. For instance, if a developer is unable to meet debt payments in the middle of construction, creditors cannot unilaterally seize the project and auction it off, and the bankrupt developer may be able to obtain additional debt, which is senior to existing senior debt, to finish the project. DIP financing is possible (with the blessing of the bankruptcy court) even if existing senior loan documents expressly prohibit any debt being senior. Again, bankruptcy law trumps contract law. The theory is that the former first mortgagee is protected, in spite of subordination of their debt, as completing the development adds sufficient value to enhance the developer's ability to pay back the original loan. But while this is the intent, it is not always the outcome.

Under Chapter 11 bankruptcy protection, the borrower does not have to pay interest on their loans, as bankruptcy law again takes precedence over loan contracts. As a result, an overleveraged company facing significant interest payments can achieve substantial cash flows while in bankruptcy. Under the oversight of the bankruptcy court the company can channel this money towards salaries, TIs, leasing commissions, capital expenditures, vendors, and other non-lenders in order to keep the business operating. Under Chapter 11 protection, the borrower also has the right to reinstate their mortgage at the original interest rate. This is particularly advantageous to the borrower in an environment where interest rates have risen since the loan was originally made.

Bankruptcy law also takes precedence over key lease terms. For example, a retailer, Modest may have signed a lease for $5 per square foot that runs an additional 15 years, with two renewal options prohibiting subleasing. Under Chapter 11 bankruptcy protection Modest can vacate the space and sublease to Ranti's Handguns for $8 per square foot, yielding a $3 per square foot profit for Modest on the lease. Under Chapter 11 bankruptcy protection, Modest has the right to sublease as long as the sublease agreement is deemed reasonable by the bankruptcy court. The landlord may even have a lease stating that Modest's lease is terminated if the company goes into bankruptcy, however, bankruptcy law trumps. Lease terms prohibiting subleasing, and causing lease termination upon tenant bankruptcy, are unenforceable without the bankruptcy court's agreement, as the lease is viewed as a tenant asset, and it is the bankruptcy court's job to supervise the attempt to maximize the value of all assets.

An office tenant, Alexis LTD, may have a lease with rent due on the 16th of the month. If Alexis goes into Chapter 11 bankruptcy on the 15th, they can decide to not pay rent while under bankruptcy protection, and the landlord has no immediate eviction right. Further, in an attempt to achieve solvency Alexis can walk away from its obligations, irrespective of the lease document. Also, bankruptcy law limits landlord back rent collections to a maximum of roughly 18 months.

Rockefeller Center in the 1990s offers a glimpse into the cold realities of the US bankruptcy process. The lender had a secured first position against the property for $1.3 billion, secured by the entire property and all its leases. There was roughly $20 million in trade debt, and some "slip and fall" insurance claims. The simplicity of the borrower's capital structure in the Rockefeller Center situation meant a "fast" foreclosure was possible. Yet even in this case it took roughly 14 months to consummate the foreclosure. With more complex capital and lease structures, this process would have taken considerably longer, with $50,000-$100,000 in legal and advisory bills piling up monthly. In contrast, if Rockefeller Center was in the U.K., the foreclosure would have been completed in a few weeks (as was the case with Canary Wharf).

BANK OF AMERICA VS. LA SALLE STREET PARTNERS

This is an important case for real estate bankruptcy, illustrating several key aspects of bankruptcy law. In this case a debtor defaulted on the mortgage secured by a property which was located between two other properties owned by the debtor. For operating reasons the debtor wanted to retain the defaulting property. While in bankruptcy, the debtor proposed a plan of reorganization under which the debtor recognized the **absolute priority rule**, which states that no junior creditor will receive consideration until all senior creditors are paid in full, and no equity holder will receive consideration until all creditors have been paid in full (including interest). The debtor proposed contributing fresh capital in exchange for the 100% ownership of the property as it exited bankruptcy. This is called the **new value exception** to the absolute priority rule.

In this case there was a significant deficiency claim. That is, the value of the property was not sufficient to repay all of the creditor's outstanding debt. If the debtor classified the deficiency claim as unsecured debt, the debtor could never receive either the 51% creditor approval, or the two-thirds creditor class approval which are necessary to obtain court approval for a reorganization plan. This is due to the fact that there are usually very few unsecured creditors for real estate. As a result, if the debtor classified the deficiency claim as unsecured debt it would allow the deficiency claimants to overpower the other unsecured creditor class members, making it very difficult to achieve the necessary reorganization approvals. To circumvent this problem the debtor placed the deficiency claim in a separate class from the unsecured creditors, while offering the unsecured creditors 93 cents for every dollar owed, which virtually assured acceptance by a sufficient number of creditor classes. The debtor offered only 3 cents on the dollar for the deficiency claim.

Not surprisingly, the secured lender objected to this plan. The debtor tried to use the **cram down rule** against the sole dissenting party, as the bankruptcy code allows the bankruptcy court to force a dissenting party to accept a plan, effectively cramming down the plan on the dissenting party.

One of the questions in the case was whether the debtor could classify the deficiency claim as a separate class rather than as unsecured debt. The second issue was the new value exception. The bankruptcy court, the US District Court, and the US 7th Circuit Court all confirmed the reorganization plan. However, the US Supreme Court overturned. The Supreme Court ruled that the original equity owners had no right to contribute this new value simply because they were the original equity holders. This ruling reduced the availability of the new value exception to current owners. The court held that the new value exception requires a market test. That is, if you want to use the new value exception, you have to offer the new equity position to the market and not simply offer it as the original owner. This market test clearly detracts from the exclusive right of the original equity holder to use the new value exception. Unfortunately, the courts have yet to establish a clear definition of "testing the market".

SECTION 11.11B

Section 11.11B of the bankruptcy code is particularly important for real estate. Most mortgages that enter bankruptcy are **non-recourse mortgages**, which means that the creditor can only look to the property to recoup principal and owed interest. The lender cannot go after the debtor's personal assets to satisfy claims, and, thus, cannot file a deficiency claim for insufficient value from the property. However, in Chapter 11 both recourse or non-recourse lenders are permitted to file for a deficiency claim. Under section 11.11B the lender can waive their deficiency claim. For example, assume you are a lender with a $10 million mortgage against a building that is only worth $5 million today. Therefore, you have a secured claim of $5 million, and also an unsecured deficiency claim worth $5 million, and receive settlements as both a secured creditor and an unsecured creditor. As the lender you can waive your $5 million deficiency claim, which results in a single $10 million secured claim. However, the return on that claim will only have a present value of $5 million. In other words, the stream of payments promised under the debtor's reorganization will only have a present value of $5 million. So why would you waive the deficiency claim? The primary reason is you believe that the debtor will fail again, in which case you retain your $10 million secured claim. If you accepted the deficiency claim and the property subsequently defaults, you only have a $5 million secured claim. This option is available only during Chapter 11 protection.

CLOSING THOUGHT

While Chapter 11 bankruptcy provides strategic opportunities unavailable via Chapter 7 liquidation, it is not an easy ride. The bankrupt entity must provide a viable plan for keeping the company alive and deal with the bankruptcy court. Keep in mind your equity holders may lose faith in you and seek your ouster as manager. There is a good chance they will get little if any of their money back. Imagine trying to raise money for future deals after that! Moreover, a bankruptcy situation may generate bad feelings with investors, who may feel that you cheated them, even if you didn't. Hence, the effect on your reputation can be substantial. Bankruptcy is a very complicated and highly nuanced legal field, and varies wildly across states and countries, with some providing absolute foreclosure rights and others having no foreclosure law. While the general principles of lending are clear enough, bankruptcy law can change everything. As a borrower you can use bankruptcy both offensively and defensively, so be sure to understand your rights and restrictions under bankruptcy laws before taking out a loan.

Chapter 12
Should You Borrow?

"Embrace the 11th Commandment: thou shalt not take yourself so seriously".
-Dr. Peter Linneman

Now that you begin to understand some of the dynamics that exist between a lender and a borrower, ask yourself "why should someone borrow?" Why would anyone go through all of the negotiations, headaches, and operating restrictions that come with lenders? There are four primary reasons to borrow:

- You simply don't have enough money to buy the asset.
- Even if you have enough money to purchase the asset, you want to diversify your investments.
- You desire the tax shield that comes with interest payments.
- You seek to enhance the return on your equity.

Let's examine each of these interrelated rationales for borrowing.

DON'T HAVE ENOUGH MONEY

The simplest reason to borrow is that you don't have enough money to purchase the asset. You have found the perfect investment opportunity, but lack sufficient capital to buy the property. Remember that buying a building with predictable cash flows costs a great deal of money. Not everyone can afford to pay for the property solely through their equity, and borrowing bridges the gap.

Alternatively, you may want to develop a property in the hope that it will generate significant cash flows upon completion. A developer incurs substantial negative cash flows before the project is completed, leased, and generating revenues, and may not have enough money to cover these costs.

In short, since real estate is a capital intensive business, it requires a great deal of capital, and debt enables you to build or buy real estate that you could otherwise not afford solely with your own money.

DIVERSIFY

You may be fortunate enough to have sufficient capital to build or buy the property on which you are focused. Suppose you have $10 million in savings and identify a wonderful opportunity to purchase a $10 million building. While you like the asset, you may not want to commit 100% of your wealth to real estate. Even if you want to put all of your wealth in real estate, you may not want it all in a single property. By using 75% non-recourse debt you can spread your $10 million across four $10 million properties. This diversification lowers your geographic, tenant, lease expiration, and asset risk, improving your portfolio risk profile.

Investing in multiple properties may also create economies of scale in terms of property operations. For instance, you can spread your back office expenses over multiple properties. Or by contracting with a painter for four buildings rather than one, the painter will give you a lower price per unit.

Investing in multiple properties may also enhance your revenues. For example, with more tenant relationships you can offer alternative space when a tenant's lease expires. By moving a tenant to a larger (or smaller) space in one of your other buildings to satisfy their expansion needs, you will retain more tenants and enhance your revenues.

INTEREST TAX SHIELD

Another reason people borrow is to shield taxable income. Of course, this reason is not unique to real estate, as the IRS allows you to deduct all interest payments from your taxable income. The greater your debt, the higher your interest deductions, and the lower is your tax bill. But remember, you are only allowed to deduct interest, not principal payments.

ENHANCED EQUITY RETURNS

If things "go right", you can enhance your equity returns via debt financing. To illustrate, assume you are considering three alternative capital structures for the $10 million purchase of Anoop Towers: Structure 1 is 100% equity; Structure 2 is 50% debt and 50% equity; while, Structure 3 is 90% debt and 10% equity, as summarized in Figure 12.1.

FIGURE 12.1

Anoop Towers Project			
	Capital Structure 1	**Capital Structure 2**	**Capital Structure 3**
Building Value	$10 MM	$10 MM	$10 MM
Equity	$10 MM	$5 MM	$1 MM
Debt	$0 MM	$5 MM	$9 MM

There are two components of total returns: capital appreciation; and, annual cash flow. **Capital appreciation** is the return you receive as the building's value increases (or decreases), while the **cash flow return** is generated by the net of debt service cash flows generated by the property.

CAPITAL APPRECIATION

Assume that you believe the property will increase 10% in value over a two-year period. Since this expected property appreciation is about the property, you expect this 10% increase regardless of the capital structure you employ. After all, the building doesn't know how much debt is on it! With a 10% appreciation, the building is expected to be worth $11 million in two years, as seen below in Figure 12.2.

FIGURE 12.2

Anoop Towers Project			
	Capital Structure 1	Capital Structure 2	Capital Structure 3
Building Value	$10 MM	$10 MM	$10 MM
Debt	$0 MM	$5 MM	$9 MM
Equity	$10 MM	$5 MM	$1 MM
Appreciation (after two years)	$1 MM	$1 MM	$1 MM
Building Value (after two years)	$11 MM	$11 MM	$11 MM
Debt Repayment	$0 MM	($5MM)	($9MM)
Equity Value	$11 MM	$6 MM	$2 MM
Equity Return	10%	20%	100%

For each Capital Structure you must repay any debt you owe from the proceeds of the anticipated $11 million dollar sale (in two years). For Capital Structure 1, there is no debt to repay because there was no debt on the building. For Structures 2 and 3 you must repay $5 million and $9 million, respectively. Thus, the residual value for you after debt repayments for Structures 1, 2 and 3 are: $11 million, $6 million, and $2 million, respectively.

At first glance the $11 million proceeds provided to you by Structure 1 seems more lucrative than the other two Capital Structures. But you cannot directly compare this with the other two Capital Structures because you initially contributed different amounts of equity capital: the entire $10 million for Capital Structure 1; $5 million for Capital Structure 2; and only $1 million for Capital Structure 3. To make an apples to apples comparison, you need to calculate the expected equity return from the expected capital appreciation. The expected equity return from expected capital appreciation is equal to the money you expect to receive on sale, minus the money you put into the deal, divided by the money you had in the deal, as illustrated in Figure 12.3 and 12.4.

FIGURE 12.3

Equity Return From Capital Appreciation
Equity Return From Capital Appreciation = (Residual Value at Sale – Original Equity Investment)/ Original Equity Investment

FIGURE 12.4

Calculations (in MM)
Equity Return $_{\text{Structure 1}}$ = ($11 - $10) / $10 = 10%
Equity Return $_{\text{Structure 2}}$ = ($6 - $5) / $5 = 20%
Equity Return $_{\text{Structure 3}}$ = ($2 - $1) / $1 = 100%

Remember that the anticipated return from expected capital appreciation was for a two-year period. You can calculate the annual equity capital appreciation using the present value calculations, as summarized in Figure 12.5.

FIGURE 12.5

Calculations*	
Two Year Return	**Annualized Return**
10%	4.9%
20%	9.5%
100%	41.4%

*Formula: (1+Two Year Return)^(1/2) - 1

Note that the greater the proportion of debt, the higher is the expected equity appreciation return. This is because the expected total gain on the property ($1 million) is the same for each Capital Structure, while the equity you have in the project is lower with greater debt. Thus, debt provides you the opportunity to leverage the property's expected appreciation into a greater equity appreciation, as seen in Figure 12.6.

FIGURE 12.6

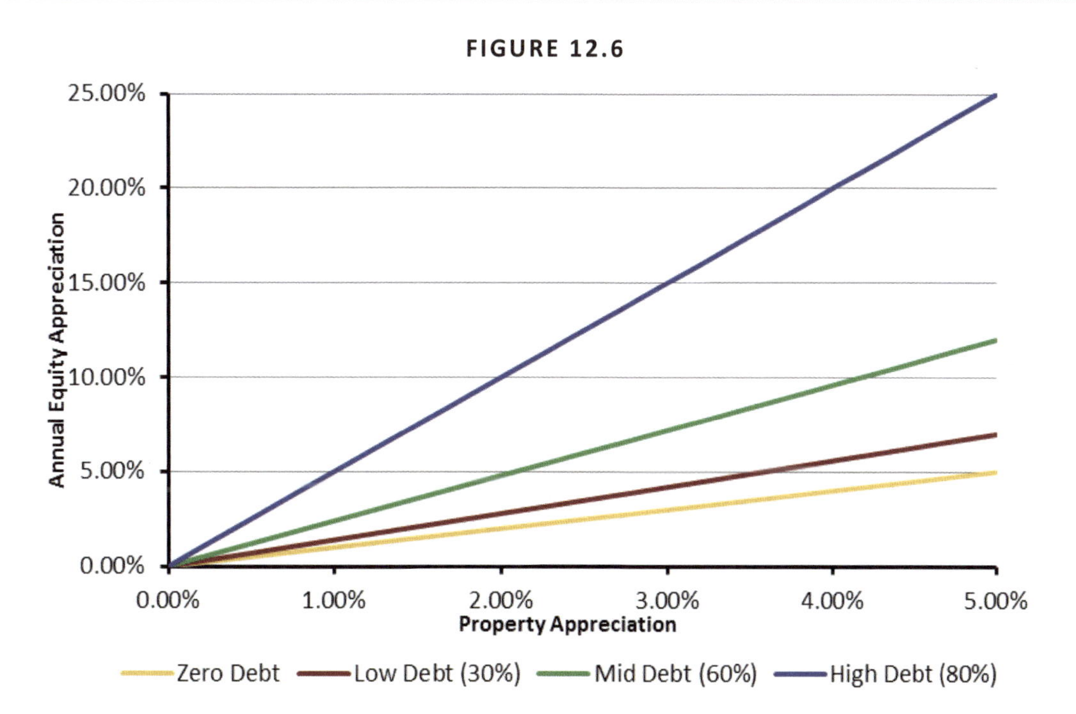

One of the great mistakes that plagues real estate borrowers is that when debt is plentiful, many borrowers forget that debt has both a price (the interest rate) and risk. That is, these greater expected leveraged equity returns are not risk free! To see this, ask what happens if instead of the anticipated 10% increase in value, the property actually decreases in value by 10% over 2 years due to an unexpected downturn in the economy. If this occurs, after two years of hard work you will only be able to sell the property for $9 million, even though you originally paid $10 million. This means the property realizes a loss of $1 million in value, irrespective of the Capital Structure. The residual value to the equity holder will then be $9 million, $4 million, and $0 for Capital Structures 1, 2 and 3, respectively. So a 2 year decline in property value of 10% generates total equity appreciation returns of negative 10%, negative 20%, and negative 100% for Structures 1, 2 and 3, respectively over the 2 year period. This is illustrated in Figure 12.7. These 2 year losses amount to annualized loss rates of negative 5.1%, negative 10.6%, and negative 100% for Structures 1, 2 and 3, respectively.

FIGURE 12.7

Anoop Towers Project (Poor Economy Scenario)			
	Capital Structure 1	**Capital Structure 2**	**Capital Structure 3**
Building Value	$10 MM	$10 MM	$10 MM
Debt	$0 MM	$5 MM	$9 MM
Equity	$10 MM	$5 MM	$1 MM
Appreciation (after two years)	($1MM)	($1MM)	($1MM)
Building Value (after two years)	$9 MM	$9 MM	$9 MM
Debt Repayment	$0 MM	($5MM)	($9MM)
Equity Value	$9 MM	$4 MM	$0 MM
Equity Return	(10%)	(20%)	(100%)

So if the property goes down in value, the more debt you had on the property, the worse your equity appreciation returns, as illustrated below in Figure 12.8. In fact, relatively small and temporary value declines can wipe out all equity value when high leverage is employed. And if the debt comes due or violates a covenant during such temporary value declines, the borrower will be unable to successfully refinance the property. The result is that either fresh equity must be infused in a down market (when capital is generally expensive) or they will lose a good long term property through foreclosure by the lender.

FIGURE 12.8

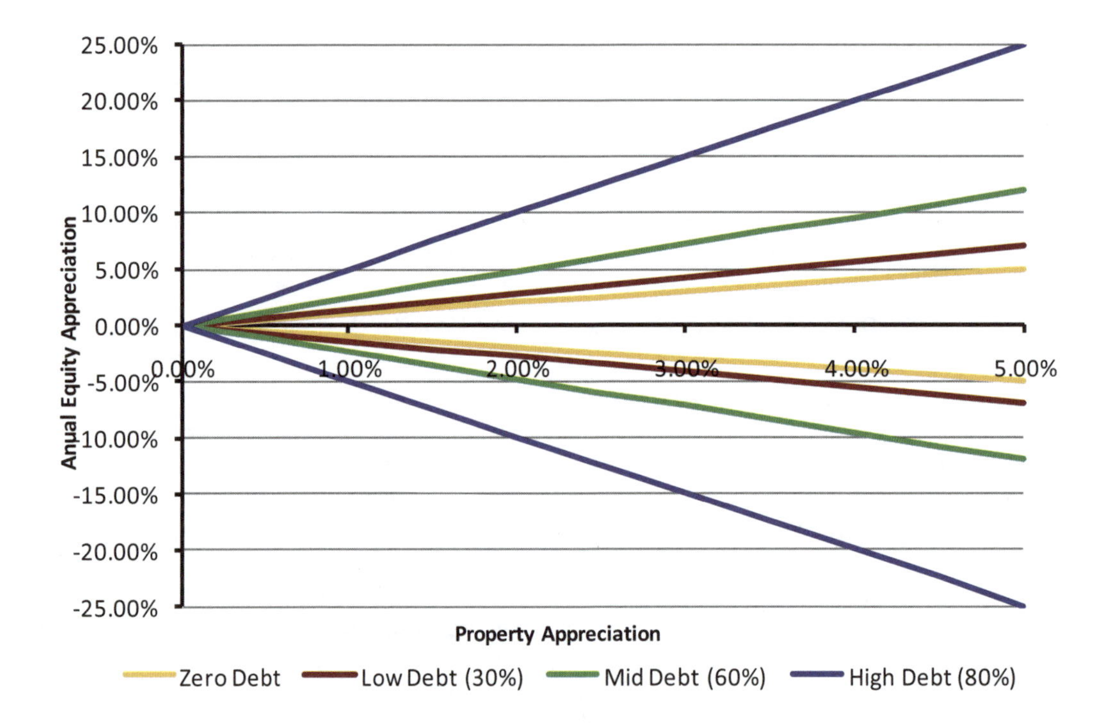

The key insight about leverage and equity appreciation returns is that in good times debt is cheap and juices your pro forma equity returns; but during downturns your losses are magnified. Stated differently, debt substantially increases the investment risk for the equity holder. For this reason you must demand a substantially higher equity return as your leverage increases. The reason debt increases equity risk is because the lender gets paid first, leaving the equity holder's cash flows in a second payment position, which is riskier. In fact, until the lender gets paid in full, the equity holder receives nothing. It is critical for you to remember that financing decisions and project investment decisions are not the same. Instead, they are separate, critically important, issues. Always calculate both unlevered and levered expected returns so that you can understand if your expected equity return derives from property performance or leverage.

POSITIVE LEVERAGE

Now let's look at the second component of equity returns: the equity cash flow return. The real estate industry frequently uses the terms **positive and negative leverage** to describe the effects of debt on cash returns. Positive leverage simply means that the property cash flow yield (NOI after standard reserves) is greater than the interest rate paid to the lender. For example, if you borrow at a 5% interest rate for a property whose cash flows are 10%, you realize a 5% (10%-5%) positive spread on every dollar borrowed. Negative leverage refers to situations where the property generates a lower cash flow yield than the interest rate. An example is borrowing at a 10% interest rate for a property with a 5% cash flow, resulting in 5% negative leverage.

To illustrate the effects of positive and negative leverage, we return to the $10 million Anoop Towers purchase. Assume that based on your analysis and negotiations with the lender you decide to use 50% loan-to-value debt ($5 million) to purchase the property, and the lender charges you an interest rate of 5% on the loan. As a result you must pay $250,000 in interest each year ($5 million * 5%). If you purchase the property at an 8 cap rate (after reserves), it generates $800,000 in annual NOI ($10 million * 8%). In this case, you have positive leverage, as the 8% property return exceeds the 5% interest rate. Effectively, you are borrowing a dollar at 5% and investing it at an 8% cash return, generating a 3% cash spread on every dollar borrowed.

How does positive leverage affect your current equity return, which is referred to as your **cash-on-cash** yield? In our example, subtracting the $250,000 interest payment from the projected NOI of $800,000 leaves a before-tax cash flow to equity (net of interest payments) of $550,000. In this case the equity investment is $5 million ($10 million-$5 million), so the cash-on-cash yield is 11% ($550,000 / $5 million), which is substantially higher than the property's 8% yield, as seen in Figure 12.9.

FIGURE 12.9

Cash-on-Cash Yield Calculations	
NOI	$800,000
Interest	$250,000
Profit after Interest Before Taxes	$550,000
Equity Investment	$5 million
Cash-on-Cash Yield	550,000/5,000,000
Cash-on-Cash Yield	11.0%

Positive leverage increases your cash-on-cash yield if the investment meets your pro forma expectations, with your $5 million equity investment earning an 11% return even though the property only generates an 8% return. Combining this expected annual cash-on-cash yield (11%) with the expected annualized capital appreciation gives you a quick estimate of your anticipated annual return. For example, if you use Capital Structure 2, you can quickly estimate your equity's expected total annual return as 11% from cash flow plus 9.5% from expected appreciation, for a total of 20.5%. If this quick calculation yields an equity return that is sufficient in view of the risks of the property and capital structure, you then construct a detailed financial model to more closely analyze the risks and opportunities of the investment. Since NOI is generally expected to grow over time, the expected IRR will be higher, but this quick calculation serves as a sanity check, and saves valuable time and energy.

What happens if you have negative leverage? Assume that the property is a hotel purchased for an 8 cap rate on September 1, 2001, with $5 million in equity, and $5 million of debt carrying a 5% interest rate ($250,000 in annual interest payments). However, instead of the 8% property level return you anticipated, the property is struggling to generate a 1% NOI return, as after the terrorist attacks of September 11, vacancy skyrocketed, room rates fell by 25%, the food and beverage business deteriorated, while most of your operating expenses such as maids, doormen, electricity, security, and other expenses continued. Because of these fixed costs and declining revenues, the building is only generating $100,000 in NOI (1% * $10,000,000). So your before-tax cash flow to equity is negative $150,000 ($100,000-$250,000). Hence, your cash on cash yield is negative 3% (-$150,000 / $5,000,000). As a result of the negative leverage you have a negative 3% return on your cash, versus the property's 1% NOI return. This means that you must come out of pocket an additional $150,000 annually to cover the difference between the property's NOI and your interest payments. In this case, the negative leverage forces you to inject additional equity in order to keep your equity position alive, while you hope that NOI improves. Each $150,000 check you write is additional equity, and as such increases your equity investment above the original $5 million. As a result, the denominator for all subsequent equity return calculations is higher than the original $5,000,000.

If you do not have the $150,000 required to fund the shortfall in this example, you can seek an equity partner. But your negotiating position will be weak, as few want to invest in a deal where they are losing money out of the gate. Particularly if this shortfall occurs unexpectedly, and you need money in a hurry in order to survive, you will not have much negotiating power. This is a major risk associated with debt, and particularly with negative leverage.

Having negative leverage is not necessarily a bad thing. For instance, development is almost always a negative leverage business, as initially your NOI is negative (i.e. no income and lots of costs) and you incur interest payments throughout construction. But you borrow because you believe the property will ultimately yield sufficient cash flows and capital appreciation to offset the risk of debt and negative leverage.

JAPAN AND POSITIVE LEVERAGE

The Japanese real estate market from 1997-2007 offers a vivid example of positive leverage at work. This example also helps you understand that declining cash streams are tricky to evaluate, but can still have substantial value. In fact, even a property with little or no residual value can still be extremely valuable. An analogy is selling a valuable painting collection. Even though you have no asset value left at the end of the sale process, your collection has value and can be a good investment if you were able to pay a low enough acquisition price for the collection.

The Japanese economy experienced basically no growth from 1990-2007. As a result, real estate demand was basically stagnant during this period. However, the real estate supply in Japan grew by about 2% per year during this time. What happens to rents if supply grows while demand remains basically flat and there is no economy-wide inflation? Rental rates decrease. Of course, it was not guaranteed that net rents would continue to decline, as many believed that the Japanese economy was about to turn around. But let's assume that the expectation was that net rents would fall by about 2% annually as the economy continues to stagnate.

Assume that in late 2002 you purchased $100 million of Japanese real estate at a 7 cap rate, so your expected NOI for next year was $7 million. If the economy performs as you expect, net rents will decline by about 2% annually. Figure 12.10 displays the expected NOI for each of the next 4 years.

FIGURE 12.10

Japanese Economy				
Year	**2003**	**2004**	**2005**	**2006**
NOI	$7.00 MM	$6.86 MM	$6.72 MM	$6.59 MM

If you financed 85% of the total purchase price with a 4% interest rate (which was very possible), you invested $15 million ($100 million-$85 million) in equity, and your annual interest payment was $3.4 million (assuming no amortization).

Let's first evaluate the expected cash-on-cash yield for 2003 (first year of ownership). You expected to earn $3.6 million after making your $3.4 million interest payment. On the $15 million equity, this is a 24% annual cash-on-cash yield! This is positive leverage at work, as you are borrowed at 4% and invested in a building that was generating a 7% cash flow. With 85% leverage you are able to leverage the 7% property return into a 24% cash-on-cash yield.

Calculating the expected cash-on-cash yield for each additional year, you see in Figure 12.11 that the cash-on-cash return was expected to decline as the NOI declined due to the decreasing net rents. In fact, the cash-on-cash yield was expected to decrease to 21.3% by 2006. But that's still a nice equity yield. After all, the Japanese long term Treasury bond yielded barely 1%, so if you expect to earn a 21.3% cash-on-cash yield on your property purchase in 2006 it seemed like an attractive yield.

FIGURE 12.11

Japan Example				
Year	**2003**	**2004**	**2005**	**2006**
NOI	$7.00 M	$6.86 M	$6.72 M	$6.59 M
Interest	$3.40 M	$3.40 M	$3.40 M	$3.40 M
Before Tax Cash	$3.60 M	$3.46 M	$3.32 M	$3.19 M
Cash on Cash Yield	24%	23%	22%	21%

But you have a problem, as the property is probably declining in value as NOI falls. Assume that you believed you could sell the building for a 7 cap at the end of 2006. To determine the eventual sales value, you capped pro forma 2007 NOI, which equals 2006 NOI grown one year at negative 2%. This implied an expected sale price of $92.3 million (($6.59 million*(1 + -2%) / 7%). After you repaid the $85 million debt, you expected to only have $7.24 million of your original $15 million equity investment left. That is, you expected to lose more than half ($7.76 million) of your initial equity investment, so your expected equity return from capital appreciation over the four year hold is negative 51.6%, or an annual expected equity capital gain of negative 16.6%. In this case, leverage severely hurt you in terms of capital appreciation, while positive leverage greatly enhanced your cash-on-cash yield. Figure 12.12 shows the expected total equity return for each year, assuming the property is sold in that year at a 7 cap.

FIGURE 12.12

Equity Returns			
	Before Tax Cash	**Before Tax Sales Proceeds**	**Before Tax Equity IRR**
2003	$3.60 M	$13.00 M	10.67%
2004	$3.46 M	$11.04 M	11.05%
2005	$3.32 M	$9.12 M	11.46%
2006	$3.19 M	$7.24 M	11.90%

This example provides a glimpse of the dilemma that the Japanese market presented to property investors: eroding property values but attractive cash-on-cash returns derived from highly positive leverage. If the economy was to rebound or cap rates fell, it would be a home run. On the other hand, if the market deteriorated more than expected, or cap rates rose, you were dead.

HOW MUCH SHOULD I BORROW?

How much debt should you use to fund your real estate projects? There is no single answer. Instead, the decision to borrow depends on both who you are, and the nature of the property. For instance, if you are a developer, the tax shields from debt are less useful than for properties with strong NOIs, as development generates little in the way of taxable income to shelter. On the other hand, a developer may need debt because they do not have enough money to fund the development and additionally desire to diversify their risk exposure. A developer may also borrow in order to enhance the expected capital appreciation when he or she sells the building.

Alternatively, since pension funds are non-taxable entities they have no use for the interest tax shield of debt. Further, cash rich pension funds often do not need debt in order to fund their investments. Since pension funds do not actively operate properties, potential economies of scale are not particularly important. But pension funds often borrow non-recourse to diversify, as well as to enhance their expected returns.

In contrast, a real estate private equity fund may borrow to finance deals they could otherwise not afford, and utilize leverage to enhance expected equity returns. Furthermore, since these funds are usually structured as tax pass-through partnerships, their taxable investors benefit from the debt tax shelter. Thus, such funds historically tend to use leverage in the 65-75% range.

The reasons for borrowing are not mutually exclusive. If you answer the question "why do you want debt", you will be able to determine how much and what type of debt you should use. But if you fail to understand what you are trying to achieve with debt, you are ultimately headed for disaster, as you are taking leveraged risks without a clear purpose. By understanding why you want debt, you can customize your financing to meet your needs.

MEZZANINE FINANCE

Mezzanine finance is a highly customized area of financing. But what is mezzanine finance? It helps to understand mezzanine finance if you know the origins of the term mezzanine. In the department stores built between 1900 and 1929, such as John Wanamaker, Marshall Fields, and Macy's, the first floor was extremely spacious, with high ceilings and elaborate décor to wow customers. On the first floor was high-end women's clothing, while the second floor was high-end men's clothing, and the basement was marked down goods. The second floor was a long climb because of the high ceilings on the first floor, and since there were originally no elevators or escalators, people actually had to walk up the stairs! Since people would get tired walking up three flights of stairs to get to the men's department, many stores incorporated a mezzanine balcony around the interior wall of the first floor. People could stop and catch their breath while shopping on the mezzanine, before continuing up to the men's floor. The store did not put the best women's clothing on the mezzanine because they were on the first floor. And there was insufficient space to put all of the quality men's clothes on the mezzanine. So the mezzanine was used for a bit of everything in between.

That's the spirit of mezzanine financing, except the "first floor" is senior debt (which is exclusively secured by the real estate itself), first priority, while the "second floor" is straight common equity (secured by nothing but the potential success of the legal entity owning the property, as equity is a residual claim on cash flows after all of an entity's liabilities have been satisfied). And mezzanine is every other imaginable type of financing that is not secured by the real estate. Mezzanine is any type of junior debt, whether holding the second position, the seventh position, or unsecured. Mezzanine is also preferred equity where you have specified rights above common equity, but below senior debt. Mezzanine is also convertible debt where you are debt, but you have the right to convert into common equity at specific terms. Mezzanine is also participating debt, where you receive an interest payment each year, and also participate in any property income above a specified level. Of course, if the borrower gives the mezzanine lender a share of income or a portion of the capital appreciation, the lender has to give something in return, such as a lower interest rate, higher LTV (Loan-to-Value), or more favorable covenants.

The only things that limit the type of mezzanine products are your creativity and the market. After all, the market can reject a creative financing product, just as customers can reject department stores selling Christmas lights on the mezzanine on March 1st. For such an offering you're probably not going to find too many buyers. So too with most mezzanine financing products for most properties. Remember, the bulk of real estate financing is generally either straight senior secured debt or common equity. But sometimes your needs merit a customized mezzanine financing.

Mezzanine financing is used mainly by borrowers seeking higher LTVs and who are able to creatively negotiate mezz terms. However, the benefits of mezzanine financing come with both greater risk and higher cost. For example, assume you are purchasing a $10 million office property, but you only have $1 million in equity and need to borrow the rest. The straight senior secured lender offers you a 75% LTV mortgage ($7.5 million) at a 6% interest rate. Thus, you need a $1.5 million mezz piece to purchase the property. The mezzanine lender is willing to provide you with the remaining 15% LTV, but at an 11% interest rate, as the mezzanine lender is taking additional risk due to their subordination to the senior secured lender. Based on this capital structure your weighted average cost of debt capital is 6.83% (as calculated by .83*6 + .17*11), as summarized in Figure 12.13.

FIGURE 12.13

Debt Capital Structure			
Building Value	**$10,000,000**		
	% of Total Debt	Value	Interest Rate
Straight Senior Secured	83%	$7,500,000	6%
Mezzanine Loan	17%	$1,500,000	11%
Total/ Weighted Average	**100%**	**$9,000,000**	**6.83%**

Thus, mezzanine financing is helpful in satisfying your borrowing needs, but raises your weighted average borrowing costs from 6%, if you had only used straight senior secured, to 6.83%. In addition, at the higher leverage inclusive of mezzanine financing, you are more exposed to equity erosion should property values decline.

To calculate your weighted cost of capital for this capital structure, assume you require a 14% annual return on your equity capital. This results in a weighted average cost of capital for the project of 7.55% as summarized in Figure 12.14.

FIGURE 12.14

Debt Capital Structure			
Building Value	**$10,000,000**		
	% of Total Capital	Value	Interest Rate
Debt	90%	$9,000,000	6.83%
Equity	10%	$1,000,000	14%
Total/ Weighted Average	**100%**	**$10,000,000**	**7.55%**

CLOSING THOUGHT

Debt can be your friend in good times, but is an unforgiving enemy in bad times. Real estate's relatively stable cash streams lend themselves to the prudent use of leverage to enhance your returns and diversify your portfolio. However, never forget that real estate is a long term asset, and as such your capital structure should have a sizable slice of the longest form of liability – equity. This equity cushion is essential to see you through the tough times that will inevitably and unexpectedly occur. At least 3 times in the last 35 years, real estate has failed to meet the stress test of maintaining equity value when financed in excess of 55-65% LTV. Yet the industry continually strives to achieve higher leverage levels, and is surprised each time extreme economic and capital market distress wipes out large numbers of equity holders and their lenders. It is true that those who ignore real estate history are condemned to relive it.

Chapter 13
The Use of Debt and Mortgages

"Stick to what you know, but keep learning".
-Dr. Peter Linneman

Thus far we have intentionally largely ignored financing decisions. This is because you need to understand the fundamentals of the real estate business before you can select the appropriate financing structure. If you do not understand the risks and opportunities of a property, you will never be able to efficiently select your financial structure.

Ask yourself, "What is the best financial outcome a secured first mortgage lender can expect from their loan"? The very best a first mortgage lender can expect is to get all of their money back and the timely payment of interest. Their upside is limited to the complete receipt of the principal plus their lending spread, (generally 110-250 basis points over comparable maturity Treasury) in interest payments. Too often lenders forget that if the building vastly outperforms expectations, the lender receives nothing more than their money back plus the timely payment of the agreed upon interest payments. But if the property fares worse, they may not do this well, and could lose much of their money. This yields the very asymmetric lender risk/reward distribution displayed in Figure 13.1 for a loan made at Treasury plus 180 basis points.

FIGURE 13.1

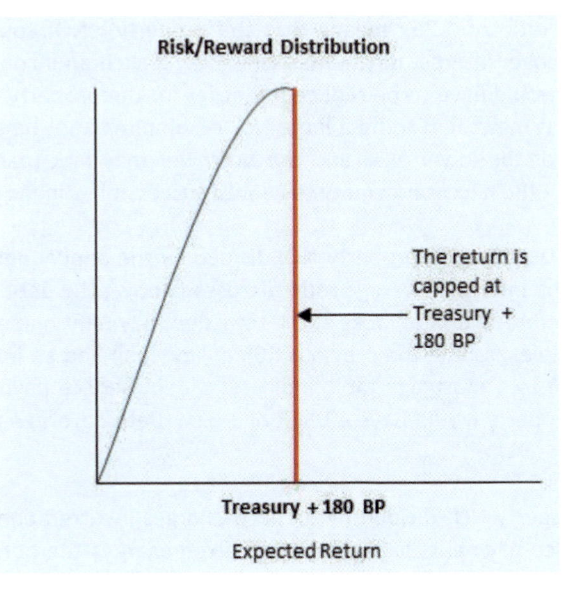

KEY RATIOS

Given their limited upside, lenders must focus on limiting their downside. As a result, a secured lender will underwrite a loan based on many key ratios. The four most commonly used ratios are: loan-to-value, interest coverage, debt coverage, and fixed charges.

Loan-to-Value (LTV) is the principal amount of the loan divided by the believed property value. The loan-to-value ratio reflects how much equity cushion the lender believes they have before value has fallen to the point that the property's value is less than the loan. For instance, if the lender believes the value of the property is $100 million and they wish to maintain a maximum LTV of 65%, they will lend the borrower up to $65 million. Typically, the LTV for secured first mortgages ranges from 50-70%.

A major problem facing lenders is "what is the property's value"? If the loan is being made to support a purchase, they will generally utilize the purchase price as the value. Of course, if the buyer is overpaying (a common problem in hot markets), this value cushion can quickly disappear. Even more problematic is the assessment of value for refinancing (refi); as there is no arms length purchase transaction to establish value. In this case an appraisal is usually done in order to provide a basis for valuation. However, these appraisals are always wrong, as they are nothing more than (hopefully) informed and unbiased professional guesses. The result is that valuations tend to be notably overstated in hot capital markets, as lenders are eager to put out money to both aggressive buyers and refinancers. Hence, when capital markets cool, much of the apparent equity cushion can quickly evaporate, leading to larger than expected lender losses.

Interest Coverage Ratio is the property NOI divided by the annual interest payment. This ratio indicates how many times NOI can cover the interest obligation, and gives the lender an idea of how much of an income cushion you have to cover your interest obligation. The higher the ratio, the greater the cushion you have for paying your interest obligations. For instance, a property with a $10 million NOI and $6.25 million in annual interest payments has an interest coverage ratio of 1.6x. Lenders will often establish a minimum interest coverage ratio. If the lender underwrites to a minimum interest coverage ratio of 1.2x for a property generating $10 million NOI, the maximum interest payment is $8.33 million ($10 million NOI / 1.2 interest coverage ratio). Typical interest coverage ratios are 1.2 to 2.0x for secured first mortgages.

An interest coverage ratio of 1.25x means that the property's NOI could fall by 25% and would still generate sufficient income to cover interest payments. However, if such an income decline occurs as the loan is coming due, the loan amount would have to be reduced in order for the property to achieve a 1.25x coverage on its reduced income. Thus, what may seem to be a large NOI cushion may not be as comfortable as it appears as the loan is not refinanceable at the lower NOI, and the borrower may lack (particularly in times when NOI is plummeting) the ability to inject the necessary equity to allow a successful refinancing.

Debt Service Coverage Ratio (DSCR) is the property NOI divided by the annual debt service payment. While this may seem to be the same as the interest coverage ratio discussed above, the debt service coverage ratio includes amortization of the loan. Therefore, the ratio looks at the total debt payment made each year, rather than just the interest component. For example, assume the previous $65 million loan had an interest rate of 7% and a 20 year amortization period. Referring to a mortgage table indicates a debt service payment of $6.14 million annually. With $10 million in NOI, the property would have a DSCR of 1.63x. Debt coverage ratios generally exceed 1.2x for secured first mortgages.

Fixed Charges Ratio is the property NOI divided by all fixed charges incurred annually. Thus, the fixed charges ratio will include all debt service payments as well as other fixed charges the borrower incurs, including ground lease payments, operating leases, and payments on unsecured debt. Assume that in addition to the $6.14 million debt service in the previous example, the borrower pays $1 million in annual ground lease payments and another $1 million interest on a second mortgage on the property. With $10 million in NOI, the property has a 1.23x fixed charges ratio ($10 million in NOI / ($6.14 debt service + $1 million ground rent + $1 million second mortgage interest)).

What are the "right" LTV, interest coverage ratio, DSCR, and fixed charges ratios? That depends on the lender, the borrower, and the property. For instance, some lenders are willing to exceed the industry norms, while others lend very conservatively. For each ratio, the lender will analyze the fundamentals of the property and lend according to their risk profile and return expectations. And the borrower must always remember that while higher LTVs and lower coverage ratios generate larger loan proceeds, they also increase the risk of financial distress and foreclosure will occur. There is no free lunch.

OTHER KEY LOAN TERMS

While these ratios are important, **loan covenants** are often far more important and contentious. In order to limit the downside of the risk profile illustrated previously, lenders demand as many loan covenants as possible. Covenants are the terms or clauses of the loan agreement. There are **positive** ("things you must do") and **negative** ("things you cannot do") covenants in a loan agreement. Lenders hope these covenants never become an issue, as if they do, it means there is a problem. It is much like parenting. You do not want to impose a lot of restrictions on your children as you would prefer they voluntarily behave like angels. Yet good parents must impose certain restrictions to help avoid instances where children might act inappropriately. Despite your teenage protests, if your parents had not imposed a 4 a.m. curfew, too often you would have come home at 7 a.m. The lender is in the same position.

Lenders must consider situations that help them avoid losses that might arise from a borrower's careless behavior. While the numbers (the interest rate, amortization, fees, and loan amount) are important, you are going to spend much of your time negotiating covenants with the lender. In fact, it is relatively easy to identify an excessively "hot" debt market, as standard loan covenants disappear in the rush by lenders to get money out the door. While this might seem advantageous to borrowers, such overheated markets (like the early 1970s, late 1980s, and 2005-2007) are usually followed by ice cold loan markets, with little debt available to refinance maturing loans or support property prices. As a result, the seemingly great loan on offer in a red hot loan market may simply lure the borrower to overpay for a property, only to default into the teeth of the subsequent ice cold debt market.

COMMON NEGATIVE COVENANTS

Prepayment Penalty: If the borrower pays off a fixed interest rate loan prior to the maturity, they must generally pay a pre-determined cash penalty. This covenant protects lenders from massive prepayments if interest rates drop, as if such prepayments occur the lender effectively loses the difference between the original interest rate and the lower interest rate. The penalty generally ensures that the lender receives the originally agreed upon interest rate (or better). In some instances the loan may contain a lock out clause, which is the complete prohibition of early repayment for a specified period of time.

Distributions: The lender may restrict the distributions paid to equity holders. For example, assume a building is generating $8 million NOI annually, and interest is absorbing $3.5 million of that income. The lender may require you to set aside an additional $3.5 million in reserves or in an escrow account in case you are unable to meet future interest payments or capital expenditure needs. These reserves provide the lender a cushion for hard times.

Operating Restrictions: The lender will frequently specify certain operating levels that the property cannot fall below without the loan becoming due upon the lender's request (so called, **loan acceleration**). For example, occupancy cannot drop below 80%, or rents cannot fall below specified levels. The reason is that lenders worry that a desperate borrower might sign below market leases, hence deteriorating the value of their collateral. Why would a borrower ever sign a below market lease? Because the borrower may derive leasing commissions and management fees from the lease which may exceed their loss in equity value. This is particularly a concern when the property is in trouble and there is little remaining equity value. In anticipation of such possibilities the lender imposes loan covenants that protect their collateral by making it difficult for the borrower to act inappropriately.

Operating restrictions may also restrict tenant quality. For example, assume a landlord wants to lease to Wish And Prayer Inc because of high rents and an upfront leasing commission. The problem is that Wish And Prayer is a very low credit company. Remember that debt holders do not benefit from property's upside, but are exposed to the property's downside risk. To mitigate their collateral risk, lenders may require the building be leased to specific tenants or tenants of a specified minimum credit quality.

Additional Debt: The lender may not let you obtain additional financing without their permission. Even if the lender has a secured first position they worry about you taking on additional debt which is subordinate to their mortgage, as this additional debt burden may prohibit you from making future loan payments. In addition, the second loan could have payments due a day before the first lender's payments are due. As a result, although the lender has a secured first position, critical cash flow could go to the second lender due to timing.

In general, loan documents specify that if any covenant is violated, the lender has the right to accelerate the loan, i.e. make it be due "now" if they so choose.

COMMON POSITIVE COVENANTS

Deposits: The lender might require you to maintain a minimum deposit balance with them. Or the lender could require you to keep the corporate checking account at their bank with a minimum balance.

EBIT, Cash Flow, or NOI: These restrictions require that the property maintain minimum levels of EBIT, Cash Flow, or NOI. These minimums provide the lender with a cushion and check on the status of the collateral.

Leases: The lender may require that the borrower provide copies of all new leases prior to execution in order to allow the lender to check the borrower's leasing execution versus the business plan.

LOAN TERMS

Secured: A secured loan is secured by recourse to the assets of the property. If the borrower fails to repay the loan, the secured lender is entitled to foreclose on the secured assets to satisfy their claim. What assets? The lender will secure against the building, the improvements, the land, and the leases. In the event the lender takes control of the property, they will need to claim the leases because they are the sources of cash flows. Remember that the cash flows, to a large extent are derived from the leases, rather than the bricks and mortar.

Recourse: If the loan is solely secured by the property's assets, it is referred to as a **non-recourse** loan. This means the lender only has recourse to the property's assets, and cannot seize any of the borrower's personal assets to mitigate losses. Absent additional collateral, the outstanding loan balance effectively becomes a put option for the borrower. That is, if the property value falls below the loan balance, the borrower can de facto sell the property to the lender for forgiveness of the loan balance. As a result, lenders need to bear in mind that their loan balance is effectively a standing offer to purchase the asset at the loan balance.

Alternatively, the lender might secure against personal assets of the borrower. In this case, if the borrower does not repay the loan, the lender can look to the borrower's personal assets in order to cover any losses on their loan, with the specifics of the process covered by state and federal bankruptcy codes. This is called **recourse** lending. Even if you structure your company as a limited liability entity, you can choose to place your personal assets at risk with a recourse loan. Legal structures that limit your liability to the assets involved in the project only mean the lender cannot unilaterally go after these personal or other assets. But the borrower can contractually agree to pledge personal or other assets. Most first mortgages are non-recourse except for specifically carved out "bad boy" acts (e.g. fraud or theft) by the borrower, and completion guarantees for development.

Guarantees: Lenders sometime require that the borrower guarantee certain events such as construction completion or leasing to a specific level of occupancy. For example, lenders often require that the developer guarantees the receipt of a certificate of occupancy for their property. Once this certificate is received, the borrower is relieved from recourse to their personal assets. However, failure to complete the project allows the lender to go after the borrower's personal assets.

Receivables: In addition to the leases, the lender may have rights to outstanding lease payments, meaning that any monies owed by tenants to the landlord accrue to the lender in order to satisfy their loan losses.

Draws: For construction loans, you must generally present the lender with supporting documentation on the use of loan proceeds. Any money you ask for must have a documented legitimate purpose (such as receipts of bills paid or copies of permits) before the loan draw, or funding, will be approved.

Amortization: Instead of only paying interest, most loans also have a specific **amortization schedule**. The borrower makes a payment each month (or quarter) that is composed of both interest and principal. It is common, though not always the case, that the payment total is the same for each payment. For example, you may have a $50 million loan with 6% annual interest rate, which matures in 10 years, with a 30 year amortization schedule. The amortization schedule specifies the number of years over which the principal is repaid. In the case of a 30 year amortization schedule, your payments will have completely paid off the loan at the end of 30 years. But how does this work if the loan matures in 10 years? You calculate the constant monthly payment, called the loan constant, as if the loan will be completely paid off over 30 years, but the final payment at the end of the tenth year is equal to the usual payment plus a **balloon payment** equal to all remaining principal which is owed.

Calculating loan constants used to absorb a great deal of time utilizing a complicated equation. However, the advent of cheap computing power and the internet make such schedules easily available. Just go to Google and enter "mortgage constant calculator" and click on one of the free and easy to use calculators. All you need to do is enter the loan amount, interest rate, loan term, and desired years to amortize, and the monthly (or annual) payment throughout the life of the loan is calculated.

Insurance: This is a critical issue, particularly since the September 11, 2001 terrorist attacks. A common loan covenant is that the borrower must maintain all insurance on the property that is "customary and typical", in an amount sufficient to cover the loan balance. Such insurance means that in the event of an insurable disaster, the borrower will receive insurance payments that are sufficient to repay the loan in full. The lender generally does not care if you insure beyond this amount. They just want their money back.

Before September 11th, few paid much attention to terrorism insurance, which was largely provided as part of the property's umbrella insurance coverage. After September 11th, many building owners were unable to obtain terrorism insurance, or could only obtain terrorism insurance at a premium payment of perhaps 2% of the value of the property. This implies a probability of roughly one out of every fifty buildings being blown up each year! If the borrower cannot get terrorism insurance or is unwilling to pay the premium, are they in breach of the loan covenant requiring "customary and typical" insurance? Yes, in the eyes of the lender, and if the borrower has breached the contract the lender may have the right to accelerate the loan. At first, some borrowers thought they wanted lenders to accelerate the loan so they could refinance the building at a lower interest rate without a prepayment penalty. However, borrowers quickly realized they would also need terrorism insurance before a new lender would make a loan. Similar problems frequently occur with respect to hurricane and earthquake insurance following major disasters.

Sweep: Any money that comes into the property must generally be paid to the lender until contractual loan obligations are satisfied. Imagine that the rent is paid on the 15th of the month, and the loan payment is due on the 16th of the month. If the owner knows they are about to default, they will deposit the rent check elsewhere on the 15th, and then default on the loan on the 16th. One way the lender protects against such behavior is with a sweep provision, which allows the lender to take all cash inflows until their loan is satisfied.

LOAN POINTS

The lender will generally charge a fee, commonly called **loan points**, for processing the loan. This is designed to cover the lender's costs associated with performing due diligence, conducting credit checks, environmental analysis, and the time and energy of its employees. The lender will charge the borrower a fee that is quoted in basis points to cover these costs. The typical loan fee is 30-100 basis points of the total amount of the loan. Do not confuse this fee with the interest rate paid on the loan. The loan points are paid at closing for making the loan. The interest rate is charged for the use of the lender's money for the term of the loan. From a cash flow perspective, loan points are an upfront outflow. From an accounting perspective you generally amortize the loan points over the life of the loan.

THE REFI DECISION

Refinancing is the replacement of one debt facility with another. Deciding whether to prematurely refinance your mortgage can be a very difficult decision. By refinancing, you may be able to withdraw cash from your property without paying any capital gains taxes. In addition, by refinancing you can lock in today's interest rate on a new long-term mortgage. But you also give up the option that rates may be even lower when your current mortgage matures. Further, early refinancing entails fees, and may trigger substantial prepayment penalties. Also, to the extent that you borrow more money than the remaining principal at the time of the refinancing, you will have a higher mortgage payment than on your existing loan. On the other hand, the new loan will generally provide a better tax shield as it will have a repayment schedule with greater interest expense, as you will once again be in the early years of the amortization schedule. In short, the early refinance decision requires you to carefully consider what objectives are most important to you, as well as to determine the desired risk-return profile for your property ownership.

There are two common reasons to undertake an early refinancing. The first is that your property has risen substantially in value, allowing you to notably increase the amount of debt on your property. Consider if you have a $70 million mortgage on a property which was worth $100 million seven years ago, when you took out a 10 year mortgage. Today the property is worth $170 million and after 8 years of amortization, the outstanding loan balance is $60 million. Thus, your current loan to value ratio is a mere 35%. By refinancing the property at a 70% loan to value, you could receive a $119 million mortgage. Thus, after retiring your existing $60 million loan balance, the refinancing generates $59 million in net proceeds. If the loan is non-recourse, this money goes into your pocket absent any taxes, irrespective of what happens to the property in the future. Your problem is that absent a refinancing, the existing $60 million mortgage, which has two years to maturity, locks in your first collateral position at a massively underleveraged level. While you could use mezzanine financing to tap into this underleveraged value, the fact that you cannot access your first lien position means that the pricing on a mezzanine financing will not be as attractive as if you could pay off your loan and refinance using the first lien right on the full $170 million value.

The second common reason for premature refinancing is that mortgage interest rates have fallen significantly relative to your existing mortgage. For example, if you have a 10 year mortgage with two years to maturity at an 8% interest rate, while the current interest rate on a 10 year mortgage is 5.7%, every dollar borrowed at the old rate costs you 2.3% in additional interest (pre-tax). If you refinance at the current lower rate, and lock this rate in for 10 years, you substantially lower the cost of your debt. If the amount of the loan and all other terms were the same, and refinancing were costless, you would always refinance when interest rates fall. Thus, the questions are: how expensive is it to refinance relative to the savings you achieve from refinancing at the current rate, and are other loan terms (including the amount borrowed) equal or better on the new loan?

The most common problems associated with prematurely refinancing are: the time and energy involved; fees; more stringent loan terms; and prepayment penalties. However, time, energy and fees, while substantial, are really a matter of time shifting. That is, you are going to have to refinance when your loan matures, so an early refinancing simply means you are doing it sooner. As a result, it is only the time value of these items which are of relevance. Hence, these factors tend to be relatively unimportant in the decision to prematurely refinance.

In general, there is no reason to believe that terms and covenants for the new loan will be systematically more onerous than the existing loan. Some will be better; others worse. But since debt markets are sometimes either overheated or super cold, terms must be carefully evaluated on a case by case basis in order to ascertain whether the new loan is more attractive in this regard.

Prepayment penalties are usually the major problem facing premature refinancing. Fixed rate mortgages with maturities greater than three years generally have substantial prepayment penalties. These penalties come in many forms, but all variants effectively require that the lender receives (at least) the present value of the future interest payments over the remaining term of the loan. The discount rate used in these present value calculations is the short term U.S. Treasury rate, resulting in a refinancing payment substantially in excess of the true present value of future mortgage payments (because the Treasury rate is lower than rate on a newly minted comparable loan the loan's interest rate). These prepayment penalties reflect the lender's desire to receive the payment stream specified in their loan.

In spite of the fact that there is generally little opportunity for interest payment savings via premature refinance, a premature refinancing may still make sense. There are four general cases where this is true. The first is when you are able to convince the lender that issuing you a new long-term fixed-rate loan, which generates origination fees and places money for the lender, is better for them than you refinancing your loan with a competitor when your current loan matures. But you will only refinance with them now if the lender waives the prepayment penalty. This sometimes happens in a highly competitive lending market, particularly when your current mortgage has only a short term remaining, as the loan officer may be pressed to place new funds in order to meet personal compensation production targets.

A second scenario is that you believe (perhaps correctly, perhaps incorrectly; only time will tell) that interest rates are at unsustainably low levels. As a result, in spite of the prepayment penalties associated with the current loan, you decide to lock in today's long-term rates before they disappear. This tends to be relevant only when the remaining term on your mortgage is short. For example, you may be willing to suffer the prepayment penalty for the remaining year on your current loan, in order to lock today's very attractive interest rate for the subsequent nine years. Essentially, you are only moderately worse off for the next year, and believe you will be much better off for the ensuing nine years, as you believe that if you wait until maturity to refinance, interest rates will be much higher. The shorter the remaining term of the existing loan, and the more unsustainable you believe today's rates are, the more likely you are to execute an early refinancing.

A third case is that, in spite of prepayment penalties, you desire to pull out capital on a non-taxed, non-recourse basis, in order to access substantially underleveraged appreciation in your property. In this case, you are making a decision to take your money off the table tax-free, and the prepayment penalties associated with the premature refinancing are simply the cost of doing so.

A fourth case is that as the new owner of the property, you can borrow at notably lower rates due to a superior credit rating or access to cheap capital. For example, if GE purchases a property, they may achieve a lower interest rate due to their superior credit. Alternatively, perhaps you were a young start-up when you took out the mortgage, while today you are a preferred customer of the lender. It is important to keep in mind that these four possibilities are not mutually exclusive. For example, it is possible you want to refinance because you believe rates are too low, and your credibility with banks has also improved, plus you desire to take cash out of the property to fund other investment activities.

Early refinancing decisions are challenging, and require understanding of what you are trying to achieve, as well as number crunching to see if the benefits outweigh the costs.

REFINANCING IN A DOWN MARKET

Refinancing in a down property market, which usually coincides with a cold debt market, is a serious challenge. Not only may the property be worth less than the loan balance i.e., be "underwater", but higher underwriting standards will often make it impossible to refinance the loan balance. In such cases, tedious and often hostile negotiations will transpire between the borrower and lender. The tenor of these discussions is usually the lender saying "just pay me" and the borrower saying "I can't and it's not my fault; just give me time". This is a highly nuanced area, and never pleasant. But often re-striking a deal with an honest and competent borrower is a better solution than foreclosing and conducting a distressed property sale in a down property market. About once a decade this type of systemic problem arises and is solved by a combination of extended maturities and equity infusions. In the (2008-2010) cycle, many lenders "extended and pretended", extending loan maturity as long as borrowers made debt payments. Why? Because the properties were cash flowing enough to cover monthly payments and they hoped that capital markets understated the value of the properties, making an accurate valuation of the property impossible. As a result, many insolvent borrowers remained in business and survived the frozen capital markets.

CLOSING THOUGHT

Will the lender get all of the terms they desire? Probably not. But given the secured lender's asymmetric return profile, you should expect them to get most. Frequently, the terms discussed above are "take it" or "leave it". However, when lenders get aggressive, they frequently compromise the restrictiveness of their covenants. Similarly, when borrowers feel that they cannot lose on their projects, more restrictive covenants are accepted and recourse guarantees are frequently provided.

Chapter 14
Commercial Mortgage Backed Securities

"The machine is rarely the problem; the people operating the machine are the problem".
-Dr. Peter Linneman

Thus far we have discussed debt financing only in the context of a single mortgage secured by an individual asset. However, the process of loan origination does not always stop with property level underwriting. In fact, a substantial secondary market exists. The evolution and subsequent collapse of the commercial mortgage backed security (CMBS) market reflects significant changes in capital sources.

CAPITAL EVOLUTION

In 1970, if you were looking for money for your real estate project, you would primarily look to commercial banks and life insurance companies. Commercial banks held federally insured deposits, and in return the federal government imposed numerous regulations on the commercial banking industry. One of the most important regulations barred commercial banks from investing in equity, as equity was considered too risky. Despite modern portfolio theory's views of diversification, government regulators viewed a 100% debt portfolio as safer than having any equity. Therefore, commercial banks could only receive federal insurance on their deposits if their investments were debt, generally secured loans to local borrowers.

Banks issued debt secured by accounts receivable, cars, single-family homes, and commercial real estate. Commercial banks have short term liabilities, as depositors can withdraw their deposits at any time. Therefore, in 1970 banks were primarily responsible for originating construction loans, as the short term and finite nature of the construction period matched their short term deposit liabilities.

At that time, banks were generally not permitted to have more than one office location. Even in the most progressive states, banks could only have a few branch locations within their home county. With only a single office location, most banks primarily originated local loans, as they had staff only in that area to evaluate prospective loans. So if you owned a bank in Grand Island, Nebraska, it was unlikely you made any loans outside of your county, let alone New York, Los Angeles, Philadelphia, or D.C. The large banks located in major US cities had the same constraints, but had larger deposit bases and served a larger local market. Senior bank managers knew the local borrowers and personally conducted business with them. Even if better opportunities existed in other markets, regulatory restrictions made it difficult to lend outside of the bank's immediate area, so most local banks simply attempted to develop lending relationships with the "best" local borrowers.

The other major sources of money at that time were the large life insurance companies. Life insurance companies take in policy premiums, invest to earn a return spread, and return the money when a policyholder dies. Actuarially a person's lifetime is a long term liability. Therefore, life insurance companies were logical long term lenders (3 to 20 years), as they sought to match their long term liabilities with long lived assets. Life insurance companies have historically been heavily regulated by the states as a result of the fear that an insurer will collect premiums from policyholders and bet on very risky assets. If the bets pay off, the insurer wins; if they lose, the insurer will be unable to pay on its policies. As a result, most state regulators require insurers limit equity investments to roughly 25% of total investments, with the remainder of their portfolios primarily composed of long term debt.

Given the heavily regulated nature of these two major sources of capital, an abundance of money flowed into real estate lending. While there were other capital sources, such as university endowments, charitable foundations, high net worth individuals, and a few pension and mutual funds, commercial banks and life insurance companies were the dominant sources of capital. In fact, US pension funds had few assets in 1970.

Today, the structure and regulation of capital sources has changed dramatically. For instance, banks operate nationally and freely invest in equities. While in real terms, banks and life insurance companies control more assets than ever, they are no longer the primary sources of capital. Instead, today if you are looking for money for your projects, you will also look to pension funds, mutual funds, endowments, and sovereign wealth funds. Pension funds and mutual funds control roughly 65% of all assets in the US, while banks and life insurers have gone from roughly 70% of all assets in 1970, to less than 35% of all assets today.

Pension funds and mutual funds are also regulated, but these regulations are primarily "prudent man" and disclosure regulations. Specifically, mutual funds are allowed to invest in anything as long as fund managers fully disclose and abide by their stated investment criteria. For example, if a mutual fund manager discloses that they will only invest in AAA bonds, the mutual fund cannot invest in lower rated bonds. Mutual funds have proliferated, investing in a variety of debt and equity investments, including real estate debt and equity.

Since pension funds are tax-exempt entities, the IRS is concerned with pension funds taking over businesses and wiping out corporate tax revenues. Therefore, pension funds are generally prohibited from actively owning businesses. As a result, most pension funds primarily invest via securities and private equity funds.

FOLLOW THE MONEY

Real estate needs to follow the money because it is a very capital-intensive business. So it is not surprising that the nature of real estate financing has changed dramatically as the sources of capital changed. With 65% of the money in the United States held by pension funds and mutual funds, the real estate industry had to figure out a way to access these deep pools of capital with a preference for securitized investments. CMBS is the vehicle used to achieve this goal with respect to real estate debt. The CMBS market did not exist in 1970, and still does not exist in most countries, as if banks are the only source of debt capital, CMBS serve little purpose.

HOW IS A CMBS CREATED?

Suppose you are a commercial mortgage lender. You have contacts and relationships with numerous borrowers, as well as the capacity to underwrite loans. However, having originated fifty, $10 million mortgages, you exhaust your $500 million capital base. If you could package your 50 mortgages and sell them to the countless fixed income mutual funds and pension funds, you could use the sale proceeds to originate more loans, allowing you to capitalize on your underwriting expertise. Pension and mutual funds generally lack loan origination and underwriting capacity, but are major investors in fixed income securities. So if you can match your mortgage origination skills with their deep pockets, you can underwrite a lot of mortgages.

Each mortgage you issue is secured by a warehouse, apartment, mall, or other real property. Assume that the average loan-to-value ratio is 65% with an interest coverage ratio of 1.4x. Of course, these ratios vary across the individual loans, but none of the loans has an LTV above 70% or a debt coverage ratio below 1.3x. Further assume that the weighted average interest rate across the 50 mortgages is 7%, and that, for simplicity, all the loans have prepayment prohibitions, no amortization, 10-year terms, with the same beginning date and maturity date. Each of these simplifying assumptions illustrates the incredible nuances that one ultimately encounters with actual CMBS packaging, as to the extent that these assumptions do not hold, the bookkeeping and math becomes much more complex, as in reality, all mortgages will not have the same maturity, interest rate, amortization schedule, LTV, or covenants.

Each mortgage is secured by the property's leases and loan documents. This is a tremendous amount of paper! This is why you see increasing standardization in the loan documents for loans that are part of a CMBS securitization. For example, no loan in a CMBS issuance may be allowed to have a DCR below 1.3x, or to exceed

70% LTV, and no one borrower can have more than a few properties in the pool. These standardized terms make it easier for the pension funds and mutual funds looking to invest in your CMBS issue to understand the pool of mortgages.

Given the assumed loan pool, you expect to receive $35 million in interest payments each year for the next 10 years ($500 million * 7% interest rate), and at the end of the 10th year the $500 million principal will be repaid. Remember that your core competence is as a loan originator. If you have the underwriting capacity to originate $500 million in loans each quarter, but only have $500 million available to lend, you cannot lend beyond your current portfolio. Therefore, rather than tie up your $500 million for the next 10 years, while your origination expertise sits idle, you decide to package and sell your existing loans in order to capitalize on your underwriting skills by originating more loans with the sale proceeds.

HOW DO YOU SELL?

To facilitate the sale of your mortgage pool you create a new special purpose company that will ultimately own the pool of mortgages. You first transfer your 50 mortgages to this new **bankruptcy remote** company in exchange for 100% ownership of the new company. The new company's bankruptcy remote structure means that, other than fraud, if something goes wrong with the assets in the new company, investors cannot generally come after either you or your loan origination company. You then put your ownership of the new company, which owns the 50 mortgages, up for sale to the highest bidder. Specifically, you will try to convince the fixed income desks of pension funds and fixed income mutual funds to buy the ownership of the new company. By focusing on these large institutional fixed income capital sources which desire long term assets, you will generally obtain a better price for the new company than if you only marketed to dedicated real estate money sources.

Your $500 million mortgage pool generates $35 million on $500 million, or a 7% yield. If you can sell the ownership claims on new company to investors for a pro forma 6.5% IRR on their investment in the new company, you can reap substantial profits. After all, the buyers of the new company do not care what interest rate you received on the mortgages, as to them it is just a company with $35 million in cash flow (with underwritten expected shortfalls) each of the next 10 years, with an additional $500 million in cash flow at the end of the 10th year. The buyers will compare this investment with others of similar risk that can generate $35 million in expected cash flow each year with $500 million at the end of 10 years. As the seller, you will try to get the buyer to offer as high a price (accept as low a return) as possible.

You will generally engage a CMBS sales and marketing specialist, such as an investment bank, to market to potential buyers to determine how much each buyer will pay for an ownership claim in the new company. If the market purchases the company for a 6.5% IRR over the 10 year hold, you will sell the company for $518 million.

PROFIT FROM THE CMBS PACKAGING

What was the cost of this process? First, you had to make the $500 million in loans. You also had to pay lawyers and accountants to create and certify the new company, and you have to pay fees to the sales agent for marketing the securities. If the costs of creating and selling the securities are $8 million, you net $10 million in profit, as seen in Figure 14.1.

FIGURE 14.1

The Calculation	
Sold For	$518 million
Loans Made	($500 million)
Costs	($8 million)
Net Profit	$10 million

As a result of the sale, you can pull out $10 million in profit and still have $500 million for new originations. If you originate, package, and sell $500 million in mortgages each quarter, you can generate $40 million in profits from sales, as well as the profit from loan origination fees on $2 billion in annual loan originations. At a 20 basis point loan origination fee profit, this amounts to an additional $4 million profit (4*$500 MM*.002) annually. Thus, your total annual net profit from this business is $44 million ($4 million from origination fees and $40 million from the four sales). Note that you only require $500 million in capital to fund your $2 billion in annual mortgage originations. In our example, securitization allows you to generate $44 million in profit, while if you originated the $500 million in loans and held them, you will only generate $36 million in profit in the first year, and $35 million for the remaining 9 years. Hence, the more frequently you can originate and sell, the greater are your profits.

IT'S ABOUT SPECIALIZATION

Securitization allows returns to specialization, with you specializing in origination, someone else in packaging, someone else in marketing the deal, and somebody else in holding the loans. Prior to the emergence of CMBS, you had to make the loan, hold it, and do all the bookkeeping until maturity. CMBS allows different people to serve different functions. You can originate the loan without holding it. You can hold it without originating it. You can manage it without either originating it or holding it.

The management of the entity is typically outsourced for a fee to two different specialists. One company (the **servicer**) is responsible for assuring that the borrowers are in compliance with their loan documents, and taking appropriate actions if the borrower is in default. This servicer also makes sure that investors and the IRS receive all pertinent information in a timely manner. The other management specialist is the **special servicer**, who takes control of the administration of any non-performing loans. The special servicer receives a small fee for being prepared to take over non-performing loans as well as an incentive-related fee for dealing with any defaults that arise.

The CMBS process is the creation and sale of new special purpose companies that own pools of mortgages. The more companies you can profitably sell in a year, the more money you can make. The business model attempts to take advantage of your specialization skills whether you are the servicer, the special servicer, the originator, the packager, or the ultimate investor. A profit occurs if there are enough buyers willing to invest in these companies. This ultimately requires quality mortgages, efficient packaging and marketing, and effective servicing. In this sense, CMBS is no different from soda bottling. You could make your own bottles, but there are companies that specialize in bottling, and you buy from them because they can do it more efficiently than you. And if the soda inside the bottles is of poor or erratic quality, ultimately people will stop buying the product, no matter how effective the marketing.

Originally, government agencies and banks with disastrous balance sheets primarily utilized the CMBS process to securitize existing mortgages. The next step was to originate mortgages with the intent of quickly securitizing the loans. Wall Street stepped in, using their sales and marketing skills, to create an active CMBS market. From 1997-2007, many investment banks purchased mortgages from banks, life companies, and mortgage brokers, as well as directly issued loans. This allowed them to pool large volumes of mortgages and quickly sell and recycle their available capital. From a marketing perspective, investment banks were ideal issuers as they specialize in selling securities, with sales teams and research support to push the securities. Of course, some CMBS purchasers employed independent research analysts to help sort through the many available CMBS offerings.

Perhaps the key marketing tool for debt securities is a bond rating from a major rating agency, such as Moody's or S&P, which theoretically independently assesses the likelihood of the debt holder receiving interest and principal as promised. It is not a rating of whether the securities are a good investment. The CMBS packager pays the rating agencies a fee to rate the securities. These rating agencies are incredibly important, as many buyers can only invest in AA or better rated securities.

CREATING TRANCHES

The rating agencies are critically important when the CMBS issuance is targeted towards multiple buyers of different risk profiles. In our original example, you created a company which sold a single class of ownership claim to pension funds and fixed income mutual funds. However, if the loan pool is large enough, it is possible to sell multiple ownership classes in an attempt to appeal to a much broader set of investors. This is referred to as **tranching** the CMBS pool. Tranching, which is the CMBS industry norm, involves the creation of 8-15 separate ownership claims of differing priority on the commingled stream of cash flows from the underlying pool of mortgages. For example, you can create a highly preferred ownership claim ("super senior"), a second ownership claim subordinate to this first claim, another ownership claim subordinate to this second ownership claim, and so on. In this case, the first ownership claim is entitled to its contracted cash flow before the subordinate investors receive any money from the pool. That is, if there is insufficient cash flow as a result of defaults or non-payments on the underlying mortgages, CMBS investors will not share the loss equally. Rather, the most senior claims will receive their money first, while the most subordinated ownership claim only receives their contractual payments if there are enough proceeds to pay all senior tranches. If the most subordinated ownership claim is insufficient to cover the entire shortfall, then the next lowest ownership claim incurs subsequent shortfall losses. This continues up the ownership classes.

Clearly the most senior ownership claim has the most protection from not receiving their contractual payments because of the subordinated owners. The actual structuring of the different tranches is highly technical, as some ownership claims may be entitled to only interest payments, while others receive only principal payments, some contractual payments may float with LIBOR, etc. Nevertheless, the idea is very simple. You create and sell ownership rights of varying seniority rather than a single ownership right to the company as in our original example.

The rating agencies apply simplistic models in an effort to determine the likelihood of losing money for the various ownership claims. In 2002, the 60% most senior claims on CMBS cash flows typically received AAA ratings, with another 10% rated AA, 10% rated A, 10% rated BBB, and roughly 8% in the BB range. The last 2% was the most subordinated ownership claim, effectively the common equity of the company. Namely, they received all the money not promised to the more senior ownership classes, and were in the first loss position. This is the most risky ownership position.

The lower the subordination, the lower the rating. The higher the rating, the lower the contractual payment rate promised to the investor (i.e., the tighter the yield spread over comparable US treasury yields). That is, the higher the ownership claim, the more the investor is willing to pay for its contractual cash flow stream. Cutting up the underlying cash flows (the $35 million annual payment) does not create or destroy risk, as the cash flow stream itself is unchanged. However, while the LTV on the overall pool is unchanged by tranching, you have created a de facto higher LTV and interest coverage for the most senior ownership claim, as they receive their money first, at the expense of the more subordinate ownership claims.

Tranching will generally generate a better price than the $518 million you realized by selling a single ownership claim, as you will find investors who are willing to pay for the customized ownership claims, particularly the most preferred ownership claim. Returning to our original example, assume the super senior 60% of the $500 million was sold at an IRR pricing of 5.8%. This 60% is rated AAA and offers the lowest risk to investors, justifying a lower required rate of return. The remaining $200 million consists of a $50 million AA rated tranche selling at a 6.2% IRR, a $50 million A rated tranche selling at a 6.4% IRR, a $50 million BBB rated tranche selling at a 6.8% IRR, a $30 million BB rated tranche selling at a 7% IRR, while the last $20 million is a unrated tranche that sells for a 9% IRR, as summarized in Figure 14.2.

FIGURE 14.2

CMBS Tranching			
Rating	% of Total Pool	Value	IRR
AAA	60%	$300 MM	5.8%
AA	10%	$50 MM	6.2%
A	10%	$50 MM	6.4%
BBB	10%	$50 MM	6.8%
BB	6%	$30 MM	7.0%
UR	4%	$20 MM	9.0%
Total/Average	100%	$500 MM	6.2%

Based on this information, the tranched CMBS sells for $529.1 million (back solve how much you would pay for $35 million for 10 years and then a $500 million principal and achieve a 6.2% IRR with a spreadsheet). The weighted average expected IRR for this tranched issuance is 6.2%. The yield (7%) is higher than the IRR as the investors pay above par for the cash flow stream and expect to receive only $500 million in aggregate in the 10th year. This pricing structure assumes that the 10-year Treasury yield is 5%.

If you are able to successfully tranche and sell this CMBS issuance at a 6.2% weighted IRR, you generate $29.1 million in proceeds in excess of the $500 million face value of the loans. Compared to our initial example, where you sold the single CMBS ownership claim for a 6.5% IRR for $518 million, you are able to generate an additional $11.1 million from tranching the ownership claims. You may have an additional $3 million in fees due to the increased marketing costs, additional documents, a more involved rating process, and extra servicing costs due to the added complexity of the deal. As a result, the tranching results in a net increase of $8.1 million in profits. In total, this process generates $19.1 million in profits ($529.1 million in sales minus the $511 million costs of creating and selling, plus the $1 million in originating fees). If you generate four turns on your $500 million during the year, you earn a total of $76.4 million net profit. This is a 15.3% return on your $500 million in assets. At five turns a year you could generate $95.5 million in total profits, for a 19.1% return. At six turns you could generate $114.6 million total net profit, for a 22.9% return. Thus, the more frequently you can create and sell a CMBS pool, the more profit you earn.

Thus far, we have assumed no defaults on the underlying mortgage pool. Assume instead that 2% of the total pool defaults at the end of the 10th year when the $500 million principal payments are due. That is, $10 million of the $500 million in mortgages do not pay according to the loan agreement. In this case the non-payments have no impact on the AAA, AA, A, BBB, BB, but will wipe out half of the $20 million non-rated tranche due at the end of the 10th year. While the non-rated tranche would have received all of their annual payments in this example, they lose half of their investment in the final year. This example illustrates the benefits of subordination for the higher rated tranches. If each class had the same ownership rights, each tranche would have suffered a 2% loss of their initial investment, while with subordination only the lowest rated tranche incurs a loss.

Tranching conceptually works because there is a deep pool of money seeking AAA rated paper. For instance, many corporations invest their cash exclusively in such securities. Similarly, many mutual funds and money market mutual funds are restricted to very highly rated debt securities. Even funds that are not limited to very highly rated bonds invest their cash positions in the AAA and AA securities. This high demand tends to generate attractive pricing for the highly rated tranches. This is similar to a beer distributor on a college campus. The liquor store can charge (within reason) higher prices as students are willing to spend their parents' hard earned money for their preferred "asset".

On the other hand, there are very few buyers of the lower rated tranches, especially those tranches rated below BBB (investment grade). You are basically selling these highly subordinated tranches to specialized real estate investors, as the lowest tranche is the first loss position after the equity in the property. Thus, investors in the most subordinated tranche need to understand the security as a real estate investment.

CLOSING THOUGHT

For a CMBS issue to succeed, it must be large enough to appeal to fixed income buyers, who are generally interested only in relatively large issues. Most bond desks will not buy unless the CMBS offering is at least $200 million. Size also helps in that it provides a more diverse pool of properties, markets, and maturities.

On the other hand, dumb mortgage lenders can kill the CMBS market. If the broad set of fixed income investors demand a 6.5% IRR for the associated risk, you work backwards and determine that you need borrowers to accept a 7% interest rate on their loans if you are to profitably originate and package a CMBS. But if lenders are willing to lend to borrowers at 4%, the CMBS issue will never take place because no one will borrow from you at 7%, and you cannot profitably sell the CMBS issue for a 6.5% IRR if you are only receiving 4% in interest income. For example, the evolution of CMBS in Germany was hindered by their old state-owned Landesbanks. You can imagine that government owned banks were not terribly efficient, and that considerable political lending took place. In this lending environment, CMBS did not generally work because the Landesbanks offered significantly lower mortgage rates than were available through CMBS issuances. In addition, there were few pension or mutual funds in Germany to purchase CMBS securities. So for years there was little in the way of a CMBS market in Germany.

The CMBS market crashed spectacularly in late 2008 after an equally spectacular run from 2003 through mid-2007. The cause of this crash and subsequent CMBS market freeze was remarkably simple: low quality mortgage pools were oversold by investment banks, and overrated by the rating agencies. In this regard, the failure of CMBS was no different than the demise of any company which oversells a product of ever deteriorating quality. By mid-2007, super senior ratings were being awarded to the most senior 80-90% of the ownership claims even as interest coverage ratios eroded to below 1.15x while underlying mortgage LTVs rose to 85 percent and the majority of mortgages having no amortization. Yet even as product quality deteriorated, pricing increased as investors took undue comfort in the AAA ratings assigned by the conflicted and overwhelmed rating agencies.

The lesson is not that the concept of CMBS is flawed, but rather that the key for long term success is to under promise and over deliver. The failure to do so erodes confidence in the product and destroys demand until the problem is clearly resolved.

A final word is in order on the diversification advantage of a CMBS pool. Never forget that if the underlying mortgages are worthless, a CMBS pool is just a diversified worthless pool. Further, if a mortgage default arises due to circumstances which are unique to the individual property, the CMBS mortgage pool provides diversification benefits for investors. However, the bulk of mortgage defaults are historically due to cyclical, rather than property specific, problems. As a result, the diversification advantages of a large mortgage pool are largely illusory, as when an economic recession occurs, all properties tend to be battered by the economic storm.

Chapter 14 Supplement A

How We Got to the Credit Crisis

The many and various factors that led to the current credit crisis.

Dr. Peter Linneman – The Linneman Letter – Spring 2008

The capital market crisis has people asking, "How did we get here?" The last time things were this messy—in the early 1990s, with the disastrous commercial real estate situation exacerbated by the savings and loan collapse—the cause was simple: there was no money available in the system. By contrast, plenty of money exists today; nevertheless capital markets are unstable, and the origins of today's problem are poorly understood.

The answer to "How did we get here?" lies in three phenomena that arise at least once a decade. First, people are always torn between greed and fear. That is, our greed is fundamental, but we are also easily frightened. Think back to the time when American neighborhoods were filled with thirty-foot television antenna towers. Your mother told you never to climb the tower because it was dangerous. But you climbed it to demonstrate your bravery—a child's version of greed. With each foot higher you climbed, the more fearful you became. At some height, fear trumped greed—you stopped, and quickly scrambled down to the ground. Something similar happened in 2005 through early 2007. Although risk premiums and credit spreads narrowed, greed kept investors in the market. The lower spreads became, the more fearful intelligent investors became. Still, most stayed in the market because they didn't want to miss out on an opportunity (Figures 14A.1-14A.3).

FIGURE 14A.1: Monthly spreads in the CMBS market

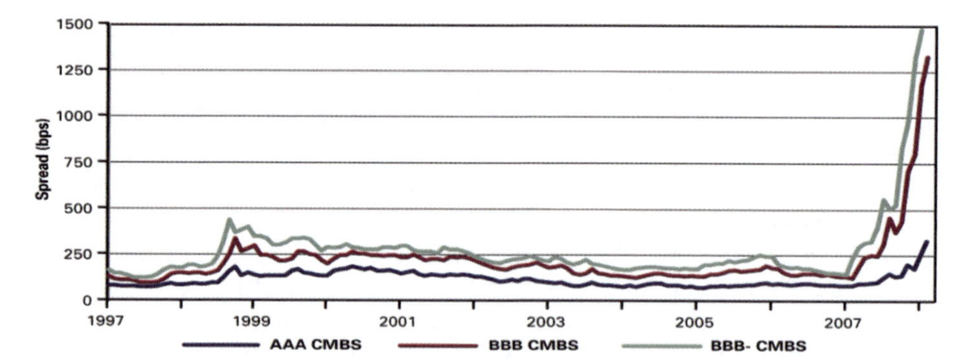

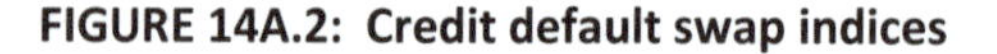

FIGURE 14A.2: Credit default swap indices

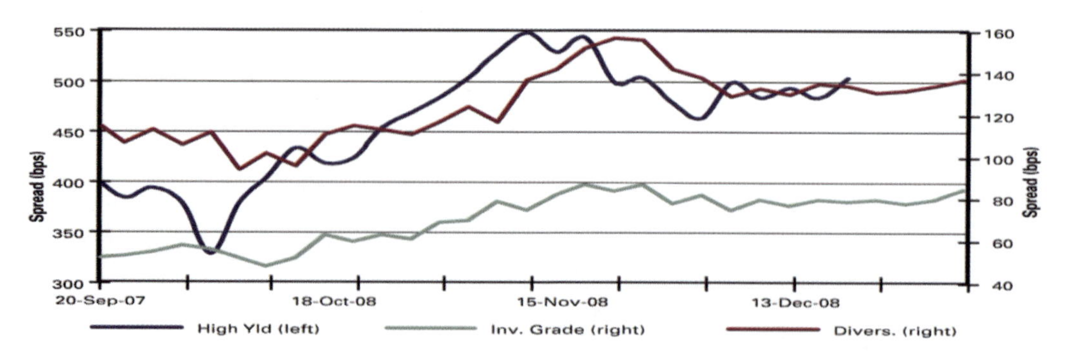

FIGURE 14A.3: High yield credit spreads

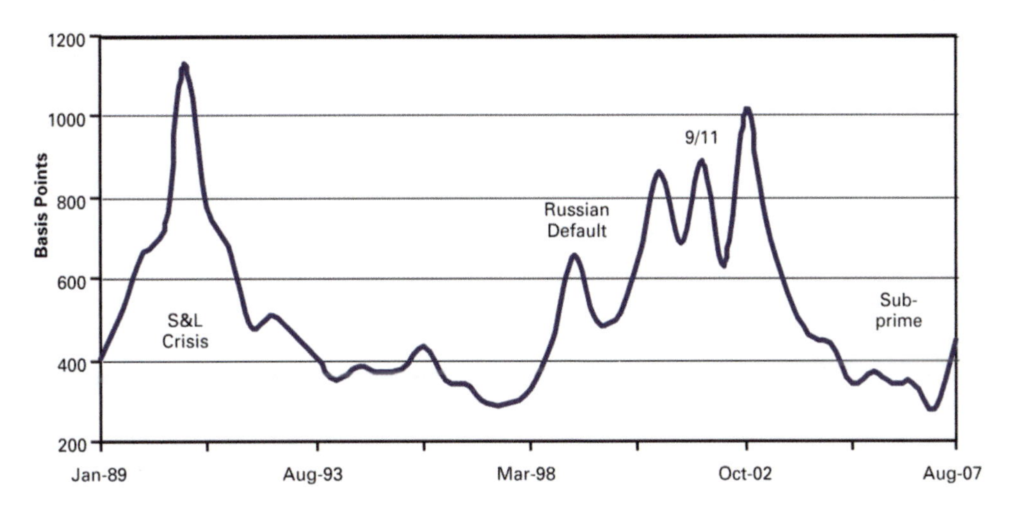

In the last twenty years, greed has been defeated by fear five times. The first time was the stock market crash of 1987 (Figure 14A.4). Thanks to fear's victory, investors ended the day 23 percent poorer than they had been that morning. Fear spread on a grand scale and optimism quickly turned to pessimism. But the financial system survived and the economy escaped without a recession. The second time that greed was defeated by fear was the savings and loans collapse of 1990, which almost brought down the American financial system and also threatened other countries. But again, we survived. The third episode was the Russian ruble crisis of 1998, which sparked widespread investor fear. At first glance, this episode is hard to explain; after all, Russia had never in the past paid its debt (there was still debt outstanding from Czarist Russia!). But the crisis wasn't really about Russian debt—it was about the basic realization that if lenders are willing to lend at low spreads to borrowers who have never paid their debts, then greed had been winning far too long. The Russian announcement that they would not service their debt merely underscored the extent of greed's victory. As a result, it was easy for fear to rout greed. But soon enough, greed returned in force during the Tech Bubble. The fourth time pervasive fear won was immediately after September 11, 2001, which was understandable. But again, by early 2003 greed was back.

FIGURE 14A.4: S&P 500

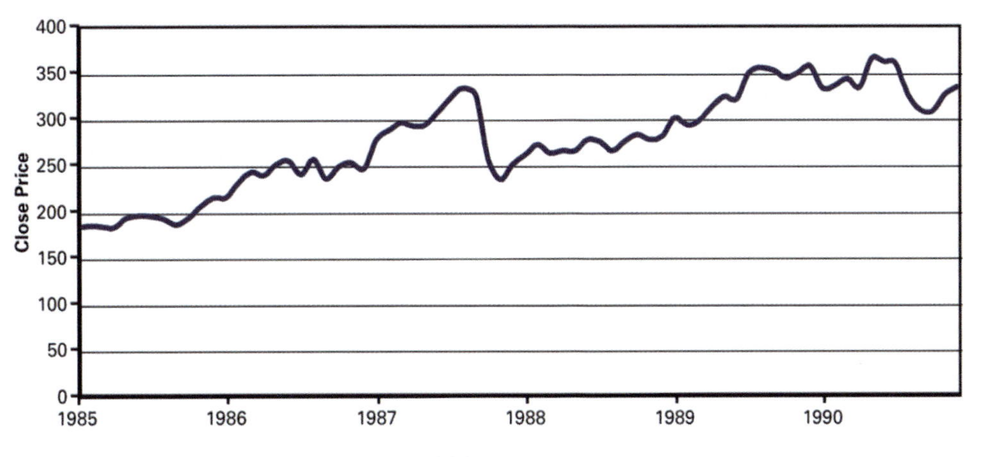

Now, fear is triumphing for a fifth time in twenty years, led by concerns about subprime residential debt. By April 2007, investors came to the realization that if lenders were willing to lend at high LTVs, razor-thin interest rate spreads, and without credit checks, to borrowers with bad credit records, greed had gone too far. If borrowers could obtain mortgages (many on speculative homes), it meant that all good lending options had been exhausted. Fear soared as people realized how low underwriting standards had fallen. But if the pattern of history holds, greed will be victorious within two years.

GREED RETURNS

The seeds of greed's return are already being sown. Historically, the first investors to return during a fearful period are contrarian non-institutional investors. These tend to be "fundamentals" investors who rely on their own counsel. Their investments are usually relatively small and fall below the radar screen. But rumors of their bottom-feeding profits stiffen the resolve of institutional investors, some of whom will invest via opportunistic funds. Already billions of dollars have been raised for distressed debt funds, with more in the pipeline. The capital for these funds comes not only from high-wealth investors, but also from university endowments and large pension funds. The purchases by distress funds set floors for asset prices, providing comfort to more conservative institutional investors.

A unique feature of the current situation is the nearly $30 billion invested in U.S. financial institutions (and probably more via distressed debt funds) by sovereign wealth funds. Although not historically contrarian investors, these sovereign wealth funds have boldly gone where lesser investors fear to tread. Their equity infusions are recapitalizing major financial institutions, speeding the resumption of normal capital market operations.

Retail investors and the mass of institutional investors will be the last to return to the fray. These investors are "herd followers". They return only after their consultants certify that others have made money. Frustrated by low yields on treasuries, and fearful that they might miss out on the next upswing, they will begin to return by mid-to-late 2008. And the return of greed will be in full swing.

MORE MONEY THAN BRAINS

A second phenomenon explains "how we got here". Consider that in the history of measured economic growth, the world economy never grew as rapidly as it did between 2002 and 2007 (Figure 14A.5). Wealth was created faster than at any other time in history, but the investment infrastructure lagged the expansion of investable wealth. In other words, there was more money than brains. In such a situation, investors commonly take two shortcuts. The first is to rely on rating agencies, rather than due diligence, to determine investment risk. But the fact is that rating agencies have never correctly forecast a major credit collapse until after the fact! The second common shortcut is to skip independent due diligence, and merely rely on "who else is investing". After all, "so-and-so is a smart investor, and they're in, so it must be a good investment". Many investors used this shortcut for "small" investments (say $50 million), focusing their diligence efforts on larger investments (say $500 million). The problem is that when lots of investors trust other investors to do the diligence, frequently no one ends up doing diligence. So, there were not enough chairs when the music stopped, and a lot of "small" $50 million errors quickly added up to billions in losses.

FIGURE 14A.5: Increase in world real GDP

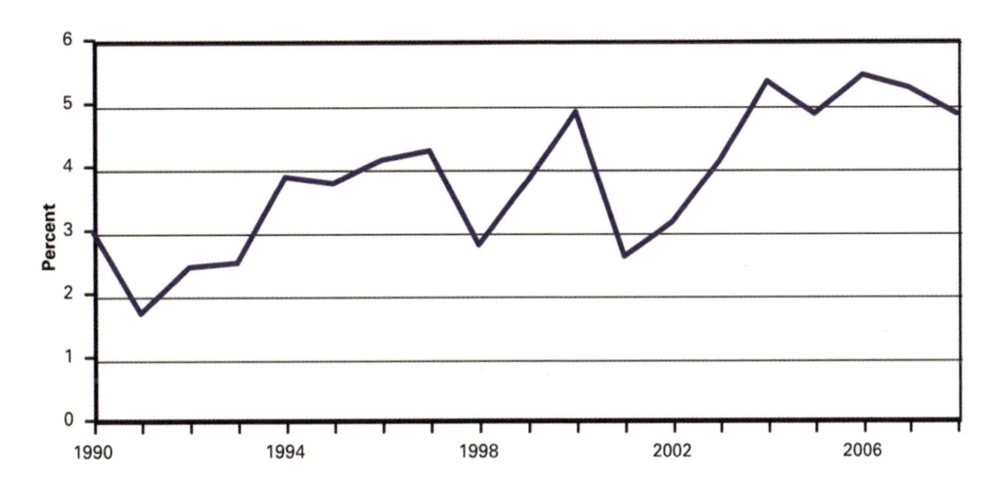

ASSET-LIABILITY MISMATCH

The third phenomenon that explains "how we got here" is that most assets, such as cash streams on buildings, the returns to homeownership, and corporate profits, are long-term, but most liabilities, such as bank deposits, are short-term. Since most assets are long-term in nature, there is a fundamental mismatch of assets and liabilities in the financial system. Mismatched investors run the risk that their debt will be subject to a margin call, or that they will be unable to roll their debt upon maturity. As long as greed is winning, this mismatch is not a systemic problem since values generally increase when greed prevails, which allows comfortable refinancing and few margin calls. But when fear defeats greed, and asset values drop, mismatched short-term debt presents a serious systemic problem. As asset values fall, investors with mark-to-market debt must sell assets to pay down their debt. As they sell, they further force asset prices down, causing a ripple effect, until the process reaches balance sheets that are strong enough to withstand margin calls, or until greed begins to win again.

The credit crisis underscores a fundamental challenge of mark-to-market pricing: many (probably most) assets trade only by appointment. This is true even of securitized assets. The concept of mark-to-market revolves around the idea that there is a "price". But for the vast majority of assets (including almost all debt, homes, private companies, and many stocks) there is no "price". Rather, there is a bid price, and an ask price. For most assets, the bid and ask prices rarely converge, as witnessed by the fact that most assets rarely trade.

When greed is winning (which is about 80 percent of the time), price "marks" tend to reflect ask prices, as the bean-counters lack the expertise to counter claims by asset owners that they would not sell for less because asset prices are trending upwards. But as fear takes hold, the bean-counters gravitate to price "marks" in line with bids, fearful of legal liability if they overstate "prices". The result is that "marks" plunge not only because fundamentals may have reduced both bid and ask prices, but also because "marks" shift from ask prices to bid prices. Such a shift can create 10 percent to 30 percent "mark" declines for illiquid assets.

But it is wrong to view either the bid or the ask as the "price", as a market price requires the presence of a willing buyer and a willing seller—that is, for the bid and ask prices to converge. Owners should not be forced to accept write-downs to prices at which they would never sell. "Marks" should be made using a consistent method, and never shift from using the ask to using the bid, as such inconsistency creates a misleading value picture. We suggest that for accounting purposes, the asset owner should always use their ask price, subject to fraud prosecution for using "marks" that systematically mislead investors. In other words, asset holders should consistently explain the worth of their assets. If investors feel misled by these disclosures, fraud statutes provide sufficient protection. But switching between ask and bid prices increases misinformation. Auditors must not be asked to divine the "price" of illiquid assets. Their job should only be to audit and certify the consistency with which illiquid assets are marked.

THE SUBPRIME MESS

As the unprecedented growth of global wealth was already fueling record demand for safe assets, the Fed made a well-intentioned, but enormous, mistake. After September 11, 2001, they cut rates, flooding the market with liquidity (Figure 14A.6). Then for four years they held rates so low that investors were guaranteed real losses of 1 percent to 2 percent on short-term safe assets. Faced with guaranteed real losses on short-term safe assets, investors chose to invest long and risky, while borrowing short, as at least this strategy offered the chance of a positive real return. The Fed forced investors to go longer and riskier than their expertise, and to mismatch their asset-liability positions, in effect issuing an economy-wide mandate to climb up the risk ladder. As investors steadily climbed this ladder, it was only a matter of time until fear prevailed; the trigger was the subprime residential mortgage market.

FIGURE 14A.6: Real Fed funds rate

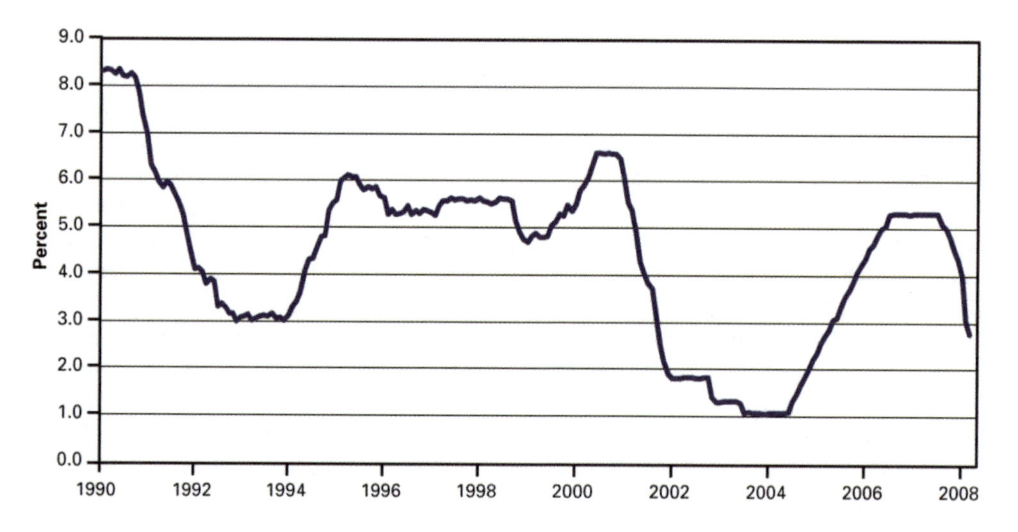

Historically, the typical subprime borrower was a small storeowner, or a service worker such as a waitress, golf caddy, cab driver, or charter boat captain. What these workers have in common are large amounts of unreported cash income. Consequently, as borrowers they have mortgage ratios that are "out of formula". In other words, their maximum mortgages, calculated according to their reported incomes, are less than what they can actually afford. The solution is to take a subprime loan and pay an extra 100 to 250 basis points on their mortgages. This premium is necessary because default rates have always been high on subprime mortgages, as fraud is easy on loans with little documentation. But these high cash-income households prefer to pay a mortgage premium rather than pay 40 percent in taxes on their unreported income.

High cash-income household borrowing does not explain why subprime borrowing skyrocketed in 2005 and 2006, however. Who were the new subprime borrowers? The answer (which is rarely mentioned in the media) is simple: speculative homebuyers. From 2004 to 2006, some 500,000 homes were bought by speculators, who were schooled by late-night television infomercials to put 5 percent down and triple their money in six months by flipping the house. Pure unadulterated greed led these speculators to buy with 95 percent LTV mortgages, secured from greedy lenders seeking a few extra basis points of spread. To avoid requesting commercial loans, for which they would not have qualified, these speculator-lenders misstated that the properties were their primary residences. But as greed rampaged, speculators had access to abundant high LTV, low (and no) doc mortgages.

If you lend $285,000 to a family member who wants to purchase a $300,000 home, and you do it without a credit check, that's imprudent. But if you make such loans to hundreds of thousands of people whom you've never met, that's idiotic. And idiots deserve to lose their money. At its heart, the subprime "problem" is the result of idiots lending to idiots.

Subprime defaults are higher than their historical norm, because once speculators realized they couldn't flip their homes for quick profits, the game was over (Figure 14A.7). Many made just one payment on their mortgage. This is particularly true in Florida, Las Vegas, Phoenix, and southern California. These areas have high default rates because they had stunning levels of speculative buying. For example, Miami absorbed some 10,000 condos in ten years, but roughly 40,000 "pre-sold" units are under construction. In large part, idiot speculators put down deposits on these units, with money provided by idiot lenders.

FIGURE 14A.7: Mortgage delinquency rates (90+ days)

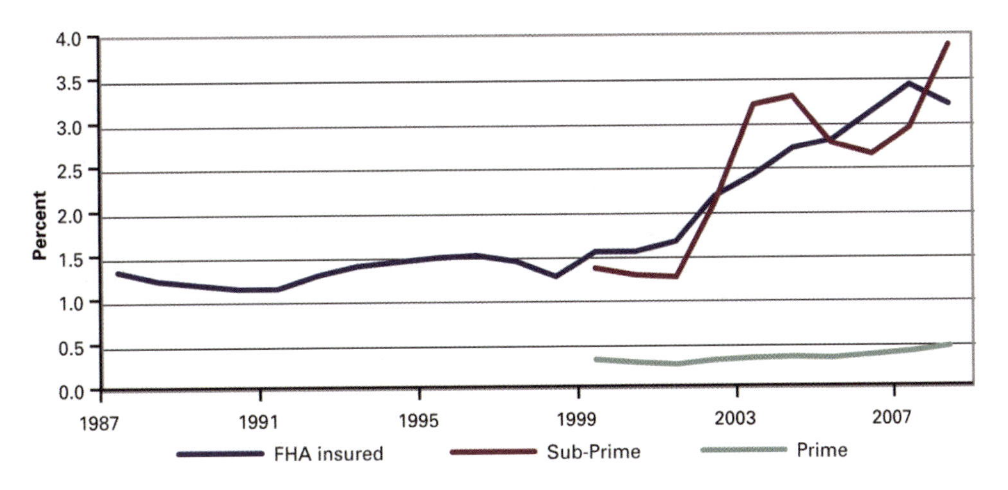

FIGURE 14A.8: Subprime mortgages as a percent of originations

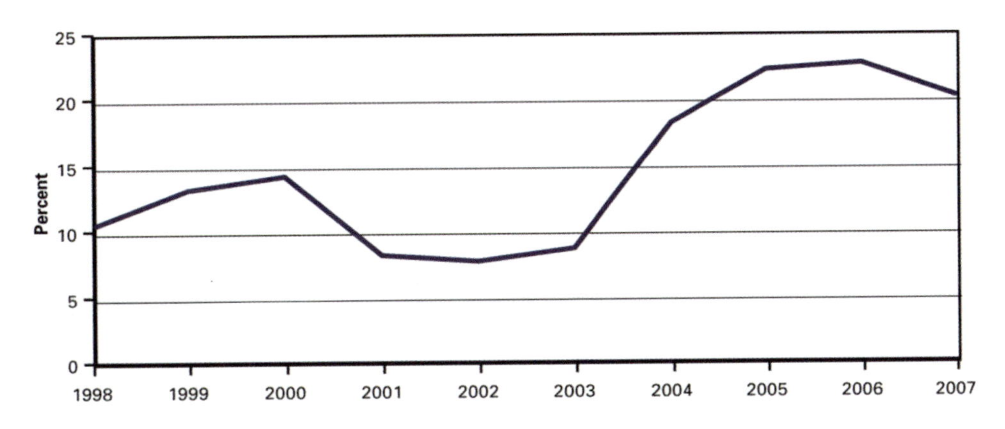

Is it surprising there are a lot of delinquencies by speculative buyers? After all, why make mortgage payments on an empty investment home you were planning to flip for a big profit, once you know it can't be done? You don't feed the beast: you stop paying and make the lender take the home. We believe most mortgage defaults in strong economic regions of the country are by speculative owners. This is consistent with the rapid rise in 2000 through 2007 of subprime borrowers with high credit scores (Figure 14A.9). In 2000, 60 percent of all subprime mortgage borrowers had credit scores of less than 620, but by the first quarter of 2007 only about 40 percent were below that threshold. During that period, the market share growth primarily occurred in the 620 to 659 and the 740+ credit rating categories, which increased from 17 percent to 26 percent and from 3 percent to nearly 9 percent, respectively. Then the trend reversed in the second quarter of 2007 when fear began to surpass greed, and about 60 percent of subprime borrowers were once again below the 620 threshold. Similarly, in the first quarter of 2007, nearly 20 percent of subprime loans were to borrowers with credit scores of 700 or greater. This has since dropped to about 5 percent, versus the 10 percent "norm" in 2000.

FIGURE 14A.9: Subprime borrower credit scores

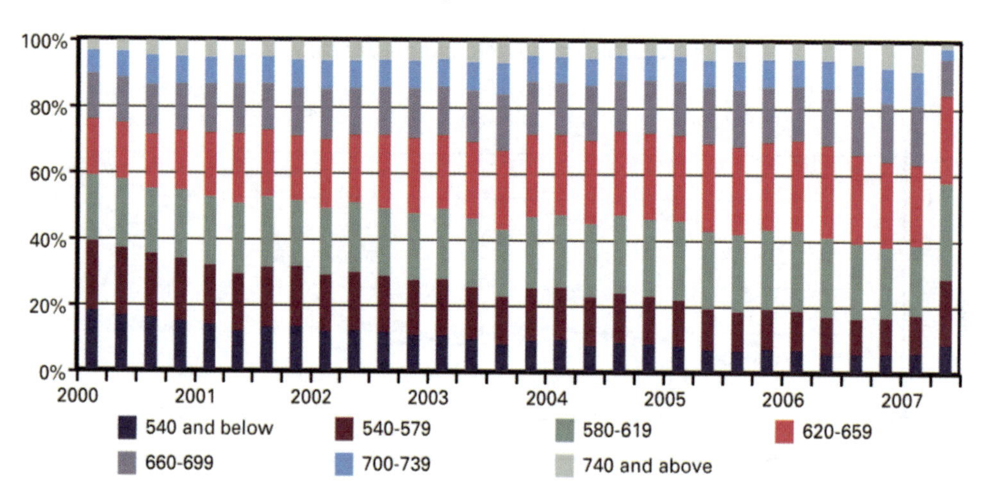

Not all mortgage defaulters are idiot borrowers. In Ohio and Michigan, defaulters are people who actually live in their homes and have been ravaged by a local recession. Borrowers in these recession areas have lost the value of their equity, but they will not lose their homes. The reality facing lenders in Ohio and Michigan is that no one other than the defaulters wants to live in these homes. These loans will generally have to be restructured, as there is no other option. Defaults are also very high in Louisiana and Mississippi, where many homes no longer exist, or have been abandoned due to Hurricane Katrina. Why pay a mortgage on a home that no longer exists? Stop paying and let the mortgage and insurance companies work it out. The lender cannot foreclose on a home that does not exist anymore.

FACT AND FANTASY

As speculative owners defaulted, the extent of poor underwriting became clear. Investors became fearful, and asked what else had been oversold and overrated. After all, the same people were packaging everything: subprime mortgages, mortgage-backed securities, and collateralized debt obligations. As fear took hold, investors effectively went on strike and stopped buying these assets. As margin calls occurred due to rising credit spreads, fear spread, and investors demanded much larger returns until they figured out what else was badly underwritten.

Today is very different from the early 1990s. In the 1990s people did not have money to invest; today, they do. But they demand a much higher return. Consider the example of the Abu Dhabi Investment Authority, which in order to stay cash-neutral must invest approximately $2 billion each week. Their recent investment in Citi amounted to just three and a half weeks of cash flow.

Financial fantasies are being written by revisionist financial historians. These fantasies claim that if only the lenders had held on to the debt they issued, rather than securitizing and selling the debt, excessive lending would have been avoided. They call for the return of whole loan lending for one's own account. But this version of past lender behavior is as overly romanticized, as are revisionist urbanist memories of the joy of children playing amid street traffic in the days of old. Just as children playing in New York City streets was dangerous, not romantic, the history of lenders who kept their loans was far from prudent. Remember the Japanese bank loans for real estate in the 1980s? Or Latin American lending by U.S. banks in the late 1970s and early 1980s? Or commercial real estate lending in the 1980s? All of these lending excesses occurred even as lenders retained their debt. In fact, retention of these loans only meant that the losses were far more concentrated and easier to hide from investors.

It is greed, not whether institutions hold or sell their loans, that generates excessive lending. Debt securitization evolved in the 1990s in response to the checkered history of whole loan lending, in order to diversify losses (among greedy investors) and to require more rapid resolution of problems. Human nature, not securitization, is the real culprit.

Unfortunately the idiots who lent to idiots have created a serious political problem. Congress and the administration feel compelled to "do something", even though the right thing to do from an economic standpoint is nothing. It is very dangerous when something is right politically, but wrong economically. It is clear that a bailout of idiot borrowers and idiot lenders is a major mistake, as idiots who lend to idiots do not deserve to be bailed out, especially as there is no feasible way to distinguish the "innocent" (whatever that means) from the idiots. But although a bailout is unwise economically, it is probably a political necessity. The fear is that such legislation will seriously undercut the integrity of our capital markets.

The U.S. economy is performing well, even though we have been told for the last six years that it is on the brink of disaster. The U.S. economy continues to grow because consumers, who make up the bulk of economy, only need to access capital markets to buy cars and houses. The typical consumer buys a new car every four years, and a home about once every eight. Consider the capital "need" for a car: unless you've totaled your car, you can forestall your purchase until spreads on auto loans return to normal. But while reduced car buying hurts the auto industry, it does not hurt the economy; consumers will spend the money they would have spent on a new car on other things. The same is true of housing purchases. Mortgage spreads are quite high, especially on jumbos, so homebuyers are deferring their home purchases. This is bad for the housing sector, good for apartment owners, and neutral for the economy. Since the majority of present homeowners locked in long-term mortgages at historically low rates in 2003 through 2005, bidders have to bribe owners to sell their houses. Young prospective homebuyers will continue renting for another year or two. Again, this does not hurt the economy, as they spend the money earmarked for housing on other things. Consumers are shifting consumption across categories, not stopping consumption.

BUT WHAT ABOUT THE LOSSES?

The newspaper headlines say, "Merrill Lynch lost $8 billion", or "Citi lost $11 billion". How can the economy withstand such massive losses? It is important not to confuse losses among participants in the economy with losses to the economy itself. If one player at a poker table loses $11 billion, the table hasn't lost a dime. The money simply transferred among the players. Similarly, subprime lenders lost tens of billions of dollars, but the U.S. economy did not lose a dime, since these losses were transferred to borrowers. The difference is that the lenders must report their losses, while private borrowers do not have to report their gains. But every lender loss is exactly offset by a borrower gain.

In fact, it could be argued that the United States made money from the subprime excess. U.S. lenders probably gave $100 billion too much to subprime borrowers, which is to say, $100 billion more than they can pay back. Thus, for U.S. borrowers, there was an offsetting gain. But U.S. lenders sold $30 billion to $40 billion of their losses to Germans, French, Japanese, and Italian investors—anybody who would buy the overrated paper. Greed led these foreign buyers to buy loans they could not possibly understand, in exchange for 5 to 20 basis points higher spread. Bad for them, but a net gain for the United States, as $100 billion in gains went to U.S. borrowers, but only about $60 billion to $70 billion of the losses were ultimately suffered by U.S. lenders.

There are two real losses associated with poorly underwritten loans. First, we built too many homes, and empty homes cannot generate a return. The economic loss is not the cost of the empty homes, but the carry cost until occupancy. There are currently 400,000 to 500,000 empty homes beyond the normal inventory. That is about $100 billion worth of housing. It will take three to twenty-four months for this surplus to be absorbed, depending on the strength of the local economy. While some empty homes will have longer carry costs than others, we calculate roughly a year's carry on $100 billion, or about $8 billion to $10 billion, is the social loss. Not much in the $13 trillion U.S. economy, with its $57 trillion net household wealth.

How can we be sure that the excess inventory of homes will be absorbed in roughly a year? Will immigration stop, or even slow, because of a credit crisis? Will couples decide not to have children, because of a credit crisis? No. Births, deaths, and immigration will be unaffected, meaning a U.S. population growth of about three million in 2008. This population growth translates into about 1.2 million new households—and every household needs a home. Add to that 100,000 second homes (the average in a normal year), and the 500,000 to 600,000 homes that are destroyed each year, and we will need about 1.8 million homes in 2008, about 70 percent of which will be owner-occupied. This amounts to 1.2 million to 1.3 million owner-occupied units demanded in 2008. The current run rate of single-family housing production is 800,000. Adding this new production to the 400,000 to 500,000 excess home inventory yields a supply of 1.2 million to 1.3 million available in 2008. So in 2008, demand will push housing inventories back to normal. Hence, home prices do not have to plummet, as many suggest, to restore market balance. All that is needed is a year of normal-demand growth.

The effect of the credit crisis on housing is affected by the fact that homeowners react differently to price changes than owners of other assets. Imagine that you learned that your stocks were 10 percent overvalued. You would be smart to sell. If you learned that your bonds were 10 percent overvalued, you'd also sell. But if you learned that your home was 10 percent overvalued, would you sell? Probably not. Selling costs are about 6 percent to 8 percent of your home's value, selling takes time, and moving is a huge headache. In addition, your home provides a guaranteed dividend: the joy of living there.

The second major economic loss associated with the capital market crisis is the erosion of the credibility of U.S. capital markets. As securitization, ratings, underwriters, hedge funds, collateral, and liquidity were shown to be incomplete, incompetent, conflicted, and occasionally corrupt, the world's trust in U.S. capital markets declined. And trust is easy to lose, but hard to regain. The loss of U.S. capital market credibility—underscored by the fact that major banks "suddenly" discovered billions in losses—is reflected in the decline in the value of U.S. dollar and the reduced U.S. trade deficit. In spite of being enormously undervalued in terms of purchasing power parity, the dollar has tumbled during the credit crisis, as foreign investors reduced their demand for U.S. assets. After all, if U.S. assets are as illiquid and flawed as those at home, why pay a "safety" premium for U.S. assets?

The weak dollar is good for U.S. exporters, but bad for American financial markets and financial firms. The decline of the U.S. trade deficit reveals that foreign investors have dramatically reduced their demand for U.S. assets, which have turned out not to be as liquid, safe and transparent as advertised. Thus, the decline of our trade deficit is bad for the U.S. economy, as it reflects a decline in the desire of foreigners to invest in the United States (Figure 14A.11). This economic loss associated with lost capital market trust is probably much larger in magnitude than the loss on our empty houses.

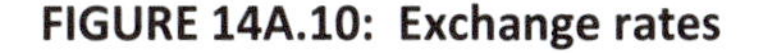

FIGURE 14A.10: Exchange rates

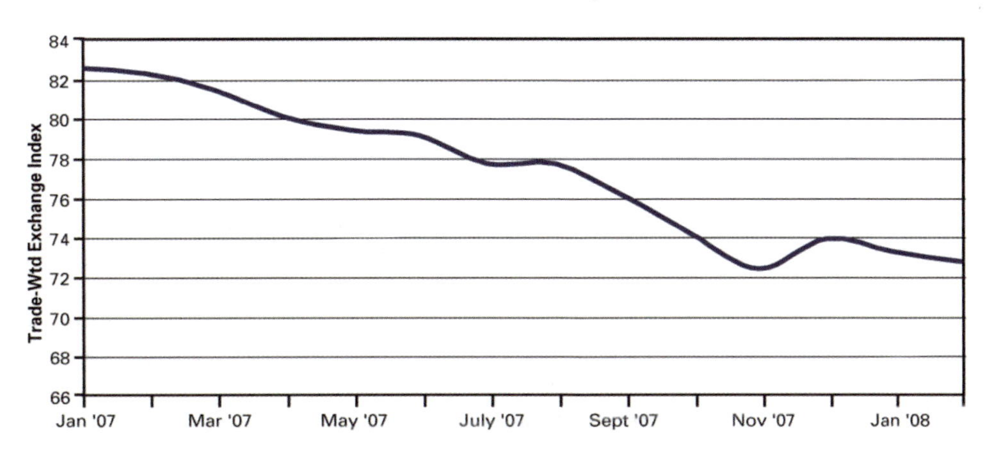

FIGURE 14A.11: The declining U.S. trade deficit indicates decreasing foreign investment

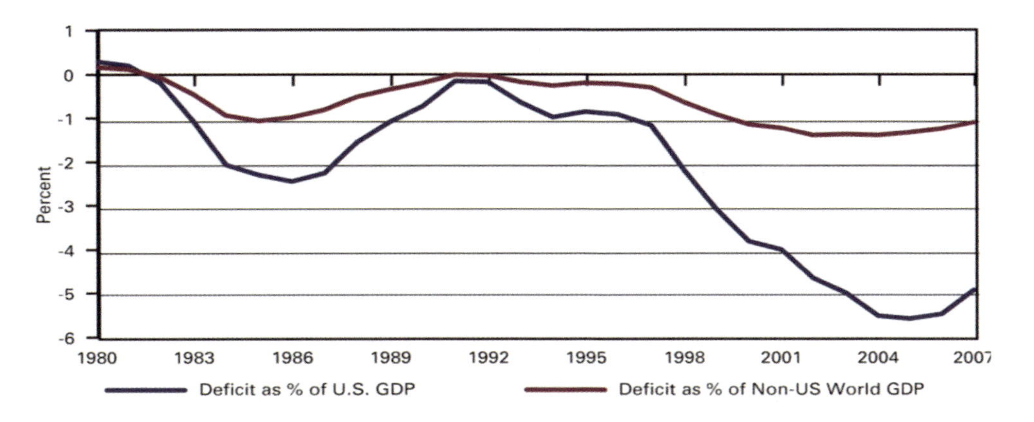

CONCLUSION

The U.S. economy will grow until the new government (regardless of which party wins) attempts to make good on their promises to "do something" about capital market excesses, health care, taxes, Iraq, and global warming. Their attempts will likely cause uncertainty, leading consumers and businesses to pause. As people and businesses pause, the economy will go flat. This means there will be too many workers, since the hiring that took place in 2008 was in anticipation of growth that did not occur in 2009. Hence, cost structures will be too high in 2009, causing employment to be cut and the unemployment rate to rise. The recession of 2009 will be billed as the worst ever, but as certainty returns, the economy will again move forward.

In the meantime, growth in 2008 will be a pleasant surprise, unless the government does something really dumb (always a possibility). This government, which loves to spend, will spend even more in this election year. While this is not good in the long term, it will be good for 2008. Also in 2008, many investors who thought they were smart will be shown up for just having had money, as they struggle with their maturing mismatched short-term loans. But in five to seven years, asset prices will be at new highs, overriding concerns about asset/liability mismatches. You can count on this because greed wins 80 percent of the time.

Chapter 14 Supplement B

The Capital Markets Disarray

When fear conquers greed, unpleasant things can happen.

Dr. Peter Linneman – Wharton Real Estate Review – Fall 2007

What is occurring today in global capital markets is the combination of two fundamental problems. The first is that most assets are long-term in nature, while most available capital is short-term. As a result, there is a fundamental bias toward asset-liability mismatches. As long as people believe in the rising values and liquidity of long-term assets, this is not a problem. However, when people lose faith, this mismatch is exposed, causing short-term illiquidity, and asset prices to tumble. The second problem is that in the eternal struggle between fear and greed, pessimism and optimism, trust and skepticism, fear occasionally wins. Through March 2007, greed was winning hands-down. It was one of the greatest victories of greed over fear, not just in real estate, but in almost every investment category. Credit spreads were very thin, the stock market was booming, and pricey buy-outs were everywhere. Although an undercurrent of fear grew as each new height was achieved, optimism abounded and capital providers focused on the good things that could happen. Six months later, fear is routing greed, as capital providers are obsessed with the bad things that might happen. This swing from greed to fear has triggered a flight from risk, leaving mismatched investors drowning in a sea of losses.

It all started with sub-prime residential loans, where egregiously poor underwriting has existed for two years, fueled by capital sources with mismatched portfolios. The poor underwriting of sub-prime debt in 2005-06 was extraordinary versus historical norms, as households that would have never qualified for a mortgage got one, with little money down, and with minimal credit spreads. This generated a great wealth transfer from sub-prime lenders to the borrowers. The good news is that roughly 70 percent of sub-prime borrowers locked in their transfers via fixed-rate mortgages. But 30 percent did not.

FIGURE 14B.1: High yield credit spreads

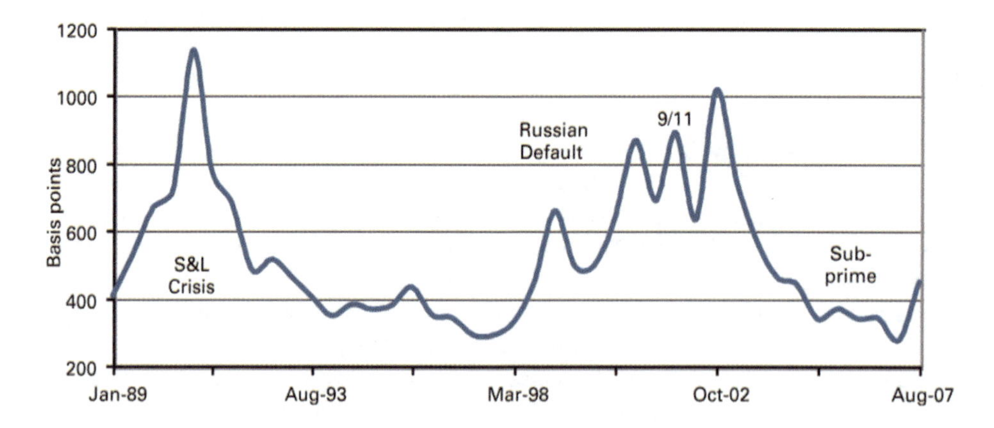

For a short time, most sub-prime lenders passed the hot potato before the poor underwriting came to light. They were aided and abetted by ratings agencies that did not understand what they were underwriting, and whose ignorance was salved by rating fees. And, as always, the rating agencies dropped ratings only well after the disaster. Not much of an "early warning" system for investors! Today's capital market crisis was triggered as it became clear that the losses on sub-prime were going to be much larger than anticipated. This not only increased spreads on sub-prime debt, but also caused investors to wonder what other credits had been poorly underwritten and overrated, which started the ball rolling for widespread widening of credit spreads and falling asset prices.

Asset prices fell as investors worried that they would lose money due to poor underwriting, and anyone who mismatched long-term assets with short-term liabilities was forced to meet margin calls. So, to cover what will ultimately be about $90 billion of losses on sub-prime loans, mismatched owners had to sell assets. The more leveraged they were, the quicker and more dramatic were the margin calls. As assets were sold (including other credit instruments and stocks) to cover margin calls, credit spreads widened further, and stock prices fell. This triggered margin calls on more mismatched asset owners, causing another round of sales. And as fear widened, the knock-on effect broadened. This is what happens when fear wins out over greed.

FIGURE 14B.2: Sub-prime mortgage volume

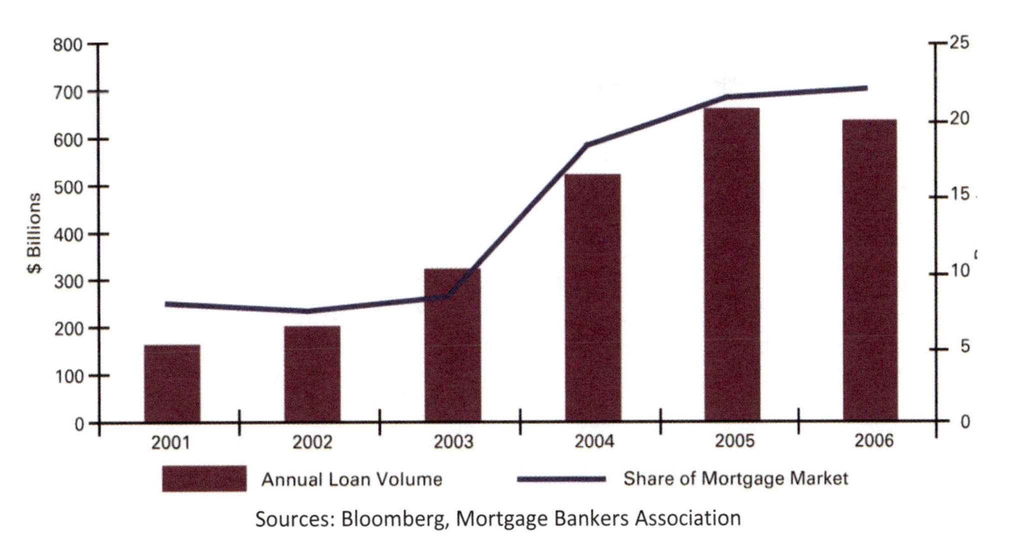

Sources: Bloomberg, Mortgage Bankers Association

This process can be expected to continue until assets are held by investors with strong enough balance sheets to take price hits without margin calls, and when asset prices fall to the point that they comfortably compensate for underwriting losses. We are nearing this turning point after four months of snowballing fear. As smart, liquid investors step up saying "at these prices these assets are a steal," greed begins its counterattack. From that point, it is just a matter of time until greed once again prevails.

IT ISN'T THE FIRST TIME

In the past twenty years, fear has defeated greed four times. The first was in October 1987, when the stock market crashed in the middle of a strong economy. At that time everyone worried—when stocks fell by more than 20 percent in two days—that the capital market turmoil would create a recession. But it did not hurt the economy, with the exception of New York City. And within about eighteen months, things had returned to normal, with greed wining and capital markets again moving forward.

In 1990-1991, we were in a recession, when capital markets experienced turmoil due to the savings and loan crisis. Ground zero was commercial real estate. Credit spreads widened, and capital rationing occurred. This episode worked itself out in the capital markets within about eighteen months, although it took about five years for real estate to work through its excess supply.

The next credit crisis was the 1998 Russian ruble crisis, which occurred in a strong economy. Russian debt was a fairly esoteric credit instrument that had been very poorly underwritten (again with the aid of the rating agencies). Margin calls hit the owners of these highly-leveraged instruments, and rippled through credit markets as all types of assets were sold to satisfy margin calls. Observers again wondered if this capital market crisis would spill over to the economy. But it did not, except (again) in New York City. And once again it took about eighteen months for credit spreads and pricing to normalize.

The fourth episode where fear defeated greed was after September 11, 2001. At that time, we were in the midst of a recession that had begun in March. Not surprisingly, in an environment where fear defeated greed credit spreads widened, and asset prices fell. Yet after about eighteen months, credit spreads and pricing had rebounded, and a new round of greed was under way.

We are now experiencing the fifth credit crisis in the past twenty years, with sub-prime debt as the trigger. As was the case in 1987 and 1998, this credit crisis is occurring in a strong economy and will not harm the general economy, except perhaps New York City. As in the past, it will take roughly eighteen months for pricing to return to normal. In the meantime, it is a horrible time to have to borrow or sell.

Fortunately most people, and most firms, do not have to access capital markets during this window. But firms in the capital business such as banks and investment banks have no choice, and their suffering will harm New York (and London). However, over the long-term, capital providers are optimists. Otherwise they'd never take a shower for fear of slipping; never drive a car for fear of dying in a wreck; and never eat for fear of food poisoning. Given time, optimism always wins. In fact, over the last twenty years, greed's record is fifteen wins and five losses.

The economic activity of firms and households with no need to access capital markets during the next eighteen months will be largely unaffected. But in financial cities, job growth and space demand will suffer in the near-term, as capital market activity declines. For example, what hedge funds—even winning hedge funds—will decide to expand their office space now? And condos in New York will struggle, since what bankers believe they're going to get a huge year-end bonus? And, as people avoid capital markets, layoffs will occur at banks and investment banks. New York and London will be impacted, as always happens during these financial crises, just as Des Moines and Iowa City suffer during corn and wheat crises. But the rest of the economy will not be harmed. The good news is that both London and New York have very little construction under way and have low vacancy rates. But they will experience near-term weakness.

THE FED DID IT

The Fed bears considerable responsibility for the current capital market crisis. During the period 2002-04, it kept the Fed Funds rate at a ridiculously low level. This low rate guaranteed a negative real return for anyone who invested short and safe, artificially encouraging investors to invest long and risky in an attempt to avoid guaranteed real losses. At the same time, the Fed's excessively low rate encouraged borrowers to borrow short-term using floating rates, taking advantage of the excessively steep yield curve. The Fed's 1.00 to 1.25 percent interest rate essentially for a short-term loan to the U.S. government, when inflation was about 2 percent, guaranteed pre-tax negative real return of at least 1.00 percent. This is hardly an attractive, or even a natural, proposition.

Long-term asset values rose across the board as capital providers went long because of this strange incentive created—and prolonged—by the Fed. Better to potentially lose later on an overpriced long asset, than to lose for sure immediately on a short investment. Eventually, the Fed realized they had kept the rate too low for too long, and rapidly raised it, changing the real short-term rate from roughly minus 1 percent to about 2.75 percent in just eighteen months. The Fed raised the Fed Funds rate to 5.25% in an attempt to soak up some liquidity, but even as the inflation rate fell, the Fed kept interest rates at that absurdly high level. And if you don't believe it was too high, ask why someone deserves a 2.75 percent real return to effectively lend the U.S. government money for six months. The answer is: "They don't".

FIGURE 14B.3: Fed Funds rate net of core CPI

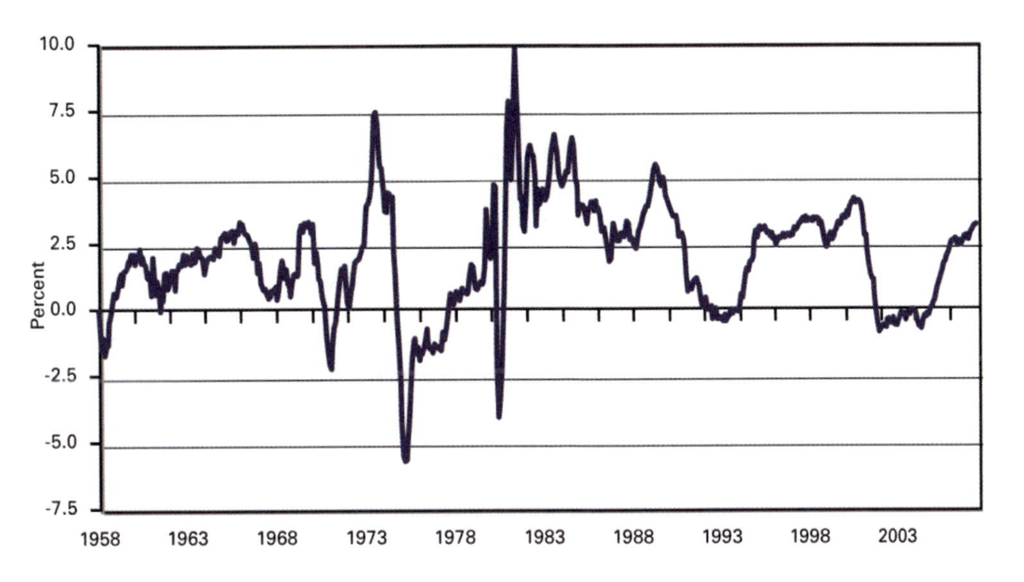

Now, three to four months too late has the Fed admitted their error with a grudging drop of 50 basis points on September 18. However, we believe it is still too high by 75 basis points. A year ago, when the Fed increased the rate to 5.25 percent, it took credit markets some time to figure out the attractiveness of investing short and safe, as they had previously unleashed their hounds in search of long assets. But now capital markets are once again reacting in dramatic fashion, abandoning long assets and moving into short-term safe investments. And as they have switched, asset prices have been whipsawed. So in the same way the Fed artificially encouraged capital sources to go long, it is now encouraging them to go short.

The Fed's errors have created a serious problem for anyone who borrowed short-term floating rate money to fund long investments, including many sub-prime borrowers and debt holders. The Fed has kept the short rate at least 125 basis points higher than borrowers should have reasonably expected. By keeping the short rate high, the Fed is punishing these borrowers (and their lenders), creating more delinquencies and defaults than necessary.

The Fed should have cut rates to 4.25 percent to 4.50 percent months ago, and certainly on August 10. It is not a matter of "bailing them out", but rather creating a neutral capital market environment. Even at 4.75 percent, anyone who says that the Fed Funds rate is now correct must explain why, when inflation is only about 2 percent, investors deserve a 2.75 percent return for effectively holding short-term government paper. It makes no sense, and seriously distorts capital markets. While the Fed has cut the discount rate and injected some funds, they need to further cut the Fed Funds rate.

Unfortunately, the Fed doesn't seem to "get it". They seem more worried about "moral hazard" bailout risk rather than creating a neutral capital market environment and continue to talk as if there is a trade-off between low unemployment and rising inflation. But Nobel Prize winners Milton Friedman and Edmund Phelps proved some forty years ago that inflation does not rise as the unemployment rate falls. Yet the Fed seems to cling to this debunked idea. If the Fed keeps the rate high much longer, it will adversely impact long-term investment activity. This will not hurt the economy during the next quarter or two, but will hurt two years from now, as we will not have put sufficient productive capital in place. That is, we will not have planted enough seeds for future growth. In short, the Fed is fueling a recession in 2009-2010.

IT COULD HAVE BEEN ANOTHER TRIGGER

The trigger for the current disarray was sub-prime debt. But if it hadn't been sub-prime, it would have been something else. As long asset prices rose and spreads fell, poor underwriting was causing too-narrow credit spreads in a number of areas. And (hidden) fear was rising as asset prices rose, just waiting for "something" to trigger panic. But given the extent of mismatched assets and liabilities, it was only a question of where and when.

Collateralized debt obligations (CDOs) get bad rap, but they have been an enormous stabilizer during this crisis, as they allowed better asset-liability matching. Thanks to CDOs, commercial mortgage-backed securities (CMBS) holders have not seen runs, as investors did a decent job matching their long-term CMBS and mortgage positions with non-mark-to-market long-term CDO debt. Hence, CDOs have prevented a CRIMIE Mae meltdown, such as transpired in 1998 when spreads widened.

Due to extraordinary spread volatility, no one believes they can profitably issue a CDO today. As a result, fixed-rate CMBS issuance is currently dead. This will resolve only as the CDO market recovers over the twelve to eighteen months as markets stabilize.

The current credit crisis has had a lesser impact on floating rate CMBS issues. For floating CMBS, AAA spreads went from 7 bps over LIBOR in June to 50 bps in August. Since LIBOR rose by about 50 basis points in early September, this has resulted in increased yield of about 93bps. In mid-September, spreads on five-year AAA floating-rate CMBS issuances stood at 52 basis points over LIBOR, versus a 52-week average spread of 14 basis points. Similarly, five-year AA floating tranches priced at 75 basis points over LIBOR, versus a 52-week average of 28 basis points, while BBB tranches were priced at 210 basis points over LIBOR, versus a 2007 low of 65 basis points and a 52-week average of 97 bps. These enormous swings reflect the fact that matched financing is near impossible in times of great volatility.

FIGURE 14B.4: Monthly spreads in the CMBS market

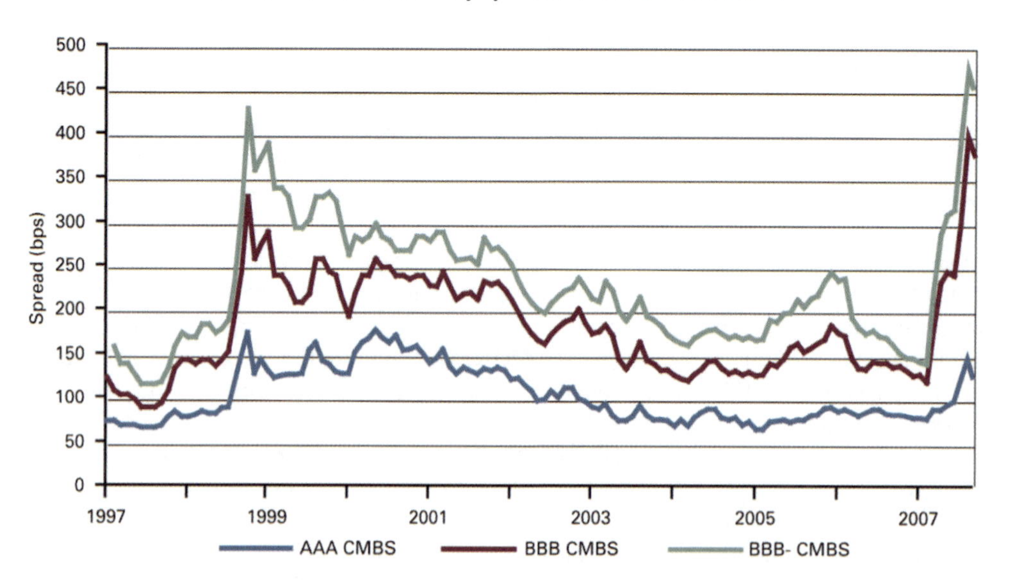

IMPACT

Although it's a terrible time to have to borrow or sell, few commercial real estate players have to sell or borrow. Instead, like most companies (and households), they will simply avoid the capital markets until things stabilize. And if they must borrow, they will borrow short and refinance when credit markets calm.

What about troubled sub-prime borrowers? Most took fixed-rate mortgages, locking in cheap money. But floating rate borrowers, who purchased some 300,000 homes as speculative investments, will suffer as these investments sit empty for the next two years (or decades in the case of Miami condos!). Society's real sub-prime loss is that the capital that built these properties could have been used for something more productive. As to the idiots who lent (often without down-payments or documents) to the idiots who bought speculative homes: they deserve to lose. We owe many thanks to German taxpayers for bailing out our idiots by German bail-outs of the German institutions holding U.S. sub-prime paper.

Many hedge funds with high water marks will shut down, because their assets (not just sub-prime paper) have fallen to the point where their high water marks are unreachable in the near-term. They will shut down and reopen under a new name. This could create some additional selling pressure in the near-term.

In terms of commercial real estate pricing, through most of 2006, pricing was about right in both public and private markets. But by late 2006, real estate pricing was beyond anything explainable by using CAPM or compared to BBB credit spreads. And by March 2007, the overpricing reached 15 percent to 20 percent. That changed very rapidly in April and early May in the REIT market, as REIT pricing reacted very quickly to widening credit spreads and reduced LTVs. REITs repriced, going from 15 percent to 20 percent overpriced in June, back to fairly priced after the stock market run-up in the third week of September.

FIGURE 14B.5: Real estate (under) over pricing using:

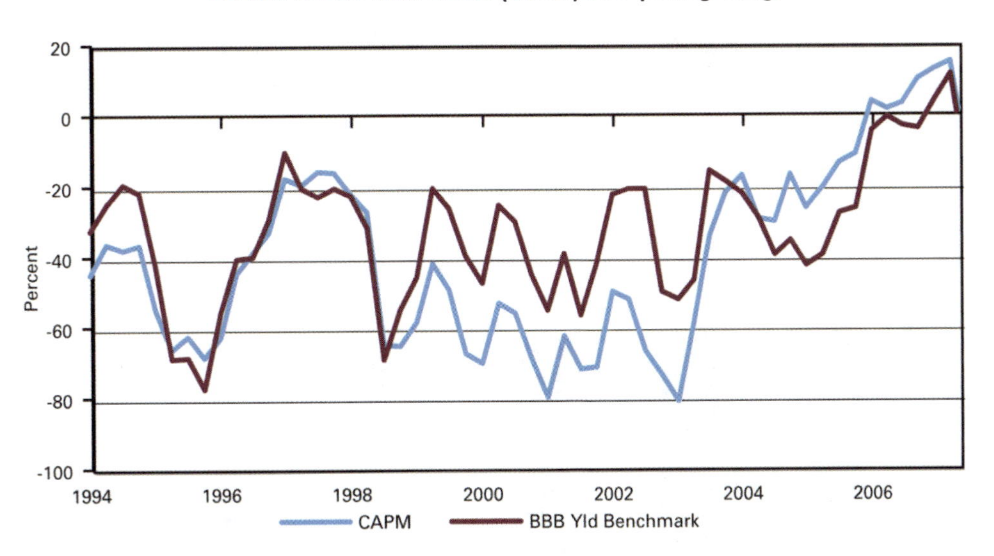

In April, May and early June, the private real estate market continued as if nothing had changed, even though credit spreads were widening, and LTVs were falling. Hence, deals made in April, May, and June, which had ninety to 180 days to close, are now struggling. Many buyers are discovering they cannot achieve the low spread 85 percent LTVs they projected. They can obtain 70 percent to 75 percent LTVs, with 1.10 to 1.25 coverage ratios, at much higher spreads. As a result, super leveraged deals are dead, a victim of fear. In today's environment, if you have to borrow, you probably should float, hoping to refinance when markets stabilize. But that's risky. These buyers are something new: "distressed buyers". To close they need more equity, and many are purchasing at prices 15 percent to 20 percent above values today. But if they walk, they lose their deposits. Those trying to re-trade find sellers who say "The only reason I was selling the property was because of the outrageous price you agreed to pay". Most sellers have no incentive to re-trade, especially in view of capital gains taxes. So do not expect a tremendous amount of re-trading.

Most funds in this situation have sufficient capital to infuse the required equity, and will close rather than walk from deposits. If they walk, they will have to explain to their investors why they walked away from money, guaranteeing the complete loss of this money. If instead they close by putting more equity in the (possibly overpriced) deal, it generates a much lower pro forma rate of return, meaning six years from now, they may have to report worse returns than projected. But better to do it six years from now than to report a complete loss at their upcoming investors meeting (especially as they pitch raising the next fund).

FIGURE 14B.6: CMBS loan to value

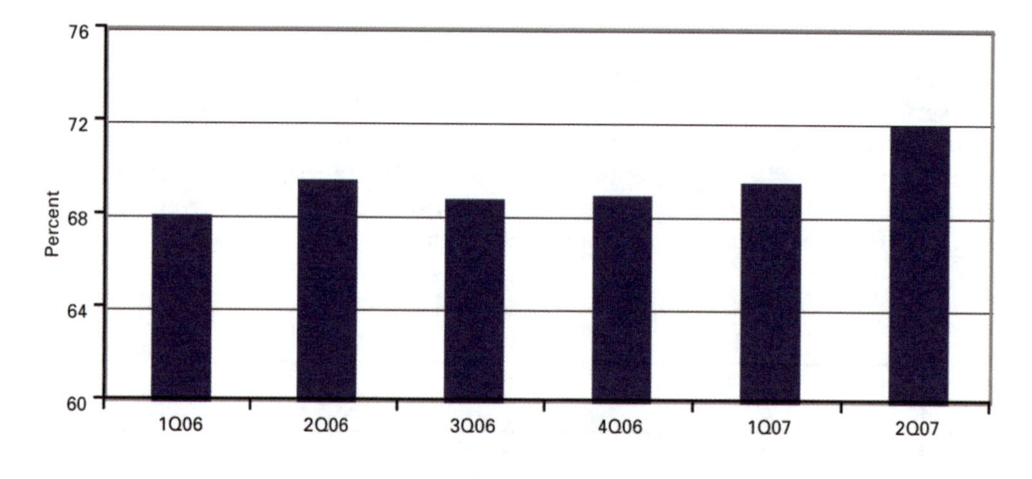

FIGURE 14B.7: CMBS debt service coverage ratio

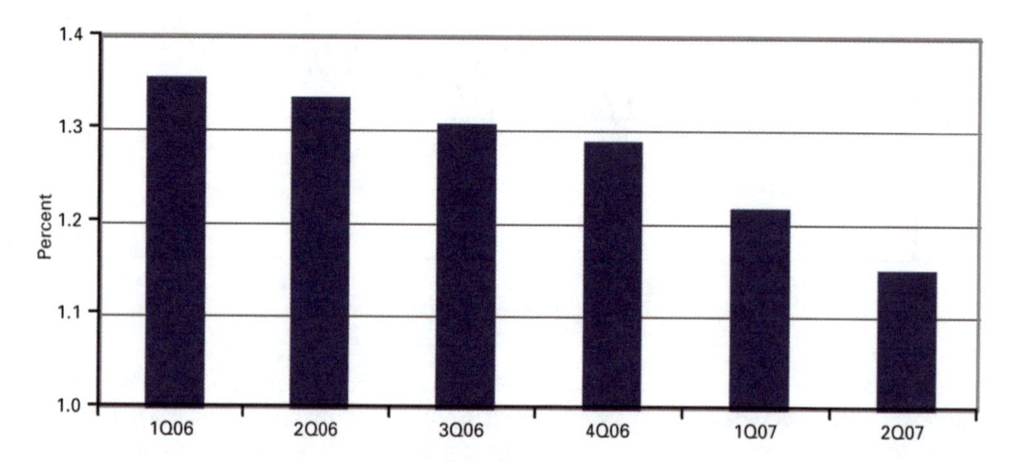

FIGURE 14B.8: Conduit CMBS subordination to BBB– (excl. I/G loans)

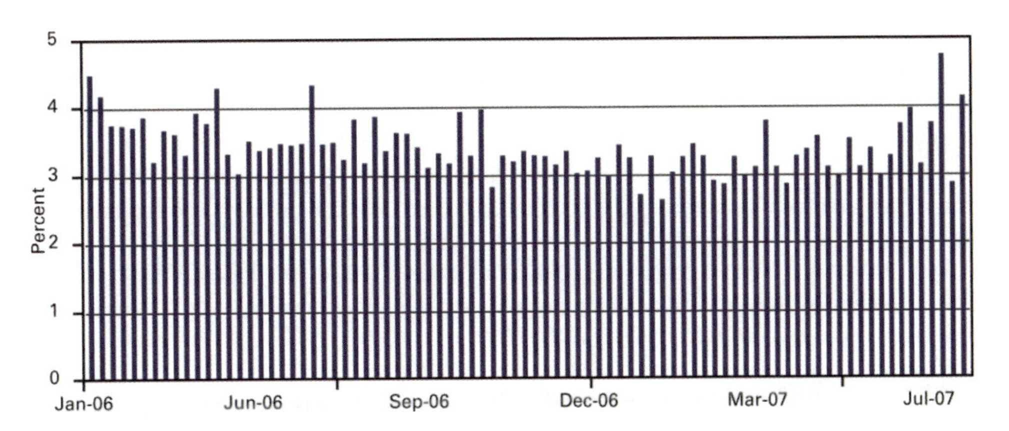

FIGURE 14B.9: CMBS full interest only loans

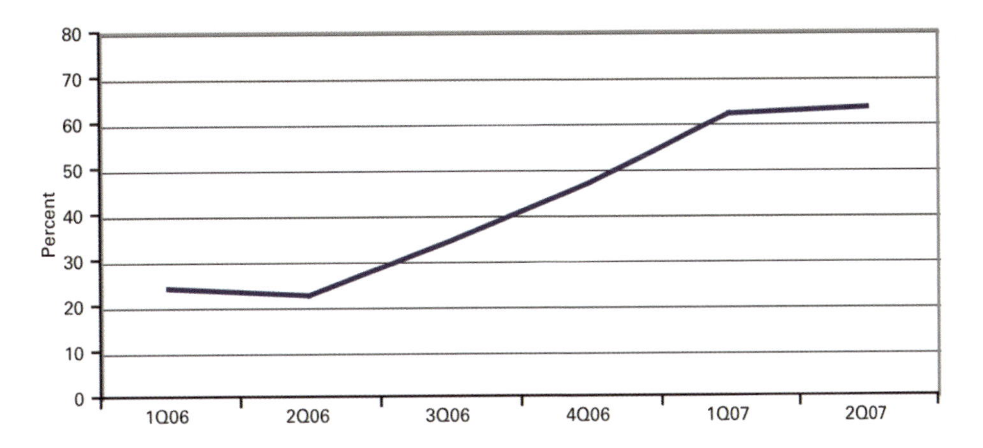

It is smart to pursue this strategy. Remember that it is only six years since 9/11. If you think of all the things that have happened since then, it is wise to say, "Who knows what six years from now will be like in terms of this investment?" Even if it's not a spectacular deal today on paper, they have the option of hanging on until greed makes its triumphant return. And greed can turn marginal investments into stellar performers. So it makes sense to stay alive to 2013.

Deals in the pipeline that were bridged by investment banks will be interesting to watch. Three times in my career I have watched Wall Street get aggressive and guarantee bridges. All three times, the bridges were enormously profitable—right up until they almost bankrupted the firm. We are witnessing the same thing as in 1987 and 1992 with bridges. Specifically, bridge makers who thought they would place the paper at a quick profit are stuck holding bridge commitments that challenge their balance sheets. Some banks have bridges that I do not know how they can bridge, as they do not have enough capital. And no one is going to take the bridge out in the near-term, except at a huge discount. This is more prevalent with big buyout deals than in real estate.

IT'S GOING TO BE ALL RIGHT

The economy is strong, job growth is solid, and most people rarely tap capital markets. While some of us are in the capital market regularly, if you go to the people running companies around the country, they're not terribly sensitive to capital market events. They rarely tap capital markets, and do not really focus on this "Wall Street stuff". They do not have Bloomberg's, and they do not read the Wall Street Journal or the Financial Times. They read their local paper, USA Today, and trade magazines. If credit spreads stay wide and the Fed keeps the rate high for more than eighteen months, it will hurt them, as eventually they will use the capital markets—but not in the short-term.

Housing is obviously a weak sector. But it should be a weak sector. The industry built 400,000 to 500,000 homes (about 0.3 percent of the existing housing stock) that they should not have built. And now they have to burn-off this excess inventory, which will take until late 2008.

Such adjustments are healthy in that they re-introduce underwriting discipline. Like jogging, it's painful, but healthy. Now is a great time to buy credit spread. But buy it with long-term money, as it could get worse before it stabilizes.

I anticipate few new transactions through the end of the year. But by the latter half of 2008, and certainly in '09, transaction velocity will resume at cap rates that are 40 to 60 basis points higher than prevailed in early 2007. In the meantime, don't panic. Just avoid capital markets. Corporate America has a very strong balance sheet and large cash balances. We are just living through another case of fear conquering greed. But count on greed returning sooner than you think.

Chapter 15
Ground Leases as a Source of Finance

"Judgment is far more important than intellect".
-Dr. Peter Linneman

Ground leases are a relatively rare, but interesting, dimension of real estate finance. Generally, real estate transactions involve the purchase of a fee interest, that is the purchase of both the building and the associated land. However, in some instances the land is leased by the building owner from a third party. For example, in Hawaii, China and London, many buildings are owned subject to ground leases. The separation of the ownership of land and structure can create problems and leads to some twists in the financial analysis.

In a ground lease structure, the party that owns the building leases the land from an unrelated landowner. To illustrate the dynamics of a ground lease, assume you are interested in purchasing the apartment building, Mona Reshma Apartments, summarized in Figure 15.1. If the land were owned fee simple, there would be a single ownership claim on the property's NOI.

FIGURE 15.1

Information for Mona Reshma Apartments	
NOI	$8 MM
Property Value*	$100 MM
*includes land value	
Debt	$65 MM
Interest on Debt	5.4%
Land Information	
Land Rent	$3 MM
Term	70 years
Ground Rental Growth	3% every 10 years

Based on your analysis, you determine that the $8 million stabilized NOI for the property (including the land) is worth $100 million (an 8 cap or 12.5 multiple). To finance your purchase of the building, you obtain a 10 year, $65 million, interest only, first mortgage on the property. With the 10-year Treasury rate at 3.6%, you negotiate a 5.4% interest rate (180 basis points above Treasury), which means $3.51 million annually in interest payments. In this example, you have a loan-to-value ratio of 65% ($65 million mortgage / $100 million believed property value) and a 2.28x interest coverage ratio ($8 million NOI / $3.51 million interest payment).

Assume that instead of a fee simple ownership for the property, the apartment complex is subject to a $3 million annual ground lease payment to the landowner. If you fail to make the $3 million ground lease payment, the ground lease specifies that the landowner has foreclosure rights on your building. Generally, the terms of the ground lease allow the landowner to take ownership of the building in order to satisfy their claim if you fail to meet the terms of the ground lease. Post-foreclosure, only if the value of the building exceeds the present value of the landowner's lease claim will the building owner receive the excess value. In some ways a ground lease is similar to a mortgage, as both have fixed payment streams that have priority over equity claimants, and failure to pay causes a contractual default that triggers specific remedies.

Ground leases generally specify that the landowner receives any structures remaining on the land at the end of the lease. That is why ground leases tend to have very long terms, for example, 99 years. They are not infinite because of legal technicalities. Ground leases tend to be renegotiated every 10-20 years, because as the expiration date approaches, the landowner may have little incentive to extend the lease. If you encounter a situation where the landowner takes control of the building due to lease expiration, you can be certain that one of the parties misplayed their hand many, many years earlier. Either someone was very sloppy or procrastinated too long.

Most ground leases have relatively simple rental payment structures. However, even if a ground lease does not provide a mechanism for increasing the ground rent over the term of the lease, the rent usually rises over time. If you are only obligated to pay $3 million per year for 90 years, why would you ever agree to an increase? Because the landowner has the right to take your building at the end of the lease. Therefore, you will renegotiate the ground lease from time to time to extend the maturity and protect the value of your building. You don't play Russian roulette with the ground lease for a valuable building, as a modest ground rent increase is preferable to losing the entire building. So even if the property has a 70 year ground lease with a 3% increase in the ground rent every ten years, you will more than likely renegotiate new terms for the ground lease sometime in the next 20 years.

What NOI is realized by the building owner given the terms of this ground lease? After the $3 million ground lease payment, the relevant NOI is $5 million ($8 million - $3 million), rather than the full $8 million NOI associated with fee simple ownership. In essence, the ground lease is an operating expense, as in order to operate the property you must pay your ground lease. An advantage of the ground lease structure is the ground rent payment is tax deductible, while if you own the land it provides no tax shelter via depreciation.

How do you value a building subject to a ground lease? Note that while the land is still valuable, you have no claim to that value. There are a couple of alternative methods to estimate the value of your building. One is to calculate the value of the land through a DCF analysis of the ground lease payments over the 70 year term (incorporating expected renegotiations), and subtract this value from the value of the property fee simple. This approach is illustrated in Figure 15.2. The discount rate to use on the ground lease payments is lower than the discount rate for the fee simple ownership structure, as the landowner owns a priority slice of the property's cash stream. Therefore, the landowner's expected rental stream has much less risk than the property under a fee simple structure. Remember that you have to pay your ground lease or lose your building! Although the ground lease payments are not riskless, the landowner should receive payment as long as the NOI remains above $3 million. In our example a 7.3% discount rate is assumed to be sufficient to compensate for the risk of the leasehold interest. Applying the Gordon Model, for a 3% increase in ground lease payments every ten years (a 0.3% annual growth rate), the terminal value in year 30 is equal to $46.83 million ($3.28/(7.3% - 0.3%)). Discounting the ground lease payments and the terminal value to the present, results in a land value of $42.48 million. This implies a value to the structure owner of $57.5 million ($100 million - $42.48 million).

FIGURE 15.2

Discount Cash Flow Analysis - Ground Lease Payments for Mona Reshma Apts.							
	Year 1	...	**Year 10**	...	**Year 20**	...	**Year 30**
Ground Lease Payment	$3.00 MM		$3.09 MM		$3.18 MM		$3.28 MM
Terminal Value							$46.83 MM
Discounted Value @ 7.3%	$2.80 MM		$1.53 MM		$0.78 MM		$6.05 MM
Value of Land	$42.48 MM						

Alternatively, you could simply cap the stabilized ground lease rental payment and subtract this value from the value under a fee simple ownership structure. Again applying the Gordon model with a 7 cap (lower than the property 8 cap due to lesser risk) on the $3 million per year payment, indicates the ground lease is worth $42.9 million ($3 million / .07). Note that this is quite close to the $42.48 million achieved by DCF analysis.

FIGURE 15.3

Ground Lease Cap Rate Calculation	
Revenue	$3.0 MM
Cap Rate	7.0%
Value	$42.9 MM

Subtracting this estimated value from the value of the property fee simple implies that the building subject to the ground lease is worth approximately $57.1 million.

Alternatively, you could cap the building's $5 million stabilized NOI ($8 million net of the $3 million ground lease payment) in order to estimate the building's value subject to the ground lease. The cap rate to apply to the $5 million NOI must be higher than the cap rate for the property fee simple, as the landowner's lease payments are stripped away with greater certainty than the remaining cash flow. In this case, using an 8.75% cap rate (higher than the 8% for the fee simple ownership) we arrive at the same $57.1 million building value as derived above.

FIGURE 15.4

Property Cap Rate Calculation		
Information		
NOI		$5.0 MM
Land Value		$42.9 MM
Structure Value	$100 MM - $42.9 MM = $57.1MM	
Calculation		
Formula		5/X = 57.1
Cap Rate		8.75%

Finally, you could do a DCF analysis of the NOI after ground lease payments, using a relatively high discount rate. For this analysis, you assume the building's NOI grows roughly with inflation, 1.5% annually. Therefore, you project 30 years of NOI for the property and subtract the ground lease payments. Given the 7.3% discount rate used to value the ground rent payments, a 10.75% discount rate for the NOI after ground lease payments is sufficient to compensate for the added risk of the building owner's interest. For the building owner's terminal value in year 30, you use a 9.25% exit cap rate, which is 50 basis points higher than the cap rate used above. This premium captures the physical deterioration of the building after 30 years. The 9.25% exit cap rate is also higher than the 8% fee simple cap rate given the additional risk of the building owner's position. Discounting the 30 years of expected NOI after ground rent and the terminal value in year 30 at the 10.25% discount rate results in a $57.75 million building value, as illustrated in Figure 15.5. This is close to the results of the alternative methods.

FIGURE 15.5

Discount Cash Flow Analysis - NOI after Ground Lease Payments							
	Year 1	**...**	**Year 10**	**...**	**Year 20**	**...**	**Year 30**
Property NOI	$8.00 MM		$9.15 MM		$10.62 MM		$12.32 MM
Ground Lease Payment	$3.00 MM		$3.09 MM		$3.18 MM		$3.28 MM
Terminal Value							$97.75 MM
Subtotal	$5.00 MM		$6.06 MM		$7.43 MM		$106.79 MM
Discounted Value at 10.75%	$4.51 MM		$2.18 MM		$0.96 MM		$4.99 MM
Value of Building	$57.75 MM						

You can analyze the situation using any of these methods, but the cap rates and discount rates selected for the alternative analysis must be internally consistent. Which answer is "right"? None of them; after all they are all just models. Only time will tell the true value.

A word to the wise: do not subtract the ground lease liability twice! That is, if you subtract the ground lease expense from revenues as an operating cost, do not subtract land value from that building valuation. Remember the land and property are worth $100 MM together. The figure below breaks down the valuation in our example. Of course, as the ground lease payment changes so too will the building's value.

FIGURE 15.6

Summary	
NOI	$5.0 MM
Cap	8.75%
Value of Building	$57.1 MM
Ground Lease Payments	$3 MM
Cap (not accounting for growth)	7.00%
Value of Land	$42.9 MM
Total Value	$57.1MM + $42.9MM = $100 MM

Now consider financing the property's acquisition. The terms you agreed upon with the lender for a fee simple purchase are completely out of whack for the purchase of the property subject to the ground lease. If you attempt to borrow $65 million to purchase the building subject to the $3 million annual ground lease it is a 113.8% LTV ($65 million / $57.1 million), as the $42.9 million land value is not yours to give as collateral. In addition, the interest coverage ratio for such a loan is only 1.42x ($5 million / $3.51 million), as $3 million of the $8 million NOI goes towards ground lease payments. Of course, the lender will know about the ground lease obligation and will use $5 million, not $8 million, as the relevant NOI when calculating interest coverage for your purchase subject to the ground lease. As a result, lenders will not lend as much to purchase a property subject to a ground lease as for fee simple ownership.

The good news is that since you are purchasing the property subject to a ground lease, instead of purchasing fee simple, you only need about $57 million to purchase the building, rather than the $100 million required for the purchase of the building and the land. If you purchase the building for $57 million subject to the ground lease using a 65% LTV mortgage, you will receive a $37 million ($57 million * 65%) loan. But the lender will charge a higher interest rate or impose tougher covenants on this loan due to the fact that the ground lease payments increase the building's NOI risk. Assume the lender charges 30 basis points higher interest rate (hence a 5.7% interest rate, 210 basis points above Treasury), for a $2.12 million annual interest payment each year. With $5 million pro forma NOI net of $3 million in ground lease payments, the pro forma interest coverage ratio is 2.36x.

The lender may demand that the landowner agree to **subordinate** their ground lease claim to the mortgage. This subordination means that the landowner accepts a lower position in terms of rights to the collateral and the cash flows throughout the life of the loan. Subordinating their land means that if you default on your mortgage, the lender not only has recourse to your building but also to the landowner's land to satisfy their mortgage claim. This highlights the fact that the details of a loan contract are everything. Even though the interest coverage ratio mathematically remains at 1.42x, such contractual terms with the lender make the coverage ratio effectively much higher.

Such a mortgage proposal might be acceptable to both the borrower and the lender. But what about the poor landowner!? You want the landowner to agree to receive his ground lease payment after the lender, and in the event that you default on your mortgage, they could lose their land to the lender. What do you think the landowner is going to say to this proposal? A good bet is "No Way"!

You begin to see the problems involved with separate owners of the land and the building. You can only give one absolute first lien, but both the lender and the landowner want that position. When you split ownership of the land and the building, it is hard to make everyone happy. That is why the ground lease structure is relatively rare and usually inefficient.

CLOSING THOUGHT

Although ground leases are not involved in most real estate transactions, understanding the complexities they create makes you a more informed analyst. Be sure to carefully evaluate the details of the ground lease before investing in a situation where they are involved.

Chapter 16
Real Estate Exit Strategies

"Get rich slowly".
-Dr. Peter Linneman

Smart investors spend considerable time thinking about their exit strategy prior to acquiring or developing a property in an attempt to avoid the "roach motel" phenomenon: you can get in, but you can't get out. And sometimes you have to free up your equity and move on to (hopefully) better things!

WHY EXIT?

Why might you decide to exit? After all, you spent a lot of time assessing whether you wanted to invest, and even more time working the property after the purchase. But if you are a developer, for example, you are in the business of creating buildings, and may need equity for new developments. So developers need an exit strategy which allows them the opportunity to free up their capital for future developments. Thus, once the property is stabilized and generating a solid return, a developer may need to exit in order to build again. Another entity, such as a REIT or local operator, may have a comparative advantage in managing stabilized properties.

Another reason to exit is to alter your risk-reward profile. For example, a developer specializes in taking development risks. However, once the building is stabilized, this risk is gone. Similarly, an older building in need of repositioning has more risk than a new building. If you are unwilling or unable to deal with the complexities, costs, and challenges posed by an older building, you will want to exit. If you are purchasing a new strip center because it is the best in the market, as demographics, the local economy, consumer preferences, competitive centers, and tenants change, at some point you may need to exit, as the building no longer will be the best property in the market.

Another example is that opportunistic investors generally desire to exit once the value has been added, in order to generate higher IRRs. All private equity funds must have an exit strategy as they have finite lives of 7-12 years.

There are also "old-fashioned" reasons to exit. For example, people exit inherited estate properties, as the beneficiaries rarely want the headaches of managing real estate. In addition, situations such as divorces and partnership dissolutions frequently force people to exit their investments. These human aspects of investing force you to have an exit strategy.

HOW TO EXIT

What is the best exit strategy? To illustrate the pros and cons of several alternative exit strategies, assume that 3 years ago you bought a poorly managed property, Jessica Crest, for $100 million with the expectation of substantially enhancing property value through active management and re-leasing. You purchased the building with $40 million of your equity and a $60 million mortgage. For tax purposes, you allocate $75 million of the purchase price to structure (depreciable), and $25 million to land (non-depreciable).

FIGURE 16.1

Jessica Crest			
Cost	$100	**Cost**	$100
Equity	$40	Land	$25
Debt	$60	Structure	$75

After three years of hard work, you have successfully repositioned the property and its value has indeed risen to the expected $140 million, increasing your equity from $40 million to $80 million ($140 million - $60 million of debt).

Having successfully executed your business plan, you now have a problem: it is highly unlikely you can double your equity via this property over the next 3 years. Meanwhile, you have identified another mismanaged property and want to repeat the repositioning strategy. Purchasing the identified property requires that you come up with $40 million in equity, but you do not have $40 million available, as all of your money is tied up in Jessica Crest. How do you access this built-up equity in Jessica Crest?

FIGURE 16.2

Jessica Crest			
Initial Value	$100	**Value after Appreciation**	$140
Equity	$40	Equity	$80
Debt	$60	Debt	$60

SALE

One option is the outright sale of Jessica Crest. If you decide to sell Jessica Crest, you have to go through the process of finding a buyer. Depending on the building and market, a "typical" sales process requires three to twelve months. To prepare the property for sale you must gather your documents and contracts, prepare financial statements, have an accounting firm audit those statements, perhaps create a sales book, hire lawyers to negotiate and structure the sale agreement, possibly hire a broker to help sell the property, spend time negotiating with buyers, etc. In addition to the time and energy involved, the sales process is not free, as lawyers, accountants, and brokers do not work for free. Many of the costs of these services are relatively fixed. As a result, fees as a percentage of total sales price tend to be larger for smaller properties, and smaller for larger properties. In general, 2%-5% is a good estimate for the costs of selling a property, but keep in mind the actual percentage fluctuates with property value. If you have a large trophy asset, like Rockefeller Center, the fees as a percentage of value will be substantially less because the amount of work and value added by the brokers are not large relative to the value of the property. If, however, you have a $5 million property, then the fees can easily exceed 5%. Assume that you estimate that selling Jessica Crest will cost you $3 million in fees.

Assume that after 6 months of searching for a buyer, you successfully sell Jessica Crest for $140 million. You will use the $140 million sale proceeds to repay the $60 million mortgage. If the buyer uses debt financing to purchase the building, there are technical complications in the final closing, as the buyer will be unable to pay you until they receive their mortgage. However, the buyer's lender will not provide a mortgage until they have a first lien on the property, which cannot be given until you sell the property and repay your loan. To solve this problem you will simultaneously close the sale, repay your existing loan, and transfer of the first lien to the purchaser's lender.

Another major payment you have to make upon sale is your capital gains tax. Under US tax code there are two components of the capital gains tax. The first component is the actual gain you achieve on the building. In this case you paid $100 million for the property and you sold it for $140 million. This $40 million gain is (currently) taxed at 15%, for a total of $6 million in taxes. But remember that the capital gains tax rate changes over time as tax law evolves.

The second capital gains tax component (under current law) is that you have to pay taxes on the property's accumulated depreciation. You have been depreciating the building over the past three years to shield income from ordinary income taxes. The government (currently) requires that you pay a 25% tax rate on accumulated depreciation. Depreciating the $75 million you attributed to structure over a 40-year period ($1.875 million per year), meant that you have taken $5.625 million in total accumulated depreciation over the past 3 years. In reality, accumulated depreciation will be larger, as not all value will be attributable to structure as opposed to shorter lived improvements such as carpet, fixtures, etc. The government will tax the $5.625 million accumulated depreciation at a 25% tax rate, or $1.4 million in taxes. If you are a non-taxable entity, such as a pension fund, the capital gains tax is zero. Combining these capital gains tax components, you will pay a total of $7.4 million in capital gains taxes upon the $140 million sale.

FIGURE 16.3

Jessica Crest Capital Gains Taxes		
Structure		$75MM
Depreciation Time		40 years
Corporate Tax Rate		25%
Cap Gains Tax Rate		15%
Depreciation Tax		
Depr. per year		$1.875 MM
Depr. since we began		$5.625 MM
Depr. Tax @ 25%		$1.41 MM
Capital Gains Tax		
Appreciation	(140-100)	$40 MM
Capital Gains Tax @ 15%		$6 MM

Thus, after repaying the loan, paying all fees and paying the IRS you are left with $69.6 million of the $140 million in gross sales proceeds.

FIGURE 16.4

Jessica Crest Equity Calculation	
Sales Revenue	$140 MM
Debt	-$60 MM
Fees	-$3 MM
Capital Gains Tax	-$ 6 MM
Depr. Taxes	-$1.4 MM
Remaining Equity	$69.6 MM

In addition, you may face a pre-payment penalty for repaying your loan prematurely. This analysis assumes that you have no pre-payment penalty on the loan. In our example you probably will not incur a pre-payment penalty, because given your repositioning strategy you would have selected a loan that allowed you to sell the building after roughly 3-4 years without penalty. Specifically, you probably used a floating rate loan in order to avoid a pre-payment penalty upon early exit. This exemplifies how the type of debt selected depends on your investment and exit strategy.

Upon completion of the sale, you have sufficient funds to execute the other repositioning deal, as you have $69.6 million, and only needed $40 million in equity for the new project. However, freeing up your money came at a cost. Specifically, even though you doubled your equity from $40 million to $80 million on the investment, you only have $69.6 million in your pocket due to the substantial leakage from fees and taxes. Are there exit alternatives available which reduce these leakages from sale?

REFINANCING

An alternative exit strategy for the Jessica Crest property is refinancing, that is, taking out a new loan on the property. If the original lender was willing to lend $60 million on the $100 million Jessica Crest property prior to repositioning, a lender should be willing to lend you substantially more once Jessica Crest is stabilized and worth $140 million. If instead of selling the property you obtain a new 65% LTV ($91 million) first mortgage, after repaying the original lender you are left with $31 million in refinancing proceeds ($91 million - $60 million).

While the refinancing process is much cheaper than the sales process, as you do not have to pay the transfer taxes and brokerage fees, you probably will have a 50 basis points loan fee on the new mortgage, as well as some lawyers' and accounting fees. But even if you pay $1 million in refinancing costs, it is a notable improvement over the costs associated with the sale option. And, if you refinance you **postpone** paying capital gains taxes, as you only pay capital gain taxes upon sale. This is the major advantage of the refinance option relative to a sale. Given the time value of money, you generally prefer to defer tax liability. In fact, the longer you think you will hold the building, the more attractive is the refinance option. For example, if you plan to sell the building tomorrow, the refinancing option makes no sense because you simply pay $1 million in refinancing fees, as well as the sale related fees and taxes. But if you plan to hold the property for 60 years, the present value of the deferred capital gain tax liability is effectively zero.

FIGURE 16.5

Jessica Crest Refinance	
Equity Value (Total)	$80 MM
Building Value	$140 MM
Debt	$91 MM
Equity in Building	$49 MM
Equity to Holder	$ 31 MM
Fees	-$ 1 MM
Equity For New Projects	$30 MM

Upon refinancing Jessica Crest, you realize net refinancing proceeds of $30 million. Thus, although you avoid $2 million in fees and $7.4 million in gains taxes, the net proceeds from refinancing the property are $39.6 million lower than from selling the building ($69.6 million from sale versus $30 million from refinancing). Where did the remaining money go? The answer is that you still own a $49 million equity position in Jessica Crest in the case of refinancing, as the building is worth $140 million against a $91 million loan. Therefore, your total wealth position after refinancing is $79 million ($30 million in cash from the refinancing plus $49 million in equity in the property), which is higher than the $69.6 million from selling the building.

Yet after refinancing you still have a problem, as you need $40 million in cash for the new repositioning deal. Therefore, refinancing does not always meet your objective. Of course, if the increase in value were greater, or the refinancing LTV were higher, the refinancing option may achieve this goal. Or if you only need $30 million for your next investment, refinancing is very effective. But in our example, too much value remains tied up in Jessica Crest for refinancing to achieve your objective.

What can you do to solve this equity gap? You could take on a smaller repositioning project, or sell a slice of either Jessica Crest or the new project to an equity partner. A problem with finding an equity partner is there are relatively few buyers of minority interests in privately owned properties, as relatively few investors want an illiquid ownership stake, particularly where their vote will never impact decisions.

Of course, investing $40 million in another property is not every investor's objective, and thus the refinancing option is very attractive for investors who are happy to retain an interest in the stabilized property. For those happy to take $30 million out of Jessica Crest and keep the $49 million equity position, the refinancing option is perfect because of the lesser value leakage. Remember that there is no single objective for all investors. Numbers are important, but who you are and what you are trying to accomplish will ultimately dictate your exit strategy.

LIKE KIND EXCHANGE (1031 EXCHANGE)

There is a third exit possibility that is US specific. Under current US tax code IRS Section 1031, you can pursue a so-called **like kind exchange**, which essentially allows you to sell your property free of state and federal tax if you purchase a "similar" property, hence forestalling capital gains taxes until you ultimately break the ownership chain. Also, the 1031 exchange allows you to restart your depreciation schedule. This is particularly helpful if you have a building that is nearing the end of its depreciable life. Under the like kind exchange principle you can exchange your property partnership interest for an IRS qualified partnership interest in a different partnership. If correctly executed, this highly technical exchange process defers your tax until you sell your new interest.

In real estate, you can sometimes utilize the like kind exchange strategy to defer tax payments otherwise due upon sale. In our Jessica Crest example, you would sell the $140 million Jessica Crest building exactly as before. You will pay the sale related fees and retire the debt, but you do not pay the capital gains taxes immediately if you successfully find a building which qualifies under the tax code. Volumes of tax law dictate the circumstances under which you can effectuate a like kind exchange and defer taxes, and the nuances constantly change.

There are some general guidelines you can use to understand the application of like kind exchange as an exit strategy, but you must make certain that the new property is being held for investment or productive use. The property cannot be acquired with the intent of being resold after a short time period. One of the criteria is the items exchanged must generally be the same business. For example, you cannot sell Jessica Crest and buy an oil and gas company, stocks, or bonds and treat it as a like kind exchange. Broadly speaking, whether a property is considered "like kind" is up to the "nature and character of the property, not its grade or quality" (IRS Code Sections 1031(a)-1(b)). You may do exchanges on both unimproved and improved property. The IRS does not consider real estate outside the United States as like kind property.

There are two noteworthy margins that people try to capitalize on via like kind real estate exchanges. The first is to sell a stabilized building, while purchasing a building where there is opportunity to add value. In our example, you would look to sell your stabilized Jessica Crest property for the poorly managed, partially leased building you wanted to reposition. As long as you can get IRS blessing of the repositioning purchase as a qualified "like kind" exchange, you have satisfied your strategic objective of purchasing the new value-added project while deferring your capital gains taxes on the sale of Jessica Crest.

The second opportunity is to sell the property and buy a stabilized building that offers a better refinancing opportunity and a much reduced management burden. The poster child property in this case is to exchange an office complex for a new building with a long term lease to the US government. This is because lenders are willing to lend you more if secured against a building with the US government on a long term lease than on Jessica Crest, due to the greater tenant credit. As a result, you can net more proceeds out of the sale of Jessica Crest. Figure 16.6 illustrates such an exit strategy.

FIGURE 16.6

Jessica Crest Like Exchange	
Part 1: Sell Asset	
Sale Price	$140 MM
Debt	-$60 MM
Fees	-$3 MM
Capital Gains Tax	$ 0 MM
Depr. Tax	$ 0 MM
Equity Freed	**$77 MM**
Part 2: Buy US Gov't Leased Asset	
Purchase Price	$140 MM
Debt*	-$105 MM
Equity in project	$35 MM
Equity Freed	$77 MM
Equity in Project	-$35 MM
Fees on Purchase	-$1 MM
Equity For New Projects	$41 MM

*We can have an increased LTV because of the high grade tenant

As before, you sell Jessica Crest for $140 million, and repay the $60 million loan, and pay $3 million in fees. But you will not pay capital gains tax, as long as the "replacement" purchase of the government-leased building qualifies as a like kind exchange. You buy the government-leased building for $140 million, using a higher 75% LTV mortgage due to the credit quality of the US government lease. You use $35 million of equity from the sale of Jessica Crest and the $105 million loan (75% * $140 million) to purchase the $140 million government building. You will also incur the $1 million in fees to borrow the $105 million, allowing you to take out $41 million while retaining a $35 million equity position in the government-leased property. That is, a total equity position of $76 million. Although the $76 million derived from the like kind exchange is less than the $79 million net value from a refinancing (due to the fees associated with selling Jessica Crest), you are able achieve your objective, as the $41 million pulled out of the property provides you the $40 million necessary to purchase and reposition another property (and put $1 million in your pocket). You also are able to focus your energy on the repositioning exercise because the government leased property you own is a relatively low-headache management task. In contrast, with a straight refinancing you still have to actively manage the Jessica Crest property.

A major drawback is that other bidders looking to protect their tax position will also be attracted to the exchange property. As a result, the price of a poster child replacement property is generally bid up to the point that some of your tax savings are often passed on to the seller in the form of a higher price.

To execute a 1031 exchange you appoint an independent specialist known as a QI, or qualified intermediary, to help sell the property. The qualified intermediary's purpose is to set up an agreement, so that an escrow or closing agent transfers the property to a buyer and that the sales proceeds go directly to the qualified intermediary. If this were not so, the 1031 exchanger would be taxed on the proceeds. The exchanger has to acquire a new property within a prescribed number of days. The property must be designated as a "replacement" by the exchanger, and sent to the person from whom the exchanger will acquire the property. This is known as the "identification" process. The exchanger must identify a property that is not owned by a subsidiary or employee of the exchanger. The IRS Code has a detailed description of the people from whom the property cannot be purchased, known as disqualified persons. While there are many types of like kind exchanges, conceptually they are merely technical variants.

PUBLIC COMPANY

Another possible exit strategy is to exchange your ownership interest in Jessica Crest for a monetarily equivalent ownership interest in a publicly traded company. For instance, you could exchange the $140 million Jessica Crest property for an interest in publicly traded Boston Properties. If this transaction is structured properly, you will again be able to defer taxes and will not recognize capital gains on the transaction until you sell your Boston Properties interest. Your tax basis from Jessica Crest will carry over to your interest in Boston Properties and your capital gains will be determined based on the proceeds from its sale versus the old basis. However, to achieve such deferral of capital gains can require rather complex structuring. You will generally receive dividend rights and voting rights equal to your pro rata share of the acquiring public company. This transaction provides you with a small slice of ownership in a larger, more diversified pool of assets. However, you will not have control of the property, and will generally lose the property management fees you earned from the property.

GO PUBLIC

The alternative to selling to a public company is to go public. In order to do so, you will need a much larger pool of assets than just Jessica Crest. Your company must consist of large pool of diversified properties in a particular property type, or the investor community will probably be unwilling to purchase your stock at the initial public offering (IPO). Furthermore, the pool of assets will need to be structured in a manner the public market wants: low debt, predictable cash flows, independent governance, and high reporting transparency. If your portfolio lacks these qualities, it is unlikely you will be able to receive fair value from the public market investor community.

In addition, an IPO takes 12-18 months. If your IPO succeeds, you will incur total fees equal to about 10% of the total money raised. In fact, you will incur $500,000-$1 million in expenses whether you successfully complete an IPO process or not. If you pursue an IPO you are subject to the vagaries of timing and the market during the process. If the market weakens, you may be unwilling to issue equity at substantially reduced prices. On the other hand, if the IPO is successful, you will be able to access public capital markets, and can use the proceeds to purchase additional properties or pay down debt.

CLOSING THOUGHT

Selecting an exit strategy is critical. The optimal strategy depends on your objectives. While the numbers and calculations are important, exit is ultimately a personal decision. Two people looking at the same numbers on the sale option and the refinance option may make completely different decisions based on their objectives. Exit strategy is definitely not a one size fits all exercise!

Chapter 17
Real Estate Private Equity Funds

"Find out who you are and stay true to your values".
-Dr. Peter Linneman

Real estate private equity funds are major equity sources for the real estate business. These funds are among the largest owners of real estate in the country, holding an estimated $100 billion of real estate assets in the United States, as well as substantial portfolios abroad.

EVOLUTION

Historically, real estate was purchased and developed with lots of debt, and very small equity syndicates. For example, if you needed equity to fund a development project, you would go to your brother, your cousin, and your neighbor, and raised the necessary sliver of equity. This structure worked pretty well when lots of debt was available for real estate projects. If you had access to almost 100% debt financing, which was not uncommon in the period 1960-1990, you could probably find the necessary equity, especially if you had an established track record. For example, with 99% leverage, if you want to do a $50 million project, you only have to come up with $500,000 in equity. While that is a lot of money, an established player should be able to raise $500,000 in equity or they should not be in the business.

In addition to the availability of debt financing, from 1981-1986 depreciation laws allowed property owners to depreciate the structure over a 15-year period. Combined with even shorter depreciation schedules for improvements, you could probably write off the entire building (excluding the land allocation) in 7-10 years for tax purposes. Assuming 80% of the property was non-land and you are writing the building off in ten years, you were able to write off (for tax purposes) about 8% of the value of the property each year. This meant that the owner of an 8 cap property could completely shelter all income solely via depreciation. Combined with 90-100% LTV debt, the tax shields from interest payments and depreciation generated enormous tax losses, and modest cash flows, each year. Until 1987, you could sell these tax losses for cash to people like doctors and dentists, who valued the losses to shelter their ordinary income from taxes. You could probably get 30-50 cents for every dollar of tax loss you sold. Therefore, you were often able to raise the necessary equity through small equity syndicate sales of the tax losses, and retain most of the property's upside for yourself.

In 1986, Congress extended depreciation schedules, and generally prohibited the sale of tax losses except for low income housing and historic preservation. The swish of the President's signature on this tax bill eliminated the primary source of real estate equity. When in the early 1990s lenders finally realized they had been vastly mispricing their real estate loans, and began offering only 50-70% LTV mortgages, it meant large chunks of equity were suddenly required to own or develop real estate.

Since the early 1990s you have generally needed a large amount of equity in order to own or develop real estate. For example, a 35% equity slice on a $50 million project requires $17.5 million. This is a lot more than the old $500,000 requirement, and you cannot raise a dime of it from the sale of tax losses. Raising $17.5 million in equity is a much more difficult and sophisticated exercise than raising $500,000. You also run the risk that while you are raising the required equity for the deal, you may lose the property to a better-capitalized competitor. For example, a high net worth individual or institutional investor may write a check to fund the project while you are scrambling to raise the necessary equity. After all, one of the advantages of a multi-billion dollar balance sheet is that you generally have sufficient equity for your real estate purchases.

In this new equity environment, investors that have equity with certainty often have an advantage. This is because although the investor putting together an equity syndicate might be willing to bid more for a property, the seller may accept a lower bid from a well-capitalized bidder to ensure a quick closing. If you can achieve even a 1-3% lower purchase price on a building with an expected 11% annual return, you realize almost one-third of a year's return up-front simply by being able to quickly write a check. This advantage of readily available equity led to the creation of **real estate private equity funds**, which raise large pools of equity prior to investing in order to ensure ready access to equity.

SOME HISTORY

The real estate private equity fund business started with the first Zell-Merrill fund in 1988. Today there are perhaps 2,000 professionals working in the business (excluding accountants), versus maybe 50 in 1992. From 1992 to 2007, these funds grew from almost no assets to more than $150 billion in assets. However, the business reached a degree of maturity, with funds raising $10 to $25 billion annually in equity commitments, to be invested over roughly three years.

These funds raise money from pension funds, foundations, university endowments, and high net worth individuals. They receive specific investment commitments from these investors, drawing down the promised commitment on an "as needed" basis. The minimum investment commitment is usually at least $1 million, meaning relatively few individuals directly invest in these funds, though millions have a stake via their pension funds.

Investors invest in a limited partnership managed by the fund **sponsor**, who serves as the general partner responsible for all operations. If an investor fails to satisfy a call on their funding commitment, the investor forfeits many of its rights and economics.

The fund does not take all of the committed money upfront because it would have to invest the excess funds in low yielding cash until it was needed for the higher return real estate investments, dragging down fund return performance. Although pension funds and other institutional investors would rather the real estate opportunity fund put the committed money to work in a predictable manner, institutional investors are generally better suited to handle the excess cash position than are the funds. In addition, pension funds and other institutions have lower total expected portfolio returns than these funds.

Historically real estate private equity funds have marketed that they will generate a 20% IRR, and a 2 times equity multiple over the life of the investment. Lately these return targets are creeping down. These high target returns were originally necessary to lure investors back into a business that no one trusted in the early 1990s. However, the truth is that realized returns have been far less, often only single digit. In fact, the liberal usage of debt to generate returns means that many funds have lost money in down property markets.

The typical fund promises to liquidate all property holdings within 7-10 years, as investors like knowing when they will get their money back. The problem with this liquidation structure is while the properties may be great investments, the market could be weak as the fund's termination date nears. To resolve this problem, sponsors and investors generally can agree to an extension period of up to three years pending a vote of the majority of the limited partners. Although the weak market conditions may persist beyond three years, most investors prefer to take reduced returns and close out the fund.

The sponsors of the fund market to pension funds, university and other endowments, and high net worth individuals requesting funding commitments. The sponsor retains the right to raise less, or more, than their investment commitment target. For example, their target may be a fund size of $1 billion but they can raise more or less. Assuming they raise exactly $1 billion in commitments, the fund strategy is to invest the $1 billion in equity commitments over the subsequent 2-4 years. The fund will leverage this equity when making its real estate investments. At a 2:1 leverage target, i.e. 67% LTV, the fund will have roughly $3 billion in investment power over the 2-4 year investment period.

Once the fund has invested most of its capital, they will attempt to raise a new fund. The investors in this second fund invest in a separate limited partnership, and have no claims on the assets held in the sponsor's first fund. It takes roughly 12-18 months, and perhaps $1 million in out of pocket costs, from the time you begin to seriously plan a fund to the time you close funding commitments. And there is no guarantee that the fund will be successfully raised. There are covenants in the fund's partnership documents that permit the sponsor to raise a new fund only after roughly 85% of the fund's capital is invested. This is designed to assure that the attention of the sponsor remains on the current fund. Of course, the sponsor wants to ensure a seamless transition to its next fund, as they do not want to be "out of the market" for 12-24 months while they raise the new fund.

The sponsor generally invests in the fund. The amount that institutional investors require the sponsor to commit depends on many factors, including the capital base of the fund sponsor. For example, investors expect a large and well capitalized sponsor to put much more into its $2 billion fund than a young real estate entrepreneur that is raising a $30 million fund. This difference reflects the investor's desire to make sure the sponsor's loss is significant if the fund fails to perform. The upper end investment among sponsors is 25-50% of total equity commitments, while the low end is 1-3%.

WHO ARE THEY?

There are three broad groups of fund sponsors today: those associated with investment banks; those associated with investment houses; and, dedicated real estate players.

Investment Banks: The players in this group of funds include: Morgan Stanley (MSREF), UBS, and Credit Suisse. Investment bank sponsors attempt to exploit their access to investors (especially high net worth individuals), deal flow, and capital market expertise. No one has better access to a network of high net worth individuals than investment banks. How did they get that rolodex? Investment banks have sales groups and asset management groups that have long focused on providing investments to high net worth individuals. With these established networks it is relatively easy for investment banks to access this source of capital. Given the investment banks' competitive advantage is raising money, they frequently partner with real estate people to run their funds.

Another advantage of investment banks is access to deal flow. For example, investment banks are frequently intermediaries for companies or governments looking to sell properties. Therefore, investment bank sponsored funds see a lot of deals. The so-called "Chinese Wall" between investment principal and transaction agent in the investment bank organization structure is riddled with holes, with the private placement memorandum of every investment bank sponsored fund describing proprietary deal flow deriving from the firm's client relationships. Finally, these shops are experts in corporate finance and have the expertise to add value by creatively financing and selling complex deals.

Investment Houses: Players in this group of funds include sponsors such as: Blackstone, Carlyle, Cerberus, Apollo, Angelo Gordon, and OakTree. Funds at these investment houses are generally stand-alone vehicles which are part of a family of funds, including LBO funds, venture capital funds, hedge funds, and distressed debt funds. The advantage of having multiple funds under the umbrella of an investment company is that you are raising money for all the funds from the same investor base. To the extent they have performed well on your other funds, they have enhanced credibility with capital sources for their real estate fund, as they can go to a pension fund and say "remember how well you did in my LBO fund, why don't you invest some of the money you made there in my real estate fund". Credibility and reputation are critical in the fund raising business, and brand recognition facilitates the process, as pension funds and endowments, the two largest sources of investment capital, are not in the business of taking risks. Remember that the individuals running investments for these institutional capital sources are generally not incentivized to take risks. If a pension fund invests in an unknown fund and loses money, the employee who made the decision might get fired. But a poor return, or even a loss, via a name brand fund is more easily forgiven.

Dedicated Real Estate Players: Well known players in this group of opportunity funds include: Starwood, Lonestar, Westbrook, AEW, Lubert-Adler, Walton Street, Colony, JW O'Conner, Crow Holdings, and JE Robert. Historically the people who head these funds have worked in real estate most of their lives, and are also skilled at raising money. They tend to be relatively focused real estate investors whose comparative advantage is property level expertise.

RETURN WATERFALL

In their marketing material the sponsor lays out the cash waterfall. This cash waterfall details how fund proceeds will be split between the investors and the sponsor. Let us take as an example an investor, Prushansky Company Pension, and the fund sponsor, Bhavik Fund. The sponsors of the Bhavik Fund commit to its investors (including their own money) that the investors will receive all cash flows until all capital is returned, plus a **preferred IRR return (the "pref")** on all commitments drawn. This preferred return is usually 7-11% annually. Assume that the preferred annual return is 9%. If the investments do not generate sufficient cash flow to pay 9% on all the invested equity, all profits that are generated by operating cash flow or sale go to "the money" (including the sponsor's money) proportionate to the amount they invested. If the investments generate more than the preferred rate of return, the sponsor and "the money" split the excess profits. The fund sponsor's share of this profit is referred to as a **"promote"** or **"carried interest"**. As long as all money is returned and the 9% preferred return is achieved, profits are generally split 80/20, with "the money" receiving 80% of the profits and the sponsor receiving 20% of the profits. Keep in mind that the sponsor is part of "the money", so it receives its share of the 80% profit slice **pari passu** in proportion to the amount it invested. This structure provides an incentive for the sponsor to generate returns in excess of the preferred return, as the sponsor realizes substantial profits once the preferred return is paid to investors.

The sponsor's promote is structured in one of two ways. In the most common structure, the sponsor and "the money" split profits 80/20 as long as "the money" receives all of their money back and the annual preferred return. Alternatively, there is an 80/20 split only on profits in excess of the preferred return (after the money has been returned). Figure 17.1 illustrates the difference.

Assume that it is a $100 million fund with a 9% annual preferred return, with the sponsor contributing $10 million to the fund. Assume for simplicity that the fund liquidates in one year, after generating $25 million in total profits after all costs and repaying debt. This $25 million profit represents a 25% annual return, which exceeds the 9% preferred return. In the case of the structure where only profits above the preferred return are split, "the money" first receives $9 million, which is their 9% preferred return, while the remaining $16 million of profits is split 80/20, with 80% going to "the money" ($12,800,000) and 20% to the sponsor ($3,200,000). The Bhavik Fund and Prushanksy Company Pension (assumed to be the only other investor) split the $12.8 million going to "the money" pro rata based on the amount of money they contributed to the fund. In our example, Prushansky Company Pension receives 90% of both the $12.8 million of excess profits and the $9 million in preferred return payments, while the Bhavik Funds receive 10% of both plus their 20% split of excess profits. In total, in this example, the sponsor (who provided 10% of the equity) receives $5.38 million of the profits while the Prushansky Company Pension receives $19.62 million of the profits. So although the fund generates a 25% return, under this structure Prushansky Pension realizes a 21.8% ($19.62 million / $90 million) return on their investment and the Bhavik Fund realizes 54% ($5.38 million / $10 million).

On the other hand, as is the case for most real estate private equity funds, if the entire $25 million profit is split 80/20 so long as "the money" receives at least a 9% return, the profit split is very different. Note that in this structure with a 9% preferred return, total profits must be at least $11.25 million before the sponsor can claim a full 20% split of the profits. This is because 80% of an $11.25 million leaves "the money" with their minimum 9% preferred return. With $25 million in total profits, this structure gives "the money" $20 million of the profits, with $5 million of the profits going to the sponsor. In addition, the sponsor receives its pro rata share of the $20 million profit split going to "the money" (10% * $20 million = $2 million). This yields $7 million in total profits for the sponsor. As you can see, which fund structure is chosen drastically impacts the profit distribution. For example, this structure provides the sponsor with a total of $7 million, and the Prushansky Company Pension receiving $18 million. Thus, although the fund achieves a 25% return, the investor realizes only a 20% return ($18 million / $90 million). Not surprisingly, fund sponsors prefer the structure which splits all profits, rather than the structure which only splits profits in excess of the preferred return.

FIGURE 17.1

Bhavik Fund Waterfall with 80/20 after 9% Pref is Paid		
Option 1: Split above 9%		
Total Investment		**$ 100 MM**
Prushansky Pension		*$ 90 MM*
Bhavik Fund		*$ 10 MM*
Total Profit		**$ 25 MM**
Preferred Return on Cash: 9%	=100*.9	$ 9 MM
90/100 to Prushansky Pension	=9*.9	*$ 8.10 MM*
10/100 to Bhavik Fund	=9*.1	*$ .90 MM*
Cash Remaining for Split	=25-9	**$ 16 MM**
80% To Money (Prushansky and Bhavik)	=16*.8	*$ 12.80 MM*
90/100 to Prushansky Pension	=12.8*.9	$ 11.52 MM
10/100 to Bhavik Fund	=12.8*.1	$ 1.28 MM
20% To Sponsor (Bhavik)	=16*.2	*$ 3.20 MM*
Total Money to Bhavik Fund		
Money from Pref Return		$ .90 MM
Money from 20% Split		$ 3.20 MM
Money from Pro Rata 80% Split		$ 1.28 MM
		$ 5.38 MM
Total Money to Prushansky Pension		
Money from Pref Return		$ 8.10 MM
Money from Pro Rata 80% Split		$ 11.52 MM
		$ 19.62 MM

Bhavik Fund Waterfall with 80/20 as Long as 9% Paid to Money		
Option 2: "The Money" is above 9%		
Total Investment		**$ 100 MM**
Prushansky Pension		*$ 90 MM*
Bhavik Fund		*$ 10 MM*
Total Profit		**$ 25 MM**
80% To Money (Prushansky and Bhavik)	=25*.8	*$ 20.00 MM*
90/100 to Prushansky Pension	=20*.9	$ 18.00 MM
10/100 to Bhavik Fund	=20*.1	$ 2.00 MM
20% To Sponsor (Bhavik)	=25*.2	*$ 5.00 MM*
Return to Money	=20/100	20%
Total Money to Bhavik Fund		
Money from 20% Split		$ 5.00 MM
Money from Pro Rata 80% Split		$ 2.00 MM
		$ 7.00 MM
Total Money to Prushansky Pension		
Money from Pro Rata 80% Split		**$ 18.00 MM**

It is instructive to see the results of a waterfall structure as the total profits increase. The example below is based on a four year fund with an 80/20 split for all profits as long as the equity investor receives a 9% preferred return, and a 50/50 "**catch up**" provision. This catch up provision says that all profits in excess of the preferred return are split 50/50 until the sponsor has received 20% of all profits, after which all profits are split 80/20. This is a very typical promote structure for funds, as the catch up provision improves the return investors receive if the fund performs only modestly better than the preferred return.

FIGURE 17.2

Investor Return Summary on $10M Investment						
Total Realized	Total Profit	Investor Profit	Investor IRR	Investor Share	Sponsor Profit	Sponsor Share
$8.0 MM	($2.0 MM)	($2.0 MM)	(5.4%)	100.0%	$0.0 MM	0.0%
$10.0 MM	$0.0 MM	$0.0 MM	0.0%	100.0%	$0.0 MM	0.0%
$12.0 MM	$2.0 MM	$2.0 MM	4.7%	100.0%	$0.0 MM	0.0%
14.1 MM	$4.1 MM	$4.1 MM	9.0%	100.0%	$0.0 MM	0.0%
$16.0 MM	$6.0 MM	$5.1 MM	10.9%	85.0%	$0.9 MM	15.0%
$17.0 MM	$7.0 MM	$5.6 MM	11.8%	80.0%	$1.4 MM	20.0%
$18.0 MM	$8.0 MM	$6.4 MM	13.2%	80.0%	$1.6 MM	20.0%
$20.0 MM	$10.0 MM	$8.0 MM	15.8%	80.0%	$2.0 MM	20.0%

FIGURE 17.3

Summary					
Total Profit	**Investor Profit**	**Investor IRR**	**Investor Share**	**Sponsor Profit**	**Sponsor Share**
7 MM	5.6 MM	11.8%	80.0%	1.4 MM	20.0%

Total Cash Flows (in MM)				
Year 0	**Year 1**	**Year 2**	**Year 3**	**Year 4**
-10	0	0	0	17
IRR	14.2%			

Total Cash Flows For Investor (in MM)				
Year 0	**Year 1**	**Year 2**	**Year 3**	**Year 4**
-10	0	0	0	15.6
IRR	11.8%			

The Calculation	
Investor Profit (If IRR > 9% then (Total Profit - Sponsor Profit), but if IRR < 9% then equals total profit	5.600 MM
Total Amount To Achieve Preferred Return of 9% (this can be determined using algebra or a spread sheet)	14.105 MM
Profits Left After Split (Total Revenue - Amount Paid for Preferred Return). Only applies of pref is covered, or else is 0.	2.895 MM
50/50 Catch Up (0.5*(Total Revenue - Amount Paid for Preferred Return). Only applies of pref is covered, or else is 0.	1.448 MM
Percent 50/50 Catch up is of total profits	21%
Max Percent Catch up can be of 50/50 split	20%
Sponsor Profit (if 50/50<20% then 50/50 Catch up figure or else (0.2*(Total Profits)). Minimum this can be is 0	1.400 MM

Figures 17.2, 17.3, and 17.4 illustrate the split proceeds realized by an investor that has committed $10 million to a fund with these terms, where it takes 4 years to realize these profits. As you can see, the sponsor only receives their promote if the total profits result in a return greater than 9% for the equity investor. As the profits increase, the value of their promote increases, creating a powerful incentive for the sponsor to generate higher returns.

Figure 17.4

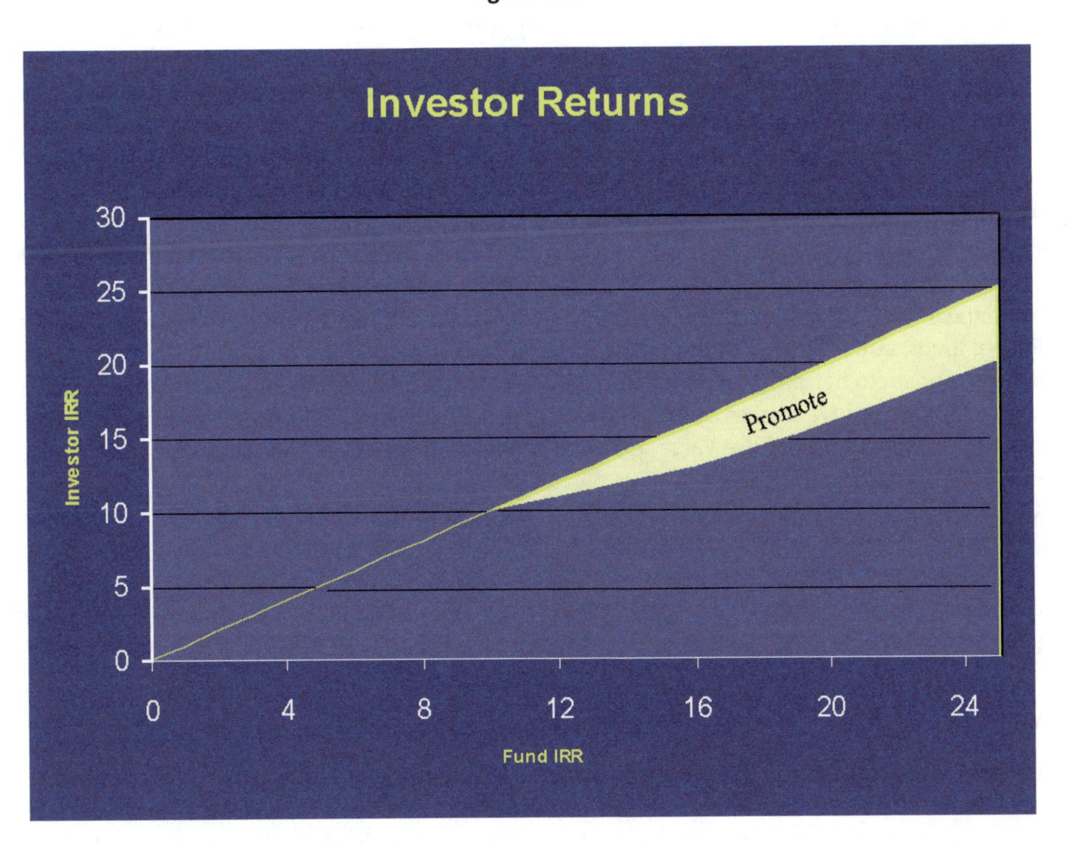

In addition to their promote, fund sponsors also receive an annual management fee. This fee is typically 1-2% of committed equity (whether the money is drawn or not). As money is returned to investors via asset sales, the base on which these fees are based declines.

CLOSING THOUGHT

Like every aspect of the real estate business, the real estate private equity fund business is highly technical and nuanced. The key to their success is their ability to formulate and execute strategies that yield returns substantially in excess of those available via public real estate companies. As is the case for all real estate investments, the private equity structure is only as good as its ability to execute.

Chapter 17 Supplement A

Revisiting Return Profiles of Real Estate Investment Vehicles

Assessing alternative real investment vehicles over time.

Dr. Peter Linneman – The Linneman Letter – Winter 2005

In "Understanding the Return Profiles of Real Estate Investment Vehicles" (*WRER* Fall 2003), we presented simulated investment returns for alternative real estate investment vehicles such as Unlevered Core (NCREIF), Core Plus, REITs (NAREIT), and Value-add funds. We assumed that $100 million was invested in each of these four vehicles for a seven-year investment horizon. For each vehicle, cash flows were estimated based on assumptions about leverage, growth rates, cap rates, management fees, and cash flow payout ratios. We found that because Value-add funds take greater up-front risks, with the expectation of greater profits late in the investment horizon, their returns are generally negative in the early years. Hence, when equivalent investments in the Value-add fund are benchmarked relative to either the NCREIF or NAREIT indices, Value-add funds will appear to under-perform in their early years, even if they exceed their business plan. The need to reserve judgment on these funds until later in their investment horizon often frustrates employees of limited partner investors, as many receive bonuses based upon annual fund performance. This delayed "day of reckoning" also allows weak Value-add managers to raise additional funds, as it is difficult to determine if the current weak performance is temporary or permanent. In short, it is inappropriate to benchmark Value-add fund performance against the other funds prior to stabilization.

Under four alternative market conditions, we determined that the Value-add vehicle tends to outperform the other vehicles. The true risk of the Value-add fund is not the prospect of "disastrous" market conditions, but the inability of the manager to "add value".

Our 2003 paper had several limitations, which we will address here. Specifically, we make four major adjustments to our analysis in an effort to more accurately compare the four investment vehicles. These adjustments include using the Value-add vehicle net cash flows to determine the investments in the other vehicles, staggering investments over three years rather than assuming all capital is invested up-front, adjusting the management fee calculations, and calculating after-promote limited partner IRRs for the Core Plus and Value-add funds.

PROS AND CONS

It is important to note the qualitative pros and cons of each vehicle (FIGURE 17A.1). For example, REITs are the most liquid, while the other three vehicles are generally considered fairly illiquid given the complex and time-consuming process of buying and selling real estate. However, this illiquidity is often mitigated, particularly by Value-add funds, through re-financing, which is a much simpler transaction, and tax-advantaged, than an outright property sale.

FIGURE 17A.1: A broader comparison

Pros and Cons				
	Core	Core Plus	REIT	Value-add
Return Potential	Low	Medium	Medium	High
Liquidity	Low	Low	High	Low
Leverage	Low	Medium	Medium	High
$ Cost-Averaging	No	No	Yes	No
Investment Transparency	Medium	Medium	High	Low
Reporting Control	Sponsor	Sponsor	SEC	Sponsor
Operating Control	Medium	Medium	Low	Low
Diversification	Low	Medium	High	Medium
Alignment of Interests	Low	High	Medium	High

Investment transparency is a matter of knowing how much capital investors will put to work, versus the investment commitment. For example, for REITs, if an investor wants to invest $100 million, then $100 million of securities (less fees) can be purchased. However, with Core, Core Plus, and Value-add funds, an investor can agree to commit $100 million, but the amount actually invested or put to work depends on the availability of desirable investments (and the ability to win control of those investments). We categorize the Core and Core Plus funds as having medium investment transparency and low transparency for the Value-add fund, because opportunistic investment properties are often more difficult to find.

With regard to reporting, REITs adhere to rigorous SEC guidelines. However, that is not to say that the other vehicles have lesser requirements, as reporting is dictated by each investor and sponsor. Separate account fund reporting can be just as demanding as SEC reporting criteria. Multiple investors in commingled funds can also dictate reporting requirements, although collaborative and consistent investor reporting is difficult. A major limitation of Value-add fund reporting is the lack of meaningful benchmarking.

By definition, the greatest investor operating control is associated with Core funds. Core assets are the most stable, and easiest to "understand" from a cash flow perspective. Core Plus and REIT funds bring a slightly higher degree of risk with moderate operating control, depending on each asset. At the other end of the spectrum, the Value-add fund brings low operating control, especially when assets have not yet been stabilized. By the same token, Core funds have less diversification because of their focus on stabilized, core assets. Diversification of the other vehicles varies, because while those vehicles have greater flexibility in which property types to invest, diversification may or may not be a primary goal. Lastly, the interests of the investor and the manager are most closely aligned under the Core Plus and the Value-add funds, because of the sponsor promote structure. If the properties perform well, then both the manager and the investor benefit.

THE SET-UP

The base case market scenario assumptions for each investment vehicle simulation are summarized in Figure 17A.2. In our earlier analysis, the investor commits $100 million of equity in each of the four real estate vehicles, which have different investment strategies, capital structures, cash flow payout ratios, management fees, and promote structures. The simulated NAREIT and Core Plus investment vehicle own the same quality properties as the unlevered Core scenario, but are levered 50 percent and 65 percent, respectively. In addition, the REIT portfolio grows over time, as the REITs retain 30 percent of their cash flow to purchase additional stabilized, core properties (that is, a 70 percent cash flow payout ratio), which are also 50 percent levered. Once stabilized, the Core Plus properties are refinanced with 70 percent debt, and net proceeds are distributed to investors.

FIGURE 17A.2: Base case investment vehicle simulation assumptions

	Base Case			
	Core	Core Plus	REIT	Value-add
Purchase Price - Year 0	$28,748,910	$82,139,743	$57,497,820	$95,829,700
Purchase Price - Year 1	$34,512,500	$98,607,143	$69,025,000	$115,041,666
Purchase Price - Year 2	$36,738,590	$104,967,399	$73,477,179	$122,461,966
Reserve for Negative CF	$0	$0	$0	$16,234,039
LTV	0.0%	65.0%	50.0%	70.0%
Equity Committed	$100,000,000	$100,000,000	$100,000,000	$102,480,769
Equity Invested	$100,000,000	$100,000,000	$100,000,000	$100,000,000
Interest Rate	n/a	6.0%	6.0%	6.3%
Going-in Cap Rate (Stabilized)	8.0%	8.0%	8.0%	n/a
Residual Cap Rate	8.0%	8.0%	8.0%	8.0%
Yr 0 Inv Residual in Yr 5	$31,741,120	$90,688,914	$69,005,082	$129,135,749
Yr 1 Inv Residual in Yr 6	$38,866,680	$111,047,658	$84,653,780	$129,135,749
Yr 2 Inv Residual in Yr 7	$42,201,091	$120,574,547	$94,686,642	$129,135,749
Cash Flow Payout Rate	100%	100%	70%	100%
Management Fee*	0.5%	1.5%	0.5%	1.5%
Carried Interest (Promote)	n/a	10%	n/a	20%
NOI Growth Rate	2.0%	2.0%	2.0%	2.0%
Pre-Promote IRR	10.5%	16.3%	13.0%	20.0%
Equity Multiple (over 7 years)	1.6x	1.94x	1.79x	2.17x
Years to Double Equity	8.7	7.2	7.8	6.5

* Management fee on committed capital for Core Plus and Value-add; on invested capital for Core and REITs.

As mentioned earlier, we make four major adjustments to our original analysis. First, we attempt to more realistically imitate the cash flows by staggering the capital outflows over three years, rather than assuming all committed capital is immediately invested. Specifically, each vehicle is assumed to have three staggered investment phases of five years each. Acquisitions occur in years zero, one, and two, which are sold in years five, six, and seven, respectively. Note that the Value-add fund experiences negative operating cash flow during the first two years of each stage of investment, before the properties are stabilized as core quality assets in the third year. That is, the properties purchased up-front experience negative operating cash flow in years one and two, and stabilize after development/redevelopment in year three. The properties purchased in year two (end of year one), experience negative cash flow in years two and three, stabilizing in year four, and the third stage investments experience negative cash flow in years three and four, stabilizing in year five. Specifically, we set the first-, second-, and third-year NOIs of each investment phase of the Value-add fund to $0, $2 million, and $9.7 million respectively.

In the base case for the Value-add fund, these NOI values are set so that combining all three investment phases generates a 20 percent gross IRR over the seven-year investment horizon (before general partner promote). Given our assumed operating cash flow, debt, and interest rate, in the base case, the three-year staggered investments of the Value-add fund generate an aggregate cash flow of -$16.2 million, which is set aside from the equity commitment as a reserve. As a result, only $86.2 million of the equity commitment is used for acquisitions. This amount is invested evenly over three years, or about $28.7 million per year.

Given this revised structure, our second critical adjustment is to use the Value-add vehicle as the starting point for the amount invested in each of the other fund vehicles each year. Because Value-add investments are unstabilized in the early years, the investor must tap into the committed capital to cover any operating cash shortfalls. These shortfalls ($5.8 million in year one, and about $8 million in year two), plus the actual capital placed by the Value-add fund ($28.7 million in each of the first three years), determine the capital placed by the other vehicles. This modification is necessary because under our original assumptions, the Value-add vehicle investor was not able to put the full $100 million to work, as he receives cash back via refinancing, prior to investing the entire $100 million. Because of this nuance, we were essentially comparing $100 million invested in the Core, Core Plus, and REIT funds to a lesser investment in the Value-add fund. Thus, in order to ensure that all vehicles actually invest the same amount ($100 million) we increased the amount of "committed" capital to the Value-add fund to allow for operating cash shortfalls and the early return of capital via refinancing.

We also adjust the management fee calculations for each vehicle, so that the Core and REIT fund fees are based on "placed" capital, and Core Plus and Value-add fund fees are based on "committed" capital. Although the actual cash investments are staggered for the Core Plus and the Value-add vehicles, the management fees for both are based upon the commitment of $100 million, not merely the amount that has been placed. As a result, in the early years, the effective management fee for these vehicles is significantly higher than 1.5 percent per year. In fact, because about $28.7 million (including operating cash shortfall of the Value-add fund) is placed in the first year, the effective management fees of the Core Plus and Value-add funds start out at about 5.25 percent of invested capital. Then as capital is returned to the investor through re-financing (for the Value-add fund) or liquidation, the management fee is adjusted accordingly, often bringing the effective management fee lower than 1.5 percent toward the end of the investment horizon.

Lastly, we further examine investor returns of the Core Plus and the Value-add funds, by netting out the sponsor promote features and fees, under alternative market scenarios.

MARKET SCENARIO COMPARISONS

Given the base case assumptions, the equity IRRs of the Core, Core Plus, and REIT vehicles over the seven-year investment horizon are 10.5 percent, 16.3 percent, and 13 percent, respectively. As indicated earlier, the Value-add vehicle is set up to generate a 20 percent IRR. Comparing the Core, Core Plus, and Value-add vehicles on an unleveraged basis, we observe that Core (10.5 percent equity IRR) outperforms Core Plus (8.7 percent equity IRR), simply because of the slightly higher management fee of the Core Plus vehicle. With an 8.9 percent unlevered IRR, the REIT fund performs slightly better than the unlevered Core Plus portfolio, but also worse than the unlevered Core vehicle. In contrast, without leverage, due to fees, the Value-add fund IRR drops to 7.8 percent.

As in the earlier paper, we model Base, Strong, Weak, and Disaster real estate market scenarios. These scenarios reflect different annual NOI growth rates and residual cap rates, as summarized in Figure 17A.3. In the Strong market scenario, NOI is assumed to grow by 3 percent (versus 2 percent in the Base case) annually, and the investor enjoys significant appreciation through a 7 percent (versus 8 percent) residual cap rate. In contrast, the Weak market scenario assumes that the annual NOI growth rate falls 100 basis points short of the base case, while the residual cap is 100 basis points higher. In the Disaster scenario, real estate market conditions soften dramatically, resulting in annual NOI growth of negative 2 percent, combined with a 9 percent residual cap rate. Each of these four real estate scenarios occur over a seven-year investment period.

FIGURE 17A.3: Scenario assumption modifications

MarketScenario Assumptions		
	NOI Growth Rate	Residual Cap Rate
Strong	3%	7%
Base	2%	8%
Weak	1%	9%
Disaster	-2%	9%

Although we have "standardized" the initial capital outlays across investment vehicles, it is still difficult to compare the four sets of cash flows from year to year, without ignoring the additional complexity of the Value-add fund of purchasing, refinancing, and selling different properties at overlapping times of the hold period. For example, in year five of the Value-add vehicle, properties purchased at the beginning of year one are sold, but properties purchased at the beginning of year three are refinanced. Thus, benchmarking the Value-add portfolio against the Core or the REIT portfolio at that time is not a fair comparison. However, we are able to consistently examine three metrics: the IRR, the equity multiple over the hold period, and the time path of the cash flows (including how long it takes to get investor capital back).

First, we examine the seven-year pre-promote equity IRRs under each of the four market scenarios, which are summarized in Figure 17A.4. In all cases, the Value-add fund yields the highest IRR, while the Core strategy (NCREIF) yields the lowest in all but the Disaster scenario. That is, unless one expects substantial value declines, the unlevered Core strategy is always dominated. Only if we change the residual cap to 10 percent (worse than the Disaster scenario), combined with a -2 percent annual NOI growth rate, the value of the Core unlevered portfolio declines by 30 percent, and generates the highest IRR (1.9 percent) of the four vehicles, roughly equal to the Value-add fund (1.7 percent IRR).

FIGURE 17A.4: Real estate scenario comparison for pre-promote equity IRRs

Pre-Promote Equity IRR (7-Year Horizon)				
Case	**Core**	**Core Plus**	**REIT**	**Value-add**
Strong	14.1%	24.3%	17.7%	29.0%
Base	10.5%	16.3%	13.0%	20.0%
Weak	7.2%	7.7%	8.5%	12.2%
Disaster	3.5%	-5.3%	0.5%	7.1%
Range in bps	1063	2964	1723	2189

Indicates best return in each case.
Indicates worst return in each case.

In the Disaster scenario (a 9 percent residual cap rate and -2 percent annual NOI growth), the Core Plus vehicle falls victim to its higher debt service and higher management fees, resulting in the lowest IRR of the four alternatives. In contrast, even though the Value-add fund uses more leverage than the Core Plus alternative, its performance is buffered by its value-add execution (assuming they successfully stabilize the portfolio). In fact, the "real" disaster situation for the Value-add fund is failure to achieve stabilization. That is, if a Value-add fund fails to add value, the returns are very disappointing except perhaps in the Strong market case, where a buoyant market may mask the lack of effective execution.

Second, we examine equity multiples by comparing the total cash outflows (regardless of timing) to the total cash inflows over the seven-year investment period (Figure 17A.5). Under all scenarios, the Value-add fund performs the best, and therefore requires the shortest amount of time to double one's equity. On the other end of the spectrum, the Core vehicle is the worst performer under all market scenarios, except the Disaster case. When Disaster strikes, the Core Plus vehicle is the weakest.

FIGURE 17A.5: Real estate scenario comparison for pre-promote equity multiples

	Pre-Promote Equity Multiple (7-Year Horizon) & Years to Double			
Case	**Core**	**Core Plus**	**REIT**	**Value-add**
Strong	1.88x 7.5	2.67x 5.2	2.2x 6.4	2.81 5.0
Base	1.6x 8.7	1.94x 7.2	1.79x 7.8	2.17x 6.5
Weak	1.39x 10.1	1.37x 10.2	1.47x 9.5	1.67x 8.4
Disaster	1.17x 11.9	.81x 17.3	1.02x 13.7	1.36x 10.3

Indicates best return in each case.
Indicates worst return in each case.

Third, absent a direct benchmark across vehicles, we examine the time path of the cash flows of each vehicle to determine how long it takes to get one's capital back. Under the Base, Weak, and Disastrous market conditions of the Core vehicle, the equity investor does not receive his full investment back until year seven when the portfolio is liquidated. However, under Strong market conditions, the Core portfolio generates sufficient cash flow to fully return equity capital at the end of year six. With the Core Plus vehicle, investors get their money back in six years, assuming Base or Strong market conditions, and seven years under Weak market conditions. However, Core Plus investors suffer a loss under Disastrous conditions. REIT investors will be in the black after six years of Base case or Strong conditions, but not until a liquidity event in year seven with Weak or Disastrous conditions. The Value-add investor's capital is fully returned in year five under Base and Strong market conditions, and year six under the Weak and Disaster scenarios. This is despite negative cash flows in the first three years of the investment period.

THE IMPACT OF SPONSOR PROMOTES

Core Plus and Value-add fund structures provide the general partner sponsor a promote (profit share) in exchange for portfolio management, asset selection, the oversight of major capital improvements, lease-up decisions, orchestrating turn-around strategies, and refinancing decisions. How do these general partner promotes alter the returns realized by limited partner investors? To evaluate this question, we analyzed a typical promote structure for a Value-add fund, using the following fund cash flow distribution waterfall:

1) A 10 percent cumulative preferred return to investors
2) The return of investor capital
3) 50 percent of remaining cash flows go to the general partner's "catch-up," until the general partner has received 20 percent of all profit distributions (not including the return on their invested capital)
4) Thereafter, profits are split, with 80 percent going to investors and 20 percent going to the fund's general partner.

For the Core Plus vehicle, the promote structure reflects the following cash flow distribution waterfall:

1) A 9 percent cumulative preferred return to investors
2) The return of investor capital
3) 50 percent of remaining cash flows go to the general partner's "catch-up," until the general partner has received 10 percent of all profit distributions (not including the return on their invested capital)
4) Thereafter, profits are split, with 90 percent going to investors and 10 percent going to the fund's general partner.

The final two profit distributions are the general partner's promote, an incentive-based compensation to the sponsor for exceeding the (cumulative) preferred return. The promote structure allows a 50 percent catch-up of cash flows to the general partner until they have received their full profit share. Beyond this "catch-up," additional cash flows are split between the limited and general partners either 80/20 (Value-add) or 90/10 (Core plus). While neither the investment's equity cash flows nor IRR are affected by the promote structure, the split of profits between investors and the general partner varies depending upon investment performance.

FIGURE 17A.6: Limited partner IRR comparison, pre- & post-promote

Limited Partner IRR Pre- & Post-Promote						
	Core	REIT	Core Plus		Value-add	
			Pre-	Post-	Pre-	Post-
Strong	14.1%	17.7%	24.3%	21.5%	29.0%	21.8%
Base	10.5%	13.0%	16.3%	14.3%	20.0%	15.2%
Weak	7.2%	8.5%	7.7%	7.6%	12.2%	9.5%
Disaster	3.5%	0.5%	-5.3%	-5.3%	7.1%	6.1%

In the Base market scenario, the Value-add limited partner's post-promote equity IRR is 15.2 percent. Even after paying the promote to the general partner, the Value-add fund still generates the highest IRR, when compared to the promoted Core Plus vehicle, and the original Core and REIT Base cases. In addition, because of the refinancing upon stabilization, Value-add investors benefit from an earlier extraction of cash flows. For the Core Plus investment, in the Base scenario, the equity IRR for limited partners is 14.3 percent, net of the general partner promote, which is still also higher than the 13 percent return for the REITs. The most conservative investment approach, unlevered Core, is by far the weakest performer for the Base case, with an IRR of 10.5 percent.

In the Strong real estate market scenario, where the residual cap rate is 100 basis points lower, and the annual NOI growth rate is 100 basis points higher each year, the Value-add fund generates a total IRR of 29.0 percent. Net of the general partner promote, the investor's IRR drops to 21.8 percent. For the Core Plus vehicle, the equity IRR is 24.3 percent, and 21.5 percent pre- and post-promote to the limited partner investor, respectively. That is, the Core Plus post-promote sponsor return in the Strong scenario is 150 basis points higher than the Value-add fund pre-promote Base market scenario return of 20 percent. In addition, the Core Plus investor still fares better after the promote than the REIT investor (who receives a 17.7 percent IRR), as well as the unlevered Core investor (who only achieves a 14.1 percent IRR) in a Strong market. In fact, with the Core (NCREIF) investment vehicle, we observe that a Strong market scenario provides unlevered investor returns less than that achieved by Core Plus investors in the Base scenario. This vividly demonstrates the severe upside limitation of the unlevered Core strategy.

Turning to the Weak real estate market scenario, returns for Core Plus are insufficient for the general partner to earn their promote until year seven. That is, performance does not exceed the preferred return hurdle until liquidation, leaving the limited partner investor with an IRR of 7.6 percent (versus 7.7 percent before the promote). In this scenario, the Value-add fund modestly exceeds the preferred return hurdle in year six, a year earlier than the Core Plus investor. As a result, the general partner earns a larger share of the profits than the Core Plus general partner under the same conditions, causing the limited partner's IRR to drop to 9.5 percent (versus a pre-promote investment equity IRR of 12.2 percent). Under the Weak market scenario, REITs generate an investor IRR of 8.5 percent, while the unlevered Core once again performs the worst at 7.2 percent. That is, even if markets are weak (higher residual cap rate of 100 basis points, and NOI growth is 100 basis points lower each year), the Value-add fund performs notably better than the alternatives, while the unlevered Core strategy substantially underperforms.

If a real estate market Disaster strikes (9 percent residual cap rate, -2 percent annual NOI growth rate), implying a portfolio value increase of about 10 percent from the Value-add fund purchase price, the promote structure does not kick in for the Value-add fund until year seven. The Value-add pre- and post-promote IRRs are 7.1 percent and 6.1 percent, respectively. For the Core Plus fund, returns are insufficient to yield profit participation for the general partner in the Disaster scenario. As a result, post-promote returns for investors are identical to pre-promote returns (-5.3 percent). In short, the Core Plus vehicle is penalized for its relatively high leverage. Note that the original $100 million Core portfolio drops in value to about $78 million after seven years in the Disaster scenario. Because of its conservative capital structure, the unlevered Core strategy generates the second highest IRR of 3.5 percent, with the Value-add fund providing a 6.1 percent post-promote IRR, as even though the Value-add fund utilizes the highest leverage ratio, its low acquisition price buffers the IRR. The strength of moderately leveraged real estate is demonstrated by the fact that the REIT strategy still ekes out a 0.5 percent IRR under this Disaster scenario.

The four simulated market scenarios (Base, Strong, Weak, and Disaster) cover a broad, yet reasonable, range of market conditions. If the Value-add fund is able to execute its stabilization strategy, it provides the best risk/return trade-off, while the unlevered Core is the worst. REITs provide the most liquid investment of the four investment vehicles, while Core Plus generally performs slightly better than REITs on the upside, but provide less liquidity. Even post-promote, the limited partner investor in a Value-add fund fares substantially better than other vehicles (assuming stabilization is successfully achieved) in the Base scenario or better real estate markets, and worst with the unlevered Core strategy.

SENSITIVITY ANALYSES

When structuring the partnership agreement, how critical is the preferred return hurdle for limited partners? As seen in Figure 17A.7a, a preferred return range of 7 percent to 10.5 percent for the Core Plus fund and 8 percent to 11.5 percent for the Value-add fund generates an equity IRR for the limited partner, ranging from 14.2 percent to 14.6 percent in the Core Plus vehicle, and 15.2 percent to 15.3 percent with the Value-add fund. In the Strong case (Figure 17A.7b), the same preferred return range corresponds to no change in the Core Plus vehicle, and a swing of only 10 basis points in the IRR for the Value-add fund limited partners. In the Weak case (Figure 17A.7c), the IRR swing resulting from a change in the preferred return hurdle varies by 60 and 30 basis points between the lowest and highest assumed preferred hurdle, for the Core Plus and Value-add funds, respectively. In the Disaster case (Figure 17A.7d), since the preferred return hurdle is never achieved for the Core Plus vehicle, it is irrelevant over the range we examine. That is, market conditions do not allow for a strong enough performance to even reach a 7 percent return hurdle. In the Value-add vehicle, the Disaster case IRR varies by 100 basis points for the given range of preferred return hurdles.

FIGURE 17A.7a: Base case preferred return sensitivity

Core Plus Base Case		Value-add Base Case	
Pref. Ret.	IRR	Pref. Ret.	IRR
7.0%	14.2%	8.0%	15.2%
7.5%	14.2%	8.5%	15.2%
8.0%	14.2%	9.0%	15.2%
8.5%	14.3%	9.0%	15.2%
9.0%	14.3%	10.0%	15.2%
9.5%	14.4%	10.5%	15.3%
10.0%	14.5%	11.0%	15.3%
10.5%	14.6%	11.5%	15.3%

FIGURE 17A.7b: Strong case preferred return sensitivity

Core Plus Strong Case		Value-add Strong Case	
Pref. Ret.	IRR	Pref. Ret.	IRR
7.0%	21.5%	8.0%	21.8%
7.5%	21.5%	8.5%	21.8%
8.0%	21.5%	9.0%	21.8%
8.5%	21.5%	9.5%	21.8%
9.0%	21.5%	10.0%	21.8%
9.5%	21.5%	10.5%	21.8%
10.0%	21.5%	11.0%	21.8%
10.5%	21.5%	11.5%	21.9%

FIGURE 17A.7c: Weak case preferred return sensitivity

Core Plus Weak Case		Value-add Weak Case	
Pref. Ret.	IRR	Pref. Ret.	IRR
7.0%	7.1%	8.0%	9.5%
7.5%	7.2%	8.5%	9.6%
8.0%	7.3%	9.0%	9.6%
8.5%	7.5%	9.5%	9.7%
9.0%	7.6%	10.0%	9.7%
9.5%	7.7%	10.5%	9.8%
10.0%	7.7%	11.0%	9.8%
10.5%	7.7%	11.5%	9.8%

FIGURE 17A.7d: Disaster case preferred return sensitivity

Core Plus Disaster Case		Value-add Disaster Case	
Pref. Ret.	**IRR**	**Pref. Ret.**	**IRR**
7.0%	-5.2%	8.0%	6.1%
7.5%	-5.2%	8.5%	6.3%
8.0%	-5.3%	9.0%	6.5%
8.5%	-5.3%	9.5%	6.6%
9.0%	-5.3%	10.0%	6.8%
9.5%	-5.3%	10.5%	7.0%
10.0%	-5.3%	11.0%	7.1%
10.5%	-5.3%	11.5%	7.1%

These simulations demonstrate that the limited partner's equity IRR is driven far more by real estate market conditions, rather than the preferred return hurdle. In short, negotiating 100 basis points higher or lower on a preferred return is not nearly as critical as some investors seem to believe, as its differential impact on the IRR comes into play only within a very narrow performance range. If a Value-add sponsor insists on a low hurdle, it may be a sign of low confidence in their performance prospects.

We also explore how changes in the general partner "catch-up" impact the limited partner's return. Recall that we assume in step three of the cash flow distribution waterfall that "50 percent of remaining cash flows (after preferred returns and return of capital) go toward the general partner's 'catch-up' until the general partner has received 20 percent (10 percent for Core Plus) of all profit distributions". What if these allocations are changed to 25 percent (or 75 percent), rather than 50 percent? How are the equity IRRs of the limited partner investing in each vehicle impacted under varying real estate market conditions?

Figure 17A.8 illustrates a range of catch-up allocations and the resulting limited partner IRRs for the Core Plus and Value-add vehicles under the Base case market conditions. On the one extreme, when 0 percent of the excess profits (after preferred return and return of capital) are allocated toward the catch-up, then the limited partner maximizes his IRR. As the catch-up allocation increases, the LP's IRR decreases. However, from the perspective of the limited partner, if enough cash flow is generated to allow the general partner to reach his maximum promote, then the limited partner's "downside" IRR is capped. In the Base case, the general partner of the Core Plus vehicle achieves his maximum 20 percent promote when 75 percent of the excess profits are allocated toward the catch-up. Even at a higher allocation percentage to the general partner, the limited partner is no worse off under the same market conditions, because the general partner allocations will have already "caught up" to the designated promote share. Similarly for the Base case Value-add fund, the general partner achieves his maximum promoted share at a 50 percent allocation. Thus, given the portfolio's performance in the Base case market conditions, the limited partner's IRR will be no less than 14.2 percent and 15.2 percent under the Core Plus and Value-add fund vehicles, respectively.

FIGURE 17A.8: LP return sensitivity to percentage allocated to the general partner catch-up

Base Case: LP 7-Year Equity IRR		
	Core Plus	Value-add
Catch-Up Alloc.		
0.0%	16.3%	20.0%
5.0%	15.3%	17.7%
10.0%	14.9%	17.3%
15.0%	14.6%	16.9%
20.0%	14.5%	16.5%
25.0%	14.5%	16.1%
50.0%	14.3%	15.2%
75.0%	14.2%	15.2%
100.0%	14.2%	15.2%

The allocation percentage that goes toward a general partner's catch-up is a way to smooth limited partner cash flows. At the extreme, if 100 percent of all excess cash flows are allocated to the general partner catch-up, then the limited partner does not receive a profit share for an extended period. This discontinuity is the most damaging situation for limited partner investors. If, on the other hand, the general partner's catch-up allocation was 25 percent or 50 percent of excess cash flows, then that would be an appreciably better position for the limited partner. However, the difference between a 25 percent and a 50 percent catch-up allocation is not as critical as avoiding the 100 percent allocation.

The Base, Strong, Weak, and Disaster scenarios are driven by real estate market conditions, specifically in annual NOI growth rates and residual cap rates. As noted, these variables have a significant impact on vehicle performance and investor returns. Figure 17A.9a and Figure 17A.9b illustrate Core Plus sensitivity tables for even more extreme market conditions. Specifically, the residual cap rate varies between 6.5 percent and 10 percent while the NOI growth rate varies between negative 3 percent and positive 4 percent (for all seven years). The resulting limited partner equity IRRs are color coded for each of the Base, Strong, Weak, and Disaster scenarios, but incremental IRRs are also shown in the matrix for combinations within those ranges.

FIGURE 17A.9a: Core plus IRR sensitivity before promote

Core Plus Equity IRR Pre-Promote								
Annual NOI Growth Rate	Residual Cap Rates							
	6.50%	7.00%	7.50%	8.00%	8.50%	9.00%	9.50%	10.00%
-3.0%	9.1%	5.4%	1.5%	-2.4%	-6.7%	-11.4%		
-2.5%	10.9%	7.3%	3.7%	-0.1%	-4.0%	-8.1%	-12.8%	
-2.0%	12.6%	9.1%	5.7%	2.1%	-1.5%	-5.3%	-9.4%	-14.1%
-1.5%	14.3%	10.9%	7.6%	4.2%	0.8%	-2.7%	-6.4%	-10.5%
-1.0%	15.9%	12.6%	9.4%	6.2%	3.0%	-0.3%	-3.8%	-7.4%
-0.5%	17.4%	14.2%	11.1%	8.0%	5.0%	1.9%	-1.3%	-4.7%
0.0%	18.9%	15.8%	12.8%	9.8%	6.9%	3.9%	0.9%	-2.2%
0.5%	20.3%	17.3%	14.4%	11.5%	8.7%	5.9%	3.0%	0.2%
1.0%	21.7%	18.8%	16.0%	13.2%	10.4%	7.7%	5.0%	2.3%
1.5%	23.1%	20.2%	17.5%	14.8%	12.1%	9.5%	6.9%	4.3%
2.0%	24.5%	21.6%	18.9%	16.3%	13.7%	11.2%	8.7%	6.2%
2.5%	25.8%	23.0%	20.3%	17.8%	15.3%	12.8%	10.4%	8.1%
3.0%	27.1%	24.3%	21.7%	19.2%	16.8%	14.4%	12.1%	9.8%
3.5%	28.4%	25.7%	23.1%	20.6%	18.2%	15.9%	13.7%	11.5%
4.0%	29.6%	27.0%	24.4%	22.0%	19.7%	17.4%	15.2%	13.1%

Strong Base Weak Disaster

FIGURE17A.9b: Core plus IRR sensitivity after promote with 50 percent catch-up allocation

Core Plus Limited Partner Equity IRR Net of Promote								
Annual NOI Growth Rate	Residual Cap Rates							
	6.50%	7.00%	7.50%	8.00%	8.50%	9.00%	9.50%	10.00%
-3.0%	8.3%	5.4%	1.5%	-2.4%	-6.7%	-11.4%		
-2.5%	9.8%	7.2%	3.7%	-0.1%	-4.0%	-8.1%	-12.8%	
-2.0%	11.3%	8.3%	5.7%	2.1%	-1.5%	-5.3%	-9.4%	-14.1%
-1.5%	12.8%	9.8%	7.4%	4.2%	0.8%	-2.7%	-6.4%	-10.5%
-1.0%	13.9%	11.3%	8.5%	6.2%	3.0%	-0.3%	-3.8%	-7.4%
-0.5%	15.1%	12.7%	10.0%	7.6%	5.0%	1.9%	-1.3%	-4.7%
0.0%	16.5%	13.9%	11.5%	8.9%	6.9%	3.9%	0.9%	-2.2%
0.5%	17.8%	15.1%	12.9%	10.4%	8.0%	5.9%	3.0%	0.2%
1.0%	19.1%	16.4%	14.1%	11.8%	9.4%	7.6%	5.0%	2.3%
1.5%	20.4%	17.7%	15.2%	13.2%	10.9%	8.7%	6.9%	4.3%
2.0%	21.6%	19.0%	16.5%	14.3%	12.3%	10.1%	8.1%	6.2%
2.5%	22.8%	20.3%	17.8%	15.5%	13.7%	11.5%	9.5%	7.8%
3.0%	24.1%	21.5%	19.1%	16.8%	14.7%	12.9%	10.9%	8.9%
3.5%	25.2%	22.7%	20.4%	18.1%	15.9%	14.2%	12.3%	10.3%
4.0%	26.4%	23.9%	21.6%	19.3%	17.2%	15.2%	13.6%	11.7%

Strong Base Weak Disaster

Gray shaded section indicates no post-promote impact on the IRR

Comparing Figures 17A.9a and 17A.9b, it is apparent that equity IRRs for the Disaster cases of the Core Plus vehicle are identical for pre- and post-promote. This is because performance under such onerous market conditions does not merit any profit participation to the general partner. However, the limited partner's Strong case equity IRR of the Core Plus strategy declines by 280 basis points between the pre- and post-promote payment. Similarly, the Core Plus Weak and Base case limited partner IRRs drop by 10 and 200 basis points, respectively.

Figures 17A.10a and 17A.10b illustrate the same analysis for the Value-add fund, with equity IRR sensitivity tables driven by changes to the residual cap rate and the annual NOI growth rate assumptions, before and after the promote payment, respectively. Once again, we examine market condition combinations, where residual cap rates range from 6.5 percent to 10 percent, and annual NOI growth rates range from negative 3 percent to positive 4 percent. Even in the Disaster case, cash flows are sufficient to achieve a general partner promote distribution, decreasing the limited partner distribution by 100 basis points. The more the performance of the Value-add fund improves, the greater the spread between pre- and post-promote IRRs. Specifically, the Weak case pre-promote IRR to the limited partner is 12.2 percent, but declines by 270 basis points to 9.5 percent upon payment of the general partner's promote. The Base Case for the Value-add fund exhibits a 480 basis point decline, with a 20 percent initial IRR and a 15.2 percent IRR net of promote. Following the same pattern, the Strong case equity IRR decreases by 720 basis points between the pre- and post-promote cash flow to the limited partner.

FIGURE 17A.10a: Core plus IRR sensitivity before promote

Value-add Fund Equity IRR Pre-Promote								
	Residual Cap Rates							
Annual NOI Growth Rate	6.50%	7.00%	7.50%	8.00%	8.50%	9.00%	9.50%	10.00%
-3.0%	23.9%	19.5%	15.4%	11.8%	8.4%	5.3%	2.5%	-0.1%
-2.5%	24.7%	20.3%	16.3%	12.7%	9.3%	6.2%	3.4%	0.8%
-2.0%	25.6%	21.2%	17.2%	13.5%	10.2%	7.1%	4.3%	1.7%
-1.5%	26.4%	22.0%	18.0%	14.4%	11.0%	8.0%	5.2%	2.6%
-1.0%	27.2%	22.8%	18.8%	15.2%	11.9%	8.8%	6.0%	3.4%
-0.5%	28.0%	23.6%	19.7%	16.0%	12.7%	9.7%	6.9%	4.3%
0.0%	28.8%	24.4%	20.5%	16.9%	13.6%	10.5%	7.7%	5.1%
0.5%	29.6%	25.2%	21.3%	17.7%	14.4%	11.3%	8.5%	6.0%
1.0%	30.3%	26.0%	22.1%	18.5%	15.2%	12.2%	9.4%	6.8%
1.5%	31.1%	26.8%	22.8%	19.3%	16.0%	12.9%	10.2%	7.6%
2.0%	31.8%	27.5%	23.6%	20.0%	16.7%	13.7%	11.0%	8.4%
2.5%	32.6%	28.3%	24.4%	20.8%	17.5%	14.5%	11.7%	9.2%
3.0%	33.3%	29.0%	25.1%	21.5%	18.3%	15.3%	12.5%	9.9%
3.5%	34.0%	29.7%	25.8%	22.3%	19.0%	16.0%	13.3%	10.7%
4.0%	34.7%	30.5%	26.6%	23.0%	19.8%	16.8%	14.0%	11.4%

Strong   Base   Weak   Disaster

* Annual growth rate applies after stabilization

FIGURE 17A.10b: Value-add fund IRR sensitivity after promote with 50 percent catch-up allocation

Value-add Fund Limited Partner Equity IRR Net of Promote								
	Residual Cap Rates							
Annual NOI Growth Rate	6.50%	7.00%	7.50%	8.00%	8.50%	9.00%	9.50%	10.00%
-3.0%	17.6%	14.8%	11.8%	9.5%	7.1%	5.3%	2.5%	-0.1%
-2.5%	18.3%	15.3%	12.3%	10.2%	7.5%	5.7%	3.4%	0.8%
-2.0%	18.9%	15.9%	12.9%	10.7%	8.2%	6.1%	4.3%	1.7%
-1.5%	19.6%	16.4%	13.6%	11.2%	8.8%	6.5%	4.9%	2.6%
-1.0%	20.3%	17.0%	14.2%	11.7%	9.5%	7.1%	5.3%	3.4%
-0.5%	21.0%	17.5%	14.9%	12.2%	10.0%	7.7%	5.7%	4.3%
0.0%	21.6%	18.0%	15.6%	12.7%	10.5%	8.3%	6.1%	4.8%
0.5%	22.3%	18.7%	16.2%	13.3%	11.0%	8.9%	6.7%	5.1%
1.0%	22.9%	19.3%	16.8%	13.9%	11.4%	9.5%	7.3%	5.5%
1.5%	23.6%	20.0%	17.3%	14.6%	11.9%	9.9%	7.9%	6.0%
2.0%	24.2%	20.6%	17.8%	15.2%	12.5%	10.4%	8.5%	6.5%
2.5%	24.9%	21.2%	18.3%	15.8%	13.1%	10.9%	9.1%	7.1%
3.0%	25.5%	21.8%	18.8%	16.4%	13.7%	11.3%	9.5%	7.7%
3.5%	26.1%	22.5%	19.2%	17.1%	14.3%	11.9%	10.0%	8.2%
4.0%	26.7%	23.1%	19.8%	17.7%	14.9%	12.5%	10.4%	8.8%

Strong Base Weak Disaster

* Annual growth rate applies after stabilization

Gray shaded section indicates no post-promote impact on the IRR

CONCLUSION

The unlevered Core vehicle only merits investment if you expect—or fear—an absolute disaster in the market, and it severely limits the upside potential. Comparing Core Plus and REITs, the two generally perform closely to each other, with Core Plus slightly stronger on the upside but less liquid, and worse on the downside than REITs. The Value-add fund generally presents the best risk-reward balance, *if* successful stabilization is achieved.

When evaluating real estate investment vehicles, it is clear that you have to run the numbers in an internally consistent manner in order to understand return profiles and risks. Because investment strategies vary so widely, including types of investment, leverage ratios, geographic risk tolerance, and countless other dimensions, an investor cannot simply rely on an "expected" base case pro forma return to evaluate the vehicle. In addition, actual execution of each strategy is critical. Anybody can say they will pursue an opportunist investment approach, but only the best investment managers can consistently generate the targeted returns. This brings us back to square one: how should we compare return performance of these alternative vehicles? We have shown that interim performance is useful for only the most conservative strategies, while more opportunistic strategies are unfortunately much more difficult to evaluate until their investments are fully liquidated. Therefore, a strong tolerance for short-term weak performance, combined with patience, is the key to pursuing more aggressive investment strategies. A key is assessing and tracking the ability to execute among Value-add funds.

Chapter 17 Supplement B

Understanding the Return Profiles of Real Estate Investment Vehicles

How four types of real estate investment vehicles fare under various market conditions.

Dr. Peter Linneman and Deborah Moy – Wharton Real Estate Review – Fall 2003

Former New York City mayor Ed Koch used to ask, "How am I doing"? For real estate private equity funds, this question is not easily answered. Despite the proliferation of these funds over the last ten years, a useful return benchmark does not exist. Does this mean the sector is not sufficiently motivated to create a useful benchmark? Or do the diverse investment strategies, most of which are very dissimilar to traditional real estate investments, preclude a useful benchmark? For example, some funds invest abroad, while others focus domestically or even in a particular region. Some funds provide development and redevelopment capital, while others execute highly leveraged acquisitions of core assets. Still others focus on distressed debt and non-performing loans, or acquiring portfolios of corporate or government assets. And to further complicate matters, most funds pursue several of these strategies simultaneously. Real estate private equity funds not only have unique investment strategies, but managers of these value-added opportunity funds target at least 16 percent to 20 percent gross returns. In contrast, "core plus" funds invest in stabilized core assets with relatively high leverage, generally targeting 13 percent to 16 percent gross returns.

What about standard real estate benchmarks, such as the NCREIF and NAREIT indices, which some argue provide useful benchmarks? Let us begin with the NCREIF index. Even putting aside the well-documented statistical problem of the roughly 18-month appraisal lag versus market pricing, for the most part this index tracks the returns for core, stabilized, domestic, unleveraged, institutional-grade properties. As a result, NCREIF returns should be relatively low and stable, as the investment objective for the properties in this index is to achieve an 8 percent to 11 percent gross return.

Turning to the NAREIT index, there is no appraisal lag, since it captures the real-time pricing of REITs. Yet returns generated by REITs are also not an appropriate benchmark for real estate private equity funds, since REITs generally own high-quality, core, stabilized, domestic real estate, as opposed to the more opportunistic assets favored by private equity funds. In addition, REIT assets are leveraged 35 percent to 55 percent, versus 60 percent to 75 percent for private equity funds. Another notable distinction is that REIT pricing reflects the value of much more than a portfolio of properties. For example, short-term variations in REIT share prices reflect changes in the value of liquidity. REIT pricing also reflects the returns associated with management, as well as properties. In contrast, management is owned separately from the properties at private equity funds. The primary investment objective for firms in the NAREIT index is to provide relatively predictable dividend streams that benefit from modest leverage, with targeted gross returns in the 9 percent to 13 percent range.

These fundamental differences of the respective NCREIF and NAREIT properties and investment objectives render these metrics futile for benchmarking the returns of opportunistic real estate private equity funds. In fact, at almost no point during their investment horizons will such funds remotely track either the NCREIF or NAREIT indices. In contrast, the returns of so-called "core plus" private equity funds can be relatively accurately tracked by NAREIT.

RETURN SIMULATIONS

To demonstrate the differences in return patterns for alternative investment vehicles, we simulate the expected performance of four different portfolios representing:
1) NCREIF; 2) core plus private equity; 3) NAREIT; and 4) opportunistic private equity funds. Assumptions and returns for each are summarized in Figure 17B.1.

FIGURE 17B.1 Base Case Simulated Investment Assumptions and Returns

	NCREIF	Core Plus	NAREIT	Opportunity Fund
Purchase Price	$100,000,000	$100,000,000	$100,000,000	$77,680,965
LTV	0.0%	65.0%	50.0%	70.0%
Equity Used	$100,000,000	$35,000,000	$50,000,000	$23,304,289
Interest Rate	n/a	6.0%	6.0%	6.3%
Going-in Cap Rate (Stabilized)	8.0%	8.0%	8.0%	n/a
Residual Cap Rate	8.0%	8.0%	8.0%	8.0%
Residual Value	$114,868,567	$114,868,567	$136,200,746	$114,868,567
Dividend Payout Rate	100%	100%	70%	100%
Management Fee	0.5%	1.5%	0.5%	1.5%
IRR	9.5%	15.2%	12.8%	20.0%
Equity Multiple (over 7 years)	1.7x	2.2x	2.1x	3.x
Years to Double Equity	8.2	6.3	6.7	4.7

The first vehicle represents a typical core NCREIF portfolio. It is unleveraged and contains $100 million of stabilized core assets, with a going-in cap rate of 8 percent, and a 2 percent per annum NOI growth rate. A 50 basis point management fee is deducted from this return stream.

The second vehicle is a portfolio of $100 million of stabilized core assets, with a going-in cap rate of 8 percent and a 2 percent annual NOI growth rate. However, this core plus strategy uses 65 percent leverage, and a 1.5 percent management fee is deducted.

The third vehicle is $100 million invested in a pool of REITs that are 50 percent leveraged and own a stabilized core portfolio that has an 8 percent cap rate and a 2 percent NOI growth rate. A 50 basis point management fee is deducted. This REIT portfolio pays out 70 percent of its cash flow in dividends, reinvesting retained funds at the same cap rate, NOI growth rate, and leverage.

Finally, the fourth vehicle models an opportunistic private equity fund, which buys unstabilized assets that take three years to stabilize. At the end of the third year, these assets are stabilized and exactly match the profiles of the core assets in the other three scenarios in years four through seven. NOI in this case in year one is negative $2 million, in year two it grows to $2 million, and in year three rises to $6 million. These assets are purchased at a sufficient discount to their stabilized value to provide a 20 percent IRR over the life of the fund, where the fund uses 70 percent leverage, and a 1.5 percent management fee is deducted.

For all four vehicles, the holdings are liquidated at an 8 cap at the end of the seventh year. For the NCREIF, core plus, and opportunistic scenarios, this liquidation yields roughly $115 million upon sale. Because of the reinvestment of retained earnings, the REIT portfolio liquidates for approximately $136 million. In the case of the opportunistic private equity fund, when the assets achieve stabilization at the end of year three, they are refinanced at 70 percent of their newly stabilized value, and excess refinancing proceeds are distributed to investors. In the case of the NCREIF, core plus, and opportunistic funds, 100 percent of available cash flow after debt service is paid out to investors.

COMPARISONS

Each of these investment vehicles generates its own cash stream, cash-on-cash return stream, and total return stream. The annual cash-on-cash return is calculated as cash flow generated by the portfolio in a given year as a percent of invested equity. Unrealized appreciation is not taken into consideration in the cash-on-cash return calculation, as the value appreciation is realized only upon refinancing or disposition. Therefore, cash-on-cash returns are back-end weighted.

In contrast, mark-to-market returns reflect both the income return and the implied annual appreciation returns. By definition, the mark-to-market and the cash flow returns are identical upon liquidation, but the timing differences in the recognition of appreciation results in varying equity returns prior to disposition. As a result, for all four investment vehicles, annual mark-to-market returns track higher than annual cash flow returns until liquidation.

The IRR for each vehicle represents the annualized rate of return for the cash flows over the duration of the investment horizon—from the initial equity investment through liquidation. The opportunity fund scenario requires the least up-front equity, but successfully stabilizing the portfolio poses a significant risk not found in the alternative investment vehicles.

Comparisons of the equity returns, both on a mark-to-market and a cash flow basis, reveal interesting patterns. Figures 17B.2 and 17B.3 illustrate the value of a $100 equity investment over the course of a seven-year investment horizon for the four alternative investment vehicles. For the "base" case assumptions described in Figure 17B.1, the opportunity fund investment grows nearly threefold to $298, while the NCREIF strategy grows to $171 over the same period. As expected, the equity returns based on cash flows lag those based on mark-to-market calculations up until year seven. The valuation pop in year three of the mark-to-market return of the then-stabilized opportunity fund and the catch-up effect in year seven for all scenarios are apparent.

FIGURE 17B.2 Base Case Mark-to-Market Index

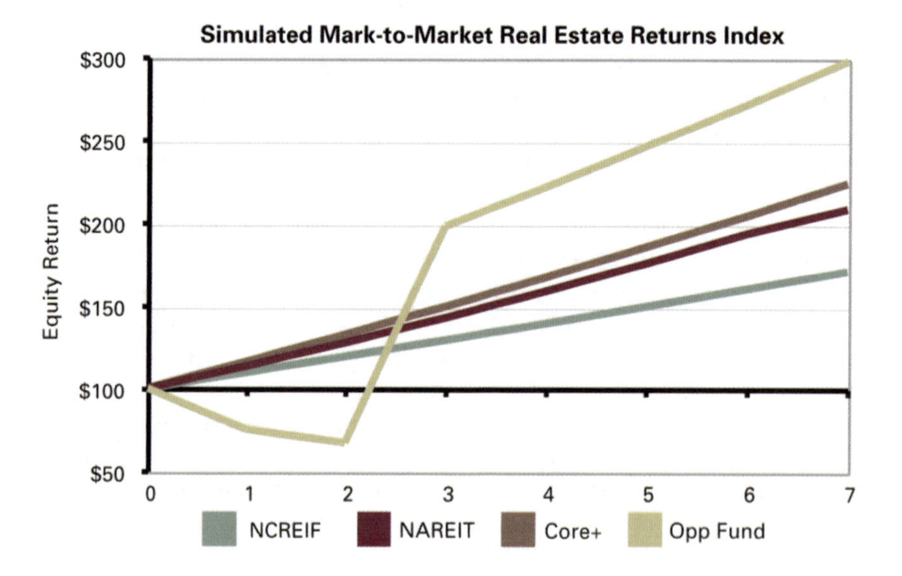

FIGURE 17B.3 Base Case Cash Flow Index

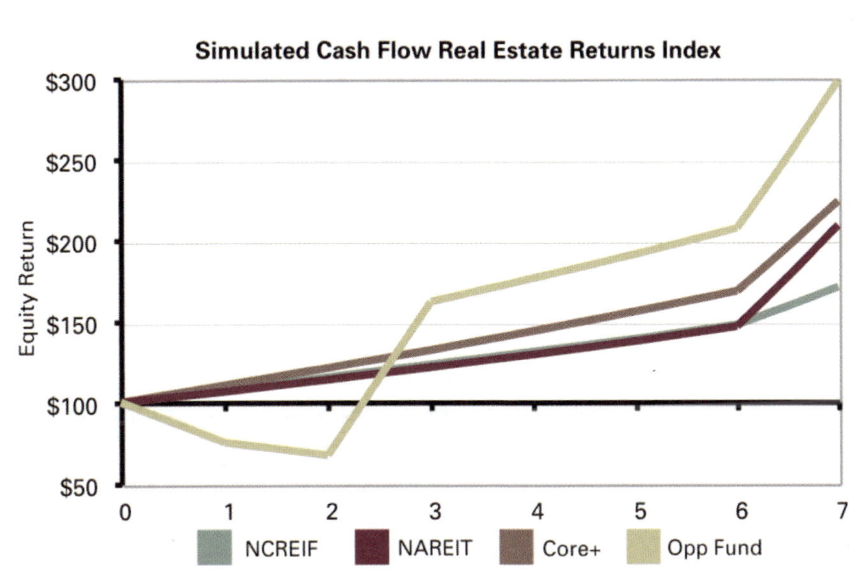

The opportunity fund profile is particularly interesting. Because of the negative NOI in the first year, its cash flows net of interest payments are negative for the first two years. Only as the stabilization is well under way in year three does the cumulative return move into positive territory. That is, its investment strategy generates a negative cumulative return in the early years, as the properties ramp towards stabilization.

The expected cumulative opportunity fund return is roughly an S-curve, with a big value pop upon stabilization of the portfolio; hence, at the end of year three, the opportunity fund investor is able to extract substantial value appreciation through refinancing. At 70 percent leverage, the initial mortgage on the newly stabilized property is paid off and excess refinancing proceeds are returned to the equity investor. As a result, the three-year cumulative return exceeds the other investment alternatives on a pro forma mark-to-market, as well as on a cash flow, basis.

Note that at almost no point during the investment horizon does the return profile for the opportunity fund resemble that of NCREIF, core plus, or NAREIT. In the first three years, the fund should under-perform the NCREIF and NAREIT benchmarks on a cumulative cash flow basis, but upon successful stabilization, it surpasses the performance of the other three scenarios.

The equity returns of the NCREIF, core plus, and NAREIT scenarios grow on a fairly linear basis, with an appreciation pop in year seven upon liquidation. The mark-to-market returns display a smoother return schedule than the cash-on-cash return stream. The slopes of the corresponding return streams are impacted by different leverage, payout ratios, and management fees, with increased leverage resulting in a steeper slope.

Studying the equity returns graphically yields another interesting observation. Comparing the simulated cash flow returns for the NCREIF and NAREIT scenarios, the two streams track almost identically until liquidation, at which point they diverge due to the return of retained and reinvested earnings.

FOUR MARKET ENVIRONMENTS

Using the "base" case assumptions, the opportunity fund vehicle achieves a 20 percent IRR, while the NCREIF alternative generates a 9.5 percent IRR over the seven-year investment period. What are the risk factors inherent to each investment strategy? While on a pro forma basis the opportunity fund vehicle achieves the highest IRR of the four alternatives, it has a different risk profile. Specifically, the opportunity fund portfolio either successfully achieves stabilization, or it does not. The interesting dynamic in this scenario is that even if stabilization does not occur on plan, the opportunity fund can still achieve a better return than the other three alternatives, assuming its cost basis is low enough. However, if the opportunity fund simply fails to achieve stabilization, then investors can lose badly.

Risk factors that affect the returns for these investment vehicles are: market pricing (i.e., exit cap rates); NOI growth rates; and delayed stabilization. In order to explore the impact of these risks, we simulate the return impacts of higher exit cap rates, lower NOI growth rates, and delayed stabilization for the opportunity fund.

Focusing first on changes in NOI growth rates and residual cap rates, we simulate three additional market scenarios, specifically, the impact of various NOI growth rates and residual cap rates on the cash flows and IRRs for the investment vehicles. Recall that the "base" case is a "normal" market with a 2 percent annual NOI growth rate and an 8 percent residual cap rate. The "strong" market case assumes a 3 percent annual NOI growth rate and a 7 percent residual cap rate, while the "weak" market case has a 1 percent annual NOI growth rate and a 9 percent residual cap rate. Finally, the "disaster" market case has a -2 percent annual NOI growth rate and a 9 percent residual cap rate. In this "disaster" case, the eighth year NOI is only about 86 percent of base year NOI. For all four scenarios, the opportunity fund is assumed to achieve stabilization at the end of year three, though only to the market level NOI. Upon stabilization, NOI growth for the opportunity fund vehicle is assumed to grow at the same rate as the other scenarios. Summary results of these market condition simulations are presented in Figure 17B.4.

FIGURE 17B.4 IRR Sensitivity to Changes in NOI Growth Rate and Residual Cap Rate

IRR SENSITIVITY				
	NCREIF	Core Plus	NAREIT	Opportunity Fund
Strong	12.1%	20.6%	17.5%	28.7%
Base	9.5%	15.2%	12.8%	20.0%
Weak	7.2%	9.4%	8.3%	12.7%
Disaster	4.2%	-0.6%	1.9%	3.5%
Range in bps	796	2125	1560	2519

Indicates best return in each case.
Indicates worst return in each case.

Due to the lack of leverage, the tightest IRR range is found for the NCREIF vehicle, with less than an 800 basis point spread between the "strong" versus "disaster" market cases. As a result, while the upside is not spectacular for NCREIF, the risk of losing capital is minimized. In contrast, the opportunity fund exhibits an IRR swing of roughly 2,500 basis points between the "strong" and "disaster" market cases. The IRR swings are 1,560 basis points and 2,125 basis points for the REIT and core plus vehicles, respectively.

What most investors fail to appreciate is the superior IRR achieved by the opportunity fund alternative, even in weak markets. In fact, it never performs the worst. In the "base," "strong," and "weak" market scenarios, the opportunity fund IRR exceeds that for core plus, which beats NAREIT, which in turn outperforms NCREIF. Only in the "disaster" market does the NCREIF vehicle record superior performance compared to the opportunity fund. Note, however, that even in the "disaster" case, the opportunity fund fares only 70 basis points worse than NCREIF. Also, the opportunity fund's "weak" market performance is still greater than NCREIF's "strong" market performance. Thus, if stabilization is executed successfully, the opportunity fund investment strategy is the most attractive, as the low acquisition price and value-added provides substantial downside protection. While opportunity fund investors do not realize their return targets in weak markets because their cost basis is so low, they still generally perform better than the alternative investment vehicles.

It is also interesting to note that in the "disaster" market case, the core plus alternative falls victim to its higher debt service and higher management fees, resulting in the lowest IRR of the four alternatives. In contrast, while the opportunity fund uses more leverage than the core plus alternative, its performance is buffered by its low acquisition price. This underscores the point that successful stabilization is critical to the opportunity fund approach. If an unstabilized portfolio is successfully repositioned, the downside is protected by the low basis inherent to the strategy. In short, the real disaster case for the opportunity fund occurs if stabilization is not achieved.

LEVELING THE PLAYING FIELD

Another way to examine the four investment strategies is to consider how low (high) must one scenario's residual cap rate (NOI growth rate) be in order for the alternative investment vehicles to generate the same IRR. For example, as displayed in Figure 17B.5, in order for a core plus portfolio to achieve the same 20 percent IRR as the opportunity fund "base" case, residual cap rates would have to move down from 8 percent ($115 million residual) to 6.6 percent ($139 million residual). Similarly, in order for the NAREIT return to be comparable with NCREIF's 9.5 percent "base" case IRR, cap rates would have to rise 120 basis points to 9.2 percent.

FIGURE 17B.5 Leveling the Playing Field

		REQUIRED RESIDUAL CAP RATE			
Scenario	Base Case IRR	NCREIF	Core Plus	NAREIT	Opp Fund
NCREIF	9.5%	8.0%	9.8%	9.2%	10.7%
Core Plus	15.2%	5.1%	8.0%	7.2%	9.0%
NAREIT	12.8%	6.1%	8.7%	8.0%	9.7%
Opp Fund	20.0%	3.6%	6.6%	5.7%	8.0%

		REQUIRED ANNUAL NOI GROWTH RATE			
Scenario	Base Case IRR	NCREIF	Core Plus	NAREIT	Opp Fund*
NCREIF	9.5%	2.0%	-0.3%	0.2%	-1.5%
Core Plus	15.2%	7.6%	2.0%	3.4%	0.3%
NAREIT	12.8%	5.2%	1.0%	2.0%	-0.5%
Opp Fund	20.0%	12.4%	4.3%	6.3%	2.0%

* Opp Fund assumes stabilization in year 3, so growth rate applies to years 4-7.
(shaded) Indicates base case assumptions and returns.

Similarly, the opportunity fund investor would realize NCREIF "base" case returns even if cap rates move up to 10.7 percent. Stated differently, residual value could drop 25 percent from $115 million to $85 million, and the opportunity fund investor would still be at least as well off as the NCREIF investor anticipates for normal markets. However, in order for a NCREIF investor to experience returns comparable to NAREIT, core plus, or opportunity fund normal market expectations, cap rates would have to fall (values rise) to 6.1 percent ($150 million), 5.1 percent ($180 million), and 3.6 percent ($255 million), respectively. Given historical market pricing, cap rates in the 7 percent to 11 percent range are not extraordinary, but cap rates that fall below 6 percent are relatively unlikely (even in today's low interest rate environment). Simply stated, the odds of the NCREIF vehicle achieving the target returns of the other vehicles are less than the odds of the other vehicles' returns declining to NCREIF levels. This limitation to NCREIF's upside is reflected in its tight IRR range.

Turning to NOI growth rates, Figure 17B.5 shows that in order for the NCREIF vehicle to generate an IRR comparable to the opportunity fund base case target, the NCREIF asset would have to enjoy an annual NOI growth rate of 12.4 percent. Conversely, the opportunity fund could experience negative year-over-year NOI growth, and still generate an IRR in line with the NCREIF base case expectation. Even if the annual NOI growth rate drops to as low as -1.5 percent, opportunity fund return performance would equal the NCREIF base case expectation. This is because the low cost basis and value-added of the opportunity fund creates enough appreciation to offset the NOI erosion. This analysis illustrates that there is substantial room for error in terms of market fundamentals (cap rates and growth rates) for the opportunity fund vehicle. In the case of the REIT investor, even if the annual NOI growth rate drops from 2 percent (residual value of $136 million) to 0.2 percent (residual value of $120 million), the REIT investor fares as well as the NCREIF investor expectation for the base case.

Using this methodology, we also examine the initial purchase price required by the private equity fund to generate IRRs comparable to the other investment alternatives. Figure 17B.6 indicates how much equity the opportunity fund must invest in order to match the returns of the other investment strategies.

FIGURE 17B.6 Opportunity Fund: Higher Prices, Lower Returns

REQUIRED RESIDUAL CAP RATE					
Scenario	Base Case IRR	Requ Purch Price	Leverage	Up-Front Equity	% Equity Increase
NCREIF	9.5%	$94,971,797	70%	$28,491,539	22%
Core Plus	15.2%	$84,980,140	70%	$25,494,042	9%
NAREIT	12.8%	$88,872,221	70%	$26,661,666	14%
Opp Fund	20.0%	$77,682,580	70%	$23,304,774	0%

Indicates base case assumptions and returns.

SENSITIVITY ANALYSIS

Sensitivity tables for a wider range of NOI growth rate and residual cap rate assumptions are presented in Figures 17B.7 through 17B.10 for the NCREIF, core plus, NAREIT, and opportunity fund investment alternatives, respectively. For the simulated NCREIF vehicle, a 25 basis point change in the residual cap rate results in a roughly 3 to 4 basis point shift in the IRR. In contrast, a 50 basis point movement in the annual NOI growth rate yields a 1 basis point movement in the IRR. Examining the impact of residual cap rate and NOI growth rate changes on the core plus vehicle results in significantly larger swings in the IRR due to the greater leverage. In fact, a 25 basis point change in the residual cap rate results in an approximately 80 basis points on a cash flow basis. Similarly, a 50 basis point swing in NOI growth rates yields 20 additional basis points on a cash flow basis. Turning to the NAREIT vehicle, a 50 basis point movement in the residual cap rate assumption elicits a change of 60 to 80 basis points on a cash basis. As for the NCREIF vehicle, 50 basis point changes in the growth rate induce movements of 50 basis points or less in the IRR. In comparison to the other three investment alternatives, changes in cap rates for the opportunity fund elicit much larger swings in the overall IRR, due to the higher leverage.

FIGURE 17B.7 NCREIF IRR Sensitivity

NCRIF IFF SENSITIVITY							
	Residual Cap Rates						
Annual NOI Growth Rate	7.00%	7.50%	8.00%	8.50%	9.00%	9.50%	10.00%
-3.0%	6.0%	5.2%	4.5%	3.8%	3.2%	2.6%	2.1%
-2.5%	6.5%	5.7%	5.0%	4.3%	3.7%	3.1%	2.6%
-2.0%	7.0%	6.2%	5.5%	4.8%	4.2%	3.6%	3.1%
-1.5%	7.5%	6.7%	6.0%	5.3%	4.7%	4.1%	3.6%
-1.0%	8.0%	7.2%	6.5%	5.8%	5.2%	4.6%	4.1%
-0.5%	8.5%	7.7%	7.0%	6.3%	5.7%	5.1%	4.6%
0.0%	9.1%	8.2%	7.5%	6.8%	6.2%	5.6%	5.0%
0.5%	9.6%	8.8%	8.0%	7.3%	6.7%	6.1%	5.5%
1.0%	10.1%	9.3%	8.5%	7.8%	7.2%	6.6%	6.0%
1.5%	10.6%	9.8%	9.0%	8.3%	7.7%	7.1%	6.5%
2.0%	11.1%	10.3%	9.5%	8.8%	8.2%	7.6%	7.0%
2.5%	11.6%	10.8%	10.0%	9.3%	8.7%	8.1%	7.5%
3.0%	12.1%	11.3%	10.5%	9.8%	9.2%	8.6%	8.0%
Strong	Base	Weak	Disaster				

FIGURE 17B.8 Core Plus IRR Sensitivity

CORE PLUS IRR SENSITIVITY							
	Residual Cap Rates						
Annual NOI Growth Rate	7.00%	7.50%	8.00%	8.50%	9.00%	9.50%	10.00%
-3.0%	5.8%	3.2%	0.6%	-2.3%	-5.4%	-9.0%	-13.5%
-2.5%	7.3%	4.9%	2.5%	-0.1%	-2.8%	-5.9%	-9.4%
-2.0%	8.8%	6.5%	4.2%	1.9%	-0.6%	-3.3%	-6.2%
-1.5%	10.2%	8.0%	5.9%	3.7%	1.4%	-1.0%	-3.6%
-1.0%	11.5%	9.4%	7.4%	5.3%	3.2%	1.0%	-1.2%
-0.5%	12.8%	10.8%	8.8%	6.9%	4.9%	2.9%	0.8%
0.0%	14.0%	12.1%	10.2%	8.4%	6.5%	4.6%	2.7%
0.5%	15.2%	13.3%	11.5%	9.7%	8.0%	6.2%	4.4%
1.0%	16.4%	14.5%	12.8%	11.1%	9.4%	7.7%	6.0%
1.5%	17.5%	15.7%	14.0%	12.4%	10.7%	9.1%	7.5%
2.0%	18.6%	16.8%	15.2%	13.6%	12.0%	10.5%	8.9%
2.5%	19.6%	17.9%	16.3%	14.8%	13.2%	11.8%	10.3%
3.0%	20.6%	19.0%	17.4%	15.9%	14.4%	13.0%	11.6%
Strong	Base	Weak	Disaster				

FIGURE 17B.9 NAREIT IRR Sensitivity

NAREIT IRR SENSITIVITY							
	Residual Cap Rates						
Annual NOI Growth Rate	7.00%	7.50%	8.00%	8.50%	9.00%	9.50%	10.00%
-3.0%	6.4%	4.6%	2.9%	1.1%	-0.6%	-2.4%	-4.1%
-2.5%	7.5%	5.7%	4.0%	2.3%	0.7%	-1.0%	-2.7%
-2.0%	8.5%	6.8%	5.1%	3.5%	1.9%	0.3%	-1.3%
-1.5%	9.5%	7.8%	6.2%	4.6%	3.0%	1.5%	0.0%
-1.0%	10.4%	8.8%	7.2%	5.6%	4.1%	2.7%	1.2%
-0.5%	11.4%	9.7%	8.2%	6.7%	5.2%	3.8%	2.4%
0.0%	12.3%	10.7%	9.2%	7.7%	6.3%	4.9%	3.5%
0.5%	13.2%	11.6%	10.1%	8.7%	7.3%	5.9%	4.6%
1.0%	14.1%	12.5%	11.0%	9.6%	8.3%	6.9%	5.6%
1.5%	14.9%	13.4%	12.0%	10.6%	9.2%	7.9%	6.7%
2.0%	15.8%	14.3%	12.8%	11.5%	10.2%	8.9%	7.6%
2.5%	16.6%	15.1%	13.7%	12.4%	11.1%	9.8%	8.6%
3.0%	17.5%	16.0%	14.6%	13.2%	12.0%	10.7%	9.5%

Strong | Base | Weak | Disaster

FIGURE 17B.10 Opportunity Fund IRR Sensitivity

OPPORTUNITY FUND IRR SENSITIVITY							
	Residual Cap Rates						
Annual NOI Growth Rate*	7.00%	7.50%	8.00%	8.50%	9.00%	9.50%	10.00%
-3.0%	9.9%	6.9%	4.3%	2.1%	0.1%	-1.7%	-3.3%
-2.5%	11.7%	8.7%	6.1%	3.8%	1.8%	0.0%	-1.6%
-2.0%	13.4%	10.4%	7.8%	5.5%	3.5%	1.7%	0.1%
-1.5%	15.1%	12.1%	9.5%	7.2%	5.1%	3.3%	1.7%
-1.0%	16.8%	13.8%	11.1%	8.8%	6.7%	4.9%	3.2%
-0.5%	18.4%	15.4%	12.7%	10.4%	8.3%	6.4%	4.7%
0.0%	20.0%	16.9%	14.2%	11.9%	9.8%	7.9%	6.2%
0.5%	21.5%	18.4%	15.7%	13.4%	11.3%	9.4%	7.7%
1.0%	23.0%	19.9%	17.2%	14.8%	12.7%	10.8%	9.1%
1.5%	24.4%	21.4%	18.7%	16.3%	14.1%	12.2%	10.4%
2.0%	25.8%	22.7%	20.0%	17.6%	15.4%	13.5%	11.7%
2.5%	27.3%	24.2%	21.5%	19.0%	16.9%	14.9%	13.1%
3.0%	28.7%	25.6%	22.8%	20.4%	18.2%	16.2%	14.5%

Strong | Base | Weak | Disaster

* Annual growth rate applies after stabilization (years 4-7).

Figures 17B.11 through 17B.16 depict equity returns (on both a mark-to-market and cash flow basis) for the four alternative investment vehicles, assuming the "strong," "weak," and "disaster" market assumptions. (Recall that Figures 17B.2 and 17B.3 illustrate the "base" case.)

FIGURE 17B.11 Strong Case Mark-to-Market Index

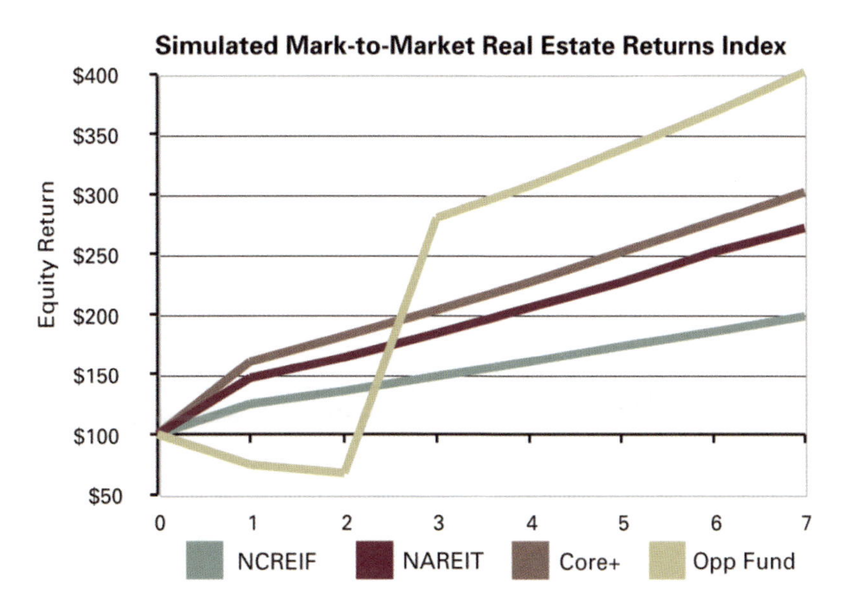

FIGURE 17B.12 Strong Case Cash Flow Index

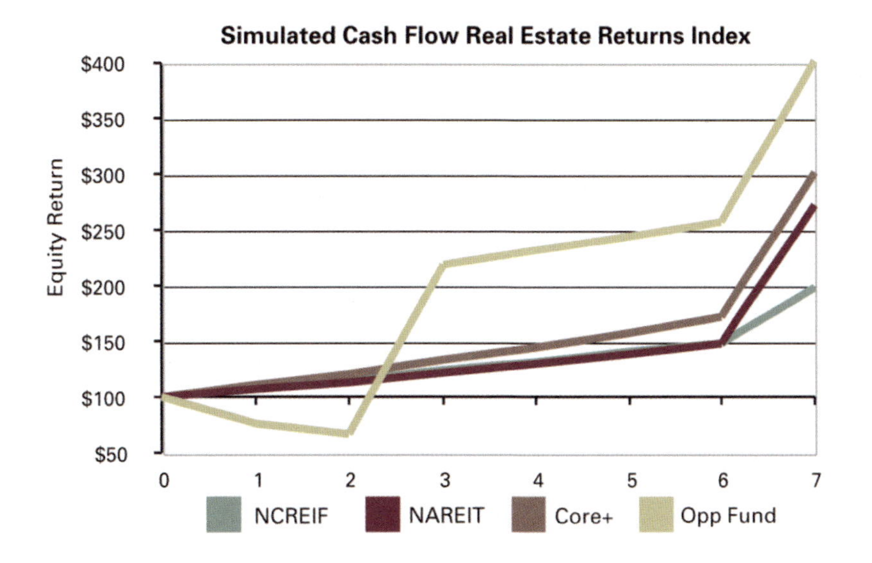

FIGURE 17B.13 Weak Case Mark-to-Market Index

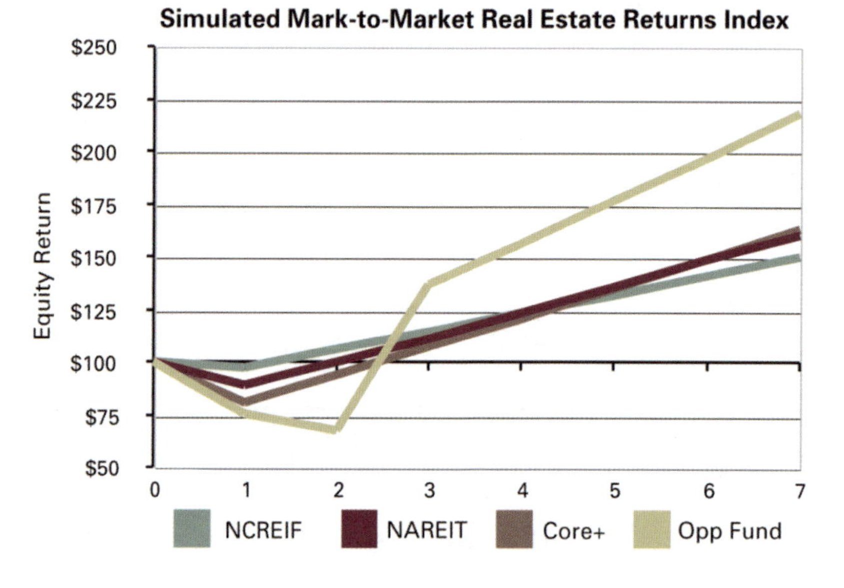

FIGURE 17B.14 Weak Case Cash Flow Index

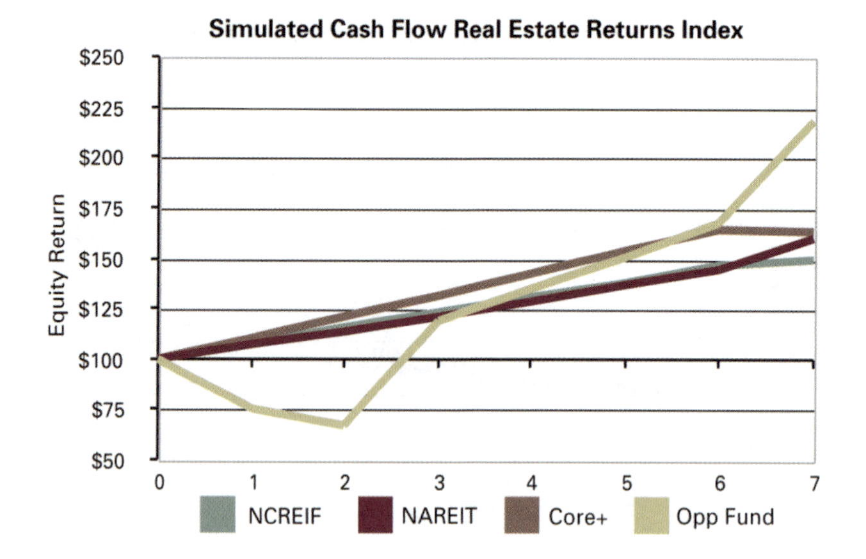

FIGURE 17B.15 Disaster Case Mark-to-Market Index

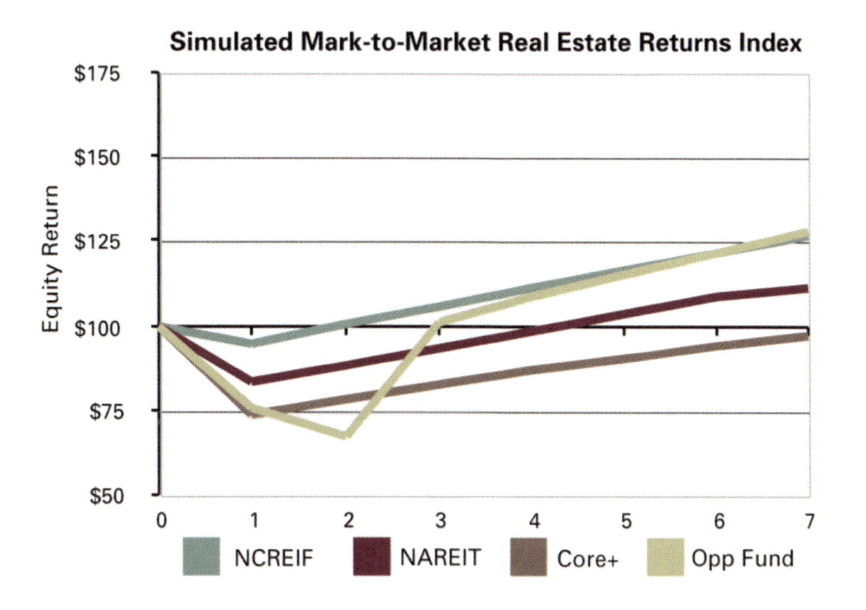

FIGURE 17B.16 Disaster Case Cash Flow Index

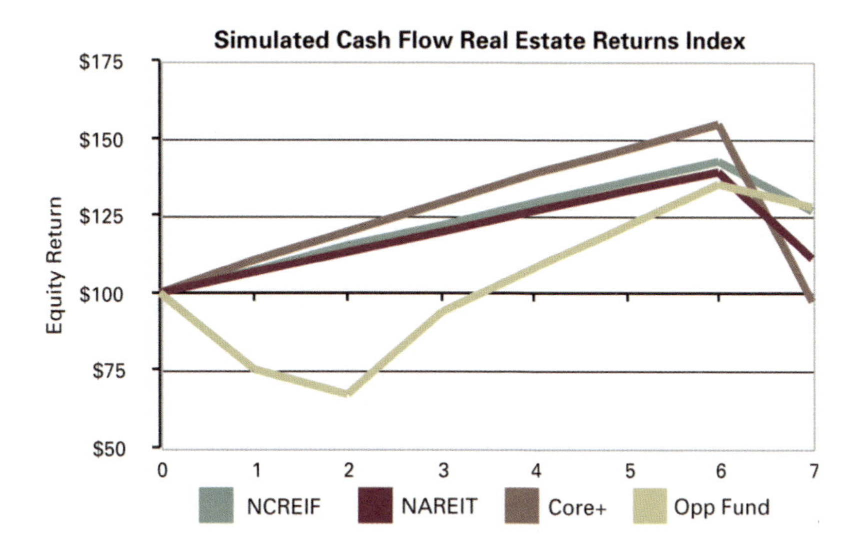

STRONG AND WEAK CASES

The strong market case assumes $100 is invested in a real estate opportunity fund, annual NOI growth is 3 percent per year, and the residual cap rate is 7 percent. As a result, the investment quadruples in value, implying a 28.7 percent IRR. At the end of seven years, the NCREIF and core plus portfolios are worth about $200, doubling in value, while the NAREIT fund is worth $272 after seven years. The NCREIF, core plus, and NAREIT vehicles generate IRRs of 12.1 percent, 20.6 percent, and 17.5 percent, respectively. The pecking order for the "strong" case assumptions track the same for the "base" case. That is, the opportunity fund performs the best, while the NCREIF fund performs the worst, even in a high growth market environment. Comparing the patterns of the "base" and "strong" cases, there is a slightly quicker step-up in the mark-to-market return calculation. This is a result of the boost in value from the lower residual cap rate, and is captured by higher appreciation returns.

In the "weak" market case, NOI is assumed to grow by only 1 percent per year and the residual cap rate is 9 percent. The same general basic pecking order is recorded across the four investment alternatives, but in a truncated manner. Total value of the initial $100 invested in NAREIT, core plus, NCREIF, and opportunity fund portfolios under the "weak" market assumptions are $150, $163, $160, and $219 at the end of seven years. The IRRs are 7.2 percent, 9.4 percent, 8.3 percent, and 12.7 percent, respectively. An interesting dynamic of the "weak" market case is that once stabilization occurs, the opportunity fund performance tracks side-by-side with the core plus fund through year six on a cash flow basis. Only upon exit does the opportunity fund "pull away". In fact, in year seven, the core plus portfolio is penalized for its greater leverage and lack of value-added.

DISASTER CASE

When "disaster" strikes, the pecking orders change. Assuming a -2 percent annual NOI growth and a 9 percent residual cap rate in year seven, the NCREIF portfolio moves to the head of the (poorly performing) class with a 4.2 percent IRR, followed closely by the opportunity fund at 3.5 percent, and the NAREIT portfolio with 1.9 percent, while the core plus portfolio actually registers a -0.6 percent return, due to the 65 percent leverage and a purchase price significantly higher than the opportunity fund's. In the "disaster" market case, retiring debt with a smaller-than-expected residual value is the problem of the leveraged alternatives. On a cash flow basis, it is easy to observe that the four scenarios track slowly, but steadily, upward (once stabilized), but cash flow gains are largely lost in all cases upon exit.

STABILIZATION SENSITIVITY

Because cash flows and timing of stabilization of the opportunity fund alternative are so critical, we explore two variables that greatly impact investment performance: initial purchase price and the years-to-stabilization. These results are presented in Figures 17B.17 and 17B.18.

FIGURE 17B.17 Impact of Purchase Price on Base Case Opportunity Fund Returns

OPPORTUNITY FUND IRR SENSITIVITY	
Purchase Price	IRR
$77,680,965	20.0%
$55,000,000	40.6%
$60,000,000	35.1%
$65,000,000	30.2%
$70,000,000	25.9%
$75,000,000	21.9%
$80,000,000	18.4%
$85,000,000	15.2%
$90,000,000	12.2%
$95,000,000	9.5%
(shaded) Indicates base case.	

FIGURE 17B.18 Opportunity Fund Cash Flow Assumptions for Stabilization

REQUIRED RESIDUAL CAP RATE					
	YEAR OF STABILIZATION				
	Year 2	Year 3	Year 4	Year 5	Year 6
1	($2,000,000)	($2,000,000)	($2,000,000)	($2,000,000)	($2,000,000)
2	6,000,000	2,000,000	-	(1,000,000)	(1,500,000)
3	8,323,200	6,000,000	2,000,000	-	(1,000,000)
4	8,489,664	8,489,664	6,000,000	2,000,000	-
5	8,659,457	8,659,457	8,659,457	6,000,000	2,000,000
6	8,832,646	8,832,646	8,832,646	8,832,646	6,000,000
7	9,009,299	9,009,299	9,009,299	9,009,299	9,009,299
IRR	23.7%	20.0%	13.5%	18.7%	6.2%

Indicates base case.

The 70 percent leverage causes changes in purchase price to have a significant impact on IRR. A $5 million change in purchase price in either direction results in a 300 to 400 basis point swing in the IRR. Yet even a $95 million purchase price (a $5 million discount to the other three alternatives) generates a return comparable to NCREIF in spite of early year negative NOI.

The risk-reward profile for the opportunity fund vehicle becomes apparent when stabilization assumptions are modified. By shifting the timing of stabilization from the second through sixth year, the resulting opportunity fund "base" case IRRs rise to 24 percent or fall to 6 percent. That is, if the opportunity fund assets are stabilized in two years (rather than three years), the IRR increases by nearly 400 basis points. Conversely, if the asset is not stabilized until year four, the IRR drops by nearly 800 basis points, resulting in returns comparable to the NAREIT vehicle, and less than the core plus "base" case scenario. If stabilization does not occur until years five or six, then the IRR for the private equity fund drops below even the NCREIF return, even for the "base" case. Thus, execution of value-added stabilization is more critical than market conditions for the return performance of an opportunity fund.

CONCLUSION

With different real estate investment strategies come different approaches to analyzing performance. This discussion has compared and contrasted four investment alternatives (NCREIF, core plus, NAREIT, opportunity fund), each within the context of four distinct sets of market conditions (base, strong, weak, disaster).

FIGURE 17B.19 Opportunity Fund Cash Flow Assumptions for Stabilization

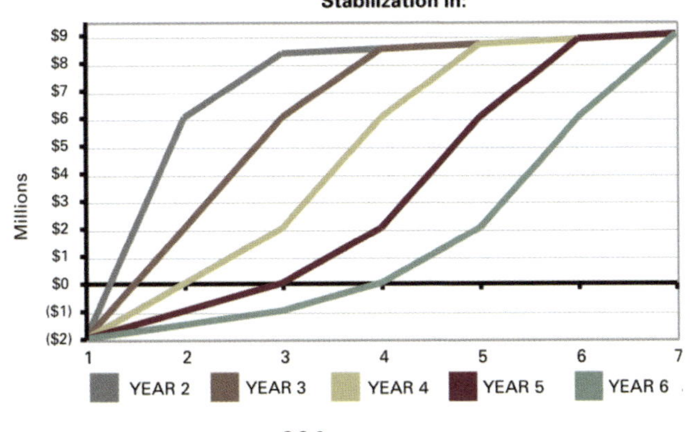

The return patterns for each investment strategy differ in different market environments, making meaningful benchmarking across investment alternatives very difficult. While good markets help all investment vehicles, the extent to which this is true varies notably. For example, the opportunity fund investor's downside return assuming successful property stabilization in a "weak" market is the same as achieved by the NCRIEF vehicle in a "strong" market. In fact, if market conditions are the main concern, then opportunity funds are generally the best alternative (ignoring liquidity considerations).

These simulations demonstrate that neither NCREIF nor NAREIT provide appropriate return benchmarks for opportunity funds. With that said, there are two critical insights that investors can utilize to prevent their fund managers from operating in a complete return vacuum. First, opportunity fund managers should regularly benchmark their performance against themselves to determine how they are performing compared to their own projections. Secondly, upon fund maturity, investors should compare the actual return spread over NCREIF and NAREIT relative to expectation. This spread should be about 700 basis points above NAREIT and about 1,000 basis points above NCREIF. While these do not answer the "How am I doing"? question, they do provide a disciplined analytical framework.

Chapter 18
REITs and Liquid Real Estate

"It is easy to raise money if you're not doing it".
-Dr. Peter Linneman

Although the real estate business has been around for a long time, large and well traded public real estate companies have only been around since the early 1990s. As of year end 2009, publicly traded US real estate companies controlled roughly $800 billion worth of (primarily) US real estate assets.

Key differences between publicly traded real estate companies and real estate private equity vehicles are: investments in private equity funds are much less liquid; private equity funds seek higher equity returns; since there are no investment minimums for public real estate companies, they provide an opportunity to invest in real estate for all types of investors; and, investors in public real estate typically own both the real estate assets and the management team.

HISTORY OF REITS

The REIT (Real Estate Investment Trust) as a legal entity was created by the US Congress in 1960 to make investments in large scale, income producing real estate accessible to all investors. REITs, however, were not a major force until the early 1990s, as banks, insurance companies, tax syndicates, and pension funds provided the bulk of capital for real estate up until then.

Until wildly undisciplined bank lending led to the collapse of real estate markets in 1990, REITs were a niche financial vehicle with a mixed history of booms and busts. For example, from 1970-1974 bank sponsored REITs made speculative development loans that ended with the mortgage REIT bust of 1974. This is because until the early 1990s, abundantly available debt meant that the major owners of real estate did not need to access large pools of equity in order to own or develop real estate. In addition, since they had tax losses due to high debt and large depreciation allowances, the REIT structure's single taxation feature offered no advantage. Only when lending rationalized and tax breaks disappeared, did many of the leading owners of real estate turn to public equity markets.

When lenders began requiring 25-50% in equity, many leading owners went public in order to efficiently access the equity necessary to delever their overlevered portfolios. This resulted in greater real estate market liquidity and transparency. The total market capitalization of REITs exploded from $12 billion at the end of 1990, to roughly $800 billion at the end of 2009, as properties shifted from private to public ownership.

There are three REIT categories: equity REITs; mortgage REITs; and, hybrid REITs. Equity REITs, the dominant format, own and operate income producing real estate, while mortgage REITs lend money directly to real estate owners, or extend credit indirectly through the acquisition of loans or mortgage backed securities. The revenue from mortgage REITs primarily derives from interest on the mortgages they own, while equity REITs derive their profits from rental streams. Hybrid REITs pursue a bit of both strategies.

Until the early 1990s, real estate was largely debt financed. If you could buy $1 billion worth of real estate for $1 of equity and finance the rest via non-recourse debt, wouldn't you take that deal, almost irrespective of the real estate? Of course! If the value of the portfolio rises by just 1%, you make a $10 million profit on a $1 investment. And if the value falls, you only stand to lose a dollar (and perhaps a bit of reputation). When 90-110% LTV loans were the industry norm, owners did not have to be particularly good at operating real estate. Instead, the critical skill was the ability to convince lenders to lend you money.

As excessive debt financing disappeared, large pools of equity and the ability to efficiently operate properties became critical ingredients for success. As a result, many real estate entrepreneurs began to specialize. After all, if you have to put significant amounts of your own money into a deal, you want to invest where you believe you have a core competency. In addition, equity sources have increasingly funneled their capital to the best operators who share an alignment of interests.

REIT IPO BASICS

As the 1990s began, there were few notable public REITs. Today, they are a big part of the "Who's Who" of the real estate business. The reason for this change is that until the early 1990s, real estate was the bastard child of the global capital markets, sustaining itself on tax gimmicks and excessive debt. Foolish tax legislation and undisciplined lending by the banks, S & Ls, and life companies led to massive overbuilding in the 1980s. As the economy softened in the early 1990s, financial regulators literally shut down real estate lending. This caused a virtual collapse in a real estate industry that was comprised primarily of highly leveraged developers reliant on continued debt refinancing to repay their maturing debt. But as these mortgages matured in the early 1990s, no new loans were available to repay these maturing obligations.

For many leading real estate operators, there were only two viable financial options: filing a Chapter 11 bankruptcy, or filing an S-11 Initial Public Offering (IPO) prospectus with the SEC. The strategy for going public was to sell the majority equity claim to your assets, and use the IPO's net cash proceeds to repay the maturing debt. For those nimble enough to successfully complete an IPO, an S-11 was far more attractive than Chapter 11. The volume of real estate public offerings was very rapid, with $19.5 billion raised in 117 IPOs from 1992-1996. Once delevered, these newly public real estate companies were able to purchase additional real estate, both by using their shares as currency to purchase properties from distressed owners unable to navigate their own IPO and via the cash raised in secondary stock offerings.

To see how the IPO process works, consider Moy Realty, which owns a portfolio worth $100 million at a 9 cap. However, this $100 million valuation was only theoretical. The actual value of these properties is highly uncertain, as the absence of debt means that there are very few viable purchasers for the properties. Hence, a large margin of error exists in assessing the value of the portfolio. This margin is easily plus or (more dangerously), minus 10 percent in market conditions. Even at the questionable $100 million valuation, the once proud multi-millionaire Ms. Moy faces a severe financing squeeze, as she has $98 million in mortgages against these properties. To make matters (much) worse, she has $56 million in debt maturing in the next 24 months, with personal guarantees on $30 million of this outstanding debt. And this $98 million debt burden is the same whether the properties were worth $100 million, or only $90 million. What can Ms. Moy do to repay this maturing debt and free herself from the personal guarantees that could leave her penniless?

If she declares Chapter 11 bankruptcy, the process will buy her perhaps 12-24 months, during which things might improve. However, absent a major market turnaround, she will eventually lose the properties securing the maturing mortgages, the management fee streams associated with these lost properties, as well as her other assets due to her personal recourse, not to mention capital gains taxes triggered by the foreclosures. Alternatively, she can attempt to sell some of her prized properties to generate enough cash to pay off the maturing obligations. But the success of this strategy is highly questionable in a market populated with few strong buyers and many distressed sellers. Further, upon sale, she would lose the management fees on these assets, have to pay capital gain taxes, and remain personally liable for any debt repayment shortfalls.

She considered selling limited partnership interests in her properties to pension funds, insurance companies, or high net-worth individuals, and she was told "No thanks, we have our own real estate woes" and "If I didn't invest in your real estate partnerships when things were supposed to be good, why would I invest now"? These potential capital sources were also troubled by the failure of real estate operators to return capital via sale, as too often these operators keep the properties in order to generate management fees, arguing that it is never the right time to sell. And no lender will provide more than a 50% LTV loan and at such an LTV she clearly lacks sufficient capital to repay her maturing debt. Since her wealth is primarily her properties, she lacks the resources to repay the loan gap with a personal equity infusion. She faces some decisions.

An answer is perhaps an IPO sale of publicly traded common equity in her properties. This solution gives individual investors the control of the return of capital decision via the sale of their individual shares. If the IPO generates sufficient proceeds, it allows her to pay off her maturing debt, eliminating personal recourse obligations, delever her portfolio, maintain control of the management fee stream, and avoid capital gains taxes. The key is that absent extreme leverage, these assets provide a relatively predictable cash flow to investors. Also, if public markets have rebounded, Wall Street will probably value the assets higher than private buyers, as private markets historically lag public real estate pricing. With a dash of transparency, a pinch of good corporate governance, a slick roadshow, and some luck, investors just might buy Ms. Moy's IPO offering in pursuit of low leveraged, relatively predictable cash streams.

So Ms. Moy rolls her property partnerships into a new entity, Moy REIT. She then (successfully) sells $60 million in publicly traded common equity claims in this new entity via an IPO, with the proceeds designated to pay off the $56 million of maturing debt and roughly $4 million in IPO fees.

How does this solve Ms. Moy's problem of salvaging her slim (and questionable) equity stake? After all, the IPO's $4 million in fees were in excess of her theoretical $2 million equity sliver. The answer is that since she did not lose control of her properties to either third party buyers or foreclosing lenders, and she still owns the fee stream associated with managing these assets. This management fee stream, which would become valueless as assets are sold or foreclosed, is also rolled into Moy REIT valued at a multiple of its fee stream. Since her management fees are roughly $650,000 (5 percent of property revenue) a year, at a 7 times multiple, Ms. Moy's fee stream is worth roughly $4.6 million. Thus, in exchange for her contribution of this fee stream to Moy REIT, Ms. Moy receives a 2% (for example) equity ownership of Moy REIT. Moy REIT was now an internally managed, public company, with Ms. Moy as the Chairman and CEO, for which she is compensated with a package of salary, bonus, and stock options. As part of the IPO, she agrees not to compete with Moy REIT, and that she will not sell her equity ownership for a period of 12 months.

FIGURE 18.1: MANAGEMENT FEE VALUATION

Value of Moy's Management Fee Stream	
Portfolio Revenue	$13M
Management Fee (5%)	$0.65M
Valuation Multiple	7X
Management Fee Stream Value	**$4.6M**

FIGURE 18.2: UPREIT STRUCTURE

Moy REIT IPO Summary	
Property Value (+/- 10%)	$100M
Management Fee Stream Value	$4.6M
Debt	$98M
Net Pre-IPO Equity	**$6.6M**
IPO Equity Raised	$60M
IPO Fees	$4M
Debt Repaid with IPO Proceeds	**$56M**
Moy REIT Debt post-IPO	**$42M**

FIGURE 18.3: UPREIT STRUCTURE

Moy REIT Post-IPO Summary	
Pre-IPO Value	$104.6M
IPO Fees	$4M
Value of Moy REIT	**$100.6M**
Debt	$42M
Equity	$58.6M

FIGURE 18.4: UPREIT STRUCTURE

Moy REIT Post-IPO Ownership	
IPO Investors	98%
Moy	2%

Thus, although the IPO drained $4 million in value due to IPO fees, it liquefies the value of Moy's management fee stream, allows all maturing debt to be repaid in a timely manner, and frees Ms. Moy of her personal guarantees. In addition, she has a well paid job, with a company that is sufficiently deleveraged to take advantage of other distressed owners. And no capital gains taxes are triggered in the process.

You may be looking at Moy REIT's ownership structure and wondering why she would settle for 2% (in this example) REIT ownership, when she formerly owned 100% of her properties and 100% of the management company which owned the property management fee stream. The answer is that 2% of something, is a lot more than 100% of nothing. Plus as an employee, she receives annual grants of restricted shares and stock options, and 2% of the dividends paid by the deleveraged company. Also, if correctly structured as an **UPREIT** (see p. 304), Ms. Moy defers paying the capital gains taxes that would have been due had she declared bankruptcy or sold the properties, as these taxes are deferred until Ms. Moy sells her ownership in Moy REIT.

Post-IPO, the Moy REIT can obtain a $16 million corporate line of credit from the lenders to whom Ms. Moy endeared herself by repaying her debt while many others were defaulting. With this line of credit, Moy REIT could purchase an additional $16 million in real estate and still maintain a 50% leverage level. When Moy REIT reaches roughly 50% debt, it plans to issue a secondary equity offering to pay down the line of credit, restoring borrowing capacity on the line of credit for further acquisitions.

To be sure, the process of Ms. Moy's IPO was hardly a walk in the park. Ms. Moy spends roughly a year preparing it, and is at risk of its failure to raise sufficient funds to repay the maturing debt. But, if successful, she is in an enviable position relative to other debt laden property owners. Post-IPO, she can approach distressed owners and offer to purchase their properties in exchange for tax deferred equity ownership interests in Moy REIT, allowing them to gracefully exit without triggering capital gain taxes, while avoiding the costs, uncertainties, and headaches of either bankruptcy or their own public offering. If Moy REIT acquires these properties for ownership interests in Moy REIT, it also generally assumes the debt on the properties. To retire this debt, the Moy REIT can either use its line of credit or float additional equity. Both routes are relatively fast, cheap, and easy because Moy REIT is now a modestly leveraged public company with a transparent balance sheet. Also, since secondary equity offerings are much faster and cheaper than IPOs, Moy REIT has a cost advantage over distressed owners contemplating survival via their own IPO. The main challenge facing Moy REIT is execution. And managing a public real estate company in a rapidly changing market means that if you screw up, you become very visible prey for bigger and savvier fish.

REIT TAX ADVANTAGES AND OPERATING RESTRICTIONS

All companies attempt to minimize their tax liability. From a tax perspective, non-real estate companies are basically C-corporations or partnerships. As a C-corp, corporate net income is taxed at the corporate level. Whatever money a C-corp has after paying corporate taxes can be retained or distributed as desired. If a C-corp decides to pay a portion of these funds in dividends, the shareholders (if they are taxable entities) pay income taxes on their dividend income. This is referred to as **double taxation**, as the government taxes profits at both the corporate and the shareholder level. If no dividend is paid, only a single corporate tax is paid.

Alternatively, partnerships do not pay taxes at the corporate level, but instead pass through all tax liabilities directly to the owners. If the property earns taxable income, the owners will be taxed pro rata on these profits, regardless of whether this income is distributed to the owners. Since there is no corporate tax payment, these structures are single taxation structures. The problem is that if the firm retains the earnings, the owners have a tax liability with no distribution to pay the taxes. As a result, these structures avoid double taxation, but owners can owe taxes without receiving any income.

The REIT tax structure offers the possibility of avoiding corporate taxes without generating tax liabilities for owners absent income distributions. This sounds perfect, right? So, why isn't every company in America a REIT? The answer is that to qualify as a REIT under the tax code, a company must satisfy a long litany of operating restrictions. Two of the most important operating restrictions are: the firm must primarily be in the business of owning and operating real estate; and, the firm must pay out at least 90% of its taxable income in dividends (though some of the required dividend may be paid in stock).

Who is impacted by the first restriction? Think about homebuilders (or builders in general). For a homebuilder to qualify as a REIT, they cannot sell the homes they build, as in order to qualify as a REIT they must own and operate their properties (i.e., homes). However, a homebuilder is in the business of building and selling, not owning and operating, homes. Similarly, developers rarely choose to be REITs, as most developers are in the business of building and selling their properties upon stabilization. In addition, the combination of relatively high debt levels and minimal taxable income during the development period generates little taxable income to shelter from corporate taxes. Therefore, there is generally little advantage, and many operating drawbacks, in a developer being a REIT.

Since a REIT's primary business must be owning and operating real estate, this tax structure is not available to most companies. For example, Microsoft owns a lot of real estate, but that is not their primary business. If Microsoft put their real estate in a separate and independent subsidiary that owns and operates those facilities, the subsidiary could qualify as a REIT. But, Microsoft cannot qualify as a REIT.

To qualify as a REIT, the firm cannot be in the business of "trading" real estate. The definition of the word "trading" is a bit ambiguous, as a REIT is allowed to sell some of their assets from time to time. This restriction can be problematic. For example, a REIT may want to purchase 12 of the 45 properties in a portfolio being sold, but the remaining 33 properties do not fit their strategy. However, to purchase the 12 desirable properties it must purchase the entire portfolio because that is what is being sold. If they acquire the entire portfolio, and sell the 33 undesirable properties as quickly as possible, they may endanger their REIT status, as the IRS may view these sales as a trading business.

If a company loses their qualified status, the IRS will demand back taxes, interest on those taxes, and perhaps penalties. The company can also be barred from becoming a REIT for at least five years. This restriction is designed to prohibit firms from constantly switching status to minimize taxes.

Another major operating restriction is that a REIT must distribute 90% of its taxable income as dividends. Hence, while it does not pass through its tax liability, a REIT must distribute a large portion of available cash flow to shareholders. Shareholders are then taxed (to the extent that they are taxable entities) on this dividend income. Remember that a REIT's taxable income will generally be notably lower than cash available for distribution due to, among other reasons, depreciation. As a result, a REIT may generally distribute as little as 50-70% of their available funds and still comply with the 90% of taxable income dividend restriction.

As a real estate operator, why might you dislike the REIT dividend restriction? Because in order to grow your business you would like to retain the capital being distributed as dividends. As a result, you pay accountants to calculate how much you must pay out in dividends to remain a REIT, and then you have to pay investment bankers to raise money to grow your business. That's expensive! Even worse is if you select REIT tax status and unknowingly violate one of the many operating restrictions. Not only did you pay out money you could have used to fund growth, but the government still collects corporate taxes, interest on those taxes, and penalties. As a result, firms generally maintain a cushion with respect to the REIT operating restrictions. In short, REITs achieve single taxation, but at a price.

FIGURE 18.5: C-CORPS VS. REITS VS. PARTNERSHIPS

Structure	Pros	Cons
C-Corp	- Can retain more cash flow for growth - Simpler corporate structure - No limitations on the types of businesses performed	- Pay corporate tax
REIT	- No corporate tax	- Large Dividend payments - More dependent upon equity specialists to raise growth capital - Numerous operating restrictions
Partnerships	- No corporate tax	- Tax liability without distribution - Cumbersome governance structure

REIT VS. PUBLICLY TRADED REAL ESTATE COMPANY

Becoming a REIT is simply a tax status election. Publicly traded REITs are governed by the same SEC and listing rules as all other publicly traded companies, and are normal companies in every way except taxation.

REITs do not have to be public companies. In fact, there are many private REITs. Choosing REIT status is a separate decision from the decision to list on a public exchange. The REIT decision revolves around the gains from single taxation (estimated at 3-5% of the value of the assets) versus the costs of the operating restrictions. If you believe more value is created by avoiding double taxation than is destroyed by the operating restrictions, you will select REIT status. One reason why most private companies are not REITs, is that to qualify as a REIT you must have at least 100 shareholders, and no 5 shareholders taken together can control 50% or more of the equity. In contrast, most private real estate companies have heavily concentrated ownership. If the controlling family wants to become a private REIT they must substantially dilute their equity stake. As a result, most owners opt for a partnership structure. To ensure compliance with these ownership restrictions, most REITs have bylaws which limit ownership concentration. This ownership structure restriction is also a key reason why companies like Microsoft do not create REITs to operate their real estate, as they would dilute their control over these operating assets.

In a similar manner, public real estate companies do not have to be REITs. For example, publicly traded developers are generally not REITs, as the tradeoff between tax benefits and operating restrictions does not favor REIT status. Never forget that REIT status is about taxes, while the decision to be public is about access to capital.

PUBLIC VS. PRIVATE

The decision to go public depends on the desire to access large pools of anonymous capital, versus the willingness to adhere to the rules imposed on public companies. What are these rules? They are many, including: reporting executive salaries; detailed audited financials; disclosing material information such as planned financings, developments, and major tenant lease expirations; describing material mistakes made in the course of business; and paying lawyers and accountants to create documents for the SEC. Not only is this expensive, time consuming, and potentially embarrassing, but it also provides information that your competitors can use against you. In addition, you have to disclose everything material (good and bad), that the company does, and everyone does stupid things sooner or later! As a private company you do not have to do any of these things. As a private company, you may write a report for your investors, but the exercise is much cheaper, shorter, less painful, and private.

IPOs are expensive. The investment banks you hire will take 6-7% of the gross proceeds of the IPO. In addition, you pay lawyers, accountants, and other related fees. In total, an IPO can easily cost 10% of the gross proceeds. Thus, if you could sell 50% of your company's equity, 5% of the value of the firm's equity disappears during the IPO process. This value loss means that you better have very productive uses for the money you raise. In addition, it costs perhaps $1 million annually in documentation and filing costs to be public. At a 10x value multiple, that represents, a further $10 million in equity value eaten up by lawyers and accountants.

If your business strategy requires substantial amounts of equity, access to the vast pool of equity capital available via public markets can outweigh the many costs of being public. For example, if your business needs $8 billion in equity to execute its business plan, being public is a viable answer, as it is very difficult to find a small group of private investors that can provide $8 billion. The beauty of the public equity market is that it efficiently pools the resources of millions of relatively small investors to achieve your otherwise unattainable $8 billion equity goal. The irony is that a group of ten very rich investors may not be able to provide the $8 billion you need for your business plan, but 100,000 not so rich investors can. In contrast, if you only need $800,000 in equity to execute your strategy, you would never incur the costs associated with being public.

Some companies incur the costs of being public without realizing the benefits of being public. This is because investors in public markets tend to avoid small companies with illiquid shares. Thus, if you are public but not large enough to effectively access large pools of public money, you bear the costs, yet receive few of the benefits of being public.

From time to time, a very dumb debate rages about whether a large real estate company is better than a small one. I supposedly began this debate started in 1997 when I wrote an article entitled *Forces Changing the Real Estate Industry Forever*. This article argued that there were economies of scale in real estate, particularly in terms of capital costs, to be exploited. My point was that economies of scale would drive consolidation until sufficient scale was achieved that diseconomies appear. I argued that visionary managers would procure financing for their projects based upon the ability to generate economic value via operating efficiency, and that the "weeding out" of small and inefficient companies would occur as they are taken over by more efficient firms. It is important to recall that this was written when the typical public real estate company had an equity market cap of just a few hundred million dollars. Over the next decade I was proven correct that a few hundred million dollars market cap was not big enough to justify being public.

Modest cost savings in real estate, as with every industry, can provide significant competitive cost advantages over the long term. It is cheaper for one firm to raise $2 billion, than for twenty small competitors to raise $100 million due to redundant fees, time, and expenses. These cost advantages provide larger public firms who own "commodity" real estate properties with a competitive cost advantage, that is particularly valuable in weak property markets.

An essential feature of being an efficient real estate company is flexibility. As leverage increases, so do loan covenants which decrease operational flexibility. Thus, in order to achieve the benefits of being a public real estate company, over the long term it pays to keep debt levels low. This is particularly true for REITs, as they realize no tax shield from interest deductions. The real estate collapse of the 2008-2010 demonstrated this simple truth, as low leveraged REITs survived, while the absence of debt killed many highly leveraged private firms.

As firms get larger, firms may be able to purchase services and supplies more cheaply. Purchasing supplies like paint, fixtures, janitorial services, landscaping, security, and power in mass quantities reduces operating costs. Also overhead may be more efficiently amortized, increasing the value of the firm. In addition, as firms become larger, they may be better able to relocate tenants to another property owned by the firm, reducing the risk of losing a prized tenant to a competitor. In addition, by having a large portfolio of assets, large real estate firms attain greater tenant and geographic diversity, generating more predictable cash streams. Against these advantages is the phenomena that larger firms are generally less entrepreneurial and far more bureaucratic. Smaller competitors often exhibit greater flexibility which offset the potential superior purchasing power, systems, and capital market access of larger firms.

For a large public company, the cost advantages of better liquidity and better access to capital do not have to be huge to be meaningful. A 1% cost reduction at a 10 multiple on a $100 million in revenue is $10 million in value added. But remember that size provides an opportunity for, not guarantee of, success. Do the economies of scale for real estate companies dissipate at some size? Probably, but surely not until a firm's market cap reaches several billion dollars. Is a $100 million REIT large enough to achieve economies of scale? Surely no. How about a $10 billion REIT? Surely yes.

The argument over whether to be a large public company or a small public company is much like asking whether a big body is better than a small body. It depends on what you want to do. If you want to be a ballerina, you are better served by a smaller, supple body; if your goal in life is to be a sumo wrestler, you will require a much larger body. Similarly, if your business strategy is to be the best owner of three garden apartments in the western Cincinnati suburbs, becoming a big public company will probably detract substantial value. On the other hand, if your business plan is to efficiently operate 70 regional malls scattered across the US, then being a large public firm is beneficial. It all comes down to your business strategy and your ability to execute that strategy.

Market Transparency: The existence of publicly traded real estate helps curtail oversupply. Why? Since publicly traded companies make numerous disclosures, market transparency is improved. These disclosures provide better information, which helps keep supply in check. But there will always be periods of excess supply, as public disclosures do not stop stupidity; they just document it. In the long run, public disclosures and the associated research will lessen excess supply risk because foolish development projects will tend to be punished upon announcement, rather than upon completion. As one sees competitors being punished for announcing foolish projects, other managements are less likely to make similar mistakes.

TAXABLE REIT SUBSIDIARY

Suppose a REIT is in the business of owning and operating top quality apartment buildings, and they desire to provide a service to tenants where pets will be walked, groomed, and fed. The REIT intends to charge tenants a fee for this service. But a qualified REIT can only offer "the customary and typical services" of a real estate company. If competitors do not offer this service, the IRS may rule that it is not "customary and typical". If strict interpretation of the "the customary and typical services" rule is applied, a REIT can never be a service leader.

In order to remedy this disadvantage, REITs can offer ancillary services as long as they do not become the company's primary business, and as long as the REIT carves out the income from such services into a taxable subsidiary. Simply stated, "non-real estate" income cannot be sheltered from taxes by REIT status.

The IRS requires that relationships between the REIT and the subsidiary reflect "market" terms. Is there room for manipulation? Of course. For example, a REIT can offer dry cleaning pick-up services to tenants via its taxable REIT subsidiary. The REIT can charge this subsidiary rent that (just coincidentally) equals the profit of the subsidiary for usage of a very tiny amount of storage space. Therefore, the REIT will attempt to push the subsidiary's rent as high as possible until the IRS says "no way".

UPREIT STRUCTURE

For most practical purposes there is no meaningful operational difference between a REIT and an UPREIT. An UPREIT is simply designed to allow a REIT to acquire buildings from partnerships without triggering capital gains taxes for the sellers. Recall that if a partnership property is acquired by exchanging buyer shares for the seller's partnership units, the transaction is a taxable event, as it is not viewed by the IRS as a "like kind" exchange. To avoid creating a capital gains tax liability on such a transaction, the UPREIT structure essentially creates a prophylactic partnership between the selling partnership and the purchasing REIT, where the REIT owns the prophylactic partnership, and exchanges units in this new partnership for the seller's partnership interests. While the legal nuances are many, when the acquisition is structured in this way, it is viewed by the IRS as a like kind exchange.

The only reason REITs use the UPREIT structure is to avoid capital gains tax for sellers of partnership properties that desire REIT equity ownership. In the early 1990s, the question existed as to whether the IRS would view this structure as acceptable. However, once the IRS blessed this structure it quickly became the industry norm. Typically, an ownership unit in the REIT's master partnership is convertible into a REIT share. Thus, if your ownership of the master partnership units represented 1% of the fully diluted shares of the REIT, you receive 1% of the REIT's dividends, votes, and upon conversion 1% of the REITs shares. As such, the master partnership is generally a pass-through vehicle. While variations of this structure exist, they are mostly legal in nature, and have little impact on either the strategy, operation, or basic governance of the REIT. Figure 18.6 is a diagram of the UPREIT structure.

FIGURE 18.6: UPREIT STRUCTURE

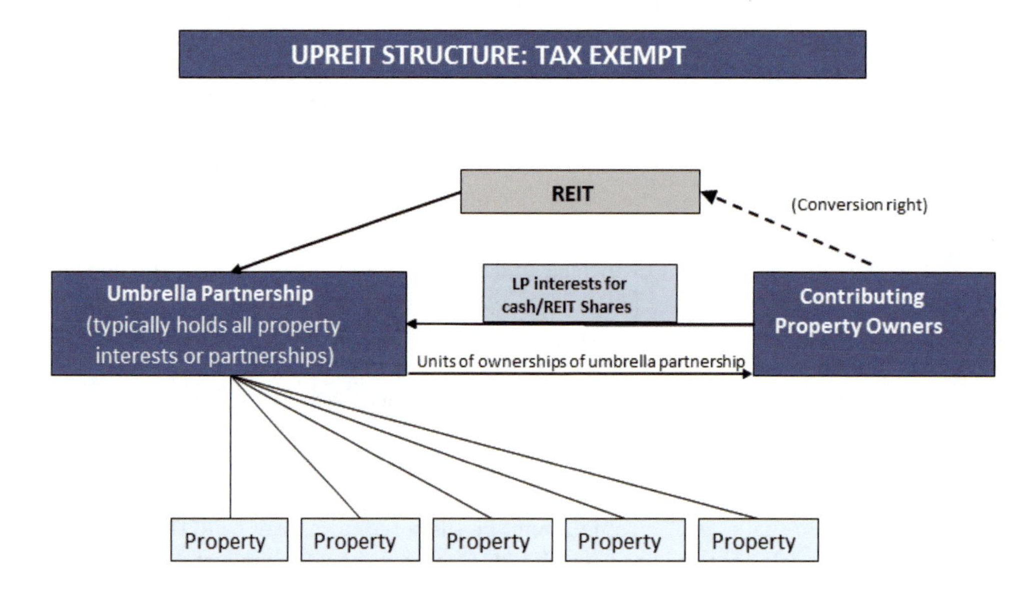

RETURN ON CAPITAL VS. RETURN OF CAPITAL

There are two commonly used investment concepts that merit attention: "return of capital", and "return on capital". Return of capital focuses on when, and with what certainty, an investor receives their invested capital back. Return on capital focuses on the return an investor earns while their invested capital remains at risk. Of course, since money is fungible, the money received by an investor is not economically earmarked as one or the other (except for tax and accounting purposes) – it's just money received. But investors typically think about how long it takes to "get their money back", how they "get their money back", and "how much they earn on their money".

Public real estate companies primarily focus on the "return on capital". This is because the individual investor substantially controls the timing of their return of capital through the decision to sell their shares. In contrast, private operators, developers, and private equity funds generally place more focus on the return of investor capital, as investors in such non-traded investments generally do not control the exit decision. While in all cases, operators attempt to maximize risk adjusted returns, public companies place a relatively greater focus on generating ongoing cash streams, while private operators must also consider when and how to exit the property.

CLOSING THOUGHT

Investor returns for equity REITs primarily come from dividend payments, with moderate long term appreciation. REITs are designed to deliver tax efficient, relatively reliable dividends. The typical dividend yield is about 5-9%. While the explosive growth of the 1990s is unlikely to be replicated, public REITs will continue to grow in importance. Today, real estate companies are included in the S&P 500, as well as other commonly utilized broad market indices. Real estate is now not only liquid, it is also de facto traded every time an S&P contract is traded. But being a REIT or publicly traded real estate is not a magic elixir. If you are a bad private real estate partnership, you will almost certainly be a bad public REIT.

Chapter 18 Supplement A

The Forces Changing the Real Estate Industry Forever

Dr. Peter Linneman - The Wharton Real Estate Review - Spring 1997

Every capital intensive industry has experienced a critical period in its evolution. This period, typically lasting 20-30 years, is triggered by factors such as the emergence of a visionary leader (petroleum and the automobile), wars (aerospace), capital requirements to meet rapid growth (steel and railroads), government regulatory changes (utilities, banks, and rail), and excess capacity (tires). These transitions were not always as quick or smooth as suggested in our high school history books. In almost every case the transition of these capital intensive industries was driven by a set of common forces and resulted in a stronger and more rational "industry". Operators who understood these forces created great wealth for their investors, while those who waged a war against the transformations experienced enormous wealth losses.

The commercial real estate industry is currently in the fifth year of its critical industrial transformation period. The evolution described below will probably take another 20-25 years to complete. The catalysts for this organizational change are many, but primary among them are the industry's collapse in the early 1990s, regulatory changes in the banking and insurance industries, and the emergence of mutual funds as a preferred investment vehicle. Real estate operators must understand the forces which are changing their industry forever if they are to benefit from this evolution.

WHAT IS THE KEY TO SUCCESSFUL REAL ESTATE OWNERSHIP?

The mantra of the industry has long been that the key to successful real estate ownership is "location, location, location". However, the recent collapse of real estate values vividly demonstrates that location does not guarantee successful ownership (witness the Rockefeller Center saga). While a bad location almost certainly ensures failure, a good location does not guarantee success.

If not location, then what? The simple answer is that the same elements which determine success in other capital intensive industries (such as petroleum, automobiles, steel, tires, rail, and aerospace) will also determine who will be successful real estate operators. Broadly speaking, successful ownership in capital intensive industries is driven by five elements:

- Visionary leadership and its ability to sell its vision
- Low long term capital costs relative to competitors
- Low overhead relative to competitors
- Enhanced revenue opportunities relative to competitors
- Successful risk management.

The most successful companies in capital intensive industries are those that can bring to bear these five elements on behalf of their investors. Firms that do not do so dissipate their investors' wealth over the long term, and exit the industry (either voluntarily or involuntarily).

MANAGERIAL VISION

A frequent topic of casual conversation at gatherings of real estate owners is the lack of visionary managers in other industries. The common view — which is probably correct — is that there are only a handful of visionary leaders in industries such as auto, steel, banking, or rails. Yet almost every operator of real estate who participates in these conversations believes that they are a visionary leader. One can only wonder at the fortunate happenstance that when the Almighty was passing out visionary leadership skills, every other major industry was only granted 3-6 great leaders, but the real estate industry was blessed with 4,192 (or at least every ULI member)! The truth is that the real estate industry has — at most — a handful of visionary leaders who also possess the ability to sell their vision to their employees and the capital markets. It is essential that the industry's assets become concentrated in the hands of this select group if it is to become a strong industry. As was the case in other industries in the early years of their transformations, the real estate industry has far too many mediocre operators, controlling too many assets.

The consolidation of capital intensive industries has historically been particularly rapid during periods of industry distress. This is because in periods of distress only the strongest can effectively access the capital needed to survive and grow. In normal times the consolidation process continues, though at a slower rate, as some weak operators see the handwriting on the wall and sell their assets while they still have real value. As a result, they receive prices greater than their assets are worth to them, but less than they are worth under the control of the strongest industry operators. These consolidation dynamics are at work in the real estate industry today. As the industry recovers, the "forced" consolidation process will slow — until the next period of industry distress. In fact, one of the reasons industry evolutions take so long is that it takes several periods of industry distress to fully shake out the weakest operators.

In capital intensive industries the relative importance of "great ideas" to the "capital required to execute these ideas" is low. Thus, in order to generate the greatest value from the limited capital allocated to the industry, it is essential to generate the biggest bang per "great idea". When capital was irrationally allocated to the real estate industry it was possible for even the most mediocre operators to survive and prosper. However, real estate has now joined the ranks of all other industries where capital is more or less efficiently rationed — perhaps for the first time in its history. Once capital demands a return, only those most skilled at predictably generating returns ultimately survive! It is particularly important in capital intensive industries like real estate to concentrate asset control under a few visionary operators.

Real estate owners should realize that collections of assets, without the ability to obtain visionary driven growth, always trade at steep discounts. The most obvious examples of this phenomenon are closed end mutual funds, which generally trade at 20-30 percent discounts to their liquidation values. This is because value derives from the visionary enhancement of assets, rather than the mere holding of assets. Those operators with the ability to add the greatest value to their assets — as Warren Buffett has done at Berkshire Hathaway — will ultimately outbid mere asset collectors for managerial talent, tenants, and additional properties.

The value of managerial vision (and the ability to sell this vision) in the real estate industry will increase as consolidation occurs, cash flow payout ratios to owners decrease, more equity is used in the capital structure, and binding debt operating and financing covenants decline. Why? If a property company borrows heavily and pays out its entire cash flow, it has little borrowing capacity, and therefore is restricted in its operations by debt covenants. This, in turn, means that when management identifies value enhancing opportunities (which generally require the deployment of significant amounts of capital), they cannot be executed without time consuming and expensive capital market activities. Since capital market "windows of opportunity" do not generally coincide with operating and investment "windows of opportunity", many value enhancing opportunities slip away for the lack of timely capital. As a result, firms constrained in their ability to exploit opportunities without going back to the capital markets will be valued at discounts, while those with ready access to capital will be priced at premiums.

As retained earnings grow due to greater size and lower cash flow payout ratios, borrowing capacity rises due to a strong balance sheet, and restrictive operating covenants decline through the use of unsecured debt with easily satisfied covenants, the value attached to the operator's ability to identify operating and investment opportunities greatly increases. This will reduce the cost of capital for these operators, further increasing the competitive pressures on mediocre operators.

The size of the company is also important. Today a large real estate company has perhaps $3 billion in assets, (comprised of 60 percent equity and 40 percent debt), an unused line of credit of $50 million, and an 80 percent cash flow payout ratio on an equity cash flow return of about 9 percent. Such a firm has annual retained earnings of roughly $32 million a year, and a maximum of $50-$80 million readily available to pursue investment opportunities without going to the capital markets. This represents only about: 900 multifamily units, 1 or 2 modest sized office properties, or several decent strip centers (not even a single good-sized regional mall). Stated most bluntly, given the small size of today's operators, funds available to act on managerially identified opportunities are too small to be of much value to shareholders — even for the largest companies. This lack of an effective opportunistic margin for value added management is even more striking among: smaller firms; operators with higher cash flow payout ratios; and, operators with less borrowing capacity. It is also a key reason why most property companies today trade as little more than collections of assets.

Now envision a real estate operator with $20 billion in assets (comprised of 70 percent equity), a cash flow payout ratio of only 65 percent on its 9 percent equity return, and a $350 million unused line of credit. This company has between $700-$800 million for opportunistic deployment each year. With this financing margin, management's ability to find opportunities, and the capital required to execute, are more in balance. An effectively managed company with this profile will have value notably in excess of the value of its assets. As such firms evolve, they will competitively dominate less efficient operators.

LOW CAPITAL COSTS RELATIVE TO COMPETITORS

Owning real estate is extremely capital intensive. In fact, given the low ratio of "ideas" to "capital", a better mantra for success in this industry is "cheap capital, cheap capital, cheap capital". As proof of this proposition consider that during the 1980s, when unlimited debt capital was literally given free to real estate operators, the most successful operators were those who accessed the greatest amount of this mispriced capital. Of course, the problem was that many of them did not get out before debt became rationally priced! That is, once capital was not free, they were not able to successfully operate — even if they had great locations.

There are three components of the cost of capital:

- the cost of debt
- the cost of equity
- the costs associated with raising capital.

The cost of debt is the most easily understood of these costs. Companies with the best histories of financial performance and the healthiest balance sheets are rewarded with lower debt costs. Firms which are able to achieve investment grade ratings for their debt, without sacrificing the risk profile of their assets, are able to realize capital cost savings associated with the greater depth and liquidity of the investment grade debt market.

An additional, often forgotten, cost of debt is the loss of operating cash flows associated with the reduced operational flexibility of restrictive debt covenants and security pledges. This hidden cost can be large, particularly in opportunistic periods. Conservatively underwritten investment grade unsecured debt imposes the least binding operating covenants, and hence the lowest hidden capital cost from debt restrictions. This is a powerful force which drives firms to use unsecured debt, and provides a substantial capital cost advantage which is not always appreciated.

A firm qualifying for a BBB+ rating for its unsecured debt has a lower interest rate and fewer operating restrictions worth perhaps 100 basis points (BP) over its strongest unrated competitors. For a company with $3 billion in assets, of which 30 percent is debt, a 100 BP debt cost advantage represents $9 million a year. At an 11 equity valuation multiple, the ability to use such debt increases equity value by $99 million (4.7 percent). Even greater value increases are obtained as the debt rating rises above BBB+.

There are two components of the cost of equity: the annual dividend and the expected annual appreciation. The pricing of equity capital reflects the pricing of risk. Factors that lower risk, lower the cost of equity capital. When all firms are privately owned and provide little in the way of standardized or detailed disclosures, no firm is at a competitive capital cost disadvantage due to the lack of disclosure. However, once major competitors provide public, standardized, detailed, and regular disclosures, equity pricing to private firms necessarily becomes relatively expensive. This is why no industry has ever reverted to private ownership once a major portion of the industry has gone public. In fact, the presence of major publicly owned competitors has always sped up the evolution of firms going public, as they need to remain competitive in terms of their equity costs.

The advantage of being a public firm grows over time, as the history of verifiable sustained financial and operational performance grows. The longer firms are public the greater the operator's understanding of the need to consistently disclose information and effectively communicate with the providers of equity capital about the risks associated with their equity.

A further advantage of public firms in terms of the cost of equity capital is enhanced liquidity. Liquidity is one way in which equity owners reduce their risks. The value of liquidity is greatest for the largest and most heavily traded companies. The industry's consolidation partially reflects operators striving for larger equity bases to lower their capital costs by increasing the liquidity of their equity.

Returning to the example of a $3 billion asset firm comprised of 70 percent equity, if the equity capital costs advantages associated with disclosure and liquidity for a public firm versus a private competitor are only 100 BP, this amounts to a $21 million equity cost savings. Again, at an 11 equity value multiple this represents an equity value gain of $231 million (11 percent) equity value enhancement.

The third component of capital costs is the cost associated with raising capital. Given the fixed cost dimension of many of these costs, clear economics of scale exist in raising capital. Ten $1 billion companies, each requiring $100 million in growth capital (debt and equity combined) a year will have a blended cost of raising funds on the order of $50 million. If instead, two $5 billion firms each raise $500 million, they will have a blended cost of perhaps $40 million. If a $10 billion firm raised $1 billion it will have blended a cost of only $25 million.

At an 11 equity multiple a $25 million savings in capital costs creates $275 in equity value for a $10 billion operator relative to the aggregate value of its ten $1 billion competitors. This amounts to 3.9 percent equity value enhancement for a 70 percent equity operator. These economies of scale of raising capital are a powerful driver of consolidation in capital intensive industries. The high costs of raising capital are also a major reason why the leading firms in capital intensive industries establish and maintain relatively low cash flow payout ratios, as no fees are paid on funds raised via retained earnings. In most capital intensive industries dividends as a percent of cash flow are on the order of 35 percent. Since REITs (Real Estate Investment Trusts) must legally payout 95 percent of their taxable income, as a practical matter they must payout a minimum of about 55 percent of their cash flow. Thus, in the absence of significant operating diseconomies of scale, real estate operators using the tax advantaged REIT structure need to grow much larger than firms in other capital intensive industries in order to increase their access to retained earnings. It also means that in order to lower their capital costs to enhance equity value, REITs will have to massively reduce their cash flow payout ratios from their current levels of 80-100 percent. Maintaining high cash flow payout ratios and remaining a fragmented industry needlessly enriches capital raising intermediaries at the expense of capital owners. This is particularly true given the fact that the best operators need to grow in order to maintain their depreciation base.

Most observers of the real estate industry fail to appreciate that capital costs (for both debt and equity) account for roughly 85 percent of the total costs of a real estate company. Consider the long term competitive outcome between two Class A garden apartment competitors. Assume that for the reasons previously described, the first has 100 BP cheaper debt costs, and 100 BP lower equity costs. If the second firm's weighted average capital costs are 11 percent, this 100 BP lower cost is a 9 percent cost advantage on 85 percent of all costs. Given the commodity nature of Class A garden apartments, this 7.7 percent total cost advantage of the lower capital cost firm represents a formidable long term competitive advantage.

The capital cost advantage of having the lowest capital costs in a capital intensive industry tends to be self-reinforcing. This is because low capital cost firms can use this cost advantage to reduce rents in order to obtain and retain tenants, make more capital expenditures on a timely basis to maintain the competitive position of their properties, purchase properties at higher prices, outbid their competitors for the best managerial talent, and engage in more advertising. Because of their lower capital costs, they can do all these things and still financially outperform their higher cost competitors! The operating advantages derived from lower capital costs are particularly valuable in times of industry distress, underscoring why industry consolidation is greatest during down cycles. Notable recent examples of this phenomenon are the tire industry in the 1980s, the banking industry in the early 1990s, and of course the real estate industry in the early 1990s.

As the real estate industry continues to evolve, firms with the lowest capital costs will competitively dominate, leaving high cost of capital operators the same three choices faced by high capital cost firms in other capital intensive industries:

- to live with needlessly low valuations for their assets and face eventual competitive ruin
- to sell their properties to lower cost operators before their properties erode competitively
- to move into non-commodity sectors where their higher capital costs do not impair their competitiveness.

The strategy of shifting away from the commodity sector of the industry to specialty niches is perhaps best exemplified by the evolution in the steel industry. The steel industry, another very capital intensive industry, turned to public capital markets and experienced rapid consolidation relatively early in its history. As it consolidated, the production of commodity steel products became completely dominated by the largest, lowest cost of capital firms. Any high capital cost firm which attempted to compete in commodity product lines was eliminated. However, many smaller (and privately owned) firms with relatively high capital costs survived and prospered by moving out of commodity steel products into specialty steel products and fabrication. Making a similar transformation is the challenge facing many of today's operators of "commodity" apartments, offices, warehouses, and retail centers. They will survive by selling their commodity assets to lower capital cost operators, and redeploying their operating skills where their high capital costs do not place them in direct competition with the low capital cost operators.

Many operators in the real estate industry, as in every industry which has gone through this transformation, will wait too long before selling their assets to more visionary operators with lower capital costs. They will convince themselves that they are doing "just fine" while markets are strong, and then be forced to sell at "fire sale" prices when their operating margins are squeezed and capital is unavailable during down markets. These high cost operators should sell sooner than later in order to realize the highest value from their assets.

Firms with intermediate capital costs face a difficult strategic problem. Initially these firms prosper competitively by beating out competitors with higher capital costs. The fact that their competitors with lower capital costs are doing even better seems of little consequence to them, as they are doing "just fine". However, as the industry's competitive process evolves, more and more high capital cost competitors are eliminated. As this occurs, intermediate capital cost firms slowly become the highest capital cost operators left in the business, and eventually it is their turn to be eliminated by competitive pressures! Industrial history is full of examples of firms which hung on too long while they were moderately successful, only to be forced out during the first downturn after they had become the highest capital cost firms left in the business. These firms would have served their owners much better had they merged with (or sold) their operations to the lowest capital cost firms during a strong market before they were the high capital firms.

It should be noted that combining real estate operation with real estate development will generally impose a capital cost disadvantage. This is because development is a 150 BP-300 BP riskier business than the operation of developed properties. Capital markets tend to price all marginal flows of capital into businesses that develop at higher rates due to the fungibility of money. That is, even though the firm may say the money will not be used for development, the fungibility of funds means the firm can effectively use the capital for development. This capital cost "penalty" associated with combining development and ongoing operations means that these activities should only be combined where the business competency advantage is sufficiently large to offset this capital cost disadvantage. This will not generally be the case in markets for commodity products.

In sum, the cost of capital is lower for larger, more liquid firms with established disclosure and financial performance records. Given the high proportion of total costs accounted for by capital costs, the need to reduce capital costs will be a major driver of a massive consolidation in the real estate industry which will occur over the next 25 years.

LOWER OPERATING COSTS RELATIVE TO COMPETITORS

Given the fact that capital costs represent by far the largest component of costs, competitive advantages associated with operating costs tend to be of secondary importance. However, in a commodity business every operating cost savings is competitively valuable. Consolidation allows for purchasing advantages in terms of supplies (paint, carpet, etc.), legal services, accounting services, insurance, systems, personnel training, employee benefits, and advertising. Obtaining a 10 percent reduction in these operating costs through effective consolidation provides a competitive advantage of approximately 1.5 percent of total costs. For a company with an operating cost of $30 million and 11 valuation multiple, a 10 percent operating cost savings creates $33 million in equity value, or an almost 5 percent equity value enhancement for a $1 billion asset operator with 70 percent equity.

LOWER OVERHEAD COSTS THAN COMPETITORS

Overhead reductions are a driver behind the consolidation in every industry. Overhead savings from consolidation are direct and substantial. One CEO, one CFO, one head of marketing, one head of acquisitions, one director of investor relations, one human resource department, one audited statement, one SEC filing, etc. All told, these costs savings easily total $5-$20 million annually. At an 11 multiple, this represents the creation of equity value of $55 - 220 million through overhead reduction. Value gains of this magnitude are the equivalent to a year or two's worth of solid cash flow growth. The gains from overhead reduction should not be dismissed lightly, particularly by high and intermediate capital cost firms, and those firms lacking visionary leaders. These firms are well advised to stabilize, and then sell during strong market periods to more efficient operators and capture a portion of the value added created via the overhead cost savings derived by the combined entity.

ENHANCED REVENUES RELATIVE TO COMPETITORS

Another force driving the consolidation of the real estate industry is potential revenue enhancement associated with consolidation. Revenue enhancements have long existed in the regional mall business, and are increasingly being realized in the strip and community center sectors, as larger real estate operators provide a national relationship base. As global tenants become more prevalent, revenue enhancement opportunities will also arise in the office and industrial sectors as larger real estate owners provide a national relationship and reputation.

It will be interesting to see if the multifamily industry is able to successfully develop brand loyalty similar to that found in the auto, tire, or hotel industries. Such branding will only be possible if large portfolios are held in a diverse set of markets over several price points. However, if successful, branding could generate substantially enhanced revenues by making the product more accessible and consumer friendly, and by reducing long term marketing costs.

An important revenue related competitive advantage of larger firms is slowly evolving in the office market. As corporate tenants move to ever shorter leases in the search for greater operating flexibility, larger portfolios of office space are required to efficiently diversify the risk of a tenant moving at the end of his short lease. Single property operators will find it difficult to hedge such leasing risks, and thus will need to charge relatively high premiums for short leases. In addition, as tenants move to shorter leases lenders will correctly tend to reduce their loan levels on secured properties. This will require single property office operators to use more equity to finance such properties.

In contrast, the operator of a large portfolio of office properties can approach the risk of shorter leases on a "statistical" basis, charging relatively low premiums for short term leases — hence making himself more attractive to corporate tenants. Also larger operators can float unsecured debt, thereby partially offsetting the need for increased equity.

One of the historic rationales for the fragmented localized ownership of real estate is that the real estate business "requires local market knowledge". This is, of course, true. But it is equally true of the automobile industry (different cars are desired in Florida and California), the tire industry (some areas need snow tires, others all-season radials), rail (which customers need shipments when), and retailing (local tastes vary). In fact, every major industry requires the utilization of extensive amounts of local market expertise. Yet other capital intensive industries are dominated by large national or international operators which have created efficient personnel methods and survey systems which allow them to incorporate local market knowledge while still reaping the benefits of size and consolidation. The creation and implementation of such methods is a major challenge facing the leaders of the industry's consolidation process.

RISK MANAGEMENT

A final source of competitive advantage is relatively efficient risk management. In the real estate industry this means that, as regional and national (and ultimately international) portfolios are assembled in areas of core competency, the cost of capital will decline. Note that the advantage of asset diversification is limited by the extent of operational competency. However, the ownership of larger portfolios in areas of core competency reduces risk by spreading tenant risk, improving informational flows, and perhaps by bestowing some degree of pricing discipline. Further, asset diversification across markets of operating competence also buffers the firm's cost of capital against movements caused by short term imbalances in local markets.

SUMMARY

On every count it is clear that the real estate industry will continue its consolidation process over the next 20-25 years. This evolution is driven by the same forces which have generated consolidation of other capital intensive industries. Real estate is not immune to these forces. In fact, its extreme capital intensity makes it particularly prone to consolidation now that capital is being effectively priced to the sector. It will take two to three more down cycles in the industry to complete this transition. However, when it is completed real estate will have an industry structure similar to that of other capital intensive industries.

Two cautionary notes are in order. First, the consolidation into larger public firms will not make the industry immune from periods of excess capacity. Periods of excess capacity exist periodically in the auto, tire, aerospace, and steel industries. However, the consolidation of these industries into large publicly owned firms has lessened the degree of excess capacity creation by reducing the number of independent decision makers. With fewer, larger decision makers, each firm is more acutely aware of its impact on market capacity. Also, the superior information flows associated with public company disclosures make it more readily transparent to providers of capital that excesses are occurring, allowing capital markets to reprice risk. This raises the cost of capital to firms in the sector, making further capacity expansion less financially attractive. Again, this disciplinary process tends to occur more rapidly in industries dominated by large public firms than in industries with fragmented private ownership.

Second, real estate operators must realize that they, like their opposite numbers in other capital intensive industries, are in the operating business rather than the trading business. As such, they need to eliminate the market timing mentality which has frequently characterized real estate operators and pension fund advisors. Their goal should be to become the best real estate operators, in both good times and bad. If investors desire to trade during different parts of the operator's or industry's cycle, this is best achieved by creating liquidity for the ownership claims which accommodate trading without disrupting the operating effectiveness of the entity. It is impossible to build a great long term operating company with a trader's mind set. This was a major flaw of the real estate pension fund advisory business which evolved in the 1980s.

Changes greater than this industry has ever seen are underway, and they will occur just as surely as they have in other capital intensive industries. These changes will absorb the rest of the careers of most readers. They will create enormous wealth for the successful, and destroy the wealth of those who unable or unwilling to adapt.

Chapter 18 Supplement B

The Forces Changing Real Estate Forever: Five Years Later

The real estate industry—what changed and what didn't.

Dr. Peter Linneman – The Wharton Real Estate Review – Fall 2002

Five years ago I wrote "The Forces Changing Real Estate Forever" (*WRER*, Spring 1997). That paper summarized my views on the future of commercial real estate markets, views that I had formulated over twelve years as an observer of the real estate industry. The reception given this paper was both surprising and rewarding. Surprising, because I felt that I was saying nothing particularly radical, but rather describing the economics that had long existed in most other capital-intensive industries. Rewarding, because the paper became part of strategic decisions being made in real time by leading real estate companies. This paper coined the now-ubiquitous phrase "real estate is a capital-intensive industry".

WHAT I SAID AND DIDN'T SAY

It is useful to summarize what I said and did not say in "The Forces Changing Real Estate Forever". I argued that economic forces were changing the structure of the real estate industry and that there was no going back. Back to what? At that time many industry leaders felt that real estate would eventually return to an environment of 95 percent to 110 percent non-recourse debt financing, thus enabling highly fragmented ownership. Also, if such debt financing, long the industry's lifeblood, returned for speculative development projects, real estate entrepreneurs could once again achieve wealth through development, regardless of economic value.

I also suggested a number of outcomes implied by the experiences of other capital-intensive industries: real estate was in the fifth year of an evolutionary transformation that would take twenty to thirty years to complete; real estate was not uniquely local in nature since *all* businesses are local; relatively modest cost advantages are important in every industry, including real estate, and being larger could provide significant competitive cost advantages; equity is an important component of appropriately capitalizing long-term assets such as real estate; the ownership and operation of "commodity" properties would be dominated by large publicly traded companies that would be able to most effectively access the large pools of capital required for ownership of sizeable pools of real estate; lower debt levels and lower payout ratios would increasingly characterize publicly traded real estate companies. I also suggested that development required a skill and risk profile different from the operation and ownership of stabilized properties, so public real estate companies would not be major developers. I also wrote that information flows would notably improve as the industry became increasingly influenced by large publicly traded companies, reducing—though not eliminating—the volatility of real estate cycles. Finally, once the real estate industry had experienced a significant movement towards publicly traded companies, I speculated, it would not return to the fragmented, privately dominated industry of the past.

Subsequent to the publication of "The Forces Changing Real Estate Forever", people attributed to me statements that I did not make, either in the paper or in companion papers and speeches. For example, I did not say that all, or even most, real estate would be publicly owned; that bigger real estate companies were necessarily better; that the cost advantages associated with size, better liquidity, and better access to capital markets were "huge"; that the industry's transition would be a rapid one; or that being a large or public company was "a silver bullet" that solved all problems and should be the goal of every property company.

It surprises me that many people thought I said these things, because I had tried to be clear about my thesis. For example, in speeches and companion papers I repeatedly used the analogy of basketball players, noting that while bigger can be better, size is no guarantee of success. I also frequently noted that "a big, poorly run company is just a big wasted opportunity".

THE "FORCES"

Five years ago I noted that primary among the "forces" that were changing real estate markets was the control of capital dramatically shifting from commercial banks and life insurance companies to pension funds and mutual funds. For example, in 1970 the combined asset base of commercial banks and life insurance companies accounted for 53 percent of all U.S. assets, while the combined asset base controlled by pension funds and mutual funds was a mere 14 percent. By 1997, assets under control had radically changed to 35 percent at commercial banks and insurance companies, and a staggering 44 percent at pension funds and mutual funds.

This dramatic shift in the control of the nation's capital is of critical importance for the real estate industry, as the industry's high degree of capital intensity means that it must constantly access large amounts of capital. Of particular significance is the fact that pension funds and mutual funds invest in both equities and debt, primarily via highly liquid, mark-to-market assets, while commercial banks and life insurance companies have historically employed primarily non–mark-to-market debt instruments. I felt that the shift of capital control from institutions that utilized non–mark-to-market debt vehicles to those that invested heavily in publicly traded equities and corporate debt was a powerful "force" that would require real estate companies to evolve in order to attract the necessary capital. The primary instruments in this regard would be publicly traded real estate company equity, commercial mortgage backed securities (CMBS), and unsecured commercial real estate company debt.

A second "force" was the considerable consolidation that had occurred in the U.S. financial sector. In fact, the number of commercial banks declined from more than 13,500 in 1970 to fewer than 9,600 in 1996. Similarly, in 1970 the largest 100 banks controlled 49.7 percent of all bank assets, while by 1996 this share had grown to 61.7 percent. The impact of this consolidation on the real estate industry cannot be overstated. It meant that there were fewer "friendly local bankers" with the mission of supporting local development. Local real estate operators no longer had an inside track to the capital they needed simply by virtue of belonging to the local country club, church, or charity. Increasingly, national, and even international, financial support bases would be essential as capital markets globalized. This was clearly a "force" that encouraged bigger, more transparent companies with strong balance sheets to emerge.

The final "force" that I felt would radically change the real estate industry was that business basics would ultimately prevail. While one could not predict exactly when this would occur, history showed that it would occur. To me, business basics meant that speculative developments could not command 95 to 110 percent debt levels priced at single A bond spreads. It meant that real estate ownership required substantial equity, particularly for development, that firms would need to focus on their core competencies, and that operators with vision, access to rationally priced capital, the lowest operating costs, and good risk management would ultimately be the most successful, eliminating the weakest competitors.

This was a harsh message to an industry raised on high levels of debt and speculative development. I stated that no longer would the industry be financed by financial gimmicks (such as unsustainable tax write-offs), mispriced debt, overleveraged properties, or inside deals with local bankers. To survive and prosper in the future would require substantial equity, exploitation of one's comparative expertise, and greater operational efficiency than one's competitors. Gone was the era when 100 percent loans allowed developers to develop and own an array of property types. In a world that required at least 25 percent equity, real estate participants would have to decide where to allocate scarce equity and how to attract large pools of it.

My message was that not all industry participants were going to survive, much less prosper, and that many players needed to figure out how and when to exit. I noted that there are only two ways to exit: when you want to or when you have to, with the former option being clearly more profitable. Ultimately, my message was that the leaders of the industry would embrace these changes while the losers would yearn for a world that would never return.

REPORT CARD

So how have events played out? A few numbers are illustrative. At the end of 1996 the largest publicly traded real estate company was Simon Property Group (after its acquisition of DeBartolo), with a total equity market capitalization of $3.1 billion and a firm value of $5.4 billion. As of year-end 2001, the largest publicly traded real estate company was Equity Office Properties, which had a total market capitalization of $10.8 billion and a firm value of $23.4 billion. Similarly, at the end of 1996, the total equity market capitalization of all publicly traded equity REITs was $78.3 billion, while as of year-end 2001 it stood at $147.1 billion. It is interesting to note that this increase in value is primarily attributable to the extraordinary increase in the number of assets owned by U.S. publicly traded companies. Since 1996 the percentage of warehouse space owned by publicly traded companies has risen from approximately 3 percent to almost 10 percent. Public ownership of office space has risen from 1.8 percent to approximately 7.6 percent, public ownership of apartments from 4.6 percent to 8 percent, and public ownership of strip retail from approximately 8.3 percent to 13.5 percent. The percentage of publicly owned hotels has grown from approximately 8.3 percent to almost 20 percent, and public ownership of malls has grown from approximately 22 percent to nearly 35 percent.

In 1996, twenty-one publicly traded real estate companies had market caps in excess of $1 billion. Today, more than 20 REITs have market caps in excess of $2 billion. Even more telling is the fact that seven (non-hospitality) publicly traded U.S. real estate firms are now listed in the Business Week Global 1000, led by Equity Office Properties, the 351st largest company in the world (179th in the United States). Similarly, the S&P 500 now includes three (non-hospitality) real estate firms, with additional representation in other broad stock indices. Publicly traded real estate companies collectively own approximately roughly 17 percent of all investable real estate asset value in the United States, and account for approximately 35 percent of the equity positions in investable U.S. real estate.

Further evidence of the role of public real estate is that the average trading volume of the NAREIT Composite index is approximately $15 billion each month. This compares to the $25 billion to $40 billion of private transactions that occur annually. Also, while a handful of public real estate companies have gone private (for example, Irvine Apartments), these have been—as I hypothesized—exceptions to the rule. Taken together, these figures demonstrate a large change in a remarkably short period of time.

In addition to the dramatic growth of publicly traded real estate companies, there has been a considerable—though more difficult to document—increase in the concentration of private real estate owners. For example, between 1996 and 2001 the largest fifty apartment companies' ownership of U.S. apartments increased from 11 percent to 17 percent. Most of these large apartment companies remain private; however, the "forces" that are creating larger public companies are also driving the creation of larger private companies.

Similarly, the equity pools controlled by the major real estate private equity funds play an increasingly important role on the real estate landscape. Real estate private equity funds are now the largest owners of privately held real estate in the United States. My estimates indicate that the real estate private equity funds of the largest twenty sponsors control approximately $100 billion of U.S. real estate, again demonstrating the "forces" driving the equitization and the consolidation of real estate capital, and the push of capital to those with scale, managerial ability, and investment vision. When I wrote "The Forces Changing Real Estate Forever," I realized that real estate private equity funds would be a permanent feature of the real estate landscape, but the maturation of the CMBS market has made these funds much more powerful than I anticipated. Real estate private equity funds and publicly traded real estate companies have equitized the industry, together accounting for roughly 50 percent of the equity ownership of U.S. real estate, and *de facto* defining the U.S. real estate equity landscape.

I was correct that the industry would not return to the days of excessive leverage. In fact, today's highly leveraged real estate owners would have been thought under-leveraged a mere decade ago. For example, the relatively highly leveraged ownership positions of real estate private equity funds utilize approximately 55 percent to 70 percent debt, while debt levels for publicly traded real estate companies hover between 40 percent to 50 percent. In contrast, a "conservatively" leveraged property in 1990 was at least 80 percent, and more typically 90 percent to 110 percent leveraged. Debt coverage ratios have improved even more dramatically, even for the most aggressive borrowers, compared to a decade ago.

The rapid maturation of the CMBS market and use of unsecured corporate bonds have also linked the pricing of real estate risks to that of the broader debt markets. The amount of outstanding CMBS debt has risen from approximately $120 billion in 1997 to approximately $325 billion today. As predicted, this growth has meant that balance sheets similar to those in other capital-intensive industries now characterize the real estate industry.

The large volumes of publicly traded real estate debt and equity have created a large analyst community that scrutinizes the supply and demand fundamentals for the major property markets. This information flow has put a damper on the optimism of developers and development lenders. The continuous public market pricing of debt and equity has also raised awareness among capital providers of the cost of capital for new developments. In this regard, real estate is becoming more like other capital-intensive industries. However, as evidenced by the excess capacity in the telecom infrastructure industry, being exposed to the scrutiny of publicly traded debt and equity markets does not guarantee that excess supply will not occur. But it has served, albeit imperfectly, to keep excess supply conditions in most real estate markets better than during past cycles.

A fundamental premise of "The Forces Changing Real Estate Forever" was that substantial levels of equity would be required for the ownership and development of real estate. This has been the case. This equity cushion is proving its worth during the current real estate market supply-and-demand imbalance. Even though vacancy rates have been driven to levels not seen since 1993, the fallout in the real estate market has been limited. Delinquency rates on mortgages are roughly 1.5 percent today versus 8.5 percent in 1993, and properties continue to throw off substantial positive cash flows to owners.

If real estate were leveraged in 2002 as it had been in 1992, the distress in the real estate industry would be substantial. When property values fell in the early 1990s, it wiped out the equity slivers of many owners. In contrast, today's reductions in cash flows and property values have reduced, but hardly eliminated, all equity value. As noted in "The Forces Changing Real Estate Forever", it is important that long-lived real estate assets be matched with substantial amounts of the longest liability—equity—because when downturns occur there is no way that owners can adjust their cost structures to maintain profitability. To harvest the long-term value of properties requires substantial equity cushions in order to see one through the inevitable hard times.

LESSONS LEARNED

Over the last five years there has been a substantial shift in institutional real estate investments to fully integrated operators, as large portfolios have shifted from the control of specialty property mangers (many of whom have either gone out of business or been merged out of existence) to public real estate companies. As superior operations became the primary way to increase value, and institutional investors were offered the opportunity to invest in the best operators via publicly traded stock, money shifted from specialty managers to operators.

Yet institutional investors continue to make direct real estate investments to a much greater degree than I predicted. This reflects the interplay of three factors. The first is that, until recently, most publicly traded real estate companies were too illiquid for major investors in real estate. However, as these companies grew and their floats expanded, they attracted a broader pool of equity investors. Similarly, their inclusion into broad stock market indices has lowered this hurdle. I saw this problem five years ago, and realized it was part of the evolutionary process.

A second reason for continued direct institutional ownership is the tyranny of the status quo: what exists has a tremendous ability to continue, since many people have vested interests in maintaining current conditions. A vivid example of this phenomenon is the promotion of the "four-quadrant" concept of real estate investing. The four-quadrant idea argues that institutional investors realize superior portfolio performance by maintaining a balanced portfolio of publicly traded real estate debt, publicly traded real estate equity, privately owned real estate debt, and privately owned real estate equity. The argument is that each category generates a unique, and largely uncorrelated, return profile. As "proof" of the unique return profiles of publicly traded versus privately owned real estate, supporters compare the NCREIF returns series for private real estate versus the NAREIT return series for public companies (see Figure 18B.1). These alternative return series appear to show that the total returns recorded for the publicly traded companies are dramatically different in every year from those recorded by privately owned properties, that the returns show very little correlation, and that privately owned property returns are notably less volatile. In fact, the closest these two series came to providing the same return was in 1994, when the difference was 320 basis points, an amount equal to the return recorded by public companies that year, and 50 percent of the return recorded by private properties. The average difference in the total returns from 1993 through 2001 was 1450 basis points, with the largest difference occurring in 1998 (3,360 basis points). From 1993 to 2001, the publicly traded index indicates a superior total return of 14 percent (or 1.6 percent per annum) relative to that of the privately owned index.

FIGURE 18B.1 Annual Total Return Indexes

	NARETT	NCREIF	DIFFERENCE
1993	19.7%	1.3%	18.4%
1994	3.2%	6.4%	3.2%
1995	15.3%	7.5%	7.8%
1996	35.3%	10.3%	25.0%
1997	20.3%	13.7%	6.6%
1998	-17.5%	16.1%	33.6%
1999	-4.6%	11.1%	17.7%
2000	26.4%	12.0%	14.4%
2001	13.9%	7.4%	6.5%

Should one conclude from these data that publicly traded and privately owned real estate have substantially different return patterns? The answer is no. A realistic comparison of these data merely reveals the irrelevance of the NCREIF series for analyzing property returns. While it is believable that publicly traded and privately owned real estate pricing are not always perfectly synchronized, it defies credibility that they could differ by as much as reported in Figure 18B.1, as large pools of "hot" money exist that would arbitrage such sizable differences across these categories. It is also unbelievable that following the Russian crisis of 1998, when the market saw a massive flight to liquidity and quality, and many real estate sales fell apart, private real estate returns were the best of the decade (16.1 percent) while public real estate returns were the worst of the decade (negative 17.5 percent). This result proves only that the appraisal driven NACREIF index does not accurately reflect the return performance of privately owned real estate, as no one really believes that private real estate owners achieved a 16.1 percent return on their assets in a year when property liquidity disappeared and prices fell.

The return characteristics of publicly traded and privately owned real estate are necessarily closely interlinked, since buildings don't know—or care—if they are publicly or privately owned. Returns are determined by the interaction of the supply and demand for space (which is the same whether the building is part of a public or a private portfolio), and the pricing of risky cash streams. The pricing of the cash streams derived from real estate are effectively the same (up to arbitrage margins) whether the cash stream is publicly or privately owned.

The NCREIF data series is a non-tradable concept, analytically similar to a Wall Street equity analyst's target valuations of publicly traded companies. However, it is important to remember that actual returns feed your family, while analyst estimates are good only for lighting the fire in your fireplace.

A final reason why many institutional investors continue to directly own substantial amounts of real estate, even though it is more burdensome and less liquid than public company ownership, is that many institutional investors desire the artificial lack of volatility associated with non-mark-to-market pricing. This demand may even grow in view of the recent increase in the volatility of public markets. While mutual funds and pension funds have driven money into mark-to-market instruments, there remains a far greater demand for non-mark-to-market vehicles than I appreciated five years ago. The existence of the NCREIF Index, which recorded low volatility and no negative returns over the last nine years, allows institutional investors who directly own real estate to claim that they have achieved lower volatility in their returns. But this is merely a sleight-of-hand trick. Will this exercise in self-deception change? Over time, of course it will, but it will take much longer than I initially thought.

IS BIGGER BETTER?

Have the last five years proven that larger firms are necessarily more efficient? Of course not. However, local real estate businesses have successfully been nationalized, and companies operate at scales previously thought impossible. The "forces" stimulated academic research that has explored real estate scale economies. Though limited, this research reveals evidence of scale economies achievable at least up to firm sizes of several billion dollars. Some direct insights on the presence of scale economies are obtained by comparing key cost components at major real estate firms back then to those of today. Figure 18B.2 compares overhead cost as a percent of revenues, net operating margins, and unsecured debt spreads for selected firms. While many other metrics are possible, these three go to the core of the scale economies I suggested in "The Forces Changing Real Estate Forever".

FIGURE 18B.2 REIT Snapshot

Year-End (as indicated)								Year-End 2001				
Company	Ticker	Year	SF or Units	# of Properties	G&A Revenue	NOI Revenue	Unsec Debt Spread	SF or Units	# of Properties	G&A Revenue	NOI Revenue	Unsec Debt Spread
Boston Properties	BXP	1997	18,177,660	92	4.29%	63.2%	LIBOR + 125	40,700,000	147	3.71%	66.1%	Euro + 105-170 bps or Prime + 75 bps
Carr America Realty	CRE	1996 (a)	13,400,000	170	9.14%	68.6%	LIBOR + 90	20,300,000	254	7.67%	70.1%	LIBOR + 70 bps
Equity Office Properties	EOP	1996	32,200,000	90	4.55%	55.9%	LIBOR + 162.5	127,000,000	165	3.50%	64.4%	LIBOR + 60-90 bps
Equity Residential	EQR	1996	67,705	239	2.06%	66.9%	LIBOR + 75	224,801	1,076	1.64%	68.7%	LIBOR + 63 bps.
General Growth Properties	GCP	1996 (a)	59,400,000	76	0.83%	57.0%	LIBOR + 100	135,000,000	163	0.75%	63.6%	LIBOR + 103 bps
SimonProperty Group	SPG	1996	64,700,000	124	3.57%	72.3%	LIBOR + 90	1187,000,000	252	3.16%	77.1%	LIBOR + 65 bps

(a) YE 1996 data, except unsecured debt spread, which is as of YE 1997.
(b) NOI = revenues plus recoveries less property expenses and G&A ~EBITDA.

Each of these companies is substantially larger in 2001 than in 1996, and each company saw its overhead as a percent of revenues decline while net operating margins increased. At a 10 multiple, 1 percent improvement represents $10 million in value per $100 million in revenue. In addition, those firms with unsecured debt instruments saw their spreads narrow where each 100 basis points is worth $10 million per $100 million in debt. In short, at least at a number of major property companies, the scale economies I described appear to be at work. The challenge for these firms is to continue this success in order to maintain and enhance their competitive positions in the marketplace.

Five years ago I argued that consolidation would occur slowly, and would be particularly forceful during bad times. My thesis was simply that when everybody makes money easily, the less efficient make smaller profits but can still survive. It is only as weak markets compress margins that the less efficient are squeezed out. We are on the cusp of the first widespread market weakness since I wrote "The Forces Changing Real Estate Forever". As vacancy rates and concessions have risen rapidly in the face of weakened property market fundamentals, company cash flows are being challenged. Office markets in Silicon Valley, San Francisco, Austin, and suburban Boston will provide tests of my thesis. The hotel market is similarly ripe for consolidation.

I anticipate that the market share of public office companies, driven by consolidation pressures created by weak property markets, will be roughly 11 percent (up from 7.6 percent in 2001) by the end of 2005, while the hotel market share of public companies will rise to nearly 25 percent by the end of 2005 (up from roughly 20 percent in 2001).

DEVELOPMENT

The new model for development remains in transition. After decades of debt-financed development, the last five years have witnessed equity requirements of 25 percent to 50 percent. As noted in "The Forces Changing Real Estate Forever", combining development with stable real estate cash streams is generally a poor financial structure. For example, I believe that the primary reason that U.K. public property companies trade at large discounts to liquidation value is that while the English lease is an extremely low-risk asset, sought after by low-risk investors, most U.K. public property companies use these very low-risk cash flows to fund high-risk developments. As a result, investors are unable to access their low-risk cash streams due to the mismatch of low-risk cash stream and high-risk development. Imagine the extreme case of a development company that utilized the proceeds from a government bond fund to fund speculative developments. Certainly such a fund would trade at a substantial discount to its liquidation value, as its logical clientele—low-risk investors—would avoid it due to the development risk.

Another major challenge for public real estate companies with substantial development activities is the need to shut down the overhead burden of development when excess supply market conditions exist. All too often, these groups become self-perpetuating overhead burdens. Firms that fail to perform this shut-down will be severely punished by capital markets.

The best model for development would be for public real estate companies and private real estate equity firms to provide the bulk of the equity side-by-side with local developers. This structure allows the larger entities to leverage both their tenant base and capital market connections, while utilizing (on an incentivized basis) the entrepreneurial skills of local developers. This structure minimizes the risk for the public companies' cash streams while providing them access to growth via the acquisition of completed developments. However, I now realize that the development of regional malls should generally be done by large public firms, since regional malls cannot be speculatively developed. Given the nationalization of retailers, only a handful of mall companies possess the expertise, credibility, and tenant connections necessary to develop a regional mall. However, in view of the maturity of this product sector, the development of new malls will remain a small part of the operations of large public mall owners.

A major unanswered question is whether a development company can successfully exist as a stand-alone public company. While real estate development offers a higher risk profile than stabilized real estate, it does not provide a massive risk premium, because many people enjoy being developers. As a result, the margins earned on developments may not be large enough to attract large-scale capital into development. For many years this was the case in homebuilding. However, as debt has become less available, homebuilding has been increasingly dominated by the largest companies. Between 1993 and 2001, the market share of the top ten homebuilders doubled from 9.2 percent to 18.4 percent. It is possible that public "pure development" companies will evolve, particularly in the multifamily and warehouse sectors, where a sufficient flow of projects exists to provide the predictable cash streams desired by public investors.

WHERE DO WE GO FROM HERE?

The "forces" of economic rationality are here to stay, and change in the real estate industry is well under way, though in fits and starts. The practices found in other capital-intensive industries will continue to provide the roadmap for the real estate industry. Within five years, a real estate company will rank among the top 50 firms in the United States, and perhaps among the top 100 globally. More operational talent will be attracted into the real estate industry, allowing the largest, most efficient, and most creative owners (public and private) to increase their margins of competitive advantage. While development will remain largely a private activity, it will require ever-greater amounts of equity, thus forcing developers to form alliances with the large equity capital pools controlled by publicly traded firms and real estate private equity funds.

Not every firm will succeed (one need only remember Patriot, Meditrust, Prime, or Security Capital). More firms will get in trouble, and new firms with strategic innovations will appear. Slowly the tyranny of the status quo will erode. This is an exciting time to be in the real estate industry, as change offers opportunity. If you think the last five years have been dramatic, stay tuned for the next decade.

Chapter 19
Corporate Real Estate Decision Making

"Why ever do less than the best you can"?
-Dr. Peter Linneman

After reading through the previous chapters, you may have decided to pursue a career in retail, medicine, or law; anything but real estate. However, you will find that in each of these careers you will still have to deal with real estate issues. For example, if you are a lawyer and the lease on your office is expiring in a month, what do you do? Where should you locate your practice? How much space do you need? Should you buy, build, or lease this space? Thus, every business faces corporate real estate decisions, not just big corporations with specialized staffs.

WHAT TYPE OF SPACE DO I NEED?

One of the key issues that arises is what type of space do you need? If you plan to service mostly family clients, such as a primary care physician, you will probably look for office space in a suburban location near a major medical center. But you might also consider space in a strip center near your home and convenient to your client base. If you work for a food distributor, you will probably look for a warehouse facility that also can be used as office space. This decision process is similar to what you went through when narrowing your list of potential colleges. You start with a list of the locations and properties based on your general knowledge, gather data, and analyze the specifics to find the right fit for you. A broker with knowledge of the space available in the market may be helpful in this process.

Determining retail space needs is particularly tricky, as many retailers are re-evaluating the decision whether to locate in a mall, a strip center, or an open-air town center. This decision has become increasingly difficult as competition and consumer preferences evolve.

WHERE SHOULD I LOCATE?

Another key decision is where to locate. The location decision depends upon the type of property you need. Assume you are in charge of real estate for Wal-Mart, and you have to select a new warehouse. The first factor you must analyze is the customer base that the warehouse will service. Specifically, the warehouse will service current and future Wal-Mart stores in the southeastern Pennsylvania market. You need to make judgments on the extent and timing of store expansions (and shrinkage) in this region. Your goal is to minimize the cost of transporting and storing the merchandise being sent from the warehouse to your stores. These costs include drive times, fuel consumption, labor costs, and rent.

To reduce costs you might combine your warehouse and retail spaces. Is this prudent? There will be two dimensions of your analysis of this alternative. The first is the relative costs of renting more space at the retail location to house the products versus the reduced shipping costs of transporting goods. The second is the cost associated with directly transporting goods from the vendor locations to the warehouse facility versus directly to your retail locations. For example, smaller lot shipments may not qualify for significant quantity discounts that are available if the vendor ships to a centralized warehouse. Your job is to minimize the combined costs and headaches of transportation and storage space, while maintaining a quality retail environment and sufficient inventory.

You will generally select warehouse facilities close to major highway interchanges in order to facilitate transportation both in, and out, of the warehouse. You will need to consider whether to utilize one large warehouse versus multiple smaller locations throughout the area. A single facility reduces the cost and effort dedicated to receiving and shipping goods, but increases the distance to store locations. Hopefully you begin to see the detailed analysis demanded by business location decisions.

Suppose you are responsible for selecting a location for a new Costco store. You will carefully analyze the accessibility of alternative sites to your target customer base. In this case, you will focus on finding a convenient location for the consumers that fit your customer profile. You need to factor in both current and future (i.e. growth) customers into your analysis. Therefore, you may decide to locate in an area that currently has a relatively small, but rapidly growing, population. Frequently you will have to decide between a site that best satisfies existing demand versus a site with greater, but uncertain, future demand. One reason why so many "mom and pop" retailers go bankrupt is because they poorly assess the best location for their store. Often they have a solid retail idea, but select a location that dooms the business.

Of course, you cannot simply locate near your customers and expect success. If you decide to locate in a heavily saturated market and you sell commodity goods, it is unlikely you will survive. Why will customers select you over existing competitors? As a result, you often select a site with less competition, even if it is accessible to a smaller customer base. The point is that both demand and supply are important in location analysis. It is no surprise that large grocery chains and retailers perform sophisticated analyses of current and future demographic trends, as well as study competitive locations when making retail location decisions.

In addition to supply and demand, you must also consider the availability of your required inputs, namely labor and finished goods. You will attempt to locate where you can find enough employees to properly staff your business, as well as a location that is accessible to deliveries from your warehouses. If it is difficult for trucks to reach your store and/or unload products, you will find it difficult and costly doing business. Hindrances to truck traffic, including weight restrictions, narrow streets, school zones, and poorly designed loading docks, must all be factored into your analysis. If trucks are forced to unload in front of your store it can significantly detract from your retail curb appeal and hurt sales. Hence, the attractiveness of retail facilities with rear loading facilities.

What if you are in the market for office space? Once again you must worry about the business coming to you, as well as delivering your services and products to customers. The people coming to your location are mostly your workers and customers visiting your office. If you are evaluating the best location of your law firm, you must make sure that your staff will be able to conveniently get to work. Otherwise you will inconvenience your employees, which over the long term will make it difficult for you to attract and retain the best talent. This becomes a significant problem in a strong labor market, when employees are more selective about where to work. Remember that a strong economy is the worst time to lose staff, as most service firms make their best profits in a strong environment, and replacing personnel is most difficult in such times.

The same is true for those customers that may travel to your office for meetings. If you are a service company, you are in the business of catering to clients, a mission that becomes infinitely more difficult if clients refuse to visit because they hate to come to your office due to location, security, traffic, poor HVAC, or other design concerns.

Another major consideration is access to your client base. For example, a plumber that is close to the residential center has a substantial advantage over competitors. Not only can he reach clients faster, but people will also notice his shop driving home. Proximity to an airport, train station (especially in Europe and Japan), and/or highway is critical if you need to travel long distances to your customers.

A key factor that often dictates office location, particularly for headquarter decisions, is CEO ego. It may be more profitable to locate in a B quality building in the suburbs, but the CEO wants a grand building with a granite lobby in the premier office district to boost their ego. While this does not always happen, it is reflective of the real world. In contrast, with the exception of shared office/warehouse facilities, ego rarely plays a role in the warehouse location selection decision. Executives frequently justify their office "ego-decisions" by saying a quality structure shows corporate quality and attracts clients. While it is true that quality space helps attract clients, many ego-driven executives go overboard.

You will also find countless studies of the optimal location for a corporate headquarters done by many firms that ultimately conclude that the ideal business location is about a mile from the CEO's residence. What a coincidence! Executives frequently act in their best interests, and often dictate location decisions that make their life convenient at the expense of the firm. Retail properties do not suffer from this problem as seriously, as they are generally driven by fundamental analysis, with the exception of mom and pop stores, who often select near-by locations simply because they do not know better.

HOW MUCH SPACE DO I NEED?

Simple calculations based on "typical" square footage used per employee will not dictate the amount of space you require. Space design and utilization are also significant factors in this process. For instance, the size of seats in sports stadiums continues to decrease (even as customer bottoms increase), while the number of seats increases. As demand for tickets increases, owners want to fit as many people in the stadium as possible. The total usable square footage of a building depends on the ability of architects and designers to maximize the number of seats within the space. So too with all space.

Design is particularly important with respect to the loss factor. The existence of load bearing columns, ducts, wiring, as well as the number and location of stairwells and elevators dictate how much usable space you will have for a given amount of gross space. The greater the loss factor, the more gross space you will need. Extravagant headquarters generally have a large loss factors. These large loss factors reflect features like large atrium lobbies, quirky angles, and round façades (it is very difficult to effectively utilize round or triangular structures).

Cost is also a factor in the space decision. In New York, there is an abundance of young workers in cubicles, effectively working in the hallway. This is because space is so expensive that employers attempt to cram as many people as possible in a given space. But in places where space is cheap, like suburban Kansas, most workers have offices, rather than cubicles. Design regulations will also impact space usage. For example, German law requires that all workers have access to direct sunlight (even though the sun rarely shines). This makes the use of interior cubicle space basically impossible.

The market will partially dictate how much space you require. For instance, when there are numerous vacancies, and market rents and lease terms are soft, landlords seek to mitigate tenant losses. As a tenant, you can exploit such conditions by stocking up on "discounted" space, assuming you have the financial ability to carry the space until you grow into it. By leasing more space in order to house future expansion you can both capitalize on the cheap rents and provide better quality space for your employees. As the market improves, demand for space generally outpaces the economic recovery, as firms actively lease before a full market recovery takes hold.

Tenants also use weak markets to move up to higher quality space, upgrading the quality of their space while the rents are low. Such quality shifts are common in office markets where tenants move from a building with slow elevators, poor HVAC, and other problems to a newer building with higher quality amenities. Warehouse upgrades consist primarily of moving closer to a major highway interchange with better clear heights.

Dramatic quality shifts for hotels can occur in a weak market environment. For example, Friday and Saturday nights are generally the weakest nights for urban hotels due to the lack of business customers. As they cut room rates in the face of a weak economic and tourism market, some urban hotels see stronger demand from high school and college students who can now afford to take their "dates" to these newly affordable, classier digs. This type of quality shift can drastically damage your profitability over the long run, as hotel customers are sensitive to the clientele, and if regular patrons notice an abundance of wild college and high school students, you can expect a rapid decline in property reputation and reduced high-end demand. Similar shifts can occur with respect to families with children shifting up into quality hotels.

The same quality shift dynamics take place at residential properties. Landlords generally prefer mature, reliable, upscale tenants. However, as rents decline in a soft market, a younger, noisier, and far more destructive tenant base can afford the property. Landlords often rent to these tenants in order to mitigate the reduction in demand from preferred customers, but an image erosion for the property can occur as the tenant mix changes. This can seriously impair the long term value of the property.

OWN VS. LEASE

Having determined what type of space you want, how much space you want, and where you want to locate, you need to determine whether to lease or buy. Many users of real estate do a miserable job evaluating the own versus lease decision, performing a fundamentally faulty analysis.

FAULTY OWN VERSUS RENT MODEL

Assume a company is interested in finding a suitable headquarters in Philadelphia. If they decide to purchase the $100 million building they are interested in occupying, it will require $40 million in equity, with the remainder financed via a non-amortizing $60 million non-recourse mortgage, which carries a 6% interest rate. This means that the company will pay $3.6 million per year in interest payments in addition to the costs of operating the building. If the company purchases the property they may engage a real estate firm to manage the property. Alternatively, the company may use in-house staff to manage the property. In either case, assume that the operation of the property costs $2 million a year.

Assuming the company is a taxable entity, they can use the mortgage interest payments as a tax shield. Assuming a 36.5% corporate tax rate, this means they will avoid $1.31 million in taxes each year ($3.6 million * 36.5%). The company can also use the property's depreciation as a tax shield. Assuming 80% of the $100 million is attributed to non-land for tax purposes, and that the combination of structure and improvements give an average depreciable life of 20 years for the non-land allocation, the company takes $4 million in depreciation a year (($100 million * 80%)/20) for 20 years, resulting in $1.4 million in annual expected tax savings ($4 million * 36.5%).

Summing the expected cash inflows and outflows as displayed in Figure 19.1, they find that in year 1 they expect a net payment of $42.89 million ($40 million equity investment + $3.6 million in interest + $2 million in operating expense - $1.31 million in tax savings from interest shield - $1.4 million in tax savings from depreciation shield). Performing this calculation for the second year results in a net payment of $2.89 million ($3.6 million in interest + $2 million in operating expense - $1.31 million in tax savings from interest - $1.4 million in tax savings from depreciation). If the company holds the property for 10 years, and ignoring inflation in operating costs, they estimate the same net outlay for each of the remaining 10 years.

FIGURE 19.1

Linneman Associates Headquarters					
	Year 1	Year 2	Year 3	...	Year 10
Total	($40 MM)				
Interest	($3.6 MM)	($3.6 MM)	($3.6 MM)	...	($3.6 MM)
Operating Expense	($2 MM)	($2 MM)	($2 MM)	...	($2 MM)
Interest Tax Shield	$1.31 MM	$1.31 MM	$1.31 MM	...	$1.31 MM
Depreciation Tax Shield	$1.4 MM	$1.4 MM	$1.4 MM	...	$1.4 MM
Total	($42.89 MM)	($2.89 MM)	($2.89 MM)	...	($2.89 MM)

The company also assumes that they can profitably sell the building at the end of the 10th year. Users almost always assume that the building will be sold for a profit, as no one ever loses money on a pro forma sale! Assuming a sale for $130 million (2.7% rate of annual appreciation), minus $3 million in selling fees, and $60 million in debt repayment, the net sales proceeds are $67 million. Since they are a taxable entity, the company calculates an expected accumulated depreciation and capital gains tax payment of $14.5 million ($4 million in depreciation *10 years * 25% accumulated depreciation tax rate, plus $30 million in actual capital gains * 15% capital gain tax rate), which results in a net cash from proceeds of $52.5 million, as summarized in Figure 19.2.

FIGURE 19.2

Linneman Associates Headquarters	
	Year 10 Sale
Sale Revenue	$130 MM
Fees	($3 MM)
Debt Repayment	($60 MM)
Accumulated Depreciation Tax	($10 MM)
Capital Gains	($4.5 MM)
Total	$52.5 MM

The company then calculates the NPV of owning the building using a 10% discount rate, yielding an NPV of -$33.88 million, (see Figure 19.3).

FIGURE 19.3

Linneman Associates Headquarters					
	Year 1	Year 2	Year 3	...	Year 10
Cash Flow	($42.89 MM)	($2.89 MM)	($2.89 MM)		($2.89 MM)
Cash Flow from Sale	$0 MM	$0 MM	$0 MM		$52.5 MM
Net Cash Flow	($42.89 MM)	($2.89 MM)	($2.89 MM)		$49.61 MM
NPV	($33.88 MM)				

Alternatively, they calculate the NPV for the rental option, assuming that a landlord rents the building at a rent that provides an 8% yield on the $100 million building, where the landlord has an 80% operating profit margin. Therefore, the annual rent is $10 million per year, with $2 million in operating costs (the same as for the user) to generate an $8 million net operating income ($10 million - $2 million) on the $100 million building. Ignoring inflation in operating costs, their rent is set at $10 million per year for the 10 years they plan to stay in the space. The estimated NPV for this rental stream over the ten years of occupancy, using a 10% discount rate, indicates a -$61.45 million NPV.

FIGURE 19.4

Linneman Associates Headquarters					
	Year 1	Year 2	Year 3	...	Year 10
Rent Payment	($10 MM)	($10 MM)	($10 MM)		($10 MM)
NPV	($61.45 MM)				

At this point all too many users say, "This is a no brainer"! Why rent at the cost of a negative $61.45 million NPV, when buying yields only a negative $33.88 million NPV? This faulty analysis is the basis for many corporations owning instead of renting.

WHAT'S THE PROBLEM?

So what's wrong with this analysis? Quite simply, enough things to almost fill a chapter in a text book. Most importantly the user did not take into consideration the opportunity cost of tying up $40 million of their equity and $60 million in borrowing capacity in a building for 10 years. The company could have used this $40 million, and borrowed an additional $60 million, to invest in their core business, rather than real estate. In the analysis above, equity is treated as free! Is it surprising that the buy option results in a massively better NPV if ownership is given a $40 million equity subsidy? But you cannot legitimately compare an investment with free capital and costs (the purchase option), with one of only costs (the rental option). You must either remove the investment aspect of the purchase option, or credit the rent option for the return realized on the equity which is utilized in core operations.

Another serious analytical error is that the ownership analysis assumes property value appreciates by 30% over 10 years, while the rental analysis implicitly assumes little or no value increase if the building is owned by a landlord (same rental income in year 10 as in year 1). Specifically, for the property value to increase by 30% one would expect rental rates would be substantially higher in the 10th year. Also, the analysis assumed the user and the landlord have the same property operating costs, even though the landlord is a real estate specialist. Taken together, these errors render the analysis hopelessly flawed, though widely employed.

CORRECTED OWN VERSUS RENT MODEL

Intuitively you should generally expect that the expected NPV for renting is better (i.e., less negative) than the own option. After all, the expected property appreciation is roughly the same irrespective of who owns the asset. Also, the user is not in the real estate business and will tend to have higher operating costs than a landlord. Also, the user should be able to generate higher expected returns from their core business operations than real estate. If not, maybe they should switch businesses! A correct analysis will incorporate this higher expected return on equity in the core business. What about the depreciation and interest deductions advantages of ownership? The landlord takes advantage of the same deductions, and if markets are highly competitive they will be forced to pass these savings along to tenants in the form of lower rents.

Returning to our example, assume that the annual opportunity cost of capital is 12% in the firm's core business. Therefore, $12 million per year in positive inflows is added to the rental option (the $100 million in retained capital investment capacity *12%) minus the 36.5% corporate tax paid on these expected profits. In addition, one must credit the tax shields they receive on the interest payments on the $60 million borrowed for the core investment. In addition, they receive a depreciation tax shield from the $100 million invested in their core business. If these core investments have a 10-year depreciable life, it generates $3.65 million in depreciation tax shield. The company will also realize a gain in the value of the investment in the core operations after 10 years. In this case, they expect to sell the business in year 10 at $53.75 million (3% expected annual appreciation). These changes to the original analysis are itemized in Figure 19.5.

FIGURE 19.5

Linneman Associates Headquarters					
	Year 1	Year 2	Year 3	...	Year 10
Investment in Operations	($40.00 MM)				
Rent Payment	($10.00 MM)	($10.00 MM)	($10.00 MM)	...	($10.00 MM)
Interest Payment	($3.60 MM)	($3.60 MM)	($3.60 MM)	...	($3.60 MM)
Interest Tax Shield	$1.31 MM	$1.31 MM	$1.31 MM	...	$1.31 MM
Depreciation Tax Shield	$3.65 MM	$3.65 MM	$3.65 MM	...	$3.65 MM
CF from Normal Operations	$12.00 MM	$12.00 MM	$12.00 MM	...	$12.00 MM
Tax on CF from Normal Operations	($4.38 MM)	($4.38 MM)	($4.38 MM)	...	($4.38 MM)
Investment in Operations Remaining	$0.00 MM	$0.00 MM	$0.00 MM	...	$53.75 MM
Total	($41.02 MM)	($1.02 MM)	($1.02 MM)	...	$52.73 MM

Since you would expect a real estate specialist to operate the property more efficiently than the user, assume the landlord's operating costs are 10% lower than if the company owns the property. This implies $1.8 million in annual operating expenses (ignoring inflation) ($2 million in operating expenses from rental option * (1-10%)). In the faulty rental analysis the landlord rents the building at a rent that yields an 8 cap. Using this same assumption in this analysis, the landlord can charge a lower initial rent and still achieve an 8 cap given the 10% lower operating costs. After all, the property value ($100 million) has not changed. To reach $8 million in NOI in year one, the landlord need only charge $9.8 million in rent ($9.8 million rent – $1.8 million operating expense = $8 million NOI).

NOI, hence rents, must increase in order to generate a 30% expected appreciation over 10 years. Given an 8 cap, the NOI in year 10 must reach $10.4 million for the property value to appreciate by 30% ($10.4 million / 8% = $130 million). This implies a rent of $12.2 million in year 10 ($12.2 million rent - $1.8 million in operating expenses = $10.4 million NOI). Assuming the rent increases at a constant rate over the 10 years, the company models a 2.46% annual rent increase each year, as shown in Figure 19.6.

With this corrected rental analysis, the company uses a 10% discount rate to calculate the expected net cash flows to determine the expected NPV of the rental option.

FIGURE 19.6

Linneman Associates Headquarters					
	Year 1	Year 2	Year 3	...	Year 10
Investment in Operations	($40.00 MM)				
Rent Payment	($9.80 MM)	($10.04 MM)	($10.29 MM)	...	($12.20 MM)
Interest Payment	($3.60 MM)	($3.60 MM)	($3.60 MM)	...	($3.60 MM)
Interest Tax Shield	$1.31 MM	$1.31 MM	$1.31 MM	...	$1.31 MM
Depreciation Tax Shield	$3.65 MM	$3.65 MM	$3.65 MM	...	$3.65 MM
CF from Normal Operations	$12.00 MM	$12.00 MM	$12.00 MM	...	$12.00 MM
Tax on CF from Normal Operations	($4.38 MM)	($4.38 MM)	($4.38 MM)	...	($4.38 MM)
Investment in Operations Remaining	$0.00 MM	$0.00 MM	$0.00 MM	...	$53.75 MM
Total	($40.82 MM)	($1.06 MM)	($1.31 MM)	...	$50.53 MM
NPV	($26.53 MM)				

As intuitively expected the rental option yields a better (i.e., less negative) NPV than the own option (negative $33.88 million for the own option versus negative $26.53 million for the corrected rent option). Based on both common sense and financial analysis you would expect most, if not all, corporate users would rent rather than own.

Why do so many companies, particularly outside of the US, own their space if it is generally economically better renting? As amazing as it may sound, one reason is that most companies have never done the correct analysis. Bad analysis leads to bad decisions.

On the other hand, some firms truly have free capital for real estate. Universities, for example, often receive capital from alumni who are willing to donate substantially more capital for the naming rights to buildings than for scholarships and academic programs. For example, if alumni are willing to donate $4 million for academic programs and scholarships, but $40 million for a named building, $36 million of the capital for the building is effectively free. Therefore, major universities are extensive owners of their real estate, as there is a large element of free capital. In addition, as tax exempt entities, universities rarely pay local property taxes, which are a major component of real estate operating costs. As a result, they may have lower operating costs than a taxable landlord in spite of their lack of real estate expertise.

Another reason universities tend to own their real estate is that few landlords are comfortable owning an asset with such a specific purpose as laboratories and classrooms. If you lease a building to a university for classrooms, and the university walks away from the lease, considerable reworking of the space will be required. In contrast, it is much easier to release a plain vanilla warehouse, office building, or apartment complex. Therefore, to the extent that the space you require is relatively unique, and your rental market is not highly competitive (meaning that rents will be relatively high), it favors the own option.

In a similar manner, users of complicated space, such as factories or casinos, often own their properties, as they believe that any realistic lease will be too inflexible to effectively deal with the constant tweaking which is essential to keep this space at maximum productivity. For example, in the case of a casino, gaming changes, the restaurant business changes, the entertainment aspects of the business change, the resort dimension changes, and the hotel changes. There is substantial value associated with the operational flexibility of ownership. In the view of most resort and casino operators, the operating flexibility and control benefits of ownership outweigh the apparent savings of the lease option.

A unique aspect of the benefits from control is the secrecy of operations. For instance, Michelin was once the only producer of radial tires in the US and they would not let any outsiders into their production plants. Their concern was understandable, but no landlord would sign a lease that states under no circumstances can they gain access to their property.

SYNTHETIC LEASES

There is a third option for meeting your corporate real estate needs, namely a **synthetic lease**. A synthetic lease allows a company with an economic and tax ownership position to hide the ownership (and the accompanying debt) from shareholders. A synthetic lease is one of a number of contracts that attempts to convince the IRS that you own the real estate, while at the same time satisfying the SEC (hence securities holders) that you rent it. You want to convince the IRS that you own the building so that you can take depreciation write-offs and use interest payments to shield your taxable income. But why would you want to convince the SEC that you do not own the building? Because you do not want put the sizeable low yielding asset (the property) and the corresponding liability (property level debt) on your balance sheet. For example, with the liability on your balance sheet you may violate corporate debt loan covenants. Also, without the asset on your books, your return on book equity and assets are higher. Sounds fishy? It is — but, it is not illegal — yet. Hiding assets and liabilities from your shareholders and bondholders simply leads to inaccurate valuations, and wasteful capital misallocations.

Synthetic leases evolve out of very detailed nuances of SEC and IRS regulations. Tax and accounting specialists have spent countless hours designing ways to satisfy both the SEC and the IRS criteria. One of the simplest techniques amounts to setting up a new special purpose entity (SPE), which is essentially a prophylactic between the corporation and the property. The SPE only exists for this purpose, and property is the only asset owned by the SPE. The SPE is financed with a minimum nominal equity contribution of say 3%, which primarily comes from the parent firm, with the remaining 97% coming from debt, which is secured by the property and also guaranteed by the corporate parent. The SPE uses these funds to purchase the building, with the parent corporation leasing the building from the SPE at a rent equal to the debt service payments and a nominal return on equity.

If structured correctly the corporation is renting the building from an independent company (the SPE). If all goes as planned, the SPE will repatriate dividends to the parent company, and make the scheduled interest payments. As long as you conform to the rules, the IRS allows the parent company to take the depreciation from the building and use the interest payments to shield their taxable income. At the same time the SEC will not require you to record either the SPE's debt or property on the parent's balance sheet as long as the lease is structured in conformity with the rules for an operating lease: the lease cannot transfer ownership; the lease cannot contain an option to purchase the building at a bargain price; the lease is less than 75% of the estimated economic life of the building; and, the present value of lease payments is less than 90% of the fair market value of the building. This will allow the company to effectively hide significant amounts of debt (and loan guarantees) and assets from both shareholders and bondholders, as individually most properties are not large enough to be material for disclosure. In an extreme example, a company with zero debt on their balance sheet could be heavily levered, with thousands of "immaterial" SPE's financed with off-balance sheet debt and corporate guarantees.

HOW LONG SHOULD I LEASE?

Assuming you have decided to lease, for how long should you lease the building? In general, the longer the lease, the better rental deal you will be able to achieve. This is similar to the price of bulk items in the grocery store. Larger quantity items generally cost less per ounce than the same product in a smaller package, as the manufacturer gets an assured sale, saves on packaging, distribution, warehousing and competition, and shares those savings with the consumer. It is no different with real estate. In general, if you sign a 10-year lease you will get a better deal than if you sign 5 two year leases, because the landlord gets assured occupancy and will save on legal costs and accounting costs and will be forced by competition to share those benefits with the tenant. However, by signing a long lease the tenant gives up the operational flexibility of exiting when they no longer need the space. If you know for certain that you will need the space for a long period of time, then you should sign a long term lease. But in a world of frequent mergers and acquisitions, bankruptcies, rapidly changing products, and increased global competition, few tenants know how long they will need their space. An exception is the US government. As a result, the US government generally signs long term leases.

Signing shorter leases provides substantial option value to the tenant, although the value of this option is difficult to accurately value. You must value the expected economic savings from the longer leases versus the expected benefit of increased operating flexibility.

CLOSING THOUGHT

The use of real estate is ubiquitous. You cannot escape its utilization. And the more successful you become in your chosen field of endeavors, the more time you will spend dealing with your real estate needs. Never forget that it is a highly specialized area, and that your expertise is running your business, not developing, owning, and operating real estate. Unless you have no viable choice, keep your scarce capital employed in your core business, and leave real estate operations to professionals.

Chapter 19 Supplement A

A New Look at the Homeownership Decision

Dr. Peter Linneman[1] – Housing Finance Review – Winter 1986

INTRODUCTION

At one time or another we have all either nodded affirmatively or personally stated "that someone in your tax bracket is better-off owning than renting". Our reasoning is usually that since the tax advantages of homeownership rise with one's marginal tax bracket, people above some critical marginal tax rate find it financially advantageous to own rather than to rent their residences. Numerous formalizations of this approach to homeownership exist in both the theoretical and the empirical literature.[2] Since these works either implicitly or explicitly extend the investment models that analyze whether an investor should purchase tax exempt municipal bonds or invest in other assets,[3] this paper will refer to this traditional approach to the homeownership decision as the municipal bond analogy of homeownership (MBAH).

The wide and almost unquestioned acceptance of the MBAH is in stark contrast to the absence of empirical support for this model. For example, the MBAH implies that the decision maker's tax bracket is a sufficient statistic for analyzing the homeownership decision. However, every empirical study of homeownership has found that variables such as family size, age of the head, and race are also significant determinants of homeownership even when income, the relative price of owning, or the marginal tax bracket are held constant. Further, many high tax bracket families rent (for example, in the Central Park area of New York City and the Gold Coast area of Chicago) while many families in low tax brackets own (particularly in smaller cities and less dense areas of major cities). These obvious failings of the MBAH have generally been dismissed as reflecting either peculiar circumstances of decision makers or intrinsic preferences for homeownership. Thus, in spite of the fact that the MBAH is at odds with the real world, economists continue to accept and "fine-tune" this model of homeownership. Swan (1984) provides a recent example of this line of analysis.

This paper builds upon previous work by this author (Linneman, 1985) and develops an equilibrium model of the homeownership decision which is consistent with observed homeownership patterns without reliance upon "peculiar circumstances" or intrinsic homeownership preferences. A simple general model of homeownership is developed which yields the MBAH equilibrium as an extreme special case. The special case of the MBAH is derived in Section III. An alternative equilibrium model of homeownership is developed in Section IV in which all families are indifferent with respect to whether they own or rent. This extreme special case is called the efficient market proposition of homeownership (EMP). An empirical analysis of the homeownership patterns in Philadelphia in 1975 and 1978 is presented in Section V. Using the Philadelphia SMSA Annual Housing Surveys (AHS) for those years, tests of the empirical relevance of both the MBAH and EMP are conducted. It is found that both of these extreme special cases of the more general model of homeownership are dearly rejected. This is the case in both years and with respect to the ownership decisions of all observations as well as the homeownership decisions of those households that have moved in the previous 12 months. Further, a household's marginal tax bracket in general has little impact on the homeownership decision when other relevant economic variables are held constant. The paper concludes with a brief summary.

[1] Originally appeared in *Housing Finance Review* 5.3 (Winter 1986). Valuable comments on previous drafts were received from Jack Guttentag, Joseph Gyourko, and participants of the Political Economy Workshop at the University of Pennsylvania. Excellent research assistance on this project was provided by Alan Mathios.

[2] See, for example, Aaron (1970), Diamond (1980), Eilbott and Binkowski (1985), Hendershott and Shilling (1982), Henderson and Ioannides (1983), Laidler (1969), Li (1977), Rosen (1979), Rosen and Rosen (1980), Roulac (1974), Struyk (1976), and White and White (1977).

[3] See, for example, Miller (1977).

GENERAL HOMEOWNERSHIP MODEL

In order to analyze the implications of a pure financial decision model of homeownership, it is assumed that consumers derive no direct utility from homeownership. Following urban economics, each consumer is assumed to choose their optimal housing quality (Q^*) as the result of a standard constrained utility maximization process. If the present value of the full cost of owning the consumer's optimal quality residence (F^O) is less than the present value of the full cost of renting (F^R) this residence, the consumer will choose to own (OWN = YES),

$$OWN_i = YES \text{ if } F_i^O \leq F_i^R, \quad (1)$$

where *i* indexes consumers. Thus, in order to understand the financial determinants of homeownership, one must analyze the determinants of the present values of these full tenancy costs.

The present value full cost of renting one's residence over the consumer's planning horizon is equal to the discounted stream of rental payments. Linneman (1985) demonstrates that in a competitive housing market the rental payment for a unit is a function of landlord production costs (C^L), property value appreciation (net of capital gain taxes) anticipated by the landlord (G^L), the opportunity cost of the landlord's equity in the property (D^L), the tax benefits of depreciation allowances given to landlords (T^L), and the production efficiency of landlords (α^L).[4] Rather than deriving these relationships for specific solutions, this section simply expresses the model in general functional form. Precise functional ownership probability relationships are easily derived if one imposes specific functional forms on the components of this model. The interested reader should consult Linneman (1985) for an example of such a solution.

In a competitive equilibrium as the costs of producing and maintaining a unit rise, other things constant, so too must the rental payments for the unit. This, of course, is a primary reason why higher quality residences command higher rents. Similarly, the greater is the opportunity cost of the landlord's equity investment, the higher rents will have to be in order to allow competitive rates of return to be earned by landlords. However, the expectation of capital gains on the property will, other things constant, reduce competitive rents. This is because higher levels of anticipated appreciation mean that more of the landlord's competitive rate of return will be realized through capital gains and, therefore, less profit will be obtained through operating profits. These rental savings associated with anticipated appreciation on the part of landlords indicate that renters in competitive housing markets effectively reap the benefits of anticipated property appreciation as these reduced rental payments are translated by renters into investments in other assets. The exact trade-off between rents and anticipated appreciation depends upon tax rates, the discount rate (r), the tax treatment of capital gains relative to operating profits, and the landlord's planning horizon (N^L_i).

Landlords are allowed to lower their federal tax burdens by deductions for the noncash item called depreciation. These deductions generally do not reflect economic depreciation patterns. In fact, to the extent that economic depreciation is forestalled by deductible cash outlays (such as painting, repairs, and janitorial maintenance), the allowed deduction for depreciation is a pure subsidy to landlords. The greater the depreciation deductions allowed to landlords, the lower will be competitive rents. Since the value of the property reflecting land is not deductible, other things constant, competitive rents will be positively related to the proportion of property value, which is (legally) attributable to land. The value of these deductions is also a function of the landlord's tax bracket.

Finally, the greater is the extent of landlord production efficiency, the lower will be competitive rents. Thus, the present value of the full cost of renting a unit of quality Q^*_i for the *i* th consumer can be summarized as

[4] The term "production efficiency of landlords" is used to refer to the efficiency with which a landlord conducts his or her operation. It is not meant to refer to the efficiency in the physical construction of the unit. Similarly, the phrase "production efficiency of owners" refers to the homeowner's efficiency in providing landlord services (rather than the physical construction of the unit) to himself or herself.

$$F_i^L = F^L(C^L, G^L, D^L, T^L, \alpha^L, r, N^O; Q_i^*) \qquad (2)$$

where N^O_i is the i th consumer's planning horizon and the cost components are for quality market Q^*_i.[5]

The full cost of homeownership is a function of: self-production costs (C^O), property value appreciation (net of capital gain taxes) anticipated by the owner (G^O), the opportunity cost of the owner's equity (primarily the down payment) in the property (D^O), the tax benefits derived from ownership (T^O), the production efficiency of owners (α^O), and the closing costs of purchasing and ultimately selling one's residence (L^O).[6] As expected, the full costs of homeownership rise with the self-production costs, the opportunity costs of the owner equity, and the closing costs of homeownership. The full cost of homeownership is negatively related to the tax benefits of homeownership, the degree of homeowner production efficiency, and expected property appreciation.

The tax advantages of homeownership derive from the fact that owners are allowed to deduct mortgage interest and property tax payments from their federal taxes, and they are not required to pay taxes on their imputed rental income. This means that homeowners receive a tax benefit equal to their marginal tax bracket (t) times the sum of mortgage interest and property tax payments (M). Other things equal, these benefits grow with one's marginal tax bracket. Unlike landlords, homeowners are not allowed any depreciation deductions.

The extent to which anticipated property appreciation reduces the full costs of homeownership depends upon the discount rate, tax treatment of capital gains, the consumer's marginal tax bracket, and the consumer's planning horizon.

The large closing costs associated with homeownership represent a substantial deterrent to homeownership. This is particularly true for consumers with relatively short planning horizons (expected tenancy durations). For example, if the sale of one's residence is not anticipated for 30 years, the present value of the closing costs of that sale are quite small relative to a consumer who expects to move from his residence in 2 years. In sum, the present value of the full cost of owning a unit of quality Q^*_i for the i th consumer can be expressed as

$$F_i^O = F^O(C_i^O, G_i^O, D_i^O, t_i M_i, \alpha_i^O, r, N_i^O, L_i^O; Q_i^*) \qquad (3)$$

The general model of homeownership is obtained by substituting Equations (2) and (3) into Equation (1),

$$OWN_i = \text{YES if}$$
$$F^O(C_i^O, G_i^O, D_i^O, t_i M_i, \alpha_i^O, r, N_i^O, L_i^O; Q_i^*) \leq F^L(C^L, G^L, D^L, T^L, \alpha^L, r, N^O; Q_i^*) \qquad (4)$$

Note that in this general model both the full costs of homeownership and renting vary for a number of reasons including variations across quality submarkets and consumers in: closing costs, production efficiencies, expected tenancy durations, marginal tax brackets, and the landlord depreciation benefits. It is noteworthy that, other things constant, several dimensions of costs tend to neutralize one another in Equation (4) since they are experienced by both landlords and homeowners. Included in this category are: the production costs of housing (net of the homeownership tax benefit on mortgage interest and property tax payments), the opportunity cost of equity in the property, and anticipated property appreciation.[7] Viewed in this light, the financial viability of homeownership for any given housing quality primarily depends upon: 1) the tax benefits of homeownership associated with mortgage interest and property tax payments relative to the value of the depreciation allowances

[5] The consumer's planning horizon has no direct impact on competitive rents but rather reflects the period over which the stream of rental payments are discounted. Both F^L_i and F^O_i must be discounted over the same planning horizon for any consumer.

[6] See Linneman (1985) for a more precise derivation of the full cost of homeownership.

[7] The exact amount of offsetting for any of these factors depends upon the discount rate, the expected tenancy duration, the nature of production efficiencies, the tax codes, and the nature of alternative investment opportunities. These relationships are explored in Linneman (1985).

given landlords; 2) the burden of the closing costs associated with homeownership; and 3) the differential production efficiency of landlords (α^L) relative to homeowners (α^O).

The tax advantages of homeownership relative to the tax advantages obtained by landlords via depreciation depend upon four factors. First, since the value of homeowner deductions rises with the homeowner's marginal tax rate, the advantages of homeownership tend to rise with the homeowner's marginal tax bracket. Also homeownership benefits increase as mortgage interest rates and property tax rates rise as these increase the value of homeowner deductions. A third consideration is the proportion of the property's valuation that is attributable to land. Since landlords receive no depreciation benefits for land, homeownership tax advantages will be relatively high for housing qualities that are land intensive per dollar of value. A final factor is the extent to which tax laws allow landlords to take early and large depreciation deductions. Large and early depreciation allowances reduce the relative tax advantages of homeownership.

Taken together these relative tax considerations provide several important qualitative insights about homeownership patterns. For example, the rises in homeownership rates through the 1970s (often accomplished through condominium conversions) were caused by a combination of the rising marginal tax rates (both legislated and "bracket creep" induced), rising property taxes, inflation induced increases in mortgage interest payments, and the increasing importance of land in housing demand, that is, increased suburbanization. These homeownership trends have been stopped and even reversed in the 1980s as the result of the lower mortgage interest payments brought about by reduced inflation, the lower property tax payments brought on by "taxpayer revolts" in many communities, the significant reductions in marginal tax rates, the very liberalized landlord depreciation allowances that have been introduced, and the renewed desirability of many dense areas in central cities that has resulted from increased fuel costs and reduced family sizes.

These tax trade-offs also help explain why, contrary to the MBAH, not all relatively high tax bracket consumers own and not all relatively low tax bracket consumers rent. Specifically, high tax bracket consumers who desire land intensive housing (for example, in distant suburbs) will tend to find owning relatively more attractive than their equally high tax bracket counterparts who desire (perhaps because of age and family size considerations) to reside in denser areas (for example, the Central Park area of New York) because of the greater value of the depreciation allowances given to landlords in the non-land-intensive locations. Similarly, relatively low tax bracket families residing in more land intensive housing (for example, rural areas and small towns) will have greater financial incentives to own than their counterparts living in dense areas (for example, core areas of big cities).

The inclusion of the closing costs of homeownership in this model further enriches the model's descriptive power. Since the present value of this homeownership burden grows as expected tenancy duration declines, the model helps explain why relatively high tax bracket consumers with short expected tenancy durations (for example, law firm associates, junior investment bankers, and assistant professors in business schools) rent while relatively low tax bracket consumers with longer expected tenancy periods (for example, full professors in the humanities) choose to own.

Finally, the general model of homeownership developed in this section stresses the importance of the production efficiency of landlords relative to homeowners. If landlords are more efficient providers of any particular housing quality, other things constant, the attractiveness of homeownership declines. As noted in Linneman (1985), differential landlord production efficiency may derive from many sources including superior credit ratings; lower tax assessments due to greater political skills, maintenance, and management cost efficiencies; and the ability of landlords to internalize many "free-rider" problems. The ability of landlords to solve "free-rider" problems by the internalization of externalities will be a particularly significant source of differential landlord production efficiency in multifamily structures and in dense neighborhoods. Partially offsetting these sources of relative landlord production efficiencies is the fact that the landlord and tenant must expend resources to monitor the performance of the other party in fulfilling the terms of the lease. For example, tenants may have to expend resources to make sure that the landlord provides adequate services, while the landlord must expend resources to prevent tenants from "skipping-out" on their rental obligations. Since monitoring lease compliance is costly and these costs can be eliminated by homeownership (that is, vertical integration), homeownership tends to offer a source of relative production efficiency.

The importance of the relative production efficiency in the homeownership decision was first noted by Linneman (1985). This concept helps further explain why many low tax bracket consumers in non dense areas tend to own, while many high tax bracket consumers in denser areas (for example, luxury central city high rise buildings) choose to rent. This is because landlord efficiency gains attributable to solving "free-rider" problems are small for low density residences and large for high density residences. It also helps explain why idiosyncratic residences (for example, large estates and units with structural modifications) are typically owned, since the additional costs associated with monitoring unusual contracts and the absence of scale economies tend to offset landlord production efficiencies.

In sum, the general model of homeownership developed here indicates that the financial dimensions of the homeownership decision may depend on a number of variables and not simply the consumer's marginal tax bracket. In particular, the type of housing the consumer desires to consume and the consumer's expected tenancy duration may also be of considerable importance. Before turning to an empirical examination of the homeownership decision, it is instructive to analyze two extreme special cases of this general model, the MBAH and the EMP. As is often true of polar cases, these extreme special cases provide clear insights into fundamental aspects of the general model. Further, since the MBAH is the dominant model in the literature, its implications deserve special attention.

THE MUNICIPAL BOND ANALOGY OF HOMEOWNERSHIP AS A SPECIAL CASE OF THE GENERAL MODEL

Traditional analyses of homeownership yield an equilibrium in which most consumers are not indifferent with respect to their ownership status. These models note that homeownership, like municipal bonds, represents an investment instrument with an after-tax yield that is dependent on the consumer's marginal tax bracket. Further, like municipal bonds; these models assume that the investment risks of homeownership are the same as other investment instruments (via portfolio diversification). These models proceed to argue that the heterogeneous population (with respect to marginal tax brackets) bids for these homogeneous investment instruments (in terms of risk)[8] and arbitrage occurs until the marginal bidder is indifferent between owning and renting.

Since very few consumers will be marginal bidders, most consumers are not indifferent with respect to ownership status in these models. Since this traditional approach to the homeownership decision is analogous to the investment models for municipal bonds, this family of homeownership models is referred to as the MBAH.

Variants of the MBAH have assumed (either implicitly or explicitly) that: 1) all consumers face the same rental cost ($F^L_i = k$ for all i); 2) production efficiencies do not vary across consumers ($\alpha^O_i = 1$ for all i); and, 3) either homeownership closing costs are zero for all consumers ($L^O_i = 0$ for all i) or the expected tenancy duration for all tenants is infinite ($N^O_i = \infty$ for all i). The two conditions in the third assumption are operationally equivalent and work to eliminate the cross-sectional importance of closing costs in the homeownership decision. Solving Equation (4), given these assumptions, for the marginal tax bracket that equates owning and renting costs (t_c) yields the familiar MBAH of homeownership condition that one owns if their marginal tax bracket is greater than or equal to this critical tax bracket and rents otherwise,

$$\text{OWN}_i = \text{YES if } t_i \geq t_c = g(C^O_c, G^O_c, D^O_c, M_c, k),$$

[8] The investment choices of relevance are either to put one's equity in one's residence (homeownership) or an alternative investment pool (renting).

where $i = c$ indicates the consumer who is financially indifferent between owning and renting. Thus, if the MBAH is correct, the consumer's marginal tax bracket will be a sufficient statistic for predicting the ith consumer's homeowner propensity.

The fact that the MBAH is an extreme and restrictive special case is seen in the assumptions underlying this model. First, to assume that all consumers face the same rental quote irrespective of the quality of housing they consume is contrary to price theory. If rents are allowed to vary across consumers, as specified in the general model, the consumer's marginal tax bracket is no longer a sufficient statistic because rents will vary to reflect the factors described in the last section. Further, to assume away the importance of homeownership closing costs simplifies the algebra of the general model but robs the model of rich predictive insights. If these closing costs are not assumed to be zero, the consumer's marginal tax bracket is no longer a sufficient statistic for predicting homeownership propensities. In Section V a strong empirical test of the MBAH is conducted by examining whether a consumer's marginal tax bracket is a sufficient statistic to predict homeownership propensity. In view of the restrictive nature of the MBAH, it is not surprising to find that the data resoundingly reject the MBAH.

EFFICIENT MARKET PROPOSITION AS A SPECIAL CASE OF THE GENERAL MODEL

One of the primary shortcomings of the MBAH is that it assumes that all consumers face the same rental quote. This implicitly requires that all consumers desire the same housing quality. However, both empirical and theoretical studies in urban economics demonstrate that consumers desire to consume different levels of housing quality. Thus, although portfolio diversification considerations may (as is argued for municipal bonds) make the investment risk component of homeownership the same as other assets, contrary to municipal bonds, the consumption dimension of homeownership is not homogeneous. That is, contrary to the case of municipal bonds, the homeownership decision is not accurately described as a population of heterogeneous consumers bidding for homogeneous assets. In fact, studies in urban economics indicate that in equilibrium the housing market tends to be described by a series of housing quality submarkets with each submarket composed of homogeneous consumers bidding for a homogeneous housing quality.

In the extreme, if all consumers desiring a particular optimal housing quality, for example $Q^*_i = 1$, are identical, then by definition all consumers in this housing quality submarket will have the same expected tenancy durations, discount rates, production efficiencies, marginal tax brackets, mortgage interest payments, and the other variables in Equation (3). That is, in this extreme case of perfect sorting into totally homogeneous housing submarkets, the present value of the full cost of owning within the submarket is constant. In this extreme special case, referred to here as the efficient market proposition (EMP), the key determinant of homeownership is whether the present value of competitive rents in this submarket are greater than or less than this constant present value full cost of homeownership. Figures 19A.1 through 19A.3 present three possible outcomes for a particular housing quality submarket under the special case of the EMP. Similar figures apply to any other housing submarket if the EMP is correct.

FIGURE 19A.1 The 100% homeownership in submarket Q*=1

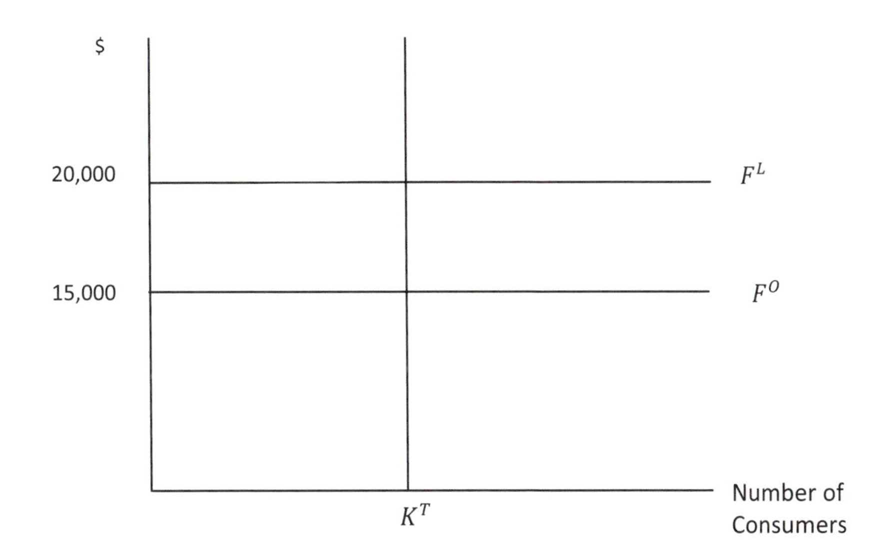

Figure 19A.1 shows one possible supply and demand configuration in submarket Q* = 1 under the EMP. The demand for this quality of housing is (for simplicity) assumed to be inelastic with K^T consumers. Since the present value of the full cost of owning is constant across consumers in the EMP, the supply curve if all consumers own is completely elastic at (by assumption) $15,000. If the present value of rental costs for units of this quality are (by assumption) $20,000, the costs of homeownership are less than the costs of renting and all K^T consumers will find it optimal to self-produce this housing at a present value full cost of $15,000. Alternatively, in Figure 19A.2 the present value of rental costs in this submarket is assumed to be less than the present value full cost of owning. In this case all consumers in this submarket would find it optimal to rent their units at a present value cost of (by assumption) $10,000. In these corner solutions cases, consumers in the submarket either all own or all rent. Hence, knowing the percentage of a random consumer's submarket that owns is a sufficient statistic to predict the individual consumer's homeownership propensity in the case of the EMP. That is, information about the consumer, for example marginal tax bracket or age, only matters to the extent that they cause consumers to choose different housing submarkets. These different submarkets will have different levels of F^L and F^O reflecting differing tax advantages to landlords and homeowners, differential production efficiencies, and differing expected tenancy durations.

FIGURE 19A.2 The 100% rental in submarket Q*=1

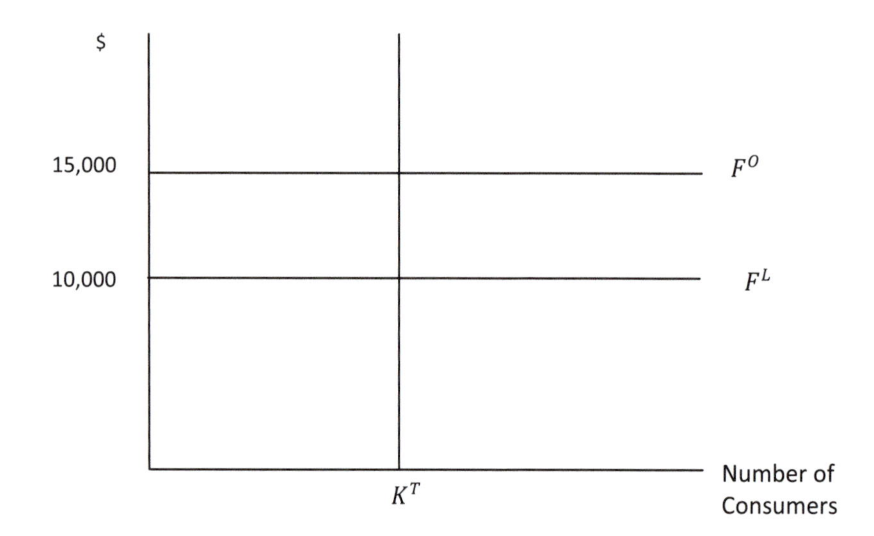

FIGURE 19A.3 An interior homeownership equilibrium in submarket Q*=1

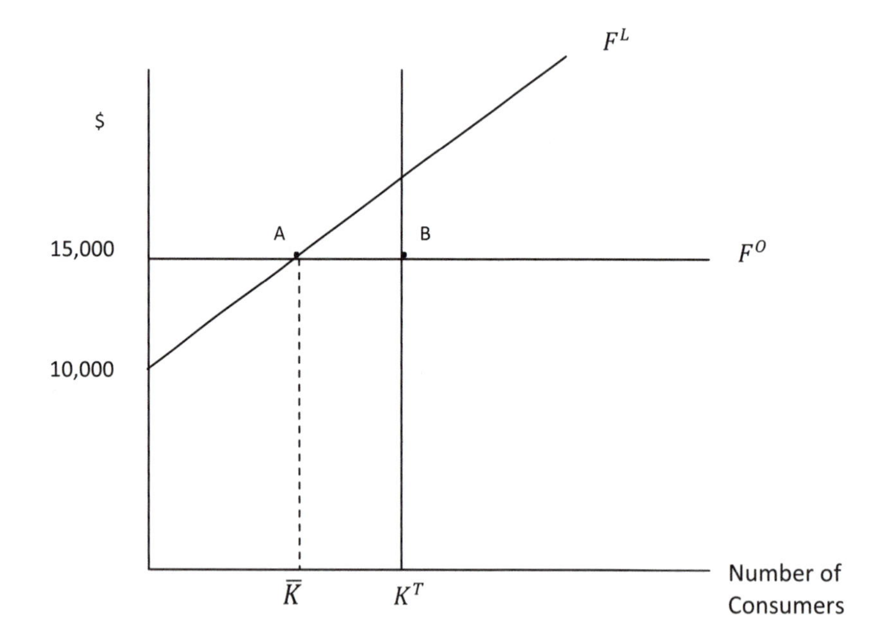

In Figure 19A.3 the present value of the full cost of homeownership is again assumed completely elastic at \$15,000. However, due to variations in landlord conditions in this submarket (for example, differential production efficiencies), the landlord supply function is assumed to be upward sloping. In the case displayed in Figure 19A.3 landlords can supply rental units at sufficiently low costs to compete successfully with homeownership up to K^- units. Beyond that, however, landlords are not sufficiently efficient to compete with self-production by homeowners. The effective supply curve in this submarket is F^L up to point *A*, and F^O thereafter. Supply equals demand (again assumed vertical for simplicity) at point *B*. The equilibrium present value of rents will, therefore, be \$15,000. Thus, in equilibrium all consumers in this quality submarket will pay a present value full cost of \$15,000 whether they own or rent. The K^- of the units will be rented and $K^T - K^-$ will be owned in equilibrium. Since all consumers in this submarket will pay the same present value full cost (including equity effects) whether they own or rent, all consumers in this market will be indifferent between owning and renting in equilibrium. Stated differently, in equilibrium there is no information about the consumer (such as marginal tax bracket or age) that would provide any additional insight about the consumer's homeownership propensity beyond the proportion

$$\left(\frac{K^T - \bar{K}}{K^T}\right)$$

of his or her submarket that is owned. Of course, if the intercept of the F^L schedule exceeds F^O, a corner solution of 100% homeownership results. Similarly, if the demand curve intersects the effective supply curve to the left of K^-, a corner solution with a 100% rental rate results.

The mathematical equilibrium conditions for the EMP are obtained by solving Equation (4) for each quality submarket. Each submarket will have a unique set of values for the variables in the homeownership cost function. If the landlord supply function is upward sloping, at least one of the variables in the rental cost function must vary across landlords. Linneman (1985) more fully analyzes the case where landlord production efficiency is distributed across landlords within a given submarket.

In sum, the distinguishing feature of the extreme special case of the EMP is that market sorting is so complete that all housing submarkets are completely homogeneous with respect to consumer characteristics. In this case the percentage of a consumer's housing submarket that one owns is a sufficient statistic for predicting one's homeownership propensity. The assumptions of this extreme special case are in notable contrast to those underlying the MBAH in that the MBAH assumes a heterogeneous consumer population bids for homogeneous assets, while the EMP assumes that completely homogeneous consumer populations bid for homogeneous assets.

EMPIRICAL ANALYSIS OF HOMEOWNERSHIP

The last two sections developed extreme special cases of the general model of homeownership which was presented in the second section of this paper. As noted, the MBAH implies that the consumer's marginal tax bracket is a sufficient statistic for predicting one's homeownership propensity, while the EMP implies that the homeownership proportion in the consumer's housing quality submarket (% OWN) is a sufficient statistic for predicting one's homeownership propensity. Stated differently, if the MBAH is correct then the consumer's marginal tax bracket should be the only significant regressor in the homeownership regression. Further, the sign of the marginal tax bracket on homeownership should be positive. Similarly, if the EMP is correct the % OWN variable should be the only significant regressor in the homeownership equation, with a positive coefficient equal to approximately infinity.

Of course, neither of these extreme special cases may accurately describe actual homeownership decisions. For example, imperfect sorting across quality submarkets or historical fixities in tenure status will cause the EMP to fail to describe homeownership patterns adequately. Similarly, if the consumers who sort into any given housing submarket are not perfectly homogeneous with respect to marginal tax bracket and expected tenancy duration, the EMP special case will not fully describe the data. For example, residences with a 1-acre lot and four bedrooms may be demanded by both high marginal tax bracket consumers with no children and much lower marginal tax bracket consumers with large families. Finally, any sorting of consumers into separate housing quality submarkets will cause the MBAH to be rejected.

Figure 19A.4 displays the means for the variables used in the empirical analysis. The data are all observations in the Philadelphia SMSA that are included in the 1975 and 1978 AHS and provide usable answers to all variables used in this study. The columns labeled "All Observations" include all such usable observations and the columns headed "Deciders" only include those observations who have lived in their residence less than 1 year. The "Deciders" samples reflect the homeownership decisions of those consumers who explicitly made such a decision in the past year, whereas the "All Observations" sample includes consumers who both explicitly and implicitly (by default of not changing tenure status) made the homeownership decision in the past year.

FIGURE 19A.4 Philadelphia Data Means

	1975 Deciders	1975 All Observations	1978 Deciders	1978 All Observations
Home ownership	0.279	0.704	0.288	0.702
Family income	13,108.2	14,929.1	14,759.8	18,055.1
Predicted duration	10.1	14.7	13.0	17.7
Age of head	33.6	48.8	34.5	49.6
Education	13.9	12.7	14.0	12.9
Black head	0.19	0.19	0.21	0.19
Male head	0.73	0.75	0.68	0.72
Unit in city of Philadelphia	0.42	0.46	0.44	0.46
Detached unit	0.21	0.37	0.20	0.36
Family size (No. of children)	2.6	3.0	2.5	3.0
Predicted net family income (taxable income)	9,739.0	10,921.0	11,311.0	13,035.9
Married	0.55	0.66	0.47	0.61
Tax bracket	0.24	0.25	0.24	0.25
Market owned (%)	0.42	0.70	0.43	0.70
Unit 2 (2 units in structure)	0.118	0.064	0.128	0.066
Unit 24 (3 or 4 units in structure)	0.099	0.041	0.105	0.041
Unit 119 (5 to 11 units in structure)	0.099	0.259	0.076	0.260
Unit 249 (more than 11 units in structure)	0.072	0.028	0.083	0.027
Story 1 (1 to 3 stories in structure)	0.922	0.963		
Story 2 (4 to 6 stories in structure)	0.041	0.016		
Story 3 (7 to 12 stories in structure)	0.024	0.010		
No. of floors in unit			2.61	2.30
1 Bath + 1 toilet	0.075	0.156	0.093	0.183
2 Baths	0.066	0.085	0.065	0.078
1 Bath + half without toilet	0.002	0.003	0.001	0.004
3 or more baths	0.085	0.109	0.072	0.115
No. of rooms (non-bath)	4.75	5.82	4.74	5.84
No. of observations	1,309	11,462	1,215	11,462

Of course, ideally the discounted value of all future expected financial variables should be included in the empirical analysis. However, data limitations restrict the analysis to contemporaneous values of financial variables. The life cycle variables partially capture differences in these expected values. Similarly, a measure of expected property value appreciation would ideally be included in the analysis. However, since there is no reason to believe that cross-sectional variations in these expectations are systematically related to the variables included in the analysis, no obvious bias is induced by the omission of a measure of expected property appreciation.

In order to test the MBAH, a measure of the consumer's expected marginal tax bracket is required. This was obtained by first predicting the consumer's expected family income, adjusting this figure for dependents using the standard deduction for dependents, and then using the Federal tax tables for 1975 and 1978, respectively, to find the consumer's expected marginal tax bracket. Expected family income was obtained by using the predicted family income yielded by the regressions of family income on the set of socioeconomic traits shown in Figure 19A.5 (for all observations). This was done in an attempt to eliminate income variations associated with transitory income; however, this method also unfortunately eliminates cross-sectional income deviations that reflect permanent deviations from the cohort mean income.

Expected tenancy duration is obtained by first estimating the regressions for how long tenants have resided in their current units (for all observations) shown in Figure 19A.6. In the absence of additional information, one expects that tenants are currently halfway through their ultimate tenancy period. Thus, a consumer's expected tenancy is equal to two times the prediction yielded by the regressions in Figure 19A.6.

FIGURE 19A.5 Family Income Predictors

	1975	1978
Constant	-16,975.50	-19,833.00
	(14.86)	(14.83)
Education	-654.00	-701.70
	(5.12)	(4.66)
$Education^2$	66.50	75.20
	(5.10)	(12.63)
Age of head	791.90	937.60
	(33.90)	(24.18)
Age of $head^2$	-7.40	-8.60
	(21.70)	(22.54)
Male head	4,257.90	4,973.00
	(12.44)	(13.56)
Black head	-2,933.60	-3,258.40
	(11.80)	(11.44)
Married	1,907.80	3,296.50
	(5.47)	(8.70)
Family size	2,663.00	2,463.10
	(13.75)	(10.59)
Family $size^2$	-182.40	-121.00
	(8.67)	(4.59)
R^2	0.312	0.340

[2]Absolute t-values are in parentheses

FIGURE 19A.6 Length of Tenancy Duration Predictors

	1975	1978
Constant	-4.696	-5.971
	(3.48)	(3.72)
Predicted family income	1.248E-04	-1.150E-05
	(1.77)	(0.18)
Predicted family income^2	-7.129E-09	-4.659E-09
	(3.94)	(3.62)
Age of head	0.500	0.631
	(9.58)	(10.68)
Age of head^2	-2.167E-03	-3.259E-03
	(4.37)	(6.07)
Black head	-1.974	-2.187
	(7.74)	(8.26)
Male head	0.598	1.795
	(1.60)	(4.51)
Education	0.198	0.279
	(1.61)	(2.08)
Education^2	-0.010	-0.008
	(1.80)	(1.35)
R^2	0.237	0.241

[2]Absolute t-values are in parentheses

In order to develop estimates of the percentage of each quality submarket that is owned, the observations were allocated to housing quality cells. Following Linneman (1985), the observations were allocated to over 100 housing quality cells on the basis of: city versus suburb, the number of bathrooms, whether the unit was detached, the number of stories in the building, the number of rooms, and whether the unit had central air conditioning. Each housing quality cell contained approximately 100 observations.[9] There are approximately 3 to 5 times as many housing quality cells used here than were used in Linneman (1985) and each cell contains approximately 3 times as many observations as in that work. Thus, the housing quality cells utilized in this study are both more internally homogeneous and have smaller sampling errors than those used in Linneman (1985). Thus, the % OWN for a consumer in a detached unit in Philadelphia with 2 bedrooms, 1 bathroom, etc., is equal to the proportion of units in that particular quality cell which are owned.

A logit functional specification is used to estimate the homeownership probability equations. For simplicity, the following tables on the estimated impacts on homeownership report the maximum value of the partial derivatives of homeownership with respect to each variable and the absolute t-values of the estimated logistic regression coefficients.[10]

Figure 19A.7 reports the maximum partial derivatives and absolute t-values for the probability of homeownership for all observations in 1978. Figure 19A.8 displays the same statistics for the 1975 "Deciders"

[9] Complete housing quality cell definitions and cell sizes are available upon request. Fewer than five cells were at corner solutions with respect to homeownership; that is, the cell homeownership percentages were generally greater than zero and less than one.

[10] The logit function specifies the probability that the i th observation owns as

$$P_i = P_r(OWN_i = 1) = \frac{e^{ax_i}}{1-e^{ax_i}}$$

where B is the vector of logistic coefficients for the variable matrix X. The partial derivative of the probability of owning with respect to X_j is given by

$$\frac{\delta P_i}{\delta X_i} = P_i(1-P_i)B_i.$$

This derivative achieves its maximum at P_i = .5. Complete logistic regression results are available upon request.

sample. Figures 19A.9 and 19A.10 report the regression results for all observations and "Deciders", respectively, for 1975.

The first column in each of these tables displays the results of estimating a traditional specification of the homeownership probability as a function of the consumer's socioeconomic characteristics. For the "All Observations" samples, the results are consistent with previous research and indicate that the probability of homeownership rises significantly with age, family size, and expected family income. The probability of homeownership in the "All Observations" samples falls significantly with education and is significantly lower for blacks, male-headed households, and unmarried consumers. Although the same sign patterns are found among "Deciders", only expected family income was significantly related to the homeownership probability in both years. The magnitude of the expected family income impact on the homeownership propensity was approximately the same for both years and sample groups. It is interesting to note that in both 1978 and 1975 black households were significantly less likely to own in the "All Observations" samples, while blacks were more likely to choose ownership among "Deciders" in both years (significantly in 1978). This may reflect that historical racial discrimination with respect to homeownership had been eliminated by the late 1970s.

The second columns in each of these tables display the homeownership propensity as a simple function of the consumer's expected marginal tax bracket and expected tenancy duration. In all four samples the impact of increased expected marginal tax bracket was significantly positive. The magnitude of this impact was approximately the same in both years and for both “All Observations” and “Deciders”. However, contrary to the implication of the MBAH, the expected tenancy duration variable was found to exert a significantly positive impact in all samples except the 1975 "Deciders".

FIGURE 19A.7

Table 4. Maximum Values of Partial Derivatives for Homeownership Probability (1978 Philadelphia SMSA, All Observations)[a]

	(1)	(2)	(3)	(4)	(5)	(6)
Age of head	0.1130			0.0053	-0.0020	0.0020
	(22.50)			(1.62)	(0.62)	(0.57)
Education	-0.0215			-0.0048	-0.0010	0.0018
	(6.62)			(0.95)	(0.20)	(0.33)
Black head	-0.0340			-0.0120	-0.0525	-0.0548
	(2.13)			(0.49)	(2.10)	(2.05)
Male head	-0.1040			0.0568	0.0360	-0.0345
	(4.84)			(1.89)	(1.21)	(1.09)
Family size	0.0288			-0.0438	-0.0368	-0.0480
	(4.60)			(4.49)	(3.87)	(4.92)
Pred. net income (per $1000)	0.0527			0.04373	0.0236	0.0260
	(15.37)			(5.50)	(3.19)	(3.27)
Married	0.1263			0.1200	0.1920	0.1833
	(5.94)			(2.84)	(4.83)	(4.29)
Predicted duration		0.0318	0.0363	0.1930	0.0440	0.0298
		(31.75)	(24.17)	(1.67)	(2.48)	(2.38)
Marginal bracket		2.3523	1.5948	-0.6223	-0.5098	-0.4853
		(27.67)	(13.40)	(1.95)	(1.82)	(1.61)
Market owned (%)			0.0150	0.0145		0.0088
			(60.00)	(58.00)		(17.50)
Unit in Philadelphia					0.1300	0.1000
					(6.88)	(4.51)
1 + 1/2 Baths toilet					0.2288	0.0860
					(8.39)	(3.07)
1 + 1/2 Baths no toilet					0.5500	0.2723
					(2.30)	(1.45)
2 Baths					0.0743	0.0123
					(2.11)	(0.33)
3 Baths					0.1430	0.0575
					(3.20)	(1.27)
No. of other rooms					0.1865	0.1023
					(25.72)	(12.39)
Detached					0.1948	0.1178
					(8.11)	(4.49)
Unit 2					-0.3158	-0.1258
					(11.18)	(4.02)
Unit 24					-0.5183	-0.2153
					(10.21)	(3.93)
Unit 119					-1.1903	-1.3085
					(6.58)	(5.08)
No. of floors in building					-0.2053	-0.0970
					(17.10)	(7.92)
-2 in L	10,733.1	12,343.9	6,777.9	6,467.2	6,535.5	5,830.2
Model Chi-squares	3,162.6	1,591.8	6,886.8	7,197.4	7,400.2	7,524.1
Degrees of freedom	7	2	3	10	20	21

[a]Absolute t-values are below derivatives

FIGURE 19A.8

Table 5. Maximum Values of Partial Derivatives for Homeownership Probability (1978 Philadelphia SMSA, 1978 Deciders)[a]

	(1)	(2)	(3)	(4)	(5)	(6)
Age of head	0.0010			-0.0563	-0.0565	-0.0638
	(0.50)			(3.69)	(3.77)	(3.98)
Education	-0.0213			0.0688	0.0570	0.0690
	(1.77)			(2.48)	(2.11)	(2.40)
Black head	0.1398			0.4035	0.3653	0.4325
	(2.50)			(4.23)	(3.99)	(4.33)
Male head	-0.0420			-0.1130	-0.0798	-0.1468
	(0.60)			(1.17)	(0.86)	(1.45)
Family size	0.0073			0.0123	0.0003	-0.0080
	(0.36)			(0.34)	(0.01)	(0.21)
Pred. net income (per $1000)	0.0625			0.0052	-0.0053	-0.0112
	(4.66)			(0.21)	(0.22)	(0.43)
Married	0.0418			0.2840	0.2905	0.3473
	(0.68)			(2.41)	(2.55)	(2.81)
Predicted duration		0.0093	0.0148	0.2038	0.2013	0.2248
		(2.47)	(2.81)	(3.88)	(3.89)	(4.09)
Marginal bracket		2.095	1.308	-0.7458	-0.6423	-0.1383
		(7.52)	(3.69)	(0.91)	(0.78)	(0.16)
Market owned (%)			0.0125	0.0125		0.0088
			(16.67)	(16.67)		(7.00)
Unit in Philadelphia					0.0900	0.0400
					(1.71)	(0.62)
1 + 1/2 Baths toilet					0.1745	-0.0190
					(2.49)	(0.26)
1 + 1/2 Baths no toilet						
2 Baths					0.0383	-0.0575
					(0.43)	(0.61)
3 Baths					0.1073	0.0150
					(1.13)	(0.15)
No. of other rooms					0.1425	0.0835
					(7.40)	(4.07)
Detached					0.2085	0.1303
					(3.31)	(1.91)
Unit 2					-0.2918	-0.1243
					(3.49)	(1.36)
Unit 24					-0.2543	-0.0053
					(2.22)	(0.04)
Unit 119					-0.7178	-0.5908
					(2.80)	(2.20)
No. of floors in building					-0.1918	-0.0683
					(5.01)	(1.75)
-2 in L	1,223.5	1,369.9	813.1	761.5	822.9	712.6
Model Chi-squares	235.5	89.1	569.4	621.0	636.1	670.0
Degrees of freedom	7	2	3	10	20	21

Absolute t-values are below derivatives[a]

FIGURE 19A.9

Table 6. Maximum Values of Partial Derivatives for Homeownership Probability (1975 Philadelphia SMSA, All Observations)[a]

	(1)	(2)	(3)	(4)	(5)	(6)
Age of head	0.0108			-0.0013	-0.0105	-0.0048
	(21.50)			(0.36)	(0.30)	(1.27)
Education	-0.0270			-0.0023	-0.0015	-0.0013
	(8.31)			(0.41)	(0.30)	(0.23)
Black head	-0.0338			-0.0093	-0.0310	-0.4530
	(2.08)			(0.32)	(1.14)	(1.45)
Male head	-0.0970			0.0098	0.0078	0.0238
	(4.26)			(0.28)	(0.25)	(0.66)
Family size	0.0415			-0.0275	-0.0310	-0.0403
	(6.92)			(3.06)	(3.65)	(4.24)
Pred. net income (per $1000)	0.0576			0.0232	0.0107	0.0172
	(16.94)			(2.57)	(1.31)	(1.84)
Married	0.1405			0.1830	0.2375	0.2045
	(6.53)			(4.36)	(6.33)	(4.78)
Predicted duration		0.0315	0.037	0.0430	0.0728	0.0525
		(25.20)	(21.14)	(3.31)	(5.82)	(3.75)
Marginal bracket		2.5300	1.3173	0.4063	-0.2055	-0.36825
		(24.32)	(8.46)	(1.07)	(0.59)	(0.95)
Market owned (%)			0.0160	0.0155		0.0128
			(64.00)	(62.00)		(25.50)
Unit in Philadelphia					0.1300	0.0900
					(6.95)	(4.04)
1 + 1/2 Baths toilet					0.2153	0.0195
					(7.36)	(0.64)
1 + 1/2 Baths no toilet					0.3948	0.1645
					(1.56)	(0.73)
2 Baths					-0.0228	-0.0718
					(0.70)	(2.16)
3 Baths					0.0928	0.0095
					(2.05)	(0.20)
No. of other rooms					0.2050	0.0768
					(27.33)	(8.77)
Detached					0.3035	0.0743
					(13.05)	(2.75)
Unit 2					-0.3233	0.0258
					(11.65)	(0.75)
Unit 24					-0.5520	-0.0690
					(10.93)	(1.21)
Unit 119					-1.1833	-0.9750
					(6.59)	(5.18)
Story 1					0.4513	-0.0358
					(5.45)	(0.44)
Story 2					-0.3915	-0.2815
					(2.75)	(2.04)
Story 3					-0.5930	-0.4265
					(3.45)	(2.57)
-2 in L	10,887.8	12,552.1	5,900.4	5,682.9	6,702.8	5,466.1
Model Chi-squares	3,004.4	1,340.1	7,319.7	7,537.2	7,189.5	7,755.5
Degrees of freedom	7	2	3	10	22	23

Absolute t-values are below derivatives[a]

FIGURE 19A.10

Table 7. Maximum Values of Partial Derivatives for Homeownership Probability (1975 Philadelphia SMSA, 1975 Deciders)[a]

	(1)	(2)	(3)	(4)	(5)	(6)
Age of head	0.0005			-0.0095	-0.0293	-0.0148
	(0.25)			(0.69)	(2.05)	(0.98)
Education	-0.0128			0.0188	0.0128	0.0145
	(1.11)			(0.82)	(0.59)	(0.59)
Black head	0.0563			0.1810	0.1700	0.1308
	(0.98)			(1.56)	(1.59)	(1.05)
Male head	0.0360			0.1238	0.0353	0.1418
	(0.44)			(1.05)	(0.33)	(1.16)
Family size	0.0110			-0.0513	-0.0700	-0.0755
	(0.56)			(1.64)	(2.33)	(2.25)
Pred. net income (per $1000)	0.0511			-0.0204	0.0207	0.0169
	(3.54)			(0.65)	(0.73)	(0.52)
Married	0.4935			0.4935	0.4935	0.4703
	(0.2678)			(3.82)	(4.17)	(3.59)
Predicted duration		0.0030	0.0063	0.0523	0.1110	0.0648
		(0.75)	(0.96)	(1.11)	(2.30)	(1.27)
Marginal bracket		2.6363	1.0748	1.2820	1.9525	1.1445
		(7.78)	(2.20)	(0.83)	(1.31)	(0.73)
Market owned (%)			0.0155	0.0160		0.0148
			(15.50)	(16.00)		(8.43)
Unit in Philadelphia					0.1300	0.1500
					(2.28)	(2.25)
1 + 1/2 Baths toilet					0.2125	-0.0125
					(2.91)	(0.16)
1 + 1/2 Baths no toilet						
2 Baths					0.1093	0.0575
					(1.37)	(0.69)
3 Baths					0.1898	0.1220
					(2.06)	(1.21)
No. of other rooms					0.1468	0.0400
					(7.53)	(1.82)
Detached					0.2123	-0.0183
					(3.61)	(0.26)
Unit 2					-0.4008	-0.0335
					(4.16)	(0.27)
Unit 24					-0.7650	-0.1433
					(3.00)	(0.53)
Unit 119					-0.8530	-0.7253
					(3.34)	(2.58)
Story 1					0.3620	-0.2015
					(1.31)	(0.69)
Story 2					-0.2288	-0.0473
					(0.61)	(0.13)
Story 3						
-2 in L	1,259.00	1,470.50	740.70	664.89	816.50	633.10
Model Chi-squares	290.50	79.00	739.30	815.10	733.00	846.80
Degrees of freedom	7	2	3	10	22	23

[a]Absolute t-values are in parentheses

Additional evidence of the failure of the MBAH is found in the third and fourth columns of these tables. Specifically, in all four samples the explanatory power of the regressions rose significantly when the proportion owned in the consumer's quality submarket (third columns) and the consumer's socioeconomic characteristics (fourth column) are incorporated in the analysis. That is, the hypothesis that the consumer's expected marginal tax bracket is a sufficient statistic for predicting homeownership propensities is clearly rejected by these data. Further, when socioeconomic characteristics are included with % OWN (fourth columns), the partial derivative of the expected marginal tax bracket is generally negative and not significantly different from zero.

The data also reject the EMP and its perfect housing quality submarket sorting equilibrium. This is because variables other than % OWN provide additional explanatory power with respect to the homeownership propensity. However, the significance and magnitude of this impact (mean partial impacts of approximately 0.01 in all four samples), combined with the notable reductions in the magnitudes and significance of other regressors when this variable is included in the analysis, clearly demonstrate that a great deal of sorting is occurring across housing quality submarkets. Thus, actual homeownership decisions appear to be represented by a more complicated equilibrium than either the MBAH or the EMP.

The final two columns of Figures 19A.7 through 19A.10 incorporate several measures of the housing quality that is consumed. These variables are intended to capture differences in landlord production efficiencies and landlord depreciation allowances, which are part of the general model. Since the AHS does not collect information on the unit's lot size, several variables are used to proxy for the land intensiveness, and hence landlord tax advantage via depreciation, of the residence. These include measures of the number of floors in the structure, the number of units in the structure, and if the unit is a detached residence. These variables also reflect the density of the unit and capture the differential landlord efficiencies associated with internalizing externalities. As predicted by the general model, the homeownership propensity declined significantly as the housing was denser and less land intensive. For example, in Table 4 the probability of homeownership is significantly higher for detached units and units in small buildings (in terms of both number of floors and number of units). Similar qualitative and quantitative results were found in the other samples.

Surprisingly, significantly higher homeownership propensities were generally found in the city of Philadelphia than in the rest of the SMSA (including Camden, NJ). This may reflect the fact that the property tax rates in the city raised the value of the property tax deduction for homeowners. The probability of homeownership also rose in all four samples (generally significantly) with the number of rooms and number of bathrooms in the unit. Since these housing traits are positively correlated with property values, this result may reflect that a substantial portion of the closing costs of homeownership were not related to property value. Alternatively, these variables may be further proxies for the land intensity of the residence or reflect differential production efficiencies related to monitoring leases for more valuable properties.

In sum, the presence of numerous significant variables other than the marginal tax bracket in the complete regressions displayed in Figures 19A.7 through 19A.10, combined with the negative and generally insignificant impact of expected marginal tax bracket when complete control variables are included in the analysis, provides definitive evidence on the failure of the traditional MBAH to describe observed homeownership patterns. Similarly, although the magnitude and significance of the % OWN variable indicates that considerable sorting is occurring with respect to housing quality submarkets, the evidence leads one to reject the perfect sorting equilibrium of the EMP. Instead of either of these simple special cases, the data indicate that a more complex decision process exists.

SUMMARY

This paper developed a simple yet powerful general model of the homeownership decision. This model stresses a number of previously overlooked dimensions of the homeownership calculus including landlord production efficiencies, the depreciation tax advantage of landlords (particularly for non-land-intensive residences), and the consumer's expected tenancy duration. It was also shown that this model was capable of explaining a number of the "puzzles" in homeownership patterns. The traditional model of homeownership, the MBAH, was derived as an extreme special case of the general model. It was shown that the assumptions required for this special case are highly restrictive and inconsistent with both price theory and urban economics. An alternative extreme special case (EMP), which requires perfect market sorting, was also presented. However, both of these extreme special cases were rejected by the data for both 1975 and 1978, and for both all observations and those who had changed their residence in the previous year. A more complex set of factors including the land intensity of the residence, the unit's housing quality, the consumer's expected tenancy duration, and the consumer's socioeconomic characteristics, were identified as the empirical keys to understanding homeownership patterns. In fact, when these other variables are included in the analysis, the impact of the consumer's expected marginal tax bracket on one's homeownership propensity was negative and generally insignificant. The more general approach to the homeownership decision presented in this paper is hopefully the first step in the evolution away from the traditional models of homeownership toward a more relevant analytic approach to this complicated and important question.

References

Aaron, H. J. Dec. 1970. Income taxes and housing. *American Economic Review* 15(5):798-806.

_____ (1978) *Shelter and Subsidiaries: Who Benefits from Federal Housing Policies?* Brookings Institution, Washington, D.C.

Diamond, D. B., Jr. Fall 1980. Taxes, inflation, speculation and the cost of homeownership. *AREUEA Journal* 8(3):281-298.

Diamond, D. B., Jr. and Tolley, G. S. 1977. Housing in the aftermath of tax reform. Mimeo, North Carolina State University.

Eilbott, P. and Binkowski, E. S. May 1985. The determinants of SMSA homeownership rates. *Journal of Urban Economics* 17(3):293-304.

Graves, P. E. and Linneman, P. July 1979. Household migration: Theoretical and empirical results. *Journal of Urban Economics* 6(3):383-404.

Hendershott, P. and Shilling, J. D. 1982. The economics of tenure choice, 19551979. *Research in Real Estate* 1:105-133.

Henderson, J. V. and Ioannides, Y. M. March 1983. A model of housing tenure choice. *American Economic Review* 73(1):98-113.

Kain, J. and Quigley, J. June 1972. Housing market discrimination, homeownership, and savings behavior. *American Economic Review* 62(3):263-277.

Laidler, D. 1969. Income tax incentives for owner-occupied housing. In *The Taxation of Income from Capital.* (A. C. Harberger, and M. J. Bailey, ed.) Washington, D.C.: Brookings Institution, pp. 50-76.

Li, M. M. July 1977. A logit model of homeownership. *Econometrica* 45(5):10811097.

Linneman, P. July 1981. An analysis of the demand for residence site characteristics. *Journal of Urban Economics* 10(1):129-148.

_____ March 1985. An economic analysis of the homeownership decision. *Journal of Urban Economics* 17(2):230-246.

McFadden, D. 1974. Conditional logit analysis of qualitative choice behavior. In *Frontiers in Econometrics. (P.* Zarembka, ed.) New York: Academic Press.

Miller, M. H. May 1977. Debt and taxes. *Journal of Finance* 32(2):261-275.

Rosen, H. S. April 1979. Owner-occupied housing and the federal income tax: Estimates and simulations. *Journal of Urban Economics* 6(2):247-266.

_____ Jan. 1979B. Housing decisions and the U.S. income tax: An econometric analysis. *Journal of Public Economics,* 11(17):1-23.

Rosen, H. S. and Rosen, K. T. Feb. 1980. Federal taxes and homeownership: Evidence from time series. *Journal of Political Economy* 88(1):59-75.

Rosen, S. Jan. 1974. Hedonic prices and implicit markets: Product differentiation under pure competition. *Journal of Political Economy* 82(1):34-55.

Roulac, S. E. July 1974. Economics of the housing investment decision. The *Appraisal Journal* 42(3):358-371.

Shelton, J. O. Feb. 1968. The cost of renting versus owning a home. *Land Economics* 42(3):63-68.

Straszheim, M. 1975. *An Econometric Analysis of the Urban Housing Market.* New York: Columbia University Press.

Struyk, R. J. 1976. *Urban Homeownership.* Lexington, Mass.: Lexington Books.

Summers, L. May 1981. Inflation, the stock market and owner-occupied housing *American Economic Review* 71(2):429-434.

Swan, C. Nov. 1984. A model of rental and owner-occupied housing. *Journal of Urban Economics* 16(3):297-316.

Tiebout, C. 1956. A pure theory of local expenditure. *Journal of Political Economy* 64(5):416-424.

Whinihan, M. J. 1981. *Taxes, Inflation, and the Equilibrium between the Rental Housing Market and the Owner Occupied Housing Market.* Unpublished Ph.D., University of Chicago.

White, M. J. and White, L. J. 1977. The tax subsidy to owner-occupied housing: Who benefits? *Journal of Public Economics* 7(1):111-126.

Chapter 19 Supplement B

Evaluating the Decision to Own Corporate Real Estate

There is no single answer as to whether a company should own or lease its real estate.

Dr. Peter Linneman – Wharton Real Estate Review – Spring 2008

One of the most important capital decisions made by corporations is whether they should own or lease their operating real estate (offices, industrial and warehouse facilities, and retail space). This decision is generally viewed by corporations as a trade-off between the present value of rental payments versus that of the operating costs of owning the real estate, net of expected capital appreciation and the depreciation tax benefits from ownership. The rule of thumb is that only if the present value of future rent is less than the present value of costs of self-ownership of the space (net of depreciation benefits, and expected property appreciation), should the firm lease rather than own. However, as this paper demonstrates, this analysis is fundamentally flawed, leading companies to own far more corporate real estate than is economically justified. This is true in countries such as Germany, where corporate users own as much as 75 percent of their real estate, as well the United States, where roughly 40 percent is owned by corporate users.

The correct model for the own-versus-lease decision must compare the present value of profits the corporation expects if it leases versus the present value of expected profits if it decides to own its real estate. The key insight provided by this corrected approach is that the own-versus-lease decision revolves around the comparison of the lost profits associated with moving corporate capital from core operations to real estate, versus the profits achieved by real estate owners. That is, capital freed up from real estate ownership generates the company's core business rate of return, while rents reflect the rate of return earned by landlords on their real estate capital. Since most companies have higher expected rates of return in their core business than are achievable through real estate ownership, this decision model indicates that the vast majority of corporate real estate should be leased. The intuition of this result is simply that by moving capital from low-yielding real estate to high-yielding core operations, companies increase profits.

WHAT DO COMPANIES DO?

Germany is the third-largest economy in the world but remains relatively inefficient in terms of capital allocation and the management of corporate capital. As a result, some 75 percent of corporate real estate is owned, one of the highest proportions in the developed world. In this decade, some tentative steps have been taken by major German companies to reduce their ownership of corporate real estate. However for the most part these efforts have followed the general pattern, which is to dispose of corporate real estate only when there is no alternative for raising capital, or to find a gimmick to remove the ownership from the company's balance sheet even though ownership remains.

For example, in 2000, Germany's leading retailer, Metro, transferred all of its 357 real estate assets, which included department stores, supermarkets, and do-it-yourself stores, into a joint venture (JV). Metro retained a 49 percent ownership, with a major mortgage bank owning 49.5 percent and a large insurance company owning the remaining 1.5 percent. The transaction was worth €2.7 billion, yielding approximately €1.3 billion in cash for Metro. This transaction resulted in Metro leasing these properties on a long-term basis from the JV and successfully moved the assets from Metro's balance sheet. In 2002 and 2003, Metro attempted to sell the entire JV to third-party investors. But after two failed attempts with buyer consortia, the attempt was abandoned. Metro ultimately repurchased the ownership shares from the insurance company and mortgage bank, resulting in a reconsolidation of the real estate onto Metro's balance sheet, largely purging the cash raised in the original sale.

State-owned Deutsche Bahn also spun off all of its land and development properties into a JV. This transaction raised approximately €1.1 billion for Deutsche Bahn and was structured almost identically to the Metro transaction. Like Metro's transaction, this transaction was also reversed when Deutsche Bahn subsequently repurchased the shares of the JV investors. The real estate assets were subsequently sold in September 2007 to a JV of the German construction company Hochtief and investor Redwood Grove International LP for €1.64 billion.

In 1999, Siemens entered into an agreement transferring eighteen properties to a newly established open-end German real estate fund. Siemens received approximately €750 million for these properties from the fund, and immediately contributed these proceeds to its corporate pension fund to cover outstanding pension liabilities. This resulted in the transfer of the real estate as well as its pension liabilities to off-balance-sheet status. The management of the open-end fund was provided for a fee by a management company wholly owned by Siemens. The open-end fund subsequently acquired additional real estate, bringing in additional shareholders beyond Siemens' pension trust. Recently, Siemens sold the fund management company to a third party. In a similar transaction, Dresdner Bank transferred a portfolio of 300 bank buildings to a newly established open-end real estate fund managed by its wholly owned subsidiary. In this case, shares in the open-end fund were never offered to other investors. In 2005, Dresdner Bank sold this fund to Eurocastle. There have also been a number of smaller transactions where one or more properties were sold to third-party purchasers in sale-lease back transactions. For the most part, however, German corporate owners continue to retain their corporate real estate.

In an effort to identify why German corporations have failed in their real estate monetization efforts and are so predisposed to corporate real estate ownership, one of the authors (Pfirsching) has conducted detailed research documenting that the problems are both technical and strategic in nature. Among key technical problems are: insufficient data quality and poor data management; unprofessional management of the transaction; the seller's lack of knowledge of the value of its assets; and demands by investors for re-trades. The key strategic problems are: lack of seller commitment to the sale; unrealistic valuations, often based on book value; seller changing of the portfolio of assets available for sale during the sale process; and changing space requirements of the seller throughout the sale process. Additional studies have identified other reasons for the failure of sale and monetization efforts of corporate real estate, including: the seller's unwillingness to take book value losses; the seller's desire for complete control over all real estate assets; concern about image and reputation damage to the seller; preservation of social peace in the company; fear of losing key properties and sites to competitors; the lack of off-balance sheet treatment if the seller retains long-term control of the asset; poor data quality; and higher perceived long-term occupancy costs.

As in any business effort, it is essential to have a clear strategy when it comes to disposing of corporate real estate. A lack of such clarity inevitably leads to an inefficient and ineffective process. But in addition, many corporate real estate executives appear to conduct faulty analysis of the benefits of leasing rather than owning their real estate.

THE CORRECT DECISION MODEL

The typical own vs. lease analysis evaluates the differential operating costs associated with owning versus leasing, net of the depreciation tax advantages and expected appreciation on the corporate real estate. But the appropriate approach to evaluating the economic benefits of leasing rather than owning corporate real estate must compare the present value of profits if they own their real estate versus profits if they lease. That is, differential expected profits—not just costs—must drive the analysis.

The present value of the after-tax profits associated with owning corporate real estate (πo) is equal to the present value of after-tax profits from core operations, ignoring the incremental costs of owning corporate real estate costs (Po), minus the present value of the after-tax incremental costs associated with real estate ownership (C), plus the present value of the tax savings associated with the depreciation allowance provided to owners of corporate real estate (D), plus the present value of the expected after-tax appreciation on the corporate real estate (A):

$$\pi o = Po\ (1\text{-}t) - C(1\text{-}t) + D + A,$$

where t is the corporate income tax rate.

The present value of core operations profitability (ignoring incremental real estate ownership costs) is equal to the rate of return (r) it achieves on capital invested in core operations, times the capital it invests in core operations (K), times the company's cash flow valuation multiple (M):

$$Po = r\ K\ M.$$

That is, core cash flow reflects a return of r percent, earned on each of the K dollars at work in the core business, and annual cash flows are translated into value via the firm's cash flow multiple (M).

The corporate owner's present value of incremental real estate costs, should it choose to own, can be expressed as the proportional costs (α) relative to property value (V), times the owner's cash flow multiple, which converts annual operating costs to value:

$$C = \alpha VM.$$

The corporate owner's after-tax present value of profits if it leases (πL) its corporate real estate, and redeploys its real estate capital (V) in core operations, are the after-tax present value difference between core profits (PL) and rental payments (R):

$$\pi L = (1\text{-}t)\ (PL - R).$$

The present value of core profits if the corporation leases (PL) are the core business rate of return (r), times capital employed in core operations (K+V), concerted to value by the corporation's cash flow multiple (M):

$$PL = r\ (K+V)\ M.$$

That is, core profits are higher because an additional V dollars are invested in core operations rather than real estate.

Turning to the present value of rental payments, it is instructive to analyze the present value of the landlord's profits (πLL). Rents must be sufficiently high for the landlord to achieve an expected required rate of return (g) on the capital invested in real estate (V). Landlord profits are equal to the expected rate of return on real estate (g), times the capital invested by the landlord in real estate (V), with this cash stream converted to present value via the real estate's cash flow multiple (N):

$$\pi LL = g\ V\ N.$$

The landlord achieves his profits via the present value of rental payments (R), plus the value of the depreciation tax shield he receives by owning the property (D), plus the present value after-tax capital gains (A), minus real estate operating costs (CL):

$$\pi LL = g\ VN = R + D + A - CL.$$

Note that for any level of landlord profit, rents decline with the tax benefits of depreciation and expected property appreciation. It is also noteworthy that the depreciation (D) and capital gain (A) components are the same irrespective of whether the property is owned by a corporate user or a third party landlord (up to differences in effective tax rates).

The landlord may (or may not) be a more efficient provider of real estate from the perspective of operating costs. For example, a landlord may achieve lower operating costs via scale economies, or detailed operating expertise derived from greater experience or specialization. In addition, the corporate owner may lack knowledge of real estate, and make "rookie" mistakes that are avoided by a professional landlord. Alternatively, the operations of the real estate may be so unique and idiosyncratic that the corporate owner has lower operating costs than a landlord. The presence of operating cost efficiency is easily captured by expressing the present value of the landlord's real estate costs (CL) as lower (higher) than those of the corporate owner by e percent:

$$CL = (1-e)\ C.$$

If e equals zero, landlords and corporate owners have the same operating costs. Alternatively, if e is greater than zero, landlords have lower operating costs by e percent, while if e is less than zero, the property is so idiosyncratic (or landlords so operationally inept) that operating costs are lower if self-provided. For example, if e equals 0.05, the landlord is 5 percent more efficient, resulting in landlord operating costs that are 95 percent of the operating costs of corporate owners.

The presence of landlord operating cost efficiencies ($e>0$) lowers rents for any given landlord rate of return (g), meaning lower landlord operating costs translate into lower rents. That is, to a large degree, the benefits of landlord operating cost efficiencies are passed on to tenants in the form of lower rents.

The nature of the relevant property market will determine the rate of return (g) that the landlord expects to earn given operating costs (CL), depreciation (D), and appreciation (A) benefits. In a highly competitive market, competitive pressures reduce rents, resulting in a lower landlord expected rate of return (g). In contrast, if the property is such that there is little landlord competition, rents will be high, allowing landlords to achieve a higher rate of return (g). This is the case for less developed property and geographic markets, as well as for highly idiosyncratic properties for which landlords require a high rate of return.

Substituting the operating costs expression ($CL = [1-e]\ C$) and rearranging the landlord profit expression ($\pi LL = g\ VN = R+D+A-CL\ 7$), yields the present value of rental payments (R) as:

$$R = g\ VN + (1-e)\ C - D - A.$$

That is, rent is established in the marketplace such that the landlord receives a g percent rate of return on operating costs, after realizing the return benefits of depreciation (D) and property appreciation (A). It may seem like a long process, but we are (after appropriate substitution and manipulation) able to use these relationships to express the differential after-tax present value profitability of leasing versus self-ownership as:

$$\Delta\pi = \pi L - \pi O = (1-t)\ V\ [(r+ \alpha e)M - gN] - t(D+A).$$

While at first blush this expression looks obscure, it is actually very transparent. The first term simply reflects the after-tax value of deploying V dollars of capital in core operations rather than real estate ownership. If the capital is employed in core operations, they generate a rate of return $r+\alpha e$, which is converted to present value by the core operation valuation multiple (M). This core return derives both directly from the g rate of return earned on core capital, plus any additional capital that is freed by arbitraging landlord operating cost efficiencies (or inefficiencies) that exist.

If the same V dollars of capital are invested in corporate real estate, they generate a rate of return of g, which is converted to present value by the real estate's cash flow multiple. Finally, set against this are the tax benefits of depreciation and capital gains achieved by self-ownership times the corporate tax rate. This later effect reflects the fact that since rents are lower due to depreciation (D) and property appreciation (A) benefits, only a fraction (t) of these benefits differentially flow to self ownership.

This differential profit expression indicates that a firm should own if $\Delta\pi>0$, that is, if renting generates greater after-tax present value profitability. Leasing is more profitable in cases when: core returns are high; landlord efficiencies exist; the core cash flow multiple is high; real estate returns are low; real estate's cash flow multiple is low; the corporate tax rate is low; depreciation benefits are low; and capital gains expectations for the real estate are low. Hence, firms with high core returns (financial service and tech firms), that are growing rapidly, while using space in highly competitive markets, where land is a large component of property costs (New York, Tokyo, and London vanilla office space), and in low-inflation environments should rent their real estate. At the other extreme, firms using highly idiosyncratic space in non-competitive markets (e.g., specialized manufacturing facilities in developing countries, and corporate headquarters in small markets), for whom core returns are modest, the firm is slow growing, while real estate appreciation is high, should own their real estate. Of course, each firm and property will have a unique combination of these factors. Further, what is optimal will change over time as capital and real estate markets change.

A key element of the ownership decision is the value arbitrage associated with draining capital from core operations. If core operations generate a relatively low rate of return (as is the case in many old-line businesses), while real estate returns are high (as may be the case for expanding operations into non-competitive property markets), ownership makes economic sense. But since core returns are typically higher than real estate returns, renting tends to be more profitable.

Another way to describe the return arbitrage associated with renting is that taking capital from assets generating 7 percent to 10 percent returns (corporate real estate) and transferring the capital to core operations that generate 10 percent to 15 percent returns generates substantial value gains. Hence, by converting dollars from EBITDA into rent, the firm can create value, as rent sells for a higher multiple than EBITDA for most companies. Of course, this entails designing a lease that allows sufficient operating control for the company to achieve the core return on its capital. If core operating ability is compromised by an imperfect lease, then the core return would reflect this lack of control. However, in markets with sophisticated legal systems this should rarely be a problem, except with the most idiosyncratic operating facilities.

A key insight is that the more competitive the real estate market is, the greater is the incentive to rent, as competition reduces rents. Thus, as more corporate real estate is sold to landlords, a virtuous cycle is created, as if all corporations own their real estate, it is unlikely that a competitive landlord market evolves. But as real estate is sold by corporate real estate owners into the landlord market, a deeper and more competitive rental market evolves, reducing landlord returns, causing lower rents, encouraging less corporate real estate ownership.

More developed capital markets and more competitive property markets, such as those found in major U.S. markets, should have greater corporate leasing due to greater competition and landlord operating cost efficiency. It also suggests that as the markets become more globally integrated, and real estate returns are reduced by greater competition, liquidity, and transparency, the ownership of corporate real estate should decline.

THREE SIMULATIONS

Three simulated cases demonstrate the own vs. lease decision (Figure 19B.1). First, consider the case of a "typical" firm. It has 35 percent corporate tax rate, a 12 percent core return, and a 13 cash flow multiple. The property return is 9 percent, and has a 13 cash flow multiple. Landlords have 10 percent lower operating costs than corporate owners due to the commodity nature of the real estate and depth of the property market, while self provision operating costs are 3 percent of value. The property is expected to appreciate 3 percent annually, and there is a 20 percent effective capital gains tax, 2.5 percent of non-land is depreciable annually, and land accounts for 30 percent of real estate value. For this company/property/market combination, leasing generates a present value greater profit equal to 24 percent of the value of the real estate. That is, every $100 million deployed in corporate real estate destroys $24 million in corporate value.

The second case is a company with a mere 8 percent core return, and a seven times core cash flow multiple. In addition, the company is evaluating a high idiosyncratic piece of real estate for which their operating costs are 10 percent lower than a landlord's operating costs, while these costs are 4 percent annually of real estate value. The property is expected to appreciate at 5 percent annually. Due to a non-competitive real estate market, the landlord's return is 12 percent. All other parameters are the same as in the first case. In this case, the ownership of corporate real estate generates a higher present value profit equal to 93 percent of the value of the real estate. That is, owning $100 million of real estate generates higher present value profits of $93 million. Note that it is difficult to envision a more attractive case for ownership, as there is substantial arbitrage, lower owner operating costs, and substantial property appreciation associated with owning.

FIGURE 19B.1: Simulation parameters

		Case 1 "Typical" situation	Case 2 Loaded towards freehold (e,g, specialized assets)	Case 3 Loaded towards rental (e,g, tech company)
$\Delta\Pi$ =	Differential Rental to Freehold	24%	-93%	41%
r =	pre-tax rate of return on core business	0.120	0.080	0.060
M =	after tax cash flow multiple	13.000	7.000	18.000
t =	effective corporate tax rate	0.350	0.350	0.350
V =	property value	1.000	1.000	1.000
B =	annual non-land depreciation allowance rate	0.025	0.025	0.025
a =	freehold property annual capital appreciation rate	0.030	0.050	0.030
N =	after tax real estate multiple	13.000	15.000	10.000
e =	landlord specialization efficiencies relative to freehold pre-tax costs	0.100	-0.100	0.200
α =	freehold real estate costs as a proportion of value	0.030	0.040	0.030
n =	discount rate for real estate appreciation	0.100	0.080	0.120
s =	capital gain tax rate	0.200	0.200	0.200
T =	years freehold property is held	40.000	40.000	40.000
g =	landlord return rate	0.090	0.120	0.050
l =	land (non-depreciable) share of value	0.300	0.300	0.300
d =	discount rate for tax shield (reflects risk of tax law change)	0.080	0.080	0.080

The third case considers a firm leasing space in a highly competitive property market (g=6 percent), where landlord efficiencies are high (e=20 percent), real estate multiples are low relative to core business multiples, and core returns are high (r=14 percent). In this instance, the arbitrage associated with shifting capital from real estate to core operations, combined with reduced rents attributable to landlord efficiencies, create a 41 percent present value profit gain associated with renting real estate. That is, $100 million of corporate real estate ownership destroys $41 million in corporate value.

FIGURE 19B.2: Simulation results

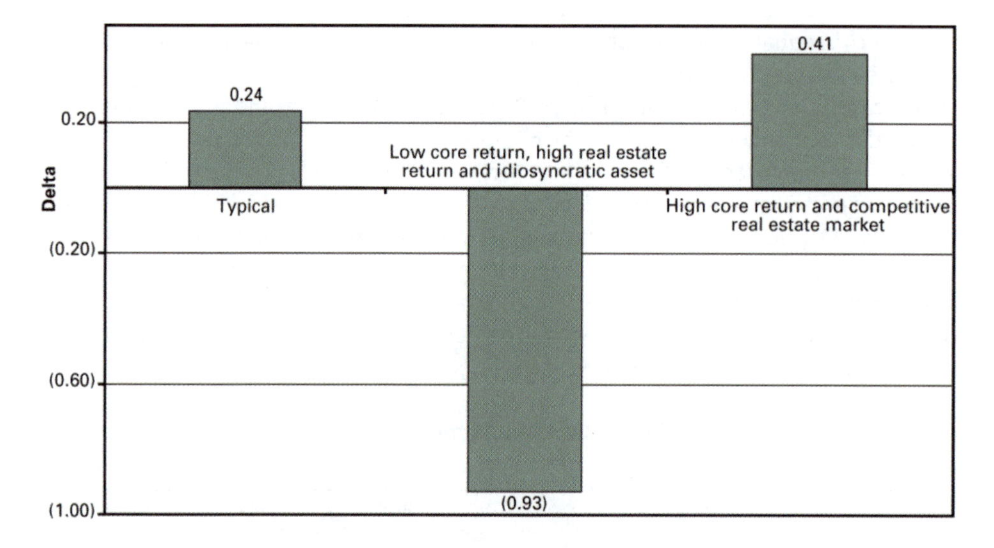

CONCLUSION

The model demonstrates that there is no single answer as to whether a company should own or lease its real estate. Instead, it depends upon the nature of the firm, the nature of the real estate market, the type of the real estate, and taxes. But the model demonstrates that high-multiple firms with high core rates of return, particularly if they are looking for real estate that is readily available in a competitive real estate environment, should lease. The model also suggests that for idiosyncratic properties in less competitive property markets, companies with low rates of return in their core business will gain by owning their real estate, particularly if the rental market is very inefficient.

Our model can be easily applied to every property to determine if the firm should own or lease the property. A critical insight is that shifting dollars from EBITDA to rent can enhance corporate value, as the capital is allocated to higher return core businesses, generating greater bang on the firm's limited capital, by freeing capital from relatively low-yielding real estate to high-yielding corporate operations. This decision also allows corporate management to focus its energies on its core competencies, which generally both lowers risk and adds value.

Chapter 20
Real Estate Cycles

"Don't lose your cool about things you cannot possibly control".
-Dr. Peter Linneman

Real estate cycles are widely misunderstood, in spite of their recurring impacts on real estate markets. The better you understand cycles, the more humble you will become about the accuracy of your beautiful financial models, as these models rarely (if ever) incorporate cycles.

You have heard discussions of real estate cycles on TV, and read about them in the newspapers. Like the authors of these stories, you probably did not really understand what these stories were saying. For example, what does it mean when someone says, "We are at the bottom of the real estate cycle"? Does it mean real estate is over-valued? Undervalued? While press pieces frequently incorporate such assertions, it is very difficult to know if a property is undervalued. The truth is that when you purchase a property with substantial vacancy in a recessionary market where capital is scarce, within a few years you will either be labeled a fool who paid too much by trying to "catch a falling knife", or a visionary who accurately foresaw a booming recovery and the return of cheap capital. You may believe that the property is cheap, but never forget that the Winner's Curse is that no one, including a lot of smart investors, is outbidding you. All that is known with certainty is that buildings take time to build; leases eventually expire; and, if things get better fast enough, property values will rise quickly. But there are considerable lags in the supply and demand responses for space, and being a contrarian investor is both risky and lonely.

WHAT ARE CYCLES?

Real estate cycles are prolonged periods of property supply and demand imbalance. Every product, from pumpkins to office towers, experiences times of supply and demand imbalance, with a long-term tendency to gravitate towards supply and demand balance. For some products this adjustment occurs in a matter of weeks; for others it requires many years. Real estate imbalances fall in this latter category. In fact, real estate markets are rarely near equilibrium.

It is a week before Halloween, a time when pumpkins experience their greatest demand. But for some reason, jack-o-lanterns are a bit out of fashion this year. Consequently, there are too many pumpkins relative to demand. What happens? Faced with an oversupply of soon-to-rot pumpkins, grocers slash their prices, inducing some additional consumers to buy pumpkins. Also, as prices plummet, some pumpkin farmers find alternate uses for their pumpkins, such as selling to pumpkin meal canners. In fact, prices may fall so much that some marginal farmers may not even harvest their pumpkins, leaving them to rot on the vine. If an excess pumpkin supply still exists after Halloween in spite of major price cuts, any unsold pumpkins will rot in a couple of weeks. As a result, the supply and demand for pumpkins is back in rough equilibrium within a few weeks.

CONTRACTUAL AGREEMENTS AND MARKET FRICTIONS

Contrast the market dynamics for pumpkins with those for real estate. Real estate, unlike pumpkins, takes years to plan, build, and lease. Further, properties do not "rot" in a few weeks if they are unused. Imagine developing a new office building in Chanmoy, Pennsylvania, where demand had grown rapidly for six years, and supply and demand were roughly in balance when you commenced construction a year ago. But sadly, the economy in Chanmoy badly weakened shortly after construction began. Thus, instead of surging demand exceeding supply (as you expected), you must lease your property into a market with notable excess supply. As a result, you are seeing almost no leasing interest (in stark contrast to your financial model's confident predictions).

What happens? The long-term nature of real estate leases means that faced with weak demand, landlords are hesitant to lease in today's depressed market for (say) a 10 year lease term. In addition, even if you drastically lowered your rents, very few tenants will move to your property in the short run, as most are locked into long term leases at their current premises. So, you lower rent a little, or offer concessions like tickets to a football game, a dinner at the best restaurant in town, or a couple of months of "free rent". After all, who knows exactly what the next decade will bring? Do you really want to lease all of your space at today's low rents, and lose the possibility of better rents for the next decade? So rents fall slowly, supply begun in good times continues to come onto the market with substantial vacancy, no old buildings "rot", and investors nervously await an uncertain market rebound.

Another important phenomenon is also at work. There is an older, sub-quality building in town that happens to be fully leased for the next six years at solid rental rates, because it had the good fortune of being fully released when the market was red hot and quality space was scarce. Interestingly, the rent paid in this lower quality building may be much higher than you can get today for space in your fabulous new building. Will the owner of this lesser quality property have to lower rents to "market levels" to keep their tenants from moving to your higher quality property? Of course not, as their building is fully leased with six year leases. So the worst building remains substantially fully leased at relatively high rent, while the best and newest building languishes with substantial vacancy and poor rents. Strange indeed.

Will this situation last forever? Probably not. Just as the least attractive pumpkins will rot, given enough time the least efficient property will be eliminated. But this can take a very, very long time, because when the leases at the weakest property expire in six years, demand may again exceed supply, giving the property a further extension on its economic life. Thus, by sheer luck of timing, inefficient buildings and owners can survive for extraordinarily long periods of time, while the newest properties can struggle for frustratingly long periods. And as long as the weakest survive, supply remains unchanged, even in the face of weak demand. This means that things move very slowly, and relatively predictably, as only demand growth will tend to close the supply-demand gap. And demand grows slowly.

DEMAND ADJUSTMENTS

Let's explore demand adjustments on a "national" level. "National" is in quotes, because there is no "national" real estate market. Nonetheless, focusing on the national dynamics allows us to easily focus on the market adjustment process.

The US population is roughly 310 million. Not everyone in the US has a job, as some people are retired, others are in prison, and many are too young to work. Consequently, there are about 136 million jobs in the US. The US annual population growth rate is about 1%, coming roughly about one-third from immigration, and two-thirds from births in excess of deaths.

A 1% growth rate for a 310 million person nation means about 3 million new people each year. Due to the age structure of the population, this means there are roughly 1.8 million new jobs each year, as these "new" people work to feed, house, etc. themselves.

Will the US add 1.8 million new jobs every year? Of course not. Some years it may add only 800,000. In another year it will add 2.4 million. Occasionally it will even lose jobs, as it did from September 2008 through December 2009, when it lost nearly 8 million jobs. But roughly 1.8 million is the sustainable job growth rate given an annual population growth of roughly 3 million people. Thus, if 6 million jobs are added over a two year period, in an economy that adds only 3 million people a year, it is great fun, but not sustainable.

In 2000, the US office supply roughly equaled demand for the first time in almost two decades. In addition, the demand for office space was growing rapidly due to economic growth fed by the last gasps of the tech bubble. Of course, supply equaling demand did not mean there was zero vacancy, as at zero vacancy, supply is too low relative to demand. In 2000, the US office vacancy rate was about 8%, and roughly 6 million jobs had been added during the preceding two years. It was the "Dotcom era", where nonsense was believed sensible. As a result, developers built financial models justifying developments that assumed that soaring job growth would quickly fill their new buildings.

Suppose that in 2000 you were the developer of a 200,000 square foot building. How many jobs do you need to fill a typical 200,000 square foot building? Think back to your office cubicle last summer. It may have been small, perhaps 9 feet by 9 feet (81 square feet). But there was also common space for boardrooms, bathrooms, hallways, copy rooms, servers, elevators, stairs, etc. In addition, your bosses had much larger offices. Taking all this space into account, a typical US office employee requires approximately 200-250 square feet. This space usage is contingent upon nation, culture, building design, and region, with offices in New York City being smaller than offices in Ashland, Ohio. However, a 200,000 square foot (leasable space) building, at 200 square feet per worker, requires roughly 1,000 workers to fill it.

With the economy adding 3 million jobs a year, you felt comfortable that you could easily find the 1,000 jobs you need to fill your new building. These may be either new workers, or employees transferring from other buildings as leases expired. But can 3 million jobs per year be added to the US economy forever? No. If you look at the total amount of office square footage completed in 2001-2003, it would have taken about 3.5 million new jobs, for each of three years to fill that space. But remember that the US only averages about 1.8 million new jobs a year. Clearly excessive development in the absence of a recession.

You may have even correctly concluded that this pace of job growth was unsustainable, but thought, "Hey, I only need 1,000 jobs. That's a drop in the bucket, even in bad times". But if you have 4,000 similar developers scattered across the country thinking the same thing, new supply quickly results in overbuilding.

So what happened in 2001-2003? Instead of the 10-11 million new jobs being created, in line with development expectations, the US lost about 2 million jobs. This is a roughly 13 million total job shortfall versus expectations, or about 10% of total US employment. As a result, the office market quickly went from about an 8% vacancy rate, to roughly 18% vacancy. That is, roughly the original vacancy rate plus the new supply excess as a proportion of total jobs. Note that the jobs "that didn't occur" were far more numerous than the jobs actually lost during the recession.

Unfortunately, this excess supply does not disappear like pumpkins at Halloween. Thus, to get back to balance, the US must add roughly 13 million jobs and halt new construction. This means that even if construction completely halts (which it never does), it will take roughly 7 years of normal job growth to restore supply-demand balance. Of course, this excess supply is not evenly spread across markets, with tech havens, such as Silicon Valley being hit the hardest. But high office vacancy was prevalent throughout the nation until 2007.

By mid-2007, vacancy rates had fallen after 5 years of strong demand growth and little new supply. So what happened? First, supply pipeline grew by about 3% of the existing stock. At the same time, the Great Recession wiped out nearly 6% of all US jobs. This demand collapse plus the supply expansion quickly pushed the US office vacancy rate from about 9% to roughly 18%. Once again new supply ceased, but it will take several years of economic growth to restore balance. Meanwhile, property owners and lenders struggle, while the original financial models look laughable.

What will happen to all this vacant office space? Eventually, it will be absorbed, destroyed, or re-used as residential or institutional space. In the meantime, the "cycle" of rental decline and recovery plays out slowly over the time path of job growth. Real estate cycles do not have to happen, but once underway, they play out slowly due to the slow nature of demand growth, long term leases, and the fixity of supply.

To better understand cycles, it's necessary to constantly gather information, and monitor trends. Publications such as the *Linneman Letter* provide such information for a variety of local markets and property types. Vacancy rates indicate whether markets are improving (vacancy falling) or weakening (rising). Another useful statistic is net absorption, which measures how much vacant supply is being leased. *Linneman Letter* and other research publications forecast market supply and demand by assessing local economic growth and the new supply pipeline. This information helps you better understand your market, and raises your awareness of the challenges "behind the numbers" in your pro forma. But it is important to remember that there will always be good investment opportunities even in bad markets, while bad deals abound in great markets.

PERMITS AND REGULATIONS

While smart developers attempt to match new supply to forecasted space demand, their efforts encounter substantial friction. A major source of friction is the time it takes to develop a building, as construction, planning, and obtaining financing are not instantaneous. As a result, new properties continue to come on-line even after markets plummet, as they were started a year or two earlier when the market looked great. If supply could easily match demand in the real estate market, you'd have them moving together, as seen in Figure 20.1.

FIGURE 20.1: SUPPLY AND DEMAND IN SYNC

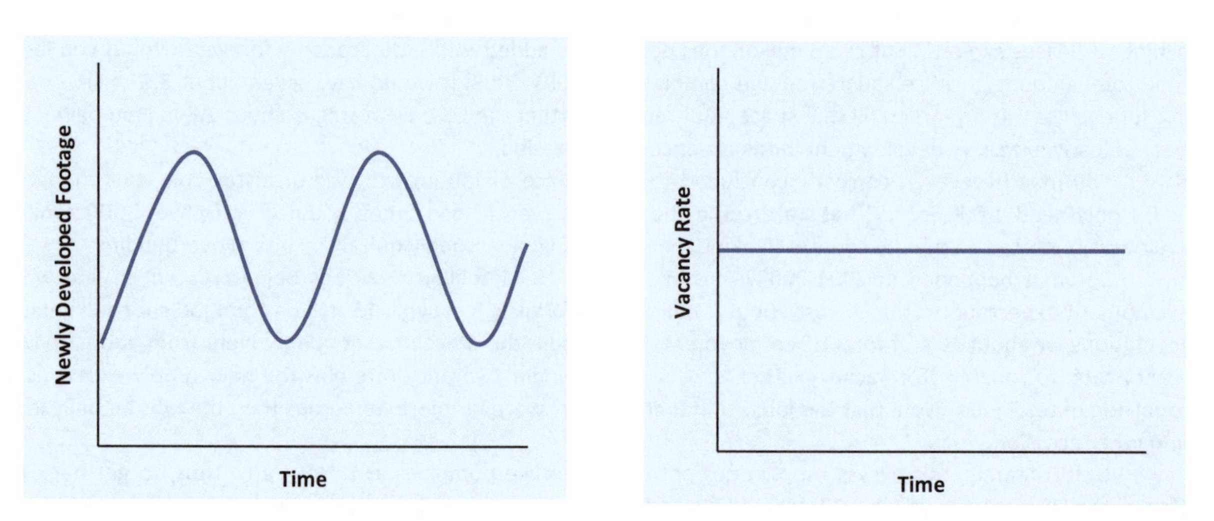

However, due to production and information lags, mismatches in the timing of supply and demand occur, with supply soaring even as demand plummets.

FIGURE 20.2 SUPPLY LAGS DEMAND

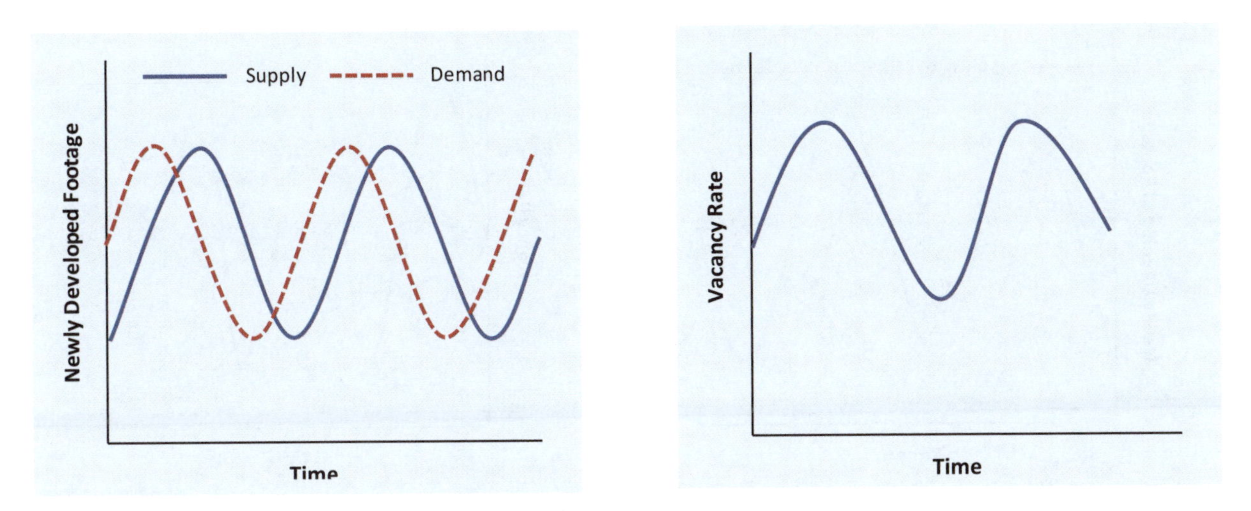

Another major source of market friction is the development regulatory process. Developers must receive many permits, certificates, and approvals before construction can commence. Even a highly skilled developer becomes entangled in a web of conflicting and changing regulations. How does this affect cycles? Imagine you have spent six months getting your financing in place, after a year was spent obtaining the necessary permits and approvals, and you are now ready to start construction. Your equity has already been invested, primarily in the land acquisition and approval process. Two years ago as you embarked on the project, the supply and demand picture looked great, and your development pro forma appeared conservative. At that time, you believed several major local tenants were going to expand and seek space in your building. Just before you commence construction, you discovered that several other developers shared your vision, and are starting 5 similar properties. Some of these competitors started their planning process at the nearly the same time as you, while others started later (earlier), but took less (more) time to clear regulatory hurdles. You know that if the local economy cools, it cannot support all of the planned developments. Should you stop? Will any of the other developers stop? Often the answer is no, as some of this space is already pre-leased. In other cases, the leases are "almost signed". In most instances, the remaining money for construction comes completely from lenders who have already legally committed their money. If this is the case, developers will generally build in spite of the clear excess supply, as their only hope to recover their equity is to spend the lender's money to complete the property, and hope for the best.

FIGURE 20.3: SUPPLY HAS GREATER VOLATILITY

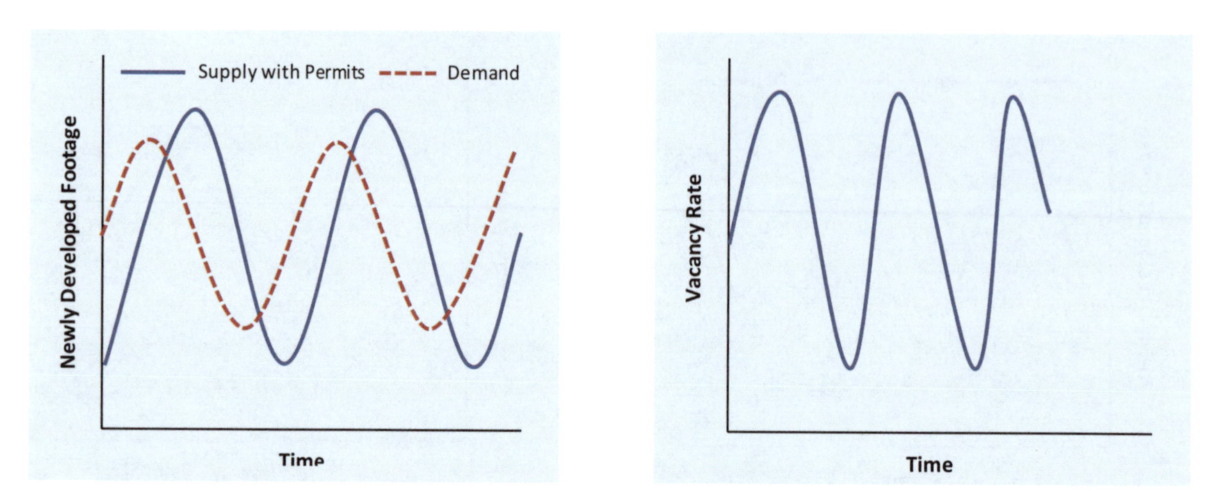

Regulations make the development process longer, more cumbersome, and riskier, meaning that the volatility of supply will generally exceed demand. Hence, it will take a long time to absorb the supply mistakes, leading to longer periods of market imbalance.

Another source of friction is complex building designs. For example, it is quicker to build the typical single family home than a complicated mixed use property. Regional malls, for which the average planning and building time is several years, compensate for this complexity by rarely developing speculatively, requiring roughly 80% pre-leasing before beginning construction. However, even pre-leasing can backfire, as many of these tenants may go bankrupt prior to the project's completion.

CAPITAL CYCLE

A fundamental truth is that if a developer gets money, they will build: a corollary is that, if debt is cheap and plentiful, real estate owners will overpay and overleverage. These two truths underscore the boom and bust of property prices.

Developers often cry that "there is no money". That is generally untrue, although there is often a shortage of funds willing to back a speculative development in a weak or recovering market. Most smart money has gone to the same schools (both academic and "of hard knocks") as you, and understands the business. They see what is going on in the market, and have their own views on whether the market will recover in 3 or 5 years. Generally, smart guys agree on the "big picture" that the market will recover. The devil is generally in the detail of a year or two.

Having substantial equity is a tremendous advantage, especially during down cycles, as equity allows you both to survive the bad times and the luxury of your upside convictions being wrong by a year or so. Having capital when lenders and institutional equity are conservative allows you to fund your developments and acquisitions, even during down cycles. Of course, if you are correct (or lucky), and an earlier than expected demand recovery occurs, your space will benefit from a rapidly tightening market. If you are wrong, you will realize sub-standard returns (at least temporarily).

If there is too much money chasing too few opportunities, investors will ultimately be disappointed. Borrowers are always lured by cheap and plentiful debt, but generally the beneficiaries of such debt markets are the sellers of land and buildings who exit into the teeth of a bidding frenzy fueled by cheap debt. Conversely, too little money may be a sign of short term illiquidity and an opportunity to purchase at bargain prices. For this reason it is important to track the supply of real estate capital. The Linneman Real Estate Index (published quarterly in The Linneman Letter) measures capital market balance by calibrating commercial real estate debt relative to the ultimate driver of space demand, economic activity (proxied by GDP). This index is near 100 when supply and demand conditions for real estate capital are in rough balance (for example 1982 and 1999). As the index rises notably above 100, it indicates an excess supply of real estate capital. For example, an index value of 110 means that there is roughly 10 percent too much capital relative to underlying real estate demand.

This index rapidly rose from 1982 through 1988, with the expansion of real estate capital outstripping demand growth by more than 40%. Not surprisingly, given this flood of capital, vacancy rates soared, as this excess capital was largely transformed into bricks and mortar. However, the index began to decline in 1989, as lending ceased and the economy gradually grew into the capital stock.

FIGURE 20.4

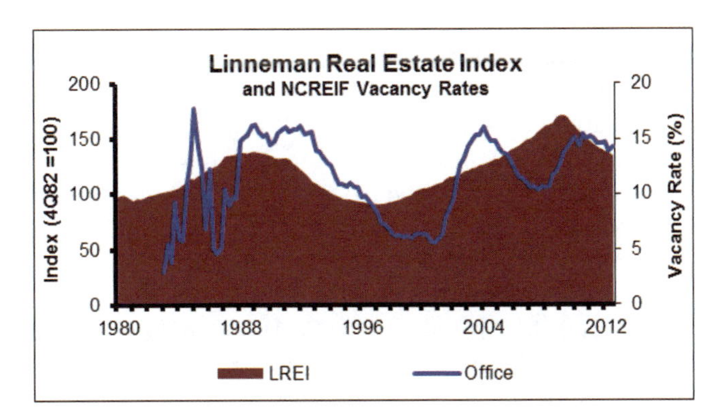

By 1994, the index indicated a moderately undersupplied real estate capital market, which lasted through 1999. Not surprisingly, this time period was one of the best periods ever for purchasing real estate, as capital availability was about 10% less than justified by demand. Even though vacancy rates fell through early 2001, capital availability had become about 10% excessive by early 2001, with most of this excess capital being used to fund new developments for Tech Bubble tenants. By year end 2001, there was a nearly 20% oversupply of real estate capital relative to underlying demand. This rose to some 45% debt excess as debt securitization created a massive excess from 2005-2007. Not surprisingly, it all ended in the Great Recession of 2009, and has since fallen.

CLOSING THOUGHT

Things are easier to analyze on a national basis, because at a local market level you have the vagaries of what specific areas are hot. For example, if Lex Wexner had started The Limited in Akron (rather than Columbus, Ohio) and if Bill Gates had founded Microsoft in Cleveland (rather than Seattle), the real estate markets of Akron, Cleveland, Columbus, and Seattle would all be very different, but the US economy would be roughly the same. Similarly, the chemical industry may be in the dumps, but if your market is primarily driven by telecom demand, you may not be greatly affected. Thus, it is easier to predict demand nationally than locally, as you know that a Comcast is going to be somewhere, but it is much more difficult to accurately predict it will locate in Philadelphia, and even more difficult to accurately forecast which Philadelphia submarket, and building, they will select.

The best market analysts are humble in the face of cycles. Remember that people rarely model a cycle in their 10 year pro-formas. But you will almost certainly experience a cycle over this time period. Surviving these down cycles is the key to a long and prosperous career in real estate. And equity cushions are the ultimate key to surviving cycles.

Chapter 20 Supplement A

Is This the Worst Ever?

A comparison of historical recessions.

Dr. Peter Linneman – The Linneman Letter – Fall 2008

Every time the U.S. economy slows, pundits claim that it is the worst recession ever and will drag on much longer than in the past. These claims are frequently made when it is not even a recession, or after the recession is over and the economy is in the early stages of a recovery. In October 1970, Representative Wilbur Mills predicted a "serious recession if inflation is not controlled" in the *New York Times*; the economy grew the next three years in spite of accelerating inflation. In April 1975, the *Times* wrote that the United States is "sliding deeper and faster into recession that is showing no signs of bottoming out"; the recession had ended a month earlier. In April 1980, an Aetna strategist wrote in the *Wall Street Journal* that "the risks of a credit crunch and a severe recession were still very high"; the recovery was a month underway. In October 1981, the *Times* reported that "the price of lower inflation is a severe recession and 10.1 percent unemployment, the highest rate since 1940... some economists also argue that the outlook for recovery is still uncertain"; the recession was actually ending. In July 1992, the *Wall Street Journal* confidently asserted that "this recession has been the longest since before World War II"—sixteen months after the recession had ended. In February 2003, AFL-CIO president John Sweeney was quoted by the *Times* as saying, "There's an economic code red for America's working families who are in the worst economic crisis in two decades"—a full fifteen months after the recession's end.

Today we have the Great Capital Strike. In August 2008, Nouriel Roubini wrote in the *RGE Monitor*, "At this point, a severe recession and a severe financial crisis is unavoidable". Do you detect a common thread? Just as many teenagers take a perverse pleasure in watching Jason killing other teens on screen in the fortieth sequel to *Friday the 13th*, many observers seem to relish the eminent demise of the U.S economy. To put the current slowdown in perspective, it has yet to be categorized as a recession, even using today's watered-down definition. But how bad is it? To separate myth from fact, we compared the economic performance during the first seven months of 2008 with U.S. recessions of the past forty years.

According to the current definition of the National Bureau of Economic Research: "A recession is a significant decline in economic activity spread across the economy, lasting more than a few months, normally visible in real GDP, real income, employment, industrial production, and wholesale-retail sales. A recession begins just after the economy reaches a peak of activity and ends as the economy reaches its trough. Between trough and peak, the economy is in an expansion. Expansion is the normal state of the economy; most recessions are brief and they have been rare in recent decades". This is a more elastic approach to defining a recession than the Bureau's previous definition of "two consecutive quarters of negative real GDP growth".

Using the current definition, there have been six recessions over the past forty years. The first five would be categorized as recessions under both definitions, while the 2001 episode was only a recession under the new definition. Specifically, only the first and third quarters of 2001—not two consecutive quarters—experienced real negative GDP growth. The key features of the six recessions, and the first eight months of 2008, are summarized in Figure 20A.1.

FIGURE 20A.1 : "Worst ever" U.S. recessions over the past 40 years

	12/69-11/70	11/73-03/75	01/80 03/80	07/81-11/82	07/90 03/91	03/01-11/01	01/08 07/08
Duration in Months	12	17	3	17	9	9	6
Change in GDP (%)	-0.4%	-3.5%	-0.7%	-2.7%	-1.4%	-0.2%	1.3%
Change in Payroll Employment (%)	-1.2%	-1.6%	0.2%	-3.1%	-1.1%	-1.2%	-0.3%
Change in Real Household Net Worth (%)	1.7%	-10.1%	-1.8%	-1.4%	-3.5%	-3.4%	0.2%
Change in Auto Sales (%)	-29.2%	-30.4%	-15.9%	-12.5%	-15.2%	-6.2%	-5.9%
Change in Industrial Output (%)	-7.1%	-15.0%	-0.8%	-8.5%	-4.4%	-4.0%	-1.4%
Change in Real Sales by Retail Stores (%)	-2.1%	-9.5%	-4.9%	-5.1%	-5.2%	-1.3%	-1.9%
Change in Construction Contracts for C&I Builidings (%)	-37.6%	-52.2%	-21.1%	-41.3%	-25.0%	-33.6%	-28.6%
Percent Real Return in S&P 500	-23.2%	-39.9%	-12.9%	-23.2%	-16.5%	-11.3%	-10.1%
Change in Real Median Home Price (%)	-15.8%	-4.0%	-3.1%	-8.7%	-6.2%	-1.1%	-3.2%
Change in Real After Tax Profit (%)	-13.3%	-30.4%	-12.7%	-6.8%	-12.3%	-8.3%	0.5%
Lowest Consumer Confidence Level (Monthly)	72.4	57.6	62.1	65.7	65.1	88.6	59.1
Change in Housing Starts	-17.5%	-30.5%	-32.7%	-25.1%	-31.6%	2.1%	13.7%
Highest Inflation Rate (Monthly)	6.4%	12.2%	14.6%	11.0%	6.4%	3.6%	4.9%
Highest Unemployment Rate (Monthly)	5.8%	8.3%	6.3%	10.7%	6.8%	4.8%	5.7%

Sources: Bureau of Economic Analysis, Bureau of Labor Statistics, Standard & Poor's, OFHEO, Linneman Associates

THE EVIDENCE

In order to quantify the severity of the seven events, we focused on fifteen important metrics of economic activity. While these metrics are not definitive, we believe they provide a clear image of each episode. The longest recessions occurred in 1973-75 and 1981-82, each lasting seventeen months. The average recession duration has been eleven months, and the shortest was three months. The shaded areas of our figures indicate recessionary periods.

The greatest decline in real GDP was a staggering -3.5 percent, and took place in the 1973-75 recession (Figure 20A.2). Per capita GDP growth was roughly 1 percent lower, or -4.5 percent, due to a 1 percent annual population growth. Through July of 2008 (hereafter referred to simply as "2008"), the current slowdown registered a healthy 1.3 percent real GDP growth. This means per capita GDP is increasing by about 0.3 percent, which belies consumer sentiment reports but reinforces the relative strength of today's economy. In 2008, payroll employment fell by 0.3 percent (Figure 20A.3). This pales in comparison to the 3.1 percent decline registered during the 1981-82 recession. The average decline in payroll employment has been 1.2 percent, with only the brief 1980 recession escaping without a decline in payrolls.

FIGURE 20A.2: Real GDP growth rate, quarterly annualized growth

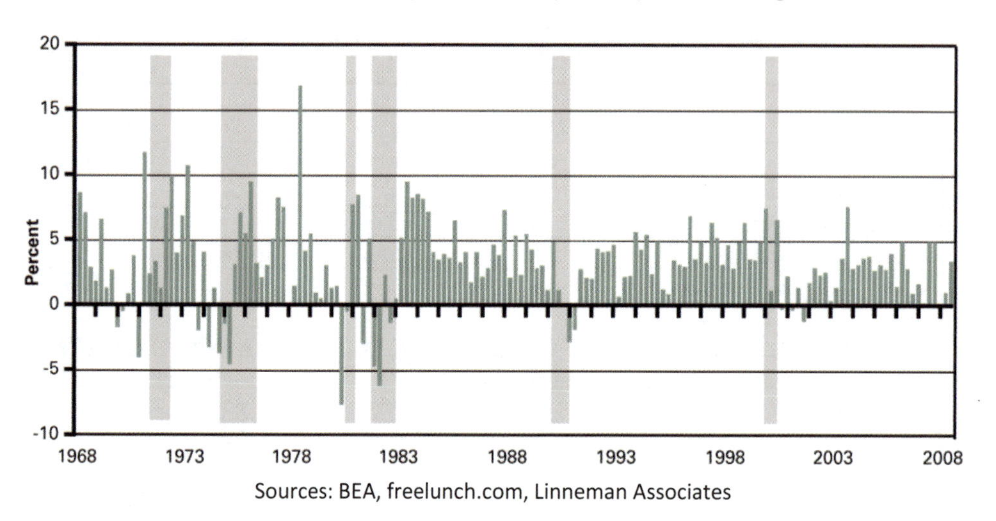

Sources: BEA, freelunch.com, Linneman Associates

FIGURE 20A.3: U.S. payroll employment, year-over-year percent change

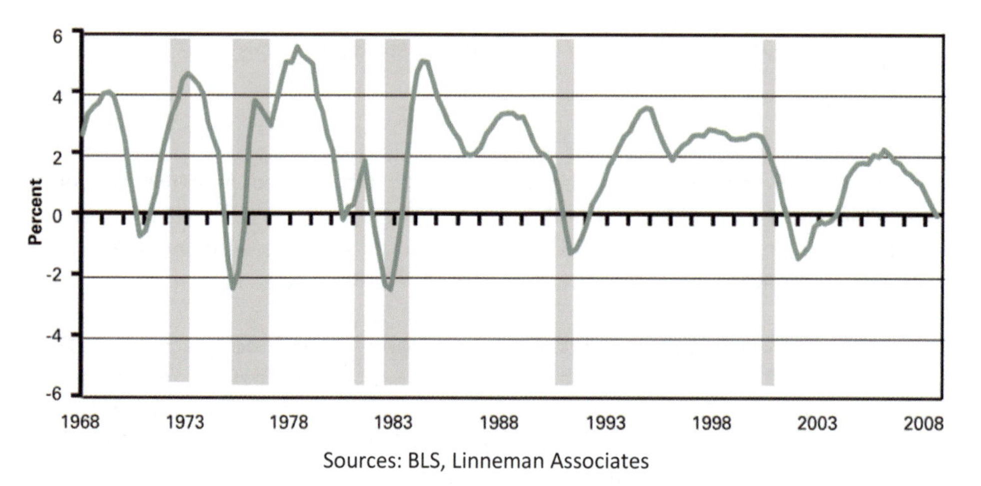

Sources: BLS, Linneman Associates

With housing prices tumbling and the stock and bond markets cracking, real household wealth has risen by just 0.2 percent in 2008 (Figure 20A.4). Thus, on a per capita basis, real wealth has fallen by 0.8 percent. In contrast, real wealth fell by a staggering 10.1 percent in the 1973-75 recession (11.1 percent per capita) and by 3.5 percent in the 1990-91 recession (4.5 percent on a per capita basis). The sales of durable goods, particularly autos, generally declined in the face of weak economic conditions, as consumers forestall purchases in the face of credit squeezes and uncertain near-term income (Figure 20A.5). The 5.9 percent decline in unit auto sales in 2008 is dramatic and painful, but only about one-fifth of the 29.2 percent and 30.4 percent declines registered in 1969-70 and 1973-75, respectively. And while real sales by retail stores have weakened, the 2008 decline is small relative to the other recessionary periods, with the exception of 2001 (Figure 20A.6).

FIGURE 20A.4: U.S. household net worth (real–2007 $)

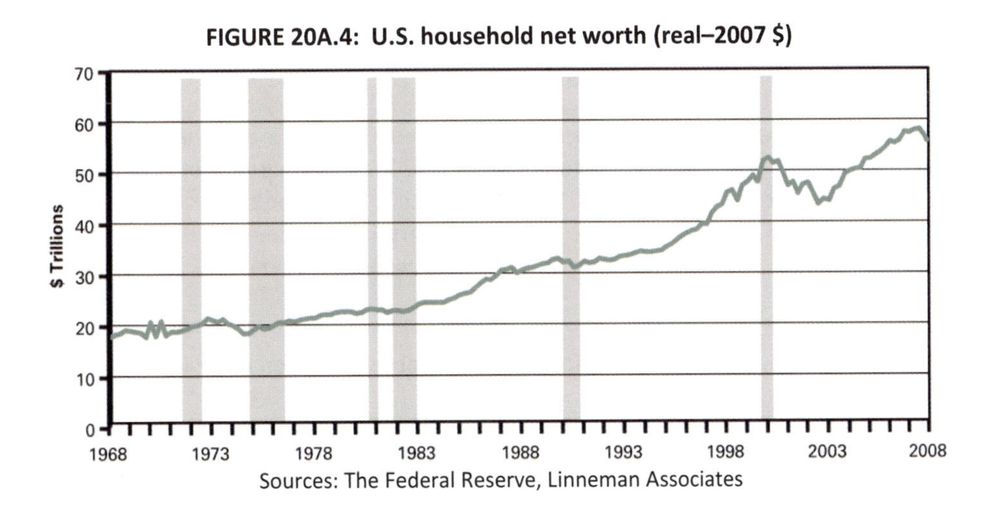

Sources: The Federal Reserve, Linneman Associates

FIGURE 20A.5: U.S. auto sales

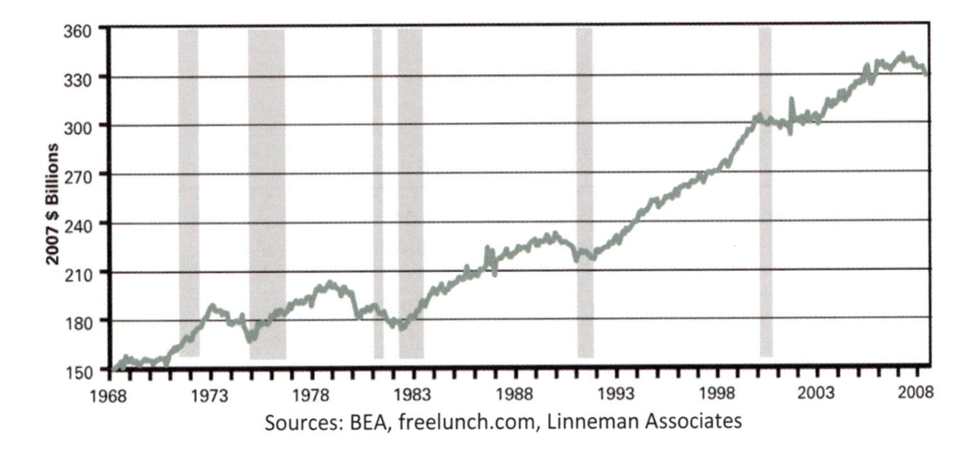

Sources: BEA, freelunch.com, Linneman Associates

FIGURE 20.A6: U.S. real retail sales

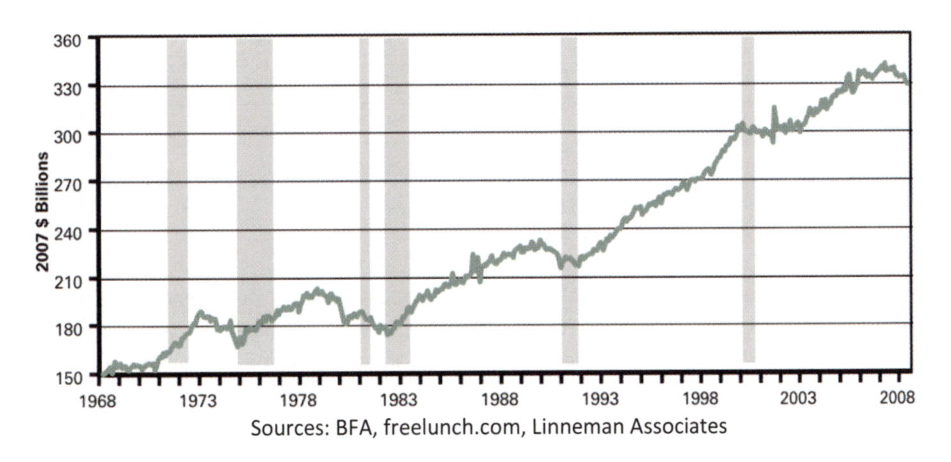

Sources: BFA, freelunch.com, Linneman Associates

New construction contracts for commercial and office buildings have invariably suffered when the economy weakens and capital market liquidity evaporates (Figure 20A.7). The decline of nearly 29 percent in 2008 is no exception. But the 2008 decline is not exceptionally large. In fact, in two recessions, contracts fell by 52 percent (1973-75) and 41 percent (1981-82) in a matter of months due to a complete absence of capital. This serves as a dramatic reminder that the Great Capital Strike of 2007-08 is hardly the first time that capital has disappeared seemingly overnight (and "forever"). The -10.1 percent return on the S&P 500 in 2008 is extremely painful (Figure 20A.8). However, such declines are par for the very difficult course called recession. The 1973-75 recession registered a negative return four times as large, wiping out 40 percent of its value in just seventeen months.

FIGURE 20A.7: Commercial and industrial construction contracts

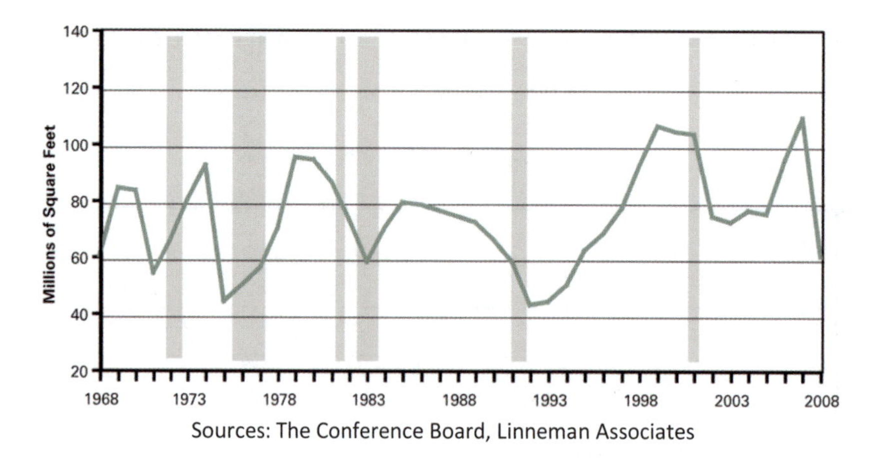

Sources: The Conference Board, Linneman Associates

FIGURE 20A.8: Annualized S&P 500 returns

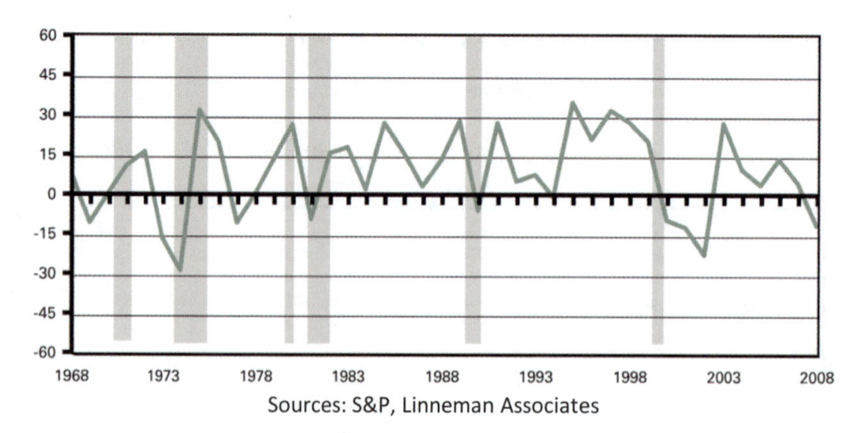

Sources: S&P, Linneman Associates

Real median home prices (measured by the Census Bureau's index of new residential sales) have fallen in all of the six previous recessions, with the 1969-70 recession registering double-digit declines (Figure 20A.9). This index is in line with the Office of Federal Housing Enterprise Oversight Housing Price index (OFHEO HPI) but this goes back only to 1975. The current home price decline is "only" 3.2 percent, which is much smaller than the decline indicated by the frequently cited Case-Shiller index (Figure 20A.10). But this latter index, like the NAR index, is unrepresentatively loaded with sales of foreclosed empty and speculatively owned homes, and focuses primarily on the most overbuilt housing markets. The corporate sector as a whole registered a modest real after-tax profit increase of 0.5 percent in 2008, in spite of staggering losses in the financial sector (Figure 20A.11). This is in contrast to the 30 percent and 13 percent real declines in after-tax profit witnessed in the 1973-75 and 1969-70 recessions, respectively. Consumer confidence in 2008 plummeted to levels not seen since the recessions of 1973-75 and 1980 (Figure 20A.12). Interestingly, all three periods share abnormally high oil and gasoline prices, serious geo-political disturbances, domestic political uncertainty, and constipated capital markets (Figure 20A.13).

FIGURE 20A.9: New single-family home median sale price

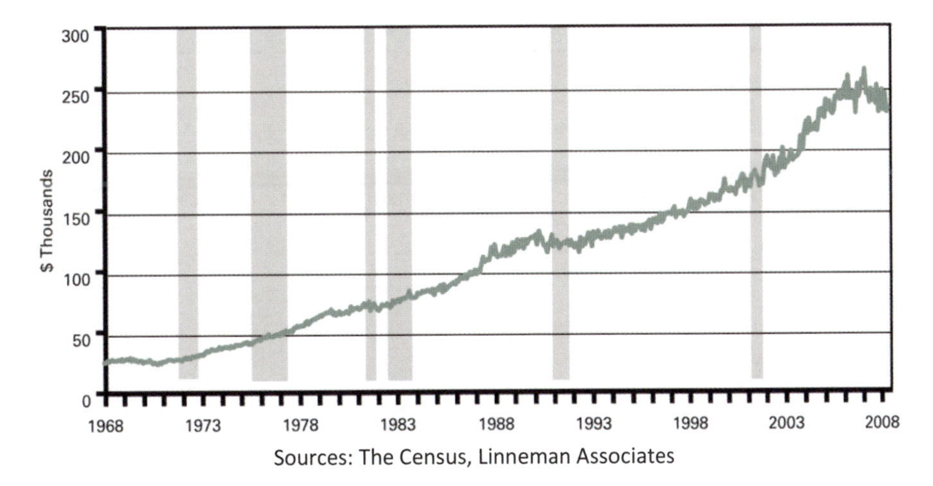

Sources: The Census, Linneman Associates

FIGURE 20A.10: Home price changes

Market	Case-Shiller		OFHEO		NAR	
	YE 2003-05 % change	YE 2006-03/08 % change	YE 2003-2005 % change	YE 2006-03/08 % change	YE 2003-2005 % change	YE 2006-03/08 % change
Atlanta	10%	-7%	10%	2%	10%	-10%
Boston	13%	-7%	18%	-3%	15%	-11%
Charlotte	9%	2%	8%	8%	19%	1%
Chicago	19%	-10%	21%	1%	20%	-9%
Cleveland	6%	-11%	6%	-1%	6%	-24%
Dallas	7%	-4%	6%	5%	7%	-5%
Denver	8%	-7%	7%	1%	4%	-10%
Detroit	6%	-20%	4%	-7%	4%	-20%
Las Vegas	61%	-27%	61%	-12%	70%	-22%
Los Angeles	52%	-23%	57%	-8%	49%	-21%
Miami	63%	-26%	54%	-4%	57%	-14%
Minneapolis	14%	-16%	17%	-2%	18%	-14%
New York	31%	-8%	33%	0%	30%	-5%
Phoenix	75%	-25%	63%	-7%	62%	-17%
Portland	34%	-3%	33%	4%	30%	2%
San Diego	35%	-22%	41%	-11%	42%	-24%
San Francisco	39%	-21%	37%	-3%	28%	-7%
Seattle	32%	-3%	30%	5%	32%	3%
Tampa	56%	-21%	48%	-9%	49%	-19%
Washington, D.C.	49%	-16%	51%	-5%	53%	-14%

Sources: Standard & Poors, OFHEO, NAR, Linneman Associates

FIGURE 20A.11: YOY percent change in real after-tax corporate profits

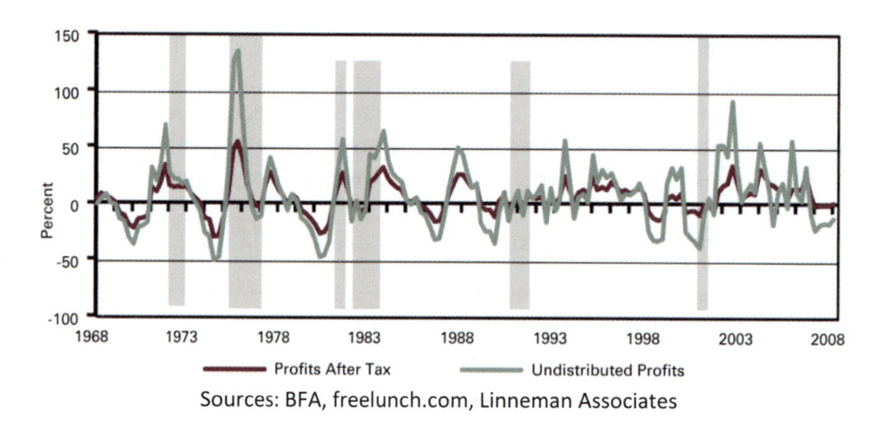

Sources: BFA, freelunch.com, Linneman Associates

FIGURE 20A.12: University of Michigan consumer sentiment, 1968 = 100

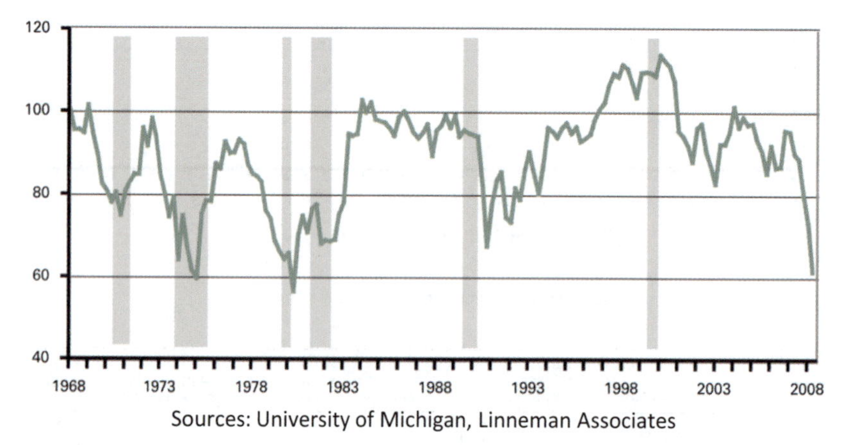

Sources: University of Michigan, Linneman Associates

FIGURE 20A.13 Historical crude oil price per barrel

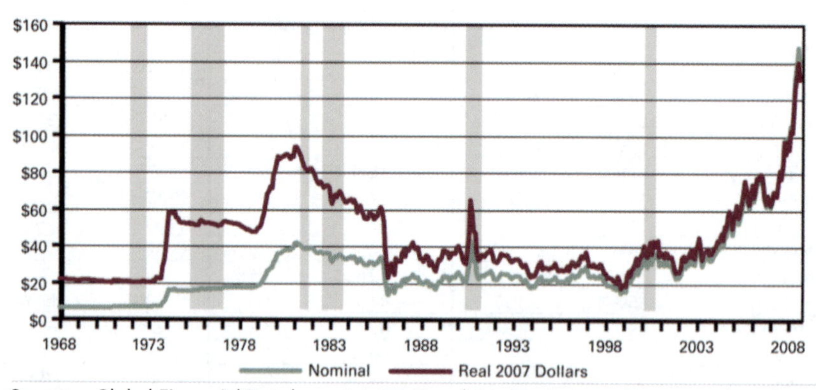

Sources: Global Financial Database, International Energy Agency, Linneman Associates

In many ways, the prolonged presidential campaign of 2007-2008, combined with the chaos in post-war Iraq and Afghanistan, echo the collapse of the Nixon-Agnew administration amidst the Vietnam War, and the global ineptness of the Carter administration (remember the Iranian hostage crisis?). Today's anemic rate of housing starts is breathtaking, particularly after the giddy starts registered just two years earlier (Figure 20A.14). However, the percentage declines in 2008 are similar to those registered in the 1969-70 recession, and about half or more of the declines in 1973-75, 1980, 1981-82, and 1990-91. Only the 2001 recession witnessed an increase in housing starts.

FIGURE 20A.14: Single-family home starts

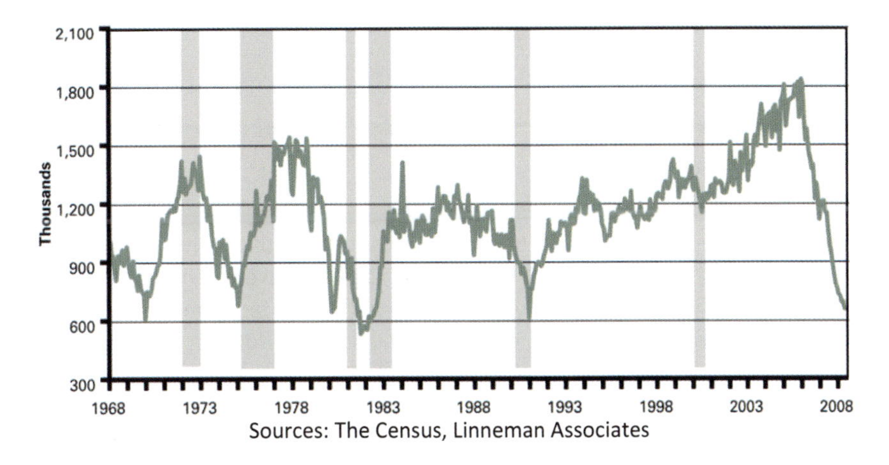

Sources: The Census, Linneman Associates

Inflation, once again, has reared its ugly head in 2008, with annual inflation reaching 4.9 percent as measured by CPI including food and energy (Figure 20A.15). But this rate is just one-third of inflation registered in the 1980 recession, and well below the double-digit rates of 1973-1975 and 1981-1982. How quickly we forget what real inflation looks like. The U.S. unemployment rate rose to 5.7 percent in 2008: high, but well below rates seen during previous recessions (Figure 20A.16). Particularly noteworthy in this regard are the continental European-like 8 percent unemployment rate registered in 1973-1975, and the double-digit unemployment rate registered in 1981-1982.

FIGURE 20A.15: All items consumer price index, YOY percent change

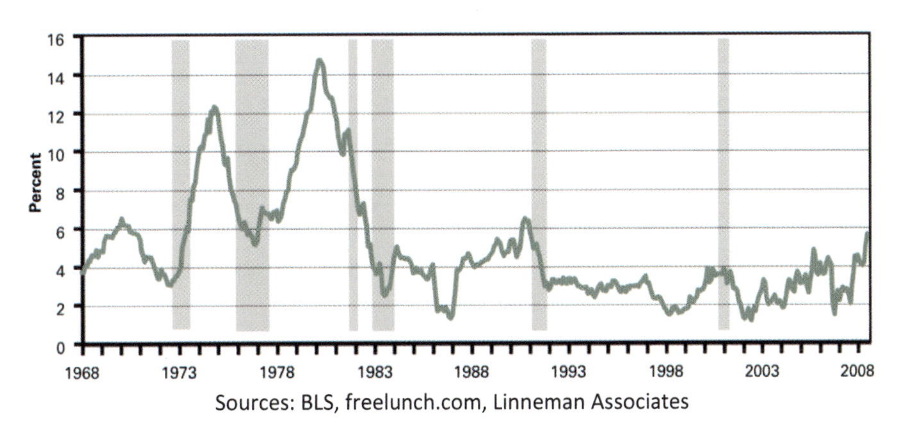

Sources: BLS, freelunch.com, Linneman Associates

FIGURE 20A.16: Unemployment rate

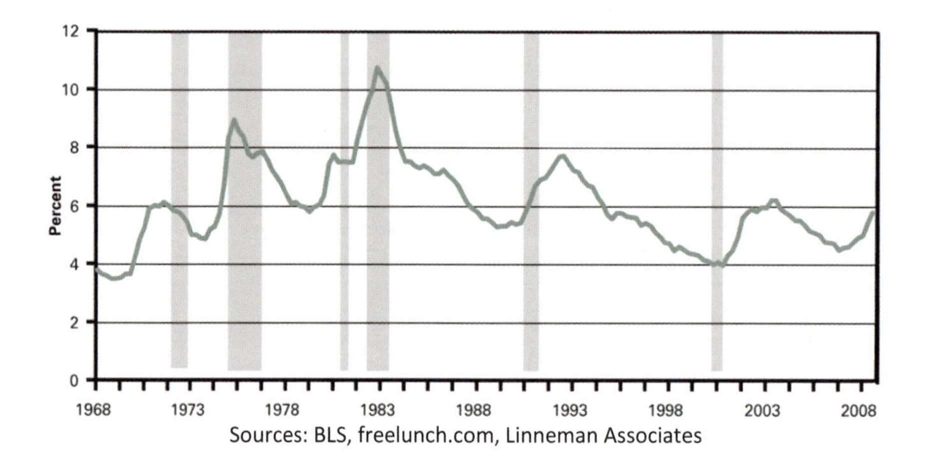

Sources: BLS, freelunch.com, Linneman Associates

When viewed as a whole, how does the current U.S. economic situation (which may still worsen) compare to past recessions? Clearly things are not good, and the Great Capital Strike merits a position on the list of worst U.S. economies of the past forty years. But it is very clearly (at least so far) far from the worst. To demonstrate this, we ranked each of the seven episodes on a scale of one to seven (seven for the worst, six for the second worst, etc.) for each of the selected fifteen metrics. The worst possible score is 105 (the worst score for each of the selected 15 metrics), while the best possible score is fifteen (the least bad on each of the fifteen selected metrics). The total score for each of the seven episodes is displayed at the bottom of Figure 20A.17.

FIGURE 20A.17: "Worst ever" U.S. recessions over the past 50 years

	12/69-11/70	11/73-03/75	01/80 03/80	07/81-11/82	07/90 03/91	03/01-11/01	01/08 07/08
	RANK ORDER (7 is Worst; 1 is Best)						
Duration in Months	5	6.5	1	6.5	3.5	3.5	2
Change in GDP (%)	3	7	4	6	5	2	1
Change in Payroll (%)	4.5	6	1	7	3	4.5	2
Change in Real Household Net Worth (%)	1	7	4	3	6	5	2
Change in Auto Sales (%)	6	7	5	3	4	2	1
Change in Industrial Output (%)	5	7	1	6	4	3	2
Change in Real Sales by Retail Stores (%)	3	7	4	5	6	1	2
Change in Construction Contracts for C&I Builidings (%)	5	7	1	6	2	4	3
Percent Real Return in S&P 500	5.5	7	3	5.5	4	2	1
Change in Median Home Price (%)	7	4	2	6	5	1	3
Change in Real After Tax Profit (%)	6	7	5	2	4	3	1
Lowest Consumer Confidence Level (Monthly)	2	7	5	3	4	1	6
Change in Housing Starts	3	5	7	4	6	1	2
Highest Inflation Rate (Monthly)	3.5	6	7	5	3.5	1	2
Highest Unemployment Rate (Quarterly)	3	6	4	7	5	1	2
Total Rank Score	**62.5**	**96.5**	**54**	**75**	**65**	**35**	**32**
Number of Worsts	**1**	**10**	**2**	**3**	**0**	**0**	**0**
Number of Bests	**1**	**0**	**4**	**0**	**0**	**6**	**4**

Sources: BEA, S&P, OFHEO, NAR, Linneman Associates

Far and away, the worst recession of the past forty years appears to have occurred in 1973-75, with the second-worst taking place in 1981-82. The 96.5 rank score for the 1973-75 recession is reinforced by the fact that it was ranked the worst in ten out of fifteen selected metrics, and was never the best in any category. In contrast, the Great Capital Strike is (so far) the mildest, with a score of 32. Though it is ranked sixth in consumer confidence, it is not the worst in any of the categories. The current period has exhibited the strongest growth in GDP, auto sales, S&P returns, and after-tax profits (all in real dollars), compared to the previous six recessions.

COMMERCIAL REAL ESTATE

Turning to commercial real estate markets, it is impossible to compile the data necessary to fully compare across these seven episodes. However, as long-time observers and participants, we offer our views. First, consistent with the sharp declines previously documented in commercial and industrial contracts, each episode was painful for developers. We lived through our first real estate recession in 1969-70. In some ways, it was just a "blip on the radar screen", in that there was "only" a short-lived 37.6 percent decline in construction activity, and no substantial change in lending activity.

Atlanta offers an interesting example of the effects of recession on real estate. In 1969-70, if you asked developers in Atlanta about the recession, most would have responded: "What recession?" Of course, things were not as rosy in the Midwest and Northeast, but all in all, it was not a deep decline. This cockiness left most developers ill-prepared for the deep recession of 1973-75. Atlanta experienced a huge construction boom post-1970, with 40,000 apartments permitted in 1972 alone. Many were condominiums and townhome developments. Then, seemingly out of nowhere, the recession of 1973-75 struck. It was such a disaster that it was 1979 before there was any appreciable construction activity in the Atlanta area for all building types. And Atlanta, Texas and California were the "boom" markets in these dark times. More than one-half of the real estate developers and home builders went bankrupt or left the business; the Atlanta condominium business was so damaged in this period that there was no appreciable condominium development until the mid-1990s. Commercial real estate values plummeted by 25 percent to 30 percent, and foreclosures and workouts (especially for condo projects) were the program du jour. There was no capital available for new construction, except for build-to-suit projects. In 1976, Post Properties permitted and closed on a 276-unit apartment development (Post Woods) financed by Manufacturers Hanover Bank—the only multifamily permit issued over a three-year period in metro Atlanta.

Economic conditions in 1980-82 were unique for the commercial real estate industry in that the recession was entirely due to monetary policy and had nothing to do with supply and demand fundamentals. There was solid pent-up demand for space on the heels of the slowdown of the mid-1970s. Unfortunately, rampant inflation caused Fed chairman Paul Volker and the Federal Reserve to use a sledgehammer in the battle against inflation. Bank interest rates for construction loans were based on a 16 percent prime rate.

Post Properties did a transaction for a small apartment project with 50 percent debt at a 19 percent interest rate. The good news was that because there was so little development and so much demand, the project worked.

In 1987, there was a change in the tax treatment for commercial real estate that set the stage for a disastrous real estate downturn nationally. Absent tax benefits and in the teeth of a difficult financing market, real estate "suddenly" became very illiquid. The savings and loan industry literally disappeared, and most banks and life companies abandoned the real estate market. Capital for commercial real estate completely evaporated. We view July 1990 through March 1991 as the second-worst recession as it pertains to commercial real estate. This recession heralded the end of an era of commercial real estate financing, requiring the evolution of entirely new sources of capital.

Like many real estate owners, Post Properties went public as a REIT in 1993 simply because there was no viable alternative capital source at that time. For many real estate owners, it was as Stan Ross once stated: "Do you want to file a Chapter 11 or an S-11?" It took some seven to eight years for a new era of real estate capital to evolve, characterized by REITs, CMBS, and private equity funds. The 2001 recession had only a limited effect on most real estate markets, primarily affecting the travel and lodging sector, Silicon Valley, SOMA in San Francisco, and New York City real estate. However, capital flows remained plentiful and real estate sales abounded.

The current episode has affected the for-sale housing markets in a way that was predictable. The generous availability of financing to home buyers (including "investment" purchasers), no-document loans, and customers walking out of closings with large sums of money clearly foreshadowed the current depression in the for-sale business. It will be many years before the for-sale markets, particularly for condos, regain such giddy heights. In fact, we suspect it will be another decade before we again have a healthy condominium business. However, thus far the Great Capital Strike has largely caused development to be put on hold as people wait to see how things evolve. Also, cap rates have increased by 5 percent to 20 percent, and there are few transactions. The apartment business remains solid, but we suspect we have yet to see the end of this cycle.

Figure 20A.18 compares the early 1990s real estate depression and the Great Capital Strike. While real estate fundamentals weakened in 2008 as the economy slowed, the run-up in construction costs during the previous two years have kept construction pipelines conservative. As a result, although vacancies have risen, vacancy spikes will be relatively muted due to limited new supply. And development plans are being scuttled everywhere, particularly in the hotel sector, due to greater market transparency. In almost every way, at least so far, the early 1990s was objectively much worse than today for commercial real estate. Real estate capital markets are very difficult today, with limited debt availability and wide debt spreads the norm. However, debt remains available for cash flow properties today, although at much higher coverage ratios, while equity remains plentiful, particularly at private equity firms (Figures 20A.19-20A.20). While it is not pretty today, it stands in stark contrast to the early 1990s, when neither debt nor equity was available at any price.

FIGURE 20A.18: Commercial real estate comparison

	1991	2008
Office vacancy	19%	13.20%
Office pipeline	4.50%	1.50%
Hotel occupancy	61.90%	63.10%
Hotel pipeline	4%	2.50%
Apartment vacancy	7.30%	8.0%
Apartment pipeline	2.50%	1%
Mortgage delinquency	7-14%	0.03-0.50%
Real cap rate spread	200 bps	300 bps
Mortgage availability	None	Cash flow only
Equity availability	None	Substantial but waiting
Sales activity	Only distressed	Limited

Sources: CBRE, Smith Travel Research, Lodging Econometrics, NCREIF, Census, HUD, Linneman Associates

FIGURE 20A.19: Real estate capital sources, 2007 ($ millions)

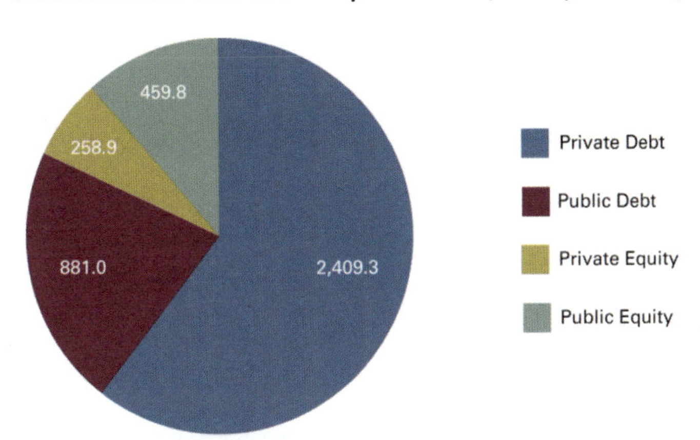

Sources: Roulac Global Places, ADLI, CMSA/Trepp Database, CMA, the Federal Reserve, FannieMae.com, IREI, NAREIT, PricewaterhouseCoopers, Real Capital Analytics

FIGURE 20A.20: Annual flows to real estate, real - 2007 $

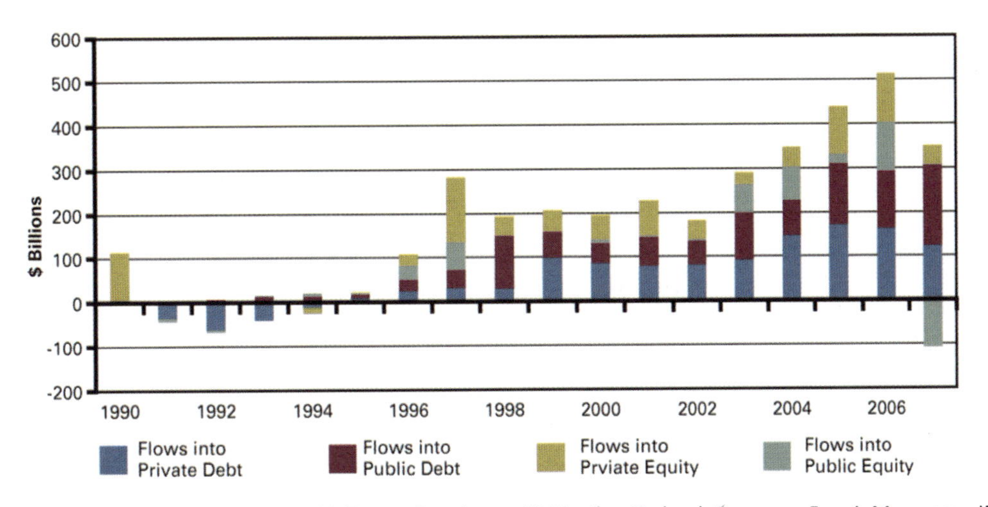

Sources: Roulac Global Places, ADLI, CMSA/Trepp Database, CMA, the Federal Reserve, FannieMae.com, IREI, NAREIT, PricewaterhouseCoopers, Real Capital Analytics

We are optimistic that the commercial real estate market will fare better during the Great Capital Strike than in either the 1970s or 1990s, as the usual culprit for prolonged real estate problems is overbuilding (Figure 20A.21). But other than single-family and condominiums, there has been relatively modest supply growth. Therefore, the market observers who predict that there is yet a "second shoe to drop" in the commercial area similar to the early 1990s appear to be either misinformed or lack an understanding of the source of commercial real estate woes. In both 1973-75 and 1990-96, we had substantial overbuilding and a severe capital shortage, which accentuated liquidity problems, and the length of and severity of these downturns. Today, we have little excess supply, and we have some liquidity to prevent widespread defaults and bankruptcies.

FIGURE 20A.21: Cash flow cap rate spreads over 10-year Treasury, 18-month lag

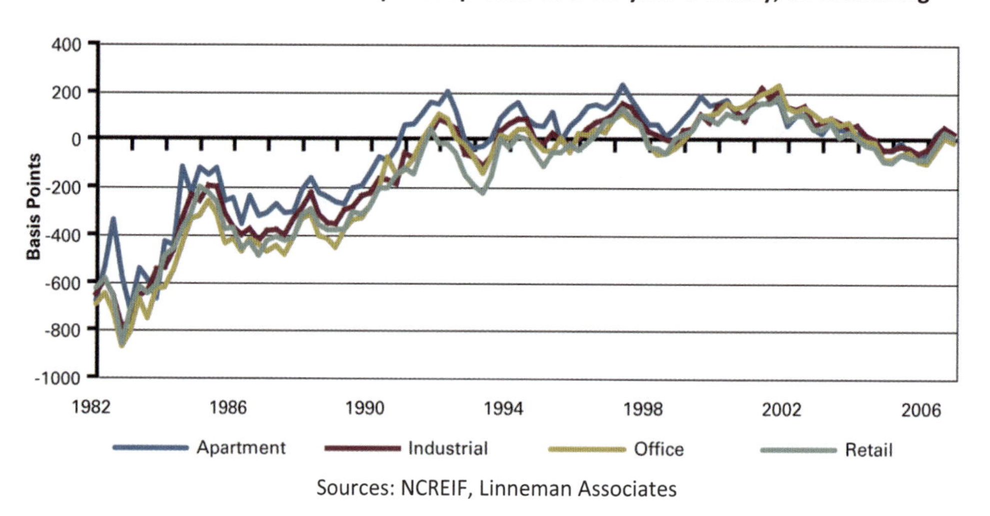

Sources: NCREIF, Linneman Associates

LESSONS LEARNED

It is tough out there, and may get tougher. But we have survived much worse economies and commercial real estate markets over the last forty years. In fact, we not only survived, but also we subsequently soared to undreamed-of new heights. Simply stated, tough economic times end, and the economy grows again, as capital creates new channels through which to flow. As domestic demand in India and China evolves, the world economy is performing better than during past U.S. downturns (Figure 20A.22). This continued foreign growth is a mild buffer to our slowdown. Also of relevance is the fact that the United States (and the world) is ever less-dependent on manufacturing.

FIGURE 20A.22: Increase in world GDP

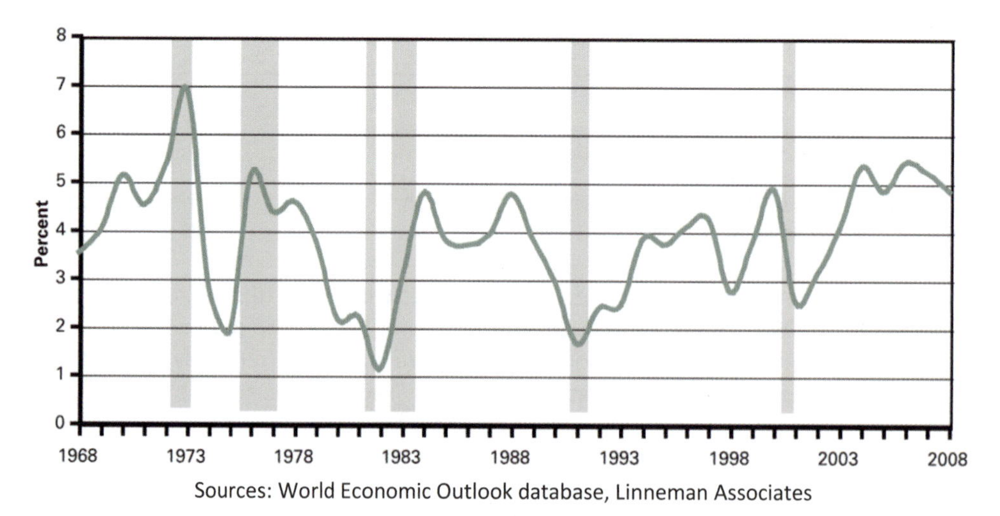

Sources: World Economic Outlook database, Linneman Associates

In the worst recessions of the past forty years, manufacturing accounted for 20 percent to 25 percent of U.S. employment (Figure 20A.23). Today, it accounts for less than 10 percent. As the importance of manufacturing declines, so too does the magnitude of the economy's cyclical ups and downs (Figure 20A.24). This is because it is far easier to incrementally expand and contract service employment (more or fewer lawyers) than it is to incrementally expand and contract manufacturing activity, where the norm is one more (or less) shift (or one more or less plant). This makes incremental increases in employment less tenuous today, and the downs less dramatic.

FIGURE 20A.23: Manufacturing as a percentage of total employment, with trendline

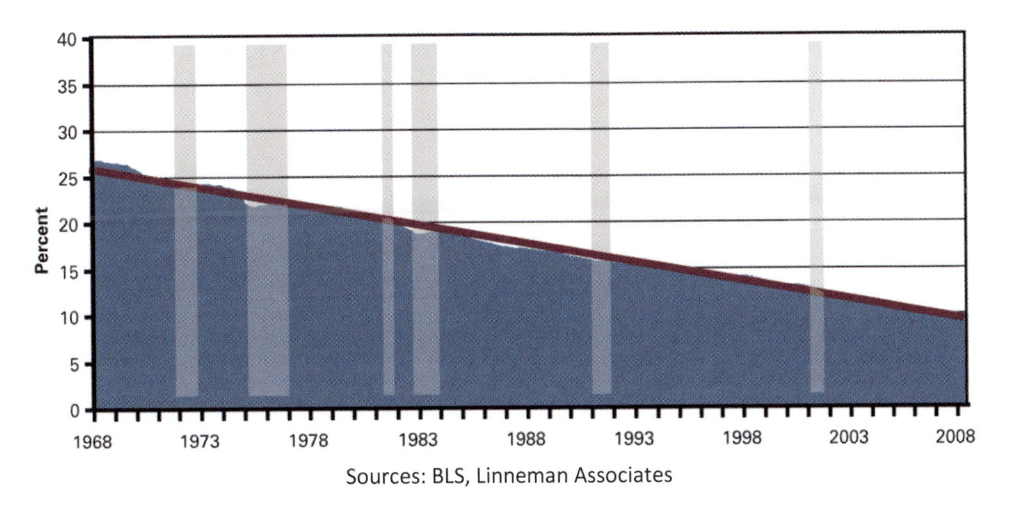

Sources: BLS, Linneman Associates

FIGURE 20A.24: Services as a percentage of total employment, with trendline

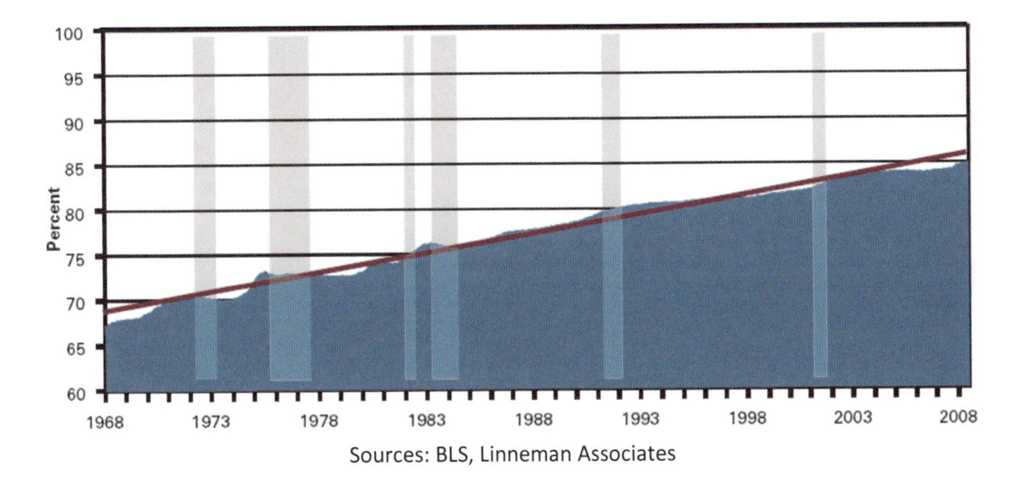

Sources: BLS, Linneman Associates

Another important lesson from the past is that recessions end well before most observers realize they are over. In particular, media accounts of unending recessions and downward spirals regularly appear as much as eighteen months after the next recovery is actually under way. In the end, "our" troubles always seem worse than problems that happened to "them" back in the long-forgotten days of yore. After all, many observers never experienced the 1973-75 or 1981-82 recessions. And most of those who did retain distorted memories. Combine this with an unhealthy dose of Boomer narcissism ("What happens to me is always the most intense") and you grasp why people today think the Great Capital Strike is the worst ever. But it is not. It is not even close to the worst of the past forty years. For example, while observers fret that the Great Capital Strike will hurt New York City employment, they forget that the recessions of 1970, 1973-75, 1980, and 1981-82 effectively wiped out New York City's largest employer: manufacturing.

History suggests that unless you think that the Great Capital Strike will yet evolve into a repeat of the Great Depression, it is a sucker's bet to bet against the U.S. economy. The United States is fueled by too much entrepreneurship and innovation to stay down for long. So stay liquid, be patient, and focus on long-term growth.

Chapter 20 Supplement B

Is This The Worst Ever Yet?

A comparison of historical recessions

Dr Peter Linneman – The Linneman Letter – Winter 2008

In the last issue of the *Wharton Real Estate Review*, John Williams and I examined how the 2008 recession compared to the six recessions of the past forty years. We noted that—as of that time—the current recession was the "least worst" of the seven episodes. An updated analysis indicates that we are in the midst of the second-worst recessionary period of the last forty years, and it is worsening fast (Figures 20B.1 and 20B.2). But do not bet against the U.S. economy. Entrepreneurs are still out there, and with a modicum of political leadership and stable economic policy, we will get through this stronger than ever. However, it will take more time than we thought, due to the needless panic that has been created by our so-called political leadership.

FIGURE 20B.1

"Worst ever" U.S. recessions over the past 40 years

	12/69-11/70	11/73-03/75	01/80 03/80	07/81-11/82	07/90 03/91	03/01-11/01	12/07 01/09
Duration in Months	12	17	3	17	9	9	14
Change in GDP (%)	-0.4%	-3.5%	-0.7%	-2.7%	-1.4%	-0.2%	0.4%
Change in Payroll Employment (%)	-1.2%	-1.6%	0.2%	-3.1%	-1.1%	-1.2%	-1.9%
Change in Real Household Net Worth (%)	1.7%	-10.1%	-1.8%	-1.4%	-3.5%	-3.4%	-4.3%
Change in Auto Sales (%)	-29.2%	-30.4%	-15.9%	-12.5%	-15.2%	-6.2%	-36.0%
Change in Industrial Output (%)	-7.1%	-15.0%	-0.8%	-8.5%	-4.4%	-4.0%	-9.9%
Change in Real Sales by Retail Stores (%)	-2.1%	-9.5%	-4.9%	-5.1%	-5.2%	-1.3%	-13.2%
Change in Construction Contracts for C&I Builidings (%)	-37.6%	-52.2%	-21.1%	-41.3%	-25.0%	-33.6%	-28.6%
Percent Real Return in S&P 500	-23.2%	-39.9%	-12.9%	-23.2%	-16.5%	-11.3%	-50.4%
Change in Real Median Home Price (%)	-15.8%	-4.0%	-3.1%	-8.7%	-6.2%	-1.1%	-7.4%
Change in Real After Tax Profit (%)	-13.3%	-30.4%	-12.7%	-6.8%	-12.3%	-8.3%	-4.3%
Lowest Consumer Confidence Level (Monthly)	72.4	57.6	62.1	65.7	65.1	88.6	57.0
Change in Housing Starts	-17.5%	-30.5%	-32.7%	-25.1%	-31.6%	2.1%	-43.4%
Highest Inflation Rate (Monthly)	6.4%	12.2%	14.6%	11.0%	6.4%	3.6%	5.5%
Highest Unemployment Rate (Monthly)	5.8%	8.3%	6.3%	10.7%	6.8%	4.8%	7.2%

FIGURE 20B.2

Ranking of U.S. recessions over the past 40 years

	12/69-11/70	11/73-03/75	01/80-03/80	07/81-11/82	07/90-03/91	03/01-11/01	12/07-12/08*
	(Rank Order (7 is Worst; 1 is Best)						
Duration in Months	4	6.5	1	6.5	2.5	2.5	5
Change in GDP (%)	3	7	4	6	5	2	1
Change in Payroll (%)	3.5	5	1	7	2	3.5	6
Change in Real Household Net Worth (%)	1	7	3	2	5	4	6
Change in Auto Sales (%)	5	6	4	2	3	1	7
Change in Industrial Output (%)	4	7	1	5	3	2	6
Change in Real Sales by Retail Stores (%)	2	6	3	4	5	1	7
Change in Construction Contracts for C&I Builidings (%)	5	7	1	6	2	4	3
Percent Real Return in S&P 500	4.5	6	2	4.5	3	1	7
Change in Median Home Price (%)	7	3	2	6	4	1	5
Change in Real After Tax Profit (%)	6	7	5	2	4	3	1
Lowest Consumer Confidence Level (Monthly)	2	6	5	3	4	1	7
Change in Housing Starts	2	4	6	3	5	1	7
Highest Inflation Rate (Monthly)	3.5	6	7	5	3.5	1	2
Highest Unemployment Rate (Quarterly)	2	6	3	7	4	1	5
Total Rank Score	54.5	89.5	48	69	55	29	75
Number of Worsts	1	6	1	3	0	0	5
Number of Bests	1	0	4	0	0	8	2

* 2008, Construction contracts, comparisons are through 2Q08.
2008 Median Home Price comparisons are through Oct. 2008.
2008 GDP, net wealth, A/T profit are through 3Q 2008.
2008 S&P Percent Real Return calculated at lowest reading on 11/20/08.
2008 Payroll employment, auto sales, industrial output, and real retail sales are through Nov. 2008.

The dotcom bubble gave rise to a belief that fabulous riches could be achieved by age thirty (thirty-five if you are dumb) through financial models, flip books and PowerPoint presentations. The goal became: fool "them" to give you big money; cash out a short time later; buy a sports franchise and never work again. "Only chumps work past thirty-five" became the prevalent culture. But great business enterprises, and the jobs and fortunes they create, are the result of decades of hard work and execution, not of fast, nifty financial models. Getting rich slowly is the American way, and most overnight successes prove to be fools' gold.

Many of us bear blame for creating the impression that flashy presentations and models, rather than grinding it out, are the sure route to riches. Business schools reinforced the idea that clever ideas trump painstaking execution. And faculty made it acceptable for students to float by as long as they had good financial modeling skills. But there is no substitute for rolling up your sleeves every day and working hard on the details. This is true even if you are a genius. We have all done capitalism a great disservice by not saying that the "get rich quick" emperor has no clothes.

WE CALLED IT – ALMOST

In December 2005, I wrote that failed political leadership, Fed policy errors, and private sector hubris would cause a recession in 2009. Did I foresee the magnitude of the Great Capital Strike or the current recession back then? Of course not. But I knew that humans being human meant that hubris would have its day. The last time it was technology, while in the 1980s it was commercial real estate, as well as Fed policy errors fueling hubris in housing and finance. And talk about hubris: financial firms operating at 35:1 debt-to-equity ratios apparently believed that they were incapable of 3 percent errors (which would have wiped out all their equity).

The serial disaster of the Troubled Asset Relief Program (TARP) turned what might have been a typical recession into a very serious recession. After failing to save Lehman from bankruptcy but supporting AIG, and forcing several shotgun mergers, President George W. Bush, Fed Chairman Ben Bernanke, Treasury Secretary Henry Paulson, presidential candidates McCain and Obama, as well as the leadership on both sides of the aisle in both chambers of Congress, triggered widespread panic when they announced on September 24 that the world would end if they did not enact legislation saving us. Overnight they managed to generate total panic on Main Street.

On the morning of September 29, this assembly of bipartisan leaders proudly announced that they had drafted legislation that would save mankind—only to watch as their handiwork was handily defeated. No true political leader should ever call for a critical vote without knowing that he or she actually has the votes. Yet the entire political leadership of both parties was clueless about the fate that awaited their proposed legislative salvation. The magnitude of this political failure was grasped by investors, who wrung their hands with a 9.7 percent sell-off between the September 26 and September 29 S&P 500 close (Figure 20B.3).

FIGURE 20B.3

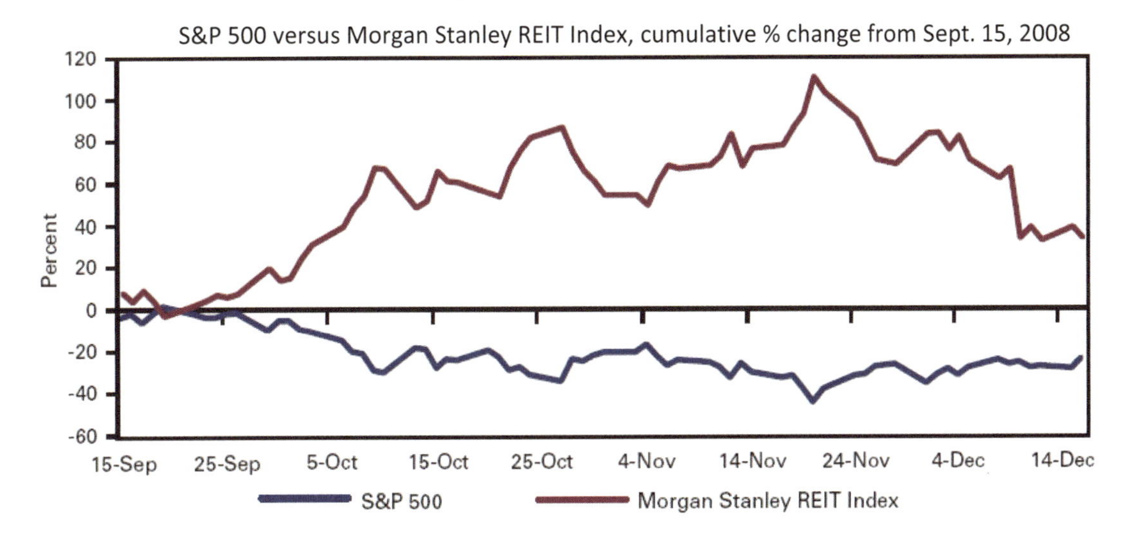

FIGURE 20B.4

Volatility is off the charts

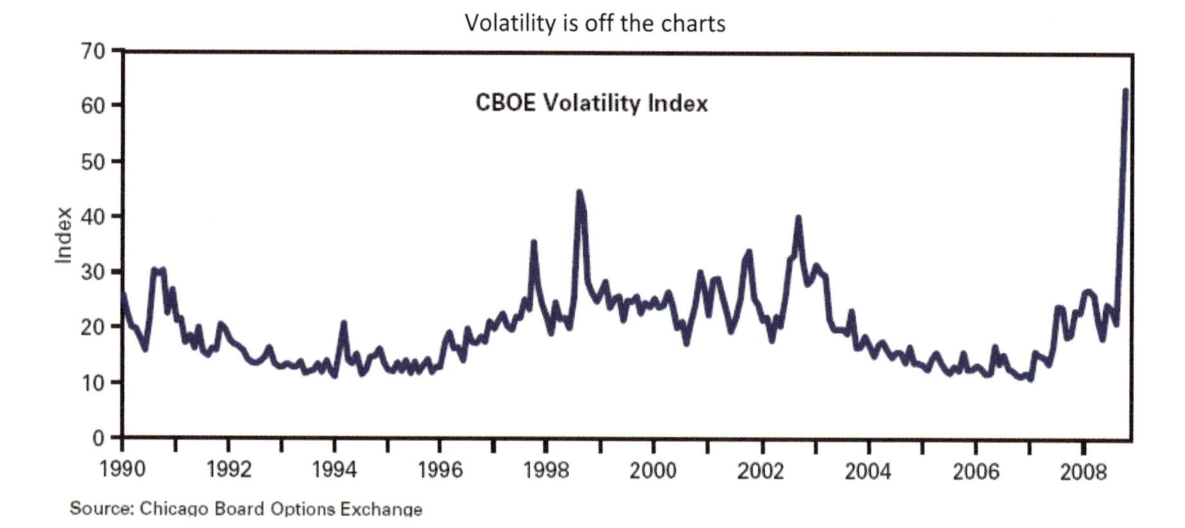

The farce did not end there. Four days later, Congress easily passed the same basic TARP proposal, supplemented with loads of pork, including appropriations for a NASCAR race track and tax breaks for a toy manufacturer of wooden arrowheads. This political travesty combined with the abandonment of economic policy for ad hoc decision making, caused a run on banks and money market funds, and a surge of hedge and mutual fund redemptions.

Instead of clear and consistent policies, the Bush Administration took on a transparency and consistency worthy of Mugabe's Zimbabwe or Putin's Russia, and abandoned considered policy for ad hoc "deals". But when the rules of the economic game disappear, so too do the people willing to play that game. So it was not a surprise that when economic rules became idiosyncratic and unpredictable, people rushed to cash and government bonds. The "deal" approach of the past six months will go down as one of the darkest eras of U.S. economic policy, creating a far deeper recession than was necessary.

The disaster continued. On October 14, Secretary Paulson (after appointing an inexperienced thirty-five-year-old to head TARP) announced that he would use $250 billion of the $700 billion to inject preferred equity in selected banks (no description was offered of how they would be selected)—after months of saying that this was not the right path. Then on November 12, he announced that he would not purchase any troubled assets, but would inject funds into banks and other companies (such as auto makers). This announcement was delivered with no apology and no apparent concern for the consequences of such a wildly changed "policy". Stocks fell another 5.2 percent and volatility grew as policy evaporated (Figure 20B.4).

As governments around the world stepped in to prop up their banks, global stock markets plummeted, registering their opinion of the long-term impact of the global drift toward socialism and of ad hoc "pragmatic decision making" rather than a reliance on markets and consistent economic policy.

BE WARY OF SAVIORS

In the past few months, we have discovered what it is like to live in a world where economic success and failure hinges primarily on government dictate rather than on markets satisfying customers and competition. As the U.S. Treasury made deals to "save" the economy, the economy reacted like a patient with a penicillin allergy who had been given penicillin. As the rules of the economic game were replaced by government fiat, people withdrew en masse from the economic game.

FIGURE 20B.5

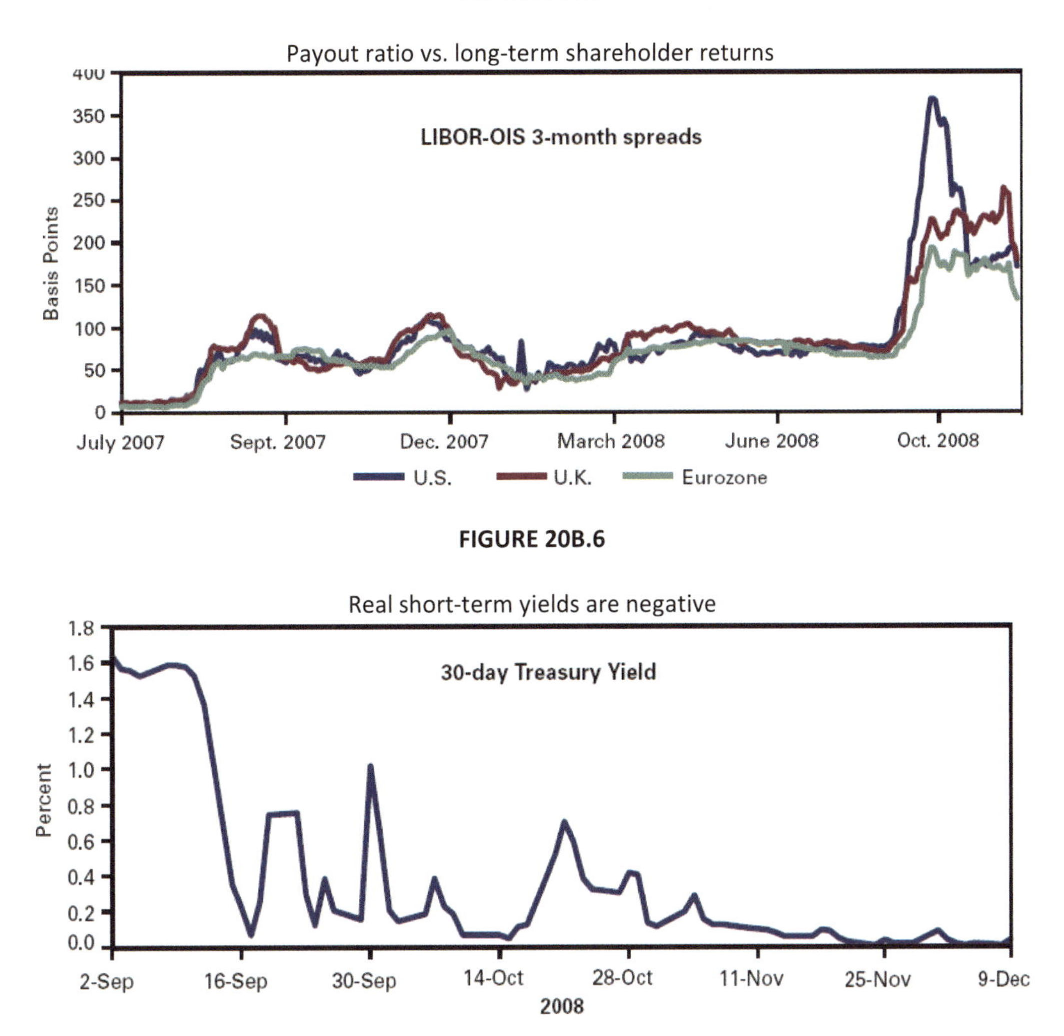

Uncertainty is the deadly enemy of efficient decision-making, and the government's daily attempts to "save us" ratcheted up the level of economic uncertainty (Figure 20B.5). As uncertainty skyrocketed, the economy collapsed. Faced with government-created panic, common citizens sought cash by runs on banks and mutual funds, while sophisticated investors sold everything they could to move into government notes. Short-term Treasury bill yields took a nosedive, resulting in negative real returns (Figure 20B.6). Just as the economic fabric is thin in government-dictated economies such as Russia, Zimbabwe and Venezuela, so too the collapse of the rule of economic law has crippled the U.S. economy.

This abrogation of rules was underscored by the lame-duck Treasury's decision to bail out the Hopeless Three automakers at unspecified terms, within twenty-four hours after U.S. lawmakers defeated a bailout bill (which was opposed by 65 percent of Americans). This decision made a mockery of the legislative process, and was the nearest thing to a political coup that we have witnessed in the U.S. during our lifetime.

The economy will rebound from a needlessly deep recession far more quickly than most anticipate. This is particularly true in view of the enormous decline in the price of oil. Using the rule of thumb that each $10 increment in oil price above $30 per barrel reduces GDP by roughly 30 basis points, the recent oil price decline provides a 3 percent stimulus.

FIGURE 20B.7

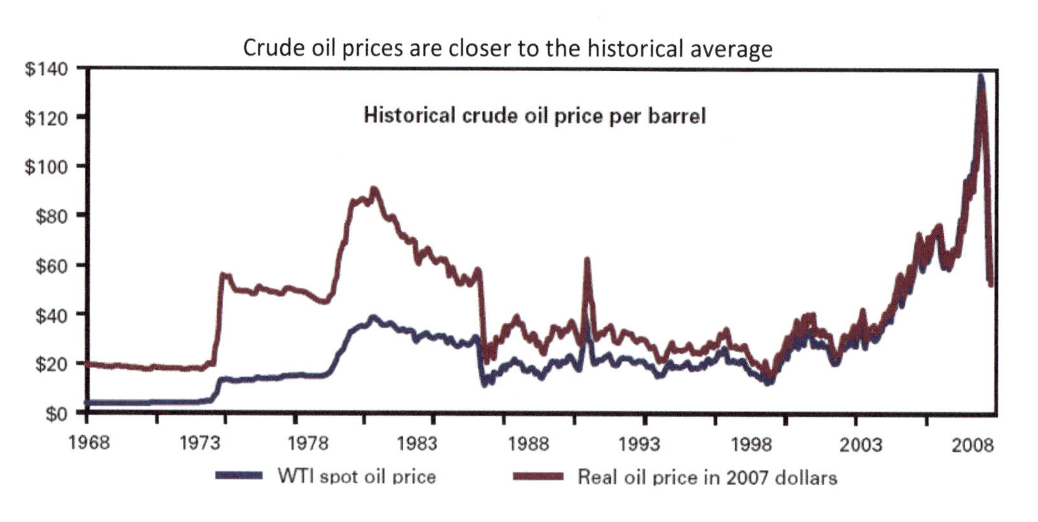

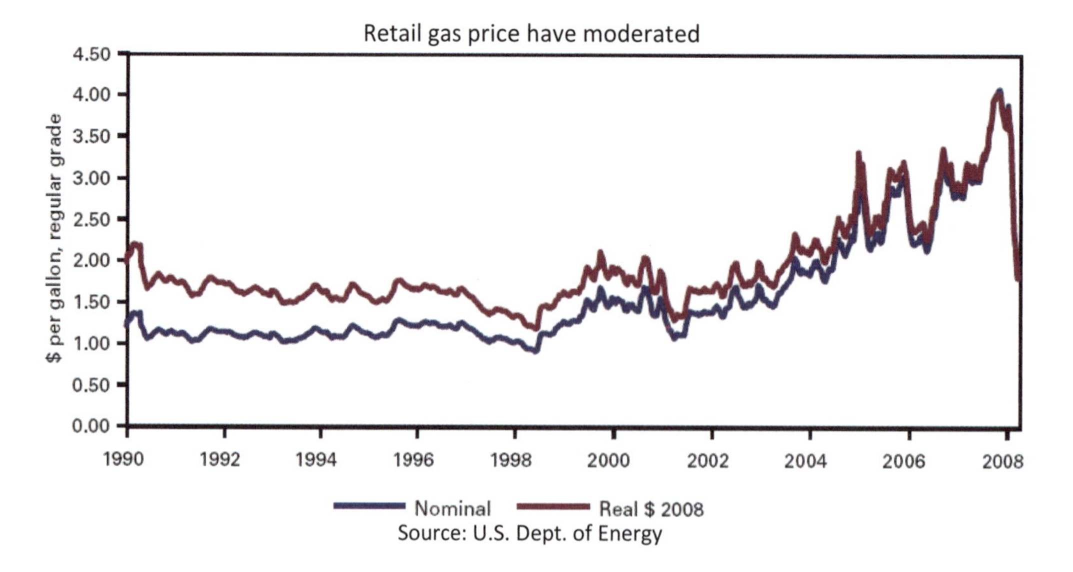

Source: U.S. Dept. of Energy

A major and widely overlooked cause of the worldwide recession was the precipitous run-up in oil prices to $147 per barrel (Figures 20B.7 and 20B.8). As rapidly elevated oil prices worked through economies around the world the economic burden became unbearable, and global growth plummeted from 4.5 percent to less than 2.5 percent.

FIGURE 20B.9

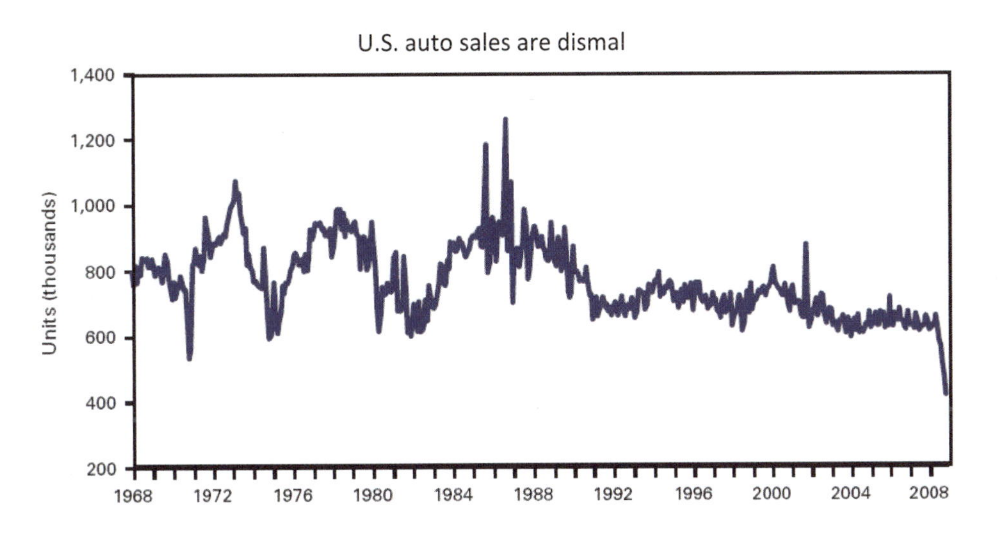

U.S. auto sales declined roughly 30 percent from their peak in the third quarter of 2005, while consumer real expenditures on gasoline and related products fell by 6 percent over the same period (Figures 20B.9 and 20B.10). In fact, monthly auto sales declined by $18.1 billion when comparing June 2007 to November 2008. Total monthly retail sales declined by $18.6 billion during that time. As was the case during the Weimar Republic, when people sought "salvation" in dubious political leaders, these are dangerous times. The fact that $700 billion in "salvation financing" was hurriedly passed by Congress only to become a blank check public welfare program for the politically connected should underscore our concern.

FIGURE 20B.10

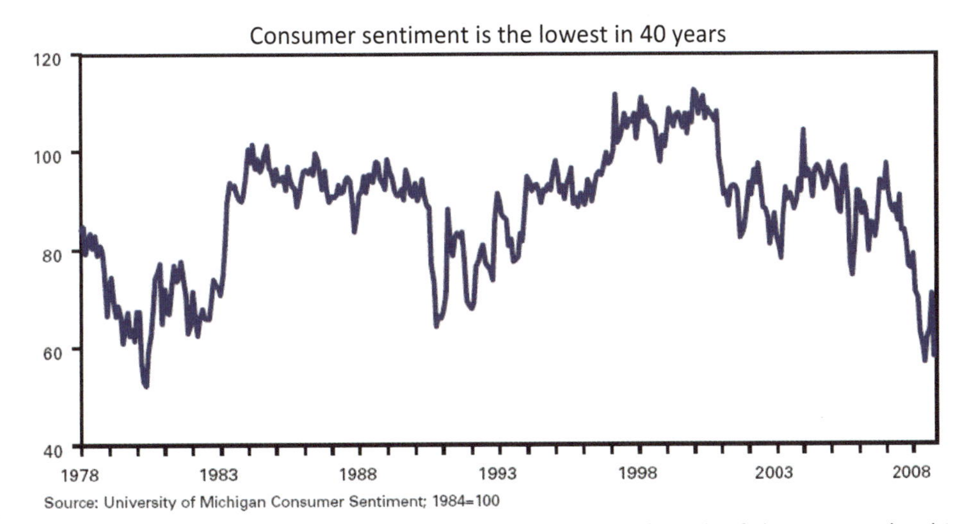

There are reasons why governments around the world sold off much of their nationalized interests over the past two decades, including: scandals arising from political lending, hiring and contracting at nationalized firms; a lack of financial and managerial innovation; a financial system run with the plodding effectiveness of the U.S.

Postal System; the lack of responsive customer service; ever growing subsidies to support inefficient financial entities; large losses suffered on loan portfolios; politicians retiring to well-paid cushy bank directorships. It was a *state-owned* German bank that was so asleep at the wheel that it wired €300 million to Lehman minutes before Lehman declared bankruptcy. Also, recall the political corruption that characterized state-owned banks in Mexico and Italy. And let us not forget the horrid underwriting record of state-owned Chinese, French, and German banks.

Why was Bear Stearns saved but not Lehman? Why were forced mergers arranged for some institutions but not others? Why was AIG saved? Why did TARP initially focus on a buy-in of assets rather than guarantees or equity infusions? Why was TARP $700 billion rather than $600 or $800 billion? Why was Citibank propped up while Indy Mac and Wachovia were set adrift? Why was the buy-in plan dropped in favor of cash injections just weeks later? Will short sales be allowed? And if so, for how long? Why was $125 billion in preferred equity earmarked for eight selected banks (as opposed to seven or nine)? Why $125 billion for all others? Why were the Hopeless Three provided access to TARP after Congress said no to subsidies? No one knows—or is willing to share—the answers to these questions.

The absence of a clearly articulated economic policy may be understandable, but it is not forgivable. This is an era in which reporters were embedded with our troops in Iraq, to assure that they "got the message out" expeditiously. The absence of a message in this case created widespread financial and economic panic, with cascading consequences.

TRUST MATTERS

Without trust, any society will degenerate into petty survivalism. One of the primary functions of government is to codify basic trust (prohibitions against theft, rape, and murder) and to punish those (thieves, rapists, and murderers) who violate societal trust. Basic financial trust revolves around the belief that debts will be repaid, that entities seeking debt and equity are truthful, and that governments will punish wrong-doers and not act capriciously. It is reflective of the serial failure of political leadership that from September 13 to November 21, not only did the stock market collapse and debt spreads substantially widen, but also that the commercial paper market all but ceased to function, and money market funds teetered. LIBOR spreads over the Fed Funds rate spiked 53 percent (from 248 basis points the day before the initial failed TARP vote to 380 basis points on October 10th); REITs fell by 76 percent; while AAA CMBS spreads rose by 138 basis points, and the S&P 500 fell by 25.9 percent. Only the strongest and most transparent non-financial borrowers have been able to overcome this widespread lack of trust.

Like children playing the old game "button, button, who has the button?", capital sources have hoarded cash as they play "losses, losses, who has the losses?" Real yields on 30-day Treasuries reached -1.57 percent (Figure 20B.11), underscoring the fact that many savvy investors were happier to experience guaranteed losses of merely 2 percent, rather than stumbling into huge losses, and as of December 19, the 30-year Treasury yield was 2.6 percent.

FIGURE 20B.11

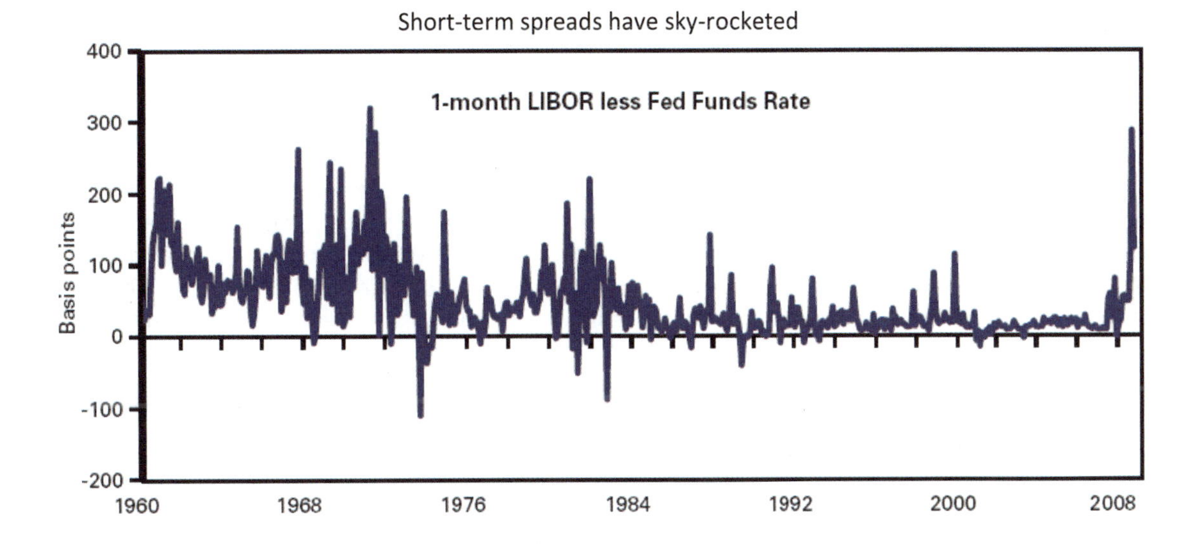

What the U.S. economy needs is the immediate and total disclosure of all assets and liabilities (with no materiality, safe harbor or off-balance sheet exceptions) from any institution with access to any form of state or federal guarantee. If you owe the donut delivery kid $10, just tell us and we'll decide whether it is a material liability. And mark-to-market valuations should only be applied to assets with active markets (for example, a bid-ask spread of less than 2 percent). A full disclosure requirement could be implemented immediately, and would allow investors to assess who holds the losses, restoring basic financial trust. It would also quickly reveal which financial institutions are insolvent, allowing public and private liquidity infusions to be given only to the living, while an RTC-like agency set about the orderly liquidation of the dead.

The losses of 2004-2007 have created a mine field. But just as there are a finite number of mines in a mine field, there are a finite number of losses. The real question is who holds the losses? The strange thing is that each time a loss-mine explodes (Bear Stearns, Fannie/Freddie, AIG, Lehman, Wachovia, Washington Mutual), we become a bit safer, as there is one less mine to be inadvertently stepped on (this is true in spite of collateral damage to those near the detonation). Yet psychologically speaking, seeing firms blown to bits erodes our confidence, makes us feel more endangered, stops us dead in our tracks, and creates public panic.

What is required to get the economy out of this minefield of losses? Leadership! A great officer with troops stuck in a mine field: does not panic; keeps the troops from panicking; identifies the location of the mines; and expeditiously clears a path so that the troops may proceed forward. Only after the troops are safely out of the mine field does the officer worry about how much is paid to the victims and who is at fault for the troops marching into the minefield. There will be finger-pointing, but first the mines must be cleared away.

The mines the economy faces are the future losses associated with poorly underwritten investments made during 2004 through early 2007. The trouble is that we do not know how big these losses are, when they will occur, which firms hold these assets, or if these losses will wipe out their equity. Unfortunately, like a young lieutenant fresh out of West Point, our political leadership panicked in the mine field. This panic quickly spilled over to the troops on both Wall Street and Main Street. And we still do not know who holds the losses. Until the location of the losses is revealed, the economy and capital will largely stand around in a worried state, rather than moving forward.

This is going to be a recession rivaling 1973-1975, and it is going to take time to work our way through it. Unfortunately, the politically-created panic coincided with the Christmas retail season. People fell into a post-9/11 mentality, where even if they had money, they did not spend because it seemed like the wrong thing to do. The result was even more bad economic news.

THE WAY FORWARD

A large stimulus package is in the offing, but the evidence on the efficacy of such packages is highly questionable at best. At a theoretical level, government borrowing and spending largely only encourages the private sector to save more to service future debt burdens, reducing spending today. Moreover, there may be substitution between public and private spending. For example, if the government decides to feed all school children as a part of the stimulus package, private expenditures on children's lunches will fall dramatically, yielding little net change in the economy. The argument for government spending as a stimulus is most compelling for infrastructure programs, where little private sector substitution occurs. However, if expenditures degenerate into massive pork allocation, there will be a social loss.

Contemporaneous descriptions of past recessions are always characterized by observations such as: "This is the worst I can remember"; "It has never been this bad"; "This one is different"; "This one will last much longer than previous ones"; "I don't see any catalyst to get us out of this one"; "There is no sector to lead us out of it"; and "This recession will fundamentally change the economy". Yet even as boardrooms, analyst reports, the media, and government officials, make such statements, a sustained recovery is generally only months away. This time will be the same.

No modern recovery has had a "catalyst" to turn things around. In each case, sustained productivity growth, population growth and a return to fundamentals were the routes to resumed economic growth. And the growth was not driven by an industry or sector, but rather by a broad based recovery, with isolated lagging sectors. And rebounds, like downturns, happened far more rapidly than anyone predicted. This time will be the same.

Commercial mortgage-backed security (CMBS) must return to its simple roots: loan-to-value ratios of 50 percent to 60 percent; simple pass-through structures; high debt coverage ratios; pools of assets with similar risk characteristics (only apartments, for example); and over-collateralization. This simplified structuring would restore transparency, and when fear is rampant, transparency and simplicity maximize value.

The best news for real estate is that new construction financings were virtually non-existent in late 2007 and 2008. This will continue into 2009, meaning that weakening demand fundamentals will meet limited supply expansion, rather than the exploding supply which usually appears at the end of an economic cycle. Housing prices are down year-over-year by 4 percent for the nation, based on the OFHEO housing price index (Figure 20B.12). By mid-2009, the housing markets will start to shift from an excess supply to the very early stages of an excess demand.

FIGURE 20B.12

Case-Shiller versus OFHEO home prices indices through 3Q08

MSA	Case-Shiller % change			OFHEO % change		
	YE 2005 to 3Q08	1-Year	3rd Qtr	YE 2005 to 3Q08	1-Year	3rd Qtr
Atlanta	(5.8)	(9.5)	(1.5)	2.4	(1.8)	(2.3)
Boston	(10.3)	(5.7)	(0.8)	(8.9)	(4.1)	(2.7)
Charlotte, N.C.	7.9	(3.5)	(2.3)	15.9	1.6	(1.7)
Chicago	(9.4)	(10.1)	(1.5)	2.2	(3.8)	(2.7)
Cleveland	(10.5)	(6.4)	0.2	(7.8)	(5.7)	(5.1)
Dallas	(0.2)	(2.7)	(0.4)	8.7	2.6	0.0
Denver	(4.8)	(5.4)	(0.5)	(1.9)	(1.0)	(2.2)
Detroit	(29.0)	(18.6)	(2.7)	(21.9)	(13.3)	(6.8)
Las Vegas	(36.1)	(31.3)	(7.5)	(26.4)	(26.8)	(12.6)
Los Angeles	(30.3)	(27.6)	(5.7)	(13.5)	(18.8)	(6.6)
Miami	(32.5)	(28.4)	(5.9)	(4.4)	(17.9)	(8.2)
Minneapolis	(17.5)	(14.4)	(0.7)	(7.3)	(6.5)	(4.3)
New York	(10.0)	(7.3)	(1.8)	1.5	(4.5)	(3.2)
Phoenix	(36.7)	(31.9)	(8.7)	(11.9)	(16.6)	(7.5)
Portland, Oregon	3.5	(8.6)	(3.1)	13.9	(2.6)	(2.3)
San Diego	(34.0)	(26.3)	(6.4)	(23.3)	(17.6)	(6.1)
San Francisco	(32.3)	(29.5)	(8.9)	(6.8)	(8.0)	(2.6)
Seattle	5.3	(9.8)	(3.1)	16.3	(3.0)	(2.2)
Tampa	(24.5)	(18.5)	(2.2)	(10.5)	(15.1)	(4.6)
Washington	(23.2)	(17.2)	(3.9)	(9.5)	(12.5)	(4.7)
United States	**(19.8)**	**(16.6)**	**(3.5)**	**1.5**	**(4.0)**	**(2.7)**

Source: Case-Shiller, Office of Federal Housing Enterprise Oversight, Linneman Associates.

FIGURE 20B.13

Mortgage delinquency rates are on the rise

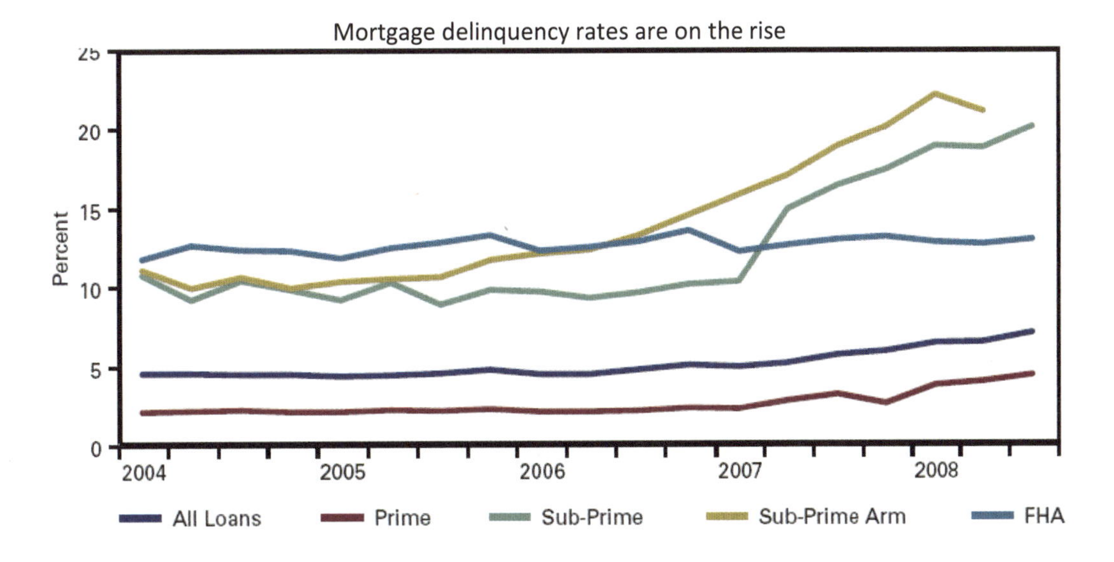

The roughly $1 billion in global losses by financial institutions are primarily associated with loans that are fully current. This means the losses are primarily conjectural losses associated with current loans. Are these staggering paper losses reflective of future cash flow losses, a greater liquidity premium, an increased risk premium, or sheer irrational panic? Probably all of the above, but no one knows for sure, as the actual losses will not be known for many years. Each time someone makes a payment on their mortgage, car loan, student loan, or credit card, the maximum potential loss declines. Only when every outstanding loan originated in 2004-2007 is either retired or settled via a post-foreclosure sale will the actual losses be tallied. This may take anywhere from three to twenty-five years. Until then, estimates of losses are a pure guessing game.

A poorly underwritten mortgage issued in February 2005 to a greedy speculative home flipper, at the behest of a snake oil salesman peddling a "can't lose" proposition, with the assistance of a slimy sub-prime broker, cannot be magically transformed into a prudent loan. If instead of disclosing the loss-mines and getting the economy moving forward, we point fingers, pass counter-productive legislation, and raise taxes, our languishing economy will create unnecessarily large future losses.

We all need to admit "I am guilty" because: I did not argue forcefully enough that the excesses were crazy; I took some of that poorly underwritten debt; I invested in money market funds that bought anything rated AAA, irrespective of real asset quality; I financed (or built) a home or condo using excessively cheap debt; I invested in the stocks of firms which carelessly used cheap short-term debt to invest in highly leveraged illiquid long-term assets; I elected politicians who required Freddie/Fannie to take ever greater risks; I put my money in insured depositories without caring if they were making sound loans with my deposits. In short, this mess is my fault. Having accepted guilt, we can focus on identifying the location of the loss-mines and providing capital transfusions (both public and private) to the living, thus getting the U.S. economy back on track without creating unnecessary damage.

Even if the present value of the losses is ultimately $1.2 trillion, the full reimbursement of these losses via the proceeds of long-term federal debt will cost us less than $1.4 trillion (including financing costs), versus aggregate U.S. GDP of roughly $150-170 trillion, and federal spending of $30 trillion to $35 trillion, over the next 10 years. That is, for a mere 0.7 percent of our income over the next ten years, we can reimburse the maximum conceivable losses. It is only a few hours of work a year by each of us, and less than a couple percent of our net worth (spread over ten years).

So please take the "I am guilty" pledge, and urge our political leaders to cover the losses as they occur out of our future income. This is most easily be done by a ten-year federal guarantee of all remaining interest and principal payments due on every loan written from mid-2004 through mid-2007. After all, we are all guilty, so we should all pay.

This loan guarantee program (subject to a good faith requirement effort to collect on loans and a fraud exception) will spread the government cash flow burden over time, as payments will occur only as the loans default. This policy can be implemented with minimal effort and will instantly raise the value of loans by converting most qualifying debt to government debt valuation, thus allowing this debt to be sold efficiently as government credit, creating cash proceeds for new loans.

Everyone agrees that the financial system was substantially over-leveraged and that we need to de-lever. But no one with debt wants to be impacted by this policy. De-lever "them", not "me". But all de-leveraging efforts must be concentrated on the debt that requires rebalancing, maturing loans, or new loans, as the lender cannot generally reduce lending on long-term debt. Hence, the de-leveraging of the system is 100 percent focused on about 20 percent of all loans. As a result, many wildly over-levered situations get a free pass, while new loans are stonewalled by lenders.

But if lenders make new loans, they will not achieve their leverage targets. It is like going from a diet of 3,000 calories a day to 900 calories a day: on such a diet, even a lot of healthy food has to be forsaken. However, once we hit our target weight, we can go to a 2,400 calorie diet. This will occur once lenders reach their target exposures.

The "de-lever them, not me" sentiment is the schizophrenic element of the lender bailout efforts. On the one hand, infusions of government money are intended to increase the asset base to more effectively match current leverage. At the same time, banks are being told to expand their lending. But the first task is to right-size lender balance sheets. Lending will resume once this objective is achieved.

A FINAL THOUGHT

We must resist the urge to save everyone—Wall Street, Detroit, homebuilders, mortgage borrowers. Everyone has a "special" case to make. We have Chapter 11 as a limbo where companies can attempt to reconstitute themselves. This protection should be extended in a simple form to consumers. But "special" bailouts do nothing but redistribute income according to political clout, undermining confidence in economic outcomes, causing economic activity to drop precipitously.

Losers must lose if winners are to prosper. If one or more of the Hopeless Three goes bankrupt, their competitors' sales will rise as consumers shift their purchases. The increased sales realized by the competitors, who make their vehicles in the U.S., will improve their operating margins, allowing them to avoid financial distress and expand output and employment. As with wildebeest in the Masai Mara, death is essential to life.

Finally, people knew that leverage was not without risk. They relished its upside, and they now must suffer its downside. The idea that a reasonably safe real estate cash stream bought at a 4-5 percent cap rate could generate a 20 percent return is absurd unless premised on carry trades and loads of ever available debt. But just as tenants do not always renew their leases, lenders do not always roll their loans. Debt is wonderful on the upside, but remorseless on the downside. This lesson will hopefully be remembered for a new generation.

Chapter 20 Supplement C

Will We Need More Office Space?

Dr. Peter Linneman – Wharton Real Estate Review – Fall 1997
This research is funded by the Wharton Real Estate Center's Research Sponsor Program.

Office markets in the United States are in much better balance than five years ago. Yet, some observers wonder whether we will need to build more office space over the next decade. Many analysts see three forces threatening the future demand for office space: technological advancement; improved space management techniques; and corporate downsizing. They argue that these forces will massively reduce the demand for office space, and that continuing technological advances will result in office tenants using less and less space while working from ever more remote locations. In this scenario, virtual offices make traditional offices obsolete, as workers interact via the Internet and video screens, rather than face-to-face in offices and conference rooms. The tenants' use of more efficient space management techniques, including home offices and hoteling, reinforces this scenario. Pessimists argue that the "1-2 punch" of technology and improved space management efficiency will be followed by a "knock out punch" — continued corporate downsizing. They maintain that as employers downsize, more and more workers will be let go, emptying vast amounts of office space. Is such a scenario likely?

SOME FACTS IN A FIELD OF CONJECTURE

Since 1980 there have been unprecedented technological and managerial advancements, including: the personal computer; massive increases in data storage capacity and efficiency; staggering data processing and assimilation expansion; cheap and accessible fax and telephonic communication; beepers; video conferencing; networking; and a stunning reduction in the real cost of information. If technological advancement reduces the demand for office space, then surely space per office worker must have fallen steadily since 1980. However, just the opposite has happened! Figure 1 displays the estimated amount of space used per worker in the office sector since 1980 based on Torto/Wheaton data. Since 1980 the estimated space per worker has actually risen from 142 ft^2 to 155 ft^2. This amounts to an increase of just under 1 ft^2 a year, or roughly 0.6 percent annually.

Office space usage fell from a peak in 1992 through 1994. This decline reflects the cyclical economic recession and subsequent strong recovery, not a technologically or managerially induced reduction in space usage. As the U.S. economy reached the peak of its business cycle in 1994, businesses cautiously expanded their space usage with an eye to more sustainable job growth. This resulted in space per worker decreasing, even as total space demanded rose dramatically due to employment growth. As the economy achieved a more sustainable level of employment growth in 1995, space per worker grew again at about 1 ft^2 per year. Similarly, the high levels of space per worker registered in 1991-1992 reflected rising space demand in anticipation of normal employment growth rates. A similar pattern occurred during the economic cycle of the early 1980s.

During the period 1980-1995, real office rents fell approximately 40 percent. Some of the increased usage of space reflects a response to falling real rents. Precise estimates of the demand elasticity for office space do not exist, however this elasticity is probably about 0.1. That is, a 10 percent reduction in real rents increases the demand for space per worker by 1 percent. Such an elasticity suggests that the demand for space per worker rose about 4 percent since 1980 due to real rental decreases. Stated differently, even after adjusting for the impact of real rental decreases, the trend in space demand is still roughly 0.4 ft^2 per worker per year.

FIGURE 20C.1

Occupied Office Space per Office Worker

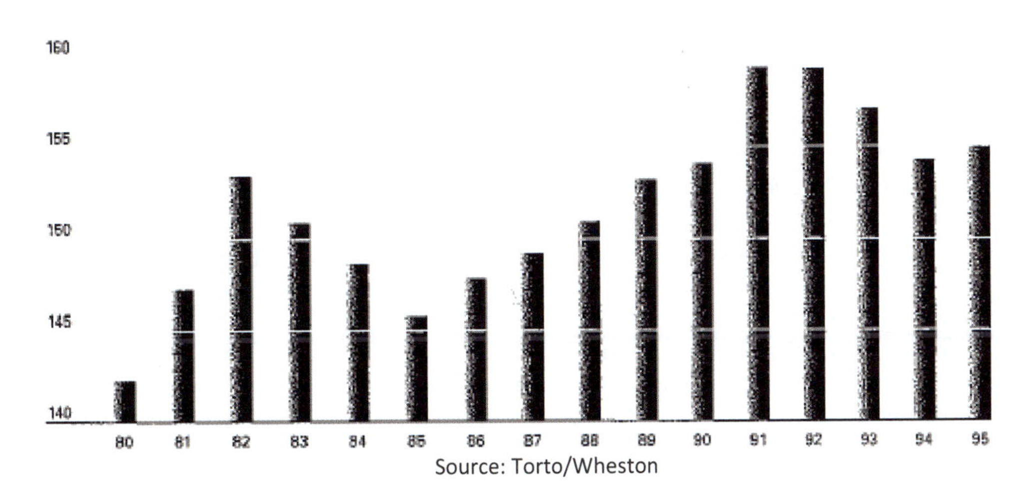

Source: Torto/Wheston

Several forces have driven space per worker steadily upwards during this period of massive technological and space management advances. First, while technology has greatly reduced the need for certain types of space (e.g. typing pools), at the same time it has increased the demand for other types of space (e.g. video conferencing facilities and trading floors). The "doctors of doom" for office demand observe the negative impacts of technology, but fail to appreciate the subtle — and more powerful — expansionary technological impacts on office space. The purpose of the technology, which appears to be to "free" executives from their offices is widely misunderstood. This technology is intended to raise productivity to acceptable levels while executives are out of the office, rather than eliminating the need for an extensive office support base. In fact, more office support staff is now required due to the executives' greater productivity while on the road. This technologically induced productivity gain increases the demand for office space.

A third factor is a change in the composition of jobs which have continuously grown more "professional" and "office intensive", in the office sector. Thirty years ago armies of clerks and typists each occupied tiny amounts of space. The emergence of a large cadre of senior management (including bankers, attorneys, accountants, and consultants) has increased space allocations per worker. The modern American firm employs more professionals (who use larger amounts of space) per support worker (who use less space) than ever before. The average space per worker has risen due to of the changing mix of workers. In fact, the average space per worker has risen even though modern space management techniques allocate less space than before to both professional and support workers. For example, if formerly two support workers used 100 ft^2 each in conjunction with one professional using 200 ft^2, where now two professionals use 175 ft^2 each in conjunction with one support worker using 75 ft^2, average space per worker rises from 133 ft^2 to 142 ft^2 even though both types of workers use substantially less space than before.

Finally, in our service-based economy it has become increasingly critical that firms provide an office environment that attracts and retains high-value-added employees. For example, the annual after-tax cost of providing an additional 200 ft^2 to a high-producing professional is a mere \$6,000, even at \$45 per ft^2 rents. However, this is a small price to pay if it attracts an employee who will generate annual net after-tax profits in excess of \$150,000.

THE IMPACT OF HOME OFFICES

A common concern regarding the future demand for office space is that people will telecommute from their homes, thus eliminating the need for traditional offices. A study by the U.S. Bureau of Labor Statistics found that in 1994 approximately 20 million Americans claimed to work at home. However, more than 99 percent of these individuals reported that they also had offices at their places of employment. In other words, only 100,000 worked at home. This low rate of exclusive home office usage is hardly surprising. Many of us work in our homes but we also have offices (frequently large and elaborate) at our places of employment.

The 100,000 Americans who work exclusively from their homes do not represent a threat to the future demand for office space. Even if this number were to triple over the next decade, it would mean that only an additional 200,000 workers would work exclusively from their homes. If each of these new telecommuters would have occupied 160 ft^2, the reduction in the total demand for office space will be only 32 million ft^2 over the next decade. While 32 million ft^2 is not a trivial amount of space, it represents less than 0.5 percent of the current U.S. office stock.

In fact, this 32 million ft^2 demand reduction probably represents the upper bound of the adverse impact of home office usage on office demand over the next decade. This is because for most Americans the home is an extremely poor work environment. Most workers cannot be productive in home offices given the distractions of their home lives. These distractions include children, pets, household chores, computer games, food, shopping, surfing the Internet, and the ever present television complete with VCR and 100 cable channels! The fact that technology has greatly increased our home entertainment choices actually makes the home an increasingly less productive work environment. Few workers possess the self discipline necessary to produce the output necessary to generate their current incomes from their homes. In addition, only highly paid employees can create home work environments of sufficient quality to allow them to exclusively work at home. Most workers simply do not have large enough — or nice enough — homes to provide quality work environments. Also, most jobs require constant interaction with co-workers for reasons of both productivity and office politics. The old phrase "out of sight, out of mind" means that the executive who chooses to work exclusively from his home will inevitably lose political power in the firm, even if his actual productivity equals that of his peers working in the office.

The viability of office space is vividly demonstrated by Microsoft, perhaps the world's most technologically advanced firm. Microsoft is currently building large amounts of office space, utilizing roughly 250 ft^2 per employee. If Microsoft cannot figure out how to use technology to eliminate office space, it will be a very long time before banks, law firms, and insurance companies figure out a way to do so!

Management continues to be about motivating and coordinating humans in teams. This is still most effectively achieved in the traditional office environment. Exclusive users of home offices tend to be those who do not work in teams (such as university professors and journalists, who are precisely those who predict the future dominance of the home office!). However, these are not typical workers. To believe that the home office is a serious threat to the future of office demand ignores the simple realities of both modern home and work life.

THE IMPACTS OF DOWNSIZING

Another common argument is that since firms are downsizing they no longer need as much office space. This claim is correct as far as it goes, however, it stops far short of a complete analysis of the impacts of downsizing. Most downsizing reflects the outsourcing of tasks previously done internally at large firms, as they focus on their core competencies.

After the downsizing occurs, roughly the same number of workers perform outsourced tasks. However, they are now employed at smaller firms possessing core competencies in the outsourced activities. Downsizing does not mean a drop in total employment, but the reshuffling of tasks and employment among firms. In fact, U.S.

employment has continued to grow by roughly 1.7 million workers per year even as downsizing has spread. Often after downsizing, the same individuals perform the same tasks as before, the difference is that they are now employees of smaller firms serving as vendors.

THE NEXT DECADE

The increase in the demand for office space over the next decade depends on the interaction between the amount of space used per office worker and the growth of the number of office workers. As noted earlier, the underlying trend in space per worker is to add roughly 0.4 ft^2 per year. Offsetting this trend is the expectation that real office rents will rise by roughly 30-40 percent over the next decade, implying a reduction in space demand of 3-4 percent per worker. Combining these factors means that over the next decade the real rental elasticity impact will essentially negate the upward trend in office use per worker. Therefore, the space per office worker will remain roughly constant over the next decade.

Approximately 32 percent of the workers in the U.S. are generally categorized as working in the office sector, up from approximately 30 percent a decade ago. Over the next decade, the U.S. economy will probably continue to shift towards the office sector. However, in order to provide a conservative office demand projection, it is assumed that the proportion of the economy employed in the office sector remains at its current level over the next decade.

Over the last 15 years, the U.S. economy, driven by the steady growth rate of the U.S. population (roughly 1 percent annually), has averaged approximately 1.7 million new jobs each year. (This annual job growth rate over the next decade actually understates the expected growth in jobs in the U.S. economy, since it ignores the effect of compounding on the growth base.) To remain conservative it is assumed that a total of 17 million new jobs will be added to the U.S. economy over the next decade. Applying the current proportion of jobs in the office sector to this job growth estimate implies that nearly 5.4 million new office sector jobs will be created over the next decade.

To obtain the estimated increase in the demand for office space over the next decade, the current amount of space per office worker (155 ft^2) is multiplied by the increase in office sector employment over the next decade (5,372,000). This yields a total estimated demand increase of about 832 million ft^2 over the next 10 years. From this, the 32 million ft^2 decline associated with increased home office use is subtracted, to arrive at a net increase in office demand of about 800 million ft^2. This represents an approximately 13 percent increase in the demand for office space, spread over the next 10 years. Stated differently, the demand for office space will conservatively grow by an annual rate of 1.25 percent over the next decade. This means that each year the U.S. will absorb roughly the entire office stocks of the Philadelphia and Orlando metropolitan areas combined. In the next decade, an amount equal to two New York City metropolitan areas plus one Chicago metropolitan area will be absorbed.

The current national office vacancy rate is roughly 13 percent. Assume that the equilibrium vacancy rate is 5-6 percent, and that on average 1 percent of the current office stock is destroyed or rendered obsolete each year. Thus, a projected increased demand of 800 million ft^2 requires that roughly 1 billion ft^2 of the new office space will have to be developed over the next decade. Due to current vacancy levels and real rental rates relative to replacement costs, the bulk of this new development will occur after the year 1999. This amounts to an annual average of approximately 1.3 percent of the existing office stock.

These estimates indicate that the demand for office space in the United States will grow substantially over the coming decade, in spite of significant real rent increases (ultimately reaching replacement cost levels) and continued managerial and technological advances. The total increase in office demand will range from 800 million-1.5 billion ft^2 over the coming decade. The challenge facing the office real estate sector will be to bring new space on line only as it is economically justified.

Chapter 21
There Are a Lot of Right Ways to Do It

"Do the right thing simply because it is the right thing to do".
-Dr. Peter Linneman

ETHICS IN REAL ESTATE?

Yes, there are ethics in real estate. In fact, you are well advised to behave ethically if you want to be a successful long-term investor. At the end of the day, "the deal" is always secondary to people and relationships. More money has been lost on "great deals" done with the wrong people, than doing the wrong deal with great people. This is particularly true in real estate, where you have relatively predictable cash streams and a smaller opportunity to create value. Therefore, if you cheat investors, constantly tie them up in knots, or make it difficult to operate, you will have a short and troubled career.

Your reputation is all you have in business. As a young person, your problem is that you have no reputation. You may believe that you do, because of the way you have lived your life, but people in the industry have not been with you and rarely can call anyone they know and respect to verify your reputation. For example, they will not call your buddies, parents, or high school teacher because they don't know them. They may call one of your professors, but since they generally do not know your professors very well, they will take their recommendation with a grain of salt. And in most cases, your professor does not know you very well. The true challenge you face early in your career is not how to do deals and make a lot of money, but rather how to build a reputation as someone with whom people want to do business.

A lot of young people ask me: "How do I get a contact base like you", or "Why do people ask you for help", or "Why do people respect your opinions"? Trust me, I did not begin my career with great (or any) contacts, nor did people ask me for help, or request to hear my opinions. A successful network is created very slowly. You do it by doing the right things for people, even if there is nothing in it for you. This includes helping their kid, or giving free advice gladly, or introducing them to someone with a common business or social interest, all performed without any expectation of reward. It is about under-promising and over-delivering. These are the foundations of a reputation.

A reputation is not a con; you cannot fake it over the long run. You must want to be the person whose reputation you create, and not just perform "good acts" when it is convenient.

As you begin your career, your goal should be that in 15-20 years, people trust you and put their faith (which you will discover is more important than money) in you. The problem with reputation is it is very slow and difficult to build, but can be lost unbelievably fast. You could do the right thing for 20-30 years, building trust and loyalty, and then do one thing that people view as wrong, and in a matter of hours you can lose your reputation. Guard it more carefully than you guard your money, because if you retain your reputation you can always regain your money.

In my experience, investors and partners are much more forgiving if you lose their money, than if you treat them badly. This is because people understand that even the smartest investors sometimes lose money. While they do not like it, they accept it. But if they feel you mistreated them, lied to them, misinformed them, or took advantage of them, they are unforgiving, even if you make money. Ethics in real estate is not just about doing what is legal; that goes without being said. It is about doing what is right.

RIGHT AND WRONG

Everyone must develop their own sense of right and wrong with respect to business. Obviously there is the golden rule of "do onto others as you would have them do unto you," but each of you has a different perspective as to what you want done to you. You must find your way, make your decisions, and attempt to behave consistently. No one expects you to be nominated for sainthood at the end of your career. But at the end of your career, you hope people do not say, "this person cheated me" or "this person mistreated me". You would like to believe that the worst somebody will say at the end of your career is "very tough, but always fair".

If you never have an ethical dilemma during your career, you are probably being unnecessarily conservative. You are in the business to make money, and making money legitimately and fairly means you are going to encounter conflicts. The point isn't to avoid all conflicts, as that is not fair to your investors, lenders, or employees. At the same time, if you have an ethical dilemma every hour, sooner or later you are going to cross the line. So if you are always having ethical problems, back off a little; and if you are never having them, push harder. A footnote is that research shows that some of you have a hard time identifying ethical challenges. Therefore, you will be well served to have a couple of people in your life that you respect and with whom you regularly touch base to see things you may miss.

Hopefully you aren't thinking, "someday I plan to cheat people". If, as a student, you are planning to con the world, you will have a very difficult career, and nothing you read here is likely to change your mind. It's the same as if when walking down the aisle to get married, you are planning a midnight rendezvous with the barmaid.

Whatever guidelines or anecdotes one provides, most of you believe such situations will never happen to you. But, unfortunately, ethical issues sneak up on you. What is the best way to deal with these problems? Be alert as to how and why they arise, and watch how people you respect resolve them. Preparation is your best defense.

BRIBES

What about corruption? Is there corruption in US real estate? Ever been to New Orleans? Bribes may get things done, but jail time and the loss of reputation are heavy prices to pay. Even if you are doing business abroad, you are prohibited by US law from bribery and the willful ignorance of your partner performing corrupt acts.

Most corruption happens when you need a permit or approval, as the regulator has the power to halt or delay profitable business activities. Thus, development is much more difficult in a corrupt environment than is operating a building, as many approvals are required to complete a development. Under US law, you are allowed to pay accommodation fees, but not allowed to pay bribes. The question is, where is the line? If you take a local politician to a basketball game, it is generally viewed as an accommodation. But if you give him a brown paper bag filled with $10 million in cash in an alley, it is a bribe! But there is a lot of ground in between. This is where tough calls arise.

In some ways investing abroad is similar to what many of you faced as college freshmen. As high school seniors you knew how to survive the system, with its many explicit and implicit rules. But as a freshman you had a hard time adjusting because you did not know what was acceptable behavior. This "freshman feeling" is a taste of what you will feel entering a foreign market. You do not know exactly who to befriend; who to avoid; what is legal; or what is acceptable. To lessen the cost of transition, many businesses form partnerships with locals, but be very careful about whom you choose as your partner.

BUT EVERYBODY IS DOING IT!

The following story is a true story, although I have changed the names, numbers, and places to protect the innocent. I was assisting a prominent US investment group, who owned the best building in the developing country of Feli. The good news was that they owned the best building in Feli; the bad news was they owned the best building in Feli, as Feli is a very rough place. Rents in Feli were about $50 net per square foot, and the newly completed building was about 15% leased, when the economy of Feli absolutely collapsed. If you had space for rent in Feli you were in trouble, because no one was renting.

Their local partner said they could rent a large block of space for about $40 a foot to a high credit tenant. The problem was that Feli had a value-added tax which applied to rent. This tax amounted to about $14 per square foot, resulting in a net rent of $26 per square foot. While this was lower than the pro forma net rent of $50, it was better than nothing. As we debated whether to wait, and see if rents picked up, or to take the $26 per square foot for 5 years, the local partner suggested that instead of calling the $40 per square foot payment rent, we should structure it as $1 per square foot rental payment and a $39 per square foot payment for "consulting-services," as consulting was exempt from the value-added tax. Structured in this manner, the net rent was just under $40 per square foot. Needless to say, our local partner swore that this was common practice.

Would you accept this structuring proposal? While this may (or may not) be tax fraud for which you risk going to jail and becoming someone's lover, the other risks associated with this transaction far outweighed the benefits. The biggest risk? Damage to our reputation!

How long did it take us to decide? Two minutes. This was not a holier than thou decision. If we used this structure, a number of people would "have us". At the very least, the tenant and our partner would know about this transaction, as would the lawyers and local brokers. Any one of these people could hold this over our heads. The reward simply did not justify the risk, as we had all worked too long building reputations to lose it like this.

PERVERSE INCENTIVES

A classic example of a real estate ethical dilemma is when you are selling a fully-leased property, while having extensive conversations with two major tenants about developing a new property for them. While you do not have a contract, you are pretty sure that these tenants will move to your planned building when their leases expire in two years. Should you reveal this information to the buyer? If you do, the deal may fall through, or you may receive a substantially lower price. Obviously, if the prospective buyer asks you "are you in discussions about tenants moving to a new property" and you lie, that is fraud. The question is whether you should volunteer this information? Should you say, "here is a building for sale, but I am pretty sure that two of the key tenants will leave soon to a new building I am developing", when you do not really know for sure what they will decide? What damage are you doing to your reputation if the tenants leave for your new project after sale? The buyer will be upset and people in business discuss relationships, especially when they are angry. These discussions are not necessarily "bad-mouthing", but rather a way for people who do not know a potential partner to find out the type of person they will be working with. If people discuss you in a negative context too often, you get the reputation as a person no one wants to deal with.

There are people who if things do not go according to plan, will sue as a part of their business strategy. They figure that they do this all the time and are used to it, while you may be intimidated by a lawsuit. They view it as just another business tool. They are like guys who in pickup basketball games call a foul every time they miss a shot. Is this the way you want to conduct your business? You have to decide if what you extract from constant lawsuits against your partners, lenders, employees, and investors is worth the damage to your reputation. Will it destroy your reputation? Probably not. Will it affect your reputation? Absolutely.

FAVORITISM

Should you favor the people that do business with you? Do you turn a smiling eye to an executive that gives you a consulting contract? Do you give favorable treatment to somebody who is paying you? Do you help somebody who is paying you, such as a tenant or investor, get their child into college? You can look at things like this in a lot of ways. You can say, "I will not be a part of that", but then people will view you as unhelpful. On the other hand, you can say that the university has to accept someone, and this applicant is as good as anyone else, and if you can be a tie-breaker and help someone you know, so be it. You will have to frequently sort through these types of issues during your career.

DON'T EXPECT THANKS

There was an instance when I was doing work for one the world's largest corporations. I had done a pretty good job, and billed them for my services. Shortly after sending the bill, I received a check for the exact amount of my invoice. I was paid, they were happy with my work, and everything was wonderful. The next day I received a second check for the exact amount as I had received the previous day. For a minute, I thought, "Gee, maybe I had actually done some other work and it was owed to me," and maybe "They were so happy with my work they decided to double my pay as a bonus!" However, the second check was clearly an error. Given the size of the corporation, they probably would never realize that they had made a mistake. It was a trivial amount for them, but a significant amount for me.

What should I do? Taking the check was not only wrong, but it was probably theft. So, I sent them a letter stating that they overpaid me and returned the second check. After sending this check I felt I was the world's most noble person, and that they would be so grateful they would send me a bonus. However, I never heard a word about the check, as no one wanted to admit it was their fault. How do you think it looks for them to tell their boss, "We double-paid Peter Linneman, but he is such a swell and honest guy that he gave it back!"? The boss would kill them and check out all their work in search of similar mistakes. While I believe I would have done the same thing had there been three more zeros at the end of the check, I fortunately did not have to face that situation.

CONFLICT OF INTEREST

You are working on a deal, and suddenly find yourself on both sides of the deal. This can happen whether you are an advisor, lender, or bidder. For example, you may be on the board of a lender, but at the same time are working with a firm that is going to that bank for a loan. If you are an active business person, you will frequently encounter conflict of interest situations. No one is upset when you have a conflict of interest. The question is how you deal with it? A word to the wise is to avoid situations where continual conflicts cannot help but regularly arise. You should know before you agree to be on the board of two major New York City office owners, that there is a high chance that these companies will frequently be bidding on the same assets.

When a conflict situation arises, declare it early, often, and clearly. Ask yourself, "What are the conflicts?", "How did they arise?", "What business do you do with the parties"? Make certain that both parties understand the situation fully, and are clearly supportive of your continued involvement. If not, either pick a side or bow out altogether. Your reputation in dealing with such situations will affect how people deal with you when the tables are turned.

CLOSING THOUGHT

The goal is not to be a saint, but rather a legitimate, respected professional. People will slowly come to understand what it means to deal with you, and they hopefully will enjoy the experience. Reputation is a rare asset that can generate great profits over the course of your career. Stay focused on your guiding principles, and carefully choose the people with whom you deal. When in doubt, it doesn't hurt to ask if your mother would be proud of how you act.

Chapter 21 Supplement A

Some Observations on Real Estate Entrepreneurship

Are real estate entrepreneurs born, or are they made?

Dr. Peter Linneman – Wharton Real Estate Review – Fall 2007

I have been a small-scale entrepreneur for twenty-eight years, and have taught real estate entrepreneurship for nearly a decade. In addition, over the past thirty years I have befriended and observed innumerable entrepreneurs, including many legendary figures. I have read numerous books about entrepreneurs, as well as scholarly papers on the topic. I offer here some observations on entrepreneurship.

"Can entrepreneurship be taught?" is a common question. It is generally asked with a knowing smirk by someone who misunderstands the purpose of education. The answer is "Of course it can". Education at its core is about efficiently passing along "what is known" on a topic. This involves a set of focused lessons that advance the student's learning process. Assuming that focused lessons are twice as efficient as trial and error, sixty hours of student time in my class (twenty in class and forty outside of class) can generate the equivalent of 120 hours of insight. Sixty hours spent on my course amounts to a mere week of full-time work, but if a course can achieve in a week what would otherwise require two weeks to learn through experience, it must be considered a success. Yet in the context of a career, two weeks is a drop in the bucket.

Another important educational goal is to assist students to discover their strengths, weaknesses, and passions, and to help them to determine if they have what it takes. If the sixty hours committed to a course can save years of pursuing false dreams, or light a fire under someone, the course has been a success. In this context, I am reminded of the Monty Python skit in which a mousey chartered accountant tells a career counselor that he wants to become a lion tamer. After the career counselor disabuses him of the idea that lions are cute little furry animals that sit on your lap and play with string by showing him a man-eating lion, the man realizes that chartered accountancy is perfect for him. Better to learn such lessons in the comfort of a classroom than to be eaten alive on the job.

Entrepreneurship can be effectively taught. But while you can teach someone to play football, say, and even to love the game, you cannot teach them to be Bret Favre. Teaching can expose and excite, but it cannot create virtuosos. Being a professional, much less a superstar, in any walk of life requires a combination of innate skill and a lifetime of honing one's game. Just as few young football players ever achieve superstar status, few entrepreneurs ever achieve the level of success of Albert Ratner, Steve Roth, or Steve Ross.

But by inspiring and helping budding entrepreneurs understand the challenges they will face, how to approach these challenges in a disciplined manner, and how to avoid making the "well-known" mistakes, it is possible to help them along the path to becoming an entrepreneur. As an educator, my goal is to move them along so they make mistakes that others have yet to make, and to allow them understand that making errors is what entrepreneurs do. And that success comes from solving, not avoiding, problems.

ARE THERE ENTREPRENEURIAL TRAITS?

All too often, people seek a cookbook approach to entrepreneurship: "Just do these things and you will become a billionaire!" But this is as foolish as saying someone will be a star quarterback if he is the right height, weight, speed, IQ, and so on. While these factors tend to be correlated with success, they are far from perfect predictors. There is no formula for great quarterbacks, as they come in many sizes and shapes. But there are no 5-foot, 120-pound great pro quarterbacks. The same is true for entrepreneurs: they come in many different packages, with certain personality traits correlating with success, and others associated with failure.

Entrepreneurs are usually intellectual arbitrageurs rather than inventors. That is, they are more likely to tweak existing ideas than to create new concepts out of whole cloth. Thus, Steve Wynn's brilliant resort/casinos appropriate and combine the best elements of large-scale resorts, boutique retail, and quality entertainment venues in a way that enhances their complementarities. Alfred Taubman's shopping malls likewise combined elements found in ancient arcades with modern merchandising concepts found in the world's best downtown shopping. Neither created entirely new concepts, but rather put together existing components in a new way.

Successful entrepreneurs generally look at things differently from other people. While most people see how things are, entrepreneurs see how they could be. As a result, entrepreneurs must be able to sell their personal vision to their audience (employees, vendors, customers, capital sources, and advisors), who does not necessarily share it. Absent the ability to sell effectively, entrepreneurs will fail to muster the resources necessary to implement their idea. Entrepreneurial sales ability involves being able to describe the vision in a simple yet sophisticated manner. A great entrepreneur is able to package his ideas into a presentation that is so simple that it can be grasped by an intelligent child. What could be simpler, for example, than Sam Walton's vision of everyday low prices built around economies of scale?

The ability to sell doesn't require PowerPoint or a thick consultant report. It does require many hours of thought about how to express a complicated idea in a simple manner. When I fail to understand an entrepreneur's pitch, it usually means that they are not ready for success. I encourage students who are preparing a pitch to think about the selling of televisions. Televisions are highly complex pieces of equipment that work due to an amazing combination of high-level electronics and physics. Yet how is one sold? The customer is told, "Push this button to turn it on and this button to change channels". No one would buy a television if the sales pitch consisted of electrical flow charts and discussions of wave theory.

The ability to present complex ideas simply is a critical trait of entrepreneurial success. But just as important is the ability to persevere after repeatedly being told "no". As social animals, we all love to be told "yes". In fact, most people do everything possible to avoid being told "no"; the easiest way to do this is to conform. Thus, entrepreneurs proposing unusual and untested ideas are constantly being told "no" by customers, vendors, potential employees, government officials, and capital sources. And yet, entrepreneurs are not deterred, which requires somewhat odd "social wiring".

Entrepreneurs believe that they can't fail because they will (somehow) figure out a way to make things work. Entrepreneurs view each "no" as a missed opportunity for the naysayer, not a personal failure. And yet most entrepreneurs are terrified of failure. This fear also forces them to be more flexible and pragmatic than most people, constantly altering their approach as they move forward. Anything to avoid the ultimate "NO!"

Successful entrepreneurs are willing to make decisions, knowing that they will need to change course many times on the fly. They are like a great quarterback scrambling for his life, yet still able to see things evolving around him so he can make a play. This adaptability is apparent in another quality of entrepreneurship. Entrepreneurs tend to believe that "the answer" is less important than the ability to quickly adapt if an initial answer leads them awry. It is perhaps the reason why most lawyers and academics are poor entrepreneurs, as their training teaches them to search for the answer rather than selecting an answer, with a mind to changing it if need be.

The entrepreneur perceives risks differently from other people. Just as a great quarterback knows he will take some big hits if he is going to throw touchdowns, the successful entrepreneur knows there will be a lot of bumps on the road to success. And like a great quarterback, his fear is not getting hit (which is what a normal person fears), but rather that he won't complete the pass. Stated differently, entrepreneurs are more afraid of failure more than they are of getting hurt.

Entrepreneurs have a rare capacity to absorb their social and business environment. This is essential, as it allows them to see opportunities that others fail to see. Entrepreneurs tend to be avaricious readers of newspapers, trade periodicals, magazines, and analytic reports. Their reading even includes seemingly unrelated fields such as novels and history. Entrepreneurs do not read to learn the "story" but to understand how things "fit together". This reading forms a mosaic of the world they live in, helping them identify the missing pieces of the mosaic that provide business opportunities.

Entrepreneurs also tend to seek the advice and counsel of various experts. This includes not only lawyers, accountants, bankers, architects, and economists, but also those in seemingly unrelated fields: doctors, scientists, historians, artists, and writers. Again, these advisors provide the entrepreneur with additional pieces for their mosaic. The ability to create a mosaic of life is one of the most consistent elements I have found in observing entrepreneurs. Interestingly, entrepreneurs are less interested in mastering the analysis provided by these inputs than in abstracting bits and pieces to form their ever-changing mosaic.

Contrary to popular belief, entrepreneurs are not dreamers. They are extreme pragmatists. They do not imagine a perfect world where everything goes right and everybody wants their product. Instead, most are brutally realistic in their appraisal of the challenges they face. When someone tells me that everyone needs their product, I know I am listening to an unsuccessful pitch; no one has a product that everyone needs. Entrepreneurs realize this and possess the flexibility and vision to take on the challenges that would frighten off others.

Entrepreneurs are an unusual blend of studied pragmatic opportunism and blind determination. Once they have identified an opportunity and determined that it is realistic, they act with a sense of urgency. In fact, what distinguishes a good entrepreneur from a good corporate executive is the sense of urgency in pursuing a course of action. A good corporate executive in a well-established firm will meticulously scrutinize a business opportunity, consulting numerous committees, before embarking on a course of action. In contrast, the entrepreneur acts quickly, as it is only a matter of time before others see the same opportunity, and will perhaps attack it with greater resources than the entrepreneur possesses. We have all observed an entrepreneur execute a project with great success, and wonder, "Why didn't I do that?" The opportunity was obvious, the market demand was obvious, and yet most people did not pursue it. The challenge for entrepreneurs is to act before established corporations get around to addressing the situation.

Entrepreneurs must be smart enough to process information and identify opportunities. But being an entrepreneur is not about being a genius. One needs an IQ of 120, but not 150. Entrepreneurs come from many different social backgrounds, ranging from scions of wealthy families to new immigrants, and from places as diverse as Manhattan and Fayetteville, Arkansas. Today, most entrepreneurs are college graduates, though in previous generations this was not the case. But entrepreneurs do not always hold advanced degrees. I know successful entrepreneurs who have studied business administration at Wharton, music at Julliard, fine arts at the University of Southern California, and English literature at Amherst. It is neither education, super-intelligence, nor heredity that typifies entrepreneurs. What is common to every entrepreneur I have ever met is a total passion for what they are doing. It is both their work and their entertainment. It is how they make friends, as well as how they make their living. It is what they live to do, rather than what they do to live.

WHAT MAKES SAMMY RUN?

Students often believe that entrepreneurship is about getting rich—getting fabulously rich, overnight. But almost every entrepreneur's story is one of an "overnight" success that took ten to fifteen years. It only seems like overnight because their stories did not appear in Forbes or Fortune until they were already established. This creates the impression that success—as opposed to notoriety—is instantaneous. This false impression is compounded by the fact that the typical person's exposure to entrepreneurs is primarily through magazines and news profiles. But the successful entrepreneurs highlighted in the media are newsworthy precisely because they are atypical. Bill Gates and Steve Jobs are not typical entrepreneurs, nor are Trammell Crow, Mel Simon, Don Bren, or Gerald Hines. It is precisely their uniqueness that makes them interesting. Their success is beyond the dreams of even very successful entrepreneurs. The truth is that most successful entrepreneurs are in their fifties and sixties and have net worth in the range of $500,000 to $10 million after years of work and struggle. While this is financially successful by any normal standard, it is far from what my students have in mind when they think of entrepreneurial success.

Entrepreneurs' passion is to be successful in what they're doing, rather than to get rich. Money is a by-product, although a comforting one. In fact, there are non-profit entrepreneurs. Sister Theresa was a great entrepreneur. She had passion, intelligence, and a vision of what could be done. She was terrified that she might fail in fulfilling her mission. Both she and Bill Gates are legendary entrepreneurs; one ended up the richest man in the world, while the other died poor. But both were extraordinary entrepreneurs.

I tell my students that, with a few exceptions, the mere fact that they are at this institution means they will be able to earn enough to live a comfortable life. But it is not clear if they will have fun. I note that if they want to be an entrepreneur in order to get rich quick, they are making a big mistake, as they can make far more—at least in the short term—by working for Goldman Sachs, Morgan Stanley, or General Electric. They will work the same hours, with less risk, and higher compensation. The question is: Will they be as happy? A real entrepreneur would not be.

I begin my course by asking students why they want to be entrepreneurs. The most typical answer is, "I want to be my own boss". This may be a necessary condition for being an entrepreneur, but it is hardly sufficient motivation. Many people want to be their own bosses, but most lack the courage, vision, and passion to be entrepreneurs. It is this passion that explains why so many entrepreneurs remain active, often almost to the end of their lives. Their jobs are what they are, who they are, and what they do for fun. As they get older and enjoy the benefits of a lifetime of entrepreneurial success, they may put in fewer and more flexible hours, but with no less passion. In fact, many entrepreneurs stay on well after the market has passed them by, and their personal mosaic is a tattered ruin. One need look no further than Henry Ford, a great entrepreneur, whose belief in the black Model T lasted a decade or more past its useful life, and who nearly destroyed the Ford Motor Company. Ford's story is a reminder that being your own boss often means having a bad boss, since most entrepreneurs are poor managers. They are so passionate about doing what they are doing that they fail to focus on the need to manage, frequently including themselves.

BETTER, FASTER, CHEAPER

Entrepreneurs do not possess identical skill sets. Some, like Gerald Hines, Steve Wynn, and Alfred Taubman, are brilliant with products. They master how real estate functions, and how to improve the physical product from a cost and usage perspective. They understand how properties will be used, and possess the rare skill of putting themselves in the place of the consumer. Consumer empathy is important, not only for high-end hotels, Class A office buildings, and luxury resorts, but also for mobile home communities, strip centers, and affordable housing. Most people lack the ability to understand, respect, and empathize with consumers' behavior, and are thus unable to fulfill and enhance the consumer's experience. But those that provide a unique and superior value experience reap great rewards. Izzy Sharpe's Four Seasons Hotel chain is a perfect example of this phenomenon.

Another defining attribute of entrepreneurs is the ability to control production processes, time schedules, and costs. Such entrepreneurs make generic products but they do it faster, more reliably, and more cheaply than their competitors. They possess the ability to control cost overruns before they occur, and to adapt to the unknowable events that will challenge timely product delivery. An example is Ron Caplan of Philadelphia Management, who consistently delivers residential re-developments at a significant cost advantage over his competitors.

Another skill that defines some entrepreneurs is an ability to sell, even if their property is inferior to, or more expensive than, that of their competitors. Great marketers not only describe their product in an appealing manner, but are also able to get customers to execute agreements. They are closers. They stand in marked contrast to most people, who are often good at describing the product of choice, but have difficulty closing the sale. Donald Trump leaps to mind as an example.

Another type of entrepreneur, although rarely found in the real estate field, excels at managing people. Such entrepreneurs are able to communicate their insights, skills, and passions to large numbers of employees. Sam Walton is perhaps the greatest example. Not only did he have a great business model but he was able to take it to extraordinary scale by creating a managerial environment that could replicate his vision. If one can make 10,000 people only 10 percent more productive, and each worker produces $50,000 annually, the value creation is $50 million annually, representing a present value of $500 million or more.

Some entrepreneurs are great risk analysts. This sounds simple, but great risk analysts are able to evaluate and manage both the upside and the downside of their vision in light of their limited capital (both financial and human). Jay Pritzker and Sam Zell come to mind in this regard. Such entrepreneurs focus on how to limit their downside, how to get out if they are unsuccessful in a way that does not cripple them, and how to identify the investments most worth making. These investment decisions are not simply based upon Internal Rates of Return and Net Present Values, but also on understanding what can go wrong and how to survive. For students, this is the most alluring type of entrepreneurship because they believe that their courses in risk analysis have prepared them for this task. But being able to calculate an IRR or NPV is very different from having a feel for the opportunities of the market, and being able to constantly adapt to changing conditions.

A final defining skill of some entrepreneurs is being a master deal maker. Deal-making is exemplified by legendary real estate entrepreneurs such as Mel Simon or Edward DeBartelo. There is seemingly no obstacle that a great deal maker cannot overcome. This takes enormous resourcefulness and social connectivity. It requires understanding what others are seeking, and how to help them to achieve their goals without compromising one's own objectives. It requires a belief that deal making is a positive-sum game. (It is also the reason that great deal makers are rare in the socialist countries of Western Europe as well as Japan, where a zero-sum mentality prevails.)

Each of the above skills is rare, even among highly intelligent and educated individuals, but entrepreneurs must possess at least one of these skills to succeed. A small group of entrepreneurs possess two of these entrepreneurship skills, and legends are made of those who possess more than two. It is unrealistic for teenagers playing high school football to believe that they will become the next Peyton Manning; a more realistic goal is to play on a college team, and if successful receive a scholarship to a Division I university, and then if extremely successful make it to the NFL as a substitute for a season or two. It is the same for entrepreneurs. The young entrepreneur's goal should not be to be the next Bob Toll, but rather to be successful in developing his skill in a pursuit about which he is passionate.

The greatest difficulty in teaching entrepreneurship is to avoid creating the impression that success as an entrepreneur is the result of having a Big Idea. Was Ray Kroc's idea to make hamburgers of consistent quality throughout the country a Big Idea? Or Sam Walton's plan to sell quality merchandise at the lowest prices in town? Or Warren Buffett's strategy to make long-term value investments? Hardly. What distinguished these entrepreneurs, and made them legends, was not their idea, but rather its execution: "It's the singer not the song". Tens of thousands of young men are big enough and strong enough to play professional football, but most cannot make it for the lack of execution—reliability, perseverance, consistency. Unlike Big Ideas, execution is neither glamorous nor easy to teach. Execution requires attention to detail, commitment, and a fanatical exploitation of one's skills. Don Bren's source of success is his commitment and attention to details. In football, great athletes who are well trained and able to repeatedly execute mediocre plays are more valuable than mediocre players who lack the skills to execute a great playbook. The same holds true for real estate entrepreneurship.

Entrepreneurial success is rarely about doing "something new". Most real estate entrepreneurs succeed by doing something better, or cheaper, or faster. If an entrepreneur can do any one of these three, he will be a winner. And if an entrepreneur can do it better, cheaper, and faster, he will win the Super Bowl.

In terms of execution, getting the right people doing the right jobs is the key to success. This entails selecting not necessarily the best talent, but rather the best talent for the assignment at hand, people who share the vision, and fit the budget. Too often managers are dazzled by résumés, and ignore the compatibility of a résumé with the task at hand. In addition, one's social networks and business relationships are critical in terms of successful execution, since entrepreneurs are not institutions and must rely on a broader network rather than their own firms. Great entrepreneurs are instinctive network builders. Most entrepreneurs treat people well irrespective of their job or status in life, and help people simply because they can. They do not engage in a "tit for tat," in marked contrast to many corporate managers who do favors only if they believe the favor will be repaid. I urge students to treat the assistants of the executives they want to interact with as well or better than they treat the executives themselves. This advice eludes most students (and most corporate employees). They do not understand that if executive assistants dislike them, the "big boss" will dislike them, too, as bosses respect their assistants' opinions. This is not to suggest that entrepreneurs are saints, or that all of them are easy to work with. After all, they are human. But entrepreneurs generally treat people with greater sincerity and respect than most corporate managers, creating a support network to offset their lack of institutional infrastructure.

The fact that entrepreneurial success depends upon execution, rather than Big Ideas, leads most academics to under-estimate entrepreneurs. But in fact in every endeavor in life, virtuosity is defined by execution rather than idea. Milton Friedman was smart and had many ideas—some of them big—but his stature as an economist derived from his skill in executing his research agenda. Even in the idea business, execution trumps ideas.

Great athletes adapt to different game conditions, weather conditions, and opponents, finding a way to prevail. The same is true of great entrepreneurs. They make decisions, fully aware that their decisions are flawed. But unlike Hamlet, entrepreneurs realize that the question is not "To be or not to be?" but rather "What's next?" It is entrepreneurs' high tolerance for change that allows them to succeed where others fail. But this tolerance for change can also become their enemy, as they can underestimate the market's resistance to change. This is because the only thing most people hate more than change itself is the person responsible for the change. Thus, to be able to continually adapt and change requires that entrepreneurs have relationships and employees that are compatible with the entrepreneur's pattern of behavior. They must constantly sell and motivate people about the necessity to change, in spite of natural resistance to change.

The entrepreneur rarely says, "It's okay because we've always done it this way", but frequently asks "Why don't we try this?" This characteristic can be risky, and has led to the downfall of many entrepreneurs, as they can find it difficult to know when not to change. This becomes more difficult the more one succeeds, as we all tend to believe our headlines. Entrepreneurs are constantly at risk of hubris, believing they can achieve anything to which they set their minds. For this reason it is essential for entrepreneurs to have advisors who are perceptive, loyal, and brutally honest (though perhaps leavening their advice with honey). The need for such advisors grows the more successful the entrepreneur becomes. The successful entrepreneur must rein in the human tendency to avoid dissent.

WHAT ARE THE RISKS?

Everyone takes a shower in the morning. Most get into a car, drive to work or play, ride in elevators, and sit in their kitchen or dining room to eat. Each of these activities presents the risk of serious bodily injury, and perhaps even death. Yet, most of us go through the day without thinking we took a risk. This underscores the difference between risk, perception of risk, and the management of risk. Many things that are quite risky are not generally perceived as risks, partially because we take steps to mitigate and manage risks (seatbelts, elevator safety features), and partially because the activities are routine. Entrepreneurs see the risks they face in a similar manner.

Entrepreneurs manage risk by specializing in a particular market or product type. Today's world is too complex for anyone to master all geographies and product types. Successful entrepreneurs who cut across geographies and product lines invariably started as a specialist in a single geography, or in a single product, slowly growing beyond that niche. Even the prolific developer Trammell Crow spent his early years building everyday warehouses in his hometown of Dallas, branching out only after establishing a competency and track record in this niche. One of the most difficult things to convey to students is that in order to be successful entrepreneurs, they will have to specialize, to develop a knowledge and skill base that allows them to effectively manage risk. This frustrates students, who are worried about being pigeonholed. But in this case, being pigeonholed is simply being knowledgeable. Great real estate entrepreneurs must know every deal in their market. They must know every tenant who is looking for space. They must know the capital sources seeking to do business in their product niche and market. They must know each building in their market, why it works, and its limitations. Although amassing this knowledge base is time-consuming, it is critical, since no one can master multiple markets, particularly early in their career. It is a common, and usually fatal, mistake of young entrepreneurs to fail to specialize.

Another way entrepreneurs manage risk is to use other people's money, exchanging their sweat for a slice of the profit they create for others who do not possess their knowledge and skill base. This underscores the need for an identifiable expertise, as without specialized knowledge, why would anyone entrust the entrepreneur with their money? But entrepreneurs also put their money at risk side-by-side with their investors because they believe in their vision. One of the quickest ways to distinguish a true entrepreneur from a fake is to determine if they have their money side-by-side with their investors. An entrepreneur's investment may not be as large as that of other people, but real entrepreneurs believe in their vision and want to put their money to work in their deals, rather than let it sit in a well-diversified portfolio of stocks and bonds.

While entrepreneurs face many risks, perhaps none is greater than the risk to one's reputation. This is because a reputation is difficult to establish, but very easy to lose. It takes a long time to build trust, but trust can be lost in an instant. And reputation is the most valuable asset an entrepreneur possesses, as it yields increasing returns over one's career. I was once asked by a student how to build a great business network and reputation. I responded that if you always do the very best you can to fulfill what you said you would do, help others simply because you can rather than because you believe it will directly benefit you, and do this for the next thirty years, you will have a great reputation and network. In short, a great reputation takes twenty-five to thirty years to create.

Young entrepreneurs will receive little cash compensation relative to what they could be earning working for a major company. They may even have to be out of pocket for payroll and operating expenses. I am constantly asked by recent graduates with high-paying jobs in management consulting or investment banking how they can receive cash compensation equivalent to their current pay, but get the upside reward of an entrepreneur. My answer is that they can't. As Ron Terwilliger tells his partners, entrepreneurship is a "get rich slow" exercise. In the beginning, this means a relatively meager lifestyle compared to one's corporate peers. Entrepreneurship is about building a business, not making a quick killing. There simply is not enough money to be made in early entrepreneurial opportunities. Instead, early entrepreneurial opportunities generally help outside investors get rich while establishing the foundation for a long entrepreneurial career. Early entrepreneurial opportunities are best viewed as investments in human capital, building the track record, reputation, and expertise that will generate more profitable opportunities in the future.

Entrepreneurs face significant political, product, and market risk. By knowing everything that is happening in their market, and by building relationships with tenants and information sources in their market, entrepreneurs mitigate their operating risk. Similarly, by becoming an integral part of their community, entrepreneurs develop a network that helps them understand what is going on in the community and how it affects them, as well as learning how to legitimately influence political outcomes. This is particularly important for developers. Entrepreneurs involve themselves in community service, as it provides them with introductions to key players in their community. This is not to suggest that they are not interested in the charities, but rather that in addition to doing good, these networks also help them do well. Again, it is a positive sum relationship.

Great entrepreneurs study competitive products and competitors, both to analyze what these competitors do well and to determine what opportunities they leave in their wake. They must understand the difference between fads and market realities, for while money can be made from fads, long-term success cannot be made by fads (unless you're Ron Popeil, the legendary inventor of gadgets sold on TV). Great entrepreneurs avoid the pitfalls of fads by concentrating on market fundamentals. Think of Warren Buffett, who during the Tech Bubble stayed true to value, investing even when it was temporarily out of favor.

Entrepreneurs seek the advice of experts, not to generate voluminous reports that can be put in a file somewhere in case a lawsuit occurs (as many large corporations do), but rather to gain insights. This input filters into their mosaic of life. Developer-entrepreneurs also understand that paper is cheap, but bricks and mortar are expensive. That is, they spend endless hours analyzing things on paper before committing to construction.

Perhaps the ultimate risk-mitigant is the entrepreneur's passion. After all, if they are not excited about what they are doing, why should others be excited? If they are unclear as to why they are doing things, how can they expect others to share their vision? In the end, entrepreneurs manage risk by doing it "for themselves" rather than doing it "for money". While most entrepreneurs desire to make money (and lots of it), money is the derivative of their success. Most entrepreneurs' passion allows them to see that there's plenty of money to go around if they can successfully execute their vision. They seek a win-win exercise for all parties involved. For only by making it a win-win exercise will they be able to have repeated success as an entrepreneur. This is particularly true, as win-lose situations do not enhance reputation as effectively as win-win situations. In an unspoken way, great entrepreneurs understand that they'll ultimately spend a lot of time trying to figure out how to effectively give away their money, so a fixation on making more at the expense of their reputation is not worth the possible short-term gain.

RAISING CAPITAL

Real estate is highly capital-intensive, since development and buying buildings and land requires capital well in excess of the entrepreneur's wealth. Hence, successful real estate entrepreneurs must raise outside capital. Raising money is rarely fun, but if the entrepreneur is passionate about the objective, has realistic goals, has a reputation commensurate with the objective, and can explain the vision in a clear manner, money will come. Failure to raise capital generally reflects failure in at least one, if not all, of these categories.

To raise money requires a reputation commensurate with the task at-hand. If an entrepreneur's reputation is small, so too must be the project. As reputation grows with success, so too will the capital that can be raised. The entrepreneur also must be able to tell his story in a clear and simple manner, in two or three simple sentences. What is the opportunity and why have others not pursued it? Why will the entrepreneur be successful in the pursuit of this opportunity? How does the plan compare with what others are already doing?

In my experience, a complicated pitch reflects a lack of understanding of the business opportunity. One of the easiest ways for an entrepreneur to convincingly convey his story is to risk a significant amount of his own net wealth in the project, side-by-side with the money of investors. The failure to do so often is—and should be—a death knell during capital raising.

Raising money takes time. While a project may be of utmost importance to the entrepreneur, it is just another capital commitment consideration for the people from whom he is seeking capital. Capital sources will rarely have the same sense of urgency about a project. Therefore, a successful entrepreneur must be respectful of the time-line of capital sources, and yet be insistent on moving the process along. Sometimes this means that fund raising will have to be concluded at a lower level than initially intended. But "declaring victory" is important when raising capital, as it allows the entrepreneur to establish that he has done something other than spend years trying to raise money.

In many ways, capital raising is less about raising money for the current opportunity than raising it for an opportunity two or three down the line, when the entrepreneur's reputation is more established. This is particularly true with respect to institutional capital sources, which are hesitant to invest with young entrepreneurs. Hence, when meeting a potential capital source, even though the entrepreneur is telling the lender about the opportunity at hand, he must realize that the lender's logical answer for this opportunity may be "no". It may take one or more proven successes before the entrepreneur can establish a successful relationship with a lender.

Entrepreneurs must master leverage, which can be either a great friend or a cruel enemy. Generally, entrepreneurs think in terms of financial leverage, with greater debt enhancing their expected returns. But great entrepreneurs understand that nothing ever goes according to plan. As a result, debt that is wonderful on the upside is very unforgiving on the downside. And the entrepreneur's key asset—reputation—is even more dependent on his behavior in bad times than in good times. Winning gracefully is easy; losing gracefully takes class.

Great entrepreneurs understand that in spite of their best efforts, they will experience difficult times, and that the key to success is to survive the inevitable downturns. They must have the relationships and capital necessary to make it through the hard times. Hence the importance of "getting rich slowly", as taking on less debt means the entrepreneur will survive the downturns.

Another type of leverage is managerial leverage: identifying the right people, putting them in positions where they can grow and succeed, motivating them effectively, and facilitating their success. Managerial leverage can be enormously profitable, but requires keen judgment and generosity. Great entrepreneurs have staffs who want them to succeed, not because if the entrepreneur succeeds they will receive better compensation, but because they are on the entrepreneur's side. Great entrepreneurs understand that they need excellent people around them. And they understand they will need these people most during the hard times. If an entrepreneur is successful in terms of both financial and managerial leverage over a prolonged period of time, he or she will become a legend.

Being an entrepreneur is not about a bank account, nor is it about prestige or headlines. It is about a life journey of enjoying what one is doing. It is about the opportunity to help people, whether they are customers, employees, partners, or capital providers. It is about developing long-term relationships. It is about retiring not when one can, but when one wants. This is what it means to be an entrepreneur.

So where does all this leave us? Entrepreneurship can be taught, with future entrepreneurs aided by such courses. But entrepreneurs will never be created by books, case studies, and lectures. Yet, entrepreneurship courses serve a vital purpose: to underscore the importance of entrepreneurs to growth and dynamism of our economy. They are agents of change who challenge existing conventions. Their successes lead to new conventions, producing greater wealth and prosperity for society. Even their failures invigorate the economy by marking the path forward. Courses in entrepreneurship demonstrate that entrepreneurs succeed not by luck (as we all have luck), but rather by the focus and determination of entrepreneurs to capitalize on their luck. Entrepreneurs are not the kings of the system, but rather constantly challenge the kings, keeping the established business class ever-vigilant. In short, they are the underappreciated drivers of progress. And this should be taught to all members of the business community.

Prerequisite I
The Basics of Discounted Cash Flow & Net Present Value Analyses

Discounted cash flow analysis (DCF) postulates that the value of a property is equal to its expected future cash flows, discounted into present dollars. DCF is built upon two basic concepts: the only source of value for a property is its ability to generate future cash flows; and, a dollar received today is more valuable than a dollar received tomorrow. But just because DCF assumes these things does not necessarily make them true. Though most of the time it's probably true that future cash flows are the sole determinants of a property's value, some investors value a property for more than its income potential. Common reasons include the psychic value as a piece of art and pride of ownership. If these reasons are reflected in future cash streams (e.g., the best building always sells for more), it fits the DCF methodology. However, as is sometimes the case with trophy properties, if an investor values the "bragging rights" of ownership, they will pay more than the value indicated by DCF analysis. Does this make them dumb? Not if they value the "bragging rights".

TIME VALUE OF MONEY

The second element is the **time value of money**, that is a dollar received today is worth more than a dollar received tomorrow. Why? Because if you have $100 today, you can invest those $100 and expect to have more than $100 in the future, as the investment is expected to yield a positive return. Thus, other things equal, you would prefer a property to produce income earlier rather than later, and "discount" dollars received in the future to reflect this preference.

How much less valuable is $100 received tomorrow than $100 received today? That is, by how much should you discount future dollars? A bit of background is helpful.

The **future value** is how much $100 today is expected to be worth some time in the future. For instance, if you invest $100 today in a low risk project generating a 4% expected annual return, you expect to have $104 at the end of one year (the original $100 plus $4 earned over the year). This $104 at the end of one year is the future value one year from now of $100 today. You would be indifferent between receiving $100 today and $104 dollars one year from now if you felt that the 4% return was a fair return for the risk associated with investing in this manner for one year. You can express the future value (FV_1) of the original $100 ($CF_0$) one year from now as:

$$\text{[Eq. PI.1]} \qquad FV_1 = CF_1 = CF_0 * (1+ r_1)$$

where r_1 is the return you need to receive in year one to make it just worth the risk of investing in this project. Equation PI.1 tells you that given an appropriate **risk adjusted** one year rate of return (r_1) you can calculate how much a particular cash flow today will be worth in one year. Figure PI.1 illustrates graphically the concept of future value where the arrow indicates how the current cash flow grows into the future at the year one rate (r_1).

FIGURE PI.1

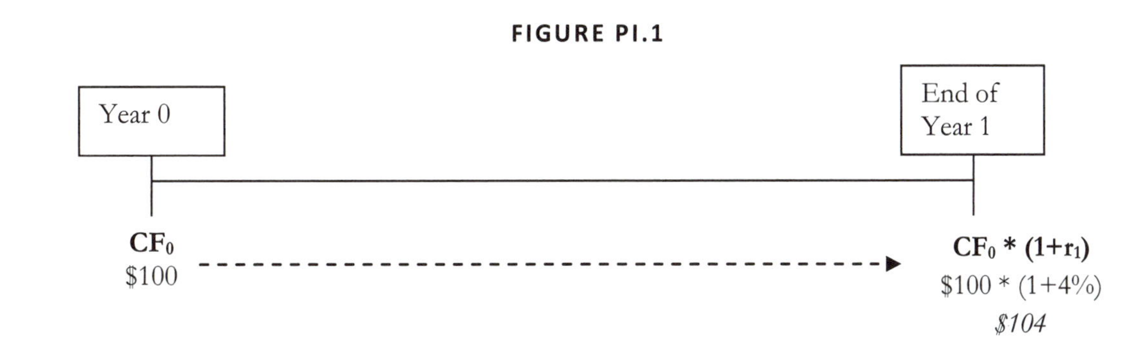

Continuing with this example, suppose that the expected annual return you required to hold onto the investment for two years is 4.5%. If you start with $100 in the investment and earn a compound return of 4.5% for two years, you will have $109.20 at the end of the second year. That is, the future value at the end of Year 2 of $100 invested in this particular risk profile for the next two years is $109.20. Note that the two year future value is higher due to the **compounding** of the return, as well as the fact that in this example you felt a modestly higher annual return was required for you to undertake a two year investment horizon. Compounding means you are generating a return on the 4.5% return earned in the first year. Specifically, the $4.50 of interest from the first year generates 20 cents of interest in the second year ($4.50 * 4.5%).

Expanding Equation PI.1 to incorporate year two, you can express the future value in year two (FV_2) of $100 ($CF_0$) today as:

[Eq. PI.2] $$FV_2 = CF_2 = CF_0 * (1 + r_2) * (1 + r_2)$$
$$FV_2 = CF_2 = 100 * (1 + 4.5\%) * (1 + 4.5\%)$$
$$FV_2 = CF_2 = \$109.20$$

where r_2 is the expected annual return you need to receive to make it worth the risk of you investing for the two years. In Equation PI.2, the $100 initial investment earns 4.5% interest in year one to generate the future value one year from today of $104.50, and this becomes the $109.20 at the end of year two. Figure PI.2 illustrates graphically the concept of compounding and future value for a two year investment.

FIGURE PI.2

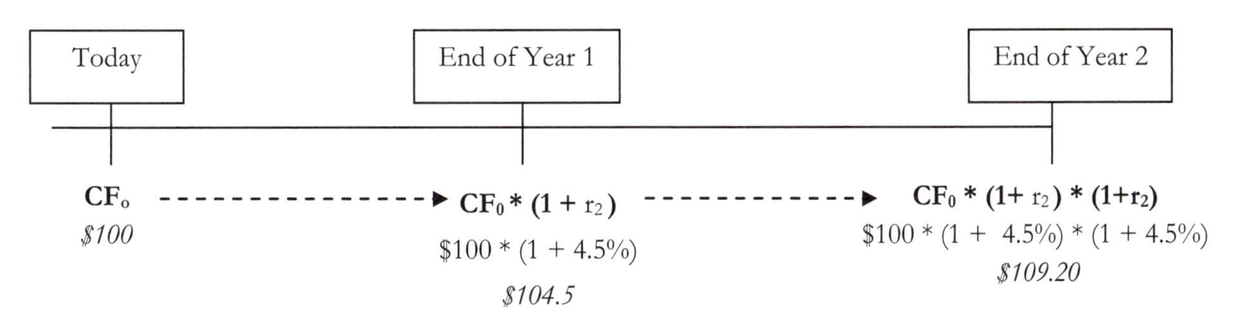

Expanding this example, assume that the required annual expected rate of return necessary to invest the $100 for 3 years is 3.9%. In this case, if you leave the $100 invested for 3 years, it grows to $112.16 at the end of the third year. Thus, the future value of $100 today given this three year risk profile is $112.16 in three years.

Expanding Equation PI.2 to incorporate the third year, you can express the future value in three years (FV_3) of $100 ($CF_0$) today as:

[Eq. PI.3] $$FV_3 = CF_3 = CF_0 *(1+ r_3) * (1+ r_3) * (1+r_3)$$

$$FV_3 = CF_3 = \$ 107.95* (1 + 3.9\%) = 100 *(1+ 3.9\%) * (1+ 3.9\%) * (1+3.9\%)$$

$$FV_3 = CF_3 = \$112.16$$

where r_3 is the expected annual return you need to receive to make it worth the risk of investing for the three years. Figure PI.3 graphically represents this third year of investing.

FIGURE PI.3

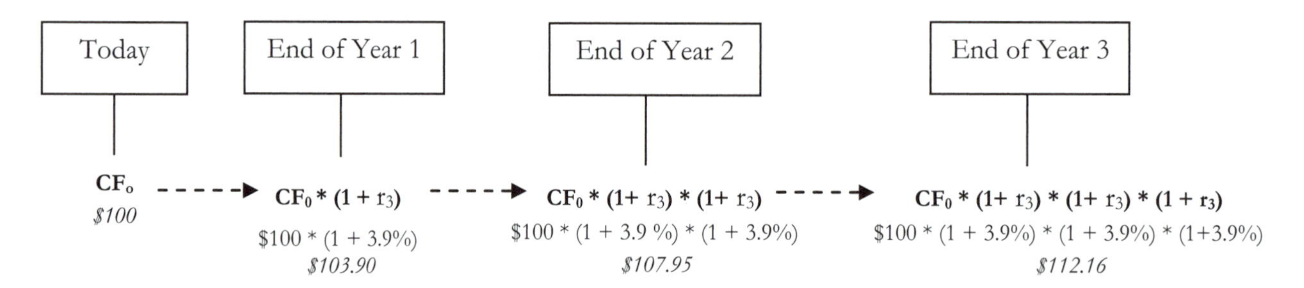

You can extend Equation PI.3 to calculate the future value for any year, where each subsequent year you reinvest at the expected annual return that compensates you for rolling over your investment. Expressed generally, the future value in year T is equal to the previous year's cash flow times the required expected annual rate of return in year T.

[Eq. PI.4] $$FV_T = CF_T = \quad = CF_0 *(1+ r_T) * (1+ r_T) * (1+ r_T) *......* (1+r_T)$$

Or

[Eq. PI.5] $$\text{Future Value (in year T)} = CF_T = CF_0 * (1+ r_T)\text{^}T$$

Figure PI.4 illustrates the general formula for future value for a constant rate r_T.

FIGURE PI.4

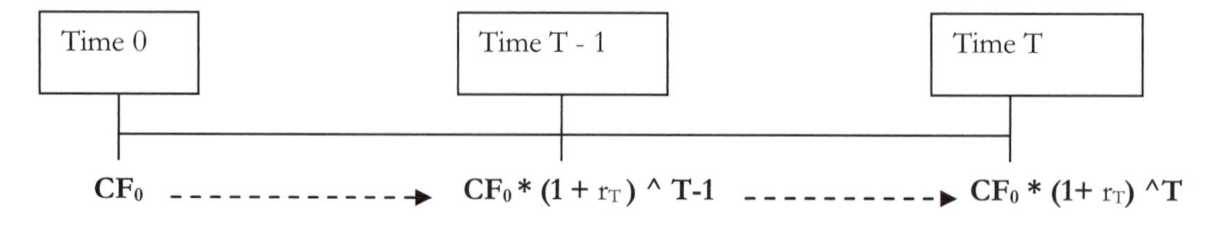

Although we have used years thus far, you can use quarters, months, days or weeks as your time unit as long as you are consistent in your application of the equation. For example, if you use months to represent time, you must apply a monthly required return to monthly cash flows.

PRESENT VALUE

With this background, you can calculate how much a dollar today is expected to be worth at any future time, for the required expected annual returns reflective of the risks of a particular investment (r_1, $r_2 ... r_T$) held for a particular time period. But how much is the **present value** of a future dollar, i.e. the value today of a future dollar? In our investment example, if you could either receive $104 in one year or $100 today, which would you pick? Since you said that 4% is the return required to make you indifferent between receiving $100 today and $104 one year from today, the options are equivalent. That is, receiving $104 one year into the future is equal to $100 today. Rearranging Equation PI.1, the present value of future cash flow received one year from today is expressed as:

$$\text{[Eq. PI.6]} \qquad \text{Present Value} = FV_1 / (1+ r_1) = CF_1 * (1+r_1)^{-1}$$

where the discount rate is r_1 and the **discount factor** is $(1+r_1)^{-1}$.

Applying Equation PI.6 to our example, $104 in one year is equal to $100 today, that is, it has a present value of $100,

$$\text{Present Value} = FV_1 / (1+ r_1) = CF_1 * (1+r_1)^{-1}$$
$$\text{Present Value} = \$104 * (1+ 4\%)^{-1} = \$104 * 0.9615 = \$100.$$

So in this example, $100 is the present value, the discount factor is 0.9615, and the **discount rate**, i.e. the required expected annual return, is 4%. Figure PI.5 illustrates graphically the concept of present value, where the arrow indicates that the future cash flows are discounted back to the present using the required rate of return (r_1).

FIGURE PI.5

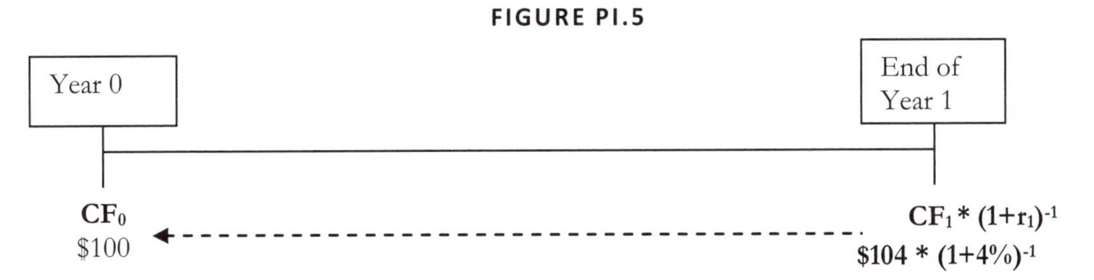

In our example, what is the present value of the future $109.20 held for 2 years? Again, you said that you are indifferent between receiving $100 today and $109.20 two years from today if you deem the required annual return is 4.5%. Therefore, the present value of $109.20 two years from now for this risk profile is $100. Rearranging Equation PI.2 and solving for the present value of cash flow received two years from today yields

$$\text{[Eq. PI.2]} \qquad FV_2 = CF_2 = CF_0 *(1+ r_2) * (1+r_2)$$
$$FV_2 = CF_2 = \text{Present Value} *(1+ r_2) * (1+r_2)$$
$$\text{[Eq. PI.7]} \qquad \text{Present Value} = FV_2 * [(1+ r_2)*(1+r_2)]^{-1} = CF_2 / [(1+r_2)*(1+r_2)].$$

In this case, the discount factor is $[(1+ r_2)*(1+r_2)]^{-1}$.

$$\text{Present Value} = FV_2 * [(1+ r_2)*(1+r_2)]^{-1} = CF_2 * [(1+ r_2)*(1+r_2)]^{-1}$$
$$\text{Present Value} = \$109.20 * [(1+ 4.5\%)*(1+4.5\%)]^{-1} = \$100.$$

So the present value of $109.20 in two years given these discount rates is $100, and the discount factor is 0.916.

Figure PI.6 illustrates the concept of discounting cash flow in year two back to the present using the required rate of return for each year.

FIGURE PI.6

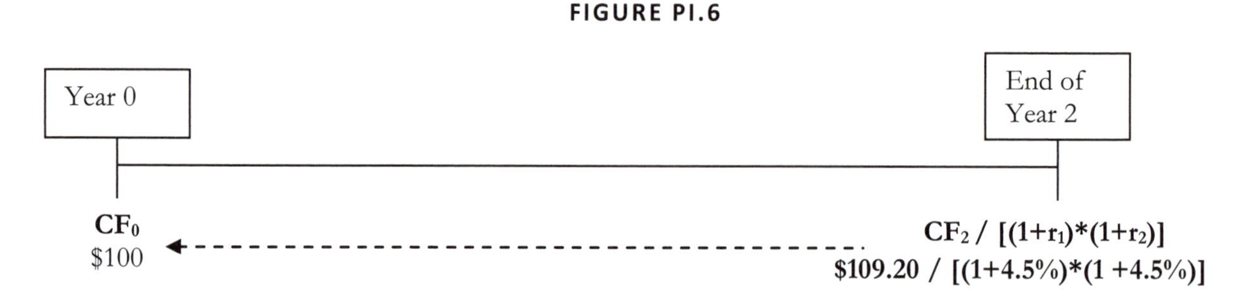

Expanding our example to the third year, if you receive $112.16 at the end of year three at the previously discussed risk profile, you would be indifferent between $100 today and $112.16 in three years. Applying our formula to this example yields $112.16 in three years equals $100 today, where the discount factor is $[(1+ r_3)*(1+ r_3)*(1+r_3)]^{-1}$.

$$\text{[Eq. PI.8]} \quad \text{Present Value} = FV_3 / [(1+ r_3)*(1+ r_3)*(1+r_3)] = CF_3 / [(1+ r_3)*(1+ r_3)*(1+r_3)]$$
$$\text{Present Value} = \$112.16 / [(1+ 3.9\%)*(1+ 3.9\%)*(1+3.9\%)] = \$100.$$

So the present value is $100, the discount rate is 3.9% and the discount factor is 0.892.

Figure PI.7 graphically depicts the discounting process for cash flow received in year three.

FIGURE PI.7

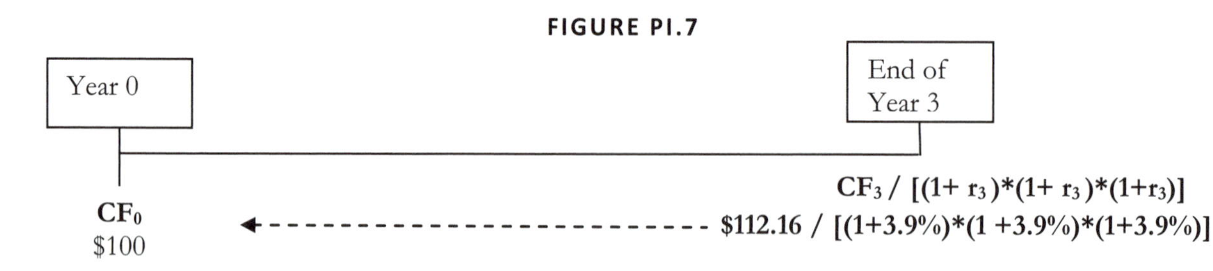

As with the future value equation, the present value equation can be expanded to express the present value of cash flow in the year T as:

$$\text{[Eq. PI.9]} \qquad \text{Present Value} = FV_T * [(1+ r_T) * (1+ r_T) * (1+ r_T) * \ldots\ldots * (1+r_T)]^{-1}$$

Or

$$\text{[Eq. PI.10]} \qquad \text{Present Value} = \text{Future Value (in year T)} * (1+r)^{-T} = CF_T * (1+ r_T)^{-T}.$$

As with future value, the time unit can be quarterly, monthly, weekly, or daily as long as you are consistent in application. Therefore, if you use months to represent time, you must also use a monthly discount rate and monthly cash flows. Figure PI.8 illustrates the general formula for present value at discount rate r_T.

FIGURE PI.8

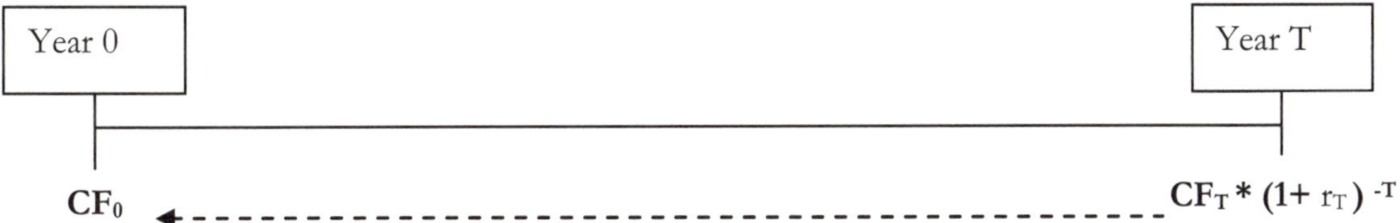

DISCOUNTED CASH FLOW (DCF)

Thus far we have only asked about the present value of the expected cash flow for a specific future year. However, most properties generate cash flows in more than one year (though not all may be positive cash flows). If you are evaluating a property, and its value is solely attributable to its ability to generate future cash flows, its value is simply the sum of the present value of all expected future cash flows.

In the following example, the present value of receiving $109.20 in two years is equal to $100, and the present value of receiving $104 in one year is equal to $100 as well. Hence, the total present value of these two future income receipts given their specific risks is:

$$\text{Total Present Value of first Two Years} = \text{Present Value (\$104 and \$109.20)} = [\$104 * 1.04^{-1}] + [\$109.20 * (1.045*1.045)^{-1}] = \$200.$$

Expanding this example for a third year, the total present value of the first three years of expected cash flows is:

$$\text{Total PV of first 3 Years} = \text{Present Value (\$104, \$109.20, \$112.16)} = [\$104 * 1.04^{-1}] + [\$109.20 * (1.045*1.045)^{-1}] + [\$112.16 * (1.039*1.039*1.039)^{-1}] = \$300.$$

Using Equation PI.12, and the addition of present values, the present value equation for a property generalizes:

[Eq. PI.11] $$\text{PV of the Property} = \text{The sum of the Present Value of all future years} = C_1 * (1+r_1)^{-1} + C_2 * [(1+ r_2)*(1+r_2)]^{-1} + C_3* [(1+ r_3)*(1+ r_3)*(1+r_3)]^{-1} + \ldots\ldots\ C_T* [(1+ r_T)*(1+ r_T)*(1+ r_T)\ldots.*(1+r_T)]^{-1}.$$

If the discount rate for each year's cash flow is roughly the same for all years, this simplifies to:

[Eq. PI.12] $$\text{Present Value of the Property} = \sum_{X=1}^{T} C_T * [(1+r)]^{-t}$$

where Ct is the cash flow expected in year t. **"Discounted"** literally means the cash flows are worth less than par value because of the time value of money, i.e., they are valued at a discount reflecting the time value of money required for the risk associated with future cash flows. For instance, the present value of the first three years of cash flows in our example, $104 in year one, $109.20 for year two, and $112.16 for year three, is a 8.45% total discount to the value of $325.36 had the three cash flows simply been valued at par. That is, the present value of $300 is $25.36 (8.45%) less than the $325.36 non-discounted 3 years sum of future values.

To evaluate property value you will use the expected pre-tax cash flows before any financing or tax liabilities. These **unlevered** cash flows allow you to calculate the value irrespective of the financing structure. This provides a value based solely on the performance of the property. In order to derive the **equity value**, subtract the property's liabilities.

REVERSION VALUE

You can plug in expected cash flows until the property is no longer able to generate any income. But this valuation process is tedious, and at some point pure guesswork. To avoid this arduous process, you generally calculate a **reversion** or **terminal value** that captures the value of all future cash flows beyond this hypothetical exit date. To estimate the reversion value you will generally apply a cap rate to a stabilized NOI.

Discount Rate: The discount rates (r_1, r_2,...r_T) are key inputs into any DCF analysis. Discount rates are always determined by your best assessment of risk of the cash stream you are discounting, that is, how high does the annual expected return have to be to make you willing to invest in something with the risk of the cash stream being discounted. For real estate projects, risk reflects many things, including: liquidity and exit risk; operating risk; political risk; lease-up risk; tenant credit risk; market risk; etc. Determining the appropriate discount rate requires judgment and is a disciplined, yet imprecise, exercise. The discount rate will not only vary between investments, but you may need to apply different discount rates to the cash flows for different years. For instance, if you are considering a development project, you will apply a lower discount rate to the initial cash outflows than to the expected future cash inflows upon completion, as the development cash outflows are fairly certain to occur, while the operating cash inflows are relatively uncertain. If, on the other hand, it is a reasonable approximation that the risk of each year's cash flow is the same, utilize the simpler present valuation formula.

To illustrate the use of discount rates, assume you could invest in a project that will stabilize by year five. The project offers the expected cash flow stream shown in Figure PI.9:

FIGURE PI.9

Project Cash Flow	
Year 1	($300,000)
Year 2	$200,000
Year 3	$0
Year 4	$100,000
Year 5	$2,100,000

Assume (unrealistically) that, you believe the entire project is basically riskless and as liquid as US Treasury bonds. You would use a discount rate approximating the US Treasury rate on these cash flows to reflect the absence of risk in each year.

Using a 4% discount rate (10 year Treasury rate) provides an estimated value of $1.7 million, as displayed in Figure PI.10.

Alternatively, assume that based on your analysis you believe the first two years of cash flows are relatively riskless due to the presence of a US government lease, but the remaining cash flows are very uncertain due to lease expirations, a very uncertain operating environment and market, and exit illiquidity. As a result, you assess the appropriate discount rate for year three is 20% and 18% for year four, while year five and all subsequent years are a less risky 15%, as you expect normal market conditions to return. Once the project stabilizes in year five, you believe NOI will grow at roughly 2% a year. Using the Gordon Model (see p. 117) you estimate the terminal value at the end of year 5 of $1.57 million ($204,000/(15%-2%)).

FIGURE PI.10

Project Cash Flows Case 1

	Year 1		Year 2		Year 3		Year 4		Year 5
Project Value=	$\frac{CF_1}{(1+r)}$	+	$\frac{CF_2}{(1+r)^2}$	+	$\frac{CF_3}{(1+r)^3}$	+	$\frac{CF_4}{(1+r)^4}$	+	$\frac{(CF_5+\text{Terminal Value})}{(1+r)^5}$
Project Value=	$\frac{(\$300,000)}{(1+4\%)}$	+	$\frac{\$200,000}{(1+4\%)^2}$	+	$\frac{\$0}{(1+4\%)^3}$	+	$\frac{\$100,000}{(1+4\%)^4}$	+	$\frac{\$2,100,000}{(1+4\%)^5}$
Project Value	**$1,707,977**								

Using Equation PI.11 to discount the expected cash flows by the appropriate discount rates, yields an estimated value of $1,154,060.

FIGURE PI.11

Project Cash Flows Case 2

	Project Value =	Project Value =	Project Value= $1,154,060
Year 1	$\frac{CF_1}{(1+r_1)}$	$\frac{(\$300,000)}{(1+4\%)}$	
+	+	+	
Year 2	$\frac{CF_2}{(1+r_1)*(1+r_2)}$	$\frac{\$200,000}{(1+4\%)*(1+4\%)}$	
+	+	+	
Year 3	$\frac{CF_3}{(1+r_1)*(1+r_2)*(1+r_3)}$	$\frac{\$0}{(1+4\%)*(1+4\%)*(1+20\%)}$	
+	+	+	
Year 4	$\frac{CF_4}{(1+r_1)*(1+r_2)*(1+r_3)*(1+r_4)}$	$\frac{\$100,000}{(1+4\%)*(1+4\%)*(1+20\%)*(1+18\%)}$	
+	+	+	
Year 5	$\frac{(CF_5+\text{Terminal Value})}{(1+r_1)*(1+r_2)*(1+r_3)*(1+r_4)*(1+r_5)}$	$\frac{\$2,100,000}{(1+4\%)*(1+4\%)*(1+20\%)*(1+18\%)*(1+15\%)}$	

This lower value, i.e. greater discount, reflects the greater risk of the cash streams.

DCF EXAMPLE

Suppose you inherit $4 million and are deciding between purchasing a New York office building, The Oberkircher Building, and a Philadelphia apartment complex, Anderson Gardens. The Oberkircher Building costs $4 million to purchase, while Anderson Gardens costs $3 million. However, you anticipate another $1 million in renovation expenditures for Anderson Gardens in order to upgrade to the property as part of a repositioning plan. You plan on selling the purchased property at the end of the fifth year. Based on your cash flow analyses, you estimate the expected cash flows from operations for the properties summarized in Figure PI.12.

FIGURE PI.12

Anderson Gardens	
Year 1	$300,000
Year 2	$500,000
Year 3	$650,000
Year 4	$875,000
Year 5	$900,000

Oberkircher Building	
Year 1	$400,000
Year 2	$430,000
Year 3	$460,000
Year 4	$490,000
Year 5	$520,000

Before conducting your DCF analysis, you must select appropriate discount rates for each year, for each property. The Philadelphia apartment complex is currently poorly run, but well located in the middle of Center City, with a 40% vacancy rate in spite of strong local market conditions. You believe that you can significantly lower operating costs, increase occupancy, and reposition the building to attract higher rents. If the repositioning is successful, you expect to recognize significant cash flow growth.

The Oberkircher Building, on the other hand, is a well-run building in Midtown Manhattan with stabilized occupancy. The building is leased to high credit quality tenants who are locked into long-term leases. Based on your analysis, comparable properties in New York should generate roughly 10.5% annual returns. However, you believe that this building will fare somewhat better given its superior tenant base, quality location, and great return history. You believe you can maintain the quality management of this property and feel it is less risky than most comparable properties. As a result, you select a 10% discount rate for the New York office building for every year, as you see no notable annual variation in the property's risk profile.

The repositioning of Anderson Gardens is a much riskier endeavor. First, there are very few comparable repositionings that have taken place in the area. Your cash flow projections assume that you will have limited success in the first year of operations, with the $300,000 in year one roughly equaling the property's current performance. Therefore, you select a relatively low discount rate for the first year, as you feel these cash flows, although weak, are relatively certain when compared to future years. Given the uncertainty over releasing, you select an 11.5% discount rate for year one (higher than that for the Oberkircher Building). For the remaining years, the cash flows are less certain due to repositioning risk. As a result, you select a higher, 13% discount rate for cash flows in years 2 through 5, believing the main risk –successful repositioning – is roughly the same for these years. Anderson Gardens therefore requires a 300 BP **risk premium** when compared to the Oberkircher Building for these years (13% versus 10%).

Given these discount rates and the expected future cash flows, you calculate the terminal value for each property upon sale in year 5. You believe that by the end of year 5, when the Philadelphia apartment building is stabilized, cash flows will roughly grow with long term inflation, which you estimate at 2% annually, as this is a highly competitive market and the leases roll over every year. Using the Gordon Model and growing year 5 cash flow to year 6 to reflect forward NOI, you calculate the terminal value for Anderson Gardens as shown in Figure PI.13.

FIGURE PI.13

Anderson Gardens Terminal Value		
Forward Year NOI_6	=	NOI_5*(1+growth rate)
Forward Year NOI_6	=	$918,000
Gordon Model:		
Terminal $Value_5$	=	NOI_6/(r-g)
Terminal $Value_5$	=	$918,000/(13%-2%)
Terminal $Value_5$	=	**$8,345,455**

To calculate the sale value for the New York office building, you similarly apply the Gordon Model. Your analysis indicates that income growth for the Oberkircher Building should slightly outpace inflation due to the strength of the market and the long term nature of the current leases which have favorable rental growth clauses. Therefore, you expect 3% annual long term growth. Given this growth rate, and 10% discount rate, you will apply a 7% exit cap rate to the year 6 NOI, as summarized in Figure PI.14.

FIGURE PI.14

Oberkircher Building Terminal Value		
Forward Year NOI_6	=	NOI_5*(1+growth rate)
Forward Year NOI_6	=	$535,600
Gordon Model:		
Terminal $Value_5$	=	NOI_6/(r-g)
Terminal $Value_5$	=	$535,600/(10%-3%)
Terminal $Value_5$	=	**$7,651,429**

Applying the selected discount rates to your expected future cash flows, and the estimated terminal values you calculate the DCF value for both properties. You estimate that Anderson Gardens is worth an estimated $6.75 million, (Figure PI.15), while the Oberkircher Building is worth an estimated $6.47 million (Figure PI.16). Of course, these valuations are based on expected cash flows and risks, and the actual outcomes will be much different. If you are wrong, you will overpay or underbid. In fact, in the big scheme of things, these two properties have about the same estimated value. That is, in the face of the many assumptions required to estimate values for these properties, their estimated values are only about 4% different. Not much of a difference.

FIGURE PI.15

Anderson Gardens Apartment					
	Year 1	Year 2	Year 3	Year 4	Year 5
Cash Flow from Operations	$300,000	$500,000	$650,000	$875,000	$900,000
Cash Flow from Sale					$8,345,455
Total Cash Flow	$300,000	$500,000	$650,000	$875,000	$9,245,455
Total Cash Flow	$300,000	$500,000	$650,000	$875,000	$9,245,455
Discount Factor	(1+11.5%)	((1+11.5%)*(1+13%))	$((1+11.5\%)*(1+13\%)^2)$	$((1+11.5\%)*(1+13\%)^3)$	$((1+11.5\%)*(1+13\%)^4)$
Value of Property	**$6,751,886**				

FIGURE PI.16

Oberkircher Building					
	Year 1	Year 2	Year 3	Year 4	Year 5
Cash Flow from Operations	$400,000	$430,000	$460,000	$490,000	$520,000
Cash Flow from Sale					$7,651,429
Total Cash Flow	$400,000	$430,000	$460,000	$490,000	$8,171,429
Discount Factor	(1+10%)	$(1+10\%)^2$	$(1+10\%)^3$	$(1+10\%)^4$	$(1+10\%)^5$
Value of Property	**$6,473,104**				

NET PRESENT VALUE (NPV)

Based on your informed, but imperfect, valuations of these properties, which building should you buy with your inheritance? A common tool that is used to help make such decisions is the **net present value** metric (NPV). The net present value of a project is equal to the present value of the cash flows the investment generates minus your initial investment.

[Eq. PI.15] NPV = Present Value – Initial Costs.

NPV tells you how much net value the investment is expected to create, i.e. how much more the property is worth than the costs of acquiring and/or building it. Other things equal (which they never are), you want to invest in the highest NPV project that is consistent with your expertise and abilities. Of course, expertise, as well as limited financial and human resources, prohibit you from investing in every positive NPV project. Therefore, you cannot invest based solely on the current investment alternatives available to you, but also must consider your expected future opportunities.

In our case, you have $4 million to invest and, thus, you can purchase only one building. Using Equation PI.15, you can calculate which of the two projects you are considering has the higher NPV, generating the greatest expected profit over your costs, as shown in Figure PI.17.

FIGURE PI.17

Net Present Value Comparison	
Anderson Gardens	
NPV=	$6,751,886-$4,000,000
NPV=	$2,751,886
Oberkircher Building	
NPV=	$6,473,104-$4,000,000
NPV=	$2,473,104

Based on these NPV estimates, it appears as if you should purchase the Anderson Gardens apartment complex. However, always be humble as the financial analyst. Don't lose sight of the many simplifying, naïve, and frequently incorrect assumptions that went into the analysis. After all that, the NPVs are "only" about 9% different. Do you feel more comfortable with your expertise in one market or project type? Does one fit your expansion strategy better? Do you feel more comfortable with the vagaries of assumptions for one than the other? Does one have a safer downside if things go wrong? As long as project NPVs are relatively close, these factors will always dominate the numbers in your decision making process.

Prerequisite II
IRR

WHAT IT IS AND WHAT IT ISN'T

The **internal rate of return (IRR)** is one of the most common metrics used to evaluate the performance of an investment. It is most certainly the most misused performance metric. It is important to understand what IRR is, and is not.

WHAT IS IT?

The internal rate of return (IRR) is defined as the annual rate of return that generates a NPV of zero for a stream of expected (or actual) cash flows. That is, the present value of the expected income exactly equals the present value of the investment. As such, it is a break even type of return. You solve for the IRR of a project lasting T periods using the NPV equation from Prerequisite I, where C_t is the expected cash flow for the period and r_t is the required rate of return for the corresponding period.

NPV = Initial Costs + Present Value of future net cash streams
NPV = Initial Costs + C_1/ (1+r) + C_2/(1+r)^2 + C_3/(1+r)^3 + C_4/(1+r)^4 +....
So by definition: 0 = Initial Costs + ∑ C_T/(1+**IRR**)^T.

What does this rate of return tell you? Only that if you were to discount your cash flows with the IRR, the project would have a NPV equal to zero. That is, the present value of the future expected net cash flows would exactly equal the initial cash investment if the IRR is the correct discount rate for every year. If this is the case, you are financially indifferent between investing in the project **only if** the IRR is the "right" risk equivalent rate (i.e., discount rate).

Never forget that the IRR does not purport to be the correct discount rate. If you believe the appropriate discount rate for the project is lower than the IRR, the project is expected to generate a positive NPV. On the other hand, if the discount rate is higher than the IRR, the project has an expected negative NPV. As such, the IRR provides a metric that can be used in conjunction with your assessment of project risk to evaluate the financial performance of an investment.

Returning to the two buildings discussed in Prerequisite I, we can calculate the IRR of the alternative investments. The total net pre-tax cash flows for both projects are shown in Figure PII.1.

FIGURE PII.1

Anderson Gardens						
	Initial Investment	Year 1	Year 2	Year 3	Year 4	Year 5
Pre-Tax Cash Flow from Operations	($4,000,000)	$300,000	$500,000	$650,000	$875,000	$900,000
Pre-Tax Cash Flow from Sale						$8,345,455
Total Pre-Tax Cash Flow	($4,000,000)	$300,000	$500,000	$650,000	$875,000	$9,245,455

Oberkircher Building						
	Initial Investment	Year 1	Year 2	Year 3	Year 4	Year 5
Pre-Tax Cash Flow from Operations	($4,000,000)	$400,000	$430,000	$460,000	$490,000	$520,000
Pre-Tax Cash Flow from Sale						$7,651,429
Total Pre-Tax Cash Flow	($4,000,000)	$400,000	$430,000	$460,000	$490,000	$8,171,429

Using calculators and computer packages that incorporate the highly non-linear IRR formula, you can quickly solve for the rate of return that generates a zero expected NPV for each project on an unlevered (exclusive of debt financing) basis. The **unlevered IRR** (also referred to as the **property-level IRR**) for Anderson Gardens is 27%, while that for the Oberkircher Building is 23%, as seen below in Figure PII.2.

FIGURE PII.2

Anderson Gardens

Initial Investment, Year 1, Year 2, Year 3, Year 4, Year 5

$$0 = (\$4{,}000{,}000) + \frac{\$300{,}000}{(1+IRR)} + \frac{\$500{,}000}{(1+IRR)^2} + \frac{\$650{,}000}{(1+IRR)^3} + \frac{\$875{,}000}{(1+IRR)^4} + \frac{\$9{,}245{,}455}{(1+IRR)^5}$$

IRR= 27%

Oberkircher Building

Initial Investment, Year 1, Year 2, Year 3, Year 4, Year 5

$$0 = (\$4{,}000{,}000) + \frac{\$400{,}000}{(1+IRR)} + \frac{\$430{,}000}{(1+IRR)^2} + \frac{\$460{,}000}{(1+IRR)^3} + \frac{\$490{,}000}{(1+IRR)^4} + \frac{\$8{,}171{,}429}{(1+IRR)^5}$$

IRR= 23%

All too often users jump to the conclusion that Anderson Gardens is the better investment, as it has a higher IRR than the Oberkircher Building. However, this is a seriously flawed usage of the IRR, as the IRR tells you nothing about the risk of these projects, the timing of the expected cash flows, your expertise in managing the properties, or any of the many other factors that go into making an investment decision.

WHAT IT ISN'T

The IRR is simply an algebraic calculation. Since it reflects no judgment, common sense suggests that it must be limited in its analytic insight. It is nothing more than an algebraic solution to the simple math question "what discount rate generates a zero expected NPV"?

The 27% IRR for Anderson Gardens does not tell you if the property is well designed and well located, about tenant risk, the risks inherent in an uncertain repositioning effort, leasing risk, cost overrun risk, or exit risk. The 23% IRR for the Oberkircher Building says nothing about the stability of the cash flows, the credit quality of the tenants, the liquidity of the New York office market, or the building's design or location. No formula can assess such risks. That is your job!

Note that an IRR also tells you nothing about the size or timing of the expected cash flows. And no IRR tells you if the numbers used in the analysis are sensible, much less correct. Consider the expected cash flows displayed in Figure PII.3.

FIGURE PII.3

	Initial Investment	Year 1	Year 2	Year 3
Cash Flows	($4,000)	$400	$650	$6,000
IRR	23%			

The IRR for this $4,000 investment is the same as the IRR of the $4 million Oberkircher Building investment. Which one should you take? Based upon your resources and assessment of risk, you may not want, or be able, to invest $4 million. Or you may find a $4,000 investment to be too small to warrant your attention. In the real world, the size of the investment is an important factor in the investment decision. Since IRR completely ignores this factor, it is clear that it is not some all-powerful investment tool.

In addition to the size of the project, IRR ignores the length of the investment period. For example, the Oberkircher Building project lasts two years longer than the alternative project shown in Figure PII.3. Whether you want your money tied up for 5 years is often a critical matter when making an investment decision. Again, IRR is silent on this issue. In fact, if you generate a 1% return on a one day investment, your annual IRR is astronomical even though your cash multiple is miniscule.

IRR does not distinguish between annual cash flows from operations and cash proceeds associated with exit. These sources of cash inflows have different timing and uncertainty. While cash flows from next year's operations are rarely guaranteed, even in the presence of long term leases, they are relatively predictable. In contrast, the exit price upon sale depends on factors which are years into the future. Therefore, it is generally much easier for investors to get comfortable with cash flows one to two years from now compared to proceeds from sale. Whether you prefer an investment with most of its cash flow generated from the property's sale depends on your risk aversion, opinion about the future, your need for ongoing cash inflows, etc. Again, the IRR says nothing in this regard.

IRR also does not distinguish between early or late cash flows. For most investors, the earlier the cash flow, the better, as a dollar received today is one less to worry about receiving in the future. Other things equal, investors generally prefer to get their money back sooner than later, as it allows them to "take their money off of the table". But IRR is of no help in this regard.

The IRR also assumes that the appropriate risk adjusted rate of return is the same for every year. But for many investments this assumption is inaccurate. Returning to the two buildings in Prerequisite I, the early operating cash flows from Anderson Gardens repositioning are relatively certain compared to the cash flow upon repositioning and sales proceeds. As a result, a higher discount rate was used to value the later operating cash flows. IRR, on the other hand, is calculated assuming these cash flows were equally risky.

IRR fails to tell you anything about financing (leverage) risk. This is particularly troubling as investors (and particularly students) often only calculate the IRR on their equity. The **equity IRR** (also referred to as the **levered IRR**) is the single discount rate that sets NPV of expected future equity cash flows equal to zero. As you saw from comparing Anderson Gardens and the Oberkircher Building, the IRR tells you nothing about property, leasing, operating, liquidity risk, etc. Now assume the $4 million total costs, (purchase and improvement), for Anderson Gardens is financed at a 75%, $3 million mortgage, with a 7% interest rate resulting in an annual interest payment of $210,000. While the $4 million purchase of the Oberkircher Building is financed at a 50% LTV, $2 million mortgage, with a 6% interest rate resulting in an annual interest payment of $120,000. Assume that both loans are for 10 years, with no prepayment penalties or amortization. Upon the sale of either property in year five, the mortgage will be repaid.

Given the information above and the pre-tax cash flows from Figure PII.1, the expected pre-tax equity cash flows are displayed in Figure PII.4:

FIGURE PII.4

Anderson Gardens						
	Initial Investment	Year 1	Year 2	Year 3	Year 4	Year 5
Total Costs of Investment	($4,000,000)					
Proceeds from Mortgage	$3,000,000					
Cash Flow from Operations		$300,000	$500,000	$650,000	$875,000	$900,000
Interest Payment		($210,000)	($210,000)	($210,000)	($210,000)	($210,000)
Cash Flow from Sale						$8,345,455
Repayment of Mortgage						($3,000,000)
Total Pre-Tax Equity Cash Flow	**($1,000,000)**	**$90,000**	**$290,000**	**$440,000**	**$665,000**	**$6,035,455**

Oberkircher Building						
	Initial Investment	Year 1	Year 2	Year 3	Year 4	Year 5
Total Costs of Investment	($4,000,000)					
Proceeds from Mortgage	$2,000,000					
Cash Flow from Operations		$400,000	$430,000	$460,000	$490,000	$520,000
Interest Payment		($120,000)	($120,000)	($120,000)	($120,000)	($120,000)
Cash Flow from Sale						$7,651,429
Repayment of Mortgage						($2,000,000)
Total Pre-Tax Equity Cash Flow	**($2,000,000)**	**$280,000**	**$310,000**	**$340,000**	**$370,000**	**$6,051,429**

Using the IRR equation you can solve for the equity rate of return that generates a zero NPV for the equity investor. The resulting expected equity IRR for Anderson Gardens is 58% while the Oberkircher Building has an expected equity IRR of 35%.

FIGURE PII.5

Anderson Gardens						
	Initial Investment	Year 1	Year 2	Year 3	Year 4	Year 5
0=	($1,000,000)	+ $\frac{\$900,000}{(1+IRR)}$	+ $\frac{\$290,000}{(1+IRR)^2}$	+ $\frac{\$440,000}{(1+IRR)^3}$	+ $\frac{\$665,000}{(1+IRR)^4}$	+ $\frac{\$6,035,455}{(1+IRR)^5}$
	Equity IRR=	**58%**				

Oberkircher Building						
	Initial Investment	Year 1	Year 2	Year 3	Year 4	Year 5
0=	($2,000,000)	+ $\frac{\$280,000}{(1+IRR)}$	+ $\frac{\$310,000}{(1+IRR)^2}$	+ $\frac{\$340,000}{(1+IRR)^3}$	+ $\frac{\$370,000}{(1+IRR)^4}$	+ $\frac{\$6,051,429}{(1+IRR)^5}$
	Equity IRR=	**35%**				

The equity IRR for both properties is higher than the property level IRRs (27% for Anderson Gardens and 23% for the Oberkircher Building). Also, the IRR for Anderson Gardens is now substantially higher than IRR for the Oberkircher Building. Where the difference between the two projects was only 4% without debt, Anderson Gardens now yields a 23% higher IRR. Based on equity IRR alone, many students are inclined to use as much debt as possible. However, the risk of the equity cash flows is much higher than for the property due to the leverage, as the lender is entitled to the first cash flows. The more debt you use to fund the acquisition, the greater is the risk of your equity cash flows. Is the additional expected return worth the risk? Maybe yes if you can afford to lose the money or the tenant has great credit quality. Maybe no if your total wealth is at risk and the economy is weak.

Stated bluntly, the IRR on equity says nothing about risk (of any type). Thus, when looking at an equity IRR you need to evaluate whether the returns are being driven by strong property cash flows, extreme leverage, or extreme operating risk.

CLOSING THOUGHT

IRR is a popular and useful metric. But it is important you know not only how to calculate it, but also understand its severe limitations. It's just one more "brick in the wall" that goes into making a sound real estate investment decision.

Prerequisite III
Amortization Fundamentals

Amortization refers to the repayment schedule for your debt. To illuminate amortization, consider Kathy Crest, a residential garden apartment complex being purchased for $6.7 million, with a $5 million loan at a 5% interest rate, and a 7 year loan maturity.

ZERO AMORTIZATION LOAN/BULLET LOAN/INTEREST ONLY LOAN

When obtaining a loan, the borrower obligates herself to pay back the principal, or capital amount borrowed, as well as the interest on the outstanding loan amount. Amortization specifies how the principal is repaid. In the case of a zero amortization loan (also known as a **"bullet"** or **"interest only"** loan), only interest is paid on the full loan amount until the final payment, when the principal is also repaid. Figure PIII.1 summarizes the loan payments and the return the lender realizes on their capital.

FIGURE PIII.1: KATHY CREST ANALYSIS OF LENDER YIELDS

Kathy Crest Analysis of Lender Yields (Zero Amortization)								
	Year	**1**	**2**	**3**	**4**	**5**	**6**	**7**
First Mortgage Holder	Closing							
Loan Proceeds Disbursed	($5,000,000)	$0	$0	$0	$0	$0	$0	$0
Debt Service Payment Received	$0	$250,000	$250,000	$250,000	$250,000	$250,000	$250,000	$250,000
Repayment of Loan Balance	$0	$0	$0	$0	$0	$0	$0	$5,000,000
Before-Tax Cash Flow	($5,000,000)	$250,000	$250,000	$250,000	$250,000	$250,000	$250,000	$5,250,000
Yield to Lender (IRR)	5.00%							

While the payment of debt does not affect NOI, as shown in Figure PIII.2, it does impact after-tax cash flows. This is because mortgage interest and amortization must be deducted from cash flow, and because interest payments reduce income taxes. As amortization increases over time, the outstanding principal decreases, as do interest payments.

While interest payments in our scenario can be paid with cash flows generated from operations, the principal will be paid off with property sale proceeds. If the property is not sold, the loan will have to be refinanced either by a new loan or an equity infusion upon maturity. If the equity holders cannot repay the principal, the lender can either forbear or foreclose on the borrower. Forbearance means that the lender gives the borrower additional time to repay the loan. If the lender forecloses, the lender will repossess the property. Figure PIII.3: displays how the principal outstanding affects the net proceeds upon sale of Kathy Crest.

FIGURE PIII.2: AFTER-TAX CASH FLOW FROM OPERATION (ZERO AMORTIZATION)

Kathy Crest: After-Tax Cash Flow from Operation (Zero Amortization)							
	Year 1	Year 2	Year 3	Year 4	Year 5	Year 6	Year 7
Net Operating Income	$518,426	$529,047	$539,741	$550,496	$561,302	$572,147	$583,017
Less: Debt Service First Mortgage	($250,000)	($250,000)	($250,000)	($250,000)	($250,000)	($250,000)	($250,000)
Before Tax Levered Cash Flows	$268,426	$279,047	$289,741	$300,496	$311,302	$322,147	$333,017
Adjustments:							
Less: Depreciation	($201,818)	($201,818)	($201,818)	($201,818)	($201,818)	($201,818)	($201,818)
Plus: CAPEX	$45,000	$46,350	$47,741	$49,173	$50,648	$52,167	$53,732
Plus: Principal Amortization	-	-	-	-	-	-	-
Less: Points Amortization	$0	$0	$0	$0	$0	$0	$0
Taxable Income (Loss)	$111,608	$123,579	$135,663	$147,850	$160,132	$172,496	$184,931
Less: Application of	*$0*	*$0*	*$0*	*$0*	*$0*	*$0*	*$0*
Suspended Losses	$0	$0	$0	$0	$0	$0	$0
Net Taxable Income (Loss)	$111,608	$123,579	$135,663	$147,850	$160,132	$172,496	$184,931
Less: Tax Liability	($44,197)	($48,937)	($53,723)	($58,549)	($63,412)	($68,308)	($73,233)
After-Tax Cash Flows	$224,229	$230,110	$236,018	$241,947	$247,890	$253,838	$259,784

FIGURE PIII.3: KATHY CREST SALES PROCEEDS (ZERO AMORTIZATION):

Kathy Crest Sales Proceeds: (Zero Amortization)	
Gross Sales Price	$ 7,423,739
Less Brokerage Commission	$ (148,475)
Net Sales Price	$ 7,275,264
Less Tax Liability	$ (399,273)
Less Outstanding Mortgage Balance	$ (5,000,000)
Net Sales Proceeds	$ 1,875,992

The Equity IRR calculation for the use of a non-amortizing loan is presented in Figure PIII.4.

FIGURE PIII.4: DCF KATHY CREST (ZERO AMORTIZATION):

DCF: Kathy Crest (Zero Amortization)				
TIME PERIOD	EQUITY INVESTMENT	ANNUAL AFTER-TAX CASH FLOW	AFTER-TAX NET SALES PROCEEDS	TOTAL AFTER-TAX CASH FLOW
0	($1,700,000)	$0	-	($1,700,000)
1		$224,229	-	$224,229
2		$230,110	-	$230,110
3		$236,018	-	$236,018
4		$241,947	-	$241,947
5		$247,890	-	$247,890
6		$253,838	-	$253,838
7		$259,784	$1,875,992	$2,135,776
	($1,700,000)	$1,693,817	$1,875,992	$1,869,809

NET PRESENT VALUE @ 10%	$429,792
INTERNAL RATE OF RETURN	14.98%

POSITIVE AMORTIZATION

Lenders generally require you to repay part of the principal with each loan payment in order to reduce their repayment risk. The loan amortization schedule does not have to equal the maturity of the loan (i.e., it can be longer, but not shorter than, the loan term). Assume the same loan terms for Kathy Crest, except that the loan is amortized over 20 years. The annual payment rises to $401,213. The way you calculate this number is to refer to a mortgage calculator, website, or by using the **annuity factor** formula in figure PIII.5, where R is the interest rate 5% and T is the amortization period, 20. The annuity factor for the Kathy Crest 20-year amortizing loan would be 12.462

FIGURE PIII.5

Annuity Factor Formula
$(1/R)-(1/(R(1+R)^T))$

Figure PIII.6 provides a summary of **mortgage constants** for a variety of mortgage interest rates and amortization periods. A mortgage constant is the percentage of the original loan principal amount, that when multiplied by that full principal amount, produces the constant annual loan payment amount inclusive of interest and principal. The mortgage constant is simply the reciprocal of the annuity factor. In our example, the mortgage constant percentage would be 1/12.462, which equals 8.024%. To calculate the annual payment, multiply the loan principal by the percentage indicated for a given interest rate and amortization period. For example, if you have a $5 million loan with at a 5% interest rate and a 20 year amortization, you will multiply 8.024% by $5 million, for a $401,200 annual loan payment. Lenders use such tables to quickly determine payment schedules. If the loan matures sooner than the amortization period, all remaining principal is due with the final payment.

FIGURE PIII.6: MORTGAGE CONSTANT SUMMARY

	Amortization Period (Years)									
Mortgage Rates	5	10	15	16	17	18	19	20	25	30
5.000%	23.097%	12.950%	9.634%	9.227%	8.870%	8.555%	8.275%	8.024%	7.095%	6.505%
5.125%	23.177%	13.029%	9.716%	9.309%	8.953%	8.638%	8.359%	8.110%	7.184%	6.598%
5.250%	23.257%	13.108%	9.798%	9.392%	9.036%	8.723%	8.444%	8.195%	7.274%	6.692%
5.375%	23.337%	13.187%	9.880%	9.475%	9.120%	8.807%	8.529%	8.281%	7.364%	6.786%
5.500%	23.418%	13.267%	9.963%	9.558%	9.204%	8.892%	8.615%	8.368%	7.455%	6.881%
5.625%	23.498%	13.346%	10.045%	9.642%	9.289%	8.977%	8.701%	8.455%	7.546%	6.976%
5.750%	23.578%	13.426%	10.129%	9.726%	9.374%	9.063%	8.788%	8.542%	7.638%	7.072%
5.875%	23.659%	13.506%	10.212%	9.810%	9.459%	9.149%	8.875%	8.630%	7.730%	7.168%
6.000%	23.740%	13.587%	10.296%	9.895%	9.544%	9.236%	8.962%	8.718%	7.823%	7.265%
6.125%	23.820%	13.667%	10.381%	9.980%	9.630%	9.323%	9.050%	8.807%	7.916%	7.362%
6.250%	23.901%	13.748%	10.465%	10.066%	9.717%	9.410%	9.138%	8.896%	8.009%	7.460%
6.375%	23.982%	13.829%	10.550%	10.152%	9.804%	9.497%	9.227%	8.986%	8.104%	7.559%
6.500%	24.063%	13.910%	10.635%	10.238%	9.891%	9.585%	9.316%	9.076%	8.198%	7.658%
6.625%	24.145%	13.992%	10.721%	10.324%	9.978%	9.674%	9.405%	9.166%	8.293%	7.757%
6.750%	24.226%	14.074%	10.807%	10.411%	10.066%	9.763%	9.495%	9.257%	8.389%	7.857%
6.875%	24.307%	14.156%	10.893%	10.498%	10.154%	9.852%	9.585%	9.348%	8.485%	7.958%
7.000%	24.389%	14.238%	10.979%	10.586%	10.243%	9.941%	9.675%	9.439%	8.581%	8.059%
7.125%	24.471%	14.320%	11.066%	10.674%	10.331%	10.031%	9.766%	9.531%	8.678%	8.160%
7.250%	24.553%	14.403%	11.153%	10.762%	10.421%	10.121%	9.857%	9.623%	8.775%	8.262%
7.375%	24.634%	14.486%	11.241%	10.850%	10.510%	10.212%	9.949%	9.716%	8.873%	8.364%
7.500%	24.716%	14.569%	11.329%	10.939%	10.600%	10.303%	10.041%	9.809%	8.971%	8.467%
7.625%	24.799%	14.652%	11.417%	11.028%	10.690%	10.394%	10.133%	9.903%	9.070%	8.570%
7.750%	24.881%	14.735%	11.505%	11.118%	10.781%	10.486%	10.226%	9.996%	9.169%	8.674%
7.875%	24.963%	14.819%	11.594%	11.208%	10.872%	10.578%	10.319%	10.091%	9.268%	8.778%
8.000%	25.046%	14.903%	11.683%	11.298%	10.963%	10.670%	10.413%	10.185%	9.368%	8.883%
8.125%	25.128%	14.987%	11.772%	11.388%	11.055%	10.763%	10.507%	10.280%	9.468%	8.988%
8.250%	25.211%	15.071%	11.862%	11.479%	11.146%	10.856%	10.601%	10.375%	9.569%	9.093%
8.375%	25.294%	15.156%	11.952%	11.570%	11.239%	10.949%	10.695%	10.471%	9.670%	9.199%
8.500%	25.377%	15.241%	12.042%	11.661%	11.331%	11.043%	10.790%	10.567%	9.771%	9.305%
8.625%	25.460%	15.326%	12.133%	11.753%	11.424%	11.137%	10.885%	10.663%	9.873%	9.412%
8.750%	25.543%	15.411%	12.223%	11.845%	11.517%	11.231%	10.981%	10.760%	9.975%	9.519%
8.875%	25.626%	15.496%	12.314%	11.937%	11.611%	11.326%	11.077%	10.857%	10.078%	9.626%
9.000%	25.709%	15.582%	12.406%	12.030%	11.705%	11.421%	11.173%	10.955%	10.181%	9.734%

As you extend the amortization period to infinity, the annual payment approaches the interest only payment of $250,000. Thus, a bullet loan (a zero amortization loan) is effectively a loan with an infinite amortization period. Figure PIII.7 displays the annual payments the lender receives for the 5%, 7 year loan with a 20 year amortization.

FIGURE PIII.7: KATHY CREST MORTGAGE AMORTIZATION (20 YEAR AMORTIZATION):

Kathy Crest Mortgage Interest Amortization (20yr Amortization)							
	1	2	3	4	5	6	7
Mortgage Amount	$5,000,000						
Interest	$250,000	$242,439	$234,501	$226,165	$217,413	$208,223	$198,573
Amortization	$151,213	$158,774	$166,712	$175,048	$183,800	$192,990	$202,640
Total Payment	$401,213	$401,213	$401,213	$401,213	$401,213	$401,213	$401,213
Year-End Mortgage Balance	$4,848,787	$4,690,013	$4,523,301	$4,348,253	$4,164,453	$3,971,463	$3,768,823

FIGURE PIII.8: INTEREST AND AMORTIZATION BREAK DOWN (20 YEAR AMORTIZATION)

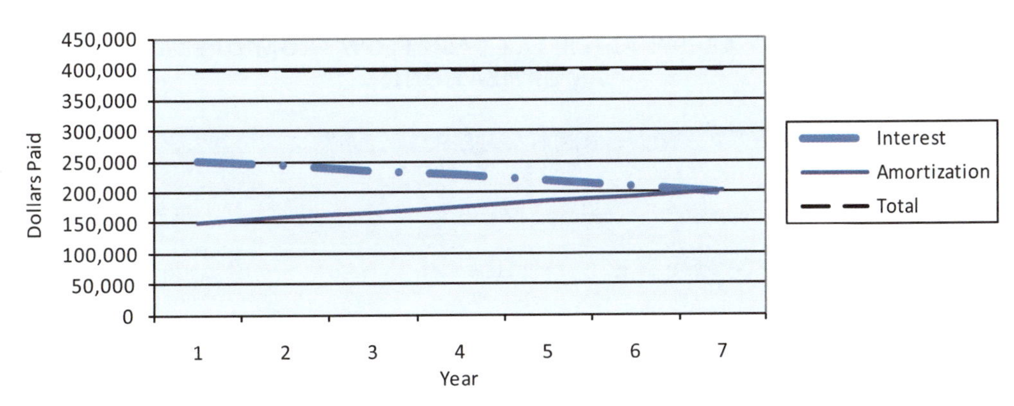

Figure PIII.8 reveals that while total payment is the same each year ($401,213), the interest portion decreases every year while the principal repayment component increases by an offsetting amount each year. This is because as the debt is repaid, the outstanding loan balance is reduced, and you only pay interest on the amount outstanding. As the amortization period increases, from 20 years to 30 years (as shown in Figure P111.9), the interest component increases each year, but since the amortization is slower, total interest payments are larger than for the 20 year amortization schedule.

Figure PIII.9 shows the amortization schedule for the same loan ($5 MM with a 5% rate and 7 year maturity) but different amortization schedules.

FIGURE PIII.9: AMORTIZATION SCHEDULE WITH VARYING AMORTIZATION SCHEDULES

Different Amortization Periods for a $5 MM Loan with a 5% Interest Rate and 7 Year Maturity															
	7 year			10 year			20 year			30 year			No Amortization		
Year	Interest Payment	Principal Payment	Mortgage Balance	Interest Payment	Principal Payment	Mortgage Balance	Interest Payment	Principal Payment	Mortgage Balance	Interest Payment	Principal Payment	Mortgage Balance	Interest Payment	Principal Payment	Mortgage Balance
1	$250,000	$614,099	$4,385,901	$250,000	$397,523	$4,602,477	$250,000	$151,213	$4,848,787	$250,000	$75,257	$4,924,743	$250,000	$0	$5,000,000
2	$219,295	$644,804	$3,741,097	$230,124	$417,399	$4,185,078	$242,439	$158,774	$4,690,013	$246,237	$79,020	$4,845,723	$250,000	$0	$5,000,000
3	$187,055	$677,044	$3,064,053	$209,254	$438,269	$3,746,809	$234,501	$166,712	$4,523,301	$242,286	$82,971	$4,762,752	$250,000	$0	$5,000,000
4	$153,203	$710,896	$2,353,156	$187,340	$460,182	$3,286,627	$226,165	$175,048	$4,348,253	$238,138	$87,120	$4,675,632	$250,000	$0	$5,000,000
5	$117,658	$746,441	$1,606,715	$164,331	$483,192	$2,803,435	$217,413	$183,800	$4,164,453	$233,782	$91,476	$4,584,157	$250,000	$0	$5,000,000
6	$80,336	$783,763	$822,952	$140,172	$507,351	$2,296,084	$208,223	$192,990	$3,971,463	$229,208	$96,049	$4,488,107	$250,000	$0	$5,000,000
7	$41,148	$822,952	$0	$114,804	$532,719	$1,763,365	$198,573	$202,640	$3,768,823	$224,405	$100,852	$4,387,255	$250,000	$0	$5,000,000

How does different amortization impact the borrower? First, the shorter the amortization period the greater are the annual payments, as you have a shorter period to repay the loan. In addition, the faster the amortization, the lower the total interest payments. As a result, the interest tax shield is lower for rapidly amortizing loans. On the other hand, higher amortization loans increase your equity position in the property more quickly.

FIGURE PIII.10:KATHY CREST: AFTER-TAX CASH FLOW FROM OPERATION (20 YEAR AMORTIZATION)

Kathy Crest: After-Tax Cash Flow from Operation (Twenty-year Amortization)							
	Year 1	Year 2	Year 3	Year 4	Year 5	Year 6	Year 7
Net Operating Income	$518,426	$529,047	$539,741	$550,496	$561,302	$572,147	$583,017
Less: Debt Service First Mortgage	($325,257)	($325,257)	($325,257)	($325,257)	($325,257)	($325,257)	($325,257)
Before Tax Levered Cash Flows	$193,169	$203,790	$214,483	$225,239	$236,045	$246,890	$257,760
Adjustments:							
Less: Depreciation	($201,818)	($201,818)	($201,818)	($201,818)	($201,818)	($201,818)	($201,818)
Plus: CAPEX	$45,000	$46,350	$47,741	$49,173	$50,648	$52,167	$53,732
Plus: Principal Amortization	$75,257	$79,020	$82,971	$87,120	$91,476	$96,049	$100,852
Less: Points Amortization	$0	$0	$0	$0	$0	$0	$0
Taxable Income (Loss)	$111,608	$127,342	$143,377	$159,713	$176,350	$193,288	$210,526
Less: Application of	*$0*	*$0*	*$0*	*$0*	*$0*	*$0*	*$0*
Suspended Losses	$0	$0	$0	$0	$0	$0	$0
Net Taxable Income (Loss)	$111,608	$127,342	$143,377	$159,713	$176,350	$193,288	$210,526
Less: Tax Liability	($44,197)	($50,427)	($56,777)	($63,246)	($69,835)	($76,542)	($83,368)
After-Tax Cash Flows	$148,972	$153,363	$157,706	$161,992	$166,210	$170,348	$174,392

Note how the after-tax cash flow is lower for the 20 year amortization than for the zero amortization case (Figure PIII.2). The difference derives from the repayment of the mortgage principal in each payment period, which lowers the cash flow before taxes to equity holders, even though NOI is the same. If the loan was fully amortized, meaning that the amortization period equaled the maturity period, the loan payments would be $864,099 each year for the 7 year term of the loan. With NOI of $518,426, the borrower would not be able to service these debt payments from property cash flows alone. This means fresh money would have to be injected via either equity or new debt.

While annual cash flows are reduced for the equity holder, when the building is sold there is less principal to retire. Figure PIII.11 illustrates the results upon the sale of the building, compared to the zero amortization case. Higher amortization shifts the equity returns from annual cash flows to the sale of the property.

FIGURE PIII.11: KATHY CREST SALES PROCEEDS

Kathy Crest Sales Proceeds: (Zero Amortization)	
Gross Sales Price	$ 7,423,739
Less Brokerage Commission	$ (148,475)
Net Sales Price	$ 7,275,264
Less Tax Liability	$ (399,273)
Less Outstanding Mortgage Balance	$ (5,000,000)
Net Sales Proceeds	$ 1,875,992

Kathy Crest Sales Proceeds: (20yr Amortization)	
Gross Sales Price	$ 7,423,739
Less Brokerage Commission	$ (148,475)
Net Sales Price	$ 7,275,264
Less Tax Liability	$ (399,273)
Less Outstanding Mortgage Balance	$ (3,768,823)
Net Sales Proceeds	$ 3,107,169

FIGURE PIII.12: DCF KATHY CREST WITH VARIED AMORTIZATION

	After-Tax Cash Flows											
Years	0	1	2	3	4	5	6	7 (with sale)	IRR	Loan Balance (Year 7)	Value of Property Year 7: $583,017/.08	LTV
0 Debt	$ (6,700,000)	$ 375,229	$ 381,110	$ 387,018	$ 392,947	$ 398,890	$ 404,838	$ 7,286,776	6.2%	$ -	$ 7,287,713	0%
10 Amortization	$ (1,700,000)	$ (173,294)	$ (175,284)	$ (177,640)	$ (180,389)	$ (183,558)	$ (187,176)	$ 4,921,350	10.3%	$1,763,365	$ 7,287,713	24%
20 Amortization	$ (1,700,000)	$ 73,016	$ 75,903	$ 78,667	$ 81,296	$ 83,772	$ 86,082	$ 3,195,375	12.7%	$3,768,823	$ 7,287,713	52%
30 Amortization	$ (1,700,000)	$ 148,972	$ 153,363	$ 157,706	$ 161,992	$ 166,210	$ 170,348	$ 2,663,128	13.8%	$4,387,255	$ 7,287,713	60%

A borrower generally prefers longer to shorter amortization, because the borrower prefers to repay their loan later than earlier. Kathy Crest starts with a 75% LTV, and over time the LTV falls as the loan amortizes and property value hopefully rises. Properties that are relatively vulnerable to value declines will tend to be granted lower LTVs and shorter amortization periods by the lender as lenders are concerned first and foremost with getting their capital back.

ALTERNATIVE AMORTIZATION LOANS

To cater to the different preferences of the lender and borrower, sometimes hybrid amortization schedules are created. For example, there may be no amortization for the first two years and then a 20 year amortization for rest of the loan term. It is also possible to have annual payments change and amortization remain constant. This means you pay down your principal by a certain amount every year. Figure PIII.13 displays an example of a **constant amortization loan**, where $500,000 in principal plus interest on the outstanding loan balance is to be paid every year.

FIGURE PIII.13: KATHY CREST MORTGAGE INTEREST AMORTIZATION (CONSTANT AMORTIZATION)

Kathy Crest Mortgage Interest Amortization (Constant Amortization)							
	Year 1	**Year 2**	**Year 3**	**Year 4**	**Year 5**	**Year 6**	**Year 7**
Mortgage Amount	$5,000,000						
Interest	$0	$225,000	$200,000	$175,000	$150,000	$125,000	$100,000
Amortization	$500,000	$500,000	$500,000	$500,000	$500,000	$500,000	$500,000
Total Payment	$500,000	$725,000	$700,000	$675,000	$650,000	$625,000	$600,000
Year-End Mortgage Balance	$4,500,000	$4,000,000	$3,500,000	$3,000,000	$2,500,000	$2,000,000	$1,500,000

NEGATIVE AMORTIZATION/ACCRUAL LOANS/CONSTRUCTION LOANS

Buildings take time to build. This means that you can go for months, even years without generating revenue, while incurring development costs. During the development phase, you may need to take on debt to cover costs. You will be charged interest on this debt, but you will not be able to pay the interest from the income the property generates until much later. Lenders understand this situation and offer **accrual construction loans**.

Because the principal is growing, accrual loans are also called **negative amortization loans**. Since interest that is not paid when incurred is added to the principal owed, new interest is charged on old unpaid interest plus the cumulative draw amount. Figure PIII.14 displays an example of an accrual loan for the conversion of an office building that will become a condominium building. Notice how until Q1 of Year 3, no revenue is reflected in the pro forma.

FIGURE PIII.14: DEVELOPMENT PRO FORMA FOR JESSICA'S CONDO DEVELOPMENT

CONDO DEVELOPMENT Project Level Cash Flows												
Initial Investment	Time 0											
Purchase of Building	($3,600,000)											
Transaction Cost	($108,000)											
Subtotal	($3,708,000)											
		Year 1 Q1	Year 1 Q2	Year 1 Q3	Year 1 Q4	Year 2 Q1	Year 2 Q2	Year 2 Q3	Year 2 Q4	Year 3 Q1	Year 3 Q2	Year 3 Q3
Revenue												
Closing Presales												
2-Bedroom										3,784,873	946,218	-
3-Bedroom										1,971,288	657,096	-
Subtotal		-	-	-	-	-	-	-	-	5,756,160	1,603,314	-
Post Construction Sales												
2-Bedroom		-	-	-	-	-	-	-	-	-	473,109	-
3-Bedroom		-	-	-	-	-	-	-	-	1,314,192	-	-
Subtotal		-	-	-	-	-	-	-	-	1,314,192	473,109	-
Total Revenue		-	-	-	-	-	-	-	-	7,070,352	2,076,423	-
Expenses												
Development & Construction		(100,000)	(200,000)	(200,000)	(300,000)	(1,000,000)	(700,000)	(60,000)	(32,000)	-	-	-
Sales Costs		-	-	-	-	-	-	-	-	(212,111)	(62,293)	-
Subtotal		(100,000)	(200,000)	(200,000)	(300,000)	(1,000,000)	(700,000)	(60,000)	(32,000)	(212,111)	(62,293)	-
Unlevered Cash Flows	($3,708,000)	(100,000)	(200,000)	(200,000)	(300,000)	(1,000,000)	(700,000)	(60,000)	(32,000)	6,858,242	2,014,130	-

The negative cash flows derive from the development and construction costs. These costs will be paid first by equity, then debt. The maximum ratio of loan to value in our example is 66%, with $2.1 million, the initial equity, paid toward the purchase of the building. Total debt required for the project is $4.2 million, which includes $421,940 in accrued interest, as shown in PIII.15.

FIGURE PIII.15: JESSICA'S CONDO DEVELOPMENT DEBT ANALYSIS

CONDO DEVELOPMENT Debt Analysis											
	Time 0	Year 1 Q1	Year 1 Q2	Year 1 Q3	Year 1 Q4	Year 2 Q1	Year 2 Q2	Year 2 Q3	Year 2 Q4	Year 3 Q1	Year 3 Q2
Unlevered Cash Flows	($3,708,000)	($100,000)	($200,000)	($200,000)	($300,000)	($1,000,000)	($700,000)	($60,000)	($32,000)	$6,858,242	$2,014,130
Debt											
Principal											
Beginning Balance	($1,608,000)	1,608,000	1,708,000	1,908,000	2,108,000	2,408,000	3,408,000	4,108,000	4,168,000	4,200,000	-
Draws	$1,608,000	100,000	200,000	200,000	300,000	1,000,000	700,000	60,000	32,000	-	-
Remaining Cash Sweep		-	-	-	-	-	-	-	-	(3,778,060)	-
Ending Balance		1,708,000	1,908,000	2,108,000	2,408,000	3,408,000	4,108,000	4,168,000	4,200,000	-	-
Interest											
Accrual Beginning Balance		-	28,186	58,922	93,058	131,444	180,880	244,766	315,112	386,240	-
Quarterly Interest		28,186	30,736	34,136	38,386	49,436	63,886	70,346	71,128	35,700	-
Cash Sweep For Interest		-	-	-	-	-	-	-	-	(421,940)	-
Accrual Ending Balance		28,186	58,922	93,058	131,444	180,880	244,766	315,112	386,240	-	-

The debt is calculated in the following manner. At time 0, the purchase price of the building, plus transaction costs, is $3.708 million. Of that amount $1.608 million comes from debt, and the rest is from equity. At this point all of the equity is invested. In quarter 1, $100,000 is used for development and construction, which is added to the principal balance, yielding a total of $1.708 million. To estimate the quarterly interest, we multiply the average of $1.608 million and $1.708 million by the quarterly interest rate, which is 6.8%/4. This calculation yields $28,186. The average of $1.608 million and $1.708 million is taken because we only pay interest on what we borrow. We will not borrow $1.708 million all at one time, so we average the two numbers to get a more realistic average balance. In quarter two we average $1.708 million and $1.908 million, and multiply that by the quarterly interest rate. The $28,186 gets carried over to the interest accrual beginning balance in quarter 2 and then is added to quarter 2 interest obligations.

When positive cash flows are generated by the property through the closing of condominium unit sales, both the loan principal and accrued interest are repaid. Once they are repaid in full, then any excess cash flows will go to the equity holders.

Supplemental I
The Return Characteristics of Commercial Real Estate

There are two commonly used real estate return indices, the NCREIF and NAREIT indices.

NCREIF

The National Council of Real Estate Investment Fiduciaries (NCREIF) index provides quarterly return data for privately owned real estate. The index is available on the NCREIF website at www.ncreif.org. It is primarily an appraisal-based index, which means the reporting property asset managers hire an appraiser to "divine" what the property "should be" (not necessarily is) worth. These non-market based estimates can be manipulated to overstate values in order to make performance look better than reality. Furthermore, appraisals are usually conducted only once a year. This results in a smoothed return series, much like stock analyst target values, and the index is known to lag market valuation changes by about 18 months. This use of appraisals also necessarily means that the NCREIF returns will be uncorrelated with stock and bond returns, even though movements in real estate market values are moderately correlated.

The index includes properties acquired and managed on behalf of large institutional managers. Properties owned by entrepreneurial owners are generally not included. The underlying assets are generally core properties, in major US markets, and include apartment, industrial, office, and retail properties. The returns are reported on an unlevered basis, which further reduces the volatility of the return series relative to more typically leveraged real estate returns.

FIGURE SI.1

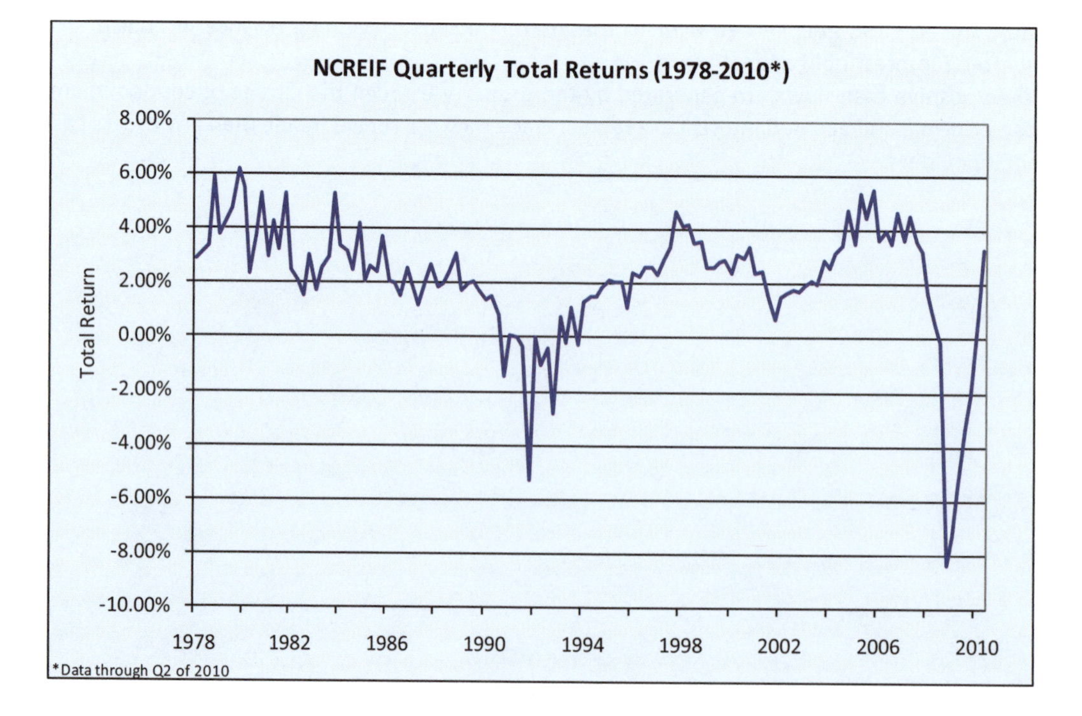

Calculations are based on quarterly returns from these properties, indexed to the fourth quarter of 1977 (when the series began). Returns (capital and income) are weighted by property value, as determined by the real estate appraisals. Figure SI.1 displays the national quarterly total returns series. Return series are also available by geographic location and property type, as well as for the income and appreciation returns.

Based on a comparison of NCREIF and other assets, it generally appears that real estate is a relatively low risk asset. Figure SI.2 provides the mean and standard deviation for NCREIF relative to the 1-year Treasury, 10-year Treasury, S&P 500, and inflation from 1978 through 2009, where annual returns reflect the year over year change in the fourth quarter.

FIGURE SI.2

Summary Statistics of Index Returns (1978-2009)

	NCREIF	1-Yr. Treas.	10-Yr. Treas.	S&P	CPI
Annual Mean Return	9.12%	6.25%	7.34%	9.40%	4.07%
Standard Deviation	8.34%	3.44%	2.87%	16.73%	2.90%

The relatively low standard deviation for the NCREIF index is primarily attributable to the appraisal smoothing and lack of leverage. This underestimation of risk is striking when comparing the NCREIF index to the 10-year Treasury return series. While the 10-year Treasury is subject to inflationary risk, its cash stream is risk-free. While NCREIF's notably lower volatility may reflect the real residual value of real estate relative to Treasury bonds, it much more likely reflects the substantial artificial smoothing of NCREIF returns. While return correlations are a useful metric for parameterizing the risk of an asset, it is largely meaningless due to the smoothing present in the NCREIF index.

NAREIT

The National Association of Real Estate Investment Trust (NAREIT) index measures the total return (appreciation and income) on the portfolio of publicly traded REITs, indexed to December 31, 1971. The index is available on the NAREIT website at www.nareit.com.

Unlike the NCREIF index, this is a stock price transaction based index. As such, the index is much more volatile, as publicly traded REITs are marked to market each trading day. The NAREIT index captures the share prices, not the underlying properties. Furthermore, since the NAREIT index tracks the return of publicly traded REITs, the index is moderately levered, with most companies utilizing roughly 50% leverage. This makes the index more volatile than a comparable pool of unlevered properties. In addition to levered property returns, the index also captures changes in the value of REIT management.

Figure SI.3 displays the historic quarterly total returns of the equity NAREIT index for REITs from 1978 to 2009. There are also NAREIT indexes for income and price appreciation.

FIGURE SI.3

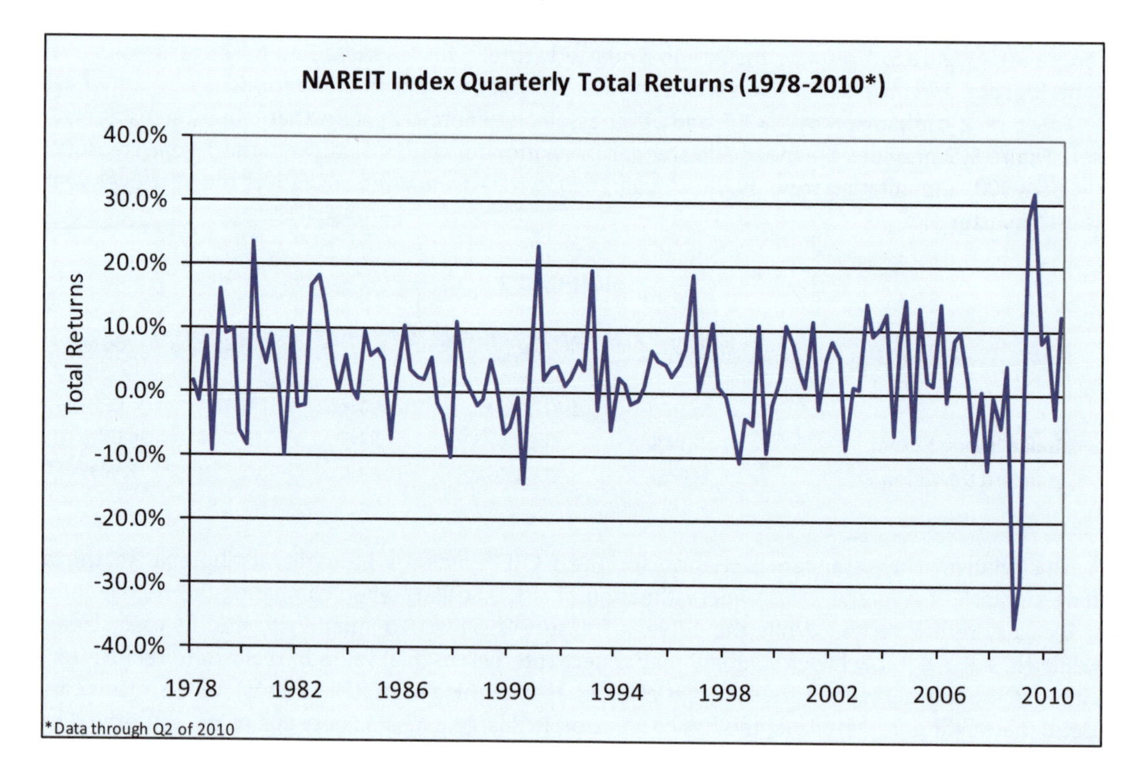

Figure SI.4 displays the annual mean return and standard deviation for the NAREIT equity index, 1-Year Treasury, 10-Year Treasury, inflation, and the S&P from 1978 through 2009, where annual returns are based on year over year change in the fourth quarter.

FIGURE SI.4

Summary Statistics of Index Returns

	NAREIT	1-Yr. Treas.	10-Yr. Treas.	S&P	CPI
Annual Mean Return	12.16%	6.25%	7.34%	9.40%	4.07%
Standard Deviation	18.89%	3.44%	2.87%	16.73%	2.90%

The NAREIT index indicates REIT stocks have about the same return volatility as S&P 500, and a modestly higher return. This risk profile is more reflective of the volatility of modestly leveraged real estate returns than the NCREIF index.

Since NAREIT is not subject to appraisal smoothing, the correlation between returns here is meaningful. Figure SI.5 displays the correlation matrix for the NAREIT, 1-Year Treasury, 10-Year Treasury, inflation, and the S&P based on quarterly returns from 1978 to 2009.

FIGURE SI.5

Correlation with NAREIT				
	1-Yr. Treas.	10-Yr. Treas.	S&P	CPI
Correlation	0.37	0.34	0.52	(0.08)

These correlations suggest a moderate relationship between real estate returns. Although REITs traded inversely to the broader equity market during the tech boom and the early stages of the tech bust, it is clear that the public REIT returns are impacted by broader market and economic fluctuations. Note that the correlation between CPI and NAREIT is on a quarterly time period. An interesting paradox is that over short intervals real estate returns have no correlation with inflation, and thus do little to hedge inflation. However, over longer periods (say every 5 years) and for large inflation rates, real estate does provide an inflation hedge.

LINKAGE BETWEEN NAREIT AND NCREIF

While the NAREIT index tracks public equity REIT returns over the long term, NAREIT returns should reflect returns on real estate. So, why are the returns and standard deviations for the NAREIT and NCREIF indexes so drastically different?

The measurement methodologies of the NCREIF and the NAREIT index explain most of this apparent disconnect. Specifically, differential leverage and appraisal valuations are the sources. Since appraisals dictate the returns for the NCREIF index, movements in the index tend to occur only when NOI changes substantially or cap rate fluctuates, and even then only when the properties are appraised. Since full-blown appraisals are costly, and of limited operational value, they are generally ordered only once a year (at the end of the fourth quarter). This explains the much lower volatility in the index, as value in quarters one through three remain relatively constant, only capturing the relatively minor movements in income for these stabilized assets. In comparison, the NAREIT index captures the countless transactions of the publicly traded REITs. The active trading of these assets provides constant pricing based on expectations about future NOI. Therefore, the NAREIT index tends to be a leading indicator for movements in the NCREIF index. Thus, the NAREIT index is a better long term indicator of return performance for a moderately leveraged high quality real estate portfolio.

BENCHMARKING

While neither the NAREIT nor the NCREIF are perfect measures of real estate returns, they are frequently used to benchmark real estate performance. To quote former NYC Mayor Ed Koch, everybody wants to know, "How'm I doin'?" For real estate private equity funds, as opposed to public REITs, that question is not simply answered. Despite the proliferation of such funds, a useful return benchmark has yet to evolve. This does not mean the sector is not smart enough to create one, but rather that these funds have diverse investment strategies, most of which are very dissimilar to traditional real estate investments. The diversity of investment strategies includes the fact that some funds invest abroad while others focus domestically. Some funds develop and redevelop, while others execute highly leveraged acquisitions of core assets. Some focus on distressed debt and non-performing loans, while still others acquire portfolios of corporate or government assets. And these differences only scratch the surface.

What about the applicability of common real estate benchmarks, such as the NCREIF and NAREIT indices? Let us begin with the NCREIF index. Putting aside the statistical problem of the 18 month appraisal lag, ask yourself what kind of properties the NCREIF index tracks. For the most part these are the returns for stabilized, domestic, unleveraged, institutional-grade properties. As a result, NCREIF returns will be relatively stable. The investment objective for the properties in this index is not to achieve a 20%+ IRR, but rather to provide a relatively safe high single digit return.

Turning to the NAREIT index, the appraisal lag issue disappears due to its real-time pricing. Yet returns generated by REITs are also not an appropriate benchmark for private equity funds, as REITs generally own high-quality, stabilized, domestic real estate, as opposed to the more opportunistic assets favored by private equity funds. In addition, REIT assets are leveraged 40%-60%, versus 65%-75% for private equity funds. The investment objective for firms in the NAREIT index is to provide relatively safe dividends, and a low double digit total return.

These fundamental differences between the respective NCREIF and NAREIT investment objectives and those of private equity funds render these benchmarks futile for comparison with real estate private equity funds. In fact, at almost no point during their investment horizon should private equity fund returns remotely track either the NCREIF or NAREIT indices. It is not just a matter of comparing apples to oranges, but rather apples to screwdrivers.

To demonstrate the differences in return patterns between the NCREIF and NAREIT indices and real estate private equity funds, we simulate the expected performance of each. The first scenario is the unleveraged purchase of $100 million of stabilized properties at a going in cap rate of 8%, with a 2% per annum NOI growth rate. A 50 basis point management fee is deducted from this return stream. This represents the typical NCREIF property. The second scenario assumes $100 million is invested in REITs, which use 50% leverage on their stabilized portfolio. The REIT properties yield 8% on NOI, with a 2% NOI growth rate and a 50 basis point management fee. The REITs pay out 70% of their cash flow in dividends, and reinvest the remainder at the same 8% cap rate and the same 50% leverage. In the third scenario, a private equity fund buys unstabilized assets that will take 3 years of hard work to stabilize. By the end of the third year, these assets achieve the same stabilized performance as those owned by REITs. Assuming NOI in years 1-3 are negative $2 million, $2 million, and $6 million, respectively, and a 20% IRR is achieved over the 7 year life of the fund, we can determine the initial purchase price for these assets. In years 4-7 (the duration of our analysis), these properties are stabilized and generate exactly the same NOI as in the first 2 scenarios. The private equity fund uses 70% leverage, and management fees are also higher, at 1.5%. Figure SI.6 summarizes key information for each strategy.

At the end of year 7, all assets are sold for an 8 cap by the investors, yielding about $115 million in sale proceeds, before debt, for scenarios I and III. Because of the reinvestment of retained earnings over the 7 years, the REIT generates a portfolio valued at about $136 million, including approximately $60 million of debt. In the case of the private equity fund, we assume that, at the end of year 3, when the assets are stabilized, they are refinanced at 70% of their stabilized value, and excess refinancing proceeds are paid out to investors.

FIGURE SI.6

Simulated Return Assumptions			
	NCREIF	**NAREIT**	**Private Equity**
Purchase Price	$100,000,000	$100,000,000	$77,740,060
LTV	0.0%	50.0%	70.0%
Equity	$100,000,000	$50,000,000	$23,322,018
Interest Rate	0.0%	6.0%	6.3%
Going-in Cap Rate (Stabilized)	8.0%	8.0%	n/a
NOI Growth Rate	2.0%	2.0%	n/a
Residual Cap Rate	8.0%	8.0%	8.0%
Residual Value	$114,868,567	$136,200,746	$114,868,567
Dividend Payout	100%	70%	100%
Management Fee	0.5%	0.5%	1.5%
IRR (Mark-to-Market)	10.0%	15.2%	25.4%
IRR	9.5%	12.8%	20.0%

Each investment scenario generates its own IRR, cash payment stream, and total return stream. The cash payment stream is simply the actual cash flow generated for each year. Realized cash flows are back-end weighted, as only a liquidation event or refinancing taps value appreciation.

In the simulated NCREIF scenario, annual total returns track slightly higher than annual cash flow returns due to appreciation, but upon liquidation the cash flow analysis will catch up with the cumulative mark-to-market return. This pattern is also the case for the REIT scenario, with a larger back-end spread due to the leveraged reinvestment of retained earnings. For the private equity fund, due to the negative NOI and high leverage, negative total returns are recorded for the first 2 years of the fund. Only as the repositioning is successful in year 3 does the return become positive.

Due to its investment strategy, the real estate private equity fund returns are negative in the early years, as the properties are ramping toward stabilization. The expected cumulative private equity fund return is roughly an S-curve. As stated earlier, at no point in time should either the cash flow or mark-to-market equity returns for the private equity fund be expected to resemble those of either the NCREIF or REIT scenarios. In the first 3 years, the fund should under-perform the NCREIF and NAREIT benchmarks on a cumulative basis, but upon successful stabilization, it surpasses the performance of the other 2 investment structures.

While the private equity fund achieves a higher IRR, there is the risk that they fail to achieve stabilization. Similarly, increased leverage by the REITs and the private equity investors results in a more volatile return stream than for NCREIF.

FIGURE SI.7

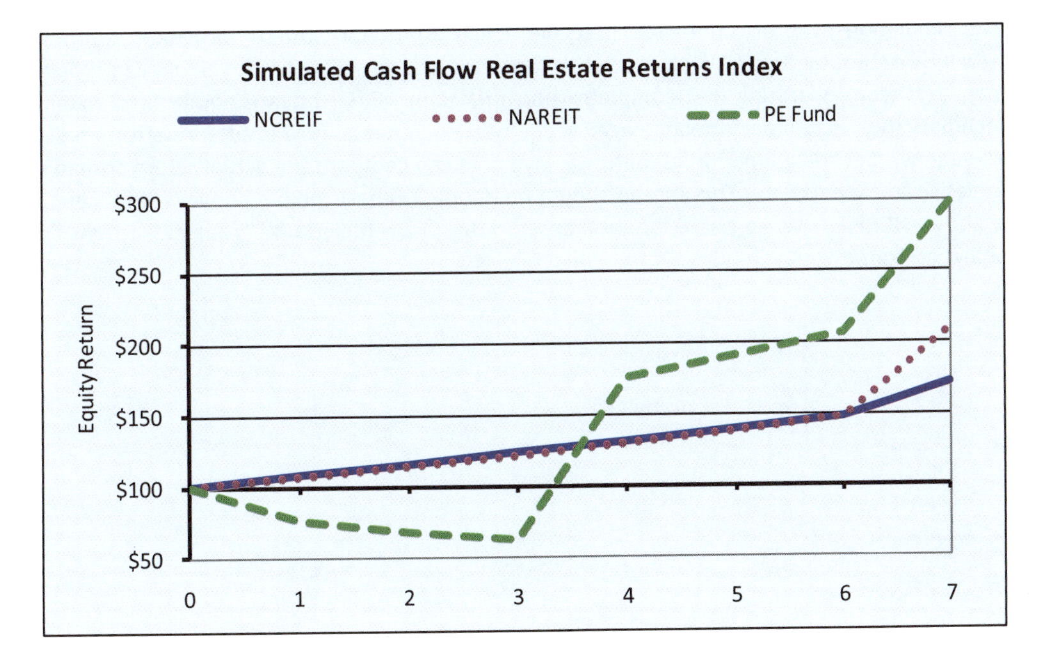

FIGURE SI.8

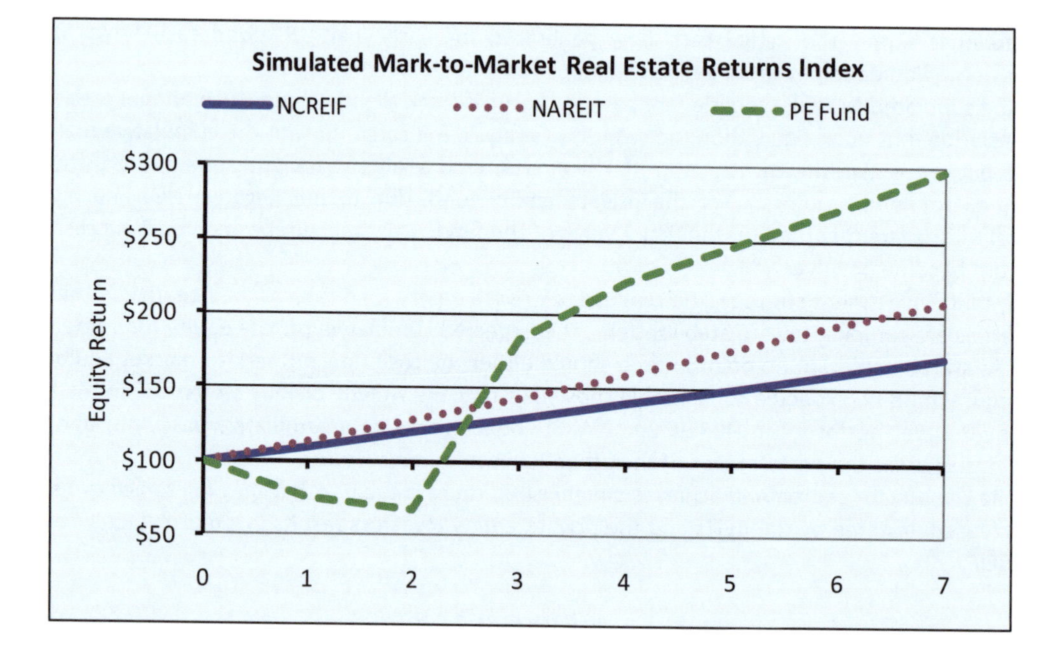

These simulations capture the fact that neither NCREIF nor NAREIT provides appropriate return benchmarks for private equity funds. With that said, there are two insights that investors can utilize to prevent their fund managers from operating in a complete return vacuum. First, private equity fund managers should regularly benchmark their actual performance against themselves. That is, how are they performing compared to their own projections? Secondly, upon fund maturity, investors can compare the actual return spread over NCREIF and NAREIT relative to expectation. This spread should be about 700 basis points above NAREIT and about 1,000 basis points above NCREIF. While these do not answer the "How'm I doin'?" question, they do provide a disciplined analytical framework.

Supplemental I Supplement A

The Return Volatility of Publicly and Privately Owned Real Estate

A comparison of historical recessions

Dr Peter Linneman – Wharton Real Estate Review – Fall 2004

THE MARKETLESS VALUE OF REAL ESTATE

The debate about whether privately owned real estate has a lower return volatility than its publicly owned counterpart has been going on for a long time. It began when academics analyzed the then-newly compiled National Council of Real Estate Investment Fiduciaries (NCREIF) return series for unlevered real estate properties in the 1980s. These studies found that the returns derived from the NCREIF index had extremely low volatility, as well as very low correlations with stock and bond returns. This led some to proclaim that privately owned real estate was a "can't lose" investment, providing portfolio diversification with almost no return volatility, and average returns not much different from stocks. Efficient investment frontier research seeped into investment practice, which suggested that privately owned real estate should comprise almost 100 percent of an "efficient" portfolio.

As the 1990s dawned, investors assumed that high-quality privately owned real estate could never fall substantially in value. But the early 1990s demonstrated that private real estate assets had substantial return volatility, with values eroding by 20 percent to 50 percent during the first half of the decade. As the chairman of Rockefeller Center, one of the nation's prime core assets in the mid-1990s, I discovered all too well the volatility of private real estate returns. Yet, the NCREIF data failed to reveal significant negative returns. Instead, the NCREIF total return in 1990 was 2.3 percent, with negative returns registered only in 1991 (-5.6 percent) and 1992 (-4.3 percent). These numbers were in stark contrast to the reality experienced by private property owners. Since the disconnect between NCREIF and the market reality was too great to be explained by differences in property or management quality, savvy observers quickly realized that the NCREIF data was at best problematic, and at worst bogus.

The early 1990s witnessed the emergence of major publicly owned REITs. Faced with the complete absence of debt, and plummeting property values, many major private owners of real estate went public in order to recapitalize their properties, paying off maturing debt with IPO proceeds. Overnight, high-quality real estate was exposed to public market scrutiny and pricing, with many of the finest property portfolios trading on the NYSE. These REITs were managed by real estate professionals with expertise equal to, or better than, NCREIF asset managers. Thus, any differential return performance between the NCREIF index and REITs could not be attributed to either product or management quality.

FIGURE SIA.1

NCREIF Quarterly Returns

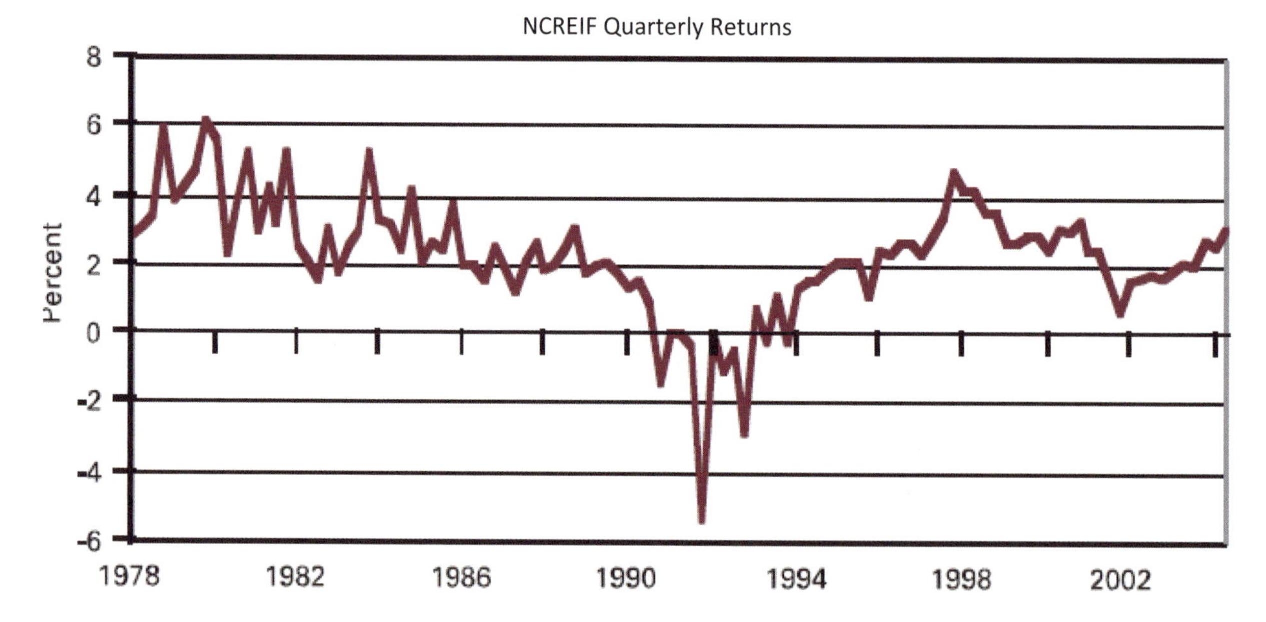

A third investment vehicle, real estate private equity funds, evolved to help equitize real estate investments. These non-traded limited partnerships, with seven-to-ten- year investment lives, use high leverage, frequently own foreign and lesser-quality properties, and often pursue development/redevelopment strategies. While the returns for these vehicles are not systematically reported, it is not surprising that the return history for these higher-risk, lower-quality, value-add investment vehicles substantially diverges from that of either NCREIF or REITs, as their returns do not generally reflect the performance of core U.S. properties.

NCREIF VS. NAREIT

NCREIF index properties are unlevered, while REITs are approximately 50 percent levered. In addition, REITs own both the company's real estate as well as the profit stream generated by management (net of executive compensation). In contrast, the NCREIF index reflects only returns on properties, with returns to managers captured by the asset management companies.

Returns to REITs, as proxied by the National Association of Real Estate Investment Trusts (NAREIT) Equity Index, and NCREIF should be highly correlated, as the key determinant of their returns is the profitability of core quality properties. REITs offer institutional investors a transparent and liquid real estate investment alternative to direct ownership. Since the mid-1990s, funds have flowed into REITs from traditional core real estate managers, causing many core managers to go out of business. Institutional investors were not only disappointed in the performance of real estate versus their expectations, but also angry with managers who hid how badly their investments performed.

Yet, based upon studies of NCREIF returns, many researchers, managers, and investors continue to believe that privately owned real estate has almost no correlation with the returns of REITs, stocks, or bonds. For example, from the first quarter of 1990 through the first quarter of 2004, the correlation of NCREIF's return with that of NAREIT was -0.04, while with S&P 500 it was 0.01, and with long bonds -0.10. In addition, the standard deviation of quarterly returns for this same period was 3.4 percent for NCREIF, versus 10.5 percent for NAREIT, 11.3 percent for S&P 500, and 6.9 percent for long bonds. As a result, many observers argue that institutional investors should own real estate both publicly and privately, with publicly owned real estate providing liquidity, and privately owned real estate providing return stability and diversification.

But these results cannot be correct, as buildings are inanimate objects, which do not know whether they are publicly or privately owned. Further, most core properties are managed by high-quality managers, whether the properties are publicly or privately owned. Therefore, large return discrepancies between public and private real estate ownership are not theoretically credible. Of course, minor return differences between public and private real estate can arise due to the valuation of management teams (which is a part of a REIT's valuation), or as a result of leverage, or because short-term capital movements are insufficient to arbitrage public versus private pricing. However, the return differences between NCREIF and NAREIT are not small, temporary, or occasional. In five of the past 14 years, the annual returns for NCREIF and NAREIT are of opposite signs. Moreover, the average absolute difference in the annual returns of these series is a staggering 1715 basis points, with this difference being fewer than 600 basis points in only two years. For example, 1998 REIT returns were shocked by the Russian ruble crisis, yielding a -17.5 percent return, while the NCREIF return was 16.2 percent, a gap of 3370 basis points!

FIGURE SIA.2

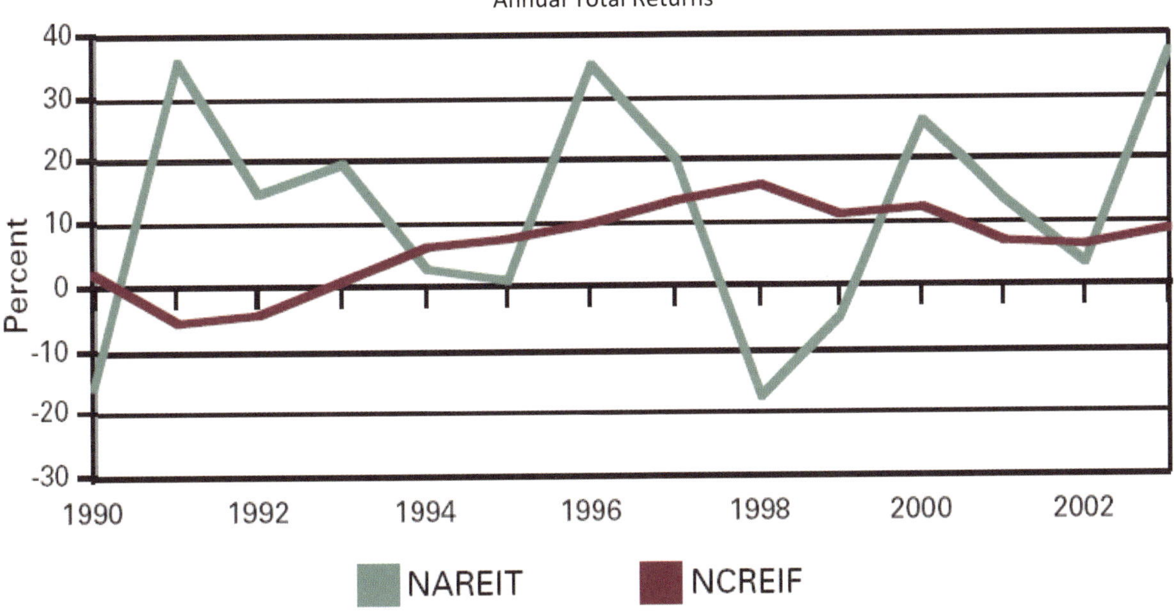

WHAT'S GOING ON?

The best research on the differences between NCREIF and NAREIT returns has been conducted by Joe Gyourko, first in a paper with Don Keim, and more recently in a paper in the *Wharton Real Estate Review.* He finds that NCREIF returns are predictable based upon historic REIT returns. Specifically, today's REIT returns foretell the NCREIF returns that will be registered roughly 18 months from now. As has been stated before, since buildings are inanimate, and since their quality of management is roughly similar, this relationship cannot be due to significant differences in property level cash flows, risk profiles, or management.

One need not be a believer in perfectly efficient markets to feel that it is inconceivable that capital markets so inefficiently value public versus private real estate cash streams. While anomalies can exist, they will be arbitraged, particularly given the large number of opportunity funds with the broad mandate to simply generate risk-adjusted real estate returns. If return differences are consistently as divergent as these series indicate, there should be no shortage of "smart money" to arbitrage the differences. In addition, REITs' property acquisitions and dispositions would arbitrage large differences in "Wall Street vs. Main Street" values. Yet, during the past 14 years, in spite of the extraordinary differences in NCREIF and NAREIT returns, few REITs were taken private, very few major positions in REITs were taken by opportunity funds, and almost no REITs liquidated their portfolios.

FIGURE SIA.3

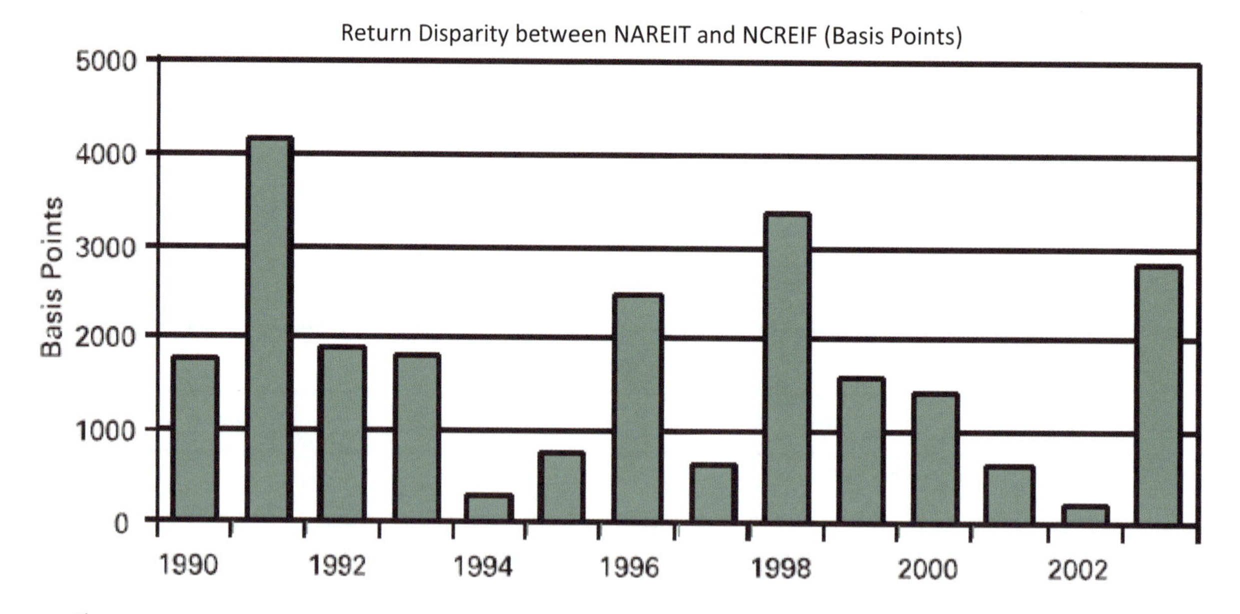

The primary reason why large return discrepancies between NCREIF and NAREIT exist is simple: the data are wrong. This was vividly demonstrated during the Russian ruble crisis, when REITs fared terribly, while NCREIF registered returns well above average. Yet almost no public to private arbitrage took place, even though the return data indicate that such activity would have been highly profitable. No opportunity funds took advantage of the option suggested by the data. Nor did entrepreneurial REIT operators see an opportunity to go private. Instead, the market clearly believed that there was no significant return differential between public and private real estate. Like Sherlock Holmes' famous "dog that didn't bark," the market's silence demonstrated that the return gap is fiction rather than reality.

VALUATION ISSUES

NAREIT pricing and returns reflect market pricing by third parties investing in publicly traded securities, and thus have no notable measurement error. It is also an investable index, with several index funds readily available for investors. In contrast, the NCREIF index is neither investable nor a market-priced index. Specifically, it is impossible to create a portfolio that contains the NCREIF properties, and NCREIF property prices are very rarely set by third-party investors. Instead, they are established by appraisals.

Many have noted the so-called appraisal lag in valuing NCREIF properties. However, the NCREIF return measurement problem is much deeper, as most observers fail to appreciate how the appraisal process, even when well done, generates meaningless valuations for evaluating return volatility and correlations. In fact, the appraisal process guarantees that NCREIF's appraisal-driven returns will have very low volatility. Since the appraisal process, rather than private-market real estate pricing, creates near-zero volatility in measured returns, near-zero return correlations with REITs, stocks, and bonds are no surprise, as these assets have considerable return volatility. Specifically, if the returns for stocks, bonds, and publicly traded real estate are essentially random walks reflecting relatively efficient market pricing, NCREIF's near-zero appraisal-induced volatility will necessarily show little return correlation.

How does the use of appraised property values produce this result? The vast majority of NCREIF properties have a value appraisal only in the fourth quarter of each year. This contrasts dramatically with private property markets, where properties are constantly valued (though not appraised) by owners. Opportunity funds, entrepreneurial owners, and high-wealth families constantly evaluate their property values. Anyone who has worked with these owners knows that, over the course of a year, the values of privately owned properties rise and fall, depending on leasing, market sentiments, rumors about new developments, macroeconomic hopes and fears, and capital market animal instincts. Many private owners exploit these value movements by either selling or refinancing their properties at opportune times, or by holding their properties while waiting for better market pricing. This is the reality of private markets. Companies such as Eastdil, Secured Capital, and Goldman Sachs make their livings from the volatility of private real estate markets.

Consider what happens to a real estate return series if the value of a core property is recorded only on the last day of each year. Since a core property's Net Operating Income (NOI) generally varies relatively little throughout the year, so too will the measured return if the property price remains unchanged for four quarters. For example, if the property has a quarterly NOI growth rate of 1 percent (4.06 percent annual rate), and an 8 percent initial cap rate, the registered quarterly returns absent quarter-to-quarter price changes over the four quarters of the year are 2.02 percent, 2.04 percent, 2.06 percent, and 2.08 percent, respectively. Hence, for NCREIF's large pool of core assets, it is almost impossible to have much quarter-to-quarter return volatility without accurately measuring quarterly value changes. But if the preponderance of core properties is appraised only in the fourth quarter, the return registered for NCREIF is by definition basically the same in the fourth, first, second, and third quarters, as NOI does not change appreciably quarter-by-quarter. The fact that the recorded returns are basically the same over a four-quarter period provides no information about whether the actual quarterly returns were the same, and merely reflects that no attempt was made to determine whether asset prices changed quarter-to-quarter. This is the first source of NCREIF's return smoothing.

Imagine what would happen if NAREIT quarterly returns were measured simply by dividing the quarterly dividend by the fourth quarter cap rate. Since NAREIT dividends change relatively little quarter-to-quarter, this approach would record little REIT return volatility. Gyourko's research notes that during the first three quarters of the year, NCREIF returns register little volatility for private real estate. But savvy private owners know this is not the case. A point of reference is provided by (incorrectly) calculating NAREIT returns as the quarterly dividend plus appreciation, divided by the closing year-end stock price. Figure SAI.4 reveals that this exercise notably reduces the volatility of NAREIT's quarterly returns.

FIGURE SIA.4

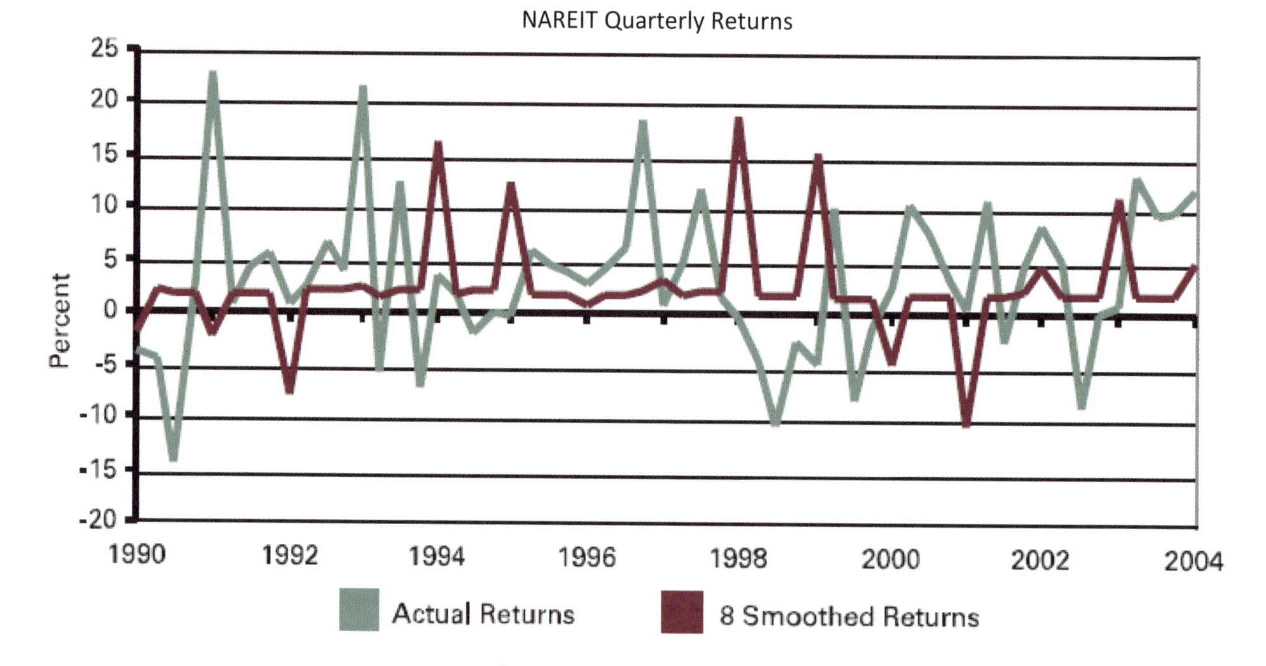

In fact, the standard deviation of NAREIT quarterly returns falls from 10.5 percent for actual NAREIT returns to 7.0 percent when this method is employed. Thus, if investors want lower REIT return volatility, and to look more like NCREIF's, they should only look at the REIT stock prices on the last day of each year!

QUADRUPLE SMOOTHING

The NCREIF measurement error story does not end here, as NCREIF's fourth quarter value generally reflects appraised—as opposed to market—property prices. To see how the appraisal process even further undercuts return measurement efforts, one must understand the appraisal process. When an "unbiased" appraiser (they may, like unicorns, exist somewhere) is engaged, their methodology for a core, stabilized property is to divide "stabilized" NOI (a second smoothing) by the cap rate of recent transactions for comparable properties. The period for which the appraiser seeks comparable sales transactions is typically 24 months. Over this 24-month period, the appraiser will generally find five to eight comparable property sales. The cap rate selected by the appraiser is usually the mean (or sometimes median) of the cap rates for these transactions. Rarely do appraisers give more weight to more recent transactions, or evaluate cap rate trends. Thus, although each comparable property sold at a specific cap rate, at a specific time, the appraisal cap rate is an average (a third source of smoothing), which eliminates the high and low valuations that existed in the market; that is, it eliminates pricing volatility. The appraiser's rationale for cap rate averaging is that the market conditions that existed when those properties were sold are better or worse than those that exist "in more typical markets." Further, the appraisal for a property this year will generally re-use approximately half of the comparable sales transactions of the previous year's appraisal. Thus, this year's cap rate is mechanically linked to last year's cap rate, introducing a fourth source of NCREIF return smoothing.

Note that the appraisal methodology adopts the position that while higher and lower cap rates than average existed, they are of no relevance to a property's appraised value. In fact, every property was transacted at a cap rate higher or lower than the average, indicative of then-current market conditions. Stated bluntly, the appraisal process eliminates—not reveals—the truth about how properties are priced in private markets. In effect, the appraised value, far from being the market value, is, in effect, a marketless value. That is, it is a value net of the vagaries of the market. Tellingly, no property is ever bought or sold at the appraiser's cap rate. Yet many researchers use the NCREIF return as if the cap rates used to value its properties reflect private property market prices. But by design, this is absolutely not the case.

The nature of the appraisal process means that even in the fourth quarter, the registered NCREIF value fails to reflect the prevailing market pricing, reflecting instead the average of market conditions that prevailed over the preceding two years. In fact, what NCREIF records as "today's cap rate" is actually the mean cap rate about 12 months earlier; that is, at the midpoint of the appraiser's time period. Hence, NCREIF fourth-quarter valuations effectively reflect "stabilized" NOI divided by the average cap rate a year ago. Quadruple-smoothed, with a lag.

This appraisal smoothing and lag not only reduces measured return volatility, but also almost necessarily eliminates any correlation with market return series. This is because if actual returns follow a random walk, inducing a one-year lag, the lagged series is uncorrelated with the original series, as the lag wipes out all correlation with all random series. Since stock, bond, and REIT returns have been shown to basically follow random walks, even if true private real estate returns were highly correlated with these series, the NCREIF appraisal lag would wipe out the correlation. The impact of lagging is vividly demonstrated by the fact that the correlation between quarterly S&P returns and the eight-quarter moving average of S&P returns is a mere 0.16 from 1990 through the first quarter of 2004. Thus, a series, which by definition is perfectly correlated with itself, is basically uncorrelated with a NCREIF-like lagged version of itself.

The fact is that while NAREIT returns reflect actual returns for an investable public real estate portfolio, NCREIF returns measure nothing remotely like actual returns for a core private portfolio. The 12-month valuation lag is accentuated over the subsequent three quarters, as NCREIF's appraised values are generally not changed during these quarters. Thus, the cap rate used in the appraisals is initially four quarters out of date, falling to five, six, and seven quarters over the next three quarters. As the property values are reappraised in the fourth quarter, the lag once again reverts to four quarters, and the process repeats. It is hardly surprising that Gyourko's research consistently finds a roughly 18-month statistical relationship between REIT returns (actual market pricing) and NCREIF's lagged returns.

IT'S ONLY REAL ESTATE

To see how quadruple-smoothing-and-a-lag mechanically affects measured returns, we calculate a variety of incorrectly measured quarterly REIT returns. First, for each quarter, the quarterly return is calculated as the sum of the actual NAREIT dividend plus percentage price appreciation, where price is defined as the moving average NAREIT price for the preceding eight quarters. This smoothing and lagging reduces the standard deviation of NAREIT quarterly returns from 10.5 percent for actual returns, to 4.9 percent. Conducting the same analysis with NAREIT price calculated as the NAREIT dividend divided by the eight-quarter NAREIT moving average cap rate results in an estimated REIT quarterly return standard deviation of 5.7 percent.

We also recalculate quarterly NAREIT returns, where for the fourth quarter the return is the actual NAREIT dividend divided by the moving average NAREIT cap rate for the preceding eight quarters, plus the percentage increase in that price over the similarly calculated price of a year earlier, where for the first, second, and third quarters there is no price change. The standard deviation of NAREIT quarterly returns for this approach is 7.7 percent.

How do these results compare to NCREIF? Recall that NCREIF is unlevered, while NAREIT is roughly 50 percent levered. To adjust for the different leverage, we calculated quarterly returns for a 50 percent leveraged NCREIF, at an interest rate of three-year Treasury plus 150 basis points. The standard deviation of this levered NCREIF series is 5.2 percent (versus 3.4 percent for unlevered NCREIF). This levered NCREIF return volatility compares to 10.5 percent for actual NAREIT, and 5.7 percent and 7.7 percent for the smoothed NAREIT series. Plus, one must remember that the use of actual, rather than "stabilized," NAREIT dividends in these calculations makes NAREIT returns more volatile than levered NCREIF, which uses "stabilized" NOI. Thus, when compared on an apples-to-apples basis, the return volatilities of NCREIF are NAREIT are basically the same.

The correlation coefficients of the alternative quarterly return series are displayed in Figure SIA.5. Note that smoothed and lagged NAREIT returns, like both NCREIF and unlevered NCREIF, show little correlation with the S&P 500 or long bonds. This is because the non-volatility induced by quadruple-smoothing-and-a-lag correlates to almost nothing. In contrast, the mean returns for the various NAREIT returns are only slightly altered by these smoothing calculations, because the time shifting only slightly alters the time period over which returns are effectively measured. Further, smoothed NAREIT returns have a much higher (though still low) correlation with NCREIF.

The best series to measure real estate returns is neither NCREIF nor the smoothed NAREIT series, but rather the actual REIT return series. This is because mark-to-market, contemporaneous, arm's-length, non-smoothed pricing is the reality of both public and private real estate. The truth is that modestly leveraged core real estate has a low correlation with stocks and bonds, but displays notable return volatility, though somewhat less so than stocks.

No one involved in private real estate markets will find these results surprising. After all, real estate ownership of core assets incorporates many of the dimensions of high-quality bonds, with superior residual value protection because it is a real (rather than nominal) asset. The result is that non-residential real estate has less cash stream volatility than the equity and debt claims on its tenants, since in good times, tenants expand their space demand more slowly than their profits increase, while in bad times the reverse is true. In addition, the supply and demand fundamentals of real estate follow unique patterns, further diminishing the return correlations with other assets. Similarly, residential real estate follows its own time patterns, as even in poor economic times, population increases and absorption generally occurs, although at a slower rate. Also, supply and demand patterns for these properties move differently from other asset categories.

FIGURE SIA.5

Quarterly Return Correlation Coefficients

Quarterly Return Correlation Coefficients						
	Smoothed NAREIT[1]	Smoothed NAREIT[2]	Unlevered NCREIF	Levered NCREIF	S&P 500	Long Bonds
Acutal NAREIT	-.16	-.21	-.05	-.05	.40	.08
Smoothed NAREIT[1]		.55	.14	.15	-.04	-.10
Smoothed NAREIT[2]			.14	.14	.12	-.24
Unlevered NCREIF				.99	.01	-.10
Levered NCREIF					.01	-.10
S&P 500						-.09

1 Based upon eight-quarter moving average NAREIT price.

2 Based upon eight-quarter moving average NAREIT price, with estimated price unchanged for four consecutive quarters.

DAY-TO-DAY REIT VOLATILITY

As is the case with a publicly traded security of any company, one is struck by the fact that in any one-hour or one-day trading period, the price of a REIT (or any) stock can go up or down by several percentage points, for no apparent reason. It is true that privately owned real estate does not have such minute-to-minute, hour-to-hour, or day-to-day price volatility, as deals are not struck in private markets on such an instantaneous basis. The presence of such price volatility for REITs means investment opportunities are available via the public ownership of private real estate that are not present with private ownership. Specifically, this volatility allows institutional owners of REITs to take advantage of momentary mispricings of their stocks by selling or shorting when prices are "too high," and incrementally buying when prices are "too low." Such trading provides an additional margin for well-capitalized institutional investors to exploit temporary pricing anomalies. Of course, just as is the case for private real estate, if one is convinced that REIT prices are too high, one can sell one's entire position. Similarly, if one believes that prices are too low, one can hold stocks until prices rise. Publicly owned real estate allows investors to incrementally alter their investment position when they believe pricing is too low or too high. In fact, aggressive institutional investors may go so far as to short assets when they believe prices are too high. Thus, far from being a negative aspect of public real estate investment, the presence of micro price volatility can only benefit well-capitalized long-term investors. At worst, the institutional investor can simply ignore such pricing variability, and simply trade out of their holdings on last day of each quarter, in which case they realize NAREIT returns.

WHAT'S IT ALL MEAN?

There is no magical potion in the private ownership of core real estate that eliminates return volatility and correlation with other assets. The fact that investors continue to believe this is the case reflects either a fundamental misunderstanding of the NCREIF data, or purposeful ignorance about the realities of real estate markets. The truth is that high-quality, stabilized real estate should be a major part of institutional investors' portfolios, and that public ownership provides the same long-term return patterns as private ownership, with the enhanced advantages of exploiting temporary mispricings and liquidity.

Core real estate provides solid long-term returns, somewhat lower volatility relative to stocks, and relatively modest correlation with the returns on other assets. However, the purported advantages of private core real estate ownership are a mirage. What matters are the quality of the property and the ability of the manager to execute a viable operating strategy, whether public or private.

Private core real estate ownership for many institutions is a narcotic that creates the "comfortably numb" illusion of non-volatility in a harsh and demanding mark-to-market world. It is one of the few remaining assets where you can pretend that your assets have not changed in price, even when they have. Hopefully, such illusions will soon be a thing of the past.

Supplemental II: A Look at a Real CMBS Issue

Let's look a little closer at an actual CMBS issue, specifically LEHMAN BROTHERS Commercial Mortgage Trust, Series 1998-C4. This particular CMBS pool originated with 286 loans, secured by 327 properties. As of May 15, 2003, two of the loans were in bankruptcy hence the loan pool was reduced to 284 loans. Note that the values of the CMBS Issue change every day, and all of the data in this Supplemental are as of May 2003. All loans were originated prior to November 17, 1998. The CMBS was priced on November 17, 1998 and closed on November 24, 1998. Since then, each tranche of this deal has traded separately. The pool is exemplary because of its size, mix of loans, concentration of low LTV loans, a low weighted average debt service coverage ratio (DSCR), and good credit history. But remember that each CMBS pool is unique, depending on its collateral and tranche structure.

The largest loan, Omni Hotels, represented about 12% of the total loan value of the pool, with the remaining 283 loans representing 88% of the pool. The discrepancy makes the pool very sensitive to a single loan.

The pool's beginning loan balance was $2,025,590,706. As a result of amortization, the loan balance as of May 15, 2003 was $1,913,478,129. Loans begin maturing in August 2003, with the last loan maturing in September 2023. Hence, not only is each CMBS pool unique but it also changes over time as loans mature, tranches expire, and as loans default.

The overall pool is referred to as a **fixed rate fusion pool**, as there are both conduit loans (58% of the pool) loans of less than $30,000,000, and large loans (39% of the pool) of more than $30,000,000. A **conduit loan** is a relatively small loan, which was made with the objective of placing it into a CMBS offering. 3.9% of the pool are net credit lease properties, which are very high LTV loans made on the basis of the high credit rating of the net lease tenant. All of the loans carry fixed interest rates.

When the tranches trade, they are priced relative to the prevailing interest rate at that time. For floating rate loans and tranches, all pricing is relative to LIBOR (London Inter-bank Overnight Rate) or short term Treasury rates at that time. The conversion from floating LIBOR to fixed Treasury can be done through a swap transaction. There are several types of LIBOR that are used: 30 day LIBOR, 90 day LIBOR, 180 day LIBOR, or 1 year LIBOR.

ORIGINATORS, SERVICERS AND ISSUERS

The originator of this CMBS pool was Lehman Brothers. They assembled the loans and constructed the pool, as well as designed the legal structure. They also marketed it for a fee. The issuer is Structured Assets Securities Corporation, a special purpose bankruptcy remote company whose sole assets are the loans. The master servicer, which is the issuer's outsourced management, for this pool is First Union National Bank. They are in charge of servicing the loans and tranches, and making sure that there are no problems with the loans. They collect the loan payments, keep the books, send disbursement checks to the tranche owners, file reports, etc. There is also a special servicer for this pool, with contractual rights and duties to deal with defaults, foreclosures, and special situations. These servicers work for fees, which are paid from the issuing entity's revenues.

GEOGRAPHY AND PROPERTY TYPES

The 327 properties are located in 35 different states and Puerto Rico, ranging from Massachusetts to Washington. The four states with the greatest loan concentration are California, New York, Florida, and Texas. There are many loans which pool properties across states.

FIGURE SII.1

Geographic Location	Number of Loans	Scheduled Balance	Based on Balance
California	22	$ 385,544,509	20.15%
Other	2	$ 283,218,211	14.80%
New York	30	$ 162,789,424	8.51%
Florida	30	$ 158,906,976	8.30%
Texas	30	$ 95,819,792	5.01%
Illinois	17	$ 76,199,735	3.98%
Pennsylvania	9	$ 70,484,781	3.68%
Indiana	8	$ 64,671,550	3.38%
Virginia	15	$ 63,697,794	3.33%
Arizona	14	$ 63,440,752	3.32%
Alabama	4	$ 58,088,633	3.04%
Georgia	12	$ 56,106,336	2.93%
North Carolina	15	$ 49,821,463	2.60%
Tennessee	7	$ 46,953,909	2.45%
Washington	7	$ 44,297,199	2.32%
Connecticut	7	$ 30,053,568	1.57%
Nevada	3	$ 25,102,254	1.31%
Ohio	6	$ 21,238,710	1.11%
Colorado	6	$ 19,719,666	1.03%
Maryland	5	$ 17,637,089	0.92%
Oklahoma	2	$ 17,459,305	0.91%
Michigan	3	$ 16,690,648	0.87%
New Jersey	5	$ 12,580,616	0.66%
Massachusetts	4	$ 10,706,285	0.56%
Missouri	3	$ 9,543,099	0.50%
Oregon	2	$ 8,909,206	0.47%
Wisconsin	2	$ 8,451,240	0.44%
South Carolina	3	$ 5,568,376	0.29%
Puerto Rico	1	$ 5,337,249	0.28%
Rhode Island	2	$ 5,023,041	0.26%
Other	8	$ 19,416,712	1.01%
Total	284	$ 1,913,478,128	100.00%

Most of the loans were originated in 1998. 2.75% of the pool matures in 2003, while the last loan matures on September 1, 2023. The vast majority of the loans (78.05%) mature in 2008, representing 10 year loan maturities.

The number of loans per property sector is shown in Figure SII.2. A weakness of the pool is the high concentration of loans in the retail sector. The problem with a large concentration of loans in one sector is that if something happens to the retail industry (e.g., the Kmart bankruptcy) during the course of the loan terms, the loan pool has a relatively concentrated potential for default.

FIGURE SII.2

Industry	Number of Loans	Percent of Pool based on Balance
Retail	134	44.25%
Multi-family	63	17.84%
Lodging	16	17.43%
Office	45	15.31%
Industrial	16	3.31%
Self Storage	5	0.75%
Health Care	1	0.70%
Mobile Home	3	0.25%
Other	1	0.16%
Total	284	100.00%

The main retail loans are secured by properties such as the Bayside Mall in Miami, FL, and Mills in Ontario, Canada which includes tenants like JC Penny, Marshall's and Burlington Coat Factory. Of the top ten loans, six of the loans are secured by retail properties; two by lodging, one by office, and one by multi-family. The largest loan in the pool is $228,681,211 to TRT Holdings, secured by 5 hotels, an office building, and a retail component.

LTVs AND INTEREST COVERAGE

The original LTVs for the loans in the pool are displayed in Figure SII.3, which was acquired from the November 1998 Moody's rating report. Usually LTVs are only updated when the loan goes into default. The high LTVs are initially not uncommon, as the value of the properties should rise as they stabilize. The majority of the loans were in the range of 90-100%, but these loans represent only 47% of the value of the loan pool. Figure SII.3 analyzes the large loans separately as their size may give them a larger impact on rest of the pool. Note how the larger loans are more conservatively levered, relative to the conduits.

FIGURE SII.3

Loan-To-Value for conduit portion		Loan-To-Value for large loans	
LTV	% based on loan balance	Loan	% based on loan balance
Less than 80%	7.70%	Omni Hotels	63%
80-90%	28.40%	Ontario Mills	69%
90-100%	46.80%	Arden Portfolio	64%
100-110%	14.50%	Fresno Fashion Fair	71%
Greater than 110%	2.60%	Bayside Market Place	74%
Total	100.00%		
Weighted Average LTV (conduit)	92%		

DSCR

The original DSCR (debt service coverage ratio) for the loans in this pool range from less than 1, to more than 2. As of May 2003, the weighted average DSCR is a relatively strong 1.88x.

FIGURE SII.4

Debt Service Coverage Ratio

DSCR	Count	Scheduled Balance	% Based on Balance
0.500 or less	2	$2,990,992	0.16%
0.500-0.625	0	$0	0.00%
0.625-0.750	4	$11,925,822	0.62%
0.750-0.875	4	$9,015,746	0.47%
0.875-1.000	13	$39,176,623	2.05%
1.000-1.125	22	$77,333,241	4.04%
1.125-1.125	19	$138,861,946	7.26%
1.125-1.375	21	$108,888,491	5.69%
1.375-1.500	32	$149,414,064	7.81%
1.500-1.625	33	$154,995,947	8.10%
1.625-1.750	34	$150,877,182	7.88%
1.750-1.875	27	$351,487,256	18.37%
1.875-2.000	23	$240,556,394	12.57%
2.000-2.125	15	$45,497,941	2.38%
2.125 & above	34	$429,453,774	22.44%
Unknown	1	$3,002,710	0.16%
Total	284	$1,913,478,129	100%

Weighted Average of DSCR: 1.88

SALE PROCEEDS

Lehman's proceeds from the sale of each tranche is proprietary information. As a result, the profit from creating and selling the company is private information.

PAYMENTS IN DEFAULT

One of the benefits of a CMBS transaction is that the risk of any one loan is mitigated by diversification. As of May 2003 there were 8 loans in delinquency, 4 of which are being handled by the special servicer. If a stand-alone loan were in default, the lender would not be receiving any payment on that loan. However, since these defaulting loans represent only 0.7% of the pool, the impact is small and impacts only the most subordinated tranche, which incorporated the possibility for defaults into their pricing. One loan was in a foreclosure/bankruptcy state, and another was in REO, meaning that the property was foreclosed and the title was taken. Figure SII.5 summarizes the default status as of May 2003.

FIGURE SII.5

Delinquency Status	
Status	**Count**
Current	277
30 Days	2
60 Days	0
90 Days	1
Foreclosure/Bankruptcy	1
REO (Real estate owned)	1
Special Servicer	4

It is important to note that delinquency status constantly changes. In addition, it is critical to know which loans are in default and why.

TRANCHES

A **tranche** is a specific ownership claim on the **issuer** company. Each tranche has a contractual priority claim on the cash flows of the issuer. The issuer is just a company that owns a pool of assets and sells claims on its future cash flows that have different maturity and priority. A tranche's priority claim may be different with respect to cash flows from interest payments, versus amortization, versus loan default proceeds. The contractual payment expectation may be fixed (even if the underlying loans float) or floating (even if the underlying loans are fixed rate), and may have different maturity than both other tranches and the underlying loans. There are 15 tranches in this particular issue, which are summarized in Figure SII.6. All of the data is as of April 2003.

FIGURE SII.6

Class	Opening Balance (000,000's)	Current Balance (000,000's)	Moodys Rating	S&P Rating	Coupon	Date of Maturity	Avg. Life (years)	Original Spread
A-1A	275.0	198.7	Aaa	AAA	5.87	08/15/06	1.72	5 yr Treas+125
A-1B	693.6	693.6	Aaa	AAA	6.21	10/15/08	5.20	Treas Curve+135
A-2	500.0	466.7	Aaa	AAA	6.30	10/15/08	4.39	Treas Curve
B	106.3	106.3	Aa2	AA	6.36	10/15/08	5.80	10 yr Treas+160
C	106.3	106.3	A2	A	6.50	11/15/08	5.50	10 yr Treas+180
D	121.5	121.5	Baa2	BBB	6.50	12/15/08	5.59	10 yr Treas+250
E	30.4	30.4	Baa3	BBB-	6.50	12/15/08	5.65	10 yr Treas+350
F	50.6	50.6	Ba1	BB+	6.00	12/15/08	5.65	
G	45.6	45.6	Ba2	NR	5.60	04/15/13	7.38	
H	15.2	15.2	Ba3	NR	5.60	08/15/13	10.25	
J	20.3	20.3	B1	NR	5.60	08/15/14	10.52	
K	10.1	10.1	B2	NR	5.60	03/15/16	12.14	
L	15.2	15.2	Caa1	NR	5.60	10/15/17	13.59	
M	10.1	10.1	Caa3	NR	5.60	06/15/18	14.94	
N	25.3	25.3	NR	NR	5.60	09/15/23	15.68	
X (IO)			Aaa	AAA	0.77	09/15/23	NA	
Total / Weight Avg	**2,025.6**	**1,916.0**			**6.18**		**5.18**	

The largest tranches received a AAA rating with par values of $275,000,000 (A-1A), $693,553,000 (A-1B), and $500,000,000 (A-2), for a total of 72.5% in AAA rated tranches. These tranches have the highest priority claims, and hence are the safest, and as a result command the highest ratings and tightest spreads. The other 37.5% of the pool is broken into increasingly junior tranches, each with a lesser priority claim to the cash flows of the issuer (which come solely from the loan pool). Note that the pricing spreads rise as the priority claim declines.

Each tranche is a detailed contract that specifies the priority claims to the issuer's cash stream. Hence, each prices uniquely. And as the pool matures, defaults occur, etc., each priority claim changes in value. For example, as amortization occurs, all tranches become safer, but especially the lower priority claims. This will often result in rating upgrades and narrower spreads as the tranches trade over time. Also as liquidity premiums and interest rates change, pricing changes.

As of May 2003, the spread for each tranche was narrower than on the closing date. The pay rate on a floating tranche floats up or down at the noted spread over whatever LIBOR is at the time. Each tranche's document will detail how the rate adjusts to the new LIBOR level. This is usually adjusted either monthly or quarterly.

One of the more significant variables that factors into the initial pricing described above is the tranches' ratings. In this CMBS issue there are levels that range from Senior secured fixed rate AAA debt, to Junior fixed rate debt that is not rated (as it wasn't worth paying a fee to a rating agency just to be told "it's really risky"). Mezzanine fixed rate debt in this pool starts with a bond rating of AA (the B tranche through E tranches).

INFORMATIONAL PROGRAMS

While this supplement summarizes a single CMBS issue, services such as Realpoint, Trepp, and Intex track all existing CMBS deals. You can access their services at www.realpoint.com for Realpoint, www.trepp.com for Trepp, www.intex.com for Intex, or you can call the issuer for a report. The benefit of these companies is in marketing deals and trading, allowing one to track information for every CMBS issue, including information on DSCR, pricing, LTV, loans in default, tranche size and rating, individual loan and property information, loans to watch, strengths and weaknesses, etc. The sources also provide pricing models for each tranche in order to facilitate trading.

Supplemental III
Careers In Real Estate

I am frequently asked by students, "I'm really interested in a career in real estate. So which investment bank do you suggest I go to work for?" I always respond that while investment banking is a great career path, there are many other career options in real estate. To say you want to be in real estate is as vague as saying you want to be in medicine. Do you want to be a cardiologist, pediatrician, nurse, professor, pharmaceutical sales rep, CFO for a healthcare company, hospital administrator, technician, researcher, or dentist? The career options discussed in this chapter are in no way comprehensive, but offer a glimpse of the variety of real estate career paths available. Opportunity funds and REITs are not discussed here, as they are described in detail elsewhere in the book.

Research: Real estate, like any industry, constantly seeks quality information. Thus, the business has many research niches. Equity research teams at major investment houses analyze market trends and company information to evaluate publicly traded real estate companies. Other research specialists, such as Linneman Associates, Torto Wheaton, and Rosen Consulting Group, provide analysis on how macro and micro events impact the real estate industry. Firms like REIS provide market rent, building permit, vacancy, and other detailed market data. Sometimes research firms are divisions of banks or money managers.

Junior level researchers gather and analyze data, work on surveys, and compile data in easy to understand formats. Writing skills are highly valued by research firms.

Brokers and Leasing Agents: Brokers are the plankton of the industry, in that they are everywhere. They range from mom and pop shops, to huge public corporations. These licensed real estate professionals assess local market values, market properties, and advise clients on the purchase, leasing, and sale of properties. Frequently corporate users engage brokers as their representatives to identify the best office, warehouse space, retail space, or housing for their needs. They also lease space for owners. Brokers generally work for fees that are primarily based upon successful deal execution.

Major firms include CBRE and Cushman & Wakefield. In addition, there are many local brokers and agents. Also, major investment banks such as Goldman Sachs and Morgan Stanley perform some of these services, as does Eastdil.

The advantage of working for a broker is that you learn about the demand side of real estate, as great brokers understand the type of space desired by different firms. For example, a financial services firm looking for office space in Manhattan has substantially different space needs than a major law or industrial firm. In addition, each property, and each suite in a property has unique usage aspects. Good brokers seek to match these traits with customers. No two markets or properties are identical, and a good broker understands who best fits what.

A junior person in this industry works on reports, marketing materials, research, leasing and space use plans, and assists in structuring leases and property sales. In this business, writing skills are useful and knowledge of programs such as PowerPoint, Argus, and Excel are essential.

Investment Banks: This sector serves the capital needs of REITs, private equity funds, private operators, etc. They raise debt and equity, provide advisory work on mergers and acquisitions, and advise on restructuring situations. Some banks also operate real estate investment funds.

Often when REITs and other large real estate firms float debt, they use an investment bank. This debt may be used to finance a large acquisition, the purchase of another firm, or refinance existing debt. Investment banks use their sales network to place both secured and unsecured real estate debt, frequently trading in the debt's after-market. The equity raising process is much the same. When an investment bank is engaged to raise capital, the bank's real estate group works with the lawyers and the capital markets group to structure the offering, which is then placed through an equity syndicate that coordinates road shows with institutional investors.

Investment banks also perform advisory work, including fairness opinions, and frequently act as brokers for major property sales. For example, the bank's technology group will be advising on a merger, which creates the need to dispose of surplus office space, and the bank's real estate group may be engaged to market this property. The bank's main expertise lies in their knowledge of capital markets.

A junior person at an investment bank creates pitch books, prepares PowerPoint presentations, and constructs detailed financial models. The hours are long and tedious.

Institutional investors: Insurance companies, pension funds, endowments, and investment companies have money to invest. Sometimes their assets are matched with their liabilities. For example, a pension fund has the relatively known long term liabilities associated with current retirees, and the less certain liability associated with current employees who will one day be retirees.

Institutional investors invest in real estate for both its diversification and return attributes. Some institutional investors invest a portion of their assets in higher risk vehicles such as private equity funds, as well as REITs, individual properties, mortgages, and CMBS.

Junior level people in this field work on asset management, due diligence, monitor investments, measure performance, prepare reports, and select managers.

Commercial Banks: Commercial banks underwrite loans, frequently acting as an intermediary between an issuer of securities and public investors. Commercial banks also engage in lending activities, sometimes holding their loans, other times syndicating them, and sometimes packaging them into as CMBS offerings. After the repeal of the Glass-Steagall Act in 1999, an integration of investment banks and major commercial banks occurred. However, local commercial banks still largely function as lenders.

Given their short term liabilities (deposits), they are typically the primary source of construction loans. Commercial banks also provide 3-7 year loans, particularly to local property owners. These loans frequently are provided to developers to fund the construction, and stabilization of new properties.

Entry level people at commercial banks assist in the due diligence process, checking financial projections, construction timelines, etc. Since many bank loans are secured by recourse to personal assets, they often analyze the personal balance sheets of the borrowers.

Developers: Developers range from large national firms like Forest City, Hines, and the Related Companies, to small local developers. Most specialize in a single property type, such as retail, hotel, residential, commercial, or resort, as each region and property type requires different skill sets, tenant relationships, and local connections. For example, a great condo developer knows how to create a buzz about his product, and is able to quickly market the units. Some developers are experts at controlling project costs, others are great at marketing, while others are masters of design. Land developers focus on pre-selling lots and obtaining the necessary zoning approvals, while mall developers pre-lease space, using their rolodex and relationships with retail tenants. Single family home development is basically a manufacturing process, where land is merely production inventory.

The best developers use their core competency to get an edge on the competition, and have the political and organization savvy to get through the regulatory maze efficiently. Many developers sub-contract architects, lawyers, general contractors, brokers, a marketing team, adding value by efficiently managing these diverse outsourced components. Others are more integrated, performing many or all of these functions in-house.

The developer's job is both about taking, and eliminating, risks. Developers seek out viable deals. While a development case may be assigned every couple of weeks in a real estate class, most developers will only find a viable development deal once every year or two. After finding such a deal, the developer lines up capital from both equity investors and lenders. The developer continually fine tunes building plans, as markets, tenants, regulatory and engineering challenges evolve. Upon completion, developers must lease and/or sell space. There is often no precise timetable, and the developer must coordinate and juggle all of these moving parts.

Junior level people at development firms create financial models, and aid in the market analysis and due diligence process. They will also assist in preparing marketing materials for tenants and capital providers, as well as presentations to planning authorities.

Architects and Planners: People think of architects such as I.M. Pei, Helmut Jahn, Kohn Pederson Fox, or Frank Gehry as creators of wonderful works of art. But most architects are in the business of designing usable and profitable space. Good architects design commercial space from the "inside out", rather than the "outside in". This is because while the exterior of the building is a great advertisement for the property and architects, the layout of the interior space must effectively meet the needs of space users to be successful. Layout and design vary across property types, users, and markets. It is the architect's job to make sure that a usable, flexible, and efficient structure is designed, which complies with zoning codes and other local regulations. Architects often specialize in different components of a project, specializing in interiors, schematics, landscaping, mechanicals, or facades.

This field attracts many young "artists" who quickly discover that it is a highly competitive business, where one prospers by efficiently executing the creative visions of developers, rather than making grand personal artistic statements.

General Contracting Firms: General contractors coordinate construction and project logistics, creating and supervising schedules and budgets for each element of the construction process. For example, should the carpenters do their work before or after the electrical contractors? The job of general contractors is to keep the construction process on time, coordinating construction details with the developer, architect, and sub-contractors. General contractors often have a specialty in one or more aspects of the construction process. They must plan for unforeseen delays and costs, and conceptualize all of the details required to complete the property in a timely and cost effective manner.

In this field, young people work on budgets, monitor project timing and costs, and facilitate negotiations with vendors and sub-contractors.

Lawyers: The real estate industry is filled with "deal guys", who buy, sell, and lease properties. This requires the assistance of many lawyers to draft, finalize, and negotiate detailed documents. Sometimes lawyers have an expertise in specialties like historic tax credits, environmental, zoning, leasing or construction.

Lawyers create the documents which will allow a developer to sell historic tax credits, or purchase a property. Lawyers also draft partnership agreements so that liability, taxes, and returns are distributed among partners as agreed. For example, non-taxable entities, such as college endowments cannot use tax credits, so complex legal structures are frequently crafted which most efficiently allocate these benefits among investors.

To be on the legal side of the real estate business, a J.D. is generally required. A young lawyer will do legal research, work on due diligence, and assist in contract drafting.

Closing Thought: These career descriptions barely scratch the surface of the possibilities in real estate. Never forget that every building and vacant piece of land is owned by someone, and that owner (including government agencies) must operate, finance, and report on the usage of the property. Real estate is ubiquitous in our world, and career paths are literally endless. Don't limit yourself to investment banks simply because your friends are working for these firms.

Supplemental IV
ARGUS Enterprise by ARGUS Software

Authors:
John Lim, Sr. Dir. Marketing
Katie Foley, Instructional Designer
ARGUS Software

WHAT IS ARGUS Enterprise™?

ARGUS Enterprise is an integrated platform for cash flow modeling, valuations, and asset and portfolio management. For 20 years, ARGUS Software has been the standard for cash flow modeling and valuations management. ARGUS models are used to facilitate transactions between real estate investors, lenders, brokers, appraisers and other commercial real estate professionals. While maintaining the robust cash flow and valuations core capabilities, ARGUS Enterprise builds on this foundation a complete asset and portfolio management solution.

ARGUS Enterprise is a global solution connecting a global commercial real estate market. Localized to handle different area measures, currencies and leasing methods, ARGUS Enterprise models can be created for any regional investor. These models can then be combined to provide a complete view across a global portfolio. Additionally, ARGUS Enterprise handles multiple valuation methods including Discounted Cash Flow, Traditional Valuations (UK) and Market Capitalisation (Australia). Meeting the increasing demand for cross border investing, models from one region can be sent to investors from another region to view and analyze in a different currency, area measure and even valuation method.

There are multiple components of ARGUS Enterprise. From the property cash flow model, property budgeting, investor and portfolio reporting, ARGUS Enterprise is a complete asset, portfolio and investment management solution. In this supplement, the cash flow modeling and valuation components are showcased to provide an overview of the inputs and the outputs that give the visibility and the results to help investors make informed decisions. ARGUS takes assured information such as contract leasing data and combines them with speculative and market assumptions to forecast cash flow projections. These results are used to calculate valuations such as the present value of the cash flows or an internal rate of return from the purchase price. Additionally, results can be changed by varying market and leasing assumptions to assess risk and make informed investment decisions.

This consistent platform connects data and business processes for acquisitions, valuations, budgeting, asset and portfolio management and investor reporting. For commercial real estate transactions, brokers, appraisers and lenders collaborate with common data points while still allowing for their own market and investment assumptions. For thousands of users, ARGUS Enterprise is the platform of choice for transacting and managing commercial real estate investments.

EXAMPLE PROPERTY

The following simple case study of a fictitious building provides an overview of the data input into ARGUS Enterprise and the results that are generated. Each aspect of the property is accompanied by a corresponding screen shot of the ARGUS Enterprise application to show how the application accepts the data required for financial modeling.

CASE STUDY – ENTERPRISE TOWER

PORTFOLIO CREATION

In ARGUS Enterprise, portfolios are collections of properties to which various scenarios can be applied. Once a portfolio has been created, properties can be added. Any changes made to a portfolio are automatically saved. Once the initial portfolio is created, it is good practice to duplicate that portfolio and make changes to the copy to test scenarios and any changes before applying them to the main portfolio.

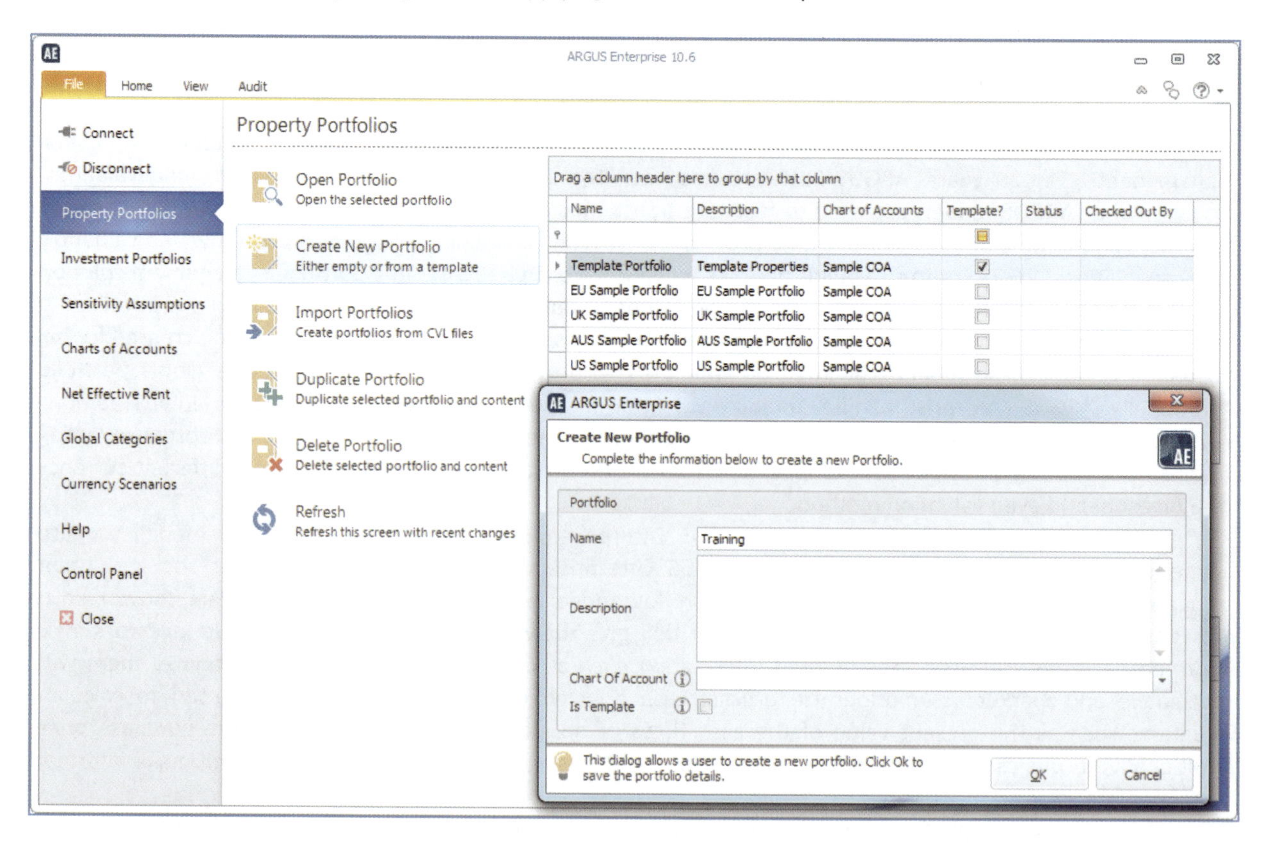

INITIAL PROPERTY ASSUMPTIONS

Enterprise Tower is a 50,000 square foot Mixed Use (Office/Retail) building located at 10 Discovery Blvd., Houston, Texas. The Analysis start date is January 1, 2016. A 5 year discounted cash flow will be used to value the property because income is expected to vary over the next few years.

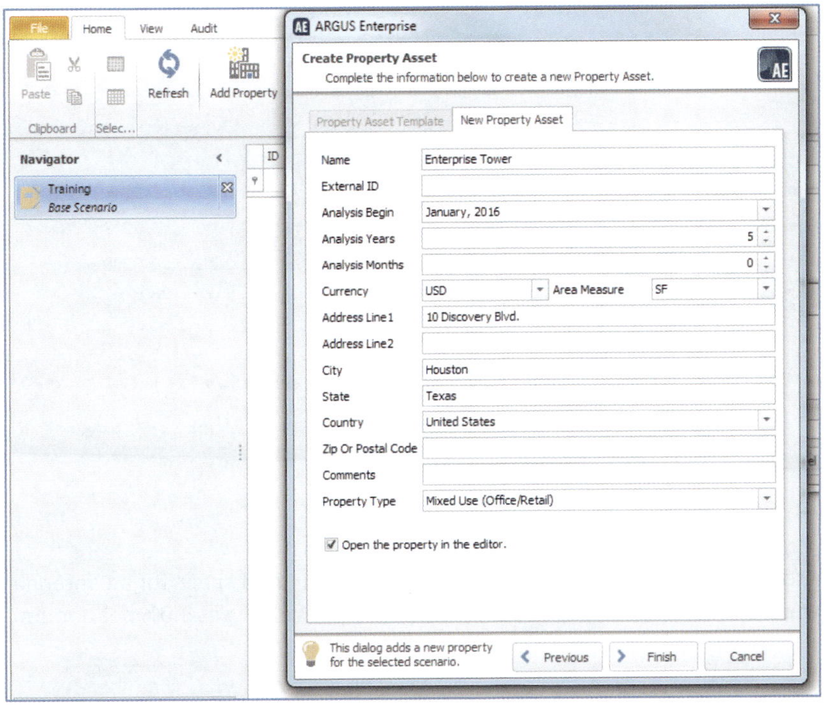

File | Home | View | Audit

Paste | Refresh | Add Property

Clipboard | Selec...

Navigator

Training
Base Scenario

ARGUS Enterprise

Create Property Asset
Complete the information below to create a new Property Asset.

Property Asset Template | New Property Asset

Name	Enterprise Tower
External ID	
Analysis Begin	January, 2016
Analysis Years	5
Analysis Months	0
Currency	USD — Area Measure: SF
Address Line1	10 Discovery Blvd.
Address Line2	
City	Houston
State	Texas
Country	United States
Zip Or Postal Code	
Comments	
Property Type	Mixed Use (Office/Retail)

☑ Open the property in the editor.

This dialog adds a new property for the selected scenario.

Previous | Finish | Cancel

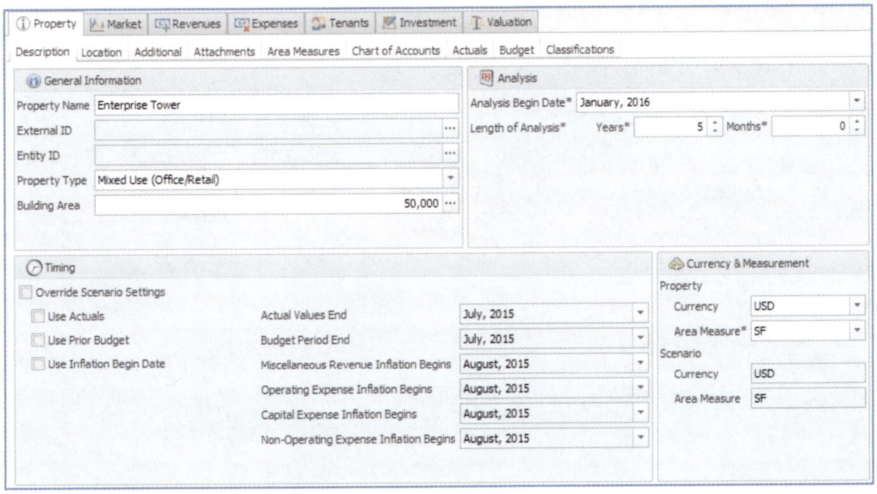

Property | Market | Revenues | Expenses | Tenants | Investment | Valuation

Description | Location | Additional | Attachments | Area Measures | Chart of Accounts | Actuals | Budget | Classifications

General Information

Property Name	Enterprise Tower
External ID	
Entity ID	
Property Type	Mixed Use (Office/Retail)
Building Area	50,000

Analysis

Analysis Begin Date*	January, 2016
Length of Analysis*	Years* 5 — Months* 0

Timing

☐ Override Scenario Settings

☐ Use Actuals

☐ Use Prior Budget

☐ Use Inflation Begin Date

Actual Values End	July, 2015
Budget Period End	July, 2015
Miscellaneous Revenue Inflation Begins	August, 2015
Operating Expense Inflation Begins	August, 2015
Capital Expense Inflation Begins	August, 2015
Non-Operating Expense Inflation Begins	August, 2015

Currency & Measurement

Property

Currency	USD
Area Measure*	SF

Scenario

Currency	USD
Area Measure	SF

In this model Inflation is calculated using a Calendar Recovery using Calendar Inflation. Both the General and Expense Inflations will be 3.00% for the Analysis. The rental market in the area is tightening at the moment, so Market Rent will inflate at 6.00% in 2017 and 2018, and then at 3.00% for the remainder of the projection.

Property | Market | Revenues | Expenses | Tenants | Investment | Valuation

Inflation | Inflation Indices | General Vacancy | Credit Loss | Market Leasing | Free Rent | CPI Increases | Tenant Improvements | Lease Commissio

Name	Inflation Basis	Dec 2016	Dec 2017	Dec 2018	Dec 2019	Dec 2020	Dec 2021
No Inflation	As Entered		0.00%	0.00%	0.00%	0.00%	0.00%
General Inflation Rate	As Entered		3.00%	3.00%	3.00%	3.00%	3.00%
Market Inflation Rate	As Entered		6.00%	6.00%	3.00%	3.00%	3.00%
Expense Inflation Rate	As Entered		3.00%	3.00%	3.00%	3.00%	3.00%
CPI Inflation Rate	As Entered		0.00%	0.00%	0.00%	0.00%	0.00%

Inflation Month: Analysis Date | Recovery Timing: Calendar Recovery using Calendar Inflation

Reset General | Reset Market | Reset Expense | Reset CPI | Reset Selected Inflation | Update

MISCELLANEOUS REVENUES

In addition to base rent, revenue is also derived from leasing roof space for an antenna. This Miscellaneous Revenue is estimated initially at $15,000 per year, increasing at 3.0% per annum.

Property | Market | Revenues | Expenses | Tenants | Investment | Valuation

Miscellaneous | Parking | Storage

Drag a column header here to group by that column

	General	Amount					
	Name	How Input	Amount1	Frequency	Amount2	Area Measure	Fixed %
1	Roof Antenna	Amount 1	15,000	Annually			100.0%

OPERATING EXPENSES

Property | Market | Revenues | Expenses | Tenants | Investment | Valuation

Operating | Non-Operating | Capital | Expense Groups

Drag a column header here to group by that column

	General	Amount							Inflation
	Name	How Input	Amount1	Frequency	Amount 2	Area Measure	Fixed %	Recoverable %	Inflation %
1	Real Estate Taxes	Amount 1	75,000	Annually			100.0%	100.0%	Custom: 2.0%
2	Insurance	Amount 1	1,000	Monthly			100.0%	100.0%	Expense Inflation Rate
3	Utilities	$ / Rentable Area	2.00	Annually		Building Area	25.0%	100.0%	Expense Inflation Rate
4	Repairs and Maintenance	$ / Rentable Area	1.00	Annually		Building Area	35.0%	100.0%	Expense Inflation Rate
5	Management Fee	% of Effective Gross Revenue	3.0%					0.0%	

Real Estate Taxes are estimated at $75,000 per year. Thereafter, the tax liability is trended at 2.0% per year for inflationary expectations. Taxes are a 100% fixed expense.

Insurance coverage including fire insurance, extended coverage, liability, and other space coverage required by a property of the subject type is $1,000 per month. This expense is increased annually with the Expense Inflation Rate, and is a fixed expense.

Utilities are estimated at $2.00 per rentable square foot per year. This is a variable expense. Only 25.0% of this expense would be incurred if the property were vacant. This expense is projected to grow at the Expense Inflation Rate.

Repairs and Maintenance is estimated at $1.00 per rentable square foot per year. This includes all interior and exterior maintenance and repairs and janitorial expenses for the building. It is estimated that the property would still incur 35.0% of this expense if the building were totally vacant. This expense is projected to grow at the Expense Inflation Rate.

Management Fee is a non-recoverable expense and will be calculated at 3.0% of the Effective Gross Revenue.

CAPITAL EXPENDITURES

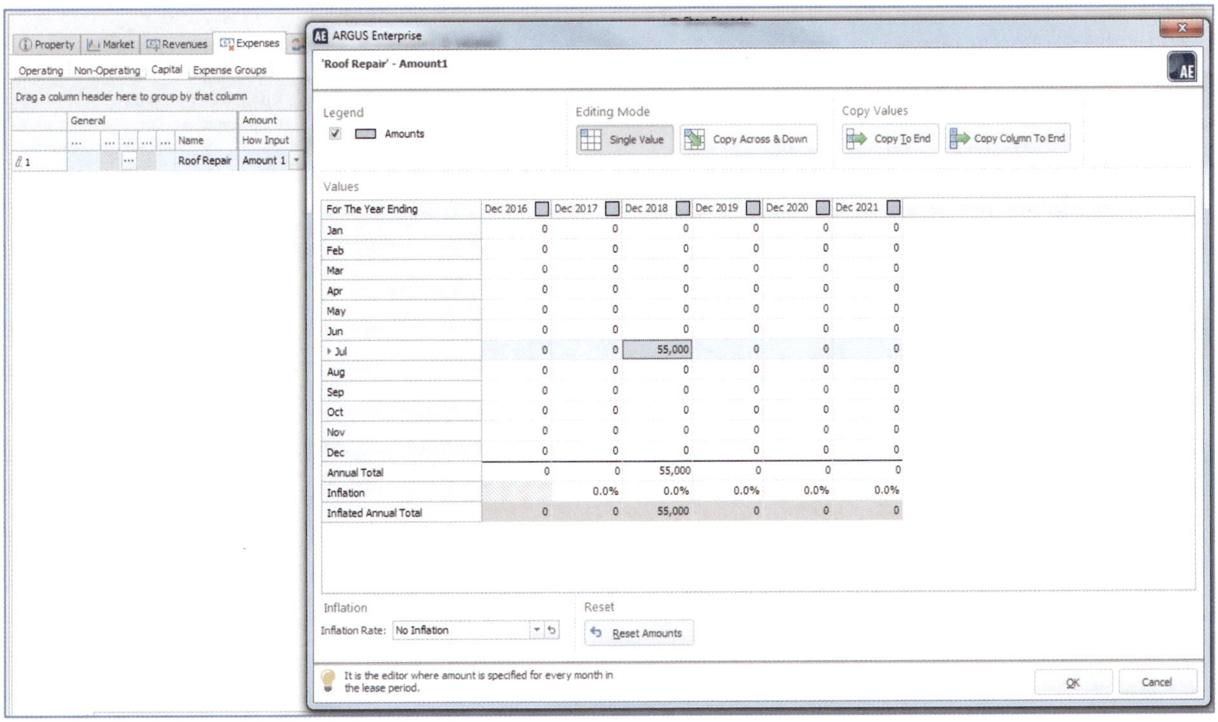

ARGUS Enterprise

'Roof Repair' - Amount1

For The Year Ending	Dec 2016	Dec 2017	Dec 2018	Dec 2019	Dec 2020	Dec 2021
Jan	0	0	0	0	0	0
Feb	0	0	0	0	0	0
Mar	0	0	0	0	0	0
Apr	0	0	0	0	0	0
May	0	0	0	0	0	0
Jun	0	0	0	0	0	0
Jul	0	0	55,000	0	0	0
Aug	0	0	0	0	0	0
Sep	0	0	0	0	0	0
Oct	0	0	0	0	0	0
Nov	0	0	0	0	0	0
Dec	0	0	0	0	0	0
Annual Total	0	0	55,000	0	0	0
Inflation		0.0%	0.0%	0.0%	0.0%	0.0%
Inflated Annual Total	0	0	55,000	0	0	0

Inflation Rate: No Inflation

The subject's roof is partially defective and it will need a major repair by 2018. Property management is currently projecting this repair for July of 2018. Current estimates from area contractors indicate the expense will be $55,000 at that time.

TENANTS – RENT ROLL

The property has four tenants listed below in the lease abstract table. Two of the leases have start dates prior to the analysis start while the other two leases are contracted leases set to begin on or after the analysis start date.

Name Suite Area	Available Date Start Date	Term / Expire	Rental Income	Other Terms
JFN Real Estate 100 3,410	Both Available and Start Dates: May 1, 2012	5 Years	$10.50/SF/Year	Recovery: Stop Amount / Area of $4.00/SF Upon Expiration: Renew
Joy Placement Center 200 6,190	Both Available and Start Dates: August 1, 2013	6 Years	$12.00/SF/Year, Increasing 3.0% per year	Recovery: Fixed Amount of $20,000 per year.
Spring Computers 300 5,400	Available Date – Analysis Begin Start Date - February 1, 2016	5 Years	100% of Market Rent	Recovery: Base Year Stop TI: $15.00/SF LC: 5.0% - Fixed %
Feighery Group 400 23,000	Both Available and Start Dates: Analysis Begin	10 Years	$10.00/SF/Year, Increasing $0.50/SF/Year	Recovery: Net TI: $15.00/SF LC: 5.0% - Fixed %

Property | Market | Revenues | Expenses | Tenants | Investment | Valuation

Rent Roll | Space Absorption | Recoveries | Tenant Groups | Ground Leases | Security Deposits | Payment Schedules

Drag a column header here to group by that column

	Name		General							
	... Name	Suite	Lease Status	Lease Type	Area	Available	Available Date	Start	Start Date
1	JFN Real Estate	100	Contract	Office	3,410	Specified Date	5/1/2012	Available Date	5/1/2012
2	Joy Placement Center	200	Contract	Office	6,190	Specified Date	8/1/2013	Available Date	8/1/2013
3	Spring Computers	300	Contract	Office	5,400	Analysis Begin	1/1/2016	Specified Date	2/1/2016
4	Feighery Group	400	Contract	Office	23,000	Analysis Begin	1/1/2016	Available Date	1/1/2016

		Rental Income			
Term / Expire	End	Base Rent Unit	Base Rent	Fixed Steps Unit	Step Amounts
5/0	4/30/2017	$ / SF / Year	10.50	None	
6/0	7/31/2019	$ / SF / Year	12.00	% Increase	3.0%
5/0	1/31/2021	% of Market	100.0%	None	
10/0	12/31/2025	$ / SF / Year	10.00	$ / SF / Year	0.50

MARKET LEASING PROFILES

Market Leasing profiles in the model are used to automatically generate assumptions and calculations for new and renewal leases. In this property, the market leasing profiles are standard for space that is less than 20,000 square feet. Quoted rates and actual recent lease terms at comparable office buildings were analyzed to determine current market rent. The building has two classifications of space. One is for tenants of less than 20,000 square feet, and the other is for tenants of more than 20,000 square feet. The Less than 20,000 Market Leasing profile is shown below.

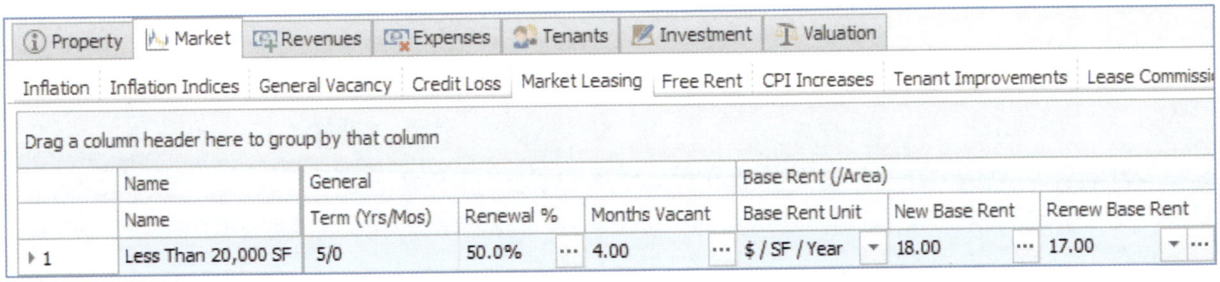

Property | Market | Revenues | Expenses | Tenants | Investment | Valuation

Inflation | Inflation Indices | General Vacancy | Credit Loss | Market Leasing | Free Rent | CPI Increases | Tenant Improvements | Lease Commissi

Drag a column header here to group by that column

	Name	General			Base Rent (/Area)		
	Name	Term (Yrs/Mos)	Renewal %	Months Vacant	Base Rent Unit	New Base Rent	Renew Base Rent
1	Less Than 20,000 SF	5/0	50.0%	4.00	$ / SF / Year	18.00	17.00

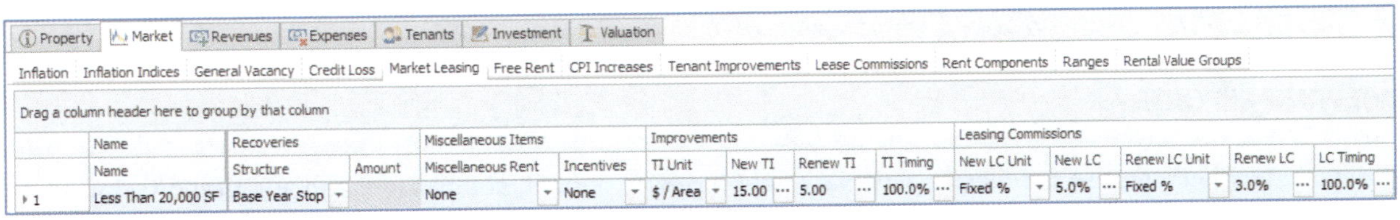

Property | Market | Revenues | Expenses | Tenants | Investment | Valuation

Inflation | Inflation Indices | General Vacancy | Credit Loss | Market Leasing | Free Rent | CPI Increases | Tenant Improvements | Lease Commissions | Rent Components | Ranges | Rental Value Groups

Drag a column header here to group by that column

	Name	Recoveries		Miscellaneous Items		Improvements				Leasing Commissions				
	Name	Structure	Amount	Miscellaneous Rent	Incentives	TI Unit	New TI	Renew TI	TI Timing	New LC Unit	New LC	Renew LC Unit	Renew LC	LC Timing
1	Less Than 20,000 SF	Base Year Stop		None	None	$ / Area	15.00	5.00	100.0%	Fixed %	5.0%	Fixed %	3.0%	100.0%

For tenants that are Less Than 20,000 SF, the term is expected to be 5 years and the Renewal Probability is assumed to be 50.0%. Months Vacant is 4 months of downtime between leases. Market Base Rent is $18.00/SF/Year for new tenants and $17.00/SF/Year for renewing tenants. Recoveries are set to a Base Year Stop. Tenant Improvements are $15.00/SF for new tenants, $5.00/SF for renewing tenants. Leasing Commissions for new tenants are set to a Fixed 5.0%, while renewing tenants are set to a Fixed 3.0%.

For tenants of More Than 20,000 SF, the term is expected to be 10 years and the Renewal Probability is assumed to be 75.0%. Months Vacant is 6 months of downtime between leases Market Base Rent $15.00/SF/Year for new tenants and renewing tenants. Recoveries are set to Net. Tenant Improvements are $20.00/SF for new tenants, $5.00/SF for renewing tenants. Leasing Commissions for new tenants are set to a Fixed 5.0%, while renewing tenants are set to a Fixed 3.0%.

SPACE ABSORPTION

Currently, 12,000 square feet are vacant in Enterprise Tower. The Less Than 20,000 SF Market Leasing profile will be used to populate the inputs for the vacant space that remains. The 12,000 square feet of vacant space will be leased out in 2,000 square foot spaces with one lease being absorbed every month. The vacant area is available at the beginning of the analysis with absorption projected to begin July 2016.

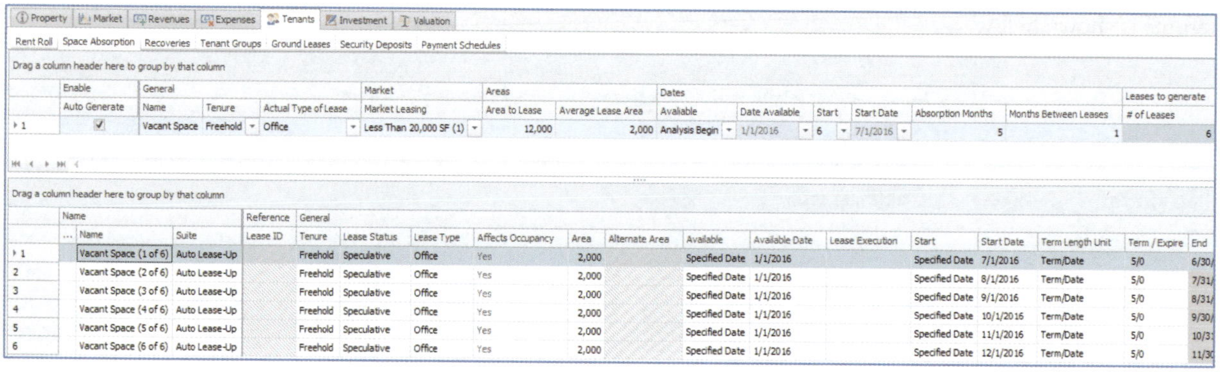

Property | Market | Revenues | Expenses | Tenants | Investment | Valuation

Rent Roll | Space Absorption | Recoveries | Tenant Groups | Ground Leases | Security Deposits | Payment Schedules

Drag a column header here to group by that column

	Enable	General			Market	Areas		Dates						Leases to generate
	Auto Generate	Name	Tenure	Actual Type of Lease	Market Leasing	Area to Lease	Average Lease Area	Avaliable	Date Available	Start	Start Date	Absorption Months	Months Between Leases	# of Leases
1	✓	Vacant Space	Freehold	Office	Less Than 20,000 SF (1)	12,000	2,000	Analysis Begin	1/1/2016	6	7/1/2016	5	1	6

Drag a column header here to group by that column

	Name		Reference	General													
	Name	Suite	Lease ID	Tenure	Lease Status	Lease Type	Affects Occupancy	Area	Alternate Area	Available	Available Date	Lease Execution	Start	Start Date	Term Length Unit	Term / Expire	End
1	Vacant Space (1 of 6)	Auto Lease-Up		Freehold	Speculative	Office	Yes	2,000		Specified Date	1/1/2016		Specified Date	7/1/2016	Term/Date	5/0	6/30/
2	Vacant Space (2 of 6)	Auto Lease-Up		Freehold	Speculative	Office	Yes	2,000		Specified Date	1/1/2016		Specified Date	8/1/2016	Term/Date	5/0	7/31/
3	Vacant Space (3 of 6)	Auto Lease-Up		Freehold	Speculative	Office	Yes	2,000		Specified Date	1/1/2016		Specified Date	9/1/2016	Term/Date	5/0	8/31/
4	Vacant Space (4 of 6)	Auto Lease-Up		Freehold	Speculative	Office	Yes	2,000		Specified Date	1/1/2016		Specified Date	10/1/2016	Term/Date	5/0	9/30/
5	Vacant Space (5 of 6)	Auto Lease-Up		Freehold	Speculative	Office	Yes	2,000		Specified Date	1/1/2016		Specified Date	11/1/2016	Term/Date	5/0	10/3
6	Vacant Space (6 of 6)	Auto Lease-Up		Freehold	Speculative	Office	Yes	2,000		Specified Date	1/1/2016		Specified Date	12/1/2016	Term/Date	5/0	11/3

VIEWING REPORTS

ARGUS Enterprise produces a wide variety of property, tenant, comparison, and audit reports, including: Dashboard Reports, Property Reports, Valuation Reports, Tenant Reports, Audit Reports, and Review reports.

We now have enough information to generate reports. The following screen capture shows the Property Reports – Cash Flow resulting from the assumptions of this property. Items to note on this report are the following: the growth of the expenses, the turnover of leases in Year 1, Year 4, and Year 6, and the calculation of the expense reimbursements based on the tenant assumptions and growing expenses.

Dashboard Reports | Property Reports | Valuation Reports | Tenant Reports | Audit Reports | Review

Cash Flow | Executive Summary | Assumptions | Budget Comparison | Month and Year-to-Date Variance | Sources and Uses

Report for Total Property

Enterprise Tower (Amounts in USD)
Jan, 2016 through Dec, 2021
8/10/2015 11:02:32 AM

	Forecast	Forecast	Forecast	Forecast	Forecast	Forecast	Forecast
	Year 1	Year 2	Year 3	Year 4	Year 5	Year 6	
For the Years Ending	Dec-2016	Dec-2017	Dec-2018	Dec-2019	Dec-2020	Dec-2021	Total
Rental Revenue							
Potential Base Rent	654,319	689,783	712,296	741,615	776,014	816,973	4,390,999
Absorption & Turnover Vacancy	-156,625	0	0	-20,894	0	-58,729	-236,248
Scheduled Base Rent	497,694	689,783	712,296	720,721	776,014	758,244	4,154,751
Total Rental Revenue	497,694	689,783	712,296	720,721	776,014	758,244	4,154,751
Other Tenant Revenue							
Total Expense Recoveries	121,380	142,441	147,800	143,092	139,670	132,170	826,552
Total Other Tenant Revenue	121,380	142,441	147,800	143,092	139,670	132,170	826,552
Total Tenant Revenue	619,073	832,224	860,096	863,813	915,683	890,414	4,981,302
Other Revenue							
Roof Antenna	15,000	15,450	15,914	16,391	16,883	17,389	97,026
Total Other Revenue	15,000	15,450	15,914	16,391	16,883	17,389	97,026
Potential Gross Revenue	634,073	847,674	876,009	880,204	932,566	907,803	5,078,328
Effective Gross Revenue	634,073	847,674	876,009	880,204	932,566	907,803	5,078,328
Operating Expenses							
Real Estate Taxes	75,000	76,500	78,030	79,591	81,182	82,806	473,109
Insurance	12,000	12,360	12,731	13,113	13,506	13,911	77,621
Utilities	86,575	103,000	106,090	107,582	112,551	111,174	626,972
Repairs and Maintenance	44,183	51,500	53,045	53,904	56,275	55,904	314,811
Management Fee	19,022	25,430	26,280	26,406	27,977	27,234	152,350
Total Operating Expenses	236,780	268,790	276,176	280,595	291,492	291,030	1,644,862
Net Operating Income	397,294	578,884	599,833	599,609	641,074	616,773	3,433,466
Leasing Costs							
Tenant Improvements	606,000	17,562	0	67,640	0	155,343	846,544
Leasing Commissions	219,175	9,217	0	25,073	0	57,583	311,049
Total Leasing Costs	825,175	26,779	0	92,713	0	212,926	1,157,593
Capital Expenditures							
Roof Repair	0	0	55,000	0	0	0	55,000
Total Capital Expenditures	0	0	55,000	0	0	0	55,000
Total Leasing & Capital Costs	825,175	26,779	55,000	92,713	0	212,926	1,212,593
Cash Flow Before Debt Service	-427,881	552,105	544,833	506,896	641,074	403,847	2,220,873
Cash Flow Available for Distribution	-427,881	552,105	544,833	506,896	641,074	403,847	2,220,873

INVESTMENT AND VALUATION

ARGUS Enterprise does the intensive calculation work, allowing the analyst to look at the yields of the property based on assumptions of the potential purchase price or achieve present value results with entries of a required rate of return.

PROPERTY PURCHASE

Property | Market | Revenues | Expenses | Tenants | Investment | Valuation

Property Purchase | Debt Financing | Other Debt

Purchase Information

Purchase Date	January, 2016	
Purchase Price	4,500,000	Enter Price
Closing Costs	0	
Total Price	4,500,000	
Less Debt Amount	0	0.0%
Equity	4,500,000	

Closing Costs

	Name
	Description

The building was purchased for $4,500,000.

DEBT FINANCING

Property | Market | Revenues | Expenses | Tenants | Investment | Valuation

Property Purchase | Debt Financing | Other Debt

Drag a column header here to group by that column

	General		Loan Details						Loan Timing			
	Name	Loan Type	How Input	Take Out Loan	Amount	Cap Rate	LTV%	Interest Rate	Loan Date	Begin Date	Loan Term (Mo)	End Date
1	Debt Funding	Amortizing	$ Amount		3,000,000			8.0%	Analysis Begin		360	December, 2045

There is a secured loan on this property. The $3,000,000 loan starts at the beginning of the analysis, amortizing over 360 months, at an 8.0% interest rate.

PROPERTY RESALE

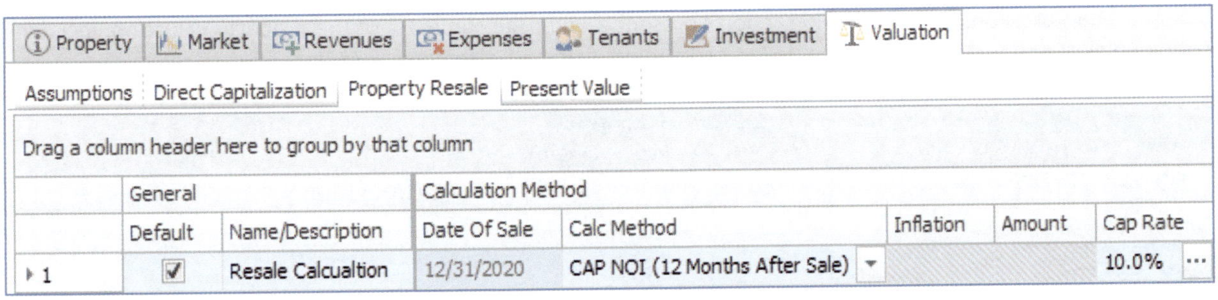

Property | Market | Revenues | Expenses | Tenants | Investment | Valuation

Assumptions | Direct Capitalization | Property Resale | Present Value

Drag a column header here to group by that column

	General		Calculation Method					
	Default	Name/Description	Date Of Sale	Calc Method	Inflation	Amount	Cap Rate	
1	☑	Resale Calcualtion	12/31/2020	CAP NOI (12 Months After Sale)			10.0%	...

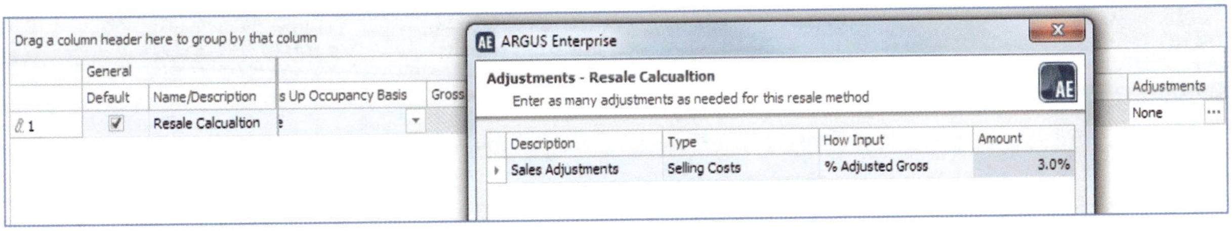

Drag a column header here to group by that column

	General				Adjustments
	Default	Name/Description	s Up Occupancy Basis	Gross	
1	☑	Resale Calcualtion			None

ARGUS Enterprise

Adjustments - Resale Calcualtion

Enter as many adjustments as needed for this resale method

Description	Type	How Input	Amount
Sales Adjustments	Selling Costs	% Adjusted Gross	3.0%

The reversion value in Year 5 is estimated by capitalizing the 6th year's Net Operating Income. The property is in a good location and is one of the better quality office buildings in the area. Therefore, a terminal capitalization rate of 10.0% is considered appropriate. Sales adjustments, including commissions and closing costs are estimated to be 3% of the gross sales and proceeds.

PRESENT VALUE

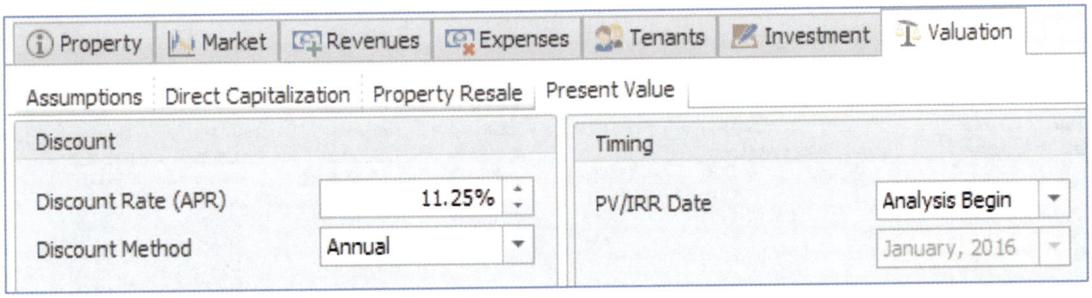

Property | Market | Revenues | Expenses | Tenants | Investment | Valuation

Assumptions | Direct Capitalization | Property Resale | Present Value

Discount		Timing	
Discount Rate (APR)	11.25%	PV/IRR Date	Analysis Begin
Discount Method	Annual		January, 2016

The subject is a modern office building constructed of very good quality materials and is well maintained. It is located in close proximity to major roadways. This area has been experiencing high occupancies (91%+). The subject is below stabilized occupancy. Given these considerations, an annual endpoint discount rate of 11.25% is considered appropriate.

PRESENT VALUE – UNLEVERAGED AND LEVERAGED REPORTS

The Valuations – Present Value reports present a one page summary of the property valuation, including valuation assumptions, the investment, leveraged and unleveraged cash flows, and cash-on-cash returns.

Dashboard Reports | Property Reports | Valuation Reports | Tenant Reports | Audit Reports | Review

IRR Matrix | Value Matrix | Resale Matrix | Valuation & Return Summary | Present Value | Yearly Valuation | Returns Over Time

Report for: Unleveraged Present Value

Enterprise Tower (Amounts in USD)
8/10/2015 11:22:08 AM
PV/IRR Date: Jan, 2016
Discount Method: Annual

Analysis Period	Period Ending	Cash Flow Before Debt Service	P.V. of Cash Flow @ 10.25 %	P.V. of Cash Flow @ 10.75 %	P.V. of Cash Flow @ 11.25 %	P.V. of Cash Flow @ 11.75 %	P.V. of Cash Flow @ 12.25 %	NOI to Book Value
Year 1	Dec-2016	-427,881	-388,101	-386,349	-384,613	-382,892	-381,186	7.46%
Year 2	Dec-2017	552,105	454,218	450,126	446,089	442,106	438,176	10.82%
Year 3	Dec-2018	544,833	406,563	401,081	395,698	390,410	385,216	11.09%
Year 4	Dec-2019	506,896	343,087	336,933	330,917	325,034	319,281	10.90%
Year 5	Dec-2020	641,074	393,564	384,760	376,191	367,850	359,730	11.66%
Totals		1,817,027	1,209,331	1,186,551	1,164,282	1,142,508	1,121,217	
Property Resale @ 10.00 % Cap Rate		5,982,696	3,672,856	3,590,693	3,510,725	3,432,885	3,357,107	
Total Unleveraged Present Value			4,882,187	4,777,244	4,675,007	4,575,393	4,478,324	

Percentage Value Distribution					
Income	24.77%	24.84%	24.90%	24.97%	25.04%
Net Sale Price	75.23%	75.16%	75.10%	75.03%	74.96%
	100.00%	100.00%	100.00%	100.00%	100.00%

Dashboard Reports | Property Reports | Valuation Reports | Tenant Reports | Audit Reports | Review

IRR Matrix | Value Matrix | Resale Matrix | Valuation & Return Summary | Present Value | Yearly Valuation | Returns Over Time

Report for: Leveraged Present Value

Enterprise Tower (Amounts in USD)
8/10/2015 11:20:56 AM
PV/IRR Date: Jan, 2016
Discount Method: Annual

Analysis Period	Period Ending	Cash Flow After Debt Service	P.V. of Cash Flow @ 10.25 %	P.V. of Cash Flow @ 10.75 %	P.V. of Cash Flow @ 11.25 %	P.V. of Cash Flow @ 11.75 %	P.V. of Cash Flow @ 12.25 %	NOI to Book Value
Year 1	Dec-2016	-692,036	-627,697	-624,864	-622,055	-619,272	-616,514	-46.14%
Year 2	Dec-2017	287,950	236,897	234,763	232,657	230,580	228,531	19.20%
Year 3	Dec-2018	280,677	209,446	206,622	203,848	201,124	198,449	18.71%
Year 4	Dec-2019	242,741	164,297	161,350	158,469	155,651	152,897	16.18%
Year 5	Dec-2020	376,919	231,396	226,219	221,181	216,277	211,503	25.13%
Totals		496,251	214,338	204,090	194,100	184,361	174,865	
Property Resale @ 10.00 % Cap Rate		3,130,600	1,921,917	1,878,923	1,837,078	1,796,346	1,756,693	
Debt Balance as of Jan-2016		3,000,000	3,000,000	3,000,000	3,000,000	3,000,000	3,000,000	
Total Leveraged Present Value			5,136,255	5,083,013	5,031,178	4,980,707	4,931,558	

Percentage Value Distribution					
Income	4.17%	4.02%	3.86%	3.70%	3.55%
Net Sale Price	37.42%	36.96%	36.51%	36.07%	35.62%
	100.00%	100.00%	100.00%	100.00%	100.00%

VALUATION & RETURN SUMMARY

The Valuation Reports – Valuation & Return Summary presents a one page summary of the property valuation, including valuation assumptions, the sales proceeds calculation, returns and distributions, leveraged, and unleveraged cash flows, cash-on-cash returns, and capitalization valuation assumptions.

Dashboard Reports | Property Reports | Valuation Reports | Tenant Reports | Audit Reports | Review | Cash Flow

IRR Matrix | Value Matrix | Resale Matrix | Valuation & Return Summary | Present Value | Yearly Valuation | Returns Over Time

Enterprise Tower (Amounts in USD)
8/10/2015 11:26:42 AM

Valuation Assumptions	
PV Calculation Date	January, 2016
Unleveraged Cash Flow Rate	11.25%
Unleveraged Resale Rate	11.25%
Leveraged Cash Flow Rate	11.25%
Leveraged Resale Rate	11.25%
Discount Method	Annual
Hold Period	5 Years
Residual Sale Date	December, 2020
Period to Cap	12 Months After Sale
Exit Cap Rate	10.00%
Gross-up NOI	No
Selling Costs	3.00%

Sales Proceeds Calculation	
Net Operating Income	616,773
Occupancy Gross-up Adjustment	0
NOI to Capitalize	616,773
Divided by Cap Rate	10.00%
Gross Sale Price	6,167,728
TI Adjustment	0
LC Adjustment	0
Adjusted Gross Sale Price	6,167,728
Sales Adjustments	-185,032
Net Sales Price	5,982,696
Less: Loan Balance	2,852,096
Proceeds from Sale	3,130,600
Pv of Net Sales Price	3,510,725

Return Summary		
Total Return (Unleveraged)		7,799,723
Total Return to Invest (Unleveraged)		1.73
PV-Cash Flow (Unleveraged)		1,164,282
PV-Net Sales Price		3,510,725
Total PV (Unleveraged)		4,675,007
Initial Investment		4,500,000
NPV (Unleveraged)		175,007
% of PV-Income		24.90%
% of PV-Net Sales Price		75.10%
IRR (Unleveraged)		12.14%
IRR (Leveraged)		17.31%
PV-Cash Flow (Unleveraged) / % Total	23.29	24.90%
PV-Net Sales Price / % Total	70.21	75.10%
Total PV (Unleveraged) $/SF	93.50	100.00%

Distributions of Net Proceeds	
Net Sale Price	5,982,696
Less: Loan Payoff	-2,852,096
Less: Equity (Investment Balance)	-1,500,000
Ending Proceeds	1,630,600

Investment & Cash Flow Summary

Year-Month	Unleveraged Investment	Unleveraged Cash Flow	PV of Unleveraged Cash Flow @ 11.25%	Unleveraged COC Return	Leveraged Investment	Leveraged Cash Flow	Leveraged COC Return
2016-January (Pd. 0)	-4,500,000				-1,500,000		
2016-December	0	-427,881	-384,613	-9.51%	0	-692,036	-46.14%
2017-December	0	552,105	446,089	12.27%	0	287,950	19.20%
2018-December	0	544,833	395,698	12.11%	0	280,677	18.71%
2019-December	0	506,896	330,917	11.26%	0	242,741	16.18%
2020-December	0	641,074	376,191	14.25%	0	376,919	25.13%
Totals	**-4,500,000**	**1,817,027**	**1,164,282**		**-1,500,000**	**496,251**	

SOURCES AND USES

The Property Reports – Sources and Uses describes the inflow/outflow of funds to the property and ends in the final years of the analysis.

Dashboard Reports | Property Reports | Valuation Reports | Tenant Reports | Audit Reports | Review

Cash Flow | Executive Summary | Assumptions | Budget Comparison | Month and Year-to-Date Variance | Sources and Uses

Enterprise Tower (Amounts in USD)
Jan, 2016 through Dec, 2020
8/10/2015 11:32:24 AM

	Forecast	Forecast	Forecast	Forecast	Forecast	Forecast
For the Years Ending	Year 1 Dec-2016	Year 2 Dec-2017	Year 3 Dec-2018	Year 4 Dec-2019	Year 5 Dec-2020	Total
Sources Of Capital						
Net Operating Gains	397,294	578,884	599,833	599,609	641,074	2,816,693
Debt Funding Proceeds	3,000,000	0	0	0	-2,852,096	147,904
Initial Equity Contribution	1,500,000	0	0	0	0	1,500,000
Net Proceeds From Sale	0	0	0	0	5,982,696	5,982,696
Defined Sources Of Capital	4,897,294	578,884	599,833	599,609	3,771,674	10,447,293
Required Equity Contributions	692,036	0	0	0	0	692,036
Total Sources Of Capital	5,589,330	578,884	599,833	599,609	3,771,674	11,139,330
Uses Of Capital						
Property Purchase Price	4,500,000	0	0	0	0	4,500,000
Total Property Purchase Price	4,500,000	0	0	0	0	4,500,000
Total Debt Service	264,155	264,155	264,156	264,155	264,155	1,320,776
Tenant Improvements	606,000	17,562	0	67,640	0	691,201
Leasing Commissions	219,175	9,217	0	25,073	0	253,465
Capital Expenditures	0	0	55,000	0	0	55,000
Debt Retirement	0	0	0	0	2,852,096	2,852,096
Defined Uses Of Capital	5,589,330	290,934	319,156	356,868	3,116,251	9,672,539
Cash Flow Distributions	0	287,950	280,677	242,741	655,423	1,466,791
Total Uses Of Capital	5,589,330	578,884	599,833	599,609	3,771,674	11,139,330
Unleveraged Cash on Cash Return						
Cash to Purchase Price	-9.51%	12.27%	12.11%	11.26%	14.25%	40.38%
NOI to Book Value	7.46%	10.82%	11.09%	10.90%	11.66%	51.22%
Leveraged Cash on Cash Return						
Cash to Initial Equity	-46.14%	19.20%	18.71%	16.18%	-165.01%	-157.06%
Unleveraged Annual IRR					12.14%	
Leveraged Annual IRR					17.31%	

* Results displayed are based on Forecast data only

LEASE AUDIT

The Audit Reports - Lease Audit is a powerful tool for reviewing key cash flow totals, such as potential and scheduled base rent, recoveries and leasing costs, on a tenant by tenant basis.

Dashboard Reports | Property Reports | Valuation Reports | Tenant Reports | Audit Reports | Review | Cas

Occupancy | Lease Audit | Percentage Rent Audit | Recovery Audit | Expense Group Audit | Loan Amortization | Property Resale | Income by Rent Review | Rent Schedule A

Enterprise Tower (Amounts in USD, Measures in SF)
Jan, 2016 through Dec, 2021
8/10/2015 11:34:31 AM

For the Years Ending	Suite	Year 1 Dec-2016	Year 2 Dec-2017	Year 3 Dec-2018	Year 4 Dec-2019	Year 5 Dec-2020	Year 6 Dec-2021	Total
Area								
1. JFN Real Estate	100	3,410	3,410	3,410	3,410	3,410	3,410	
2. Joy Placement Center	200	6,190	6,190	6,190	5,158	6,190	6,190	
3. Spring Computers	300	4,950	5,400	5,400	5,400	5,400	4,500	
4. Feighery Group	400	23,000	23,000	23,000	23,000	23,000	23,000	
1. Vacant Space (1 of 6)	Auto Lease-Up	1,000	2,000	2,000	2,000	2,000	1,667	
2. Vacant Space (2 of 6)	Auto Lease-Up	833	2,000	2,000	2,000	2,000	1,667	
3. Vacant Space (3 of 6)	Auto Lease-Up	667	2,000	2,000	2,000	2,000	1,667	
4. Vacant Space (4 of 6)	Auto Lease-Up	500	2,000	2,000	2,000	2,000	1,667	
5. Vacant Space (5 of 6)	Auto Lease-Up	333	2,000	2,000	2,000	2,000	1,667	
6. Vacant Space (6 of 6)	Auto Lease-Up	167	2,000	2,000	2,000	2,000	1,833	
Total Area		41,050	50,000	50,000	48,968	50,000	47,267	
Total Occupancy %		82.10%	100.00%	100.00%	97.94%	100.00%	94.53%	
Potential Base Rent								
1. JFN Real Estate	100	35,805	52,900	61,448	61,448	61,448	61,448	334,498
2. Joy Placement Center	200	79,789	82,182	84,648	102,467	125,365	125,365	599,817
3. Spring Computers	300	96,975	97,200	97,200	97,200	97,200	114,457	600,232
4. Feighery Group	400	230,000	241,500	253,000	264,500	276,000	287,500	1,552,500
1. Vacant Space (1 of 6)	Auto Lease-Up	35,500	36,000	36,000	36,000	36,000	39,486	218,986
2. Vacant Space (2 of 6)	Auto Lease-Up	35,417	36,000	36,000	36,000	36,000	38,905	218,322
3. Vacant Space (3 of 6)	Auto Lease-Up	35,333	36,000	36,000	36,000	36,000	38,324	217,658
4. Vacant Space (4 of 6)	Auto Lease-Up	35,250	36,000	36,000	36,000	36,000	37,743	216,993
5. Vacant Space (5 of 6)	Auto Lease-Up	35,167	36,000	36,000	36,000	36,000	37,162	216,329
6. Vacant Space (6 of 6)	Auto Lease-Up	35,083	36,000	36,000	36,000	36,000	36,581	215,664
Total Potential Base Rent		654,319	689,783	712,296	741,615	776,014	816,973	4,390,999
Lost Absorption / Turnover Rent								
2. Joy Placement Center	200	0	0	0	-20,894	0	0	-20,894
3. Spring Computers	300	-7,875	0	0	0	0	-19,338	-27,213
1. Vacant Space (1 of 6)	Auto Lease-Up	-17,500	0	0	0	0	-7,162	-24,662
2. Vacant Space (2 of 6)	Auto Lease-Up	-20,417	0	0	0	0	-7,162	-27,579
3. Vacant Space (3 of 6)	Auto Lease-Up	-23,333	0	0	0	0	-7,162	-30,495
4. Vacant Space (4 of 6)	Auto Lease-Up	-26,250	0	0	0	0	-7,162	-33,412
5. Vacant Space (5 of 6)	Auto Lease-Up	-29,167	0	0	0	0	-7,162	-36,329
6. Vacant Space (6 of 6)	Auto Lease-Up	-32,083	0	0	0	0	-3,581	-35,664
Total Lost Absorption / Turnover Rent		-156,625	0	0	-20,894	0	-58,729	-236,248
Scheduled Base Rent								
1. JFN Real Estate	100	35,805	52,900	61,448	61,448	61,448	61,448	334,498
2. Joy Placement Center	200	79,789	82,182	84,648	81,573	125,365	125,365	578,922
3. Spring Computers	300	89,100	97,200	97,200	97,200	97,200	95,119	573,019
4. Feighery Group	400	230,000	241,500	253,000	264,500	276,000	287,500	1,552,500
1. Vacant Space (1 of 6)	Auto Lease-Up	18,000	36,000	36,000	36,000	36,000	32,324	194,324
2. Vacant Space (2 of 6)	Auto Lease-Up	15,000	36,000	36,000	36,000	36,000	31,743	190,743
3. Vacant Space (3 of 6)	Auto Lease-Up	12,000	36,000	36,000	36,000	36,000	31,162	187,162
4. Vacant Space (4 of 6)	Auto Lease-Up	9,000	36,000	36,000	36,000	36,000	30,581	183,581
5. Vacant Space (5 of 6)	Auto Lease-Up	6,000	36,000	36,000	36,000	36,000	30,000	180,000
6. Vacant Space (6 of 6)	Auto Lease-Up	3,000	36,000	36,000	36,000	36,000	33,000	180,000
Total Scheduled Base Rent		497,694	689,783	712,296	720,721	776,014	758,244	4,154,751

Fixed Steps								
2. Joy Placement Center	200	5,509	7,902	10,368	6,901	0	0	30,680
4. Feighery Group	400	0	11,500	23,000	34,500	46,000	57,500	172,500
Total Fixed Steps		5,509	19,402	33,368	41,401	46,000	57,500	203,180
Recoveries								
1. JFN Real Estate	100	1,211	986	446	739	1,375	1,394	6,149
2. Joy Placement Center	200	20,000	20,600	21,218	12,748	1,155	1,189	76,910
3. Spring Computers	300	0	2,765	3,471	3,935	4,942	414	15,527
4. Feighery Group	400	100,168	111,946	114,952	116,927	121,217	121,346	686,556
1. Vacant Space (1 of 6)	Auto Lease-Up	0	1,024	1,286	1,457	1,830	921	6,518
2. Vacant Space (2 of 6)	Auto Lease-Up	0	1,024	1,286	1,457	1,830	1,074	6,671
3. Vacant Space (3 of 6)	Auto Lease-Up	0	1,024	1,286	1,457	1,830	1,228	6,825
4. Vacant Space (4 of 6)	Auto Lease-Up	0	1,024	1,286	1,457	1,830	1,381	6,978
5. Vacant Space (5 of 6)	Auto Lease-Up	0	1,024	1,286	1,457	1,830	1,535	7,132
6. Vacant Space (6 of 6)	Auto Lease-Up	0	1,024	1,286	1,457	1,830	1,688	7,285
Total Recoveries		121,380	142,441	147,800	143,092	139,670	132,170	826,552
Tenant Income								
1. JFN Real Estate	100	37,016	53,886	61,894	62,187	62,823	62,842	340,648
2. Joy Placement Center	200	99,789	102,782	105,866	94,321	126,520	126,555	655,833
3. Spring Computers	300	89,100	99,965	100,671	101,135	102,142	95,534	588,546
4. Feighery Group	400	330,168	353,446	367,952	381,427	397,217	408,846	2,239,056
1. Vacant Space (1 of 6)	Auto Lease-Up	18,000	37,024	37,286	37,457	37,830	33,245	200,842
2. Vacant Space (2 of 6)	Auto Lease-Up	15,000	37,024	37,286	37,457	37,830	32,817	197,415
3. Vacant Space (3 of 6)	Auto Lease-Up	12,000	37,024	37,286	37,457	37,830	32,390	193,987
4. Vacant Space (4 of 6)	Auto Lease-Up	9,000	37,024	37,286	37,457	37,830	31,962	190,559
5. Vacant Space (5 of 6)	Auto Lease-Up	6,000	37,024	37,286	37,457	37,830	31,535	187,132
6. Vacant Space (6 of 6)	Auto Lease-Up	3,000	37,024	37,286	37,457	37,830	34,688	187,285
Total Tenant Income		619,073	832,224	860,096	863,813	915,683	890,414	4,981,302
Tenant Improvements								
1. JFN Real Estate	100	0	-17,562	0	0	0	0	-17,562
2. Joy Placement Center	200	0	0	0	-67,640	0	0	-67,640
3. Spring Computers	300	-81,000	0	0	0	0	-62,601	-143,601
4. Feighery Group	400	-345,000	0	0	0	0	0	-345,000
1. Vacant Space (1 of 6)	Auto Lease-Up	-30,000	0	0	0	0	-23,185	-53,185
2. Vacant Space (2 of 6)	Auto Lease-Up	-30,000	0	0	0	0	-23,185	-53,185
3. Vacant Space (3 of 6)	Auto Lease-Up	-30,000	0	0	0	0	-23,185	-53,185
4. Vacant Space (4 of 6)	Auto Lease-Up	-30,000	0	0	0	0	-23,185	-53,185
5. Vacant Space (5 of 6)	Auto Lease-Up	-30,000	0	0	0	0	0	-30,000
6. Vacant Space (6 of 6)	Auto Lease-Up	-30,000	0	0	0	0	0	-30,000
Total Tenant Improvements		-606,000	-17,562	0	-67,640	0	-155,343	-846,544
Leasing Commissions								
1. JFN Real Estate	100	0	-9,217	0	0	0	0	-9,217
2. Joy Placement Center	200	0	0	0	-25,073	0	0	-25,073
3. Spring Computers	300	-24,300	0	0	0	0	-23,205	-47,505
4. Feighery Group	400	-140,875	0	0	0	0	0	-140,875
1. Vacant Space (1 of 6)	Auto Lease-Up	-9,000	0	0	0	0	-8,595	-17,595
2. Vacant Space (2 of 6)	Auto Lease-Up	-9,000	0	0	0	0	-8,595	-17,595
3. Vacant Space (3 of 6)	Auto Lease-Up	-9,000	0	0	0	0	-8,595	-17,595
4. Vacant Space (4 of 6)	Auto Lease-Up	-9,000	0	0	0	0	-8,595	-17,595
5. Vacant Space (5 of 6)	Auto Lease-Up	-9,000	0	0	0	0	0	-9,000
6. Vacant Space (6 of 6)	Auto Lease-Up	-9,000	0	0	0	0	0	-9,000
Total Leasing Commissions		-219,175	-9,217	0	-25,073	0	-57,583	-311,049
Market Rent								
1. JFN Real Estate	100	59,675	62,051	65,135	67,089	69,102	71,175	394,227
2. Joy Placement Center	200	108,325	114,825	121,714	125,365	129,126	133,000	732,355
3. Spring Computers	300	94,500	100,170	106,180	109,366	112,647	116,026	638,888
4. Feighery Group	400	345,000	365,700	387,642	399,271	411,249	423,587	2,332,450
1. Vacant Space (1 of 6)	Auto Lease-Up	35,000	37,100	39,326	40,506	41,721	42,973	236,625
2. Vacant Space (2 of 6)	Auto Lease-Up	35,000	37,100	39,326	40,506	41,721	42,973	236,625
3. Vacant Space (3 of 6)	Auto Lease-Up	35,000	37,100	39,326	40,506	41,721	42,973	236,625
4. Vacant Space (4 of 6)	Auto Lease-Up	35,000	37,100	39,326	40,506	41,721	42,973	236,625
5. Vacant Space (5 of 6)	Auto Lease-Up	35,000	37,100	39,326	40,506	41,721	42,973	236,625
6. Vacant Space (6 of 6)	Auto Lease-Up	35,000	37,100	39,326	40,506	41,721	42,973	236,625
Total Market Rent		817,500	865,345	916,627	944,126	972,450	1,001,623	5,517,672

CLOSING THOUGHT

Having completed the calculations to achieve a pro forma of the property, users have a better understanding of the property. While ARGUS Enterprise provides the form and the calculations to quickly and accurately model the property, the analysis still rests squarely on the user's shoulders.

ARGUS Enterprise takes existing assumed data, base rents, reimbursement schedules, some miscellaneous income and the operating expenses of a building to give a good representation of the property as it stands today. ARGUS Enterprise then takes the market assumptions and scenarios made by the user and creates a compete forecast pro forma. This consistent analytics and management tool provides transparency of the data for both users and investors to make informed risk and reward decisions on their property investments.

Supplemental V Cases

Case: Welcome to the Big Leagues

Introduction:

You have finally arrived! Congratulations! After leaving college, you've gone on to a successful business career, and now, after 10 years of waiting, you have succeeded your mother as the head of your family's trust fund. Your grandfather and his two brothers' estates created this trust in 1989, when they distributed the family's assets into trusts for each branch of the family. It's June 2003.

Current Trust Portfolio:

Stocks		Value	P/E	Div. Yield		Cashflow	Bid	Ask
YPF SA ADR Oil Trading Partnership	$	2,000,000	6.00 x	13.62%	$	272,400	$19.00	$20.00
BB&T Bank		15,000,000	12.43 x	3.35%		502,500	$33.59	$34.00
SCS Trucking		10,500,000	N/A	0%		-	$11.52	$11.97
Subtotal Equities	$	27,500,000		2.82%	$	774,900		

Bonds		Value		Face Amt	YTM		Cashflow	Bid	Ask
Citigroup 5 Year 5% Bonds	$	9,000,000	$	10,000,000	7.47%	$	500,000	90.00	90.50
10 Year 6.5% Treasuries		25,000,000		24,000,000	4.48%		1,560,000	104.17	104.35
5 Year Zero Coupon Treasury Strips		5,350,000		6,000,000	4.63%		-	89.17	89.30
Cash		2,150,000		2,150,000	1.25%		26,875		
Subtotal Bonds	$	41,500,000	$	42,150,000		$	2,086,875		

Note Receivable	Value	Face Amt	Interest		Cashflow	Notes
Regency Convertible Mortgage	TBD	70,000,000	8.00%	$	5,600,000	Est max CF assuming no incremental participation

- Marketable Securities: The trust has a portfolio of $70 million in stocks and bonds in primarily thinly traded securities (shown above) which currently yield about 5% per annum.

- Mortgage Note: The main asset is a $70 million participating convertible mortgage ("note") in a retail property by the name of Regency Mall ("Regency"), the single regional mall in Pueblecito, a metro area of 200,000 people. In 1980, your grandfather made his name in the local real estate community developing the Regency. The subject property is a 3 anchor, 450,000 square foot mall with outparcels of a tire store and three restaurants. Each anchor is 100,000 square foot and there is 150,000 square feet of in-line space. At the time the note was written, the property was valued at an 8% cap rate. Your grandfather structured a convertible participating mortgage that would give the trust a claim on 60% of the equity. By 1995 the property had appreciated greatly in price and it seemed like Grandpa had made a good deal. Notably, since then, a Wal-Mart super center opened in the market and Cap rates on solid stabilized regional malls in comparable cities are 8.5-10.0%.

- The details of the note are as follows.
  - The note pays 8% per annum.
  - The note is a non-amortizing mortgage due of December 31, 2008

- The note is convertible into 60% of the equity ownership of the property after December 31, 2004.
- If Regency's NOI (after a normal capital expenditure reserve) exceeds $10 million, the note receives 10% of the incremental NOI over $10 million.
- The note is the only debt on the Regency and is a secured first mortgage which prohibits any debt or preferred equity to be placed on the property without your approval.
- In 1995 Regency was appraised at a value of $100 million, with an NOI of $9 million (after cap ex reserves)
- At the end of 2002 the Regency's NOI had declined to $7 million (after cap ex reserves) and the Regency was appraised at $65 million.
- During 2004, 40% of all leases will expire, with a further 20% expiring in 2005, and 10% in 2006.

- Bank Loan:
  - When your grandfather died in 1995, your mother decided to diversify the family's portfolio into stocks and bonds. To do so, she arranged a $50 million loan for the trust with the local bank, secured by the trust's note on Regency.
  - The bank loan is interest only, matures January 1, 2005, and bears a 9% interest rate.
  - This bank loan contains a provision that if the appraised value of Regency is less than 120% of the note, the loan can be called at any time by the bank. In addition, the bank loan forbids any other debt being taken on by the trust so long as the loan is outstanding. The loan also has a sweep provision that allows the bank to take all cash inflows out of the trust until the bank loan obligations are satisfied.

Market Information:

- The 3 month LIBOR is 2.25%, the 5 year LIBOR is 4.5%, the ten year LIBOR is 6.0%, and the 30 year LIBOR is 7.0%. Floating rate mortgage spreads are between 80-125 bps.
- Short term interest rates are expected to rise over the next few years as they are historically low.
- Having spoken with Billybob Clinton, your hometown banker, he tells you that it is unlikely that you'll be able to get financing with terms similar to your $50MM loan. He notes that currently, first mortgages require a Debt Service Coverage Ratio of at least 1.2x and a Loan-to-Value of roughly 70%, though you may be able to go beyond this.
- Two years ago, a new 220,000 square foot Wal-Mart super center opened about 2 miles away from the subject property. The area approaching the Wal-Mart is surrounded by several free standing restaurants, a Circuit City, and a Bed Bath and Beyond.
- The Market occupancy rates:
  - The market occupancy for class A retail is 92%, with a total of 600,000 square foot of class A space
  - The market occupancy for class B retail is 86%, with a total of 1,300,000 square foot of class B space
  - The market occupancy for class C retail is 78% with roughly 1,000,000 square foot of class C space
- There are no other regional malls in Pueblecito.
- Market occupancy is seen as remaining stable over the next 5 years.
- Pueblecito's residential communities will probably not grow materially in the next 5 years.

The Trustees:

The principal beneficiaries of the trust are your mother (50%), your sister (25%) and yourself (25%). The beneficiaries are accustomed to total annual distributions from the trust of approximately $2-3 million to cover their living expenses.

The Proposal:

Regency's owners have approached you with concern that market conditions for Regency continue to weaken. They believe that they will be able to successfully re-lease their space as leases expire over the next few years, although at lower rents and greater concessions. The historical and their projected NOI and TIs/commissions are:

Year	NOI*	TIs/Commissions
1997	9.2M	0.5M
1998	9.3M	0.2M
1999	9.6M	0.3M
2000	9.8M	0.4M
2001	9.7M	0.1M
2002	7.0M	0.2M
2003E	6.8M	0.5M
2004E	4.0M	3.0M
2005E	5.0M	2.0M
2006E	5.8M	0.5M
2007E	6.0M	0.2M
2008E	6.5M	0.2M

*Post capex reserves but pre reserves for TI and commissions

The owners of Regency propose that they buy your note on Regency from the Trust for $47 million in cash plus a stub that converts into 35% equity ownership of Regency on December 31, 2008. They are willing to agree not to place more than 80% leverage on Regency prior to the conversion date. The owners also would agree that prior to this conversion date they will not allow the interest coverage ratio to go beneath 1:1. You have no idea if the owners are sandbagging you, but Billybob tells you that in this market, with the new Wal-Mart, these numbers seem to be 'in the ballpark'. A broker, who stands to earn a fee, says that it sounds like a great deal.

Required:

So, are you still glad to be the head of the family trust? After leaving school you've had a successful business career, but have no further real estate experience beyond having taken a real estate finance class a long time ago. You must write a business memo to your fellow trustees (the long time family minister; the family lawyer; the President of the local bank who made the loan to the trust; your 28 year old sister whose income from the trust is her primary source of income; and your retired Mother) on how you recommend the trust proceed. The memo is not to exceed 3 pages, plus no more than 2 pages of exhibits with any charts/tables/graphs you choose to use. Welcome to the big leagues!

Case: Build to Suit

Over the past 7 years you have developed 12 build to suit facilities for Convenient Marts. These facilities are generally located on strip center out parcels, are roughly 11,000 sf, and completely occupied by a Convenient Marts store. These properties have all been located along the main thoroughfares of suburban Philadelphia.

The typical lease terms on these deals have been:

- A 10 year lease term
- Rent is triple net
- Rent has provided roughly a 350 basis point spread over the 10 year Treasury rate when the deal was signed
- A 10 year renewal option
- Convenient Marts may purchase the property (Convenient Marts has the option) at any time for "fair market value"
- An option to purchase the property in year 10 (and year 20 if lease option is renewed) at a 10% discount to "fair market value"
- A right of first refusal with respect to both lease and purchase as long as the lease is in effect.

The typical Convenient Marts store is a plain "box", and petroleum product sales are prohibited in the leases.

Over the past decade Convenient Marts has expanded in the suburban areas of the major mid-Atlantic state metropolitan areas. This publicly traded company has been rated BBB+ (or better) for the past 7 years.

Convenient Marts has recently embarked upon an aggressive expansion campaign, targeting the suburban areas of secondary mid-Atlantic cities for new stores. As a result of this expansion effort, S&P has placed Convenient Mart's debt on a "credit watch", expressing concern that this effort may result in lower quality cash flows and an increased debt burden.

You have sold 10 of the 12 Convenient Mart stores you have developed. In each case, you sold them within 18 months of completion for an average cap rate that has a spread over 10 year Treasury of about 210 basis points. The two properties you have not sold have been completed with in the past 12 months. You anticipate that these properties will each sell for a spread of about 200 basis points over 10 year Treasury during the next year.

These properties you have developed for Convenient Marts have taken you as few as 10 months, and as much as 16 months to complete. Typically it requires about 12 months to develop one of these stores.

Convenient Marts has approached you, and asked you to play a major development role in their expansion effort. Specifically, they have indicated that they would like you to develop stores for them in the Allentown / Bethlehem, Pennsylvania area. They plan to add about 10 stores in this region over the next 3-4 years, and want you to be their developer in this effort.

Their first store site in this market is along the main suburban throughway in suburban Allentown. It is for a 10,000 sf store, with appropriate parking, ingress/egress, and signage requirements. Convenient Mart's real estate committee has approved the following non-negotiable (take it or walk) deal terms:

- 10 year lease
- 10 year renewal option
- Option to purchase at any time at "fair market value"
- Option to purchase in year 10 (and year 20 if lease in renewed) at 10% discount to "fair market value"
- Right of first refusal with respect to both lease and purchase as long as the lease is in effect
- Triple net rent lease
- Rent for the first 10 years is $50,000 annually
- Rent during the option years would be $65,000 annually
- Certificate of Occupancy must be in place within 13 months
- If the Certificate of Occupancy is not in place within 13 months, rent during the first 10 years is reduced to $40,000 annually
- If Certificate of Occupancy is not in place within 14 months, Convenient Marts is released from the lease and you must pay them a penalty of $60,000.

This project would represent your first effort outside of the Philadelphia area. You believe that you can acquire the site for $120,000. You believe that approval, planning, and design costs should run about $50,000, while hard construction costs are estimated at roughly $400,000.

You have a term sheet on a loan which provides 3 year financing of $440,000 at LIBOR plus 300 basis points. LIBOR is currently 1.4% (a cyclical low). The loan adjusts the interest rate quarterly. The loan has no amortization and is pre-payable without penalty. You also will receive a development fee of 5% of hard costs plus approval, planning, and design costs.

Initial discussions with your lender and local planning officials lead you to anticipate no unusual problems with the project. The equity required for this project is available, but would absorb about 30% of your equity capacity.

Should you undertake this development? You are to write a 3-page business memo to your board, with no more than 2 supplemental pages of tables/charts/graphs, explaining to them your recommendation and your rationale.

Case: The London Location Case

You have been engaged by a large U.S. financial services firm to develop a location strategy for their new European regional headquarters. They want to locate in the London metro area. You will make a 10-minute presentation (to be followed by a question and answer period) on your location proposal to their senior managers. Questions you should address include:

- Should they choose a city or suburban location?
- Which specific location(s) do you suggest?
- Should they buy, build, or lease?
- Should they consolidate all of their facilities?
- How much space will they require?
- How should they deal with their currently leased facility?
- Are there currency exposures in your proposal, and how will they be dealt with?
- How do you propose to assign their employees within the space?
- Will your proposed strategy satisfy the technological demands of a modern financial services firm?

The client is currently in the fourth year of a 25-year lease of a 75,000 square foot building (Howell Building) in the West End of London at £65/square foot, which houses all operations, including a small trading floor. There are currently 750 employees at this site. Of these, 170 are in systems and operations, 250 are in investment and merchant banking, 300 are in sales and trading, and 30 are in the European executive office. Plans for the next several years suggest the following employment levels:

	Systems/Operations	Sales/Trading	I Banking	European Exec.
2003	180	300	260	32
2004	200	310	280	35
2005	250	350	325	40
2006	300	380	360	50

The firm wants to raise its image and visibility in Europe to a level commensurate with its presence in North America. It is also important to remember that the London office will service all of Europe, and all of its functions.

Each team should be prepared to present their recommendations, although the teams that present will be selected randomly. Each team should submit a 5-page business memo plus (up to) four supporting pages of charts/graphs/maps/tables summarizing their findings and recommendations.

Case: The Condo Case

You have slaved away as an Associate for the prestigious investment banking group Gold in Stacks (GIS) for four years. You've been able to accumulate savings of $75,000, and your current lifestyle requires you to make a pre-tax gross income of $200,000. You have a two-year-old child and a working spouse.

Secretly you have always wanted to be your own boss and to build equity with your sweat. One day while walking home you notice an old, abandoned, six-story office building that is about 30,000 gross square feet.

Intrigued by the building, you do a little homework and conclude:

- the neighborhood is solid, if not spectacular
- the neighborhood is largely owner occupied high and mid-rise condos
- a typical condo in the neighborhood is about 1,400 square feet and sells for $200,000-$500,000
- you can purchase the property (not inclusive of transaction costs) for about $3.6 million
- you estimate that if all goes smoothly you can renovate the property into condos for about $3.3 million in hard and soft costs (including interest expense)
- the property is unlikely to support any ground level retail
- construction will probably take about one year.

Based upon your knowledge of financial markets, you believe that:

- you can get a combined purchase and construction loan secured by the property of roughly $4.2 million drawn down over the purchase and construction period, subject to at least $2.1 million in equity going in first
- the loan would carry an interest rate of 6.8% payable monthly, with accrual until cash coverage exists
- the lender will sweep all cash inflows not required for construction and sale of units
- the loan would be for a term of three years with no amortization
- a private equity fund would be willing to provide the necessary equity, however, they will require you to personally invest $65,000 in a subordinated equity position
- they will give you a 20% carried equity position on any profits the project earns in excess of an 11% equity IRR
- they will allow you to take a development fee of 4% of construction costs, with half paid on a pro rata basis to construction outlays, and the other half in a subordinated equity position.

Finally, though you hate to admit it, if you undertake this project you will have to work on it full time.

The Assignment:

- Provide a one-page summary of the project (how many units, how big, what target price, when sold, total cost, etc.).
- Provide a one-page spreadsheet showing (on a quarterly basis) the expected cash flows for the project.
- Provide a one-page summary of the project's unleveraged IRR, equity IRR, and your return.
- Provide a two-page summary of what you have decided to do regarding this project (and why).
- Provide a one-page floorplan summary.

All pages should be 8.5x11 and easily readable by your equity partner (who wears bifocals).

Case: The REFM Collection- The Upzoning Decision

Introduction:

115 Arts Street (the "Artist Factory") is an existing three-story 20,000 square foot historic building located in an amenity-rich neighborhood just outside the downtown core of a major US city. Under the current zoning, the property can be redeveloped another two stories into 70 residential condominiums. Under the city's zoning process, there is a chance to get the parcel upzoned to allow for 130 units. But there are conditions for getting that extra density from the city, and it is never 100% certain that a rezoning will be successfully achieved.

Background:

Donna and Terry became quick friends after meeting through a mutual acquaintance at a real estate networking event several years ago. They both worked for real estate development companies that were family businesses, but both were really entrepreneurs at heart. They eventually got fed up with working to inflate the bank accounts of these two wealthy families and decided to become business partners in a real estate development company. While it goes without saying, they named their company Modest Moguls ("MM").

After five years of successful operation, MM now has nine employees, including the two principals, and has profitably developed eight mid-size (fewer than 30 units) residential projects – all rentals, all in the close-in suburbs to the city. Each project lasted about eight to twelve months in duration and was mid-rise (6 stories or fewer) wood-frame construction.

Donna and Terry both have a keen interest in urban adaptive reuse and historic renovation projects, and crave the cachet of breathing life back into charming old buildings with the kinds of beautiful architectural details that are no longer being produced. MM had its eye on one property in particular in the city, 115 Arts Street, formerly home to an artist's workspace that produced a well-known 20th-century U.S. metals sculptor. They felt that the marketing campaign that could be tied to the history of the building could be incredibly creative and compelling, and that they could really make a splash with this as their first project in the city.

Earlier this month, MM had signed a contract to purchase the now-vacant and decrepit Artist Factory building and the land beneath it for $3.0 million (other bids also came in around that amount, but MM prevailed in the end). They put a refundable deposit down at contract signing, and were now in the 90-day due diligence period.

The Big Opportunity:

Most real estate development is accomplished "by-right" or "as a matter-of-right" (also referred to as "as-of-right"). Such development projects comply with all the standards of the zoning regulations, and there is a regular permitting process managed by the jurisdiction that does not require formal public input on design or use.

An upzoning is a planning tool that can allow for developments and associated public benefits that are superior to those that would result from matter-of-right projects. The upzoning process relaxes certain limiting regulations, such as height and FAR, in return for public benefits provided by the developer. However, an upzoning involves extensive review by public bodies and neighborhood residents and other interested groups.

MM had based its $3.0 million purchase price off of the property's 2.50 FAR by-right development potential of 70 residential units (which could be accomplished with wood-frame construction in conjunction with the existing structure), but recognized full well that they could possibly upzone the site in the future to the "BRD" (Bigger, Riskier Development) zoning designation, which had an FAR of 4.50. With this increased density, they could develop a total of 130 condominium units.

Donna and Terry knew that if they could pull off the upzoning, their land cost basis would be much lower than what it "should be" on a per-residential-unit basis for the neighborhood. With those advantageous economics, they could generate significantly higher profits than they had pitched to their investors, who had committed to providing 90% of the equity capital for the by-right project. Donna and Terry could end up being heroes and become pretty rich themselves, too, if they hit or exceeded pro forma returns, given the joint venture equity partnership promote structure they were almost done negotiating with their investors.

The Costs:

MM would have to build in concrete/steel since the building would have to be eight stories tall to accommodate the higher unit count. Additionally, they would be required to sell 7% to 9% of the residential units (they would have to negotiate) at "affordable" prices based on a government-provided pricing schedule that dealt with Area Median Incomes, or AMI (which was not negotiable) **(Exhibit A in the accompanying Excel file)**. This requirement was part of the city's mandate of "inclusionary zoning", which strove to make all neighborhoods mixed-income in nature.

While the spirit of inclusionary zoning was entirely noble, it presented an economic dilemma for the developer in that certain units would have to be sold below what it cost to bring them to market. In order for the developer to keep their targeted profit margins, the market rate units would have to become that much more expensive to make up for what would otherwise be losses.

And while every developer had the sneaky idea of just making all of the Affordable units Studios (since it was better to lose money on a lower-priced unit than on a larger higher-priced unit), the city prevented that by requiring a ratio of Affordable unit types that matched the ratio of the Market rate unit types in the building.

From preliminary conversations with the zoning office's liaison, MM understood that they would likely also have to dedicate approximately 2,000 rentable square feet on the ground floor for a city-sponsored art exhibition space (set up legally as a commercial condominium unit within the overall building condominium regime), for which they would receive no rent whatsoever. While the city would not levy real estate taxes on the commercial condominium, MM as developer, and eventually the condominium owner's association, would have to bear the art exhibit curator's $45,000/year compensation package (which provided for 3% annual increases), and also the ongoing operating expenses of the commercial condominium unit itself, which they knew would be every bit of $15 per square foot per year, naturally subject to general expense inflation.

Along these lines, Donna remembered hearing something about how condominium developers needed to also carry the costs of the individual condominium units before they were closed on by the buyers. She thought she had it already built into the pro forma but made a note to double check the downtrending of these costs as units were closed and the per-unit costs were transferred to the new unit owners.

Additionally, if they increased the number of units in the building, they would have to build underground parking to accommodate the higher parking count requirement (they were able to get away with just surface parking otherwise). They had a nagging feeling in the back of their heads that there would be lots of "dirty dirt" from 50+ years of sculpting work, and knew that the deeper they went into the ground, the more of it they could find. While it sounded like an oxymoron, they would have to have this dirty dirt carted away at a premium cost to a "special dump".

They also would need to pre-sell significantly more units to be eligible for construction financing. Right now they were hearing that construction lenders were requiring at least 30% of units be pre-sold (purchase and sale contracts signed, and 10% cash deposits taken and held in escrow) before the lenders would seriously consider funding a condominium project. At an assumed pre-sales rate of 7 units per month, they would be in for a much longer haul before they could break ground. A longer runway like that could potentially put them in danger of missing the condominium market altogether by the time they were able to deliver the larger building.

They had been over the various design and construction elements of the two scenarios with their architect and likely general contractor, and summarized them side-by-side, along with other key variables, for their and their investors' ease of reference **(Exhibit B in accompanying Excel)**.

The Big Risk:

Pursuing the upzoning would cost Modest Moguls both time and money. There would not only be significantly land use attorney's fees associated with the rezoning process, but MM would also incur various consultant's fees, as well as additional carrying costs to upkeep the property while the hearings took place. The rezoning process would certainly delay the start of construction, likely by at least 8 months, but Donna and Joan had heard horror stories that it could drag on for as many as 14 months. On the low end, they had estimated the upzoning pursuit would cost them $650,000 in additional soft costs and carry costs, and on the high end, double that amount.

Donna and Terry knew that there was a very real chance that they could go through the entire rezoning process only to have the request for additional density rejected outright. At that point they would have lost time and money, and the IRRs to their investors would likely drop relative to what they were pitched. It would be a lot to go through just to end up doing the 70-unit project that they already had in hand.

While they had not themselves been through the rezoning process before, MM knew it was quite detailed and could be tricky, especially when dealing with a potentially prickly community that was known to value the status quo, mid-rise nature of their neighborhood.

Blue Screen Of Death:

Just as Terry was making the final adjustments to the as-of-right scenario pro-forma for the upzoned scenario, his Windows computer crashed, giving him the dreaded Blue Screen Of Death **(Exhibit C in accompanying Excel)**. The machine then spontaneously combusted, melting instantly into a pile of smoldering noxious plastic. The timing couldn't have been worse! He and Donna had to present the alternatives and their decision to their investors (and potentially request more equity from their investors for the upzone scenario) on Monday, and it was Thursday night already.

To compound matters, Terry had never followed through on backing up his files to Dropbox, even though he had promised Donna that he would. After apologizing profusely to Donna, Terry found the as-of-right pro-forma file from his prior email to their investors **(accompanying Excel)**, saved it as a new file entitled "Upzone Scenario", and got back to work making the needed adjustments.

It was going to be a long weekend, but they were passionate about this deal, and were going forward with it one way or another. Plus, they reasoned, rebuilding the upzone scenario pro-forma would allow them a final opportunity to test their convictions with respect to their assumptions. In true entrepreneurial fashion, they turned on the coffee maker, ordered some pizza, and got to work in Excel on Donna's computer (an Apple with a flawless record of performance and strong graphic design capabilities).

The Assignment:

Put yourself in Donna and Terry's shoes. You need to run the upzone scenario analysis in Excel and compare and contrast the two alternatives (with appropriate sensitivity analyses for each scenario) such that you can make a decision as to which one to pursue. Then write up an Investment Committee memo recommending pursuing one scenario or the other, backed up by your quantitative and qualitative analyses.

To be clear: Donna and Terry are going forward with the development. You must take a side as to which path they should pursue, and detail why.

Assignment Deliverables:

- Two-page Investment Committee Memo in a Word file, which includes the following returns metrics:
  - IRR based off of the monthly cash flows
  - NPV based off of the monthly cash flows
  - Multiple On Equity (how many times all equity is returned to all equity holders in aggregate)
  - Profit Margin (Net Cash Flow divided by Gross Sales Proceeds)
- Up to two additional pages of Exhibits pasted as images into the Word file
- A Gantt chart of the project timeline for the Upzone Scenario from Time 0 of January 1st through the closing on the final residential unit.

The Gantt chart should have all of the activities/tasks and milestones shown in the *Project Timing And Sales Velocity Assumptions* section of Assumptions tab of the accompanying Excel.

Guidance:

For Parking Hard Costs, assume that the surface parking Hard Costs in the By-Right scenario are included in the "Residential Hard Costs" line item.

For the Underground Parking Hard Costs in the Upzone scenario, you can put those into the Retail Hard Costs line (and relabel the line). Let's assume there is no difference in cost between 2,000 SF of lobby, and the 2,000 SF of art exhibit space, so there is nothing to change on that front with respect to Hard Costs.

In both models, you can ignore the Storage Units input on the Assumptions tab, just as you can ignore the Owner Directed Hard Costs.

Assume that MM will contribute 10% of all equity invested.

You can run sensitivity analyses around some or all of the following variables:

- Hard Costs
- Sales Prices
- Upzoning Approvals duration
- Upzoning Approvals budget
- Pre Sales Absorption Rate
- Market Sales Absorption Rate

INDEX

1

A

B

C

D

E

F

G

H

I

J

K

L

M

N

O

P

R

S

T

U

V

W

Z